Burlington Route

Burlington Route

A History of
the Burlington Lines

Richard C. Overton

ALFRED·A·KNOPF

New York / 1965

L. C. catalog card number: 64–19106

THIS IS A BORZOI BOOK,
PUBLISHED BY ALFRED A. KNOPF, INC.

FIRST EDITION

For Lou and the family

_____

Foreword

THIS VOLUME IS A DISTILLATION of a 2,375-page, fully documented, typed manuscript covering the first century of the Burlington's existence. I use the word "distillation" advisedly; the present book is not simply a cut or edited version of the long draft, but rather a freshly written account based on the ideas, information, and perspectives of the parent work. It is designed for the general reader, and because it is, specialists such as economists, financial experts, labor and agrarian historians, lawyers, railway and locomotive fans, and the like may feel that more space should be devoted to their particular fields. I can assure them all, however, that they will find selected examples of their special interests.

If this book is written from any particular vantage point, I suppose it is from that of the decision-makers. Always throughout its long life the Burlington has been guided by an entrepreneurial group: during its first half century by John Murray Forbes and such associates as James F. Joy, John M. Brooks, and Charles E. Perkins. From 1901 to the end of the company's first century in 1949, James J. Hill and those working with and after him, such as Howard Elliott, Daniel Willard, Arthur Curtiss James, and Ralph Budd—to mention only a few—guided the destiny of the system. Thus I have felt it obligatory to depict the context in which these men worked in order to search out, so far as I could, their motives and techniques, and to describe their achievements as well as their failures. This does not mean that I have neglected the men and women on the line or the oft-overlooked "middle management" so essential to the smooth functioning of a massive, far-flung corporation. All these people were and are essential for making a railroad run. Yet in long-run terms it has been the entrepreneurs, usually working as a team rather than as a succession of "one-man shows," who have determined policy. That is why they occupy such a prominent part in this book.

A word should be said about the emphasis in the various chapters. This account follows, as closely as possible, a chronological pattern. But I have deliberately emphasized, by the use of detail, various functional aspects at the times when, to the men in charge of the system, they seemed of primary importance. In the early days, for example, the foremost concern was where to build the railroad and how to pay for it. During both the Civil War and the two world wars, the principal problem was how to carry an inflated traffic load despite a shortage of men and materials. In the post-Civil War years, expansion, colonization, competition from other railways, and administrative procedure were at the top of the agenda; in times of depression, financial management was necessarily the most pressing matter. Government regulation, labor relations, and personnel problems moved into the spotlight on various occasions, while at certain times improvement of equipment and service seemed of special importance. In the 1945–49 period particularly, attention was riveted on the attempt to keep mounting costs under control in an increasingly competitive transportation market. Of course, all or most of these functional factors were present in varying degree throughout the company's history, but to treat each in detail in every period would obviously be impossible within the limits of a single volume. My emphasis, I repeat, has been guided by what the men at the time believed to be most important.

To avoid cumbersome circumlocutions, I have used some "shorthand phrases." When I refer to "Burlington," I mean all roads that were at the moment of reference part of or controlled by the parent Chicago, Burlington & Quincy. I include also the two direct predecessors, the Aurora Branch and the Chicago and Aurora, as part of the Burlington. Obviously, therefore, "Burlington" means different things at different times. Similarly, in respect to the period after 1901 I refer to the Burlington, Great Northern, and Northern Pacific collectively as the "Hill Lines," as does, for example, John Moody in *The Railroad Builders*. This is not to imply that Hill personally controlled any or all of these roads at any particular time; it is simply a well-understood and current phrase which is far more convenient than spelling out all three titles.

To the best of my ability, I have let men and events speak for themselves; although I have drawn conclusions where it seemed appropriate to do so, in no case have I consciously expressed anything resembling a moral judgment on any person or policy. The mere task, however, of selecting what seemed to me the most pertinent data from eighteen or twenty tons of source material has inevitably involved a degree of subjective judgment and, since no one can read everything in several tons of manuscript material in one brief lifetime, of calculated risk. Furthermore, on occasions my genuine enthusiasm for what has struck me as a job well done, or my disappointment over opportunities missed, may be visible. I do not honestly know whether even a professional historian, fully mindful of his obligation to be impartial, can be intimately concerned with one central subject for thirty years and still avoid some identification with it. Certainly I have felt, from the beginning of my labors, that the story of the Burlington was and is significant (which is *not* the same thing as saying it was either "good" or "bad"); else I would never have stuck to this task as long as I have.

No undertaking of this sort can be the product of a single person's effort. Had it not been for the vision and faith of Ralph Budd, I would never have undertaken this history or—more to the point—have carried it to completion. He saw to it at the outset that I should have unrestricted access to the necessary records, freedom to tell the truth as I saw it, and support, when necessary, for the research and writing; his successor, Harry C. Murphy, confirmed and carried on these policies so essential to an undertaking of this sort. Ralph Budd's thoughtful and knowledgeable comments on the long draft, all of which he read with great care, saved me from countless errors. Yet never once did he even suggest that I alter my independent conclusions.

Scores of other cooperative and informed persons—academic colleagues, writers, graduate students, librarians, members of the Burlington family, and assorted friends—have helped me find elusive material, sent me nuggets from their own research, or read critically parts or all of the various manuscripts; to all of them my hearty thanks and the assurance that I alone am responsible for all the facts and interpretations in this book as well as for whatever shortcomings it may have. I am indebted to many others for their having labored long and hard in the actual preparation of guides to the material and of the many successive drafts and final copy. Finally, I owe much to my family, who have unfailingly buoyed me up with their patience and confidence. The specific contributions of these good people are summarized in "Around the Circle," on pages 583–8.

R. C. O.

The University of Western Ontario
London, Ontario, Canada
September 8, 1964

Contents

CONTENTS

Illustrations

[xiii]

[xv]

Maps

MAPS

Charts

[xix]

Note on Documentation

Adequate documentation of a single-volume work containing tens of thousands of factual statements is a difficult problem. Scholars and specialists may conceivably wish to know the source for each fact, but to provide such documentation herein (as has been done in 305 single-spaced typed pages in the long draft) would obviously be impractical. Furthermore, such complete documentation would serve no useful purpose for the general reader. On the other hand, all readers, presumably, will wish to know which major sources provided the bulk of the material for any given chapter and where direct quotations come from. Accordingly, principal sources by chapters are noted in brief form in the Chapter Bibliographical Notes, on pages 589–99; the full titles and whereabouts of these sources are indicated in the Bibliography, on pages 601–23. All direct quotations are documented by footnotes as they appear. For the sake of simplicity, names and sources frequently cited in these footnotes, in the Chapter Bibliographical Notes, and in the Index have been abbreviated as follows:

AAR	Association of American Railroads
AB	Aurora Branch Railroad
AR	*Annual Report* of company indicated
BF	Box File of original letters, C. E. Perkins to J. M. Forbes, 1884–94 (in C–O)
BMI	Burlington and Missouri River Railroad (the Iowa company)
BMN	Burlington and Missouri River Rail Road in Nebraska
Budd	Ralph Budd

BW	Richard C. Overton: *Burlington West* (see Bibliography)
C&A	Chicago and Aurora Railroad
C&NW	Chicago and North Western Railway
C&S	Colorado and Southern Railway
CB&N	Chicago, Burlington & Northern Railroad
CB&Q	Chicago, Burlington & Quincy Railroad, including those predecessors prior to 1864 using same cities in title
CB&Q/Emp	Files of the CB&Q Employment Department. Other departments similarly noted; see /Law, /Op, /Pres, /Sec, /Traffic
CB&Q/N	CB&Q archives in Newberry Library (see Bibliography)
CH	*Corporate History* of the CB&Q (see Bibliography under "Baldwin")
CM&StP	Chicago, Milwaukee & St. Paul Railway
CMT	Central Military Tract Railroad
CNB	Notebooks, primarily relating to C. E. Perkins, belonging to his daughter, the late Mrs. Edward Cunningham, of Boston (see Bibliography)
C–O	Cunningham-Overton Collection (see Bibliography); includes GM, PLB, PVB, RCO, Set A, Set M, Set X, Set Y
D&RGW	Denver and Rio Grande Western Railroad
DH	*Documentary History* of the CB&Q (see Bibliography under "Baldwin")
DRB	Duplicate Record Book, minutes of directors' and stockholders' meetings of company indicated
EC	Erastus Corning Papers in the Albany Institute of Art and History (see Bibliography)
/Emp	Employment Department files of company indicated, e.g.: CB&Q/Emp
Forbes	John Murray Forbes
FW&D(C)	Fort Worth and Denver (City) Railway
G&CU	Galena and Chicago Union Railroad
GM	*General Material*, seven bound volumes covering 1814–1907 (in C–O)
GN	Great Northern Railway
GTR	Richard C. Overton: *Gulf to Rockies* (see Bibliography)
HSJ	Hannibal and St. Joseph Railroad
IC	Illinois Central Railroad

ICC	Interstate Commerce Commission
ICC	I. L. Sharfman: *The Interstate Commerce Commission* (see Bibliography)
IC/N	Illinois Central Railroad archives in Newberry Library (see Bibliography)
JFJ	James F. Joy Papers in Detroit Public Library (see Bibliography)
/Law	Law Department files of company indicated
LDP	Land Department Papers of the BMI, BMN, and CB&Q (in CB&Q/N)
MC	Michigan Central Railroad
McM	Donald L. McMurry: *The Great Burlington Strike of 1888* (see Bibliography)
MS	Manuscript copy
MSo	Michigan Southern Railroad
NC	Northern Cross Railroad
/Op	Operating Department files of company indicated
ORB	Original Record Book, minutes of directors' and stockholders' meetings of company indicated
PLB	Personal Letter Books of C. E. Perkins (in C–O)
PLD	CB&Q presidents' letters to the directors
/Pres	Executive Department files of company indicated
PVB	Private Letter Books of C. E. Perkins (in C–O)
RCO	Seventeen notebooks of C. E. Perkins memoranda and letters (in C–O)
/Sec	Files in custody of secretary of company indicated
Set A	Three notebooks of C. E. Perkins letters (in C–O)
Set M	Four notebooks of C. E. Perkins memoranda (in C–O)
Set X	Three notebooks of C. E. Perkins memoranda (in C–O)
Set Y	Notebook of C. E. Perkins memoranda (in C–O)
TCC	Thomas C. Cochran: *Railroad Leaders 1845–1890* (see Bibliography)
/Traffic	Traffic Department files of company indicated
US	United States

Chronology

1847 *February 16:* Hannibal and St. Joseph chartered in Missouri
1849 *February 12:* Aurora Branch Railroad (Aurora–Turner Jct.) and
           Peoria and Oquawka Railroad (Peoria to Mississippi River)
           chartered in Illinois
      February 22: Stephen Gale (president of Aurora Branch) becomes
           Burlington's first president
      April 13: Northern Cross Railroad (Quincy–Galesburg) charter in
           force in Illinois
1850 *September 2:* First segment of Aurora Branch (Turner Jct.–
           Batavia) opens for traffic
      October 21: Service established over Aurora Branch (with trackage
           rights over Galena and Chicago Union east of Turner Jct.)
           between Aurora and Chicago
1851 *February 15:* Central Military Tract Railroad (Mendota–Gales-
           burg) chartered in Illinois
      February 21: Elisha Wadsworth (president of Aurora Branch) be-
           comes Burlington's second president
1852 *January 15:* Burlington and Missouri River Railroad chartered in
           Iowa
      February 21: Stephen Gale (president of Aurora Branch, later of
           Chicago and Aurora) becomes Burlington's third president
      June 22: Aurora Branch Railroad authorized by Illinois Legislature
           to change name to Chicago and Aurora Railroad and to build
           to Mendota
1853 *February 21:* James F. Joy (president of Chicago and Aurora, later

[x x v]

of Chicago, Burlington and Quincy) becomes Burlington's fourth president

October 20: Chicago and Aurora begins operations between Aurora and Mendota

1854 *December 7:* Central Military Tract begins operations between Mendota and Galesburg

1855 *February 14:* Chicago and Aurora Railroad authorized by Illinois Legislature to change name to Chicago, Burlington and Quincy Railroad

March 17: Peoria and Oquawka begins operations between Galesburg and East Burlington

1856 *January 31:* Northern Cross begins operations between Quincy and Galesburg

July 9: Chicago, Burlington and Quincy Rail Road formed by consolidation of Chicago, Burlington and Quincy Railroad and Central Military Tract Railroad

1857 *June 12:* John Van Nortwick becomes Burlington's fifth president

June 17: First segment of Burlington and Missouri River Railroad (Burlington–Mount Pleasant) opens for traffic

1859 *February 15:* Hannibal and St. Joseph Railroad begins operations over entire line

1860 *April 1:* Quincy and Palmyra Railroad begins operations

1863 *June 10:* Portion of Peoria and Oquawka west of Illinois River authorized by Illinois Legislature to reincorporate as Peoria & Burlington Rail Road

1864 *April 28:* Quincy and Chicago (successor to Northern Cross) consolidates with C. B. and Q. Rail Road

May 20: Present direct Chicago–Aurora line opens for traffic

June 24: Chicago, Burlington and Quincy Rail Road and Peoria & Burlington Rail Road authorized by Illinois Legislature to consolidate into Chicago, Burlington & Quincy Railroad (present company)

1865 *July 12:* James F. Joy becomes Burlington's sixth president

December 26: CB&Q operates first train to enter Union Stock Yards, Chicago

1867 *November 30:* Kansas City and Cameron Railroad (Cameron Jct. to North Kansas City) begins operations

1868 *August 13:* Burlington Bridge opens for traffic

November 9: Quincy Bridge opens for traffic

1869 *May 12:* Burlington and Missouri River Rail Road Company in Nebraska chartered in Nebraska

July 4: Kansas City Bridge opens for traffic

November 25: Entire line North Kansas City–St. Joseph–Council Bluffs begins operation

1870 *January 1:* Burlington and Missouri River begins operations over entire line to East Plattsmouth (operations extended to Council Bluffs over leased line January 3, 1870)

July 26: BMN begins operations between Plattsmouth and Lincoln

1871 *July 11:* James M. Walker becomes Burlington's seventh president

July 19: BMN leases Omaha and South Western Railroad (Oreapolis–Omaha) to gain access to Omaha

1872 *September 18:* BMN begins operations over entire line to Kearney Jct.

December 31: Burlington and Missouri River Railroad leased to CB&Q

1875 *July 31:* BMI consolidates with CB&Q

1876 *March 2:* Robert Harris becomes Burlington's eighth president

1878 *May 25:* J. M. Forbes becomes Burlington's ninth president

1880 *July 26:* BMN consolidates with CB&Q

September 12: Plattsmouth Bridge opens for traffic

1881 *September 29:* C. E. Perkins becomes Burlington's tenth president

1882 *May 29:* Burlington extension to Denver opens for traffic

1884 *March 11:* Burlington's *Fast Mail* service established between Chicago and Council Bluffs

1886 *August 23:* Burlington extension to St. Paul opens for traffic

1889 *January 17:* Burlington Relief Department established

1894 *March 4:* Burlington extension to St. Louis opens for traffic

October 28: Burlington extension to Huntley, Montana (junction with Northern Pacific), opens for traffic

1901 *March 1:* George B. Harris becomes Burlington's eleventh president

May 21: Consummation of sale of CB&Q to Great Northern and Northern Pacific

1908 *December 19:* CB&Q acquires Colorado and Southern Lines

1910 *January 31:* Darius Miller becomes Burlington's twelfth president

1914 *August 27:* Hale Holden becomes Burlington's thirteenth president

October 18: Burlington extension from Fromberg, Montana (junction with Northern Pacific near Billings), to Orin Jct., Wyoming (northern terminus of C&S), opens for traffic

1917 *April 11:* Hale Holden named to Railroads' War Board

December 15: Metropolis Bridge opens for traffic

1918 *July 18:* C. E. Perkins, Jr., becomes Burlington's fourteenth president

1920 *February 15:* Hale Holden becomes Burlington's fifteenth president
    September 26: Veterans' Association organized
1922 *March 14:* General Office Building fire, Chicago
1925 *May 15:* Chicago Union Station opens
    June 1: Burlington service extended into Dallas over Rock Island trackage
1929 *January 1:* Frederick E. Williamson becomes Burlington's sixteenth president
    February 14: Burlington Transportation Company incorporated in Illinois
1932 *January 1:* Ralph Budd becomes Burlington's seventeenth president
1934 *November 11:* Burlington's *Zephyr*, first Diesel streamlined train in North America, enters regular service between Kansas City and Lincoln
1935 *April 21:* Zephyr service begins between Chicago and Twin Cities
1936 *May 31:* Zephyr service begins between Chicago and Denver
    October 1: *Sam Houston Zephyr* (Ft. Worth–Houston) inaugurates Diesel-powered service in the Southwest
1937 *April 30:* *General Pershing Zephyr* enters service; nation's first train equipped with disc brakes and fluorescent lighting
1940 *May 28:* Ralph Budd appointed Transportation Commissioner on Advisory Commission to the Council of National Defense
    August 20: *Texas Zephyr* enters service between Denver and Dallas
1945 *July 23:* Nation's first Vista-Dome car enters service on Chicago–Twin Cities run
1946 *June 1:* Burlington Truck Lines replaces Burlington Transportation Company
1949 *March 20:* *California Zephyrs* enter service between Chicago and and San Francisco via CB&Q, D&RGW, WP
    September 1: Harry C. Murphy becomes Burlington's eighteenth president
1952 *October 28:* Kansas City Cut-off opens for service
1956 *October 28:* Nation's first Slumbercoaches enter service on the new *Denver Zephyrs*
1960 *October 21:* New Quincy Bridge opens for traffic
1964 *August 24:* I.C.C. Examiner recommends approval of Great Northern–Northern Pacific–Burlington consolidation

PART I

Forging a System

1849 - 75

CHAPTER 1

Modest Beginnings

1 8 4 9 - 5 2

NEARLY EVERYBODY has one trait in common: an insatiable desire to know about the beginning of things. This is not idle curiosity. There is perfectly good reason for thinking that if we know when, where, how, and particularly why a given project was started, we shall know more about its purpose and why it developed as it did.

This applies to railways as well as to anything else. Today the principal cities connected by the Burlington Lines are Chicago, St. Paul, Minneapolis, Omaha, St. Louis, Kansas City, Denver, Fort Worth, Dallas, and Houston. Yet no one in these places had anything at all to do with the beginning of the Burlington.

• THE AURORA BRANCH •

IN THE LITTLE MILL VILLAGE of Aurora, Illinois, during the winter of 1848–49, a group of determined men decided they wanted a railroad. Their resources were modest and so were their ambitions, but there is no mystery whatever as to what they wanted and why. Chicago, in that long-ago winter, was growing at a phenomenal rate. Already a crossroad for people and produce moving between the Midwest and the East, it was fast becoming a center of the lumber and grain trade, a major distributing point, and something of a magnet for eastern capital. Naturally its businessmen wanted to establish the best transportation possible between the city and

[3]

the potentially rich country to the west. Specifically, the Galena and Chicago Union Railroad had been planned to link the metropolis with the lead mines on the Mississippi River, and in 1848 the first stretch of that railway running westward from Chicago to the Des Plaines River (Maywood) was put in operation; if all went well, it would reach Turner Junction (West Chicago), thirty miles west of the Lake, in the spring of 1849.

To the alert businessmen and city fathers of Aurora and Batavia, neighboring villages located on the Fox River some thirty-eight miles west of Chicago, this was both a threat and a challenge. The rails of the Galena, passing six miles from Batavia, would be near enough to divert the trade and attract the business of surrounding territory and yet too far away for the practical commercial purposes of either river town. It would, of course, be easier to haul produce or to travel the few miles north to the railroad than to spend three days making a round trip by wagon to Chicago. But neither Aurora nor Batavia could hope to compete with the settlements directly on the railroad. The situation called for prompt action.

The first meeting to consider building a railroad north to the Galena Union was held in Batavia late in 1848. Very much in evidence at the gathering was John Van Nortwick, a resident of the town and chief engineer of the Galena. But the obvious focal point for any new scheme was the larger village of Aurora; the Batavia meeting was temporarily adjourned, to reconvene in Aurora on January 27, 1849.

Meanwhile, those most interested in the project were far from idle. On January 25, Lorenzo D. Brady, representative from Kendall County in the Illinois Legislature and a resident of Aurora, introduced a bill in the House to charter the Aurora Branch Railroad Company. Under the terms of Brady's bill, the new company would be authorized to construct a single- or double-track railroad "with such appendages as may be deemed necessary for the convenient use of the same" from Aurora to some suitable point of junction with the Galena and Chicago Union Railroad. Capitalization was fixed at $100,000, with the provision that it might be increased to $1,000,000, and five commissioners were named to accept subscriptions for stock upon a down payment of just $1 a share. When one fourth of the stock was subscribed, a meeting of stockholders could be called for the election of directors who might thereupon "commence the work." The company was given the power to make its own bylaws, rules, and regulations so long as they were not inconsistent with the existing laws and constitutions of Illinois and of the United States. Once the directors were elected, they were to have the power to choose the route, determine "by what force the carriages to be used thereon may be propelled, and the rate of toll for transportation of persons or property thereon as may be deemed suitable to their interests." They could, if they wished, unite with any other railroad company, and they would have the right to construct "such other and lateral routes" as might be necessary to connect with other rail-

[4]

roads.[1] The company was given the right of eminent domain but also had to live up to certain obligations: work on the line had to begin within two years and unless it was completed within five, the privileges granted in the charter were to be forfeited. The company was obligated to repair all public highways, bridges, or water courses that might be injured in the course of construction; on the other hand, anyone who injured the railroad was subject to triple damages and costs. The company could borrow money to the full amount of its capital stock and pledge all its personal and real property as security—provided that the individual stockholders would be liable, to the extent of their stockholdings, for the payment of all debts. Fortunate indeed that neither the Aurora Branch nor any of its successors ever defaulted on an obligation.

On the very day Brady introduced his bill, it gained a second reading and was duly referred to the Committee on Internal Improvements. Thus, when the second railroad meeting convened in Aurora on January 27, 1849, a specific proposal could be laid before the assembled citizenry. They enthusiastically endorsed the project. At Springfield, the railroad bill was reported out of committee unchanged on February 2, passed by the lower House on February 9 by a vote of 58 to 5, and on the following day accepted by the Senate. Two days later, on February 12, 1849, Governor Augustus C. French signed the charter of the Aurora Branch Railroad. At that moment the Burlington came into legal existence.

Granted, the Aurora Branch thus authorized planned to build only a twelve-mile line, and in a north-south direction at that. But it had the essential right to expand and to unite with other companies. Thus, although the original company twice changed its name during its early years and twice merged with other forerunners of the present C.B.&Q., it has enjoyed the longest continuous corporate existence of any member of the Burlington family, and hence is properly regarded as the original ingredient of the present system.[2]

No one, in 1849, could have foreseen the outcome, but then, few people could have foreseen that the Midwest, just at that moment, was poised at the threshold of a new era. Railroads, of course, were nothing new to the nation. They had been operating for nearly two decades in the East, but it had taken time for them to overcome the tremendous barrier of the Appalachian Mountains and approach the vast Mississippi Valley basin. Railway expansion into this potentially rich Promised Land depended on the resolution of one basic dilemma: the capital necessary for construction would not be forthcoming until it was reasonably certain that the proposed lines could succeed financially; on the other hand, railroads them-

[1] *DH*, Vol. I, pp. 11–14.

[2] The Hannibal and St. Joseph's Railroad was incorporated in 1847, and its name altered to Hannibal and St. Joseph Railroad in 1852, but it did not come under Burlington control until 1854, and was owned by other interests from 1871 to 1883.

selves were the only practical means of bringing in enough potential shippers and travelers to make them pay. Unless the Middle West was willing to wait until the established eastern network moved forward step by step, the only solution would lie in some plan for financing lines in advance of population. As early as 1837, the Illinois Legislature—unwilling to wait—had enacted an ambitious internal improvement bill that contemplated no less than 1,342 miles of railway for the state. Indiana and Michigan adopted similar programs, and the latter actually undertook to build the future Michigan Central and Michigan Southern, stretching westward from Detroit and from Monroe, respectively. Yet these and many other early western schemes, such as Asa Whitney's plan of 1845 to build from Lake Superior to Puget Sound, were premature. As yet there were simply not enough people nearby to justify any of these schemes.

In what Bernard De Voto terms "The Year of Decision"—1846—however, a chain of events began which radically altered the situation. The acquisition of Oregon and the outbreak of the Mexican War in that year, the Mexican Cession in 1848, and the discovery of gold in California shortly afterwards, brought hordes of vigorous people streaming into and through the Midwest. In 1848 Illinois already ranked first in the nation in production of grain, the Chicago Board of Trade was established, and the Illinois–Michigan Canal was finally completed between Chicago and La Salle, enhancing Chicago's rapidly growing importance as a natural crossroad for trade between the Great Lakes and the Illinois and Mississippi rivers on the one hand, and between the Northwest and the area east of Lake Michigan on the other.

More directly pertinent to Chicago's future as a rail center were the developments taking place in Michigan, where eastern capitalists had shouldered the task of completing the two roads the state had pushed part way across its southern counties. When the Aurora Branch acquired its charter, in February 1849, the Michigan Central had nearly completed its line from Detroit to New Buffalo on the eastern shore of Lake Michigan and had already put into service a fast steamer between Detroit and Buffalo. By the spring of that year, the railway was finished and ferry service was established to Chicago, thus providing a through route by rail and water to the East. Meanwhile, the Michigan Southern, having procured a charter to cross Indiana, was busily at work on the all-rail line between Chicago and Toledo, with steamer connections east.

Thus in the opening months of 1849 Chicago's prospects as a railway center were bright indeed. Completion of the Aurora Branch would connect Aurora and Batavia not only with Chicago, but with the entire East as well. Under these conditions, there certainly should be plenty of business to carry.

Hopes ran high as the commissioners of the Aurora Branch set out to secure stock subscriptions. So fast did they work that by February 21, 1849, over a quarter of the total issue had been subscribed, and the first board of five men was duly elected to office. The next day formal organization took place. Stephen F. Gale, already a well-known figure in Chicago and a land-owner in Aurora, was elected president, thereby attaining the distinction of becoming the Burlington's first chief executive. T. A. Hall was named secretary-treasurer, and J. L. Hanchett surveyor. Compensation for the corporate officers was passed over in silence, but in respect to the all-important surveyor, notation was made that his salary was to be fixed later. His duties, if not his recompense, were clear: the first resolution of the board authorized him to acquire a right of way and to secure lands for a western terminus at Aurora.

A second resolution directed President Gale to confer with the Galena and Chicago Union to see "upon what terms this company can unite with them."[3] The overtures of President Gale to the larger road were, however, unavailing. By what may well have been the narrowest of margins—perhaps a vote or two on the Galena board—the Aurora Branch was left to work out its own destiny and to sire, all in good time, the Burlington. This may not have been the first, and it was certainly not the last, time that the future of a mighty system hung on the outcome of a single decision.

Meanwhile, and probably quite oblivious to the inscrutable workings of corporate diplomacy, Hanchett was out in the field, busily earning the pay promised him. When the directors of the Aurora Branch met again on October 22, 1849, he was able to put before them two completed surveys; they promptly chose his line B by way of Batavia to a junction with the Galena. Provided that sufficient hard cash was forthcoming from the stock subscriptions, the board further determined to build a bridge across the Fox River and, in order to afford "ample facilities" for doing business on the east bank, to construct one or more sidetracks, together with freight and passenger buildings "of sufficient capacity to accommodate whatever amount of business may be offered." A passenger depot was authorized for Batavia, and in appreciation of Hanchett's services, the directors promoted him to the more dignified position of chief engineer.[4]

These plans were all very well, but they would require cash. A fortnight later, therefore, the board informed subscribers that twenty-five percent of their subscription would become due in five equal monthly installments beginning January 1, 1850. At the same time they announced that they would receive proposals for grading. On December 20 the work was officially awarded to four contractors at costs varying from thirteen to sixteen cents a cubic yard.

These expanding activities of the baby road obviously required more supervision than either the president or the individual members of the board could give. On December 21, 1849, therefore, three directors—

[3] AB, ORB, Vol. I, p. 1.
[4] Ibid., p. 3.

Hackney, Hoyt, and Plum—were named as an executive committee. Necessity thus created an administrative device that remains to this day an essential and effective link between the line organization and the policy-making board. The next step, taken at the annual stockholders' meeting on February 21, 1850, was to enlarge the board to nine men. In addition to Gale, Hackney, and Hoyt, who were re-elected, the stockholders named Lorenzo D. Brady, who had secured the charter; John Frink, proprietor of several prosperous stage lines radiating westward from Chicago; Elisha Wadsworth, a successful Chicago merchant; John Van Nortwick, chief engineer of the Galena road and possibly the moving spirit behind the Aurora Branch; and Allen Robbins, a New York banker. Although Robbins was the first representative of eastern financial interests to enter the directorate, no evidence suggests that he attracted funds for the company. Gale was re-elected president.

The two most pressing tasks before the new board were to secure rails, ties, and rolling stock, and to find enough money or credit to pay for them. Even as they grappled with these problems, however, they took time at their meeting of March 26, 1850, to go on record in favor of expansion "to the most feasible point on the Illinois River, as soon as practicable."[5] How soon that would be would depend, of course, on the speed with which the first twelve miles could be put into operation. Fortunately, extremely generous terms from the Buffalo and Niagara Falls Railroad enabled the Aurora Branch to obtain discarded, obsolescent strap iron, Norway pine rails on which to fasten it, and a twelve-ton locomotive. The need to pay for all this led the company to issue its first mortgage of $45,000, payable in five years at seven percent. When these bonds were all sold—largely in upper New York State—enough was left over to pay for a second-hand passenger coach and a few freight cars.

Thereupon unexpected difficulties arose from quite a different source. On May 1, 1850, some fifty men working on the roadbed struck, demanding that their existing rate of seventy-five cents a day be increased by a "shilling." Just how this first strike was settled is a mystery, but apparently it was short-lived, for on August 1 grading on the final section into Aurora was underway. By August 22 the rails were already as far south as Batavia, providing an excuse for running a special train, evidently sponsored by the Aurora Branch but operated by the Galena Road, to the end of the track and back again. Technically this was the first time that any train ran over Burlington rails, though commencement of operations is generally reckoned from the inauguration of the first regularly scheduled service.

That notable event was advertised in advance for September 2, 1850. As neither the engine nor the cars purchased by the company in the East had yet arrived, it was necessary to borrow the old "Pioneer" and a single coach from the friendly Galena for the occasion. These, then, constituted

5 Ibid., p. 10.

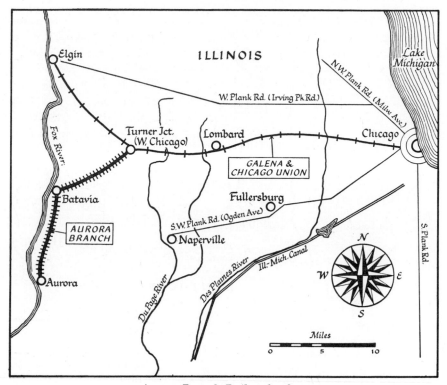

Aurora Branch Railroad, 1850

the train that left Batavia at 6:30 in the morning on September 2 to inaugurate regular service on the Aurora Branch and, as it turned out, on the
Burlington system.

Events now moved rapidly. On October 4 the rails reached Aurora;
three days later the locomotive "Whittlesey" arrived in Chicago by vessel.
Shortly thereafter, another locomotive, the fourteen-ton "Pigeon"—originally built for the Michigan Central in 1837—was added to the roster.
Where the first cars came from is less clear; perhaps they were borrowed or
came along with the "Whittlesey." In any event, on October 21, 1850, the
Aurora Branch Railroad, having secured trackage rights over the Galena,
inaugurated regular through service between Aurora and Chicago. This was
the schedule:

Lv. Aurora   7 a.m. and 3 p.m.   Lv. Chicago   8 a.m. and 3 p.m.
Arr. Chicago   11 a.m. and 6 p.m. Arr. Aurora   10 a.m. and 6 p.m.

In Chicago, the Aurora Branch shared the Galena's wooden depot at
Kinzie and Canal streets. It was 150 feet long and 50 feet wide and served
as freight house and office as well. In Aurora, trains used a temporary
structure north of Indian Creek near Pearce Street.

Midwestern Railroads, 1850

In view of the fact that the motive power and equipment of the Aurora Branch was all second or third hand, and that it had to run over strap rails—wooden beams with a strip of iron bolted along the top—these schedules represented commendably high-speed service for the day. A Chicago merchant or an Aurora farmer could leave his home after breakfast, spend several hours doing business at the other end of the line, and be home in time for supper. Compared with the three days normally required to make the round trip by stage or wagon, this constituted a veritable revolution in daily living. It is worth noting, too, that the line was completed in a little over twenty months after the charter date, more than three years ahead of schedule, and, in fact, before the latest date set by the charter for the beginning of construction. Since the work had been carried through from start to finish by homespun talent and initiative, the people of Aurora and Batavia had good cause to be proud of their achievement.

Chicago too could look upon the year 1850 as one of fulfillment. The trains of the Galena had been running through to Elgin, forty-two miles west of the city, since January 22. Then on October 30, nine days after the Aurora Branch opened regular service, the Michigan Central completed its rails from New Buffalo, the original western terminus on the lake, to Michigan City thus indicating its intention to replace the cross-lake ferry

[10]

service with a direct rail line into Chicago; in fact, it was already building its link in Indiana. Meanwhile the Michigan Southern, proceeding slowly but steadily, reached Coldwater, Michigan, in December.

In the face of these stirring events, the promoters of the Aurora Branch could hardly afford to sit still unless they wished to remain nothing more than a purely local tap line. Certainly now railroads would be built the length and breadth of Illinois, and if the Aurora Branch was to participate, it would have either to grow or to become part of a larger system. At the same time, it had to complete the facilities on its own line and establish local policies; to this task the directors turned their immediate attention.

The first order of business, carried out in the winter of 1850–51, was to gather in subscriptions on the stock. This the company accomplished by offering interest in the form of additional stock on cash promptly paid. Furthermore, now that the line was in operation, Hanchett was paid off in stock and given an assistant, and the treasurer was finally given $500 for his labors. Meanwhile, directors Gale and Wadsworth were authorized to borrow enough to meet "present liabilities." One of these, and the first of its kind on record, was the claim presented to the board by one Alvah Fuller "for damages done to his buggy in transporting the same from Chicago to Aurora." Solemnly the board agreed that the matter might be settled by an allowance of not more than $5. The question of rates had to be decided too, so Hall and Van Nortwick drew up a "tariff of prices" for the transportation of persons and property. At the same time they issued detailed instructions as to who might ride free on the railroad. The officers, federal mail agents, and, interestingly enough, the proprietors or agents of the Illinois Stage Company were to enjoy unrestricted free transportation. Station agents, clerks, engine men, and track superintendents could ride free when on company business; conductors were allowed to pass their immediate families "when accompanied by themselves."[6] Other employees could obtain single-trip passes from the station agent; casual laborers could ride for nothing when accompanied by their foremen if they traveled on freight or accommodation cars.

Important as these local matters were, however, the major concern was the relation of the Aurora Branch to surrounding railroads, both projected and built. When the stockholders met for their third annual meeting, on February 21, 1851, this question was obviously uppermost in their minds— and small wonder. During the preceding three weeks the legislature in Springfield had passed twenty-eight bills either chartering or amending charters of railways within the state. Among these, two were of immediate importance to the Aurora Branch.

In 1848 the state had chartered the Rock Island and La Salle Railroad to connect the Mississippi River with the western terminus of the Illinois–

---

[6] Ibid., pp. 17–18.

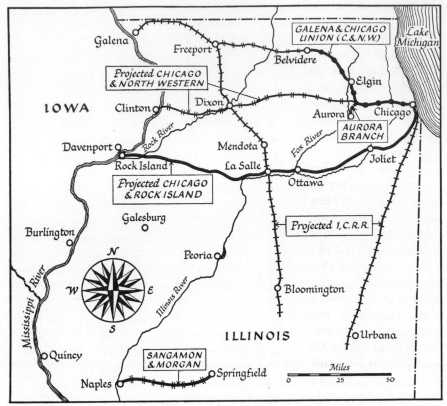

Illinois Railroads, built and projected, 1851

Michigan Canal. On February 7, 1851, this company was transformed into the Chicago and Rock Island Railroad, with authority to build between the cities designated in its title. Significantly, this amendment was sponsored by two directors of the Michigan Southern, Henry Farnum and Joseph Sheffield, who had invested in the Illinois road and were convinced that a cross-state line to Rock Island would afford a superb traffic outlet for their Michigan Southern, once it reached Chicago. Three days later, on February 10, 1851, the legislature incorporated the Illinois Central, with authority to build a Y-shaped line from Cairo to Galena, with a branch from Centralia to Chicago. Significantly, this charter was granted to a group closely affiliated with the Michigan Central. Thus it was fairly apparent to the Aurora Branch that a system of east-west alliances was in the making which might leave their little, twelve-mile branch stranded. More than ever, the Aurora felt it necessary either to ally itself with the neighboring Galena or to expand toward one of the other newly authorized systems.

Under the circumstances, the Aurora's stockholders instructed their directors to take immediate action to secure a connection either with the Cairo–Galena line of the recently chartered Illinois Central or with the Rock Island and La Salle. Accordingly, after the directors had convened and elected Elisha Wadsworth as the company's second president, they promptly told him and his predecessor Gale to negotiate once more with the Galena and Chicago Union "or any other company or companies" for the purpose of uniting or consolidating with them, or for making "any other arrangements" for the extension of the Aurora Branch.[7] For the moment the motto of the little road seemed to be: "Consolidate, expand, or die."

As the Aurora Branch had no intention of dying, the question was simply where to expand or with whom to merge. But to rush into either course would have been folly. The air was literally thick with proposed new railroads, both large and small. Until the situation crystallized further, the Aurora Branch, quite sensibly, busied itself with tasks closer to home, jobs that, in the interest of efficient operation, had to be done anyway.

In December 1851, a comprehensive long-term agreement was concluded with the strategic Galena Union. The Aurora could operate its equipment and crews into Chicago, but they had to follow the Galena's rules while on its property. Interline rates to and from points on the Aurora's own line were to be the same as those for similar distances west of the junction on the Galena. The Aurora retained, of course, all revenues earned on its own rails, but agreed to pay the Galena seventy percent of the earnings on business between the Junction and Chicago so long as that road supplied fuel and water; if and when the Aurora should build its own fuel and water facilities in the city, revenues over the joint line would be split evenly. The Aurora retained the right to provide its own depot in Chicago within a year, or thereafter on two years' notice. All these arrangements went into effect on January 1, 1852, and were to last for thirty-six years. The contracting parties provided that any differences of interpretation of the agreement should be subject to binding arbitration.

The Aurora made another, and no less important, deal with the Galena. As of January 30, 1852, it leased in perpetuity, and in return for one dollar annually, the Galena's right to build a lateral branch from the Junction to a connection with the main line of the Illinois Central. Why the Galena parted with its right for such a nominal sum is something of a mystery. Perhaps it expected to cross the Illinois Central farther west anyway, and foresaw that if anyone else built a branch, it would benefit by the additional bridge traffic at no further effort or expense. The purpose of the Aurora people is clear enough: in July 1851, they had authorized surveys to the Illinois Central at Peru, La Salle, or "such point north as expedient," and by the time the lease was negotiated with the Galena, they were ac-

[7] Ibid., p. 21.

tively purchasing rights of way.[8] To gain control in a territory they hoped to occupy themselves obviously made good sense.

Meanwhile, the ever present need for money was becoming more acute. In July 1851, the capital stock of the Aurora Branch was increased to $600,000, and the board, meeting for the first time in Chicago, issued a strong hint to the metropolis by resolving that "the City of Chicago has a deep interest in the completion of this road, and that subscriptions should be made commensurate with the advantages to be derived by same."[9] During the winter of 1851–52, the company did its best to collect cash due on stock subscriptions and, even at that early day, named a committee of the board to arrange for adjustment of taxes laid by the towns of Batavia and Winfield.

The sticking point, of course, was money. But as the annual stockholders' meeting of February 1852 approached, there was one strong ray of hope: the powerful eastern group that was building the Michigan Central around the foot of the lake and into Chicago had started to buy fairly substantial blocks of the company's securities during the winter. If this investment meant that the Aurora Branch was to be developed as a feeder for the big eastern road, then the capital stock that had been increased to finance the extension might soon be subscribed and the little road could take a new lease on life.

Just what were the Michigan Central's intentions? The answer lay not only in the value of the Aurora Branch, but also in the somewhat more nebulous prospects of no less than five more budding roads—three in Illinois and one each in Missouri and Iowa—which might conceivably be added to the Aurora Branch to form a system worthy of strong support. Just where were these other roads and how did they fit into the picture?

[8] Ibid., pp. 22, 26.
[9] Ibid., p. 23.

CHAPTER 2

Grass Roots

1849-52

· THE NORTHERN CROSS ·

BACK IN 1837, when the State of Illinois embarked on its ambitious internal improvement plan, it had chartered, among others, a Northern Cross Railroad and had appropriated over $10,000,000 to build it from Quincy on the Mississippi River through Meredosia, Jacksonville, and Springfield, and on to the Indiana state line. Work had commenced at Meredosia in 1837, and in the next year a tiny engine ran over a few miles of rail east of the town. Even though the line was extended to Springfield in 1842, the entire project was premature and failed utterly; mules replaced steam power, and eventually the dilapidated road was sold for a mere pittance to what later became the Wabash.

Some grading had been done between Meredosia and Quincy, however, and on February 10, 1849, citizens of Quincy obtained a charter to build a railroad from their town to a point on the Illinois River opposite Meredosia. With the charter went the privilege of buying the right of way and using the old name, Northern Cross. During 1850, additional work was done on the western portion of the line, and on February 1, 1851, the directors obtained permission from the legislature to construct a lateral branch northeastward to terminate at or near the southern terminus of the Illinois and Michigan Canal, provided that this branch should not run east of Knoxville. In practical terms this meant that the line stretching north-

east from Quincy would certainly go through, and possibly end at, Knoxville. The reason for this proviso lay in the ambitions of still another
embryo company destined, like the Northern Cross, to form one segment
of the C. B. &. Q.

• The Peoria and Oquawka •

By pure coincidence, the State of Illinois on the date of the Aurora
Branch incorporation, February 12, 1849, chartered the Peoria and
Oquawka Railroad. This company with such a difficult name was authorized to build a line from Peoria on the Illinois River to Oquawka, a small
village on the east bank of the Mississippi about nine miles north of
Burlington, Iowa. During the fall of 1849, enthusiasm along the route
reached a peak, and large gatherings were held at both Knoxville and
Galesburg to pledge financial support. During 1850, however, a feud broke
out between Galesburg and Knoxville as to which should be on the line.
Chauncey S. Colton, a leading merchant and citizen of Galesburg, approached the P. & O. directors with an offer to subscribe to no less than
$20,000 worth of their stock if they would build through his town. But
his overture proved fruitless, and on February 10, 1851, the citizens of
Knoxville secured an amendment to the P. & O. charter, fixing the location
of the line through Farmington, Knoxville, and Monmouth, but excluding
Galesburg. On the very same day another amendment permitted the company to build a branch west of Monmouth to a point on the Mississippi
River at or near Shokokon, directly opposite Burlington.

This second amendment provoked a lively scrap between the citizens
of Burlington, who insisted that the newly authorized branch should become the main line (as it subsequently did), and the citizens of Oquawka,
who took precisely the opposite view. But this rivalry was overshadowed by
the struggle between Knoxville and Galesburg. If, as now seemed certain,
both the Northern Cross and the Peoria and Oquawka were built to Knoxville as planned, the result would be a Y-shaped system beginning at Peoria
and forking at Knoxville, whence the two prongs of the Y would reach the
Mississippi opposite Burlington and at Quincy. This would leave Galesburg without a railroad.

• The Central Military Tract •

Faced with the prospect of being stranded, the enterprising citizens of
Galesburg promptly decided to build their own railroad. On February 15,
1851, they secured a charter for the Central Military Tract Railroad Company, which was authorized to build northeast from Galesburg to a connection with the Rock Island, presumably at or near La Salle. With the
hope that the Northern Cross might eventually be persuaded to build its

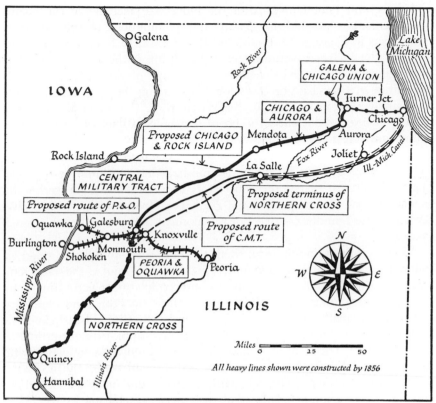

Evolution of the C. B. & Q. in Illinois, 1850–56

line to Galesburg rather than Knoxville, the Military Tract incorporators thoughtfully obtained permission to attach themselves to and form a part of the Northern Cross Railroad Company if that should prove feasible.

The sponsors of the Central Military Tract set to work at once with enormous energy to comb the country for stock subscriptions. As in a community chest fund, each director was given a section of the country to cover. The officers not only journeyed to Chicago to attend a meeting of the Rock Island directors, but also sent off a letter to that company's distinguished engineer, William Jervis, asking him whom they might hire to survey the road. Before long, two surveys were made as far eastward as Pilot Grove, and one on a line northeast from that point. The directors resolved in August 1851 to make definite locations on the northern portion and to "have the whole ready for a basis on which a contract can be made with some capitalist in aiding us in building said road."[1] This reference to capitalists made it clear that the company hoped to obtain outside aid, and indeed the hope must have been strong, for in September the engineer was instructed to begin locating the western portion of the line also, between

[1] CMT, ORB, p. 13.

[1 7]

Galesburg and Pilot Grove. After the November meeting of the board, advertisements asking bids for grading and masonry were bravely placed in newspapers in Chicago, St. Louis, and Buffalo.

But the financial picture grew dark. Although the company printed the engineer's and directors' reports in the hope of gaining new support, and authorized purchase of lands for depots along the way, cash was discouragingly slow in coming in. By March 1852, the financial crisis had come to a head. Reluctantly the board suspended all activities, and some of the contractors already hired were frankly told that the company would not pay much "until after the next harvest." The directors said they hoped to borrow $50,000 from Knox County and half that sum from neighboring Henry County, so that if the contractors wanted to continue work with "a small force," the company would gladly pay for it, together with twelve percent interest, in due course.[2] For the moment, however, all work ground to a stop.

In the early spring of 1852, then, the tally sheet for Illinois stood as follows: aside from some preliminary work near Quincy, the Northern Cross had done nothing but obtain a charter amendment permitting it to build northeast toward the vicinity of La Salle. The Peoria and Oquawka had started a small amount of grading toward Edwards, and early in 1852 had let contracts for building east from the Mississippi. Precious little else had been done. The Central Military Tract had been far more active with its surveying activities, but no more successful in attracting the necessary funds. Only the Aurora Branch, with twelve miles in actual operation and the encouraging knowledge that easterners were buying its securities, seemed in a position to go anywhere.

But what of the situation across the wide Mississippi? At the half-century mark, southern Iowa and northern Missouri, lying athwart the natural "Gulfstream of Migration" to the Great West, were already reasonably well populated. As might have been expected as a result of the reliance on river transport, the principal towns were at the eastern and western extremities of the belt; Burlington and Hannibal on the Mississippi, Council Bluffs and St. Joseph on the Missouri. Overland travel between them was so difficult that virtually all commercial intercourse followed the slow, roundabout water route. But by 1852 prominent citizens of the parallel belts in both states had formed railway companies to connect the Mississippi and Missouri and were exerting continuous pressure on Congress for land grants to aid their respective projects. These homespun enterprises were ineffective and poor at the moment, but it was inevitable that before long someone would build railroads to bridge the gap between the mighty river highways at each end of the territory.

[2] Ibid., p. 35.

• THE HANNIBAL AND ST. JOSEPH •

IN ONE SENSE the colorful Hannibal and St. Joseph, built to link the cities of its title, antedated the Aurora Branch, for it was chartered by a special act of the Missouri Legislature approved on February 16, 1847. Unlike the Illinois company, however, it was not even organized for almost four years, and therefore must forfeit any claim to being the oldest continuously functioning segment of the present Burlington. Yet the years preceding January 8, 1851, when the stockholders finally got around to electing officers, were not wasted in idleness. As early as 1846, leading citizens of Hannibal and St. Joseph began mobilizing opinion favorable to the project. The "champion and father" of the railroad, however, was without doubt Colonel R. N. Stewart, later governor of Missouri. He organized a preliminary survey of the route in 1849, defraying expenses by soliciting the necessary funds from the counties and from a number of individuals along the way. He found, as everyone expected, that construction over the gently rolling countryside presented no particular engineering difficulties; the principal problem was the lack of local capital and the hesitancy of eastern investors to put money into a railroad that would serve a still rather sparsely populated territory. Here again was the ever present dilemma of the West: without a substantial population in its territory willing and able to ship and travel, no railroad could survive as a business venture, but only a railroad could bring about a rapid development of the area. Where and how could the necessary credit be obtained?

A precedent-breaking action of Congress in September 1850 laid the basis for a possible solution. On the twentieth of that month, President Fillmore signed a bill granting more than two million acres of public domain to the State of Illinois for the purpose of aiding in the construction of a line north and south throughout the length of the state, the Illinois Central. Since 1822, Congress had aided turnpike and canal companies in sparsely settled portions of the country by offering them federal lands as an inducement to build the desired facilities. The procedure, as eventually established after some experimentation, was to grant alternate sections (each section being one square mile, containing 640 acres) for a limited number of miles on each side of the projected improvement. In the case of these early grants, and throughout the 1850's, lands were certified to the states for eventual transfer to the carriers after the facilities had been constructed. Later on, grants were made directly to the corporations. In either case, as soon as the formalities of certification were completed, the granted area could be sold or mortgaged by the company that was the eventual beneficiary, and the proceeds could be devoted to actual construction. Meanwhile, the United States doubled the usual price of $1.25 an acre on

[1 9]

the alternate sections it retained within the lateral limits of any grant, thus emerging from the deal without any loss to the Treasury. Furthermore, the United States retained the right to transport mail, troops, and government property over these facilities without charge or, as the grants were later construed, at reduced rates.

Until 1850 all such grants for transportation purposes had been to highways or canals, each having received about 3,500,000 acres up to that time. It was eminently logical, therefore, that similar aid should be extended to railroads. But despite repeated attempts to do so during the 1840's, the vagaries of sectional politics and strong doubts as to the constitutionality of such grants conspired to delay favorable action. A bill granting lands to the Hannibal and St. Joseph passed the Senate early in 1850, but died in the House. Not until the persistent Senator Stephen A. Douglas finally mustered the necessary votes for his Illinois Central grant in September was the ice finally broken.

News of this auspicious event spread like wildfire in northern Missouri, and each county along the route was urged to send representatives to a railroad convention called for October 7 at St. Joseph. There, stirred by the speeches of Colonel Stewart and others, those present resolved to make still greater efforts to secure stock subscriptions from counties and individuals along the line, "the great object being to convince Congress, in giving the land, that the people were in earnest about the railroad, and were willing to put their shoulders to the wheel, according to their strength."[3]

Despite this commendable local disposition to help as much as possible, and the subsequent pledging of several hundred thousand dollars, Congress refused to approve any railway land grants whatever during the rest of 1850 or in 1851. Undismayed, the Hannibal and St. Joseph completed its surveys at the eastern end of the line in November 1851, and in the next month undertook surveys eastward from St. Joseph. Work continued throughout the winter. On June 10, 1852, Congress, as if trying to help those who helped themselves, finally authorized the Hannibal and St. Joseph's long-sought land grant.

According to the Act, the State of Missouri was to receive every alternate section of public domain in checkerboard fashion for six miles on each side of the track. When the company should have completed a specified length of track according to proper standards, the State of Missouri was authorized to transfer the granted lands to the railroad; if a section that would ordinarily accrue to the railroad was occupied or held under some prior land act, then the company was permitted to select an equivalent acreage from a "lieu land" strip running between six and fifteen miles from the roadbed. If the quota could not be filled in this way, the railroad

[3] *Macon Weekly Argus*, February 5, 1868.

had no further claims. In return for obtaining such land as was available, the company was bound by the Act to carry the mails "at such price as Congress may by law direct," and to transport troops and government property free of charge.[4] The latter obligation remained unchanged for this particular road until 1862.

Despite the provision for the special handling of government business, the potential revenue definitely in sight for the Hannibal and St. Joseph from the sale of the land grant—which eventually amounted to some 600,000 acres—was an attractive inducement indeed for the additional eastern capital that would surely be necessary to start the project. Thus matters stood in Missouri in the late spring of 1852. What about Iowa?

• THE BURLINGTON AND MISSOURI RIVER •

IT MIGHT BE SAID without too much exaggeration that both the location and the name of the Burlington Route across Iowa owe their origin to the combined but unwitting efforts of generations of Indians on the one hand and of a nostalgic Vermonter on the other. As transportation engineers, the red men had no peers. When they had a journey to make athwart the prevailing direction of navigable streams, they unerringly located trails along the easiest grades and the most direct routes. The pathway they trod across southern Iowa between the great rivers was well established as the most feasible east-west route in the region long before the Black Hawk Purchase of 1833 threw open the eastern portion of this farmers' paradise to the white men.

Within a year after that event, a restless Vermonter named John B. Gray laid down his pack in a bustling new outpost on the west bank of the Mississippi. Perhaps the rippling waters at his feet and the steep bluffs at his back reminded him of the broad expanse of Lake Champlain and the crouching flanks of the Green Mountains he knew so well. He christened the rude settlement Burlington. The name stuck, not merely to the city, but also to the westward trail that began there and, all in good time, to the mighty railroad system that built where the Indians had trod.

The origins and development of the Burlington in Iowa during the years preceding the Civil War resemble in so many respects the story of the Hannibal and St. Joseph that both experiences can be regarded as part of a larger pattern, some of it applicable to very nearly all midwestern roads of the 1850's. Both companies applied for land grants at approximately the same time and with the same arguments, though the Hannibal enjoyed a much earlier reward for its efforts. Each railroad thought of itself from the beginning as a link between the eastern network and the inevitable Pacific road. Neither was able to make real progress until eastern

---

[4] Act of June 10, 1852, Sections 4 and 6, in *DH*, Vol. II, p. 810.

capital and a federal land grant supplemented the slender financial resources of the frontier regions it served.

In 1838, only five years after the Black Hawk Purchase, the territorial
legislature authorized surveyors to locate a highway westward from Burlington. Mount Pleasant and New London were already in existence, and the
need of the farmers for adequate roads was pressing. The highway was built
promptly enough, but its usefulness, like that of all dirt roads, depended
on the whims of the weather; before long a clamor arose for an all-weather
plank road. When, in February 1848, public sentiment was fully and
favorably crystallized, the Burlington and Mount Pleasant Plank Road
Company was organized.

William F. Coolbaugh, successful banker and merchant of Burlington, sparked this move. Early in 1849 the General Assembly of the newly
admitted State of Iowa granted him and his associates the right to condemn land for their purposes, build a good and proper road, and charge
tolls thereon. The agreeableness of the Legislature was in no small part
owing to the industrious promotion of one James W. Grimes, another
Burlingtonian, whose commercial and legal successes in his home town had
earned him a seat in the Assembly. Coolbaugh and Grimes were destined
for key roles in the railroad project that then lay just beyond the horizon.

Money, as always, was slow coming in, but finally, in December 1851,
the last white-oak planks were spiked into place, and the twenty-eight-mile
highway, with toll gates every four miles, was open for business over its
entire length. Yet on December 18, the very day that the proud citizens
met at Mount Pleasant to celebrate this event, they resolved, among other
things, that "while we regard our plank roads as emphatically the farmer's
highways to market and prosperity, yet we ardently look for the time when
the Mississippi shall be connected with the Missouri by railway, thus facili-
tating communication between remote points and constituting a part of
the railroad to the Pacific Ocean through southern Iowa."[5] Still another
resolution stated that a railway along the route of the plank road would
traverse the most populous section of the state and form a most logical
westward extension of the "Peoria and Burlington Railway," as the Peoria
and Oquawka was colloquially called. To hasten the day when this improvement would become a reality, those assembled solemnly resolved to
memorialize Congress for a federal land grant to aid in the construction
of such a line.

What worried the people at Mount Pleasant in the winter of 1851
was the fact that the newly organized Davenport and Iowa City had already surveyed its route and was getting ready to build; it would form a
logical and direct extension of the Chicago and Rock Island, which had
begun construction in Illinois some three months earlier. Like the citizens

[5] *Burlington Daily Telegraph*, December 22, 1851.

of Aurora and Galesburg before them, the people of southeastern Iowa knew that their destiny depended on a through railway of their own. To be bypassed would mean economic and social death; to be satisfied with a branch line would invite stagnation.

Consequently, on January 7, 1852, Grimes called a meeting at Burlington to transmit advice from Washington as to how to apply for a land grant; five days later, a large and enthusiastic gathering not only re-enacted the Mount Pleasant resolution seeking federal aid, but also appointed a committee of five to prepare articles of incorporation for the Burlington and Missouri River Railroad. The men chosen for this task represented the keenest business and legal talent of the area. Charles Mason, West Point graduate, had served as chief justice of Iowa during its territorial days; his younger colleagues, David Rorer and Jonathan C. Hall, had made their marks as rising attorneys. Coolbaugh, as merchant, banker, and chief incorporator of the plank road to Mount Pleasant, had showed a rare and welcome gift for raising money.

The articles "made and entered into" on January 15, 1852, forthrightly stated that the object of the "incorporation" was "to construct and use a railroad extending from Burlington to the most eligible point on the Missouri River; and along the most eligible routes." Of necessity both the western terminal and the precise route were left vague, for no survey had been made. Actually, leaving these points undecided had its advantages, for, within reasonable limits, the line could then be run through those communities willing to make the most substantial stock subscriptions or offer other tangible inducements. Logically enough, the "name and style" of the enterprise was to be "The Burlington and Missouri River Rail Road Company."[6] Its capitalization was fixed at three million dollars, with the proviso that liabilities should not exceed two million. The directors could require cash installments on stock subscriptions, but lest potential investors be scared away, they could not ask for more than twenty-five percent in any one year.

The incorporators, looking forward to the day when Congress would grant to the state federal lands specifically earmarked to aid their project, authorized the directors to make any arrangements that might be suitable and proper with the Iowa authorities to secure the benefit of such lands. The incorporators were to choose the first board of directors, and any or all of the articles of incorporation could be changed either by the unanimous consent of the directors or by a simple majority vote of the stockholders.

On January 17 the incorporators named the first board of nine directors, who promptly chose William F. Coolbaugh as first president. His first act was to "appoint a committee of three to call upon James W. Grimes,

[6] Act of Incorporation, The Burlington and Missouri River Rail Road Company, in *DH*, Vol. II, p. 5. (Name changed to Burlington and Missouri River Railroad Company in 1872.)

Esquire, and inform him of his appointment to go to Washington to use his influence to secure an appropriation of lands for the benefit of this company." The directors had no funds to finance such a trip, but the committee was "instructed to call upon the City Council to make an appropriation to defray his [Grimes's] expenses in a sum not to exceed $500."[7] Possibly the city's willingness to help out had been arranged in advance. At any rate, Coolbaugh had no difficulty in obtaining in city scrip the sum requested; the fact that it was worth only eighty cents on the dollar in no way minimized the significance of this early example of community cooperation.

Having put the wheels in motion for securing the indispensable aid of federal lands, the directors called the stockholders together on February 5. They ordered a survey of the first thirty miles made at the earliest practicable period, and a committee of ten was named to attend an Ottumwa convention scheduled for the end of the week. All told, delegates from fourteen counties converged at the bustling settlement on the Des Moines River, and once more a series of enthusiastic resolutions was passed supporting the railroad and pledging local aid even if help from Congress should not be forthcoming. Once again specific reference was made to the feasibility of an eventual connection with the "Peoria and Burlington" and thence with the Central Military Tract and Chicago.

As in Illinois and Missouri, the eager Iowans along the future Burlington Route were aflame with railroad fever in that hopeful spring of 1852. Yet all of these enthusiasts lacked one essential ingredient: adequate capital. That, in practical terms, meant eastern dollars. Would the men behind the Michigan Central, or perhaps some other groups, rise to the occasion?

[7] BMI, ORB, p. 4.

CHAPTER 3

Eastern Dollars

1 8 5 1 - 5 3

To ANYONE looking back with the 20/20 vision of hindsight, it
would seem inevitable that in the spring of 1852 the men in
charge of the Michigan Central should, without question, have
committed their funds and energy to piecing together the scattered railway
enterprises west of Chicago destined to form the Burlington system. After
all, for more than a year they had been furiously engaged in a neck-and-
neck race with the Michigan Southern to reach Chicago, and they knew
that their doughty rivals had already secured a firm working alliance with
the Chicago and Rock Island, which, ever since October 1851, had been
under construction toward the Mississippi. Why, then, hesitate? If a western outlet was essential, obviously not a moment was to be lost.

To the men on the spot, however, matters were not quite so simple.
True enough, in the winter of 1851-52 they had bought some securities of
the tiny north-south Aurora Branch, which hardly looked like a thoroughfare to the Great West. Its most valuable assets, apart from the fact that it
was actually running, were its long-term contract with the Galena assuring
entry to Chicago and its authority to extend westward. And what lay beyond? In Illinois, three destitute companies that as yet had not even agreed
upon a common junction point. West of the Mississippi, both the Hannibal and St. Joseph and the Burlington and Missouri River looked promising enough, but what good would they be unless they could be reached
over a unified Illinois system? Without question, imagination, energy, and

money would be required to translate these possibilities into reality. Did anything in the early history of the Michigan Central suggest that its promoters and builders could rise to the challenge?

Originally chartered in 1831, the Detroit and St. Joseph had been taken over in 1837 by the State of Michigan as part of an elaborate scheme to build no less than three cross-state lines. Renamed the Michigan Central, it was gradually pushed westward until, in January 1846, it reached Kalamazoo, 145 miles west of Detroit. Had this been the only railroad sponsored by the state, it might possibly have succeeded, for from the start it attracted a generous amount of traffic. But the state had become deeply and less happily involved in various other ventures, including the Michigan Southern, and by the fall of 1845, public officials concerned over Michigan's credit, as well as some enterprising individuals who thought they saw an opportunity for private capital, were urging that both the Michigan Central and the Michigan Southern be put up for sale.

As this movement gained ground, two young men grew increasingly enthusiastic over the Central's prospects. One of them, James Frederick Joy, was a rising lawyer endowed with unquenchable energy and a rare talent for persuasion. Born in Durham, New Hampshire, on December 2, 1810, he had followed his local schooling with a term as clerk in a home-town store and then had managed to work his way through Dartmouth College, where, in 1833, he was graduated at the head of his class. By coincidence, one of the younger students he tutored at Dartmouth was James W. Grimes, who was destined to play a role in the Burlington and Missouri River Railroad. Upon graduating from Dartmouth, Joy moved on to the Harvard Law School. Admitted to the bar in 1836, he was captivated by the opportunity of the West, and in 1837 went to Detroit to practice law. Thus he was on the spot while the State of Michigan went through its painful experience in railroad building and management.

Meanwhile another bright youngster was learning railroading from the technical side. John Woods Brooks, born in Boston in 1818, was trained by Laommi Baldwin, later to be honored as the "Father of Civil Engineering in America." So promising a student was Brooks that at the age of twenty-one he became assistant chief engineer of the Boston & Maine. That was in 1839. Although he spent the next four years in lumbering, he returned to railroading in 1843 as superintendent of the seventy-eight-mile Auburn and Rochester in upstate New York. Either on his own initiative or possibly at Joy's invitation, he went to Detroit late in 1845 to look over the dilapidated but promising Michigan Central. There he and Joy became convinced that if the Michigan Central could be completed across the state, it would not only secure the substantial business of the thriving farms along the route but also might well become an essential link in a rail-water route between Chicago and the eastern seaboard.

But how could they raise the necessary money? The state was willing to sell for $2,000,000, but only if the buyer would pay $500,000 cash within six months and agree to complete the line to Lake Michigan within three years. Neither Brooks nor Joy could command such funds, and certainly the local citizens were unequal to the task. Nor could they expect to get help from a state whose one thought at the moment was to get out of the railroad business. As yet the federal government was in no mood to grant either land or cash. Only one possibility remained: to go back to the eastern seaboard, where an older economy had gradually accumulated, mostly from overseas commerce and land speculation, capital for investment.

So it was that Brooks, convinced of the promise of the Michigan Central and acting for both himself and Joy, journeyed to Boston in the winter of 1845–46. Fate, no doubt assisted by a few discreet inquiries, led him to John Murray Forbes, a circumstance as important to the future Burlington as any single event in its history.

Although Forbes was only thirty-two at the time, he was already well established in Boston as a respected and successful merchant. Born in Bordeaux, France, on February 23, 1813, he was the son of a well-known New England trader and shipowner. But business reverses had caused the elder Forbes to return to America, and while John Murray was still in school, his two older brothers, Robert Bennet and Thomas, had supported the family, the former as sailor and, eventually, captain of his own ship, the latter as agent in Canton for the trading firm of his well-known uncles, James and Thomas Handasyd Perkins. When John Murray went to work in the fall of 1828, he naturally first entered his uncles' counting house and then, when his brother Thomas died prematurely two years later, went on to Canton to take his place. There John's remarkable gift for winning the confidence of the cautious Chinese and his abilities as a trader enhanced both his fortune and his reputation. When he returned to Boston to stay, early in 1837 at the age of twenty-four, he seemed destined for a bright future. For the next nine years his investments, concentrated in the East and more particularly in maritime ventures, prospered.

The proposition that Brooks put to Forbes was in a wholly new field. Perhaps that was precisely what fascinated Forbes. He was still young. Why not try something new and different? Besides, his older brother Robert Bennet, despite his brilliant seafaring career, was eager to find a more solid business connection ashore; the Michigan Central might be just the place for him. Whatever the combination of motives may have been, Forbes agreed, in the spring of 1846, to mobilize the necessary capital for the Michigan Central.

Once committed, he moved rapidly. His first step was to hire no less a luminary than Daniel Webster to draft a charter, and to send Brooks back to Michigan with it to secure its passage by the Legislature. This much accomplished, Forbes set about the much harder task of raising the purchase price, half a million dollars of which had to be in cash. During that crucial spring of 1846 he enlisted as "corporators" for the Michigan Central a distinguished group that included his uncle Thomas Handasyd Perkins, John Elliott Thayer, Robert Bennet Forbes, Josiah Quincy, Jr., William F. Weld, II, all of Boston, David A. Neal of Salem, and Erastus Corning of Albany. Perkins, of course, was best known as a China trader, but he had also financed and been president of America's first railroad, the Granite Railway Company, completed in 1826 to haul stones for the Bunker Hill monument; later he had been prominent in an effort to popularize railways, rather than canals, in Massachusetts. Thayer was a prominent banker. John Murray's brother Robert Bennet Forbes, besides being a seafarer, had been a pioneer in developing the screw propeller and iron hulls. Josiah Quincy, Jr., elder son of Harvard's president and a lawyer, had worked with Perkins as a sponsor of the "railroad scheme" for Massachusetts, had helped raise subscriptions for what later became the Boston and Albany, and then had served as treasurer of that road. Weld, once a foreign trader himself, had become an importer of iron rails and director of a handful of New England railroads. Neal was then president of the Eastern Railroad. Erastus Corning, an iron-maker and hardware merchant by trade, had been president of the Utica and Schenectady ever since 1833 and meanwhile had served as mayor of Albany and a New York State senator.

But these were by no means the only persons Forbes approached. Through family connections he obtained funds in New Bedford, where the declining whaling industry made considerable capital available for new projects. And in New York he secured substantial support from his former partner in China, John C. Green. These indeed were the most "solid men" of the East.

As he made his rounds, Forbes took with him a remarkably persuasive and prophetic document that Brooks had prepared: *Report Upon the Merits of the Michigan Central Rail-Road As an Investment for Eastern Capitalists*. The combination of Brooks's presentation and Forbes's untiring persuasion was effective. The necessary funds were raised, and on September 23, 1846, the Michigan Central Railroad took possession of its property, with Forbes as its first president.

What did all this have to do with the Burlington? Just this: the challenge presented by the Michigan Central had brought together for the first time Forbes, the mobilizer of capital; Joy, the astute lawyer; and Brooks, the energetic operating man. Furthermore, it had brought men like Thayer, Corning, and Green into the same circle as substantial investors. Their first common objective was to bring the Michigan Central into Chicago, a feat they accomplished in dramatic fashion on May 21, 1852. Was it likely that men of this caliber would stop there? Far from it. As they had already demonstrated by buying securities of the Aurora Branch, they had no intention whatever of letting the Michigan Southern (which had reached Chicago exactly one day after the Michigan Central) outstrip them in organizing a closely allied system that would link their original Michigan venture with the Mississippi and perhaps the Missouri. Indeed, in that breathless spring of 1852 they were ready and waiting to stride onto the Burlington stage.

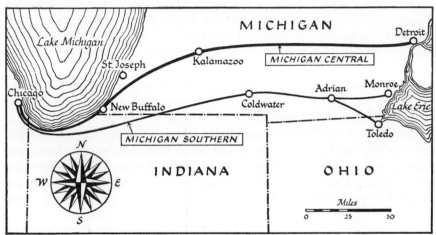

Michigan Central and Michigan Southern, May 1852

To say which particular individual first visualized the C. B. & Q. as it eventually emerged in Illinois is difficult if not impossible. Three men— Colton of Galesburg, Joy, and Brooks—all subsequently suggested that they were largely responsible for the way things turned out. Certainly each of them, then and for many years thereafter, played key roles in the development of the company, and without any one of them the story might have been far different. But Grimes, who had reasons to move quietly, and possibly others, may have had just as much to do with the eventual outcome. The simple and important facts are that half a dozen local projects scattered between Lake Michigan and the Missouri River desperately needed eastern aid; the Michigan Central just as desperately needed western feeders; by the end of 1852 the Forbes Group was committed, to a greater or lesser extent, to support them all. That this was accomplished so rapidly and on so many fronts at once simply underlines the impossibility of designating any one person as the "founding father of the Burlington." The *combined* determination of the local sponsors and the men behind the Michigan Central turned the trick.

The first tangible evidence of the easterners' entry into the Illinois situation was the election of Brooks and G. C. Davidson—a partner of Erastus Corning—to the Aurora Branch board on February 21, 1852. Significantly, although Gale was re-elected president, the directors two days later resolved once more to extend their line immediately to a connection with the Illinois Central. This time there seemed reason to believe that their action was something more than wishful thinking, for they probably knew that once Forbes and his colleagues had committed themselves to a project, further support would be forthcoming promptly.

While these events were taking place, an extraordinarily perceptive and urgent letter dated February 22, 1852, was on its way to Corning. The writer was Richard P. Morgan, chief engineer of the Peoria and Oquawka. He was stationed at the moment in Burlington, where of course he promptly learned of the memorial that the Burlington and Missouri River Railroad had sent off to Congress a few days before, praying for a grant of lands across the southern portion of the state. So it was that Morgan urged Corning to procure a good list of signatures for the memorial he enclosed and to forward it to Washington. "If by means of the extension of the Aurora Branch . . . a connection could be made with the Peoria and Burlington Railrd [sic] which I am employed to construct, and if the petition for Burlington is granted, a line from Boston through Albany and thence westward through Canada to Detroit and onward through Chicago, Aurora, Galesburg, and Burlington to [the] Platte River, would become the great route for the eastern and northern states as well as for Canada."[1]

Here was an appeal that could not fail to impress Corning. Furthermore, it would seem that the reference to Boston might well have been meant for Forbes's eyes. The main point, however, was the specific mention of Galesburg; that suggests that Morgan already had in mind the idea of using the Central Military Tract as a link between the Aurora Branch and the western portion of the Peoria and Oquawka.

The next development came from a wholly different quarter, though its timing suggests that it may not have been wholly coincidental. In mid-March 1852, the Central Military Tract, completely out of funds, had suspended all surveying activities. But a few days later, Chauncey Colton, one of its original incorporators and its untiring advocate, left for his annual spring buying trip in the East. The prospects of the Central Military Tract were much in his thoughts; as he made his calls in New York, he tried his best to enlist financial aid from his mercantile friends. What he had to say, however, failed to strike a responsive chord, and he left the city convinced that its citizens "were not the class of men to build railroads."[2]

No sooner had Colton reached Boston a few days later than matters took a different turn. Colton stopped at the old American House. There, presumably by coincidence, he chanced to run into Elisha Wadsworth of the Aurora Branch and, of all people, Grimes. After supper the three men

[1] Richard P. Morgan to Erastus Corning, February 22, 1852, EC.
[2] "Colton MS." in the Western Historical Collection in Widener Library, Harvard University, reprinted in Richard C. Overton: *Burlington West* (Cambridge: Harvard University Press; 1941), pp. 506–15.

quite naturally talked of railroad matters. To Colton it was plain as day that the interests of the lines they represented were identical, though as they stood the three roads were of no value because they had no appropriate connections or outlets. As Colton later recalled, "Mr. Grimes asked what I proposed; I said I considered it feasible to unite & harmonise our three RR enterprises, and by uniting all our influence, we could together build a railroad from *Burlington to Chicago*, via Galesburg: Further that we should endeavor to engage the Michigan Central RR Co., which was composed of wealthy people, in our united project. We could easily show them that such a railroad as ours would be a valuable feeder for their line. If the proposition was favorably received by the M. C. RR people, they could easily carry it through. I told Grimes & Wadsworth there was to be an Extra Session of the Illinois Legislature in June and that I would undertake to get the charter of the 'Central Military Tract' RR so altered & amended that the road should run northward to *connect with any railroad leading to Chicago*; Mr. Wadsworth should get the 'Aurora Branch' RR charter amended to be extended south so as to *connect* with any road, from the south, *leading to Chicago*."[3]

Colton's listeners pledged hearty support. Grimes understandably insisted that as consummation of such a plan would take all business from Galesburg and the west to Chicago instead of to Peoria, his identification with the scheme should not be made public. But he was more than ready to work behind the scenes, as he proved the next day, when he went to New York and laid the plan before John C. Green and J. N. A. Griswold, both prominent Michigan Central stockholders. These men not only expressed favorable interest, but also gave Grimes a letter of introduction to Brooks, in whose judgment, obviously, they had great confidence. Grimes's next stop was Albany, where he talked with Corning, who, likewise impressed, also wrote to Brooks, telling him to expect Grimes and to form an opinion of what he had to say. By this time, of course, Corning had had plenty of time to digest Morgan's letter from Burlington, so that quite possibly the most welcome news Grimes gave him was of Colton's willingness to dovetail the Central Military Tract into the scheme as a whole.

By April 14 Grimes had reached Detroit, and when Brooks wrote Corning again, his enthusiasm was beyond doubt. "I think it well worth our while to get that line [The Central Military Tract] to come to us [The Aurora Branch] and not to the Rock Island road." If the Michigan Central group could acquire control of the Central Military Tract, he thought, "we could raise money and sufficient aid to help carry the work through."[4]

---

[3] "Colton MS.," loc. cit., p. 508.
[4] John W. Brooks to Corning, April 14, 1852, EC.

Regardless of who first thought up the idea and when, it was clear that by mid-April 1852 both the local men most intimately interested and several key members of the Michigan Central group were thoroughly aware of a specific plan for linking together a through line from Chicago to the Mississippi. And the fact that men like Corning and Brooks were informed meant that Forbes and Joy were fully advised too, for the correspondence among them, as the overwhelming records still in existence testify, was frequent and detailed.

Agreement in principle on a scheme, however, was very different from realization. However much the Michigan Central group desired western outlets, they could hardly be expected to put up cold cash unless and until they made certain that the Illinois lines could and would actually connect with each other, and that in return for financial aid the easterners could obtain sufficient control to assure harmonious relations during construction and once the lines were put in operation.

So far as the Aurora Branch was concerned, these two requirements posed no particular problems. In respect to its route, that company already possessed the right to construct a "lateral branch" and to connect with other railroads. All that was required was specific authority to extend to a junction with the main north-south line of the Illinois Central (at Mendota, as it turned out), where a connection could also be made with the Central Military Tract. In Boston, Wadsworth had committed himself to bring this about. But he resigned from the Aurora Branch board on May 13, and the task—very probably at Brooks's suggestion—was assigned to Joy, who promptly proceeded to carry it out at the special session of the Illinois Legislature. On June 22, the Aurora Branch was authorized to build across the Fox River and to a point at least fifteen miles north of La Salle, there to connect with any railroad to be built northward from that town. At the same time, the company's name was changed to the more independent-sounding Chicago and Aurora, and permission was granted to increase capitalization to $2,000,000.

The question of eastern control of the newly christened Chicago and Aurora was already well on the way to solution. Throughout the spring of 1852, various members of the Forbes Group, with constant prodding by Brooks, had continued buying its securities. On July 6, Joy was elected to Wadsworth's place on the board, and in less than a week he too was actively soliciting further stock subscriptions in New York and Boston. In September, I. H. Burch, a Chicago financier, was appointed treasurer in place of Hall and the Company's offices were transferred from Aurora to Chicago; at the same time the directors resolved that all stock of the company still unsold should be under Joy's control, "for soliciting subscribers for the same."[5] Clearly by this time control of the company was firmly in eastern hands.

[5] AB, ORB, pp. 51-2.

Stephen F. Gale, President of the Aurora Branch (1849–51), of the Aurora Branch–Chicago and Aurora (1852–53)

Elisha S. Wadsworth, President of the Aurora Branch (1851–52)

James F. Joy, President of the Chicago and Aurora–C. B. & Q. (1853–57; 1865–71)

John Van Nortwick, President of the C. B. & Q. (1857–65)

I

James M. Walker, President of the
C. B. & Q. (1871–76)

Robert Harris, President of the
C. B. & Q. (1876–78)

John Murray Forbes, President of the
C. B. & Q. (1878–81)

Charles E. Perkins, President of the
C. B. & Q. (1881–1901)

George B. Harris, President of the
C. B. & Q. (1901–10)

Darius Miller, President of the C. B. & Q.
(1910–14)

Hale Holden, President of the C. B. & Q.
(1914–18; 1920–28)

Charles E. Perkins, Jr., President of the
C. B. & Q. (1918–20)

Frederick E. Williamson, President of
the C. B. & Q. (1929–31)

Ralph Budd, President of the C. B. & Q.
(1932–49)

Harry C. Murphy, President of the
C. B. & Q. (1949–   )

First general C. B. & Q. office building (shared with Michigan Central),
2 South Water Street, Chicago, about 1862

Inspection engine No. 1370, built by Lancaster in 1870, at Galesburg,
Illinois, about 1900

Opening of Hannibal Bridge, first over the Missouri, Kansas City, July 4, 1869

Kilpatrick's construction outfit, grading the B. & M., Custer County, Nebraska, in 1880's

Aurora (Illinois) Shops, late 1860's

Hannibal and St. Joseph Railroad packet *Colorado*, 1869

Next to the Chicago and Aurora, the most important link in the proposed Illinois system was the Central Military Tract. Without it no access was possible either to the Peoria and Oquawka or to the Northern Cross, let alone to the trans-Mississippi lines. If eastern capital was to be invested, the matters of route and of control were of prime importance.

On the first point Colton had already committed himself at Boston, and the chances are that he had kept his friends at home fully posted. At any rate, when the Central Military Tract stockholders met on April 15, they elected Colton both to the directory and to the executive committee. A fortnight later, the board authorized him to prepare a new charter for submission to the Legislature and, specifically, "to make such arrangements with other companies or individuals as may be necessary to connect with other roads and to obtain funds."[6] Clearly, the scheme outlined in Boston was in high favor in Galesburg. Accordingly Colton drew up an entirely new charter based on that of the Illinois Central. Capitalization, among other things, might be increased "to any sum not exceeding the amount to be expended on account of said road." Of prime importance at the moment, however, was the provision respecting the route. As in the original charter, the C. M. T. retained the right to build toward Chicago and a junction with the Rock Island, but a most significant clause was added: it might, if it preferred, join "any railroad or railroads connecting with or extending to the . . . City of Chicago."[7]

Thus Colton carried out his part of the Boston bargain and armed with his new charter went off in June to Springfield, where, for the first time, he met Joy. The Detroiter enthusiastically approved of Colton's changes, and despite opposition from disgruntled partisans of the Peoria and Oquawka, who still resented any advantage Galesburg and a Galesburg-Chicago line might gain over Knoxville and a route to Peoria, the desired charter containing the permissive change of route passed the Legislature on June 19.

But Joy and Colton, pleased as they were, agreed that one more step was necessary if Eastern dollars were to be coaxed into the venture. As matters stood, the Northern Cross's authority to build northeastward to LaSalle specified that the proposed road should not pass east of (but presumably should pass through) Knoxville. This meant that for a considerable distance east of that point the two lines would be virtually parallel. Colton, of course, had foreseen this possibility when, in obtaining the original Central Military Tract Charter, he had secured permission to make a connection with the Northern Cross if the latter company should build to Galesburg. But this was not enough. The Northern Cross would have to agree specifically to terminate its line at Galesburg. Joy promised that if Colton could bring this about, as Colton was sure he

[6] CMT, ORB, pp. 39–40.
[7] State of Illinois, Act of June 19, 1852, reprinted in *DH*, Vol. I, pp. 37–42.

could, then Joy would immediately open subscription lists in the East for Central Military Tract stock and, later in the summer, would go to Galesburg to work out final arrangements.

During the following month both men carried out their undertakings. At Colton's request, the Northern Cross people, doubtless hoping to secure financial aid from the well-heeled easterners, agreed to terminate their line at Galesburg, and Joy busily began selling C. M. T. stock along with that of the Chicago and Aurora. By the time Joy returned to Galesburg early in August, he and Forbes had secured subscriptions for more than $200,000 and were confidently expecting more. But these subscriptions were to be paid only on two conditions: control of the board was to be transferred to the Forbes Group; the local citizenry had to subscribe for an additional amount of stock roughly equivalent to that already raised in the East.

The first of these conditions was met promptly by contract. The second, however, was not so easy to fulfill. In an area as sparsely settled as that between Galesburg and Mendota then was, raising any substantial funds was a gigantic task. Nevertheless the local directors strained every nerve to meet the quota, and when Joy and Brooks returned to Galesburg in September they were only $50,000 short of their goal. The easterners were adamant, however; unless the remaining amount was forthcoming, they could not promise to hold their eastern subscribers. Into the breach stepped Colton and his colleague Silas Willard. Between them they pledged the desired amount and thus secured without question the desperately needed eastern support.

Here was another of those turning points in Burlington history which even the sophisticated Joy generously acknowledged years later. What is more, this last tremendous effort by Colton and Willard came not a moment too soon. As Brooks and Joy were on their way back to Chicago, they met the treasurer of the Rock Island on his way to Galesburg to subscribe for stock in the Central Military Tract and make an arrangement for that company to become a part of the Rock Island. It was a close shave, but a decisive one.

Brooks and Joy, of course, were jubilant. They reported their success at once to Corning and, incidentally, pleaded with him to double his own subscription. What happened next was almost anticlimactic. When the stockholders of the Central Military Tract met at Galesburg on October 14, the Boston group, casting three quarters of the proxies, elected four Detroiters, including Brooks and Joy, and three Chicagoans, including Burch, to the directory. This constituted a majority representing the new eastern interests, and harmonious relations with the Chicago and Aurora were assured by the fact that Brooks and Burch were serving on both boards. Colton and Willard, appropriately enough, were among the local men elected to the board. At the directors' meeting following the election,

Brooks by prearrangement was named president and consulting engineer, and it was voted to issue $800,000 in seven-percent bonds to build to Galesburg from the western end of the Chicago and Aurora.

Thus, both the route and control, as well as the preliminary financing of the Central Military Tract, were worked out in such a way as to meet fully the requirements of the Forbes Group. A through line between Chicago and Galesburg now seemed practically assured.

The status of the Peoria and Oquawka, however, was still uncomfortably vague. Although citizens of Burlington and Monmouth had reportedly acquired a majority of that company's stock, thus increasing the chances that Grimes could indeed locate the line through Galesburg, the still influential interests of Peoria and Knoxville strongly opposed such a scheme. But necessity was beginning to weaken their resistance. After all, their finances were in deplorable condition, and support from the Forbes Group would at least produce a railroad, even though not exactly where everyone wanted it. Thus, when Colton shrewdly let it be known that both Brooks and Joy would be in Galesburg for the Military Tract meetings scheduled for the morning of October 14, Grimes conveniently arranged to hold a meeting of the Peoria and Oquawka board at Monmouth that afternoon.

After a rather full morning at Galesburg, Brooks and Joy were disinclined to make the fifteen-mile trip, partly because they had never entertained too favorable an opinion of the P. & O., but more particularly because they were now certain of an outlet to the Mississippi at Quincy over the rails of the Northern Cross. In the end, however, they made the journey, and when the P. & O. directors promised that they would build through Galesburg if the easterners would take $50,000 of their bonds at par, Joy and Brooks accepted the proposition. This relatively small purchase did not, of course, give the Forbes Group control of the P. & O., but at least it settled the matter of the route and paved the way for a closer association later on.

The next step, accomplished the following day, was to lend a hand to the Northern Cross. On October 15, 1852, the Chicago and Aurora directors sought permission of the Illinois Legislature to subscribe to the stock of that company in an amount not exceeding ten percent of the C. & A.'s own capitalization, and in due course the Central Military Tract board asked for a similar authority. It would take time, however, to secure the desired permission. Consequently, on November 22, Brooks earnestly sought Corning's help in disposing of the Northern Cross bonds that company had already authorized, arguing that if this line was built, it would connect with the Hannibal and St. Joseph and thus make possible a chain of roads 478 miles long, all the way from Chicago to St. Joseph. As only the forty-two miles between Chicago and Aurora were in operation when Brooks wrote his letter, his optimism was noteworthy.

But his point was well taken. In February 1853, the Illinois Legislature allowed the C. & A. and C. M. T. to subscribe to Northern Cross stock, and later in the year Forbes succeeded in floating a substantial portion of the road's bonds with the Duke of Brunswick. Presumably Forbes took an even larger share for himself and his associates, including Corning, for as part of the arrangement the easterners secured working control of the Northern Cross directorate. Thus another link in the Illinois system was added to the chain.

Meanwhile, as Brooks well knew, from the moment the Hannibal and St. Joseph had received its land grant in June 1852, Forbes had been quietly acquiring stock of the Missouri road. Early the following year Forbes was writing enthusiastically about it to Corning, though apparently he had moments of doubt. To help reach a conclusion he persuaded Robert Bennet Forbes to travel over the proposed route in the spring of 1853 and to make, on the same trip, a survey of the B. & M. in Iowa. But his brother's report was inconclusive; he had found the country between Hannibal and St. Joseph "rolling, and rather uneven compared to that west of Burlington, and not so rich in soil, though more rich in timber; much less settled and much less appearance of drift, but still what would be called in any part of New England very fine farming land . . . ."[8]

Meanwhile, Colonel Stewart, president of the Hannibal, was doing his best to round up additional stock subscriptions both locally and in the East. At home, $630,000 had been subscribed, about two thirds of it from towns and counties, the rest from individuals. But only about $70,000 of this was in cash. The company therefore had to borrow money to meet even its modest expenses for preliminary work. Furthermore, although the state had voted $3,000,000 of its bonds to aid construction, this very substantial sum would not become available until the company itself had accumulated half a million dollars in cash. Unfortunately, Stewart's trips to the seaboard failed to secure subscriptions on terms his directors would accept. The outlook at the end of 1853 was bleak indeed.

Small wonder that in January 1854 Forbes appeared pessimistic. "As to the Hannibal thing," he wrote Corning, "I am situated just as you are: too much to do and I am not anxious to go on with it. One inducement to other parties," he went on, "has been the expectation of having you for a party to the operation & it is certainly a great one with me. If you do not come into it I should feel bound to consult with the other parties and I think we shall let the whole thing drop, which would not cause me any great regret." On the other hand, he admitted that Brooks was "very sanguine" about the road and that among its great advantages was the prospect of making a good thing of the land grant.[9] Very probably this

[8] R. B. Forbes to John Murray Forbes, June 11, 1853, in GM, Vol. I, pp. 105-6.
[9] Forbes to Corning, January 12, 1854, EC.

last consideration led him to remain, for the moment, chairman of the eastern syndicate formed to acquire the stock of the road.

What Forbes really needed was more information. Consequently he joined with Corning and Charles Gould, the other two trustees of the eastern syndicate, in engaging Edward B. Talcott, the experienced chief engineer of the Illinois–Michigan Canal, to examine the Hannibal and St. Joseph land grant and to comment upon "the general characteristics of the road, the resources of the country, and the financial condition of the company."[1] Taking all things into account, Talcott estimated that in its first year of operation the road should return more than seven percent on its estimated costs.

Without doubt this report clinched Forbes's determination to throw his full weight behind the project. On March 17, 1854, he worked out a series of agreements with the directors of the road. A Fiscal Agency was established in Boston under Forbes's control, with exclusive powers to mobilize the necessary funds; as part of the arrangement, a majority of the company's stock was assigned to the eastern syndicate. At the annual meeting of the stockholders early in November, John Murray Forbes, his brother Robert Bennet Forbes, and his old associates John Thayer and H. H. Hunnewell of Boston, along with Colonel Stewart, were elected to the directory. A $4,000,000 mortgage was placed on the land grant and an additional $2,000,000 issue on the railroad itself; both were placed in the hands of the Fiscal Agency for sale to the public. When the new board met for the first time in Boston on November 25, new bylaws were adopted and trusted lieutenants of the Forbes Group were put in charge of the essential engineering and land departments.

Colonel Stewart, whose earlier efforts to raise funds in the East had failed, was overjoyed at the turn of events. Referring to the Boston group, he exclaimed that "their interest in the work, their reputation as capitalists and gentlemen of high moral character, are a guarantee the means will be raised and the work pressed forward with vigor."[2]

Meanwhile, events had moved even more rapidly in respect to the Burlington and Missouri River. Brooks, who was just as determined to have a western outlet in Iowa as in Missouri, was an early and dedicated champion of that road. On November 22, 1852, he wrote Corning that business from Burlington would "pass over, say, forty-five miles of the Peoria and Oquawka RR, the whole of the Central Military Tract RR and Chicago and Aurora RR, and be tributary to the Michigan Central, Canada RR, and NY Central . . ."[3] Therefore, he said, Corning should urge the senators from New York to take favorable action on the land

<hr/>

[1] Edward B. Talcott: *Report upon the Hannibal and St. Joseph Railroad*, Boston, 1854, p. 17.
[2] HSJ, AR 1854, p. 14.
[3] Brooks to Corning, November 22, 1852, EC.

grant the B. & M. was seeking. Brooks well knew that if the grant were secured, support from the Forbes Group would be far more likely.

What actually jarred the easterners into action was quite another matter. In February 1853, the Rock Island secured a charter from the State of Iowa to build the Mississippi and Missouri Railroad from Davenport to Council Bluffs; at the same time it gained permission to bridge the Mississippi between Rock Island and Davenport. To Brooks and Joy this was a direct challenge from their chief rival. On behalf of the Michigan Central, therefore, of which they were both directors and officers, they promptly informed the B. & M. directors that they would favorably consider extending financial support to the Iowa line, provided of course that the latter would do all it could to help itself.

The effect of this offer on the B. & M. was electrifying. "Inasmuch as influential citizens of the East proffer to assist us with abundant means to secure the completion of the road," the Burlington board resolved on March 9, " . . . we will proceed with all energy, means, and resources in our power; . . . books of subscriptions to our stock should be offered in all counties along the line of road."[4] Furthermore, they resolved immediate steps should be taken to survey the entire route and the first fifty miles of railroad should be placed under contract at the earliest possible moment.

To speed the work, Brooks and Joy sent along Hans Thielsen, a Danish-born civil engineer of the Michigan Central, to survey the line approximately seventy-five miles west to Ottumwa on the Des Moines River. Alfred Hebard, a Vermont-born Yale graduate who had lived in Iowa for sixteen years, was commissioned to search out the most feasible route from Ottumwa to Council Bluffs. In June, Brooks and Joy journeyed to Galesburg to meet representatives from the B. & M. to discuss such arrangements as seemed best to promote their joint interests. One prompt result was the addition of Brooks and Joy to the B. & M. board on July 2 and the election of Brooks as president.

So it was that the promise of eastern dollars from the Forbes Group was extended not only to the four little companies in Illinois but also to both the Hannibal and St. Joseph and the Burlington and Missouri River. The men behind the Michigan Central had taken the first essential steps to secure themselves a western system that promised to hold its own against the strongest sort of competition. The next order of business was to build and to finance what they had undertaken to support.

[4] BMI, ORB, p. 6.

CHAPTER 4

Building a System

1852-60

• EAST OF THE MISSISSIPPI •

As MIGHT HAVE BEEN EXPECTED from the timing and extent of the Forbes Group's investment in the Illinois and trans-Mississippi companies, construction activities inevitably started at the eastern end of the system. Things really began to move on the Aurora Branch once it had received permission from the Legislature to change its name and to build to a connection with the Illinois Central. When the directors met on July 6, 1852, the company promptly authorized contracts for construction, while Davidson and Brooks were commissioned to buy the necessary rail through Erastus Corning. At the same time, arrangements were made for construction of a telegraph line along the entire length of the road, both existing and projected. To finance the new extension, the directors voted to issue not over $640,000 in seven percent, fifteen-year registered bonds. Ten days later they accepted a survey of the route to Mendota and commissioned President Gale and Brooks to buy cars and engines and to decide on the type of bridge to be built over the Fox River.

Fortunately the country to be traversed was not difficult, and such progress was made during the winter of 1852–53 that, in mid-February, President Gale reported that the roadbed would be ready for the rails as

[39]

soon as navigation opened on the Great Lakes and they could be brought in by vessel.

Before this could take place, the directors on February 22, 1853, elected Joy president of the Chicago and Aurora Railroad Company. This was altogether logical in view of the increasingly large investment of the Michigan Central group. With Joy in the saddle in Chicago and Brooks in charge at Galesburg, prompt action and harmonious relations between the two chief links of the system were assured.

As it turned out, the delay in receiving iron held up completion of the Chicago and Aurora. But on October 20, 1853, the entire 45.61 miles to Mendota were finally put into operation. The company now operated an eighty-eight mile through line between Chicago and Mendota, and not only brought "modern" transportation to a prosperous farming area, but also stood ready to carry to and from Chicago traffic of the Illinois Central's main north-south line as soon as the latter should complete its bridge over the Illinois River south of Mendota. Almost a year passed before this structure was completed, however, and the C. & A. therefore turned to building up its local business and, more importantly, to serving as a supply route for the Central Military Tract, which had had no rail contact with the outside until the arrival of the C. & A. in Mendota.

The Galesburg road, however, had already made a start. Ever since late 1852, gangs had been preparing the roadbed; from October 1853 on, the task proceeded apace. Even so, Brooks had his troubles. The years 1853–54, he subsequently reported, "were crowded with more work of this sort than any others in the history of our country. As a natural consequence, the price of common labor rose from seventy-five cents to $1.25 per day, and mechanical and other labor in proportion, followed by the usual unsteadiness of men, consequent upon high prices, which always produces incidental effects, augmenting the cost of work in a much greater degree than that indicated by the increase of wages alone."[1]

Forbes, fully alive to the situation, simply redoubled his efforts to keep the enterprise supplied with funds. Learning in the fall of 1853 that $100,000 of the Central Military Tract's bonds remained unsold, he blandly wrote the cautious Corning that he had taken the responsibility of raising by ten percent the earlier commitments each of them had made to buy a portion of the issue. The unsold block, he reasoned, was "much more likely to go freely among the stockholders and elsewhere if we stand ready to take it all than if we let it drag and if you do not like to take the chance of having to take ten percent more, let me know by return mail, and I shall consider it no particular hardship to take it myself."[2]

[1] CMT, AR 1855, pp. 3–4.
[2] Forbes to Corning, October 19, 1853, EC.

With such stout and unwavering financial support, Brooks was able to push forward as rapidly as he could solve his vexing labor problem. On December 7, 1854, just as winter was closing in, he brought to Galesburg the rails that provided a direct through line to Chicago. Thus the second of the four major links of the original C. B. & Q. in Illinois was completed.

The two remaining segments, the Peoria and Oquawka and the Northern Cross, were already presenting new problems, but in anticipation of their solution Joy was authorized by the directors of both the Chicago and Aurora and the Central Military Tract to lay two measures of basic importance before the Legislature. The first, approved on February 28, 1854, stipulated that the Chicago and Aurora, the Central Military Tract, the Northern Cross, and the Peoria and Oquawka, "or any two or more of said companies, shall be and are hereby authorized to consolidate their stocks so as to form one stock and one company, upon such terms as agreed upon, and may assume the name of either as a common name, or may adopt such new name as the consolidated company may adopt . . . and may elect the charter of either of said companies. . . ."[3] Thus the legal basis for eventual consolidation was secured, as was the right to use the liberal provisions of the old Aurora Branch charter when the proper time arrived. The advantages of a new title, however, as an advertisement of what lay in store, might well be realized sooner. Consequently, Joy persuaded the Legislature on February 14, 1855, to permit the Chicago and Aurora alone to anticipate the name-changing provision of the first measure by adopting the title "The Chicago, Burlington and Quincy Railroad Company."

As yet, however, the name was premature. The Peoria and Oquawka, chronically short of funds, had built only nineteen miles eastward from the Mississippi by the late summer of 1854, and the vital Galesburg-Burlington link could not be completed in any reasonable length of time without further financial assistance. Thus, despite the heavy financial load they were already carrying, the Chicago and Aurora and the Central Military Tract agreed, on September 22, 1854, to advance enough funds to the contractor on a fifty-fifty basis to finish the line from East Burlington into Galesburg; to protect their investment, they received a lease on that particular portion of the property. Thereupon the missing link was forged with gratifying speed, considering the rolling nature of the country and the season of the year. The forty-two miles between Galesburg and the river were completed on March 17, 1855, and arrangements promptly made for a steam ferry to carry passengers and freight to Burlington.

Completion of the road to the Mississippi marked the realization of many hopes. The Michigan Central at last had a westward feeder worthy

---

[3] *DH*, Vol. I, p. 33.

of the name, and the three Illinois companies that made up the route could look forward to becoming part of a major artery to the West. For Chicago, the line constituted a second through route, under single management, directly westward to the river and thus speeded the city toward its destined role as the railway capital of the nation. Across the river in Iowa, the citizens of Burlington and smaller villages that stretched out toward the Des Moines River saw in the Chicago line a direct eastward connection for the little local railroad they had sponsored three years before.

Clearly this called for a monster celebration, and such there was at Burlington on May 30, 1855. Riding in a "superb" ten-car train, Senator Lewis Cass of Michigan, Senator Stephen A. Douglas of Illinois, Mayor Boone of Chicago, and other luminaries arrived at the bustling river town to be welcomed by James W. Grimes, by then governor of Iowa, Mayor Silas Hudson of Burlington, and a corps of local dignitaries. According to the awed reporters who covered the event, the "selected elegance" of the East mingled happily with the "beauty and fashion, chivalry and power" of Burlington, Mount Pleasant, and way points.[4] The great feast, followed by the inevitable speeches, dancing, and music, lasted far into the soft spring night. It was an occasion long to be remembered.

But before the "C. B. & Q." could live up to its name, one more railroad had to be built. By January 1855, the Northern Cross had completed only twenty-odd miles northward from Quincy despite subscriptions to its stock by the C. & A. and C. M. T. and despite Forbes's efforts to place its bonds. Repeated delays in the delivery of rails and shortage of cash continued to plague the company. Consequently, Joy and Brooks made another arrangement, effective early in 1855, on behalf of the Chicago and Aurora and the Central Military Tract. By its terms, each company obligated itself, for a limited period, to buy $25,000 of Northern Cross eight percent bonds every six months. Joy felt called upon to explain this undertaking to his stockholders. "Your Board," he told them, "well understood how unfortunate have been the results, often, of the attempts made by one company to aid another in the construction of its road, and that generally, it is inexpedient in the highest degree." But, he argued, the Northern Cross "runs through a country, for its whole distance, second to none in the West for the exuberant fertility of its soil and the abundance of its productions." Furthermore, "it connects our line of roads with the principal city in Illinois upon the Mississippi, and the largest in the state except Chicago. . . . Under these circumstances, though with great reluctance, and knowing how difficult it would be so to place the matter before stockholders unacquainted with the country that

---

[4] William J. Petersen, "The Burlington Comes," *Palimpsest*, Vol. XIV, No. 11 (November 1933), pp. 393–4.

they would fully appreciate the reasons for the step, and having consulted and advised with some of the heaviest of them, the Board resolved to enter into the arrangement. . . ."[5]

Prior approval by the stockholders for such a step would have been desirable, but the moment had been fleeting. This was by no means the last time that Joy and his directors would have to act first and explain later.

This time all went well. Nourished by the dollars supplied by its northeastern connections, and provided at last with rails that Forbes and Corning imported from England in the spring of 1855, the Northern Cross made rapid progress during the rest of that year. On January 31, 1856, the last rail was spiked into place, and a completed chain of roads controlled by a single group connected the cities of Chicago, Burlington, and Quincy.

As yet, however, the title "C. B. & Q." belonged technically only to the former Chicago and Aurora. But as the main lines of the projected Illinois system were then completed, it was logical to consolidate at least the two eastern companies owned by the members of the Forbes Group. Consequently, on July 9, 1856, the stockholders of the C. B. & Q. and the Central Military Tract agreed to merge under the title "The Chicago, Burlington and Quincy Rail Road Company." Stockholders of the former received one and a half shares in the consolidated company for each share in the C. B. & Q.; those of the Military Tract made the exchange on an even basis. The new corporation owned 138 miles of road between Galesburg and its junction with the Galena, and operated an additional seventy-two miles: thirty between Chicago and its junction with the Galena, the rest between Galesburg and Burlington. Informally this entire through route of 210 miles was known as "The Chicago and Burlington Railroad Line," and operating statistics were regularly given for it separately in C. B. & Q. reports. It did not become a legal entity until 1864, when the troublesome title of the old Peoria and Oquawka was cleared. Furthermore, as the Northern Cross in 1856 was still operating its own railroad, the "C. B. & Q.," technically speaking, then served only one of the cities of its title. Nevertheless, for business purposes the entire Illinois system worked as a unit.

"The Chicago and Burlington Railroad Line" that emerged as a growing system in 1856 was indeed a far cry physically from the busy speedway of today. By modern standards, the roadbed was narrow and poorly drained; ties were untreated; there were neither tie plates nor rail anchors; and the rail itself was light. Water courses and swamps were crossed on wooden trestles and piling. The newest and heaviest locomotives on the line weighed only twenty-nine tons, and most of them

[5] CB&Q, AR 1856, pp. 9–10.

still burned wood. Rolling stock was proportionately light; five tons was a good freight-car load, and only forty-five or fifty passengers could be crowded into one of the hard-riding box-like coaches. Sleepers and diners did not exist, nor did air brakes, steam heat, or automatic couplers. Dispatching was according to the book of rules, and by hand signals.

Nevertheless, the men who had tried to build as well as they knew how were understandably proud of their creation. "The road," Joy told his C. B. & Q. stockholders early in 1856, "is laid with the compound or continuous rail, weighing seventy-two pounds to the yard, is generally well-ballasted with excellent gravel, and furnishes the smoothest and best track of the same distance probably in the country." There were, he pointed out elsewhere, "ample side tracks . . . substantial freight and passenger houses, brick water stations, and in all its appurtenances [the road] is believed to be as perfect as any . . . in the West."[6] When 1856 opened, the companies that operated this Chicago–Burlington line owned forty-six locomotives, all of them wood-burning. But within a month or two, one was converted to coal mined from the country through which the road ran. By the following spring, eleven of the company's fifty-four engines were burning the new fuel, a fact that Joy felt would be of great importance to the future prosperity of the road.

But there was more to a railway than simply roadbed, track, and rolling stock. The steady westward growth of the system and the increase in its business made it necessary to improve terminal facilities and connections with other roads in Chicago. Since the Aurora Branch had started operations on September 2, 1850, it had used the various depots of the Galena road. In 1855, neither company enjoyed access to the lines that entered the city from the East and South along the lake front, and the Burlington possessed no terminal properties of its own. The way had been paved for the solution of this difficulty as early as June 1852, when the Illinois Central obtained permission to build a spur westward to the south branch of the Chicago River. Doubtless Forbes, whose Michigan Central had just reached the city over the I. C. tracks, was already contemplating some such connection with his newly acquired Aurora Branch. So, at least, it would seem from the fact that the Aurora's directors on October 19, 1852, named Gale, Brooks, and Van Nortwick a committee to consider the merits of a Chicago River drawbridge to connect their line with both the Illinois Central and the Michigan Central.

More pressing financial burdens intervened, however, and the project was not taken up in earnest until 1855. The Illinois Central was then building its new lake-front depot at Randolph Street, expecting to share it with the Michigan Central, and the prospect of having the Burlington and perhaps the Galena as tenants may have provided an additional spur

[6] Quotations respectively from: CB&Q, AR 1856, p. 7; AR 1855, p. 5.

to action. In any event, the Illinois Central began purchasing the necessary rights of way early in 1855, acting on behalf of the three other interested roads as well as itself. In May 1856, both the connecting track and the bridge over the Chicago River were completed and business began to flow over what was called, then as now, the St. Charles Air Line. Thereupon, the C. B. & Q. transferred all its passenger operations and most of its freight business to the Illinois Central terminal, where they were destined to be carried on for twenty-five years. At about the same time, the C. B. & Q. acquired almost forty acres of land along the South Branch of the Chicago River at a point easily accessible to lumber vessels. The investment turned out to be a wise one, for it gave the company not only sorely needed space at the time, but also title to part of the present Union Station facilities.

Meanwhile the question of proper shops demanded attention. Those the company had been using on leased land in Chicago were inadequate, expensive to maintain, and, above all, inconvenient for serving motive power and equipment from the west end of the line. In the fall of 1855, therefore, the board resolved to construct its own facilities in Aurora. The directors hoped the necessary land could be obtained without cost, but in this they were disappointed. Late in November 1855, the company had to petition for the appointment of commissioners to fix compensation for such lands as it sought to condemn. When the judge denied the petition, Joy promptly appealed to the Supreme Court of Illinois for a mandamus to secure the desired action. One of the two opposing attorneys was Abraham Lincoln, but Justice Caton upheld the C. B. & Q. in a decision which not only granted the mandamus but also established the precedent that a railway could condemn lands for such purposes. So, at that early date, the first of the permanent shops which have served the system ever since in various capacities were built and put into operation at Aurora.

Such facilities were essential to service "the multiplied trains" that Joy reported running on the line.[7] During the calendar year 1856, the Chicago–Burlington Line transported over 400,000 tons, divided almost evenly between eastbound and westbound traffic. Principal westbound items were lumber (which made up over half the total), salt, and "sundries"; corn, wheat, and hogs led the list of Chicago-bound commodities. A quarter of a million passengers rode the line, with a few more going west than east; September and October, the harvest months, were the busiest for travel in both directions.

To build a road capable of handling that much business had been expensive, but, as Forbes wrote to a business associate in Calcutta, "it has been run by honest and intelligent men . . . and against this rather lavish

[7] CB&Q, AR 1857, p. 6.

expense I put the advantage of having it planned and managed by large minds who looked ahead, and knew the great interests they had to care for."[8] If Forbes was right, as only time could tell, the fledgling C. B. & Q. could look toward a hopeful future.

Had the prosperity that reigned when Forbes wrote his letter continued, the next two or three years might well have witnessed a prodigious growth of the C. B. & Q. and a steady increase in business. But in August 1857 the New York City branch of the Ohio Life Insurance and Trust Company failed. In the panic that followed, the areas most hard hit were the industrial regions of the East and the great wheat belt of the Middle West; in Burlington territory the basic wheat and corn crops during both 1858 and 1859 were far below normal. Nor was this all; as time went on, competition "from other sources of transit" increased, as the president explained.[9] Moreover, as the depression ran its course, the company found that a large proportion of its business consisted of cheap commodities that had to be hauled long distances at extremely low rates.

Unfortunately, only a few meaningful statistics are available for the depression years, but they indicate eloquently the impact of the panic. On a Granger road like the C. B. & Q., the six months from June to November, inclusive, were always the busiest. Revenues normally reached a peak in September and then gradually declined to a low point in January or February, the decline from the high to the low points being usually fifty percent. In 1857, the summer months reflected the region's prosperity. But once the grain crop had been moved, the paralysis in business began to show up; revenues for January 1858 were off sixty-seven percent and recovered hardly at all as spring approached. Revenues throughout the spring and summer of 1858 were only about sixty percent of what they had been in the preceding year. With the single exception of May 1859, which reflected a tiny increase over the similar month of the preceding year, it was not until September 1859 that the monthly figures reflected any improvement at all over the similar month of the preceding year. Total tonnage moved during 1858–59 was only about three quarters that of the preceding fiscal year, and although 1859–60 was better, only about half the lost ground was made up. The total number of passengers carried in 1858–59 was twenty percent below the previous year, and fell off another twenty percent in 1859–60. Not until 1860–61 did passenger business improve, and then only slightly.

In May 1857, the C. B. & Q.'s balance sheet had shown bills payable of over $700,000. Over ninety percent of this amount was on account of advances to the Peoria and Oquawka and the Northern Cross, but with business booming, the C. B. & Q. confidently expected reimbursement

[8] Forbes to George Ashburner, January 19, 1857, in Sarah Forbes Hughes, ed.: *Letters and Recollections of John Murray Forbes* (Cambridge, 1899), Vol. I, p. 162.
[9] CB&Q, AR 1860, pp. 9, 13–14.

from these companies before the bills became due early in 1858. That expectation was nullified by the crash. Moreover, prior to the outbreak of the panic, the company had agreed to buy $50,000 annually in Northern Cross bonds and had contracted for four new locomotives, 158 boxcars, and extensive depot grounds, for a total commitment of over $200,000. And during the summer of 1857 the directors had paid out a dividend of over a quarter of a million dollars.

As a result, the till was nearly empty when the depression hit with full force in December. Traffic from the Missouri and Iowa connections melted away, and the failure of the wheat crop along the Galesburg–Quincy line further depressed business. Regretfully the directors gave up all thought of the usual year-end dividend and turned their attention to economy. Even so, they did not have enough cash to carry the fixed debt without floating bonds. Despite the depressed state of the market, therefore, the company in January 1858 issued a $5,000,000 mortgage due in twenty-five years and bearing eight percent interest. Bonds totaling $563,000 were issued at once, and the proceeds, a pitiful $400,346, were applied to outstanding bills.

Despite the emergency character of this large-scale operation, it was carried through with an eye to the future. Of the total authorized, slightly more than half was earmarked to refund all outstanding bonds of the predecessor companies, and another million dollars was set aside to pay for a new, independent entry into Chicago. The remainder was placed in the treasury. Provision was made for a sinking fund designed to liquidate the entire issue on or before maturity, a conservative arrangement that was to become a standard feature of Burlington financing.

In June 1857, Joy persuaded Van Nortwick to assume the presidency of the C. B. & Q. Van Nortwick brought to the office a thorough first-hand knowledge of the property, skill as an engineer, and solid experience as a businessman. Like all the previous presidents of the C. B. & Q., Van Nortwick had a variety of outside interests. Since settling in Batavia in 1848, he had participated in the building of a dam to provide power for gristmills and sawmills in the vicinity, and later had participated in forming the First National Bank of Aurora. He was active also in manufacturing and promoting pumping engines used particularly to supply water for locomotives. The precise extent of these other interests has been impossible to determine, but his personal accounts suggest that they provided by far the largest part of his income. This is not to imply that Van Nortwick neglected the C. B. & Q.; the record of his accomplishments proves otherwise. But it is worth noting that the Burlington had not yet had, and would not for many years have, a chief executive whose only responsibility was the railroad. It can be argued that this may have been an advantage rather than a handicap. The breadth of Van Nortwick's experience was unquestionably an asset, and the fact that he was not dependent

[4 7]

on the fortunes of the road may have given him a desirable objectivity; it certainly gave him a sense of personal independence which, in due course, was to bring him into conflict with the directors.

Van Nortwick's immediate and prime responsibility when he took office in the spring of 1857 was to attend to the countless local matters, largely engineering and operating in nature, which needed careful attention. And once the effect of the panic was felt, it was his unexpected task to cut expenses to the bone and pilot the young corporation through the difficult years. That he was able to do so successfully resulted in no small part from his unshakable faith in the future of the concern. "Notwithstanding the diminished income of the road consequent upon the extreme depression in business," he told the stockholders at their annual meeting in June 1858, "and the sacrifices that have been made during the financial disturbances of the past fiscal year, the directors have undiminished confidence in the success of the enterprise in which we are engaged."[1] A year later, despite the fact that revenues had declined thirty percent, Van Nortwick reiterated his faith in the future of the company.

By the spring of 1860, moderate improvement was in sight, although less than had been anticipated. But Van Nortwick, noting the amount of grain in the company's territory and the prospects for an abundant harvest, predicted "a larger and more prosperous business" for the ensuing year than for several years past.[2] This time his faith was fully justified. Although passenger business continued in the doldrums for another year, ton-miles of freight moved in 1860–61 shot up thirty-eight percent, thus boosting revenues twenty-four percent over what they had been the previous year. For the C. B. & Q. the depression was over, but it is notable that total revenues for 1860–61 were almost exactly what they had been back in 1857–58. Literally, the company had barely been able to remain solvent. In view of the fact that important neighbors had gone into bankruptcy, this was a notable achievement.

As if the panic of 1857 and its effects were not enough to cope with, the Peoria and Oquawka continued to prove troublesome. Its owners, intent on linking Galesburg and Peoria, made a contract with Moss, Harding & Company in 1855 to build the forty miles still unfinished between those cities and to equip the entire Peoria–Burlington road. As security, the P. & O. gave the contractors not only a lien on the new portion to be constructed, but also a lease and the right to operate the *entire* line from Peoria to Burlington despite the fact that the C. B. & Q. already had a lease on the Galesburg–Burlington section and was actually operating it. On February 1, 1857, Moss, Harding & Company put the finishing touches on the Peoria–Galesburg stretch, but the P. & O., claiming that they were being overcharged, refused to pay a cent. Thereupon

[1] CB&Q, AR 1858, p. 24.
[2] CB&Q, AR 1860, p. 14.

General Harding of the contracting firm came to the conclusion that the only way he could salvage anything was to begin operating trains himself. As a result, the C. B. & Q. found itself in the unusual and uncomfortable position of sharing the forty-two miles of single track between Galesburg and Burlington with a fellow-creditor of the Peoria and Oquawka Railroad.

The directors of the C. B. & Q. immediately obtained stockholder approval to buy the P. & O. outright, and the latter promptly agreed to sell. But of course no clear title could be obtained as long as the contractors' claims were unsettled. While ways were being sought to settle them, new owners took control of the P. & O. and tried to force both the Burlington and General Harding out of the picture by petitioning for bankruptcy. To protect itself, the C. B. & Q. had no choice but to pay interest on the P. & O.'s bonds until a settlement with Harding could be effected. Not until the spring of 1860 was this brought about, and then only through the untiring efforts of Chauncey Colton. By that time, the C. B. & Q., as principal bondholder, was able to force foreclosure of the property and thus pave the way to gaining a clear title at the ensuing sale, which finally took place in 1862. Then, at long last, the P. & O.—with its vital Galesburg–Burlington stretch—was in Burlington hands, but at a cost of some two and a half million dollars.

Meanwhile, affairs on the Northern Cross were hardly less complicated. First of all, it fell into receivership late in 1856. In the following February the Illinois Legislature permitted the company to change its name to the Quincy and Chicago Railroad; the C. B. & Q., on April 1, 1857, worked out an operating agreement with this new concern to keep the line in running condition regardless of its financial situation. Thereupon Forbes, Thayer, and Von Hoffman (agent for the Duke of Brunswick), acting together as trustees for the second mortgage, took possession. But other securities were outstanding, and not until June 1860 was a plan worked out whereby the C. B. & Q. offered to exchange its own bonds for the old Northern Cross first-mortgage bonds, and scrip for the second-mortgage bonds. Under this plan the Burlington gradually acquired control of the outstanding bonds and eventually (in 1864) purchased the property at a foreclosure sale. In all, the C. B. & Q. spent over $2,000,000 to secure the line.

In summary, then, by 1860 affairs on both the P. & O. and the Quincy and Chicago had reached the stage at which eventual control by the C. B. & Q. was in sight, even though it was not consummated in either case for several years. But from a practical standpoint the Burlington could look forward to operating the entire system connecting Chicago, Burlington, and Quincy, with the knowledge that eventually it could be brought under a single corporate roof.

Throughout the depression years, of course, the Burlington tried its best to trim expenses. But despite the most heroic efforts, the operating ratio (the relation of operating expenses to operating revenues) inevitably rose as the volume of business decreased. During 1857–58, which included six months of good business, the company was able to make the most of falling prices of labor and materials; by reducing expenses more rapidly than revenues declined, it finished that year with an operating ratio of 46.13. But attempts to economize the next year were offset by heavy rains in early summer, which boosted maintenance expenses. And with the volume of business falling, the operating ratio rose to 51.79 percent. The next year the full impact of falling rates made itself felt, and for 1859–60 the operating ratio jumped to 55.58 percent. Not until 1860–61, with rising volume, could the company control expenses so as to bring the operating ratio down to 49.88 percent. "It is not believed," observed Van Nortwick, "that these expenses can be materially lessened until our road shall have attained considerable more age and permanency of construction."[3]

The performance of the operating ratio and the reasons that led to its bulge during hard times underlined two basic truths about railroading that were to be demonstrated over and over again in the subsequent history of the company. The first was the important relationship of volume to earnings, or, to put it another way, the fact that in a business such as railroading a large percentage of expenses was fixed and could not be reduced proportionately as revenues declined. A second and equally significant fact was that regardless of the gyrations of the business cycle, there was no let-up from the usual risks of bad weather, poor crops, or, indeed, the pressure of business rivals. A railroad had to keep running in good times and bad; unlike other enterprises, it could not close down to await better times or to re-tool its plant in line with changed conditions. In a growing country it was not logical even to close down portions that were not yet paying their way; and there was not, on light-density lines, much chance of reducing the amount of service then offered. Such circumstances provided constant incentives to strive for volume and to build a plant that could be operated with maximum efficiency.

During the lean early years of his administration, Van Nortwick was virtually impotent to increase volume: the economy of the Midwest was prostrate and the best he could do was to be patient and have faith. But the efficiency of the plant always could be improved, and to this end Van Nortwick addressed himself with vigor and ingenuity.

In December 1857, the Galena and Chicago Union served notice that at the end of the compulsory two-year grace period, it wished to terminate the agreement by which the C. B. & Q. was sharing its line into Chicago. Two choices were open to the C. B. & Q. Ever since 1854 it had possessed the charter right to build a direct line of its own from Aurora

[3] CB&Q, AR 1861, p. 12.

to Chicago. The company's surveys indicated that such a line would be about six miles shorter than the one currently in use, and that it could be built for some $800,000. Maintenance of the new line, together with interest on the necessary capital funds, would amount to nearly $100,000 a year, about $18,000 less than the Burlington had been paying the Galena annually over the previous two years. The other alternative would be to purchase from the Galena the south track of its double-track main line between the junction and Harlem, and a half-interest in the single-track cut-off from there to the St. Charles Air Line, with an agreement to build an additional track when needed.

As Van Nortwick put it, "the time has arrived when this company should have an independent line of their own to Chicago, or own an equal interest in that now built."[4] Despite the depression atmosphere in the spring of 1858, the stockholders heartily agreed with this position and instructed the directors to explore the entire situation. The board was in the process of doing so when, in May 1859, the Galena withdrew its termination notice and eventually extended the contract for joint operation to May 1, 1864, subject to termination on two years' notice by either party. Although the company was thus spared the necessity of a major capital outlay at a difficult time, an independent entrance to the city became a fixed goal of Burlington policy. Accordingly, in the spring of 1859, just after the Galena people had withdrawn their termination notice, the C. B. & Q. stockholders appointed a committee to explore the possibilities.

Necessarily, improvements to plant and equipment were held to the bare necessities during the lean years. One such necessity was to apply gravel along the roadbed. The company opened up a number of pits along its territory, and made constant use of the steam excavator it had received in part payment of a dishonored draft during the panic. In the realm of motive power, the most significant development during the depression years was the further testing of coal-burners. On January 1, 1858, the company began to keep accurate reports to determine precisely the difference in cost between using wood and using coal as fuel. By May 1858, fifteen of the company's fifty-eight engines were coal-burners, and Van Nortwick, at least, was convinced of "the propriety and necessity of changing all our engines into coal-burners as soon as it can be advantageously done."[5] As a matter of fact, the depression offered a splendid opportunity to test his conclusion, for business was so light that a large portion of it—some seventy-two percent in 1859–60—could be handled by coal-burners. During that year the figures showed that the cost of fuel per mile was just under ten cents for coal-burners, as contrasted to more than nineteen cents per mile for wood-burners. Small wonder that in the spring of 1860 the general

[4] CB&Q, AR 1858, pp. 19–22.
[5] Ibid., pp. 17–18.

superintendent stated flatly "that the burning of coal has been considered a fixed fact, and no longer an experiment."[6]

As of 1858, almost all the Burlington's thousand cars were either rectangular boxes (whether they carried goods or passengers), coal cars of the gondola type, or plain flatcars. The process—which still goes on—of adapting these basic forms to specialized purposes began in hesitant fashion during the depression years.

Buried in the 1858–59 *Annual Report* is this brief sentence: "Two passenger cars have been altered and fitted up for sleeping cars."[7] These were not, by any means, the first railway cars in which travelers could lie down to sleep. But they did antedate the famous "Number 9," which George M. Pullman built in the Alton shops a few months later. The Burlington's cars must have been successful: another coach was converted during the spring of 1861 and placed in the Chicago–Quincy run. Congratulating the road on this welcome innovation despite the depressed state of business, the editor of the Quincy paper waxed enthusiastic about this "new and elegant" sleeping car, which, he continued, "combines all the latest improvements—the lower berth being double and the upper a single one, making them much more roomy and convenient, while the ventilation, being done by means of a window in the roof after the manner of a steamboat cabin, renders them [*sic*], by far, the most comfortable car in use."[8] Whether the double lower berths were really as roomy as the local journalist thought may be open to question, but there can be no doubt that clerestory windows were a vast improvement. In fact, the company was busy installing them on day coaches as well as on two additional sleepers then under construction.

Freight cars were being specialized too. Early in 1860, the superintendent called for a hundred cars especially designed for the transportation of livestock, and within a year the company had built a few sample cars for this purpose and for the hauling of grain.

Significant and suggestive as these changes were in respect to quality, they were on too small a scale materially to affect business. As long as the depression persisted, additions to motive power and equipment were few. Between the spring of 1858 and the spring of 1861, only four engines were added to the locomotive roster, bringing the total to sixty-two; no additions whatever were made to the passenger-carrying fleet of thirty-one cars; the number of freight-train cars rose only from 939 to 999. The C. B. & Q. had demonstrated its ability to weather depression and to hold its own; expansion would have to await the coming of better times. Meanwhile, what was happening across the Mississippi?

[6] CB&Q, AR 1860, p. 25.
[7] CB&Q, AR 1859, p. 12.
[8] *Quincy Daily Whig and Republican*, August 24, 1861.

• WEST OF THE MISSISSIPPI •

WHEN FORBES AND HIS ASSOCIATES took over firm control of the Hannibal and St. Joseph in 1854, President Stewart was convinced that the future of the line was assured. Developments throughout most of 1855 justified his optimism. The company went ahead securing rights of way and depot grounds, and satisfactory terminal arrangements were made in both Hannibal and St. Joseph. Grading continued all along the line, and an engine house and machine shop were erected at Hannibal. By autumn, Forbes reported to Corning that "the Hannibal loan is getting into shape & I think will go *straight through*; if so we shall have a very good thing there!"[9] Unfortunately, the effects of the Crimean War unsettled the money market as the year closed, but early in 1856 the Fiscal Agency was able to place enough land bonds in Europe to purchase 13,500 tons of rail and sixteen locomotives. That fall the first twenty-five miles of railroad west of Hannibal were in operation. Furthermore, as the company had now secured enough cash to qualify it for state aid, it took possession of $3,000,000 of state bonds, which it was authorized to sell to finance completion of the line. To offset the difficulty in securing adequate labor, the company did its best to substitute machinery for hand labor wherever it could. Among other things a number of Otis steam excavators were dispatched to the hilly central region, where it was expected they would cut from six to twelve months from the time estimated as necessary to complete the road. These machines may well have been among the first steam shovels used in the West.

Matters did not go quite so well in 1857. Back in March 1854, when the Fiscal Agency had been established, it had been agreed that the contractors, Duff and Leonard, should have the privilege of operating various sections of the road as they were completed and until such time as the whole line was finished; only then would the company take over its operation. By 1857, Duff had bought out his partner, and the arrangement, from the railroad's standpoint, was far from satisfactory. As Forbes later put it: "For awhile the enterprise resolved itself into a contest between him and me, he wishing to build a cheap contractor's railroad to sell, and I a solid one adapted to being held and being used for business purposes."[1] To resolve the situation, Forbes himself went to Missouri in the spring of 1857 and, by threatening to withdraw from the enterprise entirely, got Duff to agree to limit his right of operations to a four-month period following the completion of any given stretch.

For the moment, this new arrangement cleared the air, and by June the rails were at Hunnewell, thirty-seven miles west of Hannibal, and con-

[9] Forbes to Corning, September 22, 1855, EC; italics in original.
[1] Forbes: "Reminiscences, 1857–1861," in *GM*, Vol. I, p. 187.

struction had been resumed eastward from St. Joseph. Inevitably the financial crisis of 1857 put a damper on activities, but by the following May the railhead was seventy-five miles west of Hannibal; work was resumed in earnest on the western end during the summer. Furthermore, in June construction commenced on the Quincy and Palmyra, a locally sponsored

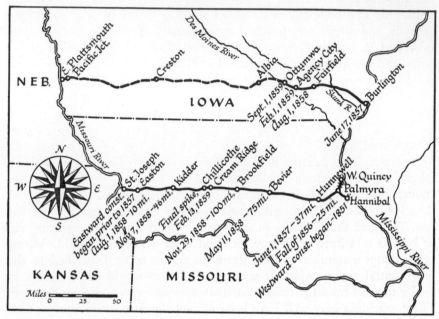

Construction Progress: the Hannibal and St. Joseph, 1851–59; the Quincy and Palmyra, 1858–60; the Burlington and Missouri River, 1854–59, with Projected Line to the Missouri River

fourteen-mile road which, as the Hannibal's general agent put it, would afford practically "an airline connection with Chicago."[2] By November 1858, three fourths of the main line of the Hannibal and St. Joseph had been completed.

The only remaining fly in the ointment was the intractable Duff. Despite his amended contract, he flatly refused to relinquish the profitable running of trains after the agreed-to four-month period. This impasse led to an actual conflict that came to a crisis when railroad forces besieged the Hannibal roundhouse where Duff had impounded the locomotives and set up a miniature fortress. By force of arms the company won the right to run its own trains, but only after the death of one of the combatants.

Once this "battle" was won, the subcontractors took their orders from the railroad company itself, and another twenty-five miles were put into

[2] J. T. K. Hayward, General Agent: *Report to the President and Directors of the Hannibal and St. Joseph Railroad Company*, June 25, 1858, p. 5.

operation before the close of the year. Late in December 1858, the C. B. & Q. directors arranged for steamboats to run between Hannibal and Quincy until such time as the Quincy and Palmyra should be completed.

On February 13, 1859, the final spike on the Hannibal and St. Joseph was driven near Cream Ridge, and on the following day the first through passenger train covered the 206-mile line from east to west. The inevitable celebration took place on Washington's Birthday in St. Joseph. With appropriate solemnity, a prominent citizen emptied a jug of water from the Mississippi into the muddy Missouri, whereupon those present repaired to the Odd Fellows' Hall for appropriate exercises and general jollification. The mighty rivers were linked by rail!

Regular service was inaugurated on February 23 on an eleven-hour schedule. Travelers from the West were assured close connections with steamboats up and down the Mississippi and with all railroad lines leading east and south. The company announced that for those heading west a line of packets would be run in connection with the railroad to Council Bluffs as soon as navigation opened and that stage lines from St. Joseph already provided service to all parts of Kansas, Nebraska, and western Iowa.

On July 12, 1859, the Hannibal and St. Joseph opened its first land office. To stimulate sales, the company distributed a sixty-page booklet containing every sort of useful information for the intending immigrant. Following generally in the footsteps of the Illinois Central, the Hannibal offered its lands for both cash and credit, fixing prices in accord with the natural advantages of each tract and its proximity to the railroad. By November more than 14,000 acres had been sold.

Business during the 1859 season was not up to expectations. The rush to the gold regions started much too early that year, and was so disappointing to those participating in it that by May and June the westward stream of travelers had been reduced to a trickle. Furthermore, competing steamboats on the Missouri River, their future in jeopardy, made a final effort to hold their business by drastically reducing rates. Nor was this all. Duff had left the road in wretched condition; much of the track was unballasted; the rolling stock was in poor shape; and at least eight of the company's engines needed complete rebuilding. Finally, the fact that almost ninety percent of the freight carried was westbound required a heavy eastward movement of empties.

Nevertheless, in the nine and a half months ending September 1, 1859, the company earned over $230,000, which, added to the $150,000 received from land sales, led Brooks to assert in November that he considered the success of the enterprise fully established. The line had had at least one distinguished customer: Abraham Lincoln rode over it on his way to Council Bluffs in August and again on his way to Kansas in November.

The year 1860 saw the Hannibal and St. Joseph come into its own. On April 1, the Quincy and Palmyra was open for traffic, and three days later a spectacular event captured the attention of the entire nation. At 12:20 p.m. on that day the C. B. & Q. brought into Quincy the first messenger from the East carrying mail for the Pony Express. Captain Taylor of the Quincy ferry got him across the river in exactly six minutes; the Quincy and Palmyra Railroad sped him to the junction with the Hannibal and St. Joseph at Palmyra in just twenty-three minutes more. There a special train with a single car was waiting to make the dash westward. Addison Clark was at the throttle of the "Missouri"; his only instructions were to make a record run that would last fifty years. This he proceeded to do by covering the 192 miles to St. Joseph in a little over four hours; total time of the messenger from river to river was four hours and fifty-one minutes, including stops. Considering that the Hannibal's roadbed was hardly seasoned, that its rails were light, its grades abrupt, and its curves sharp, it was something of a miracle that the train made it at all. In St. Joseph, an immense crowd was on hand to watch delivery of the mail sacks from the railway to the Pony Express rider, who dashed for the ferry and on to his ten-mile stint in the saddle. Nothing could have been done to bring the Hannibal and St. Joseph more into the limelight as the farthest western extension of the nation's rail network.

By September 1860, Brooks's rosy prophecies about the prospects of the road seemed on the way to fulfillment. Despite a serious drought in the spring of that year, the expected business from miners on the way to Colorado materialized; more to the point, steamboats operating on the Missouri River east of St. Joseph declined from fifty at the beginning of the year to only ten at the close of navigation. Furthermore, the company was able to sell 18,000 acres more of its granted land, along with ninety town lots. Total receipts exceeded $485,000. If only the threatening clouds of war would disappear from the horizon, the company might look forward to boom times that would more than offset the tedious years of intermittent construction.

From the standpoint of Forbes and his associates, both the Hannibal and St. Joseph and the Burlington and Missouri River were acquired to provide westward connections for the C. B. & Q. and the Michigan Central. Indeed, until the very end of the 1860's the sister roads beyond the Mississippi were regarded much like twins by their eastern sponsors. Yet there were differences between them, some of major importance for the future. For one thing, the soil of Iowa was far richer than that of Missouri; it included virtually no marshes, wasteland, or "barren knobs" unsuitable for cultivation. When Robert Bennet Forbes made his inspection trip in the spring of 1853, he described the broad acres west of Burlington as "*very fine* farming lands, all settled and cultivated. . . . We saw where the road was being graded; seemed to be several feet thick of black loam."[3]

---

[3] R. B. Forbes to his wife, June 10, 1853, in GM, Vol. I, pp. 101–2.

Yet the railroad in Iowa made a slower start and took far longer to complete than its Missouri counterpart for several reasons: trade between St. Louis and St. Joseph was far heavier and better established than between Chicago and Omaha by way of Burlington. Furthermore, from the beginning the Missouri line had been actively promoted from both ends, whereas during the early years the Iowa road was primarily the creation of the towns and villages along its eastern section. In addition, it was far harder to raise local capital in Iowa; compared with the "cities" of Hannibal and St. Joseph, Burlington was but a hamlet, and at that by far the largest on the prospective line. Finally, the Missouri line received its land grant in 1852, thus providing an early incentive for substantial eastern investment; not until 1856 did Congress take similar action in respect to Iowa. For these reasons, the B. & M. moved toward its goal only as fast as its conservative Yankee sponsors could see their way clear to making it pay. Perhaps this was just as well, for it was the only one of the four principal lines eventually built across Iowa that escaped bankruptcy in the process.

While Thielsen and Hebard were running their Iowa surveys during the summer of 1853, the local directors stepped up their drive for funds. Meetings all along the line pledged enthusiastic support, although as always it was easier to obtain promises than cash. Assistance from the City of Burlington was much more tangible. In August the mayor was authorized to lease the accretions along the river to the railroad for one dollar per year, provided that the B. & M. would erect its depot, machine shops, and other facilities there. Even though the site was partly under water at the time, it was strategically of great importance, as subsequent events were soon to prove. The discouraging reluctance of Congress to make a land grant, however, acted as a damper on activities during the rest of 1853. Nevertheless, in March of the following year the board officially adopted Thielsen's surveys to Ottumwa and in May let contracts for grading and bridging that section. Jobs were parceled out to no less than eighteen contractors, many of them local farmers, and work proceeded during the spring with considerable energy. In June, the company employed George Sumner of Boston (probably Charles Sumner's younger brother) to secure stock subscriptions in the East. But until Congress should see fit to speed matters with a grant, his task was difficult.

Not until the through rails from Chicago reached the east bank of the Mississippi in the spring of 1855 did the B. & M. take heart. Land grant or not, here at least was the long-sought link with the East. Encouraged, the B. & M. signed a firm contract on August 16 for building the first thirty-five miles of its road westward at a cost of $22,500 per mile. Work began immediately, and on New Year's Day 1856 the company's first brass-trimmed locomotive triumphantly made a round trip over the few miles of track then completed. At last the B. & M. was in business!

Problems, of course, remained. Stock subscriptions were so slow in

[5 7]

coming in that in March a $350,000 mortgage bearing interest at eight percent was placed on the first thirty-five miles of track; later on, all the company's rolling stock was pledged as additional security. The important thing was to keep moving. In May the rails reached Danville, and July found them at Mount Pleasant, where a building boom was underway; in fact, even in Ottumwa the demand for lots was so pressing that two new additions to the town were laid out forthwith.

There was indeed good cause for optimism now, for at long last, on May 15, 1856, President Pierce signed the land-grant measure providing aid to the four trans-Iowa lines then in prospect. The Burlington grant was the southernmost; to the north of it lay, in order, lands that were to accrue to what eventually became the Rock Island, the North Western, and the Illinois Central; later on, the future Milwaukee also received a grant.

As was customary at the time, the granted lands were to pass first to the state; title was not to be transferred to any railway until after the completion of each twenty-mile stretch of track. Thereupon each company was to receive every alternate odd-numbered section (square mile) for six miles on both sides of the line, provided that such land was not already occupied or subject to some prior claim. If it was, the railway could select "lieu lands" up to the full amount of the deficit from the available odd-numbered sections within fifteen miles of the track. Proceeds from land sales were to be applied solely to construction, and the federal government protected its own interests, not only by doubling the minimum price of the even-numbered sections within the six-mile limits of the grant, but also by stipulating that such roads should transport the property or troops of the United States free, and carry the mail at prices to be fixed by Congress. Generous and timely as was this aid, then, it was strictly a business proposition, and in no sense a gift. The greatest beneficiary of all was the community, which, with rail service, could develop far more rapidly than would otherwise have been possible.

Under the terms of the federal act, no lands that would accrue to the railroads could be selected until the route of each road was "definitely fixed." Since none of the beneficiary companies had met this requirement at the time, the General Land Office withdrew from private entry all public domain in the general vicinity of the grants in order to prevent speculators from rushing in and staking claims on land that would otherwise go to the railroads. Governor Grimes of Iowa then called a special session of the Assembly, which on July 14, 1856, accepted the grant and laid down conditions under which the individual roads could receive their lands. Among other things, these specified that each company had to file its permanent location by April 1, 1857, complete, and equip at least seventy-five miles before December 1, 1859, and finish its lines by December 1, 1865. Gauges of all roads had to be standard (four feet eight and one-half inches) and "of a quality equal to the average of other first-class western roads." The state reserved the sweeping right to enact "such further rules and regulations" as it might deem appropriate.[4]

In no position to quibble over details, the B. & M. directors unanimously accepted the terms of this act on September 3 and authorized Thielsen to run a final survey over the route west of Ottumwa previously spied out by Hebard. A committee was appointed to visit all towns and counties on the route in order to receive donations of land, town lots, or other property and thus secure, as far as possible, a free right of way from Ottumwa to the Missouri River. Finally, Bernhart Henn of Fairfield was sent off to Washington to look after the joint interests of the B. & M., the Rock Island, and the Illinois Central.

This last move was a wise one, for complications immediately arose. The earlier orders of the General Land Office to withdraw from private entry lands within the limits of the grants had been intercepted and thus delayed; a dispute arose between the railroads and the state as to what was meant by "definitely fixing" a route, and a prolonged argument developed over conflicting claims under the Swamplands Act of 1850. The net result was that by the summer of 1859, when the railroad calculated that it was entitled to over 307,000 acres, the General Land Office would certify only some 230,000.

While these matters were running their course, the contractors pushed the railhead forward as rapidly as they could. But as 1857 dawned, it was apparent that more funds were needed. A second mortgage of $275,000 was placed on the first thirty-five miles of line in January, and in addition the City of Burlington put up $75,000 in municipal bonds to make sure that the road would reach the Skunk River in June. Even that accomplishment would mean little unless the road could reach Ottumwa, some forty miles farther on, where it could intercept the heavy trade along the Des Moines River. Furthermore, to hold its grant the company had to complete at least seventy-five miles before December 1, 1859.

So it was that in the spring of 1857 Joy hastened east to enlist Forbes and Brooks in a new drive for additional B. & M. stock subscriptions. Forbes, whose willingness to bet on the future vitalized his innate conservatism, promised to raise no less than $1,500,000. "I had vowed a vow," he wrote Corning on May 11, "to touch nothing new; but the Iowa road with its rich and populous country, and its 300,000 acres [sic] of *free soil* seems to me so very important an extension of our line that I cannot help taking rather more than my share there. . . . *Personally* I should not be sorry to see it dropped as it may lead to some care and thought . . . but it would be as bad a mistake . . . to let it go to the enemy . . . as it *would* have been to let the Military Tract and Aurora become tributaries to the Rock Island, which we barely escaped making under similar circum-

[4] State of Iowa, Act of July 14, 1856, reprinted in *DH*, Vol. II, pp. 13–16.

stances."[5] Forbes raised the amount he had promised while Brooks appealed to the Michigan Central stockholders and brought in another substantial block of subscriptions. Meanwhile, in order to exert a more direct control over the affairs of the company in which they now had an even greater stake, the easterners elected Edward L. Baker, of New Bedford, president on May 18 and arranged that future meetings of the board be held in Boston. By the time the railroad reached the Skunk River on June 17, it looked as though the B. & M. was on the march.

At this point the panic of 1857 broke upon the nation. The "unexpected revulsion," as the directors called it, cut off the road's supply of rails and so paralyzed the business world that it was not possible to call in subscriptions that were due.[6] Not until April 1858 did work resume in earnest, and then only after Joy had persuaded the people of Burlington to put up $75,000 more in cash for an equivalent amount of the company's stock and to give the company an outright deed to the river accretions, to be delivered when the road should reach Ottumwa.

The rails reached Fairfield on August 1. Despite the inevitable celebration, the prospects were still dark, for the bad crops of 1857 were followed by another virtual failure in 1858. Once again Forbes came to the rescue. On October 1 he arranged a million-dollar, eight percent loan due in 1883; this constituted a third lien on the first thirty-five miles and a first mortgage on the additional forty under construction as well as on the entire land grant. Even though the issue brought in only $833,000 in cash, it was enough to ensure completion to the Des Moines River.

Prospects during the early months of 1859 were mixed. Excessive rains and poor business generally prompted Baker to report in April that "hope deferred has made the hearts of many sick."[7] But the General Land Office finally certified the B. & M.'s title to over 230,000 acres, growing crops gave cause for encouragement, and local reports suggested that immigration into the state was bound to improve business. Consequently, in the summer a land department was organized. On the recommendation of Forbes, Charles Russell Lowell, who had been graduated four years earlier at the head of his class at Harvard and was a nephew of the distinguished poet, was put in charge. The job, however, was too much for one person, for apart from the chore of describing each section of land and working up a sales program, there was the necessity of handling with care and tact the inevitable disputes that arose over conflicting claims. So it was that Forbes suggested to Lowell that he consider hiring as an assistant an eighteen-year-old youngster named Charles Elliott Perkins, who, at the moment, was working as an apprentice in a wholesale fruit concern in Cincinnati.

[5] Henry G. Pearson: *An American Railroad Builder: John Murray Forbes* (Boston: Houghton Mifflin Co.; 1911), p. 86.

[6] BMI, AR 1858, p. 3.

[7] BMI, AR 1859, p. 3.

The boy was a second cousin of Forbes, and Lowell had met him at Forbes's summer home. Lowell accordingly offered him the job; at the same time, June 1859, Forbes sent off a letter of his own to his young cousin:

> If I continue so unfortunate as to be concerned in railroads, I can help you on better in that direction than any other, and if you can fit yourself to manage such matters well, you can be more useful in that line than any other. There is a great want of good, trustworthy business men for the management of our railroads, and I therefore incline to have you try to get into that business when you change. You know Lowell—the B. & M. Railroad is under the direction of myself and my friends a good deal, and if you can make yourself useful there, you would certainly stand a good chance of having your services recognized by pay and promotion when the proper opening comes. . . .[8]

One might wonder how the Burlington story would have turned out had Forbes not written that letter, for the lad who was running errands for a fruit store in the sweltering streets of Cincinnati was destined to become president of the entire system and to stamp upon it, during his administration of twenty years, characteristics that have become an essential part of the institution. As it was, Perkins accepted the offer with alacrity, and sometime early in August 1859 went to work as Lowell's assistant at $30 a month.

Hardly had Perkins arrived in Burlington when, on September 1, the B. & M. opened service to Ottumwa. An excursion train made up of nearly all the cars and engines the line possessed pulled out of Burlington; by the time it reached Ottumwa, it was filled to overflowing with more than two thousand people. There were speeches, a parade, and a monster picnic, for the B. & M. had finally reached a point from which it could look forward to carrying a substantial volume of business.

Among other things, the railroad opened a new day for the traveler; if he was willing to leave Ottumwa at four in the morning, he could step down in Chicago at seven o'clock that very same evening. Of more lasting importance, freight business grew rapidly once the rails had reached the Des Moines River. As of April 30, 1860, Baker reported a fifty percent increase in receipts over those of the previous year, even though the wheat crop had not come up to expectations and the line had been open to Ottumwa only eight months. At Burlington, the accretions had already been improved, and convenient freight and passenger stations erected. This, of course, stimulated business. So did the fact that whenever the hogs or cattle accumulated at Ottumwa exceeded the capacity of the regular train, the company ran an extra; in no case was the stock allowed to lie over for a day. Traffic consisted principally of corn, flour, hay, salt, cattle,

[8] CNB, Ch. IV, pp. 10–12, quoted in *BW*, p. 112.

hogs, and coal, the last being exceedingly popular with the steamboat captains who touched at Burlington.

The B. & M. spent two and three-quarter millions to put its line into operation to Ottumwa; exclusive of equipment and surveys west of that point, the road had cost about $34,000 per mile. Stock subscriptions furnished about forty percent of the funds, bonds the balance, on which, of course, interest was due at eight percent. Thus, despite the vastly improved earnings after the road reached Ottumwa, the company wound up the year ending April 30, 1860, in the red. But Baker was far from discouraged. He attributed the company's showing to the wretched crops of 1857 and 1858 and the "general depression resulting naturally from such a misfortune in an agricultural district."[9] Sure that with normal crops the road could more than pay its way, he reminded his stockholders that the land grant then being explored represented a tremendous untapped resource.

Indeed, at that very moment young Lowell and the lad Perkins were completing the extensive preliminary work necessary before the company's lands could be put on sale. Lowell visited the offices of the Illinois Central and the Hannibal and St. Joseph, returning to Burlington with a hatful of ideas. Thielsen, meanwhile, had been sent out with the first land-examining party; he had strict orders to deal extremely tactfully with actual settlers who might be on company land. Meanwhile Lowell began composing a pamphlet that would point out the advantages of buying land from the company. "We are beginning to find," he wrote to a friend, "that he who buildeth a railroad west of the Mississippi must also find a population and build up business."[1] This was a creed that the railway never forgot in the long years of its colonization activities.

In October 1860, Lowell resigned to return to the iron business. In doing so, he strongly recommended that Perkins be appointed to succeed him. "I offer my guaranty," said he, "that both personally and B.-M.-ically you will be glad you have got him."[2] Convinced, the directors on November 9, 1860, promoted Perkins—not yet twenty—to Lowell's position as assistant treasurer and land agent. His salary was boosted to $800 a year.

What lay ahead of the B. & M. at that moment hung in the balance. The toy-like cars of the B. & M. were bringing an ever growing stream of produce across the fertile acres from Ottumwa and down the bluffs into Burlington and hauling back merchandise and miscellaneous articles. But Abraham Lincoln had just been elected President of the United States, and it was possible that the delicate sectional truce, already stretched to its limit, might break apart under the slightest additional strain.

[9] BMI, AR 1860, pp. 4–7.
[1] Charles Russell Lowell to Charles Mason, October 20, 1859, LDP, quoted in BW, p. 159.
[2] Lowell to John N. Denison, October (?) 1860, CNB, Ch. IV, pp. 38–40, quoted in BW, p. 163.

CHAPTER 5

The Impact of War

1 8 6 1 - 6 5

O N DECEMBER 20, 1860, South Carolina seceded from the Union.
Before Lincoln's inauguration, six more states had followed suit;
along with South Carolina, they formed the Confederate States
of America in February 1861. When President Lincoln made it clear that
he intended to supply Fort Sumter in Charleston Harbor, the Confeder-
ates opened fire on the fort on April 12. War had begun. Within the next
six weeks, four more states joined the Confederacy, but four border states
where slavery was legal—Maryland, Delaware, Kentucky, and Missouri—
decided to remain within the Union.

From the standpoint of economic resources, the North was in a vastly
superior position. Its twenty-three states contained 22,000,000 inhabitants,
as compared with 5.5 million whites and 3.5 million Negroes in the Confederacy. Two thirds of the nation's railway mileage and farms, three
quarters of the bank deposits and wealth produced, and four fifths of the
factories were in the North. Yet the South, recalling how the Thirteen
Colonies had gained their independence against what seemed like even
greater odds, was confident. Its soldiers were fighting on home territory,
with internal communication lines, and were brilliantly led. The struggle
promised to be a long, bloody, and costly one.

As far as the C. B. & Q. was concerned, one thing was certain: both
the northern armies in the field and the civilian population would require
the agricultural produce and livestock that made up the overwhelming

[6 3]

bulk of eastbound Burlington traffic. And the territory that produced it would continue to demand the lumber and sundries that made up well over half of the company's westbound traffic. An upward surge of freight business seemed inevitable, and the chances were that as economic activity increased in the company's territory, passenger business would rise also. For the C. B. & Q., then, the wartime problem would be to carry the augmented load. This would mean acquiring more equipment and sparing no effort to make the entire plant as efficient as possible. Meanwhile, of course, the company could not afford to overlook any logical opportunity to expand and to simplify its corporate structure. And it would have to stand ready to give what help it could to its western connections in Iowa and Missouri.

The position of these western connections was in sharp contrast to that of the C. B. & Q. Although the Hannibal and St. Joseph had completed its main line before the war, it lay in a border state and was militarily vulnerable. Furthermore, until the outcome of the war, and along with it the status of slavery, could be determined, no large-scale program for selling the granted lands on which the company was depending for a considerable share of revenue would be possible. The position of the Burlington and Missouri River, stretching only seventy-five miles westward, was equally uncertain. Although probably safe from enemy attack, it depended largely on the uninterrupted flow of commerce along the Mississippi River to provide an outlet for the grain it carried, whereas its success in originating traffic was contingent on its retaining undisturbed control of its own local territory. Time alone would tell how well either of these western connections could cope with the actual or potential threats that wartime conditions imposed.

· The Task in Illinois ·

The c. b. & q.'s prime mission—to carry the war load efficiently—was clear enough, and to it the company turned with vigor. One hold-over situation that now demanded speedy resolution was the matter of an independent entry into Chicago.

Since the spring of 1859, a committee named by the stockholders had been exploring the possibilities of building or acquiring a wholly owned line between Aurora and Chicago. On March 22, 1862, its members recommended to the stockholders by means of a special circular that the C. B. & Q. build a direct "air line" of its own. This recommendation was based on a number of compelling reasons: after three years of negotiations, the Galena people were unwilling to sell one of their tracks east of the junction. That alternative had to be dismissed. Yet operation through the junction and over the Galena was becoming increasingly impractical because of the upsurge of traffic, and increasingly expensive because payments to the Galena were based on a percentage of total revenue. It was estimated that over the next decade the cost of doing business over the Galena would average at least $110,000 annually, whereas a new line via Naperville, Downers Grove, and Lyons could be financed and maintained, and its taxes paid for $93,000 a year. In addition to this savings of $17,000 annually, local business should contribute at least $13,000 per year, so that total savings would amount to $30,000.

At a special stockholders' meeting at Boston on May 15, 1862, the committee's proposal of a brand-new C. B. & Q. cut-off was accepted, and the directors were authorized to issue the necessary bonds under the 1858 mortgage. Van Nortwick immediately notified the Galena that the joint-trackage arrangement would terminate on May 20, 1864. On July 3, 1862, the board appointed Van Nortwick chief engineer in charge of the project; work got underway about October 1.

The winter of 1862–63 was a hard one, and labor was scarce. Cost estimates had to be revised upward to $850,000. One reason was the increased price of labor and materials; another, the directors' decision to install double track over the first ten miles west of Chicago. Despite the continued scarcity of labor and the necessity of having to dump an additional 50,000 cubic yards of earth into the troublesome marshes some fifteen miles west of Chicago, the cut-off was completed and put into operation on the scheduled date, May 20, 1864. The double-tracking was delayed until late in 1865, simply because every available piece of rolling stock was required to move the ever mounting freight business, and none could be spared for construction work.

Rapidly rising prices during the last two years of the Civil War brought the final cost of the cut-off to about a million dollars. The additional $200,000 beyond the original estimates was raised by selling new stock rather than by issuing additional bonds. The wisdom of the investment was immediately apparent. The cut-off carried so much business during its first year of operation that Van Nortwick figured that rental payments to the Galena would have amounted to $236,000. Moreover, the company cleared more than $25,000 from local traffic. The new line was obviously a resounding success.

Meanwhile the C. B. & Q. set about improving its terminal facilities in Chicago. Before the war, all the company's freight and passenger business, except for lumber and some other heavy freight, had been transacted on rented premises. As traffic in and out of the city grew, this arrangement became impractical, and throughout the war years the company steadily increased its land holdings along the South Branch of the Chicago River. As 1861 gave way to 1862, first the grain trade and then all Chicago freight operations were transferred from the congested Illinois Central yards to the Q.'s own facilities. By the spring of 1864, the C. B. & Q. had acquired approximately seventy-five acres, including 3,200 feet of river and dock frontage just south of the present Union Station. On this land the company built two large stone and brick freight houses, an engine house and turntable, and the usual miscellaneous "appurtenances."

Special attention was given to the road's three chief commodities: grain, lumber, and livestock. An earlier contract whereby Armour, Dole & Company had erected the first grain warehouse and elevators on Burlington property was amended to provide twice as much storage space; meanwhile the adjacent slips were extended inward to permit easier and faster loading of vessels. These improvements came none too soon, for in the spring of 1863 Van Nortwick reported that 1,600,000 bushels of grain had filled the new facilities to capacity even before the opening of navigation. A somewhat similar situation developed in respect to lumber. Under a contract with the South Branch Dock Company, the Q constructed and operated a track connecting the Dock Company's slips directly with its yards and depot; in exchange, the railroad received 800 feet of frontage on Joy's Canal and purchased enough additional frontage to make up a full thousand feet of wharfage 300 feet deep. Completion of these facilities in 1865 concentrated the bulk of the company's heavy lumber trade on its own grounds and made possible far more efficient service to shippers.

The Burlington's part in the evolution of the Union Stock Yards is a story in itself. By the spring of 1864, the movement of cattle and hogs over the C. B. & Q. was so heavy that the directors authorized spending $80,000 to purchase forty acres just within the city limits and adjacent to the company's new cut-off from Aurora for the purpose of erecting a stockyard. This step was consistent with that taken in respect to lumber; business could be concentrated at one convenient spot. But the wisdom of having each railroad build its own yard was soon called into question. On June 28, 1864, the Chicago Pork Packers' Association went on record in favor of a single, centralized yard, and commissioned their president to confer with the rail lines serving Chicago. To both Joy and Brooks the packers' proposal made eminent good sense. Presumably after consultation with other Burlington directors in Boston, Joy advised Van Nortwick on July 25 to hold up all work and expenditures on the Burlington's own yard until a decision could be reached as to the proposed joint venture. Meanwhile, Brooks worked out a specific plan, and when the packers met again on July 30, he suggested to them that they contribute $50,000 toward building a new belt railroad from the Illinois Central's tracks on the lake front around the southern limits of the city to the Burlington's new Aurora cut-off; the proposed line would give all the roads crossing it access to the new facilities. The packers promptly accepted Brooks's proposal and promised to raise the necessary contribution toward the belt line if the railways serving the city would extend service to the consolidated yards.

To these developments Van Nortwick objected strenuously. The

C. B. & Q., he told his board, required facilities immediately to handle the fall business. When the directors finally permitted him to do only enough to meet that requirement, he promptly proceeded not only to lay out a yard, complete with alleys, tracks, scales, and necessary buildings, but also to cover twelve acres of it with heavy planking to provide an all-weather dry surface. This prompt action, which cost the company $180,000, hardly pleased the directors in the East, who were eager not to appear opposed to the idea of a consolidated yard. But what was done was done; the C. B. & Q's own facilities began operations late in the winter. Meanwhile, in February 1865, the Burlington joined other railroads serving Chicago in incorporating the Union Stock Yard & Transit Company. At the first meeting of the new company, on March 2, those present visited the still incomplete Burlington Yard and agreed to buy, at cost, the equipment and material assembled there. On the next day Joy, as Burlington representative, was elected to the first nine-man directorate of the consolidated yards. Within three months, that board approved Brooks's original suggestion of a belt line, thus establishing the present Chicago Junction Railway. Construction on the new yard began in June 1865; it was completed on Christmas Day of that year. Early the following morning the Burlington had the honor of operating the first loaded train to enter the Union Stock Yards. Its fifteen cars carried 761 hogs, and with their sale a new era dawned for Chicago, the livestock industry, and the railroads. The Q, in more ways than one, was at the very center of the new enterprise.

Circumstances made it easier for the Burlington to make permanent terminal arrangements for hogs than for people. When the agreement with the Illinois Central for the use of its depot on the lake front expired late in 1861, the Q found it impracticable to make any satisfactory alternative arrangement. Such lands as it owned were needed for freight operations, and money was too tight to finance a new passenger depot. Consequently the arrangement to use the Illinois Central facilities was extended to June 1864, when it was renewed for another three years at a 33 1/3 percent increase in rent that reflected the rapidly rising costs of the day. Apparently, neither company considered the arrangement permanent, although, as it turned out, the Burlington remained on the lake shore until 1881.

One thing that could not wait was the improvement of roadbed and track. The original line had been constructed as rapidly and economically as possible; temporary structures and second-hand materials—solid enough for the moment, but subject to rapid deterioration and obsolescence—had often been used with the thought of replacing them as soon as earnings permitted. The old Peoria and Oquawka in particular had been put together by an impatient contractor, and at its western end was subject to frequent flooding. Even the Central Military Tract had been laid pretty much on dirt, and along the whole system lengthy wooden trestles, rather than earthen fills, carried the rails over soft and marshy grounds. Before

1857, some improvements had been made, particularly in respect to rail, but during the depression years, replacement work had necessarily been limited to the barest necessities. As traffic during wartime mounted, the company began ballasting mile after mile with gravel to a depth of six inches. A second requirement was to replace wooden trestles and long bridge approaches with fill. The company found that it could put in 800 cubic yards a day with its steam excavator at a cost of only eight cents per yard. During the 1860–61 season, for example, 1,286 feet of trestles were eliminated, and the program continued throughout the war. Where narrow water courses made filling impractical, stone arches or abutments were installed to replace the original all-wood structures, and as soon as the P. & O. was securely in the hands of the company, the C. B. & Q. replaced the "drowned roadbed" near the Mississippi as well as the rest of the "frail" line with proper embankments and bridges.

When it came to bridges along the line, Van Nortwick was in favor of using iron wherever possible, but the board was more cautious and, on the old P. & O. between Galesburg and Burlington, ordered him to build half the bridges necessary of "burnetized or kyanized wood"; he might build the other half of iron provided that he was "entirely satisfied of the absolute safety of the iron bridges proposed."[1] As far as the longer spans were concerned, Van Nortwick got his way. Two bridges over Bureau Creek were built of iron; each was to have three "Bollman suspension truss" spans, supported at the ends by stone abutments and in the center by cast-iron towers resting on masonry piers.

Meanwhile, the company stepped up its program of replacing the impractical compound-type rail with the more efficient T-rail, and by 1863 had installed it throughout the system. War conditions, however, made it increasingly hard to obtain either rail or ties. Early in 1863 the directors lent $13,000 to a group of Chicago men who promised to put up a mill for rerolling iron; the amount was to be repaid at ten-percent interest in the form of a reduction of five dollars per ton on all iron thus processed. Furthermore, Van Nortwick arranged with a Chicago lumber company to go over the great oak-producing territory of southern Michigan and northern Indiana to obtain an adequate supply of ties. These measures brought prompt results. Although track work was still behind schedule in the spring of 1864, the new Chicago mill was in full operation, and 50,000 fresh ties had been cut and were ready for installation. Furthermore, fifteen miles of track were laid that year with fish-joint splices, the use of which had been determined upon "as forming a much smoother track, less liable to get out of repair, and costing less than the ordinary rubber chair."[2] Outlays for track rose from $146,000 in 1861–62 to $393,000 in 1863–64, and in the

[1] CB&Q, ORB, pp. 203–4.
[2] CB&Q, AR 1864, pp. 27–8.

next year vaulted to $709,000 owing to an average increase of forty-one percent in the combined cost of labor, rail, spikes, and splices.

Clearly it took money to make money. By the time the Civil War broke out, the C. B. & Q. was fully committed to the use of coal rather than wood in its locomotives. In order to use Illinois coal successfully—it was all that could be obtained—the company found that it had to replace its iron flues with copper. The expense of conversion was fully justified, however, by the overall savings, and in 1865 only nine wood-burning engines were left in a total roster of 105 on the system.

During the war years, the C. B. & Q. virtually doubled its supply of freight-train cars and continued the trend toward specialization. By May 1862, for example, twenty-one new cars designed especially for livestock were in regular use, and during 1862–63 the company built 180 grain and merchandise cars, "besides 30 that were built to replace that number taken for government use on a requisition from Major-General U. S. Grant."[3] Even this was not enough, and in that year a hundred more cars were bought from outside suppliers. In view of the priority for freight-train cars, the company's shops were hard put to find time for passenger equipment. But as opportunity permitted, the program of "raising the roof" and installing clerestory windows in passenger cars continued; over the three years 1862–65 the company found time to convert four more coaches to sleepers and to build two new sleepers. Nine passenger cars and five head-end cars were equipped with six-wheel trucks.

Mounting traffic obviously required the construction of a wide variety of structures of every sort, and here again the trend was inevitably toward specialization. Reviving business compelled enlargement of the Galesburg depot and erection of new passenger stations at Princeton and Oneida, for example, but it was a sign of the times when in 1865 the company built a 9,000-square-foot loading platform in Chicago for the exclusive handling of agricultural implements. The engine houses at Aurora and Galesburg were enlarged several times, and a new roundhouse put up in Chicago was heated by steam and illuminated by gas. At Aurora the wooden locomotive pits were rebuilt in stone, and an artesian well was dug and fitted with a steam pump so as to provide 65,000 gallons daily of the purest possible water for locomotives. A large, brick car shop and a brand-new machine shop erected in Galesburg in 1862–63 were matched at Aurora by special shops for repairing T-rail and for "bending truck and other iron." Meanwhile, the company built a special snowplow house at Aurora, and Van Nortwick designed a "crane and coal hod arrangement" at the minehead in Kewanee "for rapidly supplying tenders with coal while engines are en route with their trains."[4] The Burlington was fast losing its homemade

[3] CB&Q, AR 1863, p. 11.
[4] CB&Q, AR 1863, p. 31; AR 1862, p. 45; AR 1861, p. 27.

handicraft look and developing into the complex machine characteristic of a modern railroad.

The first responsibility of the C. B. & Q. during the war years was to carry the load thrust upon it, and neither time nor resources were available to embark on any systematic program of expansion. On the other hand, the company could not afford to overlook opportunities at its doorstep. Intrinsically, the two tiny companies that joined the fold during the war were hardly worth more than passing notice, for despite their immediate value as modest feeders, many years were to pass before their extension transformed them into important freight links with southern Illinois. But the manner of their acquisition established a precedent that was used repeatedly by the Burlington.

The Jacksonville and Savanna had been incorporated early in 1855 to connect the cities of its title, but by August 1861 it had graded and bridged only some twenty miles southward from Yates City, a point twenty-three miles east of Galesburg on the line to Peoria. Thereupon, unable to pay its contractors, the company quietly shut up shop.

The Peoria and Hannibal, originally incorporated under another name in 1853, had likewise lain dormant for several years, and by August 1861 had graded and bridged only ten miles between the end of the unfinished Jacksonville and Savanna and Lewistown. Thereupon it too found itself unable to pay its bills and came to a halt.

At this point, Joy and Brooks arrived upon the scene. Before them they saw the tempting roadbeds and an imposing supply of rails, ties, spikes, and chairs. Very little seemed necessary to complete the entire thirty miles that the two little companies had so bravely begun. But with the Peoria and Oquawka and Northern Cross experiences fresh in mind, the Burlington stockholders certainly would not sanction another rescue venture. If Brooks and Joy wanted to acquire the properties, they would have to figure out a way of doing it that would not commit C. B. & Q. cash and credit. This is precisely what they did.

In the capacity of agents for the C. B. & Q. directors individually, they purchased both properties in exchange for the promise to pay their debts and to complete and operate them. They then agreed to sell what they had bought to the C. B. & Q., reimbursing themselves by issuing $125,000 in Peoria and Hannibal eight percent bonds which the C. B. & Q., if it took the roads, could service and redeem by applying to that purpose fifty percent of the gross earnings on all business originating, terminating, or wholly transacted on the acquired properties. The distinctive part of this arrangement was the pay-as-you-go principle: the desired roads would be acquired wholly from the profits of the business that they were expected to create. The C. B. & Q. would not have to issue a single new bond or share of stock or contribute anything from its treasury. Furthermore, Brooks and Joy agreed to furnish all funds necessary to complete the roads

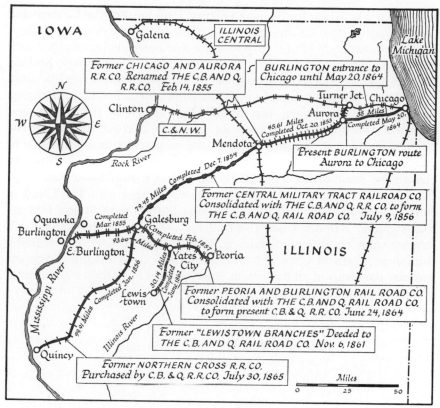

The C. B. & Q. as of July 30, 1865

by mid-1862, and said they would stand ready to operate them if the C. B. & Q. should choose not to do so.

The proposition was not presented to the C. B. & Q. stockholders until late June 1862. By then both roads were in operation. Van Nortwick explained that it had been impossible for the company itself to put up any money "even to secure a practical extension . . . into a very productive country" and then described the scheme whereby the properties could be acquired out of the profits of the business itself.[5] But he was careful to state that the arrangement was wholly contingent upon approval of the stockholders. Under the circumstances, the stockholders unanimously approved the deal on June 20, 1862. A year later, Van Nortwick had the satisfaction of telling them that the Lewistown Branch, as it was called, had fully lived up to its expectations; $37,000 of the $125,000 bonds issued had already been redeemed. A financial device had been established which was destined to serve the Burlington well many times over in the years to come.

During the war years, also, the Burlington acquired the exact corpo-

[5] CB&Q, AR 1862, pp. 24–5.

rate title it was to bear for the next century. Early in 1855 the Chicago and Aurora had changed its name to "The Chicago, Burlington and Quincy Railroad Company." When, in July 1856, that company had merged with the Central Military Tract, the title was altered to "The Chicago, Burlington and Quincy Rail Road Company." That company acquired by deed the two tiny railroads comprising the Lewistown Branch. The final change of title took place when the troublesome affairs of the Peoria and Oquawka were finally straightened out. Not long after the trustees for the bondholders of that road had acquired the property at foreclosure sale in October 1862, they secured permission from the Illinois Legislature to change the name of the P. & O. to the Peoria & Burlington Rail Road Company. On June 24, 1864, the P. & B. was merged with The Chicago, Burlington and Quincy Rail Road Company to form the Chicago, Burlington & Quincy Railroad Company, and the evolution of the Burlington's familiar corporate title was complete. Since the C. B. & Q. had acquired the former Northern Cross at foreclosure sale in April 1864, it thereupon was now the owner of all the system lines operated in Illinois, a grand total of exactly 400 miles, located as follows:

Chicago to Burlington	204 miles
Galesburg to Quincy	100 miles
Galesburg–Peoria	53 miles
Yates City–Lewistown	30 miles
Aurora–Junction	13 miles
	400 miles

Because of the way statistics were reported during the war years, it is extremely difficult to measure the operating and financial growth of the system during 1861–65 in meaningful terms. The figures available, calculated as they are from many different bases, are somewhat confusing, but taken as a whole they reflect the prodigious growth of business and earnings and indicate the added responsibilities facing management. In the year ending April 30, 1865, the 400-mile system produced over 107,000,000 ton-miles and more than 43,000,000 passenger-miles, and earned gross revenues of more than five and a half million dollars.

That position had not been achieved by a steady and continuous process. Even 1860–61—the first year in which total revenue came to predepression levels—had its anxious moments. When South Carolina seceded in December 1860, a brief crisis followed throughout the nation, and the company found it impossible to obtain funds for paying bond coupons or even temporary loans. To tide matters over, Brooks and Baker were authorized to sell sinking-fund bonds, to pledge notes, and to raise money "at such prices as they deem expedient."[6] In a matter of weeks the financial community had regained its balance, and the directors even authorized a

6 CB&Q, ORB, p. 163.

dividend of five percent on April 30, 1861, the first such payment since the summer of 1857.

Thereafter, in a period of rising prices and of labor and material shortages, recovery was bound to be slow. When gross revenues failed to register any perceptible increase and net income actually declined during 1861–62, the directors again decided to withhold all dividends, although they continued to make substantial payments into the sinking fund of the new mortgage. Not until 1862–63 did Burlington business move into high gear. In November 1862, the Q not only paid a five percent cash dividend, but also distributed an additional twenty percent in the form of a stock representing a part of the accumulated earnings of former years. At the same time, nearly half a million dollars were tucked away into the sinking fund.

But even prosperity worried the canny Baker. Writing to a friend in October 1863, he observed that the earnings of the company were very large, but that he did not deem it "politic to publish them to the world as it might provoke hostile legislation and cause a grumbling among our patrons."[7] Nevertheless, the company continued to issue its annual reports and to state its profits fully for all to see. During 1863–64, as both revenues and net income continued to rise, cash dividends of four percent each were paid in November and May, and in 1864–65, with revenues and net income jumping nearly fifty percent, the company distributed twenty percent in dividends, half in cash and half in stock.

The return of prosperity brought about one major change in financial policy. A million dollars originally had been earmarked from the 1858 bond issue to pay for the Aurora cut-off, and subsequently the directors had authorized the use of additional bonds to purchase the Peoria and Oquawka. As times improved, however, there seemed little reason to increase funded debt when cash could be raised by selling stock. Consequently, in the spring of 1864, outstanding shares were increased by a ratio of one to six. Proceeds were earmarked for the cut-off, for improved terminals (including the stockyard), for acquisition of securities of the Peoria and Oquawka and of the Northern Cross, and for a system-wide telegraph line. One new share of stock could be bought for $100 for every six shares held; as the market price at the time averaged 140½, the needed capital was attracted without difficulty. As a result of this policy, and also because of the payment of dividends in stock, the capital structure of the company was altered. On April 30, 1861, the amount of capital stock and the funded debt were almost identical; four years later, capital stock accounted for 59 percent and the funded debt for only 41 percent. Furthermore, the sinking fund reserve, which did not exist when the war began, totaled almost $650,000. Financially, then, as well as physically, the Burlington faced the postwar period in an extraordinarily sound condition.

[7] Edward Baker to Nathaniel Thayer, October 12, 1863, CB&Q/N, President's Letter Book #7.

This fact was not lost upon the investing community. A communication to the *Boston Journal* of July 25, 1865, pointed out that whereas the Chicago and North Western had cost $70,000 per mile, the C. B. & Q. had cost less than $35,000 per mile. Although this rather pointed public contrast might have annoyed a lesser man, William B. Ogden, then president of the North Western, instead pointed out to his stockholders just three months later that the "Chicago, Burlington & Quincy Railroad, through its series of consolidations, purchases, and construction, has made itself one of the largest earning and best-paying roads in the country."[8] From a worthy rival, this was praise indeed. In a sense it symbolized the C. B. & Q.'s safe passage through the tempestuous gales of the war years.

• WEST OF THE MISSISSIPPI:
THE HANNIBAL AND ST. JOSEPH •

THE WARTIME STORY of the western lines was packed with drama, discouragement, and surprising accomplishments in the face of hardships. That they survived at all and remained solvent was something of a minor miracle.

Like the Baltimore and Ohio, the Hannibal and St. Joseph was a border-state railroad, sandwiched between the principal bastions of the North and South, and therefore vulnerable to raids from either side. As early as May 1861, Corning wrote to the Secretary of War to warn him that the secession movement in northern Missouri was as strong as that in any southern state. He was convinced that one of the first things the secessionists would do would be to seize the railway and then interrupt if not suppress entirely "government and free state transportation & travel over it."[9] He urged the Secretary to furnish adequate military protection. The troops were duly furnished, and blockhouses were erected at strategic points along the line. Missouri, of course, did not secede. Nevertheless, bridges along the Quincy and Palmyra were burned late in 1861; in an effort to help, and mindful of its own interests, the C. B. & Q. put up the cash for rebuilding them. Even the gradual turn of the military tide in favor of the North seemed to bring little relief, for the rebels burned up so many passenger coaches that in the spring of 1864 not enough were left to accommodate business; Brooks pleaded with Corning to send at least five from the New York Central.

These were not the only difficulties. Land sales, slow enough before the war because of the existence of slavery in Missouri, virtually stopped altogether during the first two or three years of the conflict. Furthermore, what the federal government paid the railway for transportation of troops was hardly enough to cover costs. Although in the spring of 1861 the

8 C&NW, AR 1865, p. 39.
9 Corning to Simeon Cameron, May 1, 1861, EC.

Quartermaster agreed to deduct not more than one third from the regular rate of four cents a mile, his successor refused to pay more than two cents. This, Brooks said in December, was "much too low, but our poverty has told us to take it in order to keep the road going."[1] Also, the government was extremely dilatory in paying its accounts.

Despite these headaches, in the midst of the conflict the Hannibal and St. Joseph introduced an improvement that revolutionized a vitally important segment of overland transport. Late in July 1862, the company put into service the nation's first railway post-office car; on it the through overland mail was sorted and bagged while in transit between Quincy and St. Joseph. This time-saving innovation had been suggested by William A. Davis, assistant-postmaster at St. Joseph, and was authorized by the Postmaster General on July 7. Before the month was out, the company hastily converted a car for the purpose, and Davis himself was put in charge.

Not even the ingenuity that pioneered the railway mail-car, however, or the resourcefulness that kept the line open could bring prosperity to the Hannibal and St. Joseph during the difficult war years. Operating expenses were boosted not only by the rising costs of labor and material but also by the constant necessity of repairing property damaged by raids. The land bonds, issued under the Hannibal's largest mortgage, fell to twenty-five percent of their par value, while the company's stock brought not a penny on the market. Nothing short of a rigorous debt readjustment could save the road from bankruptcy. In 1863, all the company's bondholders except the State of Missouri, whose first mortgage, in the amount of three million dollars, could not be disturbed, agreed to a thorough reorganization. Under the provisions of the plan, they exchanged their old securities in varying proportions partly for new bonds and partly for non-cumulative preferred stock. As a result, fixed indebtedness fell from over eleven millions to just over seven, and interest requirements were cut from $700,000 to about $473,000. Net earnings of 1863 were sufficient to cover this reduced charge, and as affairs in northern Missouri gradually returned to normal, the company finished out the war years without falling into receivership.

• WEST OF THE MISSISSIPPI:
THE BURLINGTON AND MISSOURI RIVER •

WHEN, in March 1861, the United States government closed the Mississippi River to through traffic destined for New Orleans, the Burlington and Missouri River Railroad lost its principal outlet for the all-important corn trade. The price of corn at Chicago tumbled from 48 to 22 cents a bushel,

[1] Brooks to Corning, December 12, 1861, EC.

thus reducing the value of corn below the cost of shipping it from Iowa to the more distant markets of the East. "What is to be our fortune in the future," President Baker wrote in June, ". . . we cannot foresee. Our prosperity depends, we suppose, very much upon the success of the Government in putting down rebellion, and restoring peace and confidence. We can only promise the utmost vigilance in promoting the interest of the company, and the strictest economy in the management of its affairs."[2]

When the situation remained unchanged in September, Baker observed that matters might be remedied if the West would work its corn up into beef and pork, whose prices were regulated by world markets rather than by a single district of the United States. But he feared, and rightly so, that such a change could not take place in time to help the company during the current year. As a matter of fact, there was not enough money on hand to pay the semi-annual interest due October 1 on the land mortgage of 1858. Accordingly, the company arranged to pay the next two installments of the interest with income bonds and to withhold all dividends until fixed obligations could be fully met.

Even though New Orleans fell to federal gunboats early in 1862, the Mississippi was still partly in Confederate hands in the spring, and the B. & M.'s corn traffic for the year ending on April 30, 1862, was off ninety percent from the preceding year. To replace it, serious efforts were made to raise cotton. These failed, but as Baker had foreseen, the live-hog business doubled and saved the company from utter disaster. Even so, further retrenchment was imperative, and holders of the first and second mortgages were called upon, successfully, to accept interest in income bonds. Yet troubles multiplied. In 1862, the State of Iowa levied a one percent gross-earnings tax on railways, the Assembly persisted in delaying transfer of some fifty thousand additional acres of the B. & M. grant that had just been certified by the General Land Office, and both the federal government and the State of Iowa were slow to pay the company for the carriage of troops. To add insult to injury, the adjutant in charge of the military depot at Mount Pleasant persisted in issuing his own passes.

Fortunately, most of these problems were cleared up during 1862–63. The company was able to get clear title to most of its granted lands, and both the state and federal governments paid their transportation bills. More important, a steadily mounting trade in hogs, pork, and lard boosted net earnings, and the tide of immigration again began flowing into the state. Just as the situation began to brighten, however, a new threat developed: the Keokuk and Fort Des Moines Railroad, which crossed the B. & M. at Ottumwa, reached Eddyville some thirteen miles north on the Des Moines River, and thus effectively intercepted the heavy trade that funneled through the valley. This rival line had a direct con-

[2] BMI, AR 1861, p. 3.

nection eastward from Keokuk, and was therefore able to attract through business. The obvious course for the B. & M. was to build westward immediately; by doing so, it could command the business of the broad untapped lands stretching two hundred miles to the Missouri. But try as they might, the officers of the company were unable to coax the necessary funds either from the stockholders or from new investors.

Under the circumstances, the company proposed in October 1863 that the three outstanding eight percent mortgages be replaced by a new seven percent mortgage to mature in thirty years. The purpose of the new plan was not simply to reduce fixed charges, but also to provide fresh funds for extension.

Because a majority of directors of both the B. & M. and the C. B. & Q. served on both boards, this refinancing proposal of the Iowa road automatically came to the attention of the Burlington as a means of fulfilling its own long-run objectives. In June 1864, a committee of the C. B. & Q. directorate reached the conclusion that extension of the B. & M. would not only protect business the C. B. & Q. was already receiving from it, but also greatly enlarge it. In particular, the profitable cattle trade which originated at or beyond the B. & M.'s existing terminus held great promise for the future. Accordingly, in order to assure construction of an additional fifty-six miles, the committee proposed that beginning July 1, 1864, the C. B. & Q. devote half its gross earnings on business originating on or destined to the B. & M. to the purchase of that company's new extension bonds and preferred stock. Van Nortwick presented this proposal to the C. B. & Q.'s stockholders in June, taking pains to point out that the proposed participation by the C. B. & Q. would be precisely similar to that carried out in respect to the Lewistown Branch, although in this case the gains would be far greater because the B. & M., when completed, would inevitably command the trade not only of a large part of Iowa but also of the territory west of the Missouri River. Convinced, the stockholders readily gave their approval, and the bargain was struck. Van Nortwick made it clear that this proffered assistance would put the B. & M. in a position to complete its extension to the Missouri River by its own unaided efforts.

In the same month that the C. B. & Q. took this action—June 1864 —President Lincoln gave his approval to an act of Congress which permitted the B. & M. to select such additional unappropriated public lands as might be available within twenty miles of its line to the extent necessary to secure the number of acres the company would have received had it been able to obtain each alternate section within six miles under the original grant of 1856. As a result, the B. & M. acquired over a hundred thousand more acres, thus improving the collateral behind the land mortgage and giving promise of welcome additional receipts from land sales.

Just a month later, on July 2, 1864, the B. & M. received an even greater boon. On that date the Pacific Railway Act was so amended as to permit the B. & M. to connect with the main trunk of the Union Pacific Railroad by extending through Nebraska to some point not farther west than the 100th meridian. To aid construction of such a line, Congress granted every available alternate odd section of public land "to the amount of ten alternate sections per mile on each side of the line," provided that the road should be completed according to satisfactory standards within ten years.[3] Unlike any other federal grant, this one specified no lateral limits. Assuming the Nebraska road to be 185 miles long, the company could therefore reasonably look forward to receiving 2,368,000 acres, more than six times the amount of the Iowa grant. In November, despite reported Indian uprisings, a preliminary survey was run west of the Missouri as far as Fort Kearney. On the basis of this report the company accepted the Nebraska grant in January 1865. Thus, in addition to all other considerations, there was new and compelling reason for completing the road across Iowa.

As the spring of 1865 rolled around, the B. & M.'s railhead was still at Ottumwa, and nothing whatever had been done to benefit from the C. B. & Q.'s offer. The reason lay in the stubborn attitude of certain second-mortgage bondholders who vigorously objected to the 1863 refinancing plan because they were to receive fewer new bonds and more stock than any other class of bondholders. Eventually, Forbes and Brooks applied enough pressure to these recalcitrant bondholders to secure their assents to the refinancing plan by mid-June 1865. This paved the way to acceptance of the C. B. & Q.'s offer of assistance, and in July 1865 the B. & M. finally began to build west of Ottumwa.

Although the Q's stock-and-bond purchase plan was the most significant indication of the close relationship between the Illinois and Iowa companies, it was by no means the only one. So far as operations went, every train on the B. & M. of whatever sort was run in connection with those of the C. B. & Q. Furthermore, during 1863–64 all C. B. & Q. facilities at East Burlington were moved across the river and plans were laid to build a bridge over the Mississippi. Until that could be done, the Illinois company provided the necessary ferry service, improving it as time went on.

Meanwhile, despite the recurrent shortages of funds, material, and labor, the B. & M. struggled manfully throughout the war years to keep its road and equipment in proper shape. Improvements, however, were pitifully crude in contrast to those on the prosperous Illinois properties. With only half the line ballasted with gravel and broken stone in 1861, the superintendent went to work sodding the slopes along the roadbed, lest heavy rains wash it away. A good many timber bridges were rebuilt of

[3] Pacific Railway Act as amended 1864, 13 *Statutes-at-Large*, p. 356, July 2, 1864, reprinted in *DH*, Vol. III, p. 28.

stone, and a major span over the Skunk River was converted into a suspension bridge by using Roebling's wire cables. Ties were replaced with some regularity, but as rail became defective, the only recourse was to replace it with less worn iron from side tracks; in 1865 Perkins, then superintendent, bewailed the fact that only one mile of new rail had been laid in six years.

Throughout the war years, the B. & M. kept things moving with only eight locomotives; not until 1863 was the first of these converted to coal. Meanwhile, 150 freight cars sufficed to carry the load; forty more were added in 1864, another forty the next year. Apparently the Iowa line had no passenger cars of its own until it purchased two in mid-1864; until then it had borrowed equipment from the C. B. & Q. Even more indicative of the pint size of the B. & M. was the fact that as late as 1865 the average train hauled only eight freight cars and two passenger cars; its average freight-train load was forty-two tons. Even so, freight business increased fifty percent during the war years while passenger traffic as well as net earnings doubled. The B. & M., small as it was, never forgot its hopes to become part of a Great Lakes–Missouri River through line. As the C. B. & Q.'s security purchase plan of 1864 began to take effect, it appeared that the rosy future might not be so distant after all.

• THE ADMINISTRATIVE CHALLENGE •

So MUCH for the separate parts of the Burlington, east and west of the river. For seven years, counting three for the depression and four for the Civil War, the youthful system had been called upon to meet every variety of challenge under the most difficult conditions imaginable. In retrospect it is probably safe to say that no seven years in the company's long history ever posed so many novel and unforeseen challenges. Yet, one by one they were met. In Illinois, where the C. B. & Q. handled a war load for which it was hardly prepared, the physical plant had been enormously strengthened, a direct line to Chicago established, and adequate yards and terminals secured. New cars, many of them specialized, doubled the company's carrying capacity; wood was almost completely replaced by coal as fuel. The troublesome Peoria and Oquawka and the old Northern Cross had finally been brought into the fold and the C. B. & Q. corporate organization had been simplified. Meanwhile, a novel pay-as-you-go plan had been evolved for the Lewistown Branch and subsequently applied to the B. & M. of Iowa. Again, the C. B. & Q. was losing its handmade look and taking on the aspect of a heavy-duty, mass-production machine. The substitution of numbers for names on locomotive cabs was a revealing sign of the times. Finally, the roads in both Missouri and Iowa had devised and carried through debt-adjustment plans that had enabled them to remain solvent and plan for the future.

If any common denominator explained this performance, it was the administrative acumen and financial resourcefulness of the Forbes Group, which controlled the policies of the entire system. The leaders—Forbes, Brooks, Corning, Baker, and Joy—all believed, without qualification, in the eventual development of the West. Yet none of them, at least in this period, was a plunger. Rather, they were conservative investors willing and able to plan and act for the long run. Once they had decided that the Peoria and Oquawka and the Northern Cross were essential to an effective trans-Illinois system, they persevered until they acquired them. Likewise, despite the scarcity and high price of labor and materials, they pushed through their independent entrance to Chicago and played a leading part in setting up the Union Stock Yards. Every one of these moves reflected their faith in the West and their determination to pay the price to build for the future.

But more than faith and determination were needed to succeed; men of experience and know-how were required. These the Group either supplied from among its own number or sought out and put on the job. In respect to engineering and operations, Brooks was a tower of strength, and he was ably assisted on the ground by such hand-picked men as Van Nortwick in Illinois, Hayward in Missouri, and Thielsen in Iowa. Where problems were on a smaller scale, though ticklish enough, Forbes threw such youngsters as Lowell and Perkins into the breach.

When it came to negotiations and deals, Joy was inevitably called upon, whether it was a question of Chicago terminal arrangements, the Stock Yards, the Lewistown lines, or the Iowa road. When iron and other supplies were short, when additional investors were needed, or if tactful pressure seemed appropriate in political circles, Corning was the usual point of refuge; Baker, shrewd observer, acted more or less as a general counselor. Over the whole Group presided Forbes, much in the manner of a prime minister. That, of course, was not his only function, for he also acted specifically as his own diplomat and as secretary of the exchequer. Whenever the entire economic and moral weight of the Group had to be concentrated on an obdurate obstacle, such as Duff in Missouri or Harding in Illinois, Forbes brought it to bear in person. Whenever a major financial plan was brewing, Forbes gave it form and put it across. He filled another indispensable function, that of personnel director. Not only did he select and hire promising men, including Lowell and Perkins and a dozen others; he also kept such diverse spirits as the crotchety Corning and the irrepressible Joy working harmoniously together, and through it all kept the confidence of those with money to invest, whether Baring Brothers in London or some well-heeled Boston dowager.

Actually, the Forbes Group was loosely knit; no articles of partnership or association held it together: mutual confidence and common support of accepted principles and practices welded it into a smooth-working,

flexible team. Notably, none of the principals resided in Burlington territory. Actual day-to-day implementation of policy had to be carried out
by lieutenants, sometimes acting through executive committees. The
ability of Forbes to pick men he could trust and to allow them enough
on-the-spot authority was an essential ingredient of success. Sometimes,
as he wrote a friend in 1857, "honest" mistakes were made because he
and his associates were "too full of work to attend to details."[4] On the
whole, however, the system of delegation of power and constant communication worked surprisingly well.

The relation of the Burlington to politics is harder to define, primarily
because of the scarcity and elusive nature of material on the subject. As
an ordinary citizen, the company, from the moment it came into being,
had the same obligations and privileges as any person: it had to obey the
law, pay taxes, and keep the peace. On the other hand, it was entitled to
protection and, like anyone else, to state its position publicly when its interests in the community were involved. Beyond that, however, there were
special considerations affecting the political status of the company simply
because it was a public service institution. Because it possessed such special
privileges as the right of eminent domain, and because many of its policies
inevitably affected the public at large, it had to seek legislative authority—
in the form of a charter—to go into business in the first place, and further
permission to make any changes in its status. Furthermore, because, in the
eyes of the community, the Burlington even from its earliest days was a
"big business," and as such was regarded as rich and powerful, it had to
guard against overenthusiastic taxing and regulatory authorities without,
in the process, alienating the general public, on whom it depended for
business.

So it was that men like Joy, Forbes, Perkins, Holdrege, Morton,
Olney, Blythe, and others—of whom more later—kept a close eye on both
local and national political developments, whether in the councils of the
major parties or in legislative halls and committee rooms. Joy, for example,
served a term in the Michigan Legislature, Forbes was for eight years on
the National Executive Committee of the Republican Party, Morton
served as Cleveland's Secretary of Agriculture, and in the same administration Olney held, successively, the posts of Attorney-General and Secretary of State. Yet it is impossible to state, with any pretense to accuracy,
the extent and specific nature of such political influence as the railroad
or its friends exerted on its behalf. That some influence was exerted is
clear from scattered references, and when particular issues that could be
solved only by legislative or judicial action were at stake (such as, for
example, the Iowa land grant, the Kearney Gateway dispute, and the
Nebraska Maximum Rate Law, the last two to be discussed below), the

[4] Forbes to Ashburner, January 19, 1857, in Sarah Forbes Hughes, ed.: *Letters and
Recollections*, Vol. I, p. 162.

railroad was particularly active. But to generalize as to the possible beneficial or harmful effects of such activities is impossible because of the lack
of complete or even adequate evidence.

During the company's earliest years, when communities were vying
with each other to attract railroads, Joy, to judge from his speedy accomplishments, was welcomed at town and county political gatherings
and at state legislative sessions. Perkins, on the other hand, seemed not to
relish such contacts. Early in 1864 he wrote his fiancée that he was about
to leave for Des Moines to see the Iowa Legislature, "a body of wise men
who have met every two years for a length of time sufficient to have passed
all necessary and a good many unnecessary laws, so now they meet and
look around to see if some new *necessarity* [sic] for a law can't be created,
and then with great relish they *make* the law? [sic] There is a good deal
of nonsense in this very pleasant and agreeable world."[5] When he returned, Perkins reported that he had not spent any money lobbying at the
State House. Yet two years later, upon sending a political friend at Des
Moines some passes for distribution, he wrote him, rather ruefully: "I
may not approve of such means of gaining friends but, unfortunately, the
world is wicked."[6]

As the Civil War drew to a close in the spring of 1865, one all-
important question for the Burlington was whether the loosely knit Forbes
Group could and would cope with the new administrative problems that
would inevitably arise—for it was abundantly apparent that the nation
was about to embark on a new era. From a statistical standpoint, it has
been demonstrated that the rate of industrial growth, and particularly that
of the railways, fell during the years of conflict. For example, the average
national rate of new railroad construction for 1861–65 was less than 700
miles per year, compared with 2,450 miles per year over the preceding
five-year period. On the Burlington itself, the average rate of new lines
built during the war had fallen to a scant thirteen miles per year in contrast to eighty-five miles per year during 1856–60 inclusive.

But figures such as these obscure two cardinal considerations well
appreciated at the time. In the first place, despite the curtailment of the
means of production, there was a vast increase in absolute terms in output
of existing facilities. In Iowa, for example, Superintendent Thielsen of the
B. & M. managed to accommodate a 240 percent increase in traffic without a single addition to rolling stock, and in Illinois traffic on the
C. B. & Q. grew many times faster than plant and equipment. So it was
throughout the nation. Somehow the industrial East had been able to
supply sufficient coal, iron, and textiles to meet the demands of the conflict, and the West had shown, when the need arose, what it could do to
feed a growing nation. In brief, the Civil War, so tragic in itself, had

[5] Perkins to Edith Forbes, February 23, 1864, C–O, RCO Notebook #1, p. 162.
[6] Perkins to General Warren, January 9, 1866, C–O, Set A–1, p. 112.

acted as a catalyst of the nation's resources and suggested the immensity of their potential for the postwar period.

This was as true in human as in material terms. In industry, trade, and transport, as well as in banking, leaders emerged who were able and eager to develop these resources to the utmost. Some, like Jay Cooke and J. Pierpont Morgan, were primarily financiers. Others, such as Alexander Holley in steel, Philip Armour and Nelson Morris among the meat packers, Cadwallader Washburn and Charles Pillsbury, millers, John D. Rockefeller in oil, McCormick in agricultural machinery, Thomas Scott, Alexander Mitchell, and Collis P. Huntington, railroaders, had shown their capacity as business leaders in particular fields. Not far behind them were "comers" such as Andrew Carnegie, Grenville Dodge, Jay Gould, Gustavus Swift, and Cornelius Vanderbilt. True enough, these men had been hard put to it to find adequate help to do the essential pulling and hauling. The rate of immigration fell off during the early war years, but it revived again in 1863. Besides, demobilization of the armies would make available a young and energetic labor force. Furthermore, countless ordinary citizens, having put their savings into government bonds or private shares during the conflict, had become investment-conscious.

A second fact, well understood as the war came to an end, was the outstanding position of the West as a potential growth area. One had only to look at the mineral-laden hills, the vast reaches of fertile plains, and— in the Far West—the endless stretches of virgin forest, to sense the future of the miner, the rancher, the farmer, the lumberman, and the countless others who would provide essential services for them. And now, in contrast to the prewar years, the major factors that had prevented occupation of the West either had been removed or were subject to removal. Plans were afoot and the means at hand to contain and eventually eliminate the Indian menace. Thanks to the Homestead Act passed in 1862, as well as to the increasing number of railroad land grants, the door to the individual acquisition of land was open wider than ever. The promise of additional capital was there too: quite apart from surplus funds acquired in the East and looking for investment, local credit could be generated from the federal land grants, municipal and county bonds, and promises of state aid. What was needed to vitalize these factors more than anything else was railroads.

Ever since Asa Whitney had proposed building a transcontinental line before the Mexican War, this particular prospect had been very much on the national mind. Throughout the 1850's, the subject was hotly debated in Congress, as any such project would need substantial federal aid in the form of cash and lands. Sectional considerations, however, prevented agreement as to a route, and it was not until the southerners left Congress that action was possible. Then, in 1862, Lincoln signed the Pacific Railroad bill providing for a road between Council Bluffs and San

Francisco and endowing it with land grants and government loans. That bill was amended in 1864 to provide, among other things, for a number of feeder lines, including the proposed extension of the B. & M. in the State of Nebraska. When the Civil War ended, the Union Pacific was still an isolated, rickety affair that reached out only a few miles beyond Omaha. But no doubt existed that the return of peace would lead to its completion and bring construction not only of feeders to that particular line, but also of extensions elsewhere throughout the West. There was a particular reason why this should be so; although in the East both the North and the South required more railroads, these regions had long been settled and were laced with highways and countless navigable streams. In the West, on the other hand, there were precious few roads and even fewer practical water arteries. Railroads alone could open the vast untapped plains and prairies.

In such a context, the location of the Burlington was of strategic importance. At Chicago, its eastern base, it connected with the trunk lines to the Atlantic seaboard. In Illinois it constituted a through artery; the connections it controlled west of the Mississippi penetrated to the very edge of civilization. In fact, as of 1865, St. Joseph was the westernmost point on the national railway network.

Clearly and inevitably, the Burlington was on the threshold of rapid expansion. The years ahead would call for rapid decision: not the routine sort necessary to keep the road running in the black from year to year, but long-run commitments as to whether, where, and when to expand. If the company should plunge ahead too rapidly, disaster could follow. If it hesitated too long, some golden chance might be lost forever. If it stood upon principle, it might be outdistanced by more unscrupulous rivals; if it indulged in sharp practice, it might find itself with a permanently embarrassing skeleton in the closet. The future of the company would certainly depend both upon the quality and the speed of its top-level decisions.

Could the master craftsmen who had brought the system into being and seen it through the trying years of the panic and the Civil War function equally well on an accelerated mass-production basis? Would Forbes and his associates devote a proportionately smaller amount of time to each decision, or would they divide their work, relying upon each individual member to carry out some specific assignment? Would the informal means of communication so far developed prove adequate and provide necessary control?

On June 23, 1865, John Van Nortwick resigned as president of the C. B. & Q. As he explained to his colleagues, he felt that his private affairs required more of his time than would be consistent with the proper discharge of his official duties. He doubtless recognized that, with conditions and prospects as they were, the railroad would demand an increasing share, if not all, of his time. But other considerations apparently were in his mind as well. During his administration, 1857–65, the primary problem had been to achieve internal efficiency, and for this Van Nortwick had been superbly trained. As an engineer he had known how to gear his operations so as to obtain the best possible performance, whether he was faced with the thin traffic of the depression years or the huge business generated by the war. Furthermore, as an established businessman in the community, he had proved to be an able negotiator with neighboring roads and with public authorities. But as the war drew to a close and expansion became increasingly inevitable, it was clear that the centers of activity would be on the frontiers, as it were, and that expansion would take place under hotly competitive conditions. This meant that whoever sat in the president's chair would have to be clothed with ample authority. In the dispute over building a separate stockyard in Chicago for the C. B. & Q., Van Nortwick had found that his authority was hardly un-limited. And he was too experienced a man to accept increased respon-sibility without assurance of commensurate authority. So Van Nortwick resigned, taking with him the genuine respect and admiration of his colleagues.

The immediate question was whom to put in his place. Forbes, Corn-ing, Denison, and Baker were all anchored in the East, and none of them was well informed about the practical aspects of railroading. Brooks, the engineer, was a logical candidate, but he was an engineer first and an ad-ministrator second. For these reasons, if no others, all signs pointed to James F. Joy. He now had to his credit twenty years of top-level decision-making in Michigan Central affairs and was intimately acquainted on a first-hand basis with the Burlington property, on which he had held successive responsible posts. He had proved himself an astute lawyer, a natural-born negotiator, and an adept student of operating detail. Perhaps more to the point, he had demonstrated his ability to handle several complex matters at the same time, to sense new opportunities, and to devise ingenious ways to grasp them. His boldness and sophistication appeared to be precisely what the situation in the West demanded. On July 12, 1865, he was elected president of the C. B. & Q.

CHAPTER 6

Expansion Westward

1 8 6 5 - 7 3

W HEN James F. Joy took over the reins of the C. B. & Q., he had, among other things, two specific assets that were to stand him in good stead in the years immediately ahead. One was the tremendous confidence of his fellow directors. As early as 1858 Forbes assured Joy that he "had a foundation in my esteem and respect that I am sure nothing can shake."[1] The practical result of this opinion—which was shared by other members of the directory—was that Joy was to have virtually a free hand in the management of the property.

Joy's second great asset was his tremendous energy. The action of the board on October 24, 1865, for example, reflected this as well as his confidence in the future. "To keep pace with the growth of business," he asked for authority to construct two hundred cars and purchase six locomotives, to install double tracks all the way to Galesburg, and to have surveys made for a bridge at Burlington.[2] Except for limiting double tracking to a fifteen-mile stretch at first, the directors agreed. They also voted to buy extensive terminal properties in both Chicago and Quincy, to arrange for more sleeping cars, and to pay a dividend of $5 per share in cash as well as a dividend of one share of stock for every five shares held.

[1] Forbes to Joy, March 1858, quoted in M. C. McConkey: "Manuscript Biography of James F. Joy," in Michigan Historical Collections, Ann Arbor, Michigan (1933), pp. 553–4.
[2] CB&Q, ORB, Vol. II, p. 264.

At the end of his first year of office, Joy was able to report that "the progress of the western world is so rapid that in the very first year of a comparatively healthy and normal state of affairs, both the number of passengers and of tons of freight moved over the road have been larger than in any previous year, even during the war." He congratulated the stockholders upon the success of the company, but forcibly reminded them that they had a duty to "increase its ability for usefulness by completing those works which the property itself renders necessary and which no other interest is capable of accomplishing."[3] Here was Joy's philosophy in a nutshell; nor did his theme change as time went on. "In a country like the West," he told the stockholders in 1869, "it is impossible to remain stationary. If the companies owning and managing roads there do not meet the wants of the adjoining country and aid in its development, other alliances are sure to be found which end in rival roads, and damage to existing interests."[4] One thing was clear: there would be no lack of aggressiveness on the part of the Burlington if Joy could prevent it.

As of mid-1865, possibilities for expansion in Illinois existed, and before long something would have to be done to push the Burlington and Missouri River across Iowa if it was to become a major link in the system. But at the moment, and for a variety of reasons, the need for action was greatest in Missouri.

• MISSOURI, 1857–69 •

SINCE 1859, the Hannibal and St. Joseph had been in operation to the westernmost point of the nation's rail network; despite the distractions of wartime, it had sold and colonized some 77,000 acres of its land grant. Yet, more than anything else, what made the situation in the area so urgent was the tremendous possibilities of the southwestern trade beyond the Missouri, together with the determination of Kansas City to secure a direct rail connection with Chicago.

Railroad fever had struck Kansas City with a vengeance in the mid-1850's. Its businessmen had watched the Hannibal and St. Joseph with eagle eyes as it pushed across the northern part of the state. What they wanted, of course, was a direct connection to their own city. It was apparent, however, that the Hannibal and St. Joseph had neither the cash nor the time to think about branches; it was devoting all its energy to completing the original line through to St. Joseph.

So it was that a group of Kansas Cityans obtained a charter on February 9, 1857, to build the Kansas City, Galveston and Lake Superior Railroad Company. What a name! Actually, of course, all the promoters

---

[3] CB&Q, AR 1866, pp. 9, 14–15.
[4] CB&Q, AR 1869, p. 20.

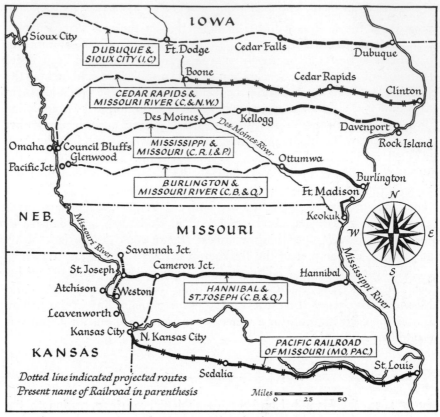

Missouri and Iowa, mid-1865

wanted was permission to link North Kansas City with Cameron on the Hannibal line, a matter of fifty-three miles. Actual performance made this plain enough. When the company was finally organized in 1860, it acquired a right of way between North Kansas City and Cameron and began grading. The war put an end to these activities. Early in 1864, the company obtained legislative permission to change its name to the more forthright "Kansas City and Cameron Railroad Company." The move constituted an undisguised bid for attention from the Burlington and served notice on such rival towns as Atchison and Leavenworth that Kansas City was in earnest about securing its link with Chicago.

This challenge to rival towns was no empty gesture. The net effect of the Pacific Railroad acts of 1862 and 1864 (which provided for building the transcontinental railroad) was to authorize feeder lines from St. Joseph by way of Atchison, from Leavenworth, and from Kansas City. If any one of these towns could contrive to be on a direct line from Chicago as well, it would have an immense advantage. Such a junction point would almost inevitably become the gateway to the Southwest.

[88]

Hopes for east-west connections were by no means the only prospects that bedazzled these hustling communities along the Big Muddy. They were eager to build north-south connections with one another, and presumably each had ideas of controlling such a line along the river. By the spring of 1861, St. Joseph was connected with Weston, thirty-five miles down the river, and with a point now known as Savannah Junction, some seventeen miles to the north. Furthermore, the energetic citizens of Council Bluffs had graded a line southward for a distance of nearly twenty-five miles. When peace returned, it clearly would be merely a matter of time until a continuous railroad would follow the east bank of the Missouri River all the way from Council Bluffs to Kansas City, thus providing a strategic link between the various Pacific-bound projects.

As far as both Kansas City and the Burlington interests were concerned, two more considerations were relevant. When the Civil War broke out, the Pacific Railroad Company of Missouri (eventually to become the Missouri Pacific) had built a line from St. Louis westward to Sedalia, a distance of 189 miles. On October 3, 1865, the tracks were triumphantly brought into Kansas City, thus linking it for the first time with the rest of the national network. Clearly, northwestern Missouri in the fall of 1865 was on the threshold of intensive railway building. This of itself was enough to attract the attention of Joy and the Burlington.

Missouri's only serious rival as a thoroughfare for east-west trunk lines was Iowa. But in that state the line farthest west at the close of the Civil War was the future North Western, which still had 145 miles to go to reach Council Bluffs. The runner-up in the race was the future Rock Island, which, having reached Kellogg, was 186 miles from the same destination. Bringing up the rear was the Burlington and Missouri River, still stalled at Ottumwa, with 212 miles to go. Not yet in the race for Council Bluffs, but making its way across northern Iowa toward Sioux City, was the predecessor of the Illinois Central, with 230 miles to cover before it reached its objective. Even though the four Iowa roads all enjoyed direct connections with Chicago, none could be expected to reach the Missouri River before a year or two at best. From the standpoint of the Burlington, northwestern Missouri rather than western Iowa therefore offered the most immediate prospect for linking the eastern network to roads bound for the Pacific. Joy understood this well.

The backers of the Kansas City and Cameron did not lack energy. Early in 1865 they obtained a charter to build a bridge at Kansas City, and as soon as the war was over they resumed grading activities. At this point, interests from Leavenworth tried their best to forge an alliance with the Hannibal, but the Kansas City interests countered by obtaining Congressional approval for their projected bridge, thus immeasurably strengthening their position.

The only way for the C. B. & Q. to decide whether to cast the lot of the Hannibal with the Kansas City or with the Leavenworth interests was to examine the situation on the spot. In the summer of 1866 Joy, with young Perkins in tow, visited both cities. After thorough investigation, Joy chose Kansas City as the southwestern terminus for the system he represented, and promptly recommended to the C. B. & Q. directors that they extend aid not only to complete the line between Cameron and North Kansas City, but also to bridge the Missouri River. So fast did Joy move that Max Hjorstberg, chief engineer of the Q, was making surveys and a preliminary report at the bridge site before the month was out. Events now moved rapidly: the Kansas City group formally changed the name of its railway, on November 12, 1866, to the Kansas City and Cameron Railroad Company (as it had obtained permission to do in 1864), and shortly thereafter completed all the grading. Later that month, the group signed an agreement giving the Hannibal the right to operate the Cameron line upon its completion. With these facts before them, the C. B. & Q. directors in December voted to apply forty percent of all gross receipts on business to or from the Cameron line to the purchase of not over $1,200,000 worth of its first-mortgage, ten percent bonds. Once again Boston dollars helped the West to live up to its destiny. Vastly encouraged, the Kansas City and Cameron people invited the future Wabash Railroad, then building from Moberly toward Kansas City, to share a portion of their line into North Kansas City as well as the bridge they contemplated building there.

All this, of course, depended on the successful bridging of the cantankerous Missouri River. To solve this formidable problem Joy, early in 1867, picked Octave Chanute, then chief engineer of the Chicago and Alton. The son of a professor at the College of France in Paris, Chanute had been active in railroading since he had been a lad of seventeen. Now, in his prime at forty-five, he tackled a job for which there was virtually no precedent and certainly no appropriate equipment.[5] Kansas City was some three hundred miles from the nearest large machine shops (at St. Louis), and farther yet from the nation's principal manufacturing centers; only one small foundry and shop existed in Kansas City. But Chanute took things as he found them and had a pile driver at work before the end of February 1867. Thereupon, the Missouri Legislature, noting that work was actually underway, granted the Cameron's request to let the North Missouri Railroad (as the future Wabash was then called) share the bridge. A paying tenant would ease the burden of heavy investment.

In November 1867, the Cameron line was finished into North Kansas City and was immediately turned over to the Hannibal to operate. Just

---

[5] During the 1890's Chanute conducted pioneering experiments in gliding which contributed to the subsequent work of the Wright brothers. Chanute Field in Chicago is named for him.

a year later, the North Missouri made its junction with the Cameron and thereupon began running its trains into North Kansas City and sharing use of the ferry across the river. All that was needed now to realize the Burlington's carefully laid plans in the area was to complete the bridge.

Even that achievement would be only one step in creating an efficient route between Chicago and Kansas City. As matters stood, the most obvious weak spot east of Kansas City was the absence of a bridge across the Mississippi at Quincy. Promoters in that area had already made plans for a bridge, but had accomplished nothing. Wasting no time, Joy in November 1866 merged several earlier projects into a new Quincy Rail Road Bridge Company and promptly negotiated an agreement whereby the C. B. & Q., the Wabash, and the Hannibal jointly agreed to lease, construct, and operate the bridge for an annual rental equal to ten percent of the actual cost of the structure. Thomas C. Clarke, a young but experienced engineer, was put in charge, and it was promptly decided to build an iron structure resting on stone piers with a pivot draw. The bridge company itself undertook the foundation work; the contract for the superstructure was awarded to the Detroit Bridge and Iron Works. By March 1867, construction was well underway.

Meanwhile, Joy was busy raising capital for the undertaking. In January 1867, the directors of both the C. B. & Q. and the Hannibal issued circulars inviting their respective stockholders to subscribe for stock in the Quincy Bridge Company. The same notice, incidentally, gave them an opportunity to invest in Cameron bonds. Nothing could have better evidenced the fact that the improvement of the Chicago–Kansas City line was a unified project.

In June 1867, Joy told his C. B. & Q. stockholders that during the preceding year the amount earned from business exchanged with the Hannibal had exceeded half a million dollars, roughly ten percent of the total gross business of the entire C. B. & Q. For that reason, he explained, a great deal of money had been spent to improve the Quincy–Galesburg line. During the fiscal year 1867–68, joint business with the Hannibal brought in more than $600,000 to the C. B. & Q. It would seem that Joy's faith in the Southwest was fully justified.

On November 9, 1868, the Quincy bridge was completed and put into operation. It had cost $1,500,000, but business between the C. B. & Q. and points west of Quincy nearly doubled during the first year it was in use.

Meanwhile, Chanute was pressing ahead with the Kansas City bridge. Although the foundations and masonry work were handled locally, the Keystone Bridge Company of Pittsburgh was given the contract for the superstructure. According to the plans accepted, the fixed spans, of the trellis girder type, were to be built partly of wood and partly of wrought iron. A draw span of more than 360 feet was deemed sufficient to accommodate all foreseeable river traffic. Provision was also made for a carriage road laid directly on the track so that horse-drawn vehicles and trains would alternate in their use of the bridge.

All sorts of difficulties arose, for the river had a way of flooding and of shifting its channel. But on June 15, 1869, the draw was swung open for the first time, and ten days later a pilot engine crossed the completed structure. Finally, on July 3, 1869, virtually the entire population of Kansas City turned out to witness the grand public opening of the first permanent bridge across the Missouri River. The job had cost $1,000,000, but the value of the investment was obvious. During the two and a half years the bridge had been under construction, Kansas City had increased its population from 13,000 to 30,000; it now boasted no fewer than seven railway lines. Among others was the through road from Council Bluffs, which reached North Kansas City on November 25, 1869, and promptly became another tenant of the new bridge. Other roads leading out to the Northwest and Southwest testified to Kansas City's strategic role as a rail center.

The opening of the Kansas City bridge not only marked a major turning point in the history of the Burlington, but also gave the Hannibal a chance to live up to its prospects. Until then its earnings had been based largely upon local business. Now it could connect with such lines as the Kansas Pacific, which ran directly westward for four hundred miles and was soon to reach Denver. It connected too with the Missouri River, Fort Scott and Gulf, stretching away to the south. Business on the Hannibal for the year ending August 31, 1869, was one third again as much as the year before; its net land sales since the close of the war had exceeded 350,000 acres. In fact, Hannibal stock was selling at such high prices on the market that at the time not even the C. B. & Q. seriously considered acquiring it and consolidating the road into the system in the corporate sense. But from a business standpoint the Burlington was firmly entrenched in Kansas City, and was there to stay.

· Iowa, 1864–70 ·

The building of the Burlington westward through Iowa and into Nebraska was accomplished by a combination of impatience and ingenuity which barely won a victory over indifference and indecision. In view of the fact that even in 1865 the destiny of the Burlington lay westward along the course of empire, one would have expected the long-planned expansion across Iowa to proceed with the same energy and singleness of purpose as had been operative in northwestern Missouri. But doubts existed, not only in 1865, but also for a good fifteen years thereafter.

Fundamentally, all members of the Forbes Group participated in the entrepreneurial alliance primarily as investors. To them, the heavy outlays that would inevitably be necessary to build an Iowa railroad more than two hundred miles to the Missouri River, and then as far again into Nebraska, appeared of highly doubtful value. The country west of Ottumwa was still sparsely settled; Nebraska was a howling wilderness except along the Missouri River itself.

Under the circumstances, the B. & M. was given, in sporadic fashion, rather grudging assistance. Had it not been for the irrepressible insistence of young Charles E. Perkins and the quiet but steady support of Forbes and Denison, the entire project might have died on the vine. Had that happened, the Burlington Lines of today would certainly have been far different. And if Perkins had been kept in the background as well, the system would have lost one of its most distinctive characters.

Admittedly, the prospects of the B. & M. when the Civil War closed were not very bright. The railhead was still at Ottumwa, and the Des Moines Valley Road (which connected with what is now the Wabash at Keokuk) had built through Ottumwa and northwestward toward Des Moines, thus draining away considerable traffic. Furthermore, to the north, the Iowa extensions of the Rock Island and the North Western were connected with their Illinois parents by bridges across the Mississippi, thus having a distinct service advantage over the B. & M. On the other hand, in June 1864 Congress had liberalized the original B. & M. grant to the extent of 100,000 acres, whereupon the C. B. & Q. directors promptly agreed to accept over a period of five years $600,000 of the B. & M.'s securities in lieu of cash for the large balances that would fall due on traffic jointly handled by the two roads. The C. B. & Q., in other words, offered substantial support to the B. & M. on the "pay as you go basis" originally worked out in respect to the Lewistown Branches. In July 1864, Congress gave the B. & M. the right to extend its line due west across Nebraska to a junction with the Union Pacific and offered as well a land grant which, if earned, might amount to two and a half million acres. On January 1, 1865, young Perkins was promoted to general superintendent of the B. & M., and in the spring of that year Forbes shrewdly persuaded four of the C. B. & Q. directors to visit Iowa to see for themselves what the prospects were.

Quite possibly as a result of this trip, the C. B. & Q. board the next month renewed its offer to buy B. & M. securities, and the Iowa company not only accepted the offer but also voted to extend the line fifty-six miles to Chariton. To help finance the extension, Joy made a quick barnstorming trip to sell additional B. & M. stock in the territory and to obtain the necessary rights of way. By early fall, construction was underway. Joy prompted the C. B. & Q. board to authorize surveys for a bridge across the Mississippi. Meanwhile, Perkins peppered the officials for new equipment and motive power, which his growing line sorely needed.

Perkins, of course, wanted more than anything else a commitment on the part of the C. B. & Q. to aid construction all the way through to the

Missouri. But even though the energetic Joy replaced Brooks as president of the B. & M. in the spring of 1866, caution seemed to be the watchword. In October 1866, however, the C. B. & Q. board offered financial aid for sixty miles beyond Chariton. Shortly afterwards, its members committed themselves to build the Mississippi River bridge. Work began the following January, with Max Hjorstberg, chief engineer of the C. B. & Q., in charge. In the light of competitive conditions, these activities came none too soon. Early in 1867, the North Western completed construction into Council Bluffs; if the B. & M. was to catch up, it would have to move with unprecedented speed.

Champing at the bit, Perkins sent Joy a detailed report of the B. & M. operations through April 30, 1867, and a summary of construction and future prospects. At the moment, he said, the road was getting along comfortably with eleven locomotives, twelve passenger cars, seven baggage cars and cabooses, and 314 freight cars of all types. Gross earnings, as in the two past years, approached the half-million-dollar mark, but Perkins thought they would move up at least thirty percent in the coming year, if, as he fully expected, the line were to be completed some twenty-five miles west of Chariton. In fact, he urged, if the road were to be built all the way through to the Missouri River, its performance would resemble that of the C. B. & Q. in Illinois during the past decade.

Joy was delighted with the report and told Perkins so. Not only that: he had it reprinted in the C. B. & Q. *Annual Report* for 1867 and added his own enthusiastic endorsement of the B. & M.; there was no doubt, he said, that it was a safe investment and would be of future value to the C. B. & Q.

Despite this apparently warm support from Joy, Denison, who was on the spot in Boston, came to the reluctant conclusion that Joy was much more interested in building a chain of railroads between Council Bluffs and Kansas City than he was in the fortunes of the Iowa line. To Denison it seemed that this would drain off Pacific railroad business for the benefit of the Hannibal and St. Joseph and perhaps for the other roads out of Kansas City in which Joy was interested.

Denison was certainly right about one thing: Joy and Nathaniel Thayer were knee-deep in projects along the east bank of the Missouri River. In July 1867, they organized the St. Joseph & Council Bluffs Rail Road Company to build between St. Joseph and the Missouri border, and became the leading spirits in the enterprise. Perkins, becoming increasingly restive, wrote Forbes in September how vital it was to push the B. & M. westward. Perkins was sure that once the B. & M. was established on the river, it could take care of itself, but until it got there nothing could be done toward selling and colonizing the land grant. Undoubtedly one reason for Perkins's impatience lay in the growing political threat both in Des Moines and in the western part of the state. He felt that many of the legislators failed to see how closely the long-run interests of the people and of the railroads were bound together, and that unless the line was put through, hostile legislation and the taxing of the company's granted lands would discourage easterners from putting up the necessary capital.

Perkins's concern was premature. On motion of Forbes, in December 1867, the B. & M. directors made a firm commitment to the Union Pacific to build to the river if the U. P. would locate its bridge so as to afford a direct connection; furthermore, the directors authorized a complete survey of the country between the railhead and the river. In April 1868, the C. B. & Q. stockholders agreed to purchase enough additional B. & M. stocks and bonds to put the line through.

The question then was what route to follow. Joy wanted to build directly from Red Oak to Council Bluffs. But Perkins favored the earlier surveys due west from Red Oak to the river, apparently for the reason that the work could be put underway at once; this choice prevailed. In the light of hindsight, the choice was unfortunate because the Union Pacific finally built its bridge at Council Bluffs rather than near Bellevue as originally planned, so that the B. & M. had to build a bridge of its own near Plattsmouth. But the latter location did eventually make possible the present short line from Iowa directly through to Lincoln, Nebraska, and beyond.

On August 13, 1868, the bridge across the Mississippi at Burlington was opened for traffic. Built entirely of iron, it was 2,237 feet long, with a drawbridge in the center, and according to Joy was a structure "of great beauty."[6] Financed entirely by the C. B. & Q., it cost approximately $1,250,000, and though it carried but a single track, was more than adequate for the moment. As far as speed of service was concerned, the B. & M. was now on a par with its principal rivals.

Early in 1868, as the B. & M. railhead moved westward and the Mississippi bridge neared completion, the company's Land Department placed on sale approximately 75,000 acres of its granted lands in the eastern part of Iowa. No great effort was made to advertise or colonize this region, and sales moved slowly. But at least it was a beginning and gave the company experience that would be useful once the railway was completed and the time arrived for a major sales and colonization effort.

By June 1, 1869, when the railhead was at Cromwell, the company's stock had risen to par. In September, the railhead passed Villisca, and on Friday, November 26, at Glenwood, Perkins noted laconically in his notebook: "Last rail laid and spiked at noon today—went through with special train to Plattsmouth."[7] Company officials and visitors were on hand to watch the meeting of the rails, but there were no formal ceremonies. As the Burlington newspaper reported it: "Everybody was satisfied to accept

6 CB&Q, AR 1868, pp. 12–13, 41; AR 1869, p. 17.
7 Perkins's diary, in GM, Vol. II, p. 110½.

the situation without the customary buncombe upon many pretentious but less deserving occasions."[8]

Fifteen years of hard though intermittent work had been required to build the B. & M. across the state. There was one notable offsetting factor, however: the B. & M. was the only one of the four trans-Iowa roads given lands in 1856 that reached its destination without going bankrupt in the process. It had at least this one distinctive accomplishment to its credit even though it had lost the race across the state to the North Western by nearly three years and to the Rock Island by six months. Regular service over the new road to East Plattsmouth began on January 1, 1870, and two days later was extended by way of Pacific Junction to Council Bluffs over the rails of the St. Joseph & Council Bluffs Rail Road Company.

At this point someone—possibly Perkins, or perhaps George M. Pullman himself—conceived the idea that although the B. & M. was not the first line to reach Council Bluffs, it might make a reputation at the start by putting dining cars on its trains between that point and Galesburg. Pullman had two of them available, the "Brevoort" and the "Cosmopolitan." Robert Harris, general superintendent of the C. B. & Q., was somewhat skeptical of the idea but rather reluctantly agreed to handle these cars over the C. B. & Q. between Galesburg and Burlington. So it was that on January 15, 1870, the first Pullman Palace cars, as well as a regular sleeper, went west over the line, and Perkins had the supreme pleasure of taking his first meal aboard a B. & M. train. Two days later, the westbound train carried the special car "Omaha" complete with an organ and all the comforts of home for a special party of newspapermen. Harris continued to fuss over the cost of the cars, but before long came to envy the excellent reputation the B. & M. was gaining. Within a few months he had persuaded Pullman to promise that as soon as sufficient cars were available, the C. B. & Q. could have two to run between Chicago and Council Bluffs, and that they would be delivered ahead of similar cars for the North Western.

Completion of the B. & M. across Iowa brought a tremendous change in the territory it served. Population along the line zoomed upward, and during the calendar year 1870 the B. & M. reported a gross of well over two million dollars, about three and one half times the amount earned in 1867. Of equal significance, direct connections were established at Plattsmouth with the Burlington's extension already underway in Nebraska. Quietly and persistently the system was laying the foundation for its latter-day trademark: "Everywhere West."

In a wholly different sphere, the system laid another foundation of incalculable value. Actual responsibility for the day-to-day welfare of the B. & M. had fallen, often by default, on the youthful shoulders of

[8] Burlington *Daily Hawk-Eye,* November 27, 1869. Cf.: BW, p. 231.

Charles E. Perkins. Indeed, he and his assistants were so young that, according to the townspeople of Burlington, the enterprise had been entrusted to "a parcel of boys."[9] Yet Perkins's energy and faith, as well as his impatience, had been the most consistent factors in pushing the road to completion. In the process he learned more about every conceivable aspect of railroading and community relations than would otherwise have been possible, and he learned something too about corporate diplomacy. Even if every dollar spent in Iowa by the Forbes Group had been charged to Perkins's education, it would have been one of the wisest investments the Burlington could have made. Not that it was planned that way, but by a quirk of fate, that is precisely what it amounted to.

• NEBRASKA, 1864–72 •

EVEN BEFORE the fate of his beloved Iowa road had been settled, Perkins began stirring up the Bostonians about the possibilities in Nebraska. Thielsen had made a preliminary survey in 1864–65, and in the following year the Secretary of the Interior had withdrawn from public sale approximately 2,400,000 acres which the company might acquire as its land grant. Because of objections by Nebraskans, the area withdrawn (though not, of course, the potential land grant) was cut in half the next year. Thus matters stood in January 1868, when Perkins urged Forbes that the time was approaching, if it had not already arrived, to get started. The Union Pacific was well on its way, and for the B. & M. to hesitate much longer would be fatal.

Brooks was skeptical. To succeed, he thought, any railroad there should have a million and a half acres of decently watered land, a fair supply of fuel, and enough additional money from Congress to cover most if not all the original cost of construction. The mere absence of coal, he said, was enough to prevent the road from carrying on a paying business and to discourage settlement for a generation. The proximity of the Union Pacific would mean incredibly stiff, permanent competition; furthermore, how could enough grain be transported all the way to Chicago on a paying basis?

The way to answer this gloomy statement, if any existed, was to get at the facts. Consequently in December 1868 Perkins and Henry Strong, an attorney of the B. & M., were dispatched to Nebraska. Their report to the B. & M. board was a glowing one: for at least a hundred miles west of the Missouri River the country was as rich in climate and soil as any portion of Iowa, and was probably even better for raising wheat. Moreover, the state capital had just been moved to Lincoln, which was situated squarely in the center of the company's grant. Already government lands along the projected line were selling at good prices, even without a railroad. Perkins and

9 Edith Perkins Cunningham, ed.: *Charles Elliott Perkins and Edith Forbes Perkins: Family Letters, 1861–69* (Boston, 1949), p. 220.

Strong were certain that southern Nebraska would provide business and that the B. & M. ought to get it. Not only that, but the state had received from the United States some 452,000 acres of land to aid in internal improvements. If the B. & M. hoped to get its share, as well as a federal grant, it would have to give proof quickly that it meant business. Specifically, Perkins and Strong suggested building the fifty-five miles from Plattsmouth to Lincoln at once. They were sure that this would bring in stock subscriptions of some $250,000 from counties and individuals along the way, and that this much construction would entitle the company to several hundred thousand acres of federal lands which could be immediately colonized.

The reaction to this report in Boston was prompt and decisive. For one thing, it was determined to form a separate company for Nebraska. Thanks to the support of senators Grimes and Harlan, Congress promptly passed a joint resolution transferring the B. & M. grant to a new corporation to be called the Burlington and Missouri River Rail Road Company in Nebraska; President Grant approved the measure on April 10, 1869. On May 12, 1869, the new corporation was duly chartered to build from Plattsmouth westward to Kearney on the Union Pacific, and in June the B. & M. of Iowa turned over its rights and privileges, including specifically the land grant, to the new corporation. Without pausing to organize a board of directors or name officers, the incorporators of the Nebraska Company decided to finance the project by offering $7,500,000 in stock to anyone who would at the same time subscribe for half as many eight-percent bonds secured by the road itself and by two thirds of the land grant; the amount of bonds to be issued was limited to a maximum of $30,000 per mile of main line. Thereupon Cyrus Woodman of Cambridge, a trusted lieutenant of the Forbes Group, was dispatched to Plattsmouth, where subscription books were opened on July 7. Perkins was with him, and the two men had a standing order to take up for the Forbes Group all stock not promptly bought by local parties. Under the circumstances, it was not surprising that the entire issue was subscribed for in fifteen minutes and that control of the project rested firmly in the hands of the Forbes Group. Meanwhile, Thomas Doane of Massachusetts, an experienced engineer, was placed in charge of construction. He was present at Lincoln, on July 1, 1869, when Governor Butler of Nebraska turned the first piece of sod. Four days later at Plattsmouth actual construction began—to the accompaniment of a brass band and a parade.

Late in October, just about when the first iron rails and a second-hand locomotive from the Michigan Central arrived at Plattsmouth, the stockholders of the Nebraska company finally got around to electing their first board of directors. Besides Forbes and Brooks, they were Sidney Bartlett, John Burnham, and Nathaniel Thayer—all established members of the Group—as well as Cyrus Woodman and Charles E. Perkins. As four of the seven were also on the board of the B. & M. of Iowa, a harmony of interests was assured. In November, Brooks was named first president of the B. & M. in Nebraska and Doane was made chief engineer.

By mid-January 1870, the first ten miles were completed. The quality of the new road was such that the federal inspectors (who had to look over the line before the grant could be certified) expressed surprise at finding it "so substantial, smooth, and perfect."[1] But more than rails and locomotives were needed to build a railroad. As usual, Forbes had an eye out for bright young men. While the fledgling road was barely underway, he sent George W. Holdrege, a twenty-two-year-old graduate of Harvard, west to Plattsmouth. Another recruit, barely twenty years old, was Thomas E. Calvert, a graduate of the Scientific School at Yale. The two lads, living at the same boardinghouse, soon formed a lasting and fruitful friendship destined to be of importance to the new railway. At just about the same time, another young man came to Nebraska. A. E. Touzalin, an Englishman by birth, had capped a few years of railroading in the United States by becoming general passenger agent of the B. & M. of Iowa in 1869. Early in 1870 he came to organize the Nebraska affiliate's passenger department. With construction proceeding apace, this was none too soon. On May 9, 1870, service opened to Ashland, and on July 4 the rails were within a mile of Lincoln.

The holiday afforded an excellent excuse for a celebration, and the company offered a free round trip from Plattsmouth to Lincoln for all who wished to go. As not enough passenger cars were available, excursionists were loaded on flatcars fitted out with benches and protected overhead by a trellis through which cottonwood branches were woven. The affair was a rousing success, and not long afterwards—on July 26—the road was finished into Lincoln itself, where two thousand inhabitants turned out to meet a special train filled with dignitaries.

By April 1871, the prospects for the B. & M. in Nebraska were promising. During the preceding twelve months the company had sold nearly 80,000 acres of its grant at an average price of about $9.50 per acre. Immigrants were pouring in, not only brightening the prospects for future land-grant sales but also, more important, giving promise of increasing business over the line itself. Encouraged, the directors voted to issue enough additional bonds and stocks to complete the railway through to the Union Pacific; by the end of the year the line was open as far as Harvard, 136 miles beyond Plattsmouth. Construction was halted there through the winter, but resumed with vigor the following spring. The rails reached Kearney, a distance of 191 miles from Plattsmouth, on September 3, 1872, and were extended to a junction with the Union Pacific on September 18.

Meanwhile, the company picked up a vitally important link. Late in

[1] *BW*, p. 278.

1869, a group of Omaha businessmen had incorporated the Omaha and South Western Railroad Company, with authority to build all the way to Kansas. By the end of 1870, it had built thirteen miles south from Omaha (along with a seven-mile branch) and had received promised bond aid from Beatrice, farther along the projected route. In the spring of 1871, the O. & S. W. offered to build south to a junction with the B. & M. at Oreapolis; to fulfill the commitment to Beatrice, it was suggested that the B. & M. acquire the O. & S. W. and then let it construct, under its own name, a thirty-mile line southward from Crete (on the B. & M.) to Beatrice. As part of the arrangement, the O. & S. W. would receive 60,000 acres of state land, which it would divide equally with the B. & M. These arrangements were carried out, so that by the time the B. & M. was completed to Kearney, it owned 191 miles of main line between that point and Plattsmouth, and forty-nine more connecting it with Omaha to the north and with Beatrice to the south.

For the moment, the essential framework of the Burlington in Nebraska was complete in the sense that it had staked out and covered the territory it hoped to make its own. Of course, other railways existed in the area. The entire Union Pacific had been in operation since May 1869, but its attention was naturally on through rather than local business. The Midland Pacific, linking Nebraska City and Lincoln, had been in operation since the early spring of 1871, but relations between it and the B. & M. were so friendly that it was more an ally than a rival. The only direct competition was that of the St. Joseph and Denver City, a U. P. project that bisected the South Platte area. Its line ran through territory in which the B. & M. controlled most of the lands, however, so that the latter was relatively free to concentrate for the next few years on building up the network it had, rather than on adding to it for competitive purposes.

Putting flesh on the bones meant colonizing the land grant. To take charge of this vital enterprise, George S. Harris, who had gained wide experience as land commissioner of the Hannibal and St. Joseph between 1863 and 1869, was put in charge of both the Iowa and Nebraska grants of the Burlington in 1869. The challenge he faced was enough to test his ingenuity. Just north of the B. & M. in Iowa, the Rock Island had more than half a million acres of granted land ready for sale. West of the Missouri, both the Kansas Pacific and the Union Pacific already had organized their land departments; the former had sold nearly half a million acres by the end of 1869, and the Union Pacific was engaging in an all-out advertising campaign that extended throughout the United States and Western Europe. More remotely, both the Northern Pacific and the Santa Fe provided competition for potential immigrants.

By the spring of 1870, Harris had a program ready. Prairie lands in both Iowa and Nebraska would be sold on a ten-year credit basis at six percent interest; both prairie and timber lands would be offered on two

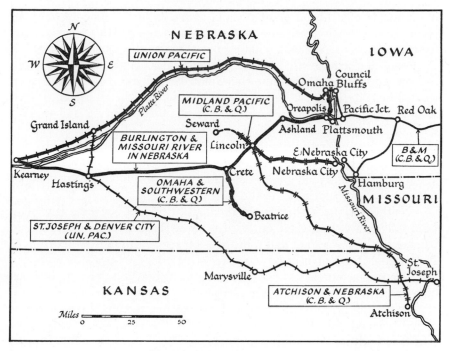

Eastern Nebraska, 1869–72

years' credit at ten percent interest or for cash at a 20 percent reduction from long-term prices. Bonds of either company would be acceptable at their face value in lieu of cash. By the ten-year credit plan, only interest would be due until the beginning of the third year, whereupon install-ments on the principal would become payable annually. But under the long-term plan, purchasers had to agree to improve at least one tenth of their land each year. Land prices were set according to the nature of the soil, proximity to the railway, the amount of available water and timber, and any other particular advantages an individual tract might have.

On the basis of his experience with the Hannibal and St. Joseph, Harris recommended that detailed pamphlets be issued describing the countryside, its resources and climatic conditions, and giving—almost like an almanac—all possible information that an intending immigrant would want to have. In addition to issuing pamphlets, he proposed using bulle-tins, car posters, handbills, circulars, and a generous supply of maps. News-paper advertisements, Harris thought, should be limited to brief notices stating the availability of pamphlets.

No one, of course, appreciated more fully than Forbes and his asso-ciates the role of the land grant in the scheme of things. As Brooks later put it, building a road entirely ahead of population and with no preexisting business to support it "would have been impracticable, except through the inducements of a liberal grant of land along its line."[2] The B. & M. in Nebraska eventually received about 2,450,000 acres. Of this, 50,000 came from the State of Nebraska (some of it through the Omaha and South Western), the rest directly from the United States. The situation, however, had one curious aspect. Because the Union Pacific and its grant had been located first, the B. & M. had not been able to find the equivalent of ten sections per mile of road in territory adjacent to the eastern and western ends of its main line. Slightly over half the land it received from the United States was more than twenty miles from the railroad itself, and some of it far to the north even of the Union Pacific. Consequently, only about half the total land granted could be used for building up permanent settlement directly adjacent to the B. & M.

Neither the precise extent nor the final title to all Nebraska lands had been fully established when, on April 1, 1870, Harris put the entire unsold balance of the Iowa grant and some 300,000 acres in the eastern portion of Nebraska—a total of over 600,000 acres—on sale. In Iowa, the company was able to give purchasers deeds at once; in Nebraska, sales were handled on a preemption basis with the understanding that the purchaser could exchange his certificate of preemption for a deed as soon as the railway was completed and title to the lands earned by the company. The pricing, credit, and advertising policies recommended by Harris were promptly put into effect. About one hundred domestic sales agencies were opened throughout the United States, two full-time agents were sent to England, and at least ten offices were opened in the British Isles. News sheets and circulars were published not only in English, but also in Scandinavian, German, French, and Bohemian.

The Burlington's colonizing campaign was so many-sided as to defy summary. Through its many agents, for example, the company kept a keen eye out for particular groups of potential immigrants who would make the best possible permanent settlers. Naturally, the bulk of purchasers came from nearby midwestern states, and they were welcome because they had already had experience in prairie farming. But the company made special efforts to attract New Englanders and Britishers. Special land-exploring tickets were issued to prospective customers, and if these people bought land within thirty days, the amount collected for travel in the state where the land was bought was credited against the purchase price. Immigrant homes were established in both Burlington and Lincoln; in these, prospective purchasers could stay with their families free of charge for a reasonable length of time while they were selecting suitable tracts. Once lands were selected, the purchasers were granted special freight rates on household goods and whatever other equipment might be needed to get established. Furthermore, Harris made it plain that if some purchaser encountered an unexpected reverse, the company would always be willing to grant reason-

[2] BMN, AR 1873, p. 6.

able accommodation until he could get on his feet. To avoid later disappointment, however, the company recommended that intending settlers have and bring with them a modest amount of capital with which to start operations, and warned against people simply taking chances on finding employment after they arrived.

The candor of the company's statements was refreshing. Perhaps the most characteristic of all appeared in a company news sheet in the spring of 1872: "No road proves a good investment unless its local trade and passenger traffic is heavy. No such traffic can exist except in a well-tilled and well-settled region. Therefore the railroad men have every inducement to advance the development of the country which their line traverses . . . it is to be expected that they will sell low to actual settlers and furnish them every facility in the way of long credit, cheap rates, etc. It is not to be supposed that railroad corporations surpass all men in disinterested benevolence, but it is beyond question that they know their own interests, and so will take some pains to help you earn a dollar whenever they can thus make two for themselves."[3]

In addition to the activities directly connected with land sales and colonization, the company shipped hundreds of Nebraska exhibits to agricultural fairs in both the United States and England. At Crete, Thomas Doane and some of the Boston directors donated enough lands and funds to make possible the foundation of an academy, which in July 1871 was transformed into Doane College. This sort of thing convinced the realistic editors of the region that the better part of wisdom was to cooperate with the railroad. "People may grumble at the railroad companies," the editor of the *Saline County Post* wrote, "but they are a necessity of the age. What should be done is, not to attempt to destroy them nor to create a prejudice against them, but to control them by law and to appreciate their work. The truth is, that the *true* interests of both the people and the companies are *identical*, and what is needed is that all concerned should be convinced of this."[4] And as the editor of the *Beatrice Express* added: "It becomes us . . . to *make the R R Cos. our allies*, by pursuing toward them such a generous policy as will make it possible for them to work for their interest and ours at the same time."[5]

The net result of the completion of the B. & M. in Nebraska and the activities of the Land Department was an increase in the gross earnings of the B. & M. in Nebraska from a quarter of a million dollars in 1871 to exactly twice that amount the next year. Despite Brooks's gloomy prediction of only a few years before, the quarter-million bushels of wheat that the B. & M. in Nebraska sent to Chicago in 1872 was of such quality as to command a price that paid the cost of its transportation easily. By the end

[3] *BW*, p. 339.
[4] *BW*, p. 340.
[5] *BW*, p. 379.

of that year, sales of the Nebraska land grant had nearly reached the 300,000-acre mark with an average net price, after all selling expenses, of close to $7.50 an acre.

Ground for the B. & M. in Nebraska had been broken on July 4, 1869. In the short space of two and a half years, it was abundantly apparent that on all counts this trans-Missouri investment was destined to be one of the most productive ever undertaken by the Forbes Group. As that fact began to dawn upon the Bostonians, their attitude toward expansion westward began to change. It was apparent, however, that what could be done in that direction would have to depend in part on what was taking place in the rest of the system. Developments in widely scattered states no longer could be regarded simply as separate enterprises. Provincialism on the Burlington was on the way out.

CHAPTER 7

The New Postwar World

1 8 6 5 - 7 5

DAY BY DAY during the years 1865–75, the company went steadily about the task of improving its plant and equipment. Meanwhile, it was plunged inevitably into the hot competitive warfare within its territory and experienced the first bitter taste of government regulation.

Between the end of the Civil War and the onset of the panic of 1873, the mileage of the Burlington family lines increased more than fourfold. This meant that heroic efforts were in order to keep the quality of the plant and equipment up to necessary standards. Nowhere was this more essential than on the main stem in Illinois, which served as a funnel for system business. Fortunately, the man directly in charge in that area was a highly competent professional. Robert Harris, born in 1830 at Portsmouth, New Hampshire, had been graduated from a local academy and had served in the navy before starting his railroad career as assistant engineer on the Hartford, Providence and Fishkill in 1852. In the following year he began work with the first of several western roads, and came to the C. B. & Q. in 1863 as assistant superintendent.

When Harris was promoted to general superintendent in 1865, the C. B. & Q. operated less than four hundred miles of railroad in Illinois.

Rails were all made of iron, and nine of the 105 locomotives still burned wood. The line had just under two thousand freight and passenger train cars. Transportation produced during 1865 amounted to 107 million ton-miles and 43 million passenger-miles. Principal produce moving eastward was hogs, cattle, and grain; westbound traffic was made up chiefly of lumber, merchandise, coal, salt, and building materials. Tonnage of eastbound traffic was nearly twice that moving westward, but passenger business was about evenly divided.

As the system expanded in the hectic postwar years, traffic and revenues shot upward. Ton-miles increased fourfold during the decade; revenues, two and a half times. Of equal importance, the character of the traffic changed. As late as the spring of 1867, six sevenths of the revenue on the C. B. & Q. came from local business. But when the bridges across the Mississippi were completed at Burlington and Quincy in 1868, through business increased rapidly, and after 1870 accounted for one quarter of the total. Furthermore, once the branch lines in Illinois were completed and those of the B. & M. in Iowa were added to the system, nearly one third of the entire gross came from them. This inevitably put a heavier burden on the original main stem from Chicago to Burlington and between Galesburg and Quincy. It was this latter that needed the most attention. When completed in 1856, it had been virtually innocent of ballast, and its rails were extremely light. During 1866, nearly half of the new iron laid by the C. B. & Q. was on this stretch, and a crash program was instituted to ballast the road with gravel.

During 1867, the Burlington laid three miles of the first steel rail on the system; this deliberately was installed where traffic was heaviest. At first the results were not encouraging, and the board even doubted the wisdom of continuing the program. By the spring of 1869, however, Chief Engineer Max Hjorstberg reported that the original rails put down two years previously showed little or no wear. A year later, the directors were inclined to recognize the superiority of steel, and by the spring of 1871 all doubts had been removed. Indeed, they resolved to lay no more iron on the main lines and were convinced that the average life of the steel rail was at least ten times that of iron. By the end of 1872, 134 miles of steel were in place; the figure rose to 389 miles by the end of 1875.

Scarcely less important than providing strong rail was the necessity for double-tracking. The Chicago–Aurora stretch was completed by the spring of 1872, along with twenty-five miles between Aurora and Mendota, to bring the total in the system to 61½ miles. More was planned, but the depression forced a postponement. There could be no waiting for additional side tracks, however. These were more than doubled and reached a total of over 250 miles by the end of 1875.

Meanwhile, countless wooden bridges were replaced with more durable iron structures. In Illinois, this sort of improvement was substantially completed by 1868, but a similar program had to be undertaken when the B. & M. of Iowa was acquired; during 1873 alone, over 7,000 feet of wooden bridging in Iowa were replaced with iron. At the same time, new stations and additional shop space were badly needed. New brick depots were erected: at Aurora in 1867, at Galesburg the next year, and several out on the line. New roundhouses were constructed at Aurora, Galesburg, and Burlington, and stockyards were opened at Quincy and Burlington. Stalls for twenty-five locomotives and a new foundry were put up in Aurora in 1872, only to be destroyed by fire the next year; they were rebuilt immediately, despite rising costs.

Equipment was chronically short throughout the decade following the Civil War. Painfully aware of this, the directors authorized a gradual increase both in motive power and in all types of cars throughout the late 1860's; one novelty on the system was the introduction of a refrigerator car early in 1871. But by the spring of 1873, with 4.64 freight cars per mile of road, there was still a shortage of equipment, and in 1874 the C. B. & Q. had to pay out over $150,000 for the rental of cars; in 1875, excess rentals dropped to some $35,000 as the freight car supply moved more into line with requirements. As the car supply increased, the operating ratio (the relation of operating expenses to operating revenues) improved. From a high of 65.39 percent for the year ending April 30, 1872, it declined markedly, to reach 54.53 percent in 1875.

Traffic remained essentially the same in character during the postwar decade, but spurted forward quantitatively. Corn and hogs, for example, the two leading eastbound commodities, increased 231 percent and 179 percent, respectively, between 1865 and 1873, while the lumber and sundries shipped westward more than doubled. The importance of the Burlington to the Chicago market was impressive indeed. During 1873, of the twelve railroads that served the city the C. B. & Q. ranked first in deliveries of cattle, sheep, hogs, wool, hides, corn, and oats; it ranked second in wheat. Westbound, it led all other roads in hauling lumber and salt, and ranked third in the carriage of shingles.

To keep up to standard, a line handling that much business required substantial sums of money. As of July 1, 1873, the C. B. & Q. had more than $11 million in bonds outstanding on its main line, and a contingent liability of more than six and a half million for branch-line bonds. To refund these issues and raise additional money for extension, double-tracking, steel rail, and equipment, the company on July 1, 1873, executed a thirty-year mortgage for $30 million; interest was to be at seven percent if paid in paper currency, six percent if paid in gold. All the Illinois lines as well as the Burlington–Keokuk branch were pledged as collateral. This was the last major financing for the C. B. & Q. until 1879.

• FAMILY TROUBLES AND COMPETITION •

ALTHOUGH BOTH TRAFFIC AND REVENUES shot upward in the postwar decade, revenues by no means kept pace with traffic. Average revenues per ton mile and per passenger mile fell steadily because of intensive competition. And as rates fell, competition simply became sharper as greater efforts were made to increase traffic volume. Each railroad or group of roads acting together was constantly on the alert to form new alliances designed to coax more traffic to its rails. As a result, the postwar decade was characterized by competitive warfare interspersed with temporary truces and alliances that shifted with bewildering frequency.

From the standpoint of organization, the Burlington family was ill-equipped to act in a unified or decisive manner. At the beginning of 1870, for example, the C. B. & Q. proper operated only in the State of Illinois. The B. & M. in Iowa and the Hannibal and St. Joseph in Missouri were organized separately, as was the Kansas City, St. Joseph and Council Bluffs. It is true that various members of the Forbes Group controlled all of these companies through stock ownership and had furnished the funds to build the B. & M. in Nebraska. When it came to competing with the Rock Island or the North Western, all these Burlington family lines could be expected to act together. But in bidding for traffic from the Union Pacific, the B & M. of Iowa automatically became a competitor of the Hannibal and St. Joseph; the Council Bluffs line could and did bargain with both the B. & M. and the Hannibal. Had there been a chief executive for the entire system, some uniformity of policy might have resulted. But Joy, who most nearly occupied that position, was financially more interested in some lines than in others. As of 1870, for example, he was president of the C. B. & Q. and the Council Bluffs, and the chief influence on the Hannibal. But Brooks was president of the B. & M. of Iowa, and later of the B. & M. in Nebraska. More specifically, Perkins at the time was concerned exclusively with the welfare of the Iowa line, and Superintendent Harris of the C. B. & Q. was inclined to think only in terms of his particular road. Harmony was lacking within the Burlington family itself.

Fortunately, the first major competitive threat to the Burlington was resolved peacefully. It arose in the latter part of 1869, when both the B. & M. and the Rock Island opened through service to Council Bluffs and thus began competing with the North Western for business to and from the Union Pacific. During the summer of 1870, these three Iowa roads, realizing that discretion was the better part of valor, formed the famous Iowa Pool. By the terms of this informal arrangement, the North Western, the Rock Island, and the Burlington each agreed to retain forty-five percent of its passenger revenues and fifty percent of its freight revenues to offset the cost of doing business. The rest was to be pooled and divided

[1 0 8]

Missouri and Iowa, 1870

equally among the three lines. Contrary to the expectations of many experts, this loose arrangement survived for approximately fourteen years and introduced an unusual degree of stability in the conduct of trans-Iowa business. For a while, the arrangement was threatened by the Council Bluffs, which was in a position to drain off business to and from the Union Pacific and hand it over to the Hannibal. But after much argument and negotiation it was agreed that Council Bluffs business to and from St. Louis should move by way of the Hannibal and that coming from or destined to Chicago should go over the B. & M. of Iowa.

No sooner had these matters been worked out than a major change occurred in the status of the Hannibal and St. Joseph. If any portion of the Burlington system seemed firmly established within the family, it was this pioneer line in northern Missouri. During the year ending April 30, 1870, the C. B. & Q. earned over $830,000 from freight business exchanged with the Hannibal, and another quarter of a million dollars from passenger business. The Hannibal was doing well on its own account too; during that same year it earned approximately three and one-third million dollars, by far the best ever. Perhaps that was why, during 1871, rumors increased that outsiders were trying to capture control; specifically, it was said that Jay Gould was at work securing proxies.

In early October 1871, both the Hannibal and the C. B. & Q. boards named committees to work out "closer and more permanent relations than at present exist between the two companies."[1] But these steps were too little and too late. When the Hannibal stockholders met on November 6, 1871, it was found that the Gould interests held control. Joy, present at the meeting as Burlington's representative, tried to make the best of the bad situation. After the ballots had been counted, he expressed the hope that the road would continue to be run for its own benefit and not for that of any other corporation. He added that any radical change in the internal management that had been built up so carefully by the Boston interests certainly would be detrimental. But that was simply a hope. The fact was that in the fall of 1871 the Hannibal and St. Joseph slipped from the grasp of the men who had backed it almost from the beginning. This did not necessarily mean that through service or close business relations would be discontinued. But presumably the Missouri road no longer could be counted upon to follow policies in harmony with those of the Burlington, particularly if they should happen to conflict with those of Jay Gould.

Had the B. & M. of Iowa suffered the same fate as the Hannibal, the Burlington system today would most certainly be far different from what it is. This was, of course, less likely to happen because of the long-standing agreement whereby the C. B. & Q. was acquiring B. & M. bonds rather than cash in payment for joint business; these bonds were convertible into stock. But the Iowa road still was not firmly in the fold, and even as late as 1870 various members of the Burlington board were none too happy with the investment. Green in particular, while admitting the value of the B. & M. as a feeder, felt that its construction cost had been exorbitant. But Forbes, for one, was convinced that the C. B. & Q. and the B. & M. belonged together and should be consolidated. By mid-1871 he had persuaded the C. B. & Q. board to meet with representatives of the B. & M. Despite his constant pressure, this joint committee accomplished little until the loss of the Hannibal jogged them into action. Finally, in October 1872, the directors of the two roads approved eventual consolidation through an exchange of stock. Because some doubt existed as to whether such a merger could be effected under the existing laws of Illinois and Iowa, it was decided that as a first step the C. B. & Q. should lease the B. & M. in perpetuity, with consolidation to follow as soon as all questions of legality were resolved. On December 24, 1872, the C. B. & Q. stockholders approved the immediate lease of and eventual consolidation with the B. & M. At the same time they voted that when the consolidation

[1] HSJ, ORB, Vol. IV, pp. 462-3.

should become effective, the name of the C. B. & Q. should be changed to Chicago, Burlington, Quincy & Pacific Railroad Company.

Just what burst of enthusiasm led to this proposed change of name is a mystery. But sober second thought over the holidays, or possibly just plain sentiment, resulted in another special stockholders' meeting on Janu-

The Burlington and Missouri River Railroad, 1872

ary 14, 1873, at which it was resolved that when consolidation should take place, the original C. B. & Q. name should be retained, unless some more appropriate title could be thought of in the interval.

The lease that became effective on December 31, 1872, included not only the 280-mile main line between Burlington and East Plattsmouth, but also a wholly owned branch between Red Oak and Hamburg (39 miles), and leased branches between Chariton and Leon (37 miles), between Clarinda Junction and Clarinda (14 miles), and between Creston and Hopkins, Missouri (45 miles). The net effect of the lease, then, was to add more than four hundred miles to C. B. & Q. operations.

The long-run benefits of this critical step can hardly be overstated. The two roads could obviously be operated much more economically and effectively as a single unit, and all possibility of conflicting interest was eliminated. For a brief moment the people of Burlington had painful doubts as to the local effect of the move, but Joy at once made a public statement to the effect that the superintendent of the B. & M. as well as the system's principal shops would remain at Burlington. For sentimental reasons, Perkins was dismayed to see the little Iowa line he had nourished so carefully from infancy swallowed up by its Illinois neighbor. Furthermore, he was not very happy when, in November 1872, he was named a vice-president of the B. & M. in Nebraska; he had become deeply attached to the city of Burlington, where his growing family was happily located. But he accepted both developments stoically and, much to his relief, was allowed to keep his headquarters in Burlington. For the next nine years, however, his professional attention was concentrated in Nebraska.

The competitive situation that greeted Perkins west of the Missouri was enough to challenge the ingenuity of the ablest railroader. The main stem to Kearney had, of course, been finished late in September 1872. Meanwhile, the Atchison and Nebraska Railroad had linked Atchison and Lincoln; Joy acquired it for the B. & M. during 1870–71. Completed at about the same time was the St. Joseph and Denver City, a line extending from a point on the Missouri River just opposite St. Joseph to Hastings, Nebraska, on the main line of the B. & M., whence its trains proceeded over the B. & M. to a junction with the Union Pacific at Kearney. As both the Wabash and the Missouri Pacific provided southern outlets for these two new roads, their construction meant that the Union Pacific now had a wide choice of routes east of Kearney for business moving to Kansas City and St. Louis. Fortunately, the B. & M. would share a portion of the haul no matter which route was used. But to the extent it did so, it would compete with the Council Bluffs road for through business that would otherwise pass between Omaha and Kansas City, thus adding to family complications.

This anomalous situation led to endless bickering and many sharp words. Because of these alternate routes, the Union Pacific could and did put pressure on the Iowa Pool lines to take smaller divisions of through rates. To prevent this, Joy attempted to prohibit the Atchison and Nebraska from carrying Union Pacific business, an action that hurt the B. & M. in Nebraska and provoked Perkins's vigorous hostility. Eventually the Pool lines did grant the Union Pacific more favorable divisions, and through business, at least between Chicago and the Union Pacific, largely returned to the Iowa roads.

More perplexing to Perkins was the fact that despite the federal law obliging the Union Pacific to exchange traffic with those lines connecting with it, the U. P. flatly refused to open the Kearney Gateway fully or for any length of time. The Burlington repeatedly sent emissaries to Washington to try to force the transcontinental to live up to its obligations, but to no avail. The Kearney Gateway never was open freely, and this was one reason why the Burlington finally lost patience and built its own line to Denver.

Perhaps the most serious family quarrel in the mid-70's swirled about the relations between the C. B. & Q. and the B. & M. in Nebraska. The question was whether the Nebraska road should exchange all its east-west business with the C. B. & Q. at East Plattsmouth or instead should carry its traffic to Omaha and there divide it with the three Pool roads. In the latter case, of course, the C. B. & Q. presumably would receive only one third as much business and revenue. On his part, Perkins felt that he was in by far the stronger bargaining position because on westbound traffic the C. B. & Q. had no alternative but to send its Nebraska-bound business westward over the B. & M. For a year and a half, Perkins on the one hand and the C. B. & Q. on the other negotiated over the question of interchange at the Missouri River. Finally, in the fall of 1873, the two roads agreed to deal with each other exclusively, and the C. B. & Q. obligated itself to pay a drawback to the B. & M. on both passenger and freight traffic as a bonus for not dealing with the Pool roads as a group. This agreement went into effect on January 1, 1874, and by it the welfare of the Iowa Pool was subordinated to the interests of one of its members. The arrangement obviously benefited the B. & M. in Nebraska and represented a substantial victory for Perkins.

To follow the intricacies of competitive warfare in the Missouri Valley in the early 70's is beyond the scope of this book; Julius Grodinsky has done it in his brilliant *The Iowa Pool*. Suffice it to say that it was extremely difficult in those years for the various segments of the Burlington family to live in harmony. The system suffered seriously when it lost control of the Hannibal, but was strengthened when the C. B. & Q. and the B. & M. of Iowa combined. Furthermore, relations with the Nebraska affiliate were stabilized by the agreement of January 1874. But it was perfectly clear even then that until that line and the Council Bluffs could be effectively controlled by the C. B. & Q., the situation would remain in dangerous disequilibrium. Several years were to pass before such integration took place.

• THE BEGINNINGS OF REGULATION •

UNTIL THE VERY EVE of the 1870's, the railways of the nation had been virtually free of government regulation. But the headlong postwar expansion, particularly of the western lines, and the consequent rate wars so disturbed normal business that a swift change in public policy took place. The western farmer was utterly dependent on the railroads and therefore particularly sensitive to the unpredictable rate situation. From the standpoint of the roads, the practices of charging more for some commodities than for others and of offering low rates on competitive runs were simply methods of meeting the market. The same reasoning held for offering lower rates to large shippers on the theory that wholesale business could be transported at lower costs. But to the ordinary farmer, the absolute power of the railways to adjust rates as they pleased was not only subject to abuse, but was actually being abused, and the fact that many of the western railways were owned by absentee easterners simply added fuel to the fire.

So it was that in the early 1870's most of the states served by the Burlington enacted stringent regulatory measures known collectively as Granger Laws. In Illinois, for example, acts were passed in 1871 and 1873.

The first set up a board of railroad and warehouse commissioners, fixed maximum passenger fares, and provided that freight rates should be based on distance. The Act of 1873 gave the commissioners power to prepare a schedule of reasonable maximum freight rates.

The first official reaction of the C. B. & Q. appeared in the *Annual Report* for 1873. Walker noted that many of the stockholders were apprehensive about the recent legislation, and he hastened to assure them that "it is not thought that it will be of a seriously injurious character."[2] He admitted that the state might regulate the railway so far as the peace, good order, health, comfort, and safety of the people were concerned, but he was confident that the Legislature could not abridge the company's charter right to fix such rates as it pleased.

In 1874 the State of Iowa passed an act which was carefully drawn and based squarely on that state's authority, reserved to it under the federal land grants, to fix rates. Walker was outraged. He wrote Sidney Bartlett that he thought the company should disregard the provisions of the act and proceed as if it had never been passed. This is just what the company did, meanwhile instituting a suit to test the validity of the law. The lower courts found against the company, which thereupon promptly appealed to the Supreme Court; Walker was sure that the C. B. & Q. would emerge victorious. As 1875 came to a close, the question of a state's right to regulate railway fares and rates had not yet been settled. But the issues were clearly drawn. The Grangers felt that businesses so closely identified with the public interest should submit to regulation. On the other hand, as the Burlington officials in general and Perkins in particular made crystal clear, the railway contended that free competition and the laws of supply and demand could and did offer the only effective type of regulation. The final word, clearly, was up to the courts.

• Crisis and Depression •

On september 18, 1873, the Philadelphia banking house of Jay Cooke failed. As the heavy doors swung shut, a distinctive era in American history came to a close. The grand splurge, the uninhibited race for power, the belief that prosperity was eternal, burst like a bubble. Never in the nation's history had there been such a devastating economic storm. And the railways were squarely in the center of it; in fact, it was the collapse of a major portion of that industry which brought the whole jerry-built economy of the day tumbling to the ground.

During 1874–77, railways operating over 20,000 miles—more than a quarter of the national network—fell into receivership. Even the C. B. & Q., despite its conservative financial heritage and superb location, was

---

[2] CB&Q, AR 1873, p. 24.

seriously affected. Like other companies, it had to resort to short-time borrowing in the closing months of 1873. Whereas C. B. & Q. stock during 1867–72 had ranged from a high of $200 to a low $124, it plummeted to $78 in November 1873. Expansion all over the system came to a standstill; no new railroad was acquired until the late fall of 1875.

Yet on the whole, both the C. B. & Q. and the B. & M. in Nebraska managed remarkably well to hold their own throughout the worst depression years. They occupied strategic territory and made ends meet because they were able to attract a substantial share of the essential business that did move over the rails. Even though average revenues per ton-mile decreased slightly, ton-miles themselves showed a very modest increase, and even freight revenues inched slowly forward. Net income per share of stock on the C. B. & Q. declined only from $11.60 to $11.22 during 1874–77. What happened, in effect, was that in contrast to the rapidly mounting earnings for the 1865–73 period, the C. B. & Q. simply stood still.

Perhaps even more indicative of what was happening to the economy was the course of land sales in the Burlington's grants in Iowa and Nebraska. In the more densely settled Iowa region it was not until mid-1875 that sales began to decline sharply; the downswing of that year was not checked until 1879. In contrast, Nebraska was affected more quickly by the panic but, with its more extensive undeveloped resources, was also quicker to recover.

But recovery was not automatic. During the worst years, land prices were reduced, premiums for improvements were increased, and larger discounts were allowed for cash purchases. Furthermore, the company reduced freight rates on immigrant movables by thirty percent and extended the bargain rates not only to purchasers of company lands, but also to anyone who would settle in a county where the Burlington had land for sale. Land buyers who had long-term contracts were carried by the company for years; to have dispossessed actual settlers would have been miserable policy. As Touzalin explained it in 1877: "Notwithstanding these large sums overdue, it has been deemed the best course to carry these delinquent contracts as the lands represented thereby are occupied and improved, and are producing business for the road. With good crops, the greater portion of the arrearage will be paid."[3] This policy eased the impact of the crisis locally, solidified community relations, and speeded eventual recovery in both Iowa and Nebraska.

The decade 1865–75 was a time of hectic expansion. Growing competition led to declining average revenue per ton mile; both ton miles and freight revenues were hit hard by the panic. By 1875, the C. B. & Q. was well on the way to climbing out of the hard times that affected the country.

[3] BMN, AR 1876, MS., pp. 28–9.

CHAPTER 8

The Complexities Of Expansion

1865-75

WHEN JAMES F. JOY became president of the C. B. & Q. on July 12, 1865, his eyes turned first to the far horizon. If the Burlington was to make good its claim to territory beyond the Mississippi, not a moment could be lost. That is why he concentrated so much attention and energy toward getting the Hannibal and St. Joseph into Kansas City, the Burlington and Missouri River across the State of Iowa, and the B. & M. in Nebraska on to a connection with the Union Pacific at Kearney.

In sharp contrast to this breathless activity on the system's outer frontier, not a foot of additional C. B. & Q. rail was laid in the home state of Illinois during the first four years of Joy's presidency. To the extent that the existing main stem could handle its established local business and serve as a funnel for traffic originating in and destined for the western portions of the system, it certainly was fulfilling its primary purpose. But with the whole country touched by railroad fever, it was virtually inevitable that the "back areas" in Illinois should demand a more intensive network to serve their particular needs. In December 1868, Joy

Illinois, 1865–75

spelled out for Forbes various proposed competing projects in Illinois which he felt sure would affect the revenues of the C. B. & Q. Under the circumstances, he assured the Bostonians that he would try his best "to keep command of the country."[1] It was in the specific context of the Illinois situation early in 1869 that he uttered his famous dictum: "It is impossible to remain stationary. If the Company's owning and managing roads there do not meet the wants of the adjoining country and aid in its development, other alliances are sure to be found which end in rival roads and damage to existing interests."[2]

[1] Joy to Forbes, December 23, 1868, CB&Q/N, 8C6.5.
[2] CB&Q, AR 1869, p. 20.

This was the thinking that prompted Joy, late in 1868, to urge extension of the Lewistown branch to Rushville, a distance of thirty-two miles. The project was completed and opened for business on July 18, 1869. Meanwhile, in October 1868, the C. B. & Q. had promised to advance funds on a "pay-as-you-go basis" to the old American Central Railway which had been chartered some fifteen years earlier to build a fifty-mile line from Galva (on the main stem of the C. B. & Q.) to New Boston on the Mississippi River. Thus nourished by C. B. & Q. dollars, the line rapidly got underway and was put into operation in October 1869. Describing these two projects, Joy told the stockholders: "Both run into sections heretofore destitute of railway accommodations and very fertile and productive . . . each of them will be valuable auxiliaries to the business of the main line. . . ."[3]

Three other branches, each one of them helped by advances from the C. B. & Q., were put underway late in 1869. As if to encase the Mississippi, one was to reach southward forty-two miles from Burlington to Keokuk along the west shore of the Mississippi, and another was located from a point on the east side of the river opposite Burlington thirty miles southward to Carthage. The third, considered at the time the most important, was a forty-four-mile link between Buda on the main line and Elmwood on the Galesburg–Peoria Road.

Such expansion, along with the cost of double-tracking the main stem, was expensive. Joy figured in the spring of 1869 that approximately one and a quarter million dollars would be needed beyond available funds. To provide it, the directors offered additional capital stock to all shareholders to the extent of twenty percent of their existing holdings "as being at once the easiest and . . . most agreeable mode of raising money."[4] Joy warned that further heavy expenditures would be required for some time to come, but was convinced that the company would gain in the long run as business increased.

Within the Burlington family, however, the very considerable burden of the new branches was not dismissed so lightly. Green in New York was particularly disturbed, and to him Joy wrote with some asperity in July 1869 that he knew of nothing "which in my opinion would be so unwise as for us to fold our hands and allow rival enterprises to occupy our domain when we can supply the want and help them out. Our expenditures," he said bluntly, "are the result of our policy, and we must enlarge our accommodations and equipment and power and all our appointments to suit our enlarged business. This is unavoidable if we mean to maintain ourselves and command the business of the country

[3] Ibid., p. 18.
[4] Ibid., p. 21.

and keep it from rival projects. . . . In the future," he concluded confidently, "all will feel that this is a safe and wise policy."[5]

On the property itself, however, Joy was singing a somewhat different tune. Painfully aware that the three branches under construction early in 1869 were progressing more slowly than expected, he reminded Superintendent Harris that the C. B. & Q. would get little if any business from them during the current year, but that interest charges on the money advanced would continue just the same. "In the circumstances," he warned, "every possible retrenchment upon those roads must be made, and nothing but the barest necessity must cause an expenditure of money. . . . I must rely upon you to stop everything which can be stopped, everywhere. . . . The absolutely necessary may be done, but what we can live without must not be done till a better time comes and we find out how we stand."[6]

By the following spring, Joy was somewhat more optimistic. The Burlington–Keokuk line had been completed late in October 1869; the branch from East Burlington to Carthage went into operation in mid-January 1870; and a fortnight later the link between Buda and Elmwood was completed. Joy promptly wrote to Green that "expenditures are at an end substantially for branches undertaken for defense, as well as profit in the future, and we shall rapidly now pay and liquidate and acquire surpluses."[7] If Joy was right, that was just as well, because the wretched corn crop of 1869 sharply reduced C. B. & Q. earnings while expenses increased. Net income for the year ending April 30, 1870, was half a million dollars less than for the preceding year; net income per share dropped from $19.35 to $12.23. Accordingly, the twenty percent dividend paid in 1869 was cut in half for 1870.

Despite what Joy had optimistically written to Green, there was to be no standing still in the West. On Christmas Day 1870, a forty-mile extension was completed between Carthage anrd Quincy, and less than a month later the Montgomery–Streator line, fifty-seven miles long, was put into operation; two days later a short five-and-a-half-mile stretch began operating between Arpee and Keithsburg. In the spring of 1871, still another nine-and-a-half-mile branch from Aurora to Geneva was completed, as was a major line of forty-five miles connecting Mendota and Prophetstown.

Throughout these hectic months of construction, Joy repeatedly sought to justify, both to other members of the Forbes Group and to the stockholders, the company's policy. He explained that since the close of the Civil War it had been extremely easy to raise capital locally for

[5] Joy to John C. Green, July 13, 1869, CB&Q/N, 8C6.5.
[6] Joy to Robert Harris, October 22, 1869, CB&Q/N, 8C6.5.
[7] Joy to Green, March 17, 1870, CB&Q/N, 8C6.5.

railroads because of the state legislation in Illinois permitting municipal corporations to incur large debts to aid such construction. Joy vigorously condemned this unrestrained system of municipal aid. As he told the stockholders early in 1870: "It has become a system of speculation by parties who are engaged in the business, and is leading to the building of many roads which will in themselves be unprofitable. . . . These roads thus built will, in many instances, yield but little revenue, while also, in many cases, they will affect the values of existing railway property. . . . It would be extraordinary," he warned, "if a revulsion did not follow. . . ."

Yet the Burlington faced a dilemma. It could either assist these roads and make them tributaries at considerable expense, and with a risk that Joy clearly understood, or else it could let them fall into the hands of rival roads. "Not so far as would have been judicious and wise," Joy wrote candidly, "but so far as at the time when the opportunity arose it was deemed expedient to do so, we have adopted the policy of rendering the needed assistance." He could simply hope that the course followed was wise and that within six or eight years the profits of the new lines would reduce the investment in them to the point at which they could stand on their own feet. "On looking over the whole ground," he assured the stockholders in the spring of 1870, ". . . the Board sees no good reason to suppose that the property of the Company will not, in the future, continue as valuable as in the past."[8] In effect, the stockholders were asked to believe, in view of the realities of the situation, that the company had chosen the lesser of two evils.

On June 28, 1871, James M. Walker was chosen president of the C. B. & Q. Like Joy a native of New Hampshire, he was born in 1821 and was graduated from Oberlin College. As a young man of twenty-one he became local attorney for the Michigan Central, and in 1853 was transferred to Chicago, where, in addition to his duties for the railroad, he was associated with a law firm and also served as president and a director of the Wilmington Coal Company.

Walker's election to the presidency of the C. B. & Q. did not herald any change of policy because, as a long-time and close associate of Joy, he looked to his predecessor for advice and guidance. Walker's salary, incidentally, was fixed at $4,000 per year, while that of the superintendent, Robert Harris, was set at $10,000. The reason was simply that Walker was not expected to be more than a part-time employee. All day-to-day decisions on the C. B. & Q. were made by Harris; Walker's principal job was to act as liaison man with the Forbes Group, and particularly with Joy, to whom the Group informally entrusted the direction of Burlington strategy.

During the first year of Walker's administration, the Mendota–Prophetstown branch was extended another seventeen miles westward to a point on the Mississippi River opposite Clinton. The Burlington had

[8] CB&Q, AR 1870, pp. 14, 19–20.

hoped that the Chicago and North Western would permit the C. B. & Q. to use its bridge at Clinton to gain access to the lines then being built toward the Twin Cities on the west bank of the river. But the North Western flatly refused. The C. B. & Q. thereupon obtained the necessary authority to build a bridge of its own, but the panic of 1873 stalled the project. Not until 1885 did the Burlington finally obtain use of the North Western's bridge.

But this outcome was far in the future when Walker made his first report to the stockholders in the spring of 1872. Following exactly in Joy's footsteps, he reiterated the hope that the various branches in Illinois would eventually become profitable, and pointed out how disastrous it would have been to let them fall into the hands of rivals.

Meanwhile, the C. B. & Q. was sponsoring still another project which, at first glance, seemed to have but little relation to its existing network. Back in 1869, the Chicago and Rock River Railroad had been incorporated to build a through line directly eastward to Chicago from Rock Falls on the Rock River opposite Sterling. As construction proceeded during 1870–71, it was apparent that if the line were completed, the eastern half of it would run virtually parallel to the Burlington. Consequently the C. B. & Q. made an agreement toward the end of 1871 by which, in return for substantial financial assistance, the Rock River agreed to build easterly only to Paw Paw, from which point it turned north to Shabbona, a town on the Chicago and Iowa Railroad between Aurora and Forreston. The entire forty-seven-mile line between Rock Falls and Shabbona was completed and put into operation on October 16, 1872. The reason why the Rock River was diverted northward to the Chicago and Iowa instead of southward to the C. B. & Q. (to which it was finally connected in 1882) lay in a phase of Joy's strategy soon to be related. The immediate significance of the Rock River was twofold: its acquisition prompted the C. B. & Q. to issue $720,000 worth of seven percent bonds, and it represented the last branch-line extension made under the Joy–Walker regime in Illinois. No further expansion in the system's home state took place until 1876.

Viewed in perspective, the cumulative effect of this piecemeal building in Illinois (including the Burlington–Keokuk line in eastern Iowa) was profound. The C. B. & Q. more than doubled its operating mileage: from 397 miles at the close of the Civil War to 820 by October 1872. Just how much this expansion cost the Burlington was variously estimated, but for balance sheet purposes the company considered the new lines to be worth approximately $10,250,000. Actual interest charges payable annually by the C. B. & Q. on account of these branches slightly exceeded half a million dollars.

How much business the branches brought and what it was worth also were estimated variously. Walker told the stockholders early in 1874 that loss of the business from the branches would seriously impair the C. B. & Q. He admitted that some of the lines were more valuable than others, but thought the program as a whole had been "a sound and judicious one."[9]

The plain fact, however, was that during the three years 1871–73, C. B. & Q. net income per share declined from $14.55 to $10.62. As gross revenues rose more than fifty percent during this period, it was apparent that the company's earning power was declining. This decline by no means could be charged wholly against expansion; intense competition had pushed average freight rates down by between fifteen and twenty percent. But certainly a major cause of reduced earnings was increased expense, much of it attributable to acquisition and completion of branch lines. The net result was to add to the natural caution of various members of the Forbes Group. Even Forbes himself had to admit that the company, faced with a dilemma, had been compelled to defend itself by acquiring or building new lines. "I don't say they were all wise nor all economically built," he told an inquiring stockholder in mid-1873, "but looking at it in the large I can see nothing fatal in the mistake so far and, give me good economical management in the future, I see good times ahead. . . . There is the pinch, and to that the owners of the property ought to turn their attention." He closed with the hope that "the *loose era* of railroad building" had come to an end.[1]

Whether the "loose era" would have come to an end if prosperity had continued is an academic question, for in September 1873 the nation was engulfed by the sharpest financial panic it had experienced up to that time. Any further expansion in the immediate future was out of the question.

The sad thing was that the damage already had been done. Forbes's concern was too little and, as it eventually turned out, almost too late. Strangely enough, the danger spot was not along the far-flung Burlington perimeter, where supervision might have been expected to be less effective, or in connection with any of the branch lines recently constructed in such haste: Perkins and Harris, respectively, had kept their houses strictly in order. Rather, the trouble that came near wrecking the entire organization grew out of a perfectly logical project that originated, like so many others, in Joy's fertile mind. He had excellent reasons for what he wanted to do. The danger lay in the way he went about it. Thereby hangs a tale.

• The River Roads: Seeds of Trouble •

At the beginning of 1870, the Burlington had established two principal through routes, one connecting Chicago and Kansas City, the other linking Chicago and Council Bluffs. That Joy should seek to box the compass

9 CB&Q, AR 1873, pp. 14–15.
1 Forbes to a stockholder, mid–1873, CB&Q/N, 8C6.5.

by looking toward the Northwest was not only logical, therefore, but perhaps inevitable. Already—during the years immediately following the Civil War—predecessors of both the Milwaukee and the North Western had penetrated the Twin Cities area, and it was abundantly apparent that a tremendous business in lumber and grain could be developed once railways were built to serve the region adequately. Joy was determined that the Burlington should have its share of this dazzling prize.

Because the existing main stem of the C. B. & Q. followed a southwesterly course across Illinois, however, any line toward the Northwest would have to branch off at some point much nearer Chicago than the Mississippi. Extension in the desired direction, therefore, would first involve expansion in northwestern Illinois.

Thanks to the ease of raising local capital, several projects in that area already were in various stages of progress. The Ogle and Carroll County Railroad, organized in 1860, began to build its line from Rochelle toward Oregon in January 1868. A second company, the Chicago and Iowa Railroad, organized in the spring of 1869, started laying rail from Aurora toward Rochelle. On June 1, 1870, the two roads agreed to merge as soon as they could be completed.

Joy made it his business to keep abreast of these developments. He knew that the Chicago and Iowa had the charter right to build all the way from Chicago to Savanna on the Mississippi; if such a line was completed and operated independently, it would preempt the route the C. B. & Q. might logically follow toward the Northwest. On the other hand, if it could be contained or absorbed, it might well form the nucleus of the desired extension toward the Twin Cities. At Joy's behest, the C. B. & Q. directors on March 30, 1870, voted to allow the Chicago and Iowa to use Burlington tracks between Aurora and Chicago in return for seventy percent of the gross earnings on C. & I. business over that stretch. They likewise authorized Joy to conclude whatever arrangements might be necessary to secure the business of the C. & I. in perpetuity.

The C. & I. completed its forty-four mile line between Aurora and Rochelle in January 1871; the Ogle and Carroll County Railroad finished the sixteen miles between Rochelle and Oregon on April 3, 1871. Thereupon the merger between those two companies became effective, and Joy promptly concluded a traffic and financial contract with the consolidated company. According to the usual pattern, the C. B. & Q. agreed to set aside forty percent of gross earnings realized over its own line from business to and from the C. & I., such sums to be invested annually in C. & I. bonds. In return, the C. & I. agreed to send all its business over the C. B. & Q. and to turn over to the latter one half of its capital stock. The other half was acquired by the Illinois Central, which, as will appear shortly, participated also in a traffic agreement involving both the C. & I. and the C. B. & Q. For Joy this was only the beginning.

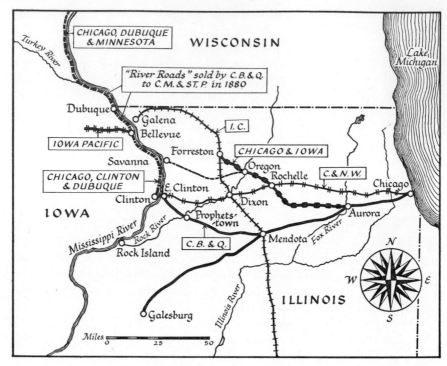

The "River Roads," 1869–75

West of the Mississippi, three railways were projected which might eventually provide a northwestern outlet for the Chicago and Iowa. One, the Chicago, Dubuque, and Minnesota, was to run northward from Dubuque to La Crescent (opposite La Crosse). A second, the Chicago, Clinton and Dubuque Railroad, was to connect with the C. D. & M. at Dubuque and run southward to Bellevue, to which point the Chicago and Iowa was already planning to build from its existing western terminal at Oregon. A third, the Iowa Pacific, was to run from Dubuque westward to Fort Dodge, Iowa. If all these projected roads could be completed and their service coordinated with that of the Burlington, the C. B. & Q. would be well on its way toward the beckoning Northwest.

As of spring 1871, however, several traffic agreements already in effect stood in the way. For one thing, freight business currently originating at Dubuque and destined for Chicago passed over the Illinois Central to Mendota and thence over the C. B. & Q. to Chicago, whereas passengers took the Illinois Central to Dixon, and thence the North Western. This meant that the Chicago and Iowa, which the C. B. & Q. hoped to use as the first leg of its route to the Northwest, was being bypassed so far as business to and from Dubuque was concerned. On the other hand, the Chicago and Iowa, on its own initiative, had already made preliminary commitments to the two "River Roads" (as the Chicago, Clinton and Dubuque and the Chicago, Dubuque and Minnesota, were called then and thereafter) to build westward to Bellevue on the Mississippi and thus provide them with a southern outlet. If this scheme was carried out, however, the only benefit to the C. B. & Q. would be the augmented business received from the C. & I. over the short haul between Aurora and Chicago.

This was a challenge made to order for Joy. "Upon learning wholly the position of affairs," he later put it in a nutshell, "I suggested to all parties to change their plans."[2] His proposals were as bold as they were ingenious:

1. Instead of continuing westward to Bellevue, the Chicago and Iowa should terminate its line at Forreston (on the Illinois Central), with the understanding that all business, both freight and passenger, originating on the rails of the Chicago, Dubuque and Minnesota would be routed via the Illinois Central to Forreston and there handed over to the C. & I., which in turn would deliver it to the C. B. & Q. at Aurora.

2. As termination of the C. & I. at Forreston would preclude provision of a southern outlet for the River Roads at Bellevue, the Chicago, Clinton and Dubuque should extend its road southward to Clinton, to which point the C. B. & Q. should build (as it promptly did) from Prophetstown, thus providing the desired southern outlet—assuming, of course, that the North Western would permit (which it did not) use of its Clinton bridge. All business originating west or north of the two River Roads (in distinction to that originating on the Chicago, Dubuque and Minnesota itself) should flow south over those two roads to Clinton and thence over the C. B. & Q. to Chicago and way points.

3. Joy would personally market $1,000,coo of Chicago and Iowa bonds and recommend that the C. B. & Q. directors execute the traffic contract described above with the C. & I. in exchange for half the stock of that road.

4. The C. B. & Q. would make a traffic contract with the C. C. & D. (on the Lewistown branch model) by which that road could redeem a portion of its adverse traffic balances with its own bonds, *provided that half the stock of the C. C. & D. be given to the C. B. & Q.*

5. The C. B. & Q. would make a similar traffic contract with the C. D. & M., *but without receiving any C. D. & M. stock in exchange.*

This fifth point deserves special scrutiny. Long-established Burlington policy had been *not* to make a traffic contract with a new road *unless* it included a provision for obtaining eventual control. In this case, however, no such arrangement was made *officially.* The *unofficial* arrangement for solving this particular problem eventually became of crucial importance.

For the moment, Joy sought approval from the interested parties for

[2] Joy to Sidney Bartlett, February 22, 1875, IC/N.

the proposals he had made. As he wrote John Newell, president of the Illinois Central, on March 27, 1871: "The thing which I wish to accomplish is to bring the North West into Chicago, to your depot and ours, and while they are young, and before they gather strength enough to go alone, to give such direction to any new and promising enterprise that we shall make it tributary to our Lines instead of a rival. Such an enterprise is the [Chicago] Dubuque and Minn[esota] Road, I am sure . . . it will be built and with a connection through to Chicago, and hostile to both of us, if we give it the cold shoulder, while by an act which will cost us practically nothing we can make it friendly and for our interests."[3] This reasoning was both familiar and, under the circumstances, warranted.

The traffic agreements that Joy had proposed were signed on April 25, 1871. The Michigan Central, as well as the C. B. & Q., was a party to the traffic contract with the C. D. & M., and, like the C. B. & Q., agreed to accept that company's first-mortgage bonds in payment of four tenths of the traffic balances arising from joint business. As far as anyone could see at the moment, there was nothing unusual or without precedent in these arrangements *except* for the *apparent* failure to provide for eventual control of the C. D. & M. In remedying this vital defect, Joy, acting without the full knowledge of the C. B. & Q. board, sowed the seeds of trouble.

As was customary at the time, the construction of the two River Roads had been entrusted by contract to construction companies shortly before Joy became interested in the roads. On October 22, 1870, the River Railroad Construction Company had agreed to acquire the necessary right of way and to build the Lower River Road between Dubuque and Bellevue (a distance of twenty-three miles) in exchange for the proceeds of the railroad's bonds at the rate of $25,000 a mile, fully paid capital stock of the railroad in the amount of $21,000 a mile, and the 38,000-acre land grant, together with such other donations as the railroad might receive. This contract had been signed by J. A. Graves, a Dubuque businessman who had become president of the railway, and J. A. Rhomberg, president of the construction company. Nothing about this arrangement was unusual.

On February 10, 1871, the Iowa and Minnesota Construction Company, of which Rhomberg was also president, had agreed to build the Upper River Road. Graves was president of that too. This line was to stretch 118 miles between Dubuque and La Crescent, and to have a twenty-nine-mile branch from the mouth of the Turkey River (twenty-nine miles north of Dubuque) southwestward to a junction with the Iowa Pacific (now Illinois Central), projected due westward to Fort Dodge. To pay for construction, the railway had agreed, as in the case of the Lower River Road, to turn over the proceeds of its bonds issued at the rate of

[3] Joy to John Newell, March 27, 1871, IC/N, quoted in TCC, p. 368.

$25,000 a mile, and also stock of the railway not in excess of $37,500 per mile, together with all tax aids, donations, or other items to be received by the railway company.

The final clause of this contract, however, was extraordinary. It provided that after the construction company should have spent its assets, including the proceeds of its own entire capital stock of $300,000, it would be released from any further liability. In other words, if the construction company should run out of money without completing the road, the line as it then stood would be turned over to the railway, with no further obligation whatever on the part of the construction company.

At this point Joy entered the picture and negotiated the various traffic contracts signed on April 25, 1871. Under their terms, as explained above, business from the Lower River Road was to flow south through Clinton and proceed thence entirely over the rails of the C. B. & Q. by way of Prophetstown to Chicago. The fact that the C. B. & Q. was willing to accept C. C. & D. bonds in lieu of cash for its share of revenues over this long haul was so favorable to the Lower River Road that the Burlington had demanded, and the Lower River Road agreed, to give half of its capital stock to the C. B. & Q.

But the situation in respect to the Upper River Road was different. To be sure, under the traffic contract of April 25, 1871, business originating *north* and *west* of the Upper River Road would indeed pass over the rails of that company and then over the Lower River Road through Clinton and on to Chicago. On the other hand, all traffic originating *on the line of the Upper River Road itself* would first travel eighty-three miles over the Illinois Central to Forreston, then about the same distance over the Chicago and Iowa to Aurora, and for only thirty-eight miles over the C. B. & Q. into Chicago. Joy therefore did not feel that the Burlington could very well demand a half-stock interest in the Upper River Road, the participation of the C. B. & Q. in the total haul from Dubuque to Chicago being so small. Even if the Upper River Road were to hand out its stock to its eastern connections, it would have to be on a pro rata basis on which the C. B. & Q. would receive far less than either the Illinois Central or the Chicago and Iowa.

But it was established Burlington policy that no traffic contract would be signed with any railroad whereby the C. B. & Q. would accept bonds in lieu of cash for traffic balances *unless* a reasonable prospect existed that the C. B. & Q. could eventually obtain control of the company with which it made such an arrangement. Joy's problem, then, was to find some alternate method for controlling the Upper River Road. As that railway had obligated itself to pay the Iowa and Minnesota Construction Company with its stock, the logical, and indeed the only, alternative seemed to be to obtain control of the construction company. This is precisely what Joy did without a moment's delay. On April 27, 1871, two days after the signing of the traffic agreements, Joy persuaded Sidney Bartlett, John W. Brooks, John A. Burnham, J. N. Denison, Nathaniel Thayer—all directors of the C. B. & Q.—and H. H. Hunnewell to join him in purchasing thirty-two out of a total of sixty shares of the Iowa and Minnesota Construction Company at a price of $5,000 a share. Because, according to the contract of February 10, 1871, the construction company was to be paid for its efforts partly in the stock of the railway company, control of its own stock was tantamount to control of the Upper River Road. That same contract, however, stipulated that the construction company was under no obligation to finish the railway once it had spent its original funds.

Men with as much experience as the Burlington directors might have been expected to familiarize themselves fully with whatever contract was in effect between the Upper River Road and the construction company in which they had invested. They testified later, however, that they had not done so, but rather had confided wholly in Joy's judgment. Joy, on the other hand, as vigorously maintained that he had made the details of the contract clear at the time, and that his fellow directors had simply suffered a wholesale loss of memory. Who was right will probably never be known. The fact was that the contract meant precisely what it said, and six members of the Burlington board bought stock in the construction company operating under it. What effect this had on what the six men did in their capacity as C. B. & Q. directors cannot be determined. Their actions must speak for themselves.

On June 5, 1871, the Burlington board approved the traffic agreements of April 25, 1871, and also approved the issuing of a circular offering to C. B. & Q. stockholders $1,600,000 of bonds of the Upper River Road. Ironically enough, the motion to offer these bonds was made by Forbes, who, of course, had no notion at the time that six of his fellow directors were stockholders of the construction company building the line.

The next step, crucial as it was, may have been known only to a few of the principals involved. On July 2, 1871, the original contract of October 22, 1870, between the Lower River Road and the River Railroad Construction Company, was amended in two significant respects. In the first place, in accordance with the traffic agreements of April 25, 1871, the construction company agreed to extend the Lower River Road from Bellevue to Clinton, although in doing so it was authorized to use any parallel railroad already in existence. Second, it was provided that after the construction company stockholders should have advanced an additional sum of $140,000—the amount of its capital stock—and after the construction company had expended this sum together with all other assets previously received (such as the proceeds of the bonds sold by the railway company), *then* the construction company was to be released from any further obligation. In other words, just as the construction company building the Upper River Road had a contract not requiring it to complete the line that it was supposed to build, the construction company building the Lower River Road now was placed in the same position. On July 29, 1871, however, the same six Burlington directors who had bought stock in the Iowa and Minnesota Construction Company purchased nine of the fourteen shares of the River Railroad Construction Company at $12,500 a share.

As proceeds from the sale of the Upper River Road's bonds became available, Denison, chairman of the C. B. & Q. board, turned them over to Graves as president of that railway. Meanwhile, however, Graves had become president also of the Iowa and Minnesota Construction Company, so that in the capacity of railway president he turned over the same funds to himself as president of the construction company, added amounts received from the sale of the construction company's stock, and went to work not wisely but too well. During the latter part of 1871 and early 1872, he built a considerable portion of the Upper Road's main line, began work on the elaborate and expensive shops at Dubuque, probably did some grading on the Turkey River branch, and (apparently unbeknown to his eastern stockholders) used some of his funds to construct the Iowa Pacific, in which he alone was interested. Eventually he diverted $173,000 to this wholly unrelated project.

To some of those in the East, only two facts were visible: the burst of activity north of Dubuque and the lack of it to the south. On January 23, 1872, Brooks wrote Joy urging him to push work on the Lower River Road promptly and vigorously. He reported that he and Thayer and Bartlett had been talking the situation over, and that they wanted to know where the necessary money was coming from, how much would be available from construction company stock, how many bonds could be issued per mile of road, and what the situation was in respect to the Clinton bridge. Finally, he inquired how much stock the Lower River Road had and who owned it. Thus it would appear that even though Bartlett, Brooks, and Thayer had bought stock in the River Railroad Construction Company, they knew little about its activities and perhaps nothing at all about its contract with the railway company.

Denison, apparently, was somewhat closer to the situation: he was remitting to Graves the proceeds of the Upper Road's bond sales. That he was alarmed by what he knew—or at least suspected—was evident in his letter of January 25, 1872 to Joy. "Mr. Graves," said he, "acted upon his understanding with you and with us here and went wild. . . . We ought never to put our money into another man's hands without constant supervision and control. Excuse our anxiety; we are very sore."[4]

[4] Denison to Joy, January 25, 1872, JFJ, quoted in TCC, p. 307.

Thus Joy was fully aware of the anxiety among those of his colleagues who had invested with him in the two construction companies. But somehow he must have quieted their fears, for when the directors of the Burlington met in Boston on February 8 (present: Brooks, Burnham, Denison, Joy, Thayer, and Walker), they authorized a circular, addressed this time not only to C. B. & Q. stockholders but also to those in the B. & M. in Nebraska, offering a second lot of $1,500,000 in bonds of the Upper River Road and a like amount of bonds of the Lower River Road. Issued on March 7, 1872, this circular made it clear that bonded debt on the two lines was strictly limited to $25,000 per mile. No mention was made of the fact that neither construction company was compelled to finish its road. Should construction not be completed, and should the roads be subsequently completed by some other agency, a bonded indebtedness substantially above the advertised limit might well result. The circular did state that business on that portion of the Upper Road already in use was fully up to expectations, and that it could be expected to grow because of the favorable traffic contracts.

On the basis of this strong endorsement, signed by Denison as chairman of the Burlington board, this second lot of bonds found ready purchasers, and in due course the proceeds were turned over to Graves, who now emerged as president of the River Railroad Construction Company as well. In other words, he was simultaneously president of both River Roads and of both construction companies.

How much money passed through Graves's hands is difficult to determine, but by the summer of 1872 he had received at least, from various sources, almost six million dollars. Even those funds proved insufficient. Between March and October 1872, the C. B. & Q. built and delivered to the two River Roads two baggage cars, eight passenger cars, and a smoking car, representing a total outlay of $64,825. Although immediate cash payment was expected, Graves was in no position to remit. Nevertheless, on October 4, 1872, the Burlington board (present: Bartlett, Burnham, Denison, Joy, Thayer, and Walker) advanced $80,000 more to the Lower River Road, taking preferred stock in exchange. Later on—the exact date is not clear—the C. B. & Q. advanced nearly $100,000 more. As if these advances and equipment and cash were not enough, Graves at about this time began to pay obligations of his construction companies with notes, signed by himself, drawn against the two River Roads. In due course this debt amounted to at least $50,000, and possibly more.

Just how much the Boston directors who had invested in the construction companies knew will probably always remain a puzzle. Apparently they knew enough by the end of 1872 to become definitely uneasy. On December 11, Brooks wrote Walker that although none of the Easterners doubted Graves's integrity, this did not dispose of the fact "that in the occupancy of a position where he ought to have known all about our affairs there, and did know that we relied solely upon him, he most fearfully misled us."[5] Brooks consequently suggested that Graves's own western associates on the boards of the two River Roads be replaced by Bartlett, Burnham, Hunnewell, Joy, Thayer, Walker, and himself. He thought that Graves might remain as president and a director, but that someone prominent should take the ninth place on the two boards. He added that Denison might be made treasurer of the two River Railroads and that, as the C. B. & Q. already owned half the stock of the Lower Road, it well might take over its management. In January 1873, the C. B. & Q. directors named by Brooks were duly elected to the boards of the two River Roads. Graves remained as president and a director of both, while the ninth place on each board was given to Rhomberg, whose only claim to prominence was his long-standing connection with the construction company.

By this time, the Iowa and Minnesota Construction Company had completed the entire 118 miles of the Upper River Road between Dubuque and La Crescent. Of the fifty-mile Turkey River branch, however, only sixteen miles were completed; the rest simply was graded. The River Railroad Construction Company had done even less well, though it had only sixty miles to go. Of this it had completed forty-eight and had graded the remaining twelve; service was maintained after a fashion by using the rails of three different companies along the uncompleted portion into Clinton. There, as the North Western Railway still flatly refused to permit use of its bridge, no physical connection whatever could be made between the River Roads and the C. B. & Q. Finally, both construction companies had exhausted their funds and therefore considered their obligations discharged. All work stopped.

The stage was set for the step which linked the fortunes of the River Roads and the Burlington even more closely. Coupons on the bonds of both River Roads had been paid regularly through December 1872, although the funds for interest had come partly from the sale of the bonds themselves; the Lower Road had used $63,500 for this purpose, the Upper Road no less than $372,000. That, unless vigorous measures were taken, both River Roads would default on their coupons due June 1, 1873, was now apparent. So it was that at the C. B. & Q. board meeting of April 19, 1873 (present: Bartlett, Brooks, Burnham, Denison, Joy, Thayer, and Walker), it was duly voted that these coupons be paid by the Burlington. On May 15, a written agreement was entered into whereby the C. B. & Q. agreed to pay not more than $237,000 on account of River Roads coupons presented; in return the River Roads agreed to

[5] Brooks to James M. Walker, December 11, 1872, CB&Q/N, quoted in TCC, p. 281.

reimburse the C. B. & Q. on or before January 1, 1874, together with interest at eight percent. No notice was given to the public of this arrangement. The offices of the C. B. & Q. and of the River Roads were both in the Sears Building at Boston. When coupons were presented, therefore, they were paid promptly by the River Roads treasurer and then turned over to the C. B. & Q. for reimbursement. Later on it was explained that this was done because the credit of the River Roads was really not impaired outside the knowledge of those in the Sears Building, and the device was a temporary expedient. Indeed, it was deemed in the interest of the Burlington to maintain the credit of the River Roads, which were closely identified in the public mind with the C. B. & Q. by virtue of the traffic contracts.

It should be noted that the C. B. & Q. directors present at the crucial board meeting of April 19, 1873, were all directors of the River Roads, except for Denison, who was their treasurer; everyone except Thayer also owned stock in the construction companies. Forbes, who was traveling in California at the time, was absent, as were Green and Griswold. How much the directors present knew about the uses to which Graves had put his funds cannot be ascertained.

• The River Roads: The Revolution of 1875 •

Thus matters stood in the summer of 1873, when Forbes was telling an inquiring stockholder of his hope that the "loose era" of railroad building had come to an end. To his fellow director Green, Forbes was far more blunt. Recent expenditures, he wrote Green on June 29, would make it imperative for the C. B. & Q. to issue, very shortly, more than $20,000,000 in bonds. He was convinced that a considerable proportion of the debt to be funded had been entered into far too casually. "We . . . have got to the point," he told Green, "where *good business management* is absolutely necessary to success. The businessmen who have been and are running this concern are our overworked Superintendent [Robert Harris] and our *lawyer* President [J. M. Walker] who certainly cannot claim any *mercantile* experience nor much, if any, knowledge of R. Road management in detail. Long years of prosperity & rich dividends usually make subordinates *loose* in spending money. I don't know whether it is so in our case, but if not it is a miracle, & reforms are probably necessary if we mean to make our property good. I was never in favor of replacing Joy, a 1st class lawyer, by Walker, a 2nd class one—neither of them pretending to experience in the details of R. Road management, but now is no time to change the presidency to other hands, and I don't suggest it, but, as men of business and trustees for others, I *do* think the time has come for us to know something more about the property of which we are the managers than any others here at the East do know. . . . I hope & believe that if *we don't* investigate the road, our stockholders at our next meeting will insist on doing it."[6]

Clearly, by the middle of 1873 Forbes was becoming increasingly concerned with the quality of C. B. & Q. management and with the way expansion was being carried out. So long as the prosperity of the postwar boom continued, there was perhaps no pressing need for specific action. But with the coming of the crash in the fall of 1873, a careful inquiry into just where the company stood could be delayed no longer. Significantly, Forbes turned his attention first to the River Roads.

In all fairness, it should be pointed out that Forbes was not alone in his concern over the perplexing developments along the Mississippi River. Brooks and Denison had been uneasy for a year and more; Walker, at least, knew that the C. B. & Q. had not been paid for the eleven cars delivered to the River Roads. Consequently, some time before October 1873, Walker demanded that Graves either pay for the cars or return them. But Graves, bereft both of funds and of business, offered instead to turn over to the Burlington sixty flatcars and three engines valued at slightly over $78,000. To this Walker agreed, and the equipment was delivered to the C. B. & Q. in October 1873. Compared with Graves's total operations, of course, this was a minor detail. The percussion cap that touched off a full-scale investigation was Forbes's discovery, purely by accident, that Burlington directors were associated with Graves in his construction companies.

Late in October 1873, Brooks, then serving as president of the B. & M. in Nebraska, journeyed west to inspect the property with Perkins, its vice-president. After going over that line, they returned eastward to meet Forbes, Griswold, and Walker, with whom they went to Dubuque. From there, on November 7, Graves took them all by special train over the Upper River Road to La Crescent and back.

Technically, of course, Perkins had no official connection with the C. B. & Q.; he was vice-president of the B. & M. in Nebraska. Perhaps that is why Graves spoke to him as freely as he did during the course of the trip. At any rate, Graves told Perkins that the River Roads were being built by construction companies in which Joy, Brooks, and various other C. B. & Q. directors were stockholders. Perkins was flabbergasted for although, as he put it later, there was nothing necessarily wrong in a construction company or even in the fact that C. B. & Q. directors were its owners and as such had recommended its bonds as a good investment for C. B. & Q. stockholders, "it was of the first importance, in view of the money advances which the C. B. & Q. had made, that there should be the

[6] Forbes to Green, June 16, 1873, CB&Q/N, 8C6.5. Cf. Forbes to Green, June 29, 1873, CB&Q/N, 8C6.4.

utmost frankness and publicity about the whole matter, and that nothing should be kept back."[7] He felt obliged to tell Forbes what he had learned from Graves. At long last, the cat was out of the bag.

When Forbes heard what Perkins had to say, he and Griswold decided forthwith to meet with Graves that evening to see what they could find out from him. As Perkins was a subordinate of Brooks, however, Forbes tactfully suggested that he withdraw from the meeting. As a result, those present were Forbes, Griswold, Brooks, Walker, Graves, and two of his assistants. The evening session was frustrating in the extreme. Neither Brooks nor Walker would divulge any information whatever, and Graves refused to reveal the names of the stockholders of the construction companies; the most he would do was promise to send Forbes a list of names later on. He did admit that he had received all the proceeds from the sale of both bonds and stock of the two River Roads and had paid them all out to the construction companies, and that no further funds remained, even though twelve miles of the Lower River Road and forty miles of the Turkey River branch still were incomplete. Finally, under severe questioning, Graves also admitted that he had spent over $170,000 of River Roads money to construct the Iowa Pacific, in which he alone was personally interested.

The moment Forbes returned to Burlington, on November 9, he sent off a lengthy letter to Sidney Bartlett, never dreaming, of course, that Bartlett himself was involved as a stockholder of the two construction companies. Forbes castigated Graves's notions of administration as "loose beyond the imagination of the ordinary mind to conceive of," and told Bartlett that the River Roads directors should meet immediately and send a competent auditor to Dubuque to make a thorough investigation.[8]

Meanwhile Graves was far from idle. He dispatched an urgent letter to Joy, marked "Private and Confidential," in which he told Joy that at all costs Forbes must be kept from finding out which C. B. & Q. directors were stockholders of the construction companies. To this end he implored Joy to mail to him at once the stock certificates of the construction companies, which had been made out originally in the names of the local directors from whom the C. B. & Q. men had bought them. Graves's idea was to send these names to Forbes rather than those of the C. B. & Q. men who currently held the stock. Otherwise, Graves feared, Forbes, Griswold, and Perkins would demand "a change of affairs in Boston."[9]

When Bartlett received Forbes's letter, he wrote Graves at once in a way that indicated that he was as shocked as Forbes. He directed Graves to send to Boston at once copies of the construction company contracts

[7] Perkins, Memorandum, November 2, 1901, PLB, Vol. XVIII, pp. 600-9.
[8] Forbes to Bartlett, November 9, 1873, GM, 1865-73, pp. 202-5.
[9] J. K. Graves to Joy, November 8, 1873, CB&Q/N, 8C6.5.

and a statement of what River Roads money had been applied to construction company debts. He told Graves under no circumstances to apply any future earnings of the railways to the construction companies. On the same day he wrote Joy enclosing Forbes's letter, which, he said, had given him "great anxiety."[1]

Joy's first move was to show Bartlett's letter, along with the enclosed letter from Forbes, to Brooks. Brooks undertook to reply to Bartlett; he laid the blame for squandering money squarely on Graves, and among other things stated unequivocally that he never had seen the construction company contracts with their incredible clauses releasing the two companies from their obligations once their funds were spent. Thus it would appear that, as in the case of Bartlett, Brooks had been blissfully unaware of what was going on.

Joy's reaction, however, was very different. He sent to Walker Bartlett's letter as well as those from Forbes and Graves. "I replied to Graves' letter," he told Walker, "that generally I did not care for the hostility of Perkins or Forbes, and had long known that they were no friends of mine. . . . I said, however, that Forbes had not strength enough to revolutionize C. B. & Q. and that if he had, I cared personally little about it, and not at all except on your account. I said to him [Graves] also that that was the only transaction of my business life which could be criticized morally, if that of itself could, and that I did not feel disposed to change the position of things so far as I was concerned. But I said I would send his [Graves's] letter to Boston and they might discuss it there and adopt such policy as they pleased. I have given it to Mr. Brooks who sent it to Mr. Bartlett."[2]

Clearly Joy had no intention whatever of retreating, and this stubborn position made a fight within the Burlington board inevitable. Perhaps if Forbes had approached Joy directly, a conflict might have been avoided. Certainly Perkins thought so, for many years later he wrote that if Joy instead of Brooks and Walker had been at the Dubuque meeting when the trouble began, "there never would have been any trouble because Mr. Joy would have told the whole story with the frankness and courage which characterized him. It was the refusal of the others to tell anything which changed the current of history!"[3]

For one thing, Joy's unwillingness to admit that mistakes had been made or to cooperate in cleaning house in the fall of 1873 put Forbes in a miserable dilemma. His immediate inclination was to return from his own pocket the money he had received on the River Roads coupons in June 1873 and demand that everyone else on the board do likewise. But Griswold, who fully agreed in principle, realized that such a course would

[1] Bartlett to Joy, November 14, 1873, CB&Q/N, 8C6.5.
[2] Joy to Walker, November 17, 1873, CB&Q/N, 8C6.5.
[3] Perkins to Henry B. Ledyard, February 1, 1897, GM, 1896–1905, p. 27.

hopelessly split the C. B. & Q. directory and that some effort should be made first to resolve the matter amicably and equitably. For the moment, Forbes agreed to abide by Griswold's advice, but he kept insisting that at the very least the stockholders of the River Roads (notably the C. B. & Q. directors who had acquired the stock through their holdings in the construction company) should turn over their certificates to the bondholders so that the latter could protect their interests. But this Forbes's fellow directors on the C. B. & Q. board refused to do. Nor would they even remove Graves as president of the two River railways. For one reason, he was fully occupied in Washington trying to force the Chicago and North Western to open its bridge at Clinton to C. B. & Q. traffic, an effort doomed to failure.

Not until August 1874 did Joy and Walker offer a concrete plan for clearing up the muddle. They then proposed that the River Roads should repay to the C. B. & Q. the (approximately) $250,000 spent for paying the coupons of June 1873, and that the Turkey River branch should be completed. They also suggested that the River Roads be leased to the C. B. & Q. until their net earnings were sufficient to pay off all debts to the Burlington. But they inserted an important condition: the River Roads bondholders should promise not to foreclose, for if they were to foreclose, they would wipe out the stock held by Joy, Walker, and their associates.

In principle, Forbes agreed to this, and on October 1, 1874, the C. B. & Q. took possession of the River Roads and began to manage them. During the next few months, the Burlington spent over $100,000 on the Turkey River branch and tried to bring order out of chaos. But Forbes still was uneasy. He was bothered that Graves continued to occupy the presidency of the River Roads, and he was convinced that the only fair thing to do was for the River Roads stockholders to turn over their shares to a committee of bondholders, who could then control all the assets and manage the road for the benefit of those who had bought bonds on the recommendation of the Burlington.

In mid-January 1875, the River Roads, obviously bankrupt, were placed in the hands of a receiver. A committee of bondholders immediately was formed. Now more than ever it was important that the Bartlett–Joy faction should cooperate by turning over their stock to this committee so that all interests could unite in presenting a plan of reorganization to the court. During the early days of February, Forbes literally worked day and night to try to persuade Bartlett, Brooks, Thayer, and Hunnewell to follow this course. He backed his plea by pointing out that the outside bondholders (that is, bondholders not also connected with the C. B. & Q.) were clamoring for a complete and independent investigation, which would undoubtedly greatly damage the Burlington. His efforts were in vain. So it was that on February 14, 1875, Forbes came to the reluctant conclusion that the only solution, for the sake of the Burlington, was "a reform of the C. B. & Q. board on which more talent and force has long been needed."[4]

Once Forbes had made this crucial decision, events moved with startling rapidity. Working closely with Griswold and Green, he organized a whirlwind campaign for proxies to be voted at the annual stockholders' meeting of the C. B. & Q. scheduled for Chicago on February 24, a scant ten days off. Meanwhile he labored over the composition of the board that he and his allies hoped to elect.

For the sake of harmony and continuity, Forbes was eager to make as few changes as possible, but he was adamant that Joy, Thayer, and Burnham would have to go. As Walker's name did not appear on the construction company contracts, he might be kept because of his knowledge of law and politics. And Forbes was willing to let Brooks and Bartlett continue if they made a clean breast of the affair and indicated without qualification their willingness to cooperate. He was inclined also to let Erastus Corning and Chauncey Colton stay, but was determined to strengthen the board by adding either Perkins or one or two other men of his choice from Boston.

While the battle lines were being drawn, the bondholders of the River Roads met in Boston on February 17 to hear a report from their own investigating committee. Item by item the sorry story was revealed, much of it from material that Forbes had turned over to the committee. Joy, with his customary courage, was present. Eloquently he explained why he had adopted the method he had to obtain control of the River Roads, and he pointed out how much he and his associates had invested personally in the stock of the enterprises. He even gave a warm endorsement to Graves, although he did say that Graves had not fully informed him of everything that had taken place. Despite sharp questioning by Forbes, Joy refused to admit that he had concealed any relevant facts.

When Joy had finished speaking, the chairman of the meeting asked that the construction company contracts be read in full. As the terms were spelled out, Forbes's indignation mounted. Jumping to his feet, he characterized the contract then being read not as one to build a road, but as one not to build it; those present burst into applause. Griswold carried on the attack by asking why the construction companies had issued more bonds per mile than they had agreed upon in the mortgage, and why they had not finished the work. Flatly he pointed out that Joy had been in the position of a trustee for the protection of the Burlington and yet had led the company into a trap while knowing fully what he was doing. As Forbes wrote Green the next day, the bondholders' meeting proved to be a ringing endorsement for swift and immediate reform within the C. B. & Q.

There was another sequel to that meeting. On February 18, Brooks,

[4] Forbes to John N. A. Griswold, February 14, 1875, CB&Q/N, 8C6.5.

Bartlett, Burnham, Hunnewell, Thayer, and Denison published a long statement in a Boston paper in which they placed the blame for the imbroglio squarely on Joy. Specifically, they disclaimed any knowledge of the odious construction company contracts. Joy's reaction was private rather than public: on February 22 he sent a lengthy letter to Bartlett in which he rehearsed the entire background of the River Roads situation, his defense being purely and simply that he had acted in the only way possible to guarantee control of the River Roads and access for the Burlington to the Northwest. Joy, in effect, nailed his flag to the mast. Thus matters stood as the climax approached.

The tense Burlington stockholders' meeting of February 24 was packed, and was covered in every detail by the press. Two slates were offered for the thirteen positions available. Nine names appeared on both: Bartlett, Brooks, Colton, Corning, Forbes, Green, Griswold, Thayer, and Walker. On the "old ticket" were also the names of Burnham, Denison, Joy, and Moses Taylor of New York. On the "new ticket" were T. Jefferson Coolidge, William J. Rotch, J. H. Clifford, and Charles J. Paine, all of Boston.

The outcome was a foregone conclusion. Except for the election of Denison rather than Coolidge, the entire "new ticket" was swept into office, and Denison won only because Griswold had misunderstood Green's instructions. But that was a detail; Joy and his closest henchmen were out. Forbes and his like-minded associates were in firm and complete control of the Chicago, Burlington & Quincy.

Before the meeting adjourned, Joy asked for the floor and, eloquent as always, made a touching speech of retirement. He called up memories of early days on the property and of the sacrifices so many of those present had made. He hoped the new administration would do as well as the old, and assured his listeners that if it did, he would rejoice as much as if he were still connected with the property. So saying, he bade his farewell. A motion expressing the stockholders' "undiminished regard" and thanks for the past services of James F. Joy was passed unanimously.[5] That very evening Joy left the city for his home in Detroit.

His departure marked the end of an era. However his involvement with the River Roads might be characterized, he more than anyone else had figured out how, in 1852, to gather together the disconnected short lines in Illinois and weld them into the original Chicago, Burlington and Quincy. His organizational energy, persuasiveness, and quick figuring had mobilized the efforts of local businessmen and brought forth consistently favorable action from state legislatures. He had staked out the territory that the Burlington should control and then had devised means for occupying and holding it. He had thought in large terms and acted accord-

---

[5] *Chicago Tribune,* February 25, 1875.

ingly. Now his overly intricate schemes and impatience had cost him his leadership. Whether the Burlington management could bind up its wounds and recover its stamina fast enough to hold its own and move ahead remained to be seen. Only one thing was certain: never again would Joy have a voice in shaping the destiny of the Burlington.

Yet the "Revolution of 1875" was far more than a struggle between two strong men, Joy and Forbes. The sort of thing that had happened with the River Roads was a good deal more characteristic of the age than it was exceptional, but for the Burlington, at least, such dubious practices now stood condemned. The Revolution had shaken the administration and broken long-standing friendships, but in the process it had established a new and higher standard of integrity.

PART II

Growth and Integration

1875 - 1901

CHAPTER 9

Reappraisal and Revival

1 8 7 5 - 7 8

• THE PROBLEM OF LEADERSHIP •

AT THE BURLINGTON STOCKHOLDERS' MEETING on February 24, 1875, the "reform group" headed by Forbes won the decisive battle of the "Revolution." The next question was whether these men, and the ideas they represented, would win the peace. For even though Joy was vanquished permanently, the problems he had sought so hard to solve in his own way were as pressing as ever: acute competition, rivalry among the "family lines," the question of whether to expand and where, continued depression, and the mounting threat of regulation. Requiring immediate attention were the inevitable wounds left by the Revolution itself: the defeated minority on the board would have to be brought into line, and some decision would have to be reached about disposition of the River Roads.

What was needed at the moment was strong, effective leadership. But the prospects for obtaining it, particularly in the near future, were hardly encouraging. Although Walker, the incumbent president, was reasonably well acquainted with the company's legal affairs, corporate relationships, and finance, he had been "close to," if not "in," the River Roads affair and, even more to the point, he possessed a subordinate turn of mind. For years he had been content to accept Joy's decisions and, indeed,

[143]

had been willing to do so without even knowing the reasons behind them. Furthermore, he was only a part-time employee; although his outside interests did not necessarily conflict with those of the Burlington, they kept his attention divided.

The most experienced operator available was Robert Harris. Adept at getting trains over the line and seeing to it that plant, operations, and labor relations were handled efficiently, he also was familiar with the hard realities of competition. But he had had little training in the formulation of policy or in dealing with the board of directors; that had always been Joy's exclusive domain, and Harris had showed little interest in it. John W. Brooks, seasoned engineer, able administrator, and a man well known to all the directors, might, under different circumstances, have provided the needed leadership. But he no longer enjoyed Forbes's full confidence. Neither did he have a reputation for training lieutenants. Of more immediate importance, his health had been increasingly uncertain; it would take a man of rugged vitality to lead the company over the months and years to come.

Charles E. Perkins, of course, was a "comer" whose marked abilities and tremendous energy even Joy, sometimes with exasperation, had recognized. But Perkins, whose earlier fierce loyalty to the B. & M. of Iowa had now been transferred to the B. & M. in Nebraska, was regarded as something of a "young Turk" by the more conservative members of the board, especially those who had been close to Joy. In view of the fact that harmony within the board would now be more vital than ever, this was no time to give Perkins a larger voice in the affairs of the system.

In many ways, John Murray Forbes himself appeared to be the logical man for the presidency. He had been concerned with the affairs of the company since its early days and was the acknowledged leader of the entrepreneurial alliance that guided its destiny. But with all his other interests he felt overburdened. Furthermore, he could hardly leave his base of operations in Boston, and he believed strongly that at least for the immediate future the man directly in charge should be on the property itself; he simply was not familiar with the many details that required handling in company territory. He was prepared—in fact, he had no other choice—to devote long hours and hard thinking to the problems of the Burlington, but he would have to do this in Boston as an active member of the directorate and through correspondence with officers on the line.

By a process of elimination, then, the simplest thing was to retain Walker as president in name. The board as a whole, however, would have to assume actual responsibility for leadership until such time as some one person with the necessary talents who possessed the unquestioned confidence of the entire directory could be found.

For the board as a whole to exert administrative leadership meant a radical change. During the preceding decade, the directors by and large had deliberately left the initiative pretty much to Joy. Now they would have to assume an active role. Moreover, unless their meetings were to degenerate into endless debates, it would be necessary to persuade Brooks, Bartlett, Denison, Thayer, and Walker—all long-time followers of Joy—to cooperate with the reform majority. This promised to be no easy task. As Denison complained to Corning on February 25, 1875, "I am regarded with anxiety by my friends and with doubts by C. B. & Q. stockholders."[1] Brooks appeared even more outraged. Writing Joy on March 11, he testily pointed out that during 1868–72, the C. B. & Q. had acquired 370 miles of branch roads under contracts which, in his estimation, were "not very unlike those of the River Roads. . . ." And, he continued, "loosely as these things were done, they as a whole have proved the salvation of the C. B. & Q. . . . We who do not claim to be immaculate, beyond expediency, but are content with right intentions and good results obtained on the whole will not be so much troubled about our defense."[2]

Brooks had a point. Certainly some of the contracts he referred to had been loosely drawn, and many a time the directors, faced by immediate competitive pressures, had had to act first and obtain authorization from the stockholders later. In none of these earlier cases, however, has evidence come to light that C. B. & Q. directors were also acting as contractors with conflicting interests. That was the issue on which Forbes had based his fight, the one point his opponents persistently refused to discuss. But all that was past history. The question now was whether the still disgruntled minority would prevent the board from discharging its increased responsibilities.

Fortunately for the company, this very real threat was liquidated far more rapidly than anyone dared hope at the time. At the March 4, 1875, meeting of the board—the first after the stockholders' battle—the reform majority carried all points without difficulty, even though Bartlett was inclined to quibble about each detail. Thayer and Brooks, on the other hand, seemed almost over-eager to go along with the majority. A month later, no doubt by prearrangement, Clifford quietly resigned; on April 2, Perkins was unanimously elected to fill his post. When Green, who had been a tower of strength to Forbes, suddenly died on May 7, his place was taken by Peter Geddes, long a severe critic of the Joy regime. And when Thayer resigned in December, Clifford returned to the directory.

At the annual meeting on February 23, 1876, Chauncey S. Colton, who had done so much to establish the C. B. & Q. a quarter of a century before, retired on account of failing health. The bylaws were thereupon amended to reduce the board to eleven. In an uncontested election, only three "Joy men" were returned: Bartlett, Brooks, and Walker. Six of the others (including Perkins) had consistently supported Forbes, and the two

---

[1] Denison to Corning, February 25, 1875, EC, quoted in TCC, pp. 308–9.
[2] Brooks to Joy, March 11, 1875, JFJ, quoted in TCC, p. 282.

new men elected were T. Jefferson Coolidge of Boston, a friend of Forbes, and Robert Harris. Finally, when Brooks resigned because of ill health a month later, his seat was given to Denison. Even so, the "reform group" could still count on a thumping eight-to-three majority. With surprisingly few changes, the directory remained for many years essentially as it then stood. Somewhat incredibly, Sidney Bartlett refused to speak directly to Forbes for twelve years after the Revolution, despite the fact that they met regularly at directors' meetings. But that was a purely personal matter. For all practical purposes sufficient harmony reigned within the board from the first meeting after the Revolution to enable it to follow a strong and consistent policy.

The most difficult administrative problem during 1875–76 arose not within the board or in respect to the presidency, but at the next lower level. Back in 1865, Robert Harris had become general superintendent of the C. B. & Q., and Perkins had stepped into a similar post on the B. & M. of Iowa. At the time there was a vast difference between the two men and their responsibilities. Harris, ten years older and more experienced, presided over some four hundred miles of railroad. Perkins, not yet twenty-five, was in charge of a seventy-five mile line that was then hardly more than a branch. As the B. & M. crossed Iowa, however, Perkins's responsibilities grew along with his experience. Among other things, he succeeded in building up and training an exceptionally able core of lieutenants, to whom, as a team, he delegated increasing responsibilities. Outstanding in this group were W. B. Strong, general manager; A. E. Touzalin, general passenger agent; T. J. Potter, superintendent; and George S. Harris, land commissioner. When, in 1872, the B. & M. of Iowa, then comprising more than four hundred miles, was leased to the C. B. & Q., this group, much to Perkins's dismay, largely was dispersed. He took many of his "old" men with him to Nebraska, but others went into the C. B. & Q. organization. Strong, in particular, became assistant general superintendent under Harris, an arrangement that proved unhappy because Walker, himself unfamiliar with operating affairs, aroused Harris's jealousy by relying heavily on Strong. Thus when Joy, as president of the Michigan Central, needed a competent general superintendent for that road in the fall of 1874, Harris willingly let Strong go. Walker, beholden as always to Joy, felt in no position to object. The net result was that in 1875 Harris was simply overworked, partly because of his own insistence on handling details, and partly because, since Joy's removal, he had to do many things that Walker should have handled.

To Perkins, running a tightly knit organization in Nebraska, and now also a director of the C. B. & Q., this situation seemed to require immediate attention. The board agreed, and in November 1875 a committee was appointed to look into the matter. Harris, Walker, and Perkins made various detailed suggestions, each differing from the other. The solution

[1 4 6]

the directors finally reached on March 2, 1876, was something of a compromise as well as a calculated risk. Harris was named president, and Walker stepped aside to serve as general counsel; the salary of each man was fixed at $12,000. Perkins was named vice-president of the C. B. & Q. at a salary of $7,500 (in addition to his stipend on the B. & M.), and Strong, with Harris's blessing, was brought back from the Michigan Central to serve as general superintendent of the C. B. & Q. at $10,000 a year. Walker, Harris, and Perkins, constituting a Western Executive Committee, were authorized to handle all affairs of the road on the spot. Any expenditure exceeding $25,000, however, and all matters on which the committee could not agree unanimously were to be referred to the board in Boston. Strong, in whom Perkins had great confidence, would have both the Operating and Traffic departments under his control; Perkins, as his superior, would serve as insulation between Harris and Strong.

This arrangement did not remove one potential danger spot. Perkins still was vice-president directly in charge of the B. & M. in Nebraska. Although this affiliate was controlled by the men who owned the C. B. & Q., its interests were not necessarily identical, particularly with respect to the Union Pacific and the complex competitive situation in the Missouri River Valley. Perkins would have to walk a tight rope in his dual capacity as vice-president of the B. & M. in Nebraska and of the C. B. & Q. It is notable that he repeatedly offered to forego any active role in the management of the C. B. & Q. and to devote all his energy to the property west of the Missouri River. The plain fact, however, was that he was needed on the C. B. & Q., and Forbes insisted on keeping him there. With fingers crossed, everyone hoped for the best.

• CAUTIOUS REGROUPING •

AT THE VERY FIRST MEETING of the reconstituted directory on March 4, 1875, it was resolved, on motion of Forbes, that the president be instructed "to notify every person in the service of the company that to receive any commission or gratuity of any kind . . . upon any negotiation or purchase in its behalf, directly or indirectly, should be followed by immediate expulsion from its service. . . . "[3] During the same month George Tyson, long a partner in Russell & Company, China traders, was appointed to the newly created post of general auditor. He was ordered to make a detailed examination of books and accounts in all departments, to investigate all "suspended accounts," including those of the River Roads, and to make recommendations. All this he promptly did, and as one result the board transferred to Boston all cash beyond that required for current business, "with the view to bring it more directly under the responsibility and super-

[3] CB&Q, ORB, Vol. II, p. 416.

vision of the Board of Directors."[4] Thus the old casual ways of doing business were brought to an abrupt end.

The next question, far from simple, was what to do with the River Roads. At the time of the Revolution everyone apparently assumed that the C. B. & Q. would complete and take over the lines. Indeed, in April 1875 Perkins wrote Forbes that if the properties were managed carefully, they should gross about half a million dollars a year. He thought that it would be a mistake to let them go, and suggested that the Burlington build a bridge at or near Sabula and construct a line to East Clinton. "After having built the Prophetstown Road," he asked, "are you not bound to get all the business you can for it?"[5] But when Perkins was offered the opportunity to manage the River Roads, he declined. By the middle of 1877, after all parties had agreed to dismiss pending suits and cancel old traffic contracts, sentiment on the Burlington shifted toward disposing of the properties. Accordingly, they were reorganized, consolidated early in 1878, and on July 1, 1880, sold to the Chicago, Milwaukee & St. Paul.

A combined accountant and detective would need months, if not years, to determine how much, if anything, the C. B. & Q. lost on the entire River Roads transaction; probably not more than $150,000, and perhaps nothing at all. What the River Roads had cost in time and anguish, however, was another matter.

Understandably, therefore, the directors addressed themselves with extreme caution to other current problems facing the company. As became standard practice thereafter, special committees were named by the board to examine a wide range of matters so that all facts could be in hand before action was taken. The question of constructing a new depot in Chicago, for example, already had been discussed with the Illinois Central and Michigan Central during 1874. A new committee was named in April 1875 to review the whole situation. A month later, grounds were purchased on the west side of the Chicago River, but the I. C. and M. C. seemed reluctant to leave the lake front. Not until the spring of 1880 were contracts completed with the Pennsylvania and the Pittsburgh, Fort Wayne & Chicago for a Union Station on the west side at Canal and Adams streets. A year later, the structure was completed, and once again, as ever since, Burlington passenger operations were centered west of the Chicago River.

A matter that had been pending since 1872 was the formal merger of the C. B. & Q. and the B. & M. of Iowa. During the summer of 1875, the necessary legislative authority was obtained. The consolidation was effected July 31, 1875, on a share-for-share basis. Eventually the C. B. & Q. issued $8,679,900 of stock for this purpose.

4 CB&Q, AR 1875, p. 28.
5 Perkins to Forbes, PLB, Vol. II, April 27, 1875, pp. 252–8.

Relations with the Hannibal and St. Joseph, once such a close member of the family, posed new problems. The road was experiencing chronic financial difficulties, and so essential was it as a connection to Kansas City that Perkins was put on a committee to consider whether the C. B. & Q. could afford to rely on it or should seek alternate means wholly under C. B. & Q. control. While this matter hung fire (as it was destined to do for several years), Perkins served on another committee with Walker and Harris to review the shop situation; very probably their investigations led to the establishment, in 1877, of the testing laboratories at Aurora which have functioned continuously ever since.

Since the fall of 1872, the Burlington had not laid or acquired a mile of new railroad anywhere on its system; like all other businesses, it had had to husband its resources in the lean years following the crash of 1873. When, however, it was learned that a group of businessmen in St. Louis and Quincy was projecting a new road northward toward Des Moines which would invade some of the company's very best territory, defensive action seemed imperative. Fortunately a solution was readily at hand, for Governor Merrill of Iowa was projecting a thirty-three mile line from a junction with the Burlington at Albia northwestward to Knoxville. Consequently the C. B. & Q. leased that line in perpetuity in November 1875, but not until, at Forbes's insistence, the nearby Rock Island was consulted and mollified. Late in 1875 a somewhat similar situation arose in respect to the Quincy, Alton and St. Louis Railway, which extended forty-six miles between Quincy and Louisiana, with a branch to Hannibal. Fearful that some other major competitor might acquire it, and eager to secure a direct connection at Hannibal with the Missouri, Kansas & Texas, the C. B. & Q. executed a perpetual lease of the road, effective on February 1, 1876.

The directors were none too happy about acquiring either of these roads. Walker frankly told the stockholders that these acquisitions were "not in accord with their general purpose" but that competitive circumstances had made action necessary.[6] "The true policy of the roads from the West, terminating at Chicago," the board resolved late in 1875, "ought to be to discourage further railroad building until absolutely necessary, and where such necessity arises, to endeavor to understand with each other that they will then equitably divide the territory naturally belonging to each of the present roads as now existing."[7] To a surprising degree (and to an extent not generally recognized since), this policy was diligently followed. For nearly a decade after 1875, the Burlington, the Rock Island, and the North Western lived in relative peace and harmony.

On October 1, 1876, the C. B. & Q. acquired the St. Louis, Rock Island and Chicago Railroad in the western portion of Illinois, a 270-mile

[6] CB&Q, AR 1875, p. 19.
[7] CB&Q, ORB, Vol. II, pp. 411, 441, December 2, 1875.

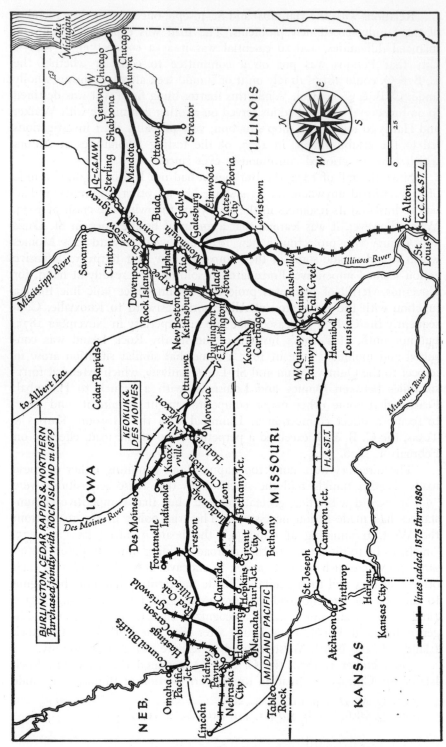

Growth of the C. B. & Q. in Illinois and Iowa, 1875–80

property shaped like a T. From a junction with the Chicago and North Western near Sterling, it ran almost due west to Rock Island; from the midpoint on this line, the main stem ran due south to East Alton, from which point it had trackage rights into St. Louis. It also had a short branch from Gladstone, just east of Burlington, to Keithsburg. The road had originally been built to serve local needs, but it crossed the main line of the C. B. & Q. at five places, diverting business and reducing rates. The Burlington felt that it could be converted into a useful feeder, that rates could be stabilized, and, of prime importance, that it would provide an entry into St. Louis. The price paid was approximately $2,000,000, and to raise that amount, together with enough to make necessary improvements, the C. B. & Q. issued $2,500,000 in five percent bonds.

In order to maintain friendly relations with the Rock Island, the Q offered that company an option to buy part of the road, and even discussed joint ownership. At first the Rock Island was inclined to resent Burlington's aggressiveness and, to offset it, sought control of both the Midland Pacific, a small line connecting Nebraska City and Lincoln, and the Keokuk and Des Moines. The C. B. & Q. was interested in these two roads, but in respect to the Midland Pacific in particular, Forbes cautioned Perkins to be extremely tactful, lest any further offense be given the Rock Island. Eventually, patience and mutual forbearance won the day. The Burlington leased the Midland Pacific (by then renamed the Nebraska Railway) in 1876, and the Rock Island leased the Keokuk and Des Moines early in 1879. Thus the two major companies remained on friendly terms. Indeed, the whole idea of mutual accommodation might well have been extended to the area west of the Missouri had it not been for Jay Gould's insatiable ambition. But that is another story shortly to be told.

System business during 1875–76 gave little grounds for rejoicing. Of 1876, Harris observed that the company had passed through a year of great dullness. But there were encouraging signs. Crops had been good; the usual dividend of ten percent had been paid; on the main line in Illinois nearly all iron rail had been replaced by steel, and the equipment had been put in good order. Land sales, both gross and net, however, fell off moderately in Iowa and sharply in Nebraska; in the latter state cancellation of contracts almost equalled gross sales. Although this was discouraging, it was not unexpected; the important point was that the B. & M. in Nebraska continued to carry rather than to evict actual settlers who were improving the land. On the whole, the system weathered the two depression years extremely well.

• REGULATION •

DURING 1875, the position of the Burlington in respect to the regulatory laws in Illinois and Iowa remained uncertain. Walker felt sure, at the end of that year, that in Illinois the courts would uphold the company's contention that the charter right conferred on the Aurora Branch to set its own rates and fares would be upheld; the controversy with Iowa moved up to the United States Supreme Court, and again Walker "confidently believed" that the decision would be in favor of the company. Furthermore, he was hopeful that the Iowa Legislature of 1876 would modify the legislation in that state as a result of what he characterized "the change in public sentiment, and the growing tendency to more reasonable views relating to the rights of private property invested in the railroads of the state."[8]

It would be interesting to discover what steps, if any, the Burlington took to encourage these "reasonable views." In 1874, Walker told an official of the Union Stockyards that as far as the C. B. & Q. was concerned, "it is a fundamental principle with us that none of our Officers or men shall have anything to do with politics, because it cannot fail to be injurious to our interests. We can always make it a ground of dismissal to employees of the Road."[9] Perkins expressed somewhat the same thought when he wrote his fellow director Griswold in December 1875: "The *Company*, I have always thought, should keep entirely out of politics. It is therefore merely a question of my personal influence, which is very small. I doubt if I could change a vote if I should try, and it would not do for me to try because the railroad would get the odium."[1] In other words, C. B. & Q. policy appeared to be that neither the company nor its employees, at least in an official capacity, should meddle in politics.

Yet, as Cochran points out and documents in his *Railroad Leaders* in respect to railways in general, specifically including the Burlington, "these general principles appear to have been subject to occasional more or less open exceptions."[2] Certainly Perkins lent his influence to Senator Allison's re-election in 1878, and, writing to Forbes in 1880 to express his dismay that Senator Paddock had turned out to be "a sort of washer of dirty linen for Conkling," he concluded: "I regret to say we put him there."[3] Whether or not the Burlington was equally active in Iowa in the mid-70's in particular must await further historical detective work.

During 1876, no final decisions concerning the challenged regulation were forthcoming from the courts, but Iowa enacted a so-called "Amnesty Law" which relieved railways there from any prosecution for non-observance of the 1874 tariff, *provided* they operated their roads for a period of two years in accordance with the schedules prescribed under it. The di-

---

[8] CB&Q, AR 1875, p. 26.

[9] Walker to G. Williams, April 1, 1874, CB&Q/N, quoted in TCC, p. 192.

[1] Perkins to Griswold, December 14, 1875, C–O, Set A–1, p. 176. Underlining in original.

[2] TCC, pp. 192–3.

[3] Perkins to Forbes, July 31, 1880, CB&Q/N, quoted in TCC, p. 193.

rectors obviously thought that strategic retreat in this instance was the better part of valor for two reasons: the fines and penalties for non-compliance with the 1874 law were extremely severe, and it was always possible that the United States Supreme Court might decide that the 1874 act was valid.

To the profound dismay of the directors, their caution was amply justified. In February 1877, the Supreme Court of the United States decided what became known collectively as the "Granger Cases." The most celebrated of these was *Munn v. Illinois,* in which the owner of a warehouse claimed exemption from an Illinois law fixing the rates he charged, on the ground that he was engaged in interstate commerce and that the rates deprived him of property (that is, reasonable profits) without due process of law. The court ruled against him on both counts and, as to the latter, laid down the famous maxim that the owner of any property "clothed with a public interest . . . must submit to be controlled by the public for the common good."[4] Having established this general doctrine, the court went on to apply it to the railway cases before it. The first one decided was *C. B. & Q. v. Iowa.* Speaking for the majority, Chief Justice Waite asserted that whereas the company could establish its own bylaws and conduct its business as it saw fit, these rights were subject at all times to the rules and regulations of the General Assembly of Iowa. Furthermore, he struck down the company's contention that the Iowa law constituted an undue burden on interstate commerce, saying that the business of the company was carried on in Iowa and therefore was a matter of "domestic concern." Waite admitted that the C. B. & Q. was in interstate as well as in intrastate business, but held that until Congress should act, "the state must be permitted to adopt such rules and regulations as may be necessary for the promotion of the general welfare of the people within its own jurisdiction, even though in so doing those without may be directly affected."[5]

In a stinging dissent, Justice Field thundered that the decision "practically destroys all the guarantees of the Constitution. . . . That decision will justify the legislature in fixing the price of all articles and the compensation for all services. It sanctions intermeddling with all business and pursuits and property in the community, leaving the use and enjoyment of property and the compensation for its use to the discretion of the legislature."[6] Ironically, Field's views were to become those of the court many years later, but that did the Burlington little good in 1877. In reporting the decision to the stockholders at the end of the year, Harris simply stated that the board did not deem it "desirable to discuss the decision or the principles upon which it is founded. The decision es-

[4] 94 US 113.
[5] 94 US 161–4.
[6] 94 US 186–7.

tablishes for the present the law under which the road in Iowa must be operated." But, he added, "there is quite a general movement throughout the state to repeal or to materially modify the law."[7] In this he was correct; on March 23, 1878, the Iowa Legislature repealed the law of 1874 insofar as it affected freight rates. Instead, it established a board of railroad commissioners empowered to prevent discrimination and unreasonable charges.

These developments ushered in a new stage in railway history. The basic principle that government could regulate a business clothed with the public interest was established for all time. In due course the Burlington was to object strenuously to the extent of such regulation. But regulation itself in one form or another had come to stay.

• Gould v. Perkins •

Enough has been said about the Burlington's ideas, and those of Forbes in particular, to warrant the generalization that, despite the giddy competitive atmosphere and the constant temptation to expand, the company's policy was basically prudent and peaceful. The company had every intention of guarding its established territory and of maintaining the special arrangements with its family lines. But it was prepared to respect the feelings of its neighbors and to limit its own expansion to territory that already was or logically could be earmarked as its own. This policy was predicated upon the assumption, often expressed, that a rapidly growing country would supply enough business for everyone, and that it was much wiser to handle such business in the most efficient and profitable way possible than to dissipate energies and resources in unnecessary competitive warfare.

This, indeed, was the long-run view of business that Forbes had always championed. He had never been interested in building what he contemptuously called a "speculator's railroad." That is why he, as well as men like Brooks and Van Nortwick, had built their physical properties as solidly as they knew how; that is why Forbes and Perkins consistently took such a deep interest in the land grants. They were concerned with building up a community with which they and their railroads expected to be permanently identified.

Another word must be added: as the outcome of the Revolution of 1875 conclusively demonstrated, the men who had so patiently pieced together the Burlington and won for it a secure and respected place among western railroads put a high value on integrity. To their thinking, it was not an idea that one could honor adequately by lip service. It meant dealing honorably within the company, with other railroads, and above all

[7] CB&Q, AR 1877, p. 22.

with the community. This, they firmly believed, was the only way to insure success in the long run.

To these men of the Burlington and their ideas, Jay Gould stood in sharp, defiant contrast. As his perceptive business biographer, Julius Grodinsky, makes abundantly clear, Gould was first, last, and always a trader. His special talent, amounting to a compulsion, was for detecting opportunities to seize control. Gould, Grodinsky says, was a "competitive bull thrown into the stabilized china shops," a man who "obtained results on one property by exploiting another," and who "could not resist the temptation to look upon railroad projects as an opportunity for beating his competitors." During his brief sojourn on the Erie, he weakened its finances, leaving the road in a precarious condition. He suborned judges and broke agreements. His countless deals involving the Union Pacific are legendary; he nearly ruined that road, as well as the Wabash. In railroading, Gould was a wrecker who, as Grodinsky says, "made stabilization impossible."[8] The fact that he led an exemplary family life simply brought into sharper focus his utterly ruthless business dealings.

This was the man who gained working control of the Union Pacific in the spring of 1875. Among other things, he was determined to break up the Iowa Pool by pitting its members against each other in bargaining for transcontinental business. Nor was that all; he reserved a special kind of wily hostility against the powerful Boston-led Burlington. He resented the fact that the system's lines between Kansas City and Council Bluffs and the B. & M. in Nebraska stood in the way of his gaining complete control of the Missouri Valley area; he was angered by the prolonged efforts of the C. B. & Q. to force open the Kearney Gateway. Finally, and perhaps as important as anything, he was galled not only by the steady habits and persistent prosperity of the Burlington, but also by the fact that Forbes and Perkins, far from being impressed or intimidated by his spectacular threats and forays, regarded him with undisguised and unalloyed suspicion.

The Burlington met Gould's moves in a variety of ways. The company vastly preferred peace and, in particular reference to Iowa, maintenance of the effectively functioning Pool on through business. Lest Gould succeed in disrupting the Pool, however, Griswold in the late summer of 1876 sounded out the Central Pacific as to whether that road would act impartially in case the Burlington felt compelled to build its own line directly west to Ogden. This, incidentally, may have been the first time the C. B. & Q. seriously turned its thoughts toward crossing the Rockies; it was certainly not the last. Although the Central Pacific in this particular case gave assurance of its neutrality, thus providing a useful extra string to the Burlington's bow, nothing more was done at the moment, and an uneasy truce descended over the Missouri Valley area. But

[8] Julius Grodinsky: *Jay Gould: His Business Career, 1867–1892* (Philadelphia: University of Pennsylvania Press; 1957), pp. 165, 212, 222.

not for long. Almost at once Gould began making pointed overtures to the Rock Island and North Western in an obvious attempt to isolate the C. B. & Q. Promptly the Burlington directors authorized Walker, Harris, Perkins, and Coolidge to meet with the officers of those two roads "to consider the relations of the three companies to each other, and to see whether means can be devised for . . . mutual and permanent development."[9] These efforts, early in 1877, were successful, and the three lines agreed to continue their fruitful cooperation in the transaction of Iowa business. In the meantime, Perkins went to Washington to urge Congress to force open the Kearney Gateway; as a first step he obtained a favorable report from the Judiciary Committee of the Senate.

These moves, of course, simply spurred Gould to further action. In March 1877, he attempted to gain control of the Council Bluffs and to increase his holding of Hannibal stock. He failed in both attempts, but acquired enough stock in both the North Western and the Rock Island to gain election to their directorates. Thereupon, characteristically, he suddenly changed his tactics. Instead of using his new advantage to harass the C. B. & Q., he suggested that the Union Pacific lease the B. & M. in Nebraska, provided that the B. & M. abandon its fight to open the Kearney Gateway.

Harris, and indeed most of the members of the C. B. & Q. board, felt that Gould's offer was a golden opportunity to achieve peace in the Missouri Valley. At the March 24 meeting of the board, Harris proposed its acceptance, provided only that existing arrangements for the exchange of business between the B. & M. and the C. B. & Q. be preserved. Only Forbes and Griswold dissented, but because they did, and because Perkins was not present, the action of the board was reconsidered and laid on the table. Even so, it was apparent that the majority of the directorate was in a mood to trade with Gould. At a series of conferences late in March, held in New York among the Pool roads, the Union Pacific, and the B. & M. in Nebraska, the Pool lines and the Union Pacific jointly proposed that if the B. & M. would share all its traffic equally with the Pool lines and would agree not to extend its Nebraska lines for a specified period of years, they then would jointly guarantee interest on its debt.

When Forbes gave a report of these meetings to the board in Boston on April 2, Harris strongly favored naming a committee to negotiate along the lines suggested. Perkins, however, vigorously opposed that step. He insisted that from the outset the Nebraska road had been built as a feeder to the C. B. & Q. and that there was no reason why it should be forced to share its traffic with the other Pool roads. Furthermore, he thought it extremely unwise to tie the B. & M.'s hands against extension. Nevertheless, the C. B. & Q. board named a committee with full power to con-

9 CB&Q, ORB, Vol. II, pp. 502–3.

clude the proposed arrangement. Forbes and Perkins abstained from this crucial vote, first because of their double relationship as directors of both C. B. & Q. and the B. & M., and second because "of their doubts as to the [proposed] conference being for the interests of the company, as a peace measure or otherwise."[1] The board, however, had spoken; its committee met that afternoon with representatives of the Union Pacific and the Pool lines, who thereupon offered to buy a million dollars worth of B. & M. bonds and to guarantee interest on the B. & M.'s debt to the extent of fifty percent of the earnings on joint business, *provided* the B. & M. drop its fight to open the Kearney Gateway, and agree not to extend.

The B. & M. board accepted these propositions in principle but, either because of innate caution or because of Perkins's and Forbes's well-known opposition, reserved the right to make various suggestions as to details. The whole matter was then referred to Chicago to be settled by the managing officers and lawyers of the various companies. This was Perkins's opportunity. He demanded and obtained so many concessions in the course of these lower-level discussions that neither the Rock Island nor the North Western, on second thought, would accept the overall understanding. Furthermore, the impatient Gould overreached himself. To put pressure on the Pool lines to accept his proposals, he caused the Union Pacific to route some of its eastbound traffic over the Council Bluffs and the Hannibal. This merely strengthened the opposition of the Rock Island and the North Western to the entire deal. Harris nonetheless persisted in trying to arrive at an agreement; in mid-May he urged upon Perkins that there be new conferences, a new committee, and a fresh approach. Perkins flatly refused. The Quintuple Contract, as it was called, was dead. And Perkins had killed it.

The effects of these negotiations were significant. Even while they were in progress, the C. B. & Q. and the B. & M. were discussing renewal of the traffic agreement governing exchange of business at Plattsmouth. Once the Quintuple Contract was out of the way, this agreement was promptly concluded, on June 21. At the same time, and in view of Gould's threats, Forbes headed a committee of directors named to bring the Council Bluffs road more securely into the system. Thus Gould was checked on every front; for another brief interval, relative peace reigned west of the Missouri River. And informally, at least, there emerged a gentlemen's understanding between the B. & M. and the Union Pacific by which the former agreed to stay south of the Platte River and the latter was to have a free hand to develop the region north of it.

Within the board, the developments of the spring of 1877 witnessed an ever widening rift between Perkins and Harris. They had been diametrically opposed throughout the negotiations with Gould, and Perkins

---

[1] CB&Q, DRB, Vol. II, p. 511.

felt more than ever that his own anomalous position as vice-president of both the C. B. & Q. and the B. & M. was untenable. In May, he wrote Tyson, president of the B. & M., that he would vastly prefer to give up his C. B. & Q. affiliation because, as he put it, its ownership was scattered and its leadership timid. A month later he told Forbes that he had lost all patience with Harris and his vacillating way of doing things. To bring matters to a head, therefore, in July he submitted to Griswold, chairman of the C. B. & Q. board, his resignation as vice-president and director of that company. Privately he told Forbes that he sincerely wanted to withdraw entirely from the C. B. & Q., but that as a middle course and to please Forbes he would be willing to remain a director if he could be relieved of his responsibility as vice-president. Clearly the administrative reorganization so hopefully entered upon when Harris became president and Perkins vice-president in March, 1876, was unworkable. Any doubt on this score was removed by an entirely new set of circumstances just then coming to a head.

• THE STRIKE OF 1877 •

IN AMERICAN LABOR HISTORY, 1877 is remembered for the bitterly fought strikes in the railway industry. The Burlington, like virtually every other major road, was affected. Mercifully, the struggle, though bitter, was brief. Its most important effects on the Burlington were the impetus it gave to better labor relations and its bearing on the fragile relationship between Perkins and Harris.

Still suffering from the prolonged depression, the Pennsylvania on May 24, 1877, announced a ten percent wage cut to become effective June 1. Other eastern lines promptly followed suit. In view of the fact that the C. B. & Q. directors felt that they would have to cut the usual ten percent dividend at least to eight percent, the C. B. & Q. board voted on June 21 to reduce wages as of July 10. Harris opposed a fixed percentage cut, pointing out that a good deal of trimming and readjustment of pay already had occurred. Successfully he urged that further reductions be made only as individual cases seemed to warrant it.

When, on July 1, the New York Central and Union Pacific, among others, announced wage cuts on their lines, Griswold was more certain than ever that the reduction scheduled for the Burlington on July 10 should be carried out "with a proper show of firmness. The men affected," he added, "must accept it cheerfully or leave."[2] Harris responded by pointing out how much lower the average monthly earnings of the C. B. & Q. engineers were than those of the Rock Island engineers, and warned that

[2] Griswold to Harris, July 7, 1877, quoted in Robert V. Bruce: *1877: Year of Violence* (Indianapolis: Bobbs-Merrill; 1959), pp. 55–6.

any system of "pauperizing" was bound to fail.[3] But Perkins, from his post in Burlington, Iowa, was of a different mind. When the first of a series of nationwide strikes broke out on the Baltimore and Ohio on July 16, he wrote that railroaders out in Iowa were well paid "and as a rule satisfied. If the strike extends to Iowa, it will be because of the influence of bad men who are neither loyal to good government, nor true to the men they urge to take the foolish and fatal step of giving up good places."[4] In his estimation, the president of the United States should be called upon to preserve order.

Striking became a reality in Chicago on Tuesday, July 24. Around noon on that day, a mob swirled through the Burlington yards calling on the men to quit. Most of them did. Whether the board knew this when they met on the same day in Boston is not clear. At any rate, they resolved that, effective August 1, all salaries of board appointees should be reduced by ten percent. Furthermore, Harris and Forbes were placed on a committee to draw up a plan to pay a year-end bonus to all officers and employees who had performed satisfactory service, the amount to be dependent upon any dividends declared in excess of eight percent. The committee also was instructed to work out a plan for a benevolent fund for widows and orphans of company employees and for disabled employees. Simultaneously, Harris cautioned Perkins to be careful. "We cannot," he said realistically, "stock this road with as good trainmen as we now have before a large part of the coming carrying season will have passed."[5] And on the same day he told a workers' committee from Aurora that the company would try to adjust any grievances they might wish to discuss.

These conciliatory moves came too late. On July 25, the C. B. & Q. trainmen and switchmen struck both at Galesburg and in Iowa. Harris promptly closed the C. B. & Q. shops and discontinued all freight service, although he continued to run passenger trains. Perkins had different ideas. He advised Harris to close up the railroad at once and "to keep the patient quiet and to show the men we could stand it if they could." When Harris refused to do that, Perkins, acting entirely on his own, shut down the B. & M. in Iowa completely. For three days no trains of any kind were operated. The strike in that region collapsed. "We made," said Perkins afterwards, "no concession of any kind. . . . Anything like vacillation and unsteadiness, in dealing with these men, is fatal."[6]

Harris, with notable courage, followed his own course in Chicago. Despite the fact that a train was fired on and a Burlington switchman

[3] Harris to J. Sterling Morton, July 21, 1877, CB&Q/N, quoted in TCC, pp. 351–2.
[4] Perkins, Memorandum, between July 14 and 22, 1877, PLB, Vol. III, p. 388.
[5] Harris to Perkins, July 24, 1877, CB&Q/N, quoted in TCC, p. 352.
[6] Perkins to Forbes, August 2, 1877, PLB, Vol. III, pp. 389–93.

instantly killed on July 25, Harris determined to keep passenger trains running if he could; at the same time he offered to discuss grievances with any committee that wished to see him. More violence occurred on the next day, but with the arrival of federal troops, peace gradually returned.

The experience prompted Perkins to write one of his many essays on labor relations. In brief, he was convinced that the labor question was primarily one of supply and demand and that any deviation from this "natural law" should simply be on a practical basis to make employment more attractive. Harris, on the other hand, was equally convinced that for the company to try to obtain labor at the lowest possible price would be a mistake in the long run. He repeated this idea to Perkins and added that the board had now given him authority to consider all grievances. He ordered Perkins to re-employ the old men at the former rate and emphasized that the amnesty should be "a real and thorough" one.[7]

Meanwhile, the board went ahead investigating a profit-sharing plan, which it eventually gave up as too difficult to administer. The possibility of a benevolent fund, however, seemed to have more promise, and Harris immediately began exploring schemes in effect on other railways and in other countries. Meanwhile, and far ahead of his day, he suggested that men be hired under written contracts effective for a year or more. These agreements, he thought, could provide for a ninety-day warning for strikes or firings, spell out all grounds for discharge, and guarantee a set rate of pay at a minimum annual wage. Griswold, incidentally, favored such a scheme both then and later. But Perkins strongly disapproved. To him any such notions were pure paternalism. That is probably why nothing more was done in this direction for a decade.

• AGAIN, ADMINISTRATIVE CHANGE •

IT WAS NOW ABUNDANTLY APPARENT that Harris and Perkins held such different views on the key matters of strategy and labor relations that further administrative reorganization was essential. Perkins urged that his resignation from the C. B. & Q. be actively considered, and on August 17 a committee of the board was named to consider it. At this point Perkins was growing doubtful even of Strong's loyalty, and dreaded bucking both him and Harris. Yet he could not resist expressing to Forbes his own ideas of how the C. B. & Q. should be run. If necessary, he said, he was ready "to take his coat off" and assume full responsibility.[8]

On September 19, 1877, the board of directors laid Perkins's resignation on the table. Within a fortnight thereafter, Strong received and accepted an offer from the Santa Fe to become its vice-president and general manager. Thereupon Perkins took charge of C. B. & Q. operations, and

[7] Harris to Perkins, August 9, 1877, CB&Q/N, quoted in TCC, p. 176.
[8] Perkins to Forbes, September 14, 1877, GM, 1874-8, p. 183.

Chicago–Downers Grove suburban train, about 1880

Passenger station, Burlington, Iowa, built 1882, burned January 1943

The *Denver Flyer* at Downers Grove, August 26, 1899

Diner of "Old Eli," Chicago-Kansas City Flyer, 1899

Conductor doing "book work," 1900

Express from Savanna at Galesburg, Illinois, 1905, with Class K-3 locomotive

Chicago Union Station, 1905

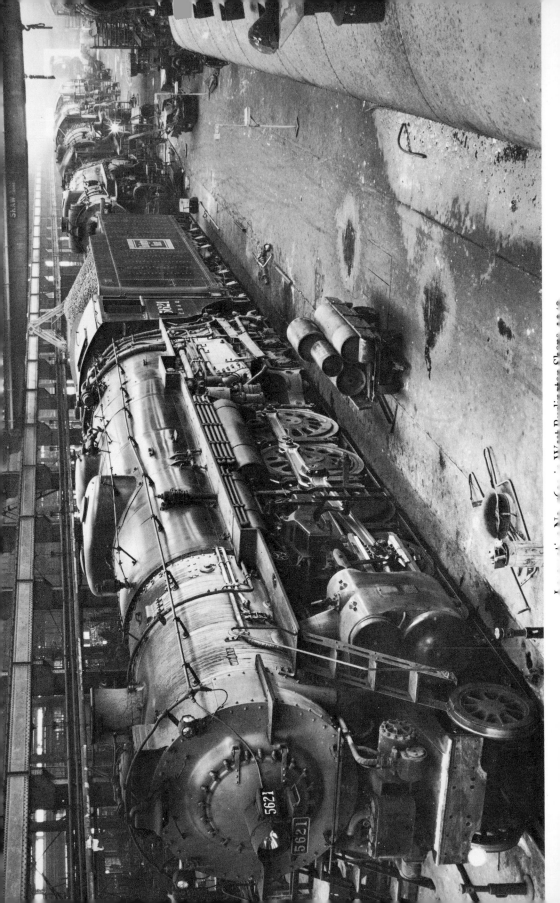

Locomotive No. 5621 at West Burlington Shops, 1940.

Pioneer Zephyr at Aurora, Illinois, on its 785-minute, nonstop run from Denver to Chicago (1,015 miles), May 26, 1934

Locomotives Nos. 6168 and 6161 hauling Train 80—3,185 tons—at Sheridan Hill, Wyoming, March 9, 1938

Two steam locomotives hauling oil tank cars, Wind River Canyon, Wyoming, 1944

Locomotive No. 5622 hauling a freight along the Mississippi,
Maiden Rock, Wisconsin, 1948

late in November persuaded Harris to appoint George Manchester assistant general superintendent. As the time for the C. B. & Q. annual meeting of 1878 approached, Perkins tried his best to prevail upon Forbes to take over the presidency; on his part, Forbes tried to convince Perkins that he should remain the operating head of the C. B. & Q. even with Harris as president. At the time of the February annual meeting, no decision had been reached. Consequently, at the directors' meeting on April 4, 1878, all officers of the C. B. & Q. were re-elected. A six-man committee of the board, however, was appointed to consider changes. This was obviously a stop-gap; only an ultimatum from Forbes cleared the air. He said that either both he and Perkins should be relieved of all responsibilities for the C. B. & Q, or else, if Forbes accepted the presidency, he should have the right to name a western manager of his own choosing. Such a manager would obviously be Perkins, even though a considerable part of the board still felt strongly that if Perkins was to take over the C. B. & Q., he should no longer be an active officer of the B. & M. in Nebraska. This Perkins opposed vigorously, for aside from his personal involvement, he thought that it would be a serious mistake, in view of the competitive situation, to separate the management of the C. B. & Q. and that of its Nebraska affiliate.

Eventually Forbes had his way. On May 25, 1878, he was named president; Harris was appointed consulting engineer at no reduction in salary. By a very close vote Perkins was permitted to remain as both general manager of the C. B. & Q. and vice-president of the B. & M. Finally, Forbes was commissioned to draw up a plan for the future organization of the company. As the result of this last motion, it was agreed that the offices of vice-president and general manager should eventually be separated, but only when an appropriate person for the latter post could be found. Until then, Perkins would be in charge of both C. B. & Q. and B. & M.

These developments were obviously a bitter blow to Harris. Whereas Walker, also a former president, had been willing to step aside and employ his considerable talents as general counsel, Harris, an operating man of long experience, was fully aware that his post of consulting engineer was simply ornamental. Consequently, and to the surprise of no one, he resigned in mid-October to become general manager of the Erie. His resignation was accepted on November 7. Of Harris's zeal and fidelity no doubt was possible. His knowledge and integrity never had been in question, nor did he ever compromise his own principles. It was simply a matter of fate that he had had to compete for the pleasure of the board, and of Forbes in particular, with Perkins, whose efficiency matched his own and whose aggressiveness was more marked. As long as the two men, each with a strong will, could not work together harmoniously, one had to go. Certainly Harris was by no means the vacillating person Perkins thought him to be. Two years after he left the Burlington, he became vice-president of the Erie, and in January 1884 was elected president of the Northern Pacific. Four years later he moved up to the chairmanship of the board and remained as a consultant of the Northern Pacific until his death in 1894.

The election of Forbes to the presidency of the C. B. & Q., the departure of Harris, and the installation of Perkins as chief executive on the property marked the end of the first stage of the Burlington's administrative reorganization and achieved the harmony that had been lacking directly after the Revolution. The years 1878–81 witnessed the operation of a smoothly functioning two-man team: Forbes in the East, Perkins in the West. Each had his share of problems, but the fact of prime importance to the railway was their extraordinary confidence in each other and their ability to work together.

CHAPTER 10

Regaining Initiative

1 8 7 8 - 8 1

• MOUNTING ACTIVITY, 1878–79 •

ONE OF THE SEVERAL DIFFICULTIES under which Harris had labored was an inadequate supply of cars. In the Fall of 1877 the company could not obtain enough to handle the crops, and even though nearly nine hundred were added late in the year, the C. B. & Q. had to pay over $150,000 in rentals to other companies. Repeal of the Iowa law regulating freight rates in March 1878, however, along with an encouraging upturn in business prompted the board to increase expenditures for both plant and equipment. More steel rails than ever were substituted for iron. By the end of 1878, the entire main line in Illinois and 216 miles in Iowa had been laid with steel. During the summer, Perkins obtained authority to cut grades on the main line in Iowa, and over the next two years he spent more than half a million dollars doing so. The company ordered 2,400 freight cars (at an average price of less than $500 each) and placed orders for additional locomotives (at about $7,000 each) and passenger cars ($5,000 each). Negotiations were completed with the City of Burlington to acquire eight acres adjoining the company's track, and the board spent $60,000 for a new depot.

Throughout 1878–79, the minutes of the board were sprinkled with phrases beginning: "Voted to let the Vice-President buy. . . ." Perkins's shopping list was a long one: new telegraph wire between Chicago and Burlington; heavier steel rails; bridges and culverts; a new roundhouse, rebuilt freight yards, and another elevator and dock at Chicago; and still more locomotives and cars.

The repeal in March 1878 of Iowa's law regulating freight rates not only stimulated this activity but also gave the green light for further expansion. As Forbes explained it, "until the subsidence of the Granger mania and the returning sanity of the Western people seemed to give us assurance that certain branches, which can be built at very low cost, will not only pay a fair return upon the cost but become valuable feeders over a long extent of road, besides averting injurious competition," the board had held back from further expansion. But repeal of the law seemed to make it safe "to satisfy . . . the reasonable demands of the region naturally tributary to the main line of road." The fact was that Forbes at heart had always been as much of an expansionist as Joy; he was simply more conservative financially and less impulsive. In the *Annual Report* for 1878 he expressed the hope that both the people of the West and the railroad owners had "learned something by the sharp lesson of past disaster; but to stand entirely still would, perhaps, be as bad a mistake as to make a too rapid advance." He foresaw steady expansion, but warned that the company must limit itself "strictly to *the unquestionable wants* of our road, and to its means of payment."[1]

So it was that early in 1878 the C. B. & Q. embarked upon a branch line building program in Iowa that reached a peak during the next two years. North of the main stem, Governor Merrill's line from Albia to Knoxville was extended to Des Moines. From Chariton, a branch was built to Indianola, Creston was linked to Fontanelle, Red Oak to Griswold, and Hastings to Carson. South of the main stem, a short link connected Albia with Moravia, and the line from Chariton to Leon was extended first to Mount Ayr, then on to Grant City, Missouri, and then southward to Albany. Farther west, the road to Clarinda was extended both southward toward Bigelow and southwestward toward Northboro; still another branch connected Hastings with Sidney. All told, approximately 280 miles were put into operation in this brief period. Each of these lines was incorporated as a separate company; the C. B. & Q. accepted their first-mortgage bonds, and presumably their stock as well, in exchange for the funds necessary for construction. When completed, they were leased to the C. B. & Q.

The approximate cost of this building program was two and a quarter million dollars. To pay for it, the company could have issued additional seven percent bonds under the 1873 mortgage. But that would have increased funded debt in proportion to stock, and as interest rates had de-

---

[1] CB&Q, AR 1878, pp. 15, 17–18, 21. Italics in original.

clined markedly since 1873, the board voted in December 1878 to raise what it could by offering at par one share of new stock for each ten held by C. B. & Q. shareowners. At the same time, the directors decided to set aside a portion of the year's profits as a renewal fund. So successful was this program that $2,782,261 was raised by selling stock at par in January 1879; another $1,000,000 became available from the renewal fund. The company's funded debt then stood at approximately $24,500,000; total capital stock amounted to about $30,750,000. The new money thus raised took care of capital needs through part of 1879, but it was not enough to finance improvements and further extensions. Hence late in the fall of 1879, the C. B. & Q. issued $600,000 in five-percent, forty-year bonds dated October 1. An annual sinking fund of one and a half percent was provided, and the mortgage was secured by a first lien on all the Iowa lines except the short Burlington–Keokuk branch. Thus it was possible to finance expansion on a far more conservative basis than under the Joy regime.

Throughout its building program in Iowa, the C. B. & Q. sought to maintain harmonious relations with the Rock Island. As a matter of fact, a merger between the two companies was considered seriously in 1879, but the price of Rock Island stock, currently inflated because of high dividends, made it impractical. Close relations, however, continued. The Burlington was permitted to extend into Des Moines in peace, and it built its branches to Griswold and to Carson only after satisfactory conferences with the Rock Island.

Another joint project was acquisition of the Burlington, Cedar Rapids, and Northern. Most of this property, extending 253 miles from Burlington northward through Cedar Rapids and on to Albert Lea, Minnesota, had been completed in the early 1870's. The panic of 1873 had pushed the company into default, and it was operated by a receiver until its reorganization in the summer of 1876. The Rock Island and Burlington purchased the line jointly in the summer of 1879. Because their intention then was to let the North Western or the Milwaukee or the Illinois Central acquire the line north of Cedar Rapids, the two lines shared the expense of that portion of the property equally. It was agreed that south of Cedar Rapids the forty miles north of Burlington lay in C. B. & Q. territory, the remaining 156 in Rock Island territory. Accordingly, the costs of that portion of the line were divided on a pro-rata basis. From that moment on, the jointly owned line became part of a well-established through route for both freight and passengers between St. Louis and the Twin Cities. Early in the twentieth century, the C. B. & Q. disposed of its interest to the Rock Island at a handsome profit.

All in all, 1879 marked a period of revival for the C. B. & Q. Even though earnings per ton-mile continued to decline (as they had ever since 1866), tonnage increased rapidly, and operations became more efficient as plant and equipment were improved. Net income rose from a little over three and a half million dollars in 1878 to nearly five million in 1879. The C. B. & Q. was doing well in its own bailiwick. But its future was becoming increasingly identified with the fast-moving competitive developments originating west of the Missouri River.

• COMPETITIVE STRATEGY, 1878–81 •

FROM THE TIME OF ITS COMPLETION to Kearney in September 1872 until August 1876, the B. & M. in Nebraska added no new mileage to its 238-mile system. On August 1, 1876, however, it leased the Nebraska Railway (former Midland Pacific), which operated about a hundred miles from Brownville, on the bank of the Missouri, northward to Nebraska City and thence west to Lincoln and Seward; a twenty-seven mile extension to York was completed in the next year, the short link from Brownville to Nemaha in 1878.

The B. & M. had been hard hit by the depression. A virtual crop failure and a plague of locusts in 1874 had compounded its difficulties and contributed to the drop in its land sales in the succeeding years. But by 1877 good crops, revival of immigration, and the extension of the Nebraska Railway brought an increasing amount of business back to the rails. Net earnings in 1877 were 162 percent greater than in 1873. Nebraska clearly was growing fast, and the B. & M. stood ready to share in its development. The question was whether the C. B. & Q., some of whose board members looked askance at their lusty Nebraska affiliate, would provide the necessary support and cooperation.

Ever since 1869, the C. B. & Q. had thought of itself primarily as a link between the Missouri River and Chicago. As such, it had been able to exchange business with all the lines west of the river without itself becoming embroiled in their competitive ambitions. Originally, investment in the Nebraska road on the part of the C. B. & Q. stockholders had been largely on the basis of the land grant, the local feeder business its colonization would provide, and the prospect of exchanging transcontinental traffic with the Union Pacific at Kearney. Matters had not turned out that way. Although the B. & M. had furnished a gratifying amount of business, its prolonged fight with Gould had embittered relations with the Union Pacific and at times had made it difficult for the C. B. & Q. to stay on friendly terms with the Rock Island and the North Western. Furthermore, the pronounced differences of point of view between Harris and Perkins had not eased relations between the C. B. & Q. and the B. & M. On the other hand, the death of the Quintuple Contract, confirmation of the traffic agreement between the C. B. & Q. and the B. & M. in 1877, and, particularly, the accession of Forbes to the C. B. & Q. presidency in the spring of 1878 all pointed toward increasing cooperation between the two companies. These developments, together with the apparent willingness of the Union Pacific to let the B. & M. dominate the area south of the Platte River, set the stage for further expansion in Nebraska.

The most promising area lay along the valley of the Republican River. The B. & M. had extensive granted lands there, and the region was ripe for colonization. On March 28, 1878, the Republican Valley Railroad Company was incorporated to build from Hastings, on the main stem of the B. & M., to Red Cloud and thence directly west to the western boundary of Franklin County. Stock of the new company was sold to the B. & M. shareholders, and the B. & M. took a long-term lease on the property and agreed to operate it. The forty miles to Red Cloud were ready for business early in November 1878, and by the following March, service was opened to Bloomington, twenty-eight and a half miles beyond Red Cloud. The company's 250,000 acres of land sold like hot cakes.

This modest building was hardly enough to provoke retaliation from Gould. But the strategic situation west of the Missouri River was like a pile of jackstraws. Whatever happened at one place might bring repercussions in another. The successive steps in Burlington expansion during 1878–81 can be understood only in reference to the dizzy development of the whole western area.

In the spring of 1878, the key to the situation lay in Colorado, where the railroad pot was bubbling merrily as usual. Ever since 1870, Denver had been connected with the nation's rail network by way of the Denver Pacific to Cheyenne and the Kansas Pacific to Kansas City. Two years later, Palmer completed his Denver and Rio Grande to Pueblo, and in the same year Governor Evans organized the Denver, South Park and Pacific to build toward Leadville. The arrival of the Santa Fe in Pueblo in March 1876 threatened trouble, but the following year that road, the Union Pacific, the Kansas Pacific, and the Rio Grande agreed among themselves on a division of traffic originating in the area. Peace, however, was short-lived. Early in 1878, the Santa Fe captured the strategic Raton Pass leading into New Mexico, and shortly afterward the desperate struggle began with the Rio Grande for occupancy of the Royal Gorge, the shortest pathway to Leadville. As the Santa Fe momentarily gained the upper hand, it leased the Rio Grande in December 1878. Meanwhile, in the spring of 1877, the Colorado Central, with Gould's help, was built directly north from Denver to a point on the Union Pacific four miles west of Cheyenne, thus providing another outlet for Denver in competition with the Denver Pacific.

These disconnected developments all had a bearing on Gould's struggle with the Burlington. As things stood in 1878, the Burlington could transact business with Denver by only three routes: the Kansas Pacific, the Santa Fe–Rio Grande, and the Union Pacific. Because Gould controlled the Union Pacific, he had nothing to worry about in that direction. And as the Santa Fe was standard gauge, whereas the Rio Grande was narrow gauge, the joint route those companies offered the Burlington hardly seemed attractive. By a process of elimination, the Kansas Pacific was by all odds the preferred connection, and because it was, both Forbes and Gould in the spring of 1878 took active steps to acquire it. The contest was brief. While Forbes was making his usual careful investigations, Gould stepped in and captured the prize.

Perkins fully understood the implications. He warned Forbes that perhaps the Burlington had let its opportunity go by and had strengthened Gould in the spring of 1878 took active steps to acquire it. The contest was enemies left against him. . . . In short, he is more dangerous than ever."[2] No truer words were ever spoken. Less than a week later, Perkins learned that the Union Pacific was planning to extend one of its subsidiaries into virtually every county in southern Nebraska. Thereupon Perkins suggested that the B. & M. might do well to survey the country between York and Grand Island. "We are in a position to hurt the U. P.," said he, "and I don't know that we shall ever have peace until we convince Gould that we mean to do it if he hurts us." A brief postscript was significant: "Parties in Colorado are anxious to talk with us, and say there is a better route to Ogden than the U. P. How would it do," he asked Forbes, "to keep up that talk and perhaps send someone out there?"[3] Clearly, a major thrust westward was very much on Perkins's mind, and well it might have been, for early in 1879 Gould leased the Colorado Central on behalf of the Union Pacific, and rapidly increased his holdings and influence in both the South Park and the Rio Grande.

The immediate danger, however, was closer to home. Despite Perkins's warnings, Gould captured the St. Joseph and Western, (former St. Joseph and Denver City), which cut squarely across the Burlington's rich South Platte territory. As a counter move, the Republican Valley Railway made plans to build just beyond the present city of McCook, and to construct a branch from Hastings to York, as well as a line eastward from Red Cloud to Wymore, Table Rock, and Nemaha. The York–Aurora segment was completed in November 1879, and on May 23, 1880, the main line reached Indianola, 107 miles west of Red Cloud. Meanwhile, construction was underway toward Table Rock.

On May 30, 1879, Perkins wrote Forbes that he doubted that the Burlington could long depend on any business not controlled by its own line, "and if that is what it is coming to, we ought perhaps go through to the mountains." He thought that if an agreement could be made with the Rio Grande and the Santa Fe for a friendly division of Colorado business, there could then be "no question whatever as to the extension of the B. & M. at once."[4] He pointed out that the B. & M. could provide a

[2] Perkins to Forbes, May 6, 1878, PLB, Vol. IV, pp. 78–80.

[3] Perkins to Forbes, May 12, 1878, PLB, Vol. IV, pp. 84–7.

[4] Quotations respectively from: Perkins to Forbes, May 30, 1879, PLB, Vol. IV, insert following p. 260, and Perkins to George Tyson, May 31, 1879, PLB, Vol. IV, p. 265.

through route between Chicago and Denver approximately a hundred miles shorter than the Kansas Pacific, 125 shorter than the Union Pacific, and nearly two hundred miles shorter than the Santa Fe.

While this possibility was pending, the competitive situation exploded on the eastern side of the Missouri River. In the spring of 1879, Gould acquired control of the Wabash, and in the fall extended that system into Omaha, thus providing another direct outlet for the Union Pacific which constituted a serious threat to the Iowa Pool roads.

Nor was this all. Extending westward 250 miles from Atchison lay the Central Branch Union Pacific, which, despite its name, had no relation to the transcontinental. Although both the Missouri Pacific and the Burlington were considering buying it, Gould again moved more rapidly than anyone else and gained control of the property at a fancy price. Just south of the Central Branch lay the Kansas Central, which stretched more than a hundred miles due west from Leavenworth. The Missouri Pacific acquired it in the spring of 1879, but to no avail, for in the late fall Gould acquired the entire Missouri Pacific. He had now forged a ring around the Union Pacific and the B. & M., with the result that he could and did force the transcontinental to buy not only the Kansas Pacific and the Denver Pacific, which it controlled, but also the Central Branch, the Kansas Central, and the St. Joseph and Western. By the end of January 1880 the transaction had been completed. Gould was paid off on a share-for-share basis in stock of the Union Pacific.

This development meant, in effect, that west of the Missouri River the Burlington was completely surrounded by the Union Pacific; of the roads reaching west toward the Rockies, only the B. & M. and the Santa Fe remained independent. For months, Perkins had foreseen this outcome and had been planning accordingly. "I have long been of the opinion," he wrote late in 1879, "that sooner or later the railroads of the country would group themselves into systems and that each system would be self-sustaining. . . ." And, more specifically: "Each line must own its feeders. This law, like other natural laws, may work slowly, but it is the law nevertheless. Hence my judgment is so decided that the C. B. & Q. should take the B. & M. and the Atchison, and make up its mind to lose a large part (of course not all) of the U. P. and K. P. and other business west of the Missouri controlled by the Wabash or its owners. If we had the Santa Fe and the B. & M. today, would not the Rock Island people be open to argument and be glad to join us in forming a great system?"[5]

One thing certainly was obvious: the C. B. & Q. and the B. & M. should consolidate without delay. A closer physical link was already underway: in August 1879, the B. & M. had started building a bridge at Plattsmouth. It was opened for traffic on September 12, 1880. Furthermore, in

---

[5] Perkins to Peter Geddes, November 24, 1879, PLB, Vol. IV, insert after p. 374.

September 1879 each road appointed a special committee to negotiate for consolidation. While these groups were deliberating, the C. B. & Q., in November 1879, seriously considered acquiring the Missouri–Kansas–Texas. But the price asked by the Dutch bondholders seemed too high, and the entire deal was put aside until an agreement could be reached with the B. & M.; all else was of minor importance. The committee representing the B. & M. hesitated, despite the fact, as Perkins warned, that Gould was making an all-out effort to force all roads east of the Missouri River to pool all trans-Missouri River business. Gould's threats injected such an air of instability into the situation that the officials of the C. B. & Q. and B. & M. scheduled a conference with him for January 1880 in an attempt to work out a viable truce. Perkins used the prospect of this meeting to exert pressure on his colleagues in the B. & M. to speed consolidation with the C. B. & Q. "Gould," he wrote at the end of December, "is determined to keep us out of Denver if he can, and questions are certain to come up in the discussion with him which the B. & M. and C. B. & Q., if they remain single, may, indeed I fear must, disagree about . . . . The two companies united will be strong enough to fight Gould if that seems best, or to make an advantageous truce if there seems to be more money in doing so than in fighting."[6]

Confronted with these realities, the B. & M. directorate accepted, on New Year's Day 1880, the C. B. & Q. offer of consolidation. The contract was signed on February 18. It provided that six shares of C. B. & Q. should be issued in exchange for every five shares of the B. & M. and for such shares of the Republican Valley Railroad as had been distributed previously by the B. & M. to its stockholders. Eventually the C. B. & Q. issued over $13,000,000 in stock to acquire these two roads; meanwhile, as of January 1, 1880, the B. & M. leased both the Atchison and Nebraska and the Lincoln and North Western so that, in effect, the C. B. & Q. acquired all the affiliated lines in Nebraska, a total of 836 miles of railroad. These agreements were overwhelmingly ratified by the C. B. & Q. stockholders on February 28, 1880, and at the same time a twenty percent stock dividend was distributed to represent a part of the surplus C. B. & Q. earnings up to that time. In May, the B. & M. stockholders ratified the merger, and formal consolidation of the two properties took place on July 26, 1880. The aggressive forces within the Burlington management, notably Perkins and Forbes, had prevailed. The C. B. & Q., a united company, now stretched from Chicago to western Nebraska, ready to fight it out with Gould if necessary.

In March 1880, Forbes was re-elected president of the C. B. & Q. In order to provide adequate administrative supervision for the enlarged system, the directors voted in May to separate the offices of vice-president and

[6] Perkins to Tyson, December 27, 1879, PLB, Vol. IV, p. 394.

general manager (both then held by Perkins) and, indeed, to appoint two general managers, one for all roads east of the Missouri River, another for those west of it. Two members of Perkins's original "Iowa team" were promptly named to these posts: T. J. Potter for Lines East and A. E. Touzalin for Lines West. These moves were significant: an organizational pattern was set that remains to this day. Of immediate importance, Perkins had two trusted lieutenants in direct charge of the property. His own salary, as vice-president, was raised to $25,000.

Despite the C. B. & Q.–B. & M. consolidation, Perkins refused to be lulled into an attitude of false security in respect to the strategic situation. "Gould is intoxicated with his extraordinary success," he wrote Forbes in February 1880. "He is rich and can afford to gratify his dislikes, and his getting into a position to rake our works strengthens him as against us west of the Missouri River . . . where we—that is the C. B. & Q. and its friends, the Boston people including the Santa Fe—are his only antagonists. My theory therefore is that Gould will buy anything that will help him to hold a sword over our heads. . . ."[7]

Even the fact that Gould was busily making peace in Colorado was ominous; in March 1880, he prevailed upon the Union Pacific, Santa Fe, and Rio Grande to make a tripartite agreement for the division of Colorado traffic. This left him free to concentrate on the eastern front, where he launched a systematic campaign to acquire the Council Bluffs. Perkins immediately warned Forbes, for the strategic value of the Council Bluffs to the C. B. & Q. was beyond question. This time Forbes acted without hesitation; although the C. B. & Q. was forced to pay $125 a share for the stock and income bonds of the Kansas City–Council Bluffs line, no alternative remained. By May, enough securities had been obtained to keep the property out of Gould's hands forever and thus to retain at least one sure entrance into Kansas City.

Control of the Kansas City, St. Joseph and Council Bluffs was achieved formally on July 1, 1880. In addition to its main stem, that company also owned a line between Amazonia and Hopkins, Missouri, at which point it connected with the C. B. & Q. line to Creston. Another branch north from Bigelow (completed in September 1880) connected with the Q's branch extending south from Clarinda, Iowa. Finally, in January 1882, a link was completed between Corning, Missouri, and Northboro, to meet an alternate C. B. & Q. branch to Clarinda. Thus several secondary routes could be used for business between the C. B. & Q. main line and Missouri River points, including Kansas City. All told, the Council Bluffs road included approximately 309 miles of line.

No sooner had this strategic company been acquired by the C. B. & Q. than Gould announced his intention to extend the Missouri, Iowa and

---

[7] Perkins to Forbes, February 11, 1880, PLB, Vol. IV, pp. 463–8.

Nebraska—running from near Keokuk to Humeston in mid-Iowa—all the way to the Missouri River, thus invading the Burlington's rich southern Iowa territory. The proposed road, in conjunction with the Wabash, would make a short route between Omaha and such points as St. Louis, Peoria, and Toledo. Perkins promptly warned the Wabash that if the proposed construction took place, the C. B. & Q. would build a parallel line. The Wabash retorted that in such an event it would build roads in Nebraska. Perkins thereupon proposed that the Wabash and Burlington together build a line between Humeston and Shenandoah, a town on the Omaha extension of the Wabash in western Iowa, to be managed for the joint benefit of the two owners. He also suggested that a general agreement be worked out as to future building in order to stabilize the situation on both sides of the Missouri River. Accordingly, a peace conference was held in New York in October 1880, among the Burlington, Wabash, and Union Pacific. The joint Iowa line was agreed upon and eventually built as Perkins had suggested. Far more important, however, the C. B. & Q. agreed to permit the Wabash to build a limited number of small branches in Iowa and, of paramount importance, also agreed not to extend the B. & M. to Denver. In return, the Wabash promised not to build any main or through lines in southern Iowa; *both* the Wabash and the Union Pacific agreed not to build into southern Nebraska.

Stretching this treaty to the utmost, Gould, early in 1881, built a north-south line into Des Moines directly across the main stem of the Burlington. This was hardly a minor branch, and was a violation of the spirit if not the letter of the 1880 agreement, but for the moment the Burlington elected to overlook the incident. What it could not overlook was Gould's decision in the late spring of 1881 to extend the Missouri Pacific from Atchison northward, on the west side of the Missouri River, to a connection with the Union Pacific at Omaha. Perkins was furious. "Gould," he wrote late in June, "is building his Missouri Pacific into Nebraska notwithstanding his agreement last summer as head of the Union Pacific not to do so."[8] Accordingly, on July 20, the C. B. & Q. board authorized Perkins to notify the Union Pacific that it regarded the building of the Missouri Pacific into Omaha as an abrogation of the agreement of October 1880. Dillon, president of the U. P., stoutly maintained that the Missouri Pacific construction had been undertaken without his consent and despite the protest of the Union Pacific directors in Boston. He said it would be unfair of the Burlington to hold the U. P. responsible "for action taken which it could not and cannot prevent, and which it did not and does not favor."[9] At the same time, W. H. Vanderbilt of the New York

[8] Perkins to W. J. Palmer, June 26, 1881, PLB, Vol. V, pp. 402–3.
[9] Sidney Dillon to Perkins, July 28, 1881, and Dillon to Bartlett, July 28, 1881, quoted in Grodinsky: *Jay Gould*, pp. 246–51.

Central, who held substantial securities in both the U. P. and the Burlington, tried to mollify Forbes.

But the day for compromise had passed. In a vigorous letter reflecting Perkins's views as well as his own, Forbes told Vanderbilt that agreements had to depend "not on their legal or technical validity, but upon the honest purpose and determination of the persons participating . . . to live up to them."[1]

Aware at last that the Burlington would not tolerate the proposed Missouri Pacific extension, Gould resorted to his familiar tactic of making even further threats. If the C. B. & Q. extended to Denver, he warned, he would, among other things, build an independent Missouri Pacific line into Chicago and extend a series of lateral branches in Nebraska. Perkins refused to budge and defied Gould to do his worst. If there was to be a war, said he, it was solely because Gould and his associates were building a railroad in eastern Nebraska where the October 1880 agreement specifically intended that none was to be built. "As to who has been the peacemaker in the past, and who is responsible for the present difficulty," he concluded, "the record speaks for itself."[2]

Thus the battle was joined in no uncertain terms. On August 19, 1880, on motion of Forbes, the C. B. & Q. board authorized the Denver extension. The step was ratified by the stockholders at a special meeting on September 28, and the Burlington was on the way to Denver.

Engrossed as the C. B. & Q. was in the trans-Missouri situation, the problem of insuring adequate control of a Chicago–Kansas City route continued to demand attention, as it had ever since the loss of the Hannibal in 1871. True enough, business was still exchanged between the C. B. & Q. and the Hannibal, but in 1879 additional competitors for the business entered the area. Until then, only the Wabash, with its very roundabout route, could be considered a rival. But on May 1, 1879, the future Alton opened service into Kansas City over its own line; later in that same year the Rock Island reached Cameron. As the latter obviously would build into Kansas City in any event, the Hannibal directors granted it trackage rights between Cameron and Kansas City.

Meanwhile, and particularly after 1877, Gould threatened to increase his holdings in the Hannibal and, perhaps, to upset its long-standing exchange of traffic with the C. B. & Q. Accordingly, in that year Perkins drew Forbes's attention to the Burlington and Southwestern, which had been constructed during the early 70's between Viele, a town on the C. B. & Q. twenty-five miles due south of Burlington, and Laclede, Missouri, a point on the main line of the Hannibal 117 miles east of Kansas City. The

[1] Forbes to W. H. Vanderbilt, July 30, 1881, quoted in Grodinsky: *Jay Gould*, p. 247.

[2] Perkins to Gould, August 8, 1881, quoted in Grodinsky: *Jay Gould*, pp. 247–51.

Southwestern at the moment was in bankruptcy, but nevertheless harbored plans of extending eventually to Kansas City; it was willing to make a deal with the Burlington, but only at a fancy price. Partly, therefore, to improve his bargaining power, Perkins had a direct line of his own surveyed from Viele to Kansas City, which, he told Forbes, would shorten the distance between Chicago and Kansas City to approximately 450 miles. He thought this line could be built with easy grades for approximately $10,000,000. Second, construction on the Chariton–Leon branch was resumed southward in the spring of 1879, and arrangements were made to acquire the narrow-gauge St. Joseph & Des Moines between St. Joseph and Albany. By widening the latter, a through, though roundabout, route to Kansas City could be obtained by way of Chariton and St. Joseph. Thus by the spring of 1880, the C. B. & Q. was in a better bargaining position in respect to the Burlington and Southwestern. On the other hand, the Southwestern was now flirting with the Santa Fe, and the Hannibal— with Gould on its board—was trying to work out an arrangement with the Alton to carry its business into Chicago. Thus pressed, the C. B. & Q. leased the Burlington and Southwestern (renamed the Chicago, Burlington and Kansas City Railway) effective September 1, 1881, as insurance against a possible parting of the ways with the Hannibal. Actually, Perkins did not stop there: he urged on Forbes the advantage of acquiring outright control of both the Hannibal and the Santa Fe. "Had we not better trade now while all hands are in the humor and take the risk necessarily involved in buying . . . than to wait and take the other risks of having to pay much more? . . . It is a big question and has yet to be treated in a big way and swallowed whole as it were!"[3] But such a bold scheme was too much for the directors in Boston. With the Hannibal fenced in, the C. B. & Q. adopted for the moment a policy of watchful waiting.

The C. B. & Q. did make another major acquisition during 1881. This was the so-called St. Louis, Keokuk and North Western, extending from Mt. Pleasant, Iowa, southeast to Keokuk, Hannibal, and Dardenne, where it joined the Wabash, over which it enjoyed traffic rights for thirty miles into St. Louis. This not only constituted a through route between St. Louis and the main stem of the Burlington in Iowa, but also formed part of a feasible though roundabout route between St. Louis and Kansas City. Furthermore the new property, in conjunction with the recently acquired Burlington, Cedar Rapids and Northern, could and did form part of a through line between St. Louis and St. Paul.

This road, as well as the Council Bluffs line, the Burlington and Southwestern, and the narrow-gauge St. Joseph & Des Moines were not, until much later, formally consolidated with the C. B. & Q. These, as well as some other roads, such as the Chicago and Iowa, were simply designated

3 Perkins to Forbes, November 4, 1880, PLB, Vol. V, pp. 182–6.

as Proprietary Lines, and although they were firmly controlled by the C. B. & Q., they were separately managed, their figures generally not being included in C. B. & Q. totals. Thus between 1880 and 1900, the "C. B. & Q." did not technically include from 700 to approximately 1,300 additional miles of extremely important railroad that were in fact a part of the system. Quite apart from this mileage, from July 31, 1875, to September 1881 the C. B. & Q. proper more than doubled—from 1,263 to 2,838 miles. Of this increase of 1,575 miles, 355 were accounted for by the St. Louis, Rock Island and Chicago, approximately 285 by Iowa branches, and about 35 by Missouri branches. The rest was made up of the Burlington and Missouri River Railroad in Nebraska, the Republican Valley Railroad, and their various branches.

As system mileage increased, so did equipment and traffic. Gross revenues on the C. B. & Q. exceeded $20,000,000 for the first time in 1880, and in the same year the car mileage account showed a credit instead of a debit; in other words, equipment was sufficient to carry the company's business and to bring in a small return from cars lent to other lines. More efficient management brought the operating ratio down from 55.75 in 1878 to 47.8 in 1880. The replacing of iron rails with steel continued, and by the end of 1881 the entire main line in both Illinois and Iowa was thus equipped, as was about half of the main line of the B. & M. in Nebraska. The company's dividend rate varied between eight and ten percent during 1877–80, but was stabilized at eight percent in 1881. There it remained for the next seven years.

In broad terms, the strength of the Burlington in 1881 lay essentially in four basic factors. In the first place, its strategic position had been vastly improved by consolidation with the B. & M., the decision to build to Denver, acquisition of the Council Bluffs road, and the gaining of new access to St. Louis. Only the Kansas City situation remained something less than satisfactory, but even there various possibilities were in sight. In the second place, the physical property and operating methods were vastly improved. Third, sound financing had put the capital structure in a much more manageable status. As Forbes put it in 1880: "We have, under a conservative policy, so far improved our credit that we may expect to refund upon very favorable terms any part of our loans which it is best to extend."[4] The fourth basic source of Burlington strength was a solution, at long last, of the thorny problem of administrative leadership.

[4] CB&Q, AR 1880, p. 20.

CHAPTER 11

Perkins and Expansion

1 8 8 1 - 8 8

• CHARLES E. PERKINS •

BY THE SUMMER OF 1881, Perkins had proved himself to the satisfaction of Forbes, who needed no convincing, and to that of the rest of the directors. Accordingly, as of October 1, 1881, he was elected president of the C. B. & Q.

This was the most important part of a wholesale revamping of top management at the Burlington. At the same time, Touzalin was transferred to Boston to serve as first vice-president and chief liaison officer with the directors. James Peasley, as second vice-president and treasurer, was to concern himself with the growing financial affairs of the corporation. T. J. Potter, third vice-president, assumed charge of operating the entire system. Forbes moved up to the chairmanship of the board. At least in Perkins's mind, this was to be no ornamental post. "I do not know that he [Forbes] can be said to have any well defined duties," he wrote, "but . . . in our case he is the head man."[1]

The important point was that as of the fall of 1881, in name as well as in fact, Forbes was the Burlington's strong man of the East, Perkins of the West. Potter, of course, was in charge of operations; in November,

---

[1] Perkins to Frederick Billings, November 19, 1884, CB&Q/N, quoted in TCC, p. 437.

Henry B. Stone, who had worked up through the mechanical departments, was made general superintendent of Lines East, and George W. Holdrege, general superintendent of Lines West. At long last, Perkins was undisputed head of a team of his own choosing, and this fact marked the end of the critical period in Burlington administrative history. After having four presidents in the short space of six years, the company had achieved stability of organization.

Perkins, only forty when elected, was destined to serve as president for almost twenty years, longer than anyone else in the history of the system. Except for Robert Harris, he was the first professional railroader to devote full time to the company entrusted to him. Like all other presidents, of course, he was elected by the board of directors and was subject to it. But real executive leadership, which previously had oscillated between the board and the chief executive, was thenceforth firmly in his hands. He was expected to initiate and formulate policy and did so; by and large, the directors who served with him acted primarily in an advisory and stabilizing capacity.

It is probably correct to say that Perkins actually exercised more power than any other Burlington president before or since. Throughout his tenure, ownership of the C. B. & Q. was widely dispersed, and the average holding by each stockholder was small. As the shareowners were usually satisfied with the actions of the board and the board in practice left matters largely in Perkins's hands, he literally ruled as well as reigned. His predecessors had been either unable or unwilling to wield so much power. After the sale of the C. B. & Q. to the Great Northern and Northern Pacific in 1901, both the Burlington board and the president, despite wide grants of autonomy on most matters, still were subject to the ultimate control of the two proprietary companies and, indirectly, to their owners. Thus the Perkins administration was unique in respect to the amount of power granted to and accepted by the president.

Long before Perkins became chief executive, he had acquired the habit of writing extensive memoranda on every facet of railroading. As a matter of fact, he seemed bent on applying the principles of scientific management to railroading long before they were generally recognized or applied to industry as a whole. His usual approach was to establish a number of general propositions (which he often designated as "natural laws") and then show how they applied to the specific problem at hand. In no sense of the word, however, was he doctrinaire. His favorite quotation was from John Locke: "The greatest part of true knowledge lies in a distinct perception of things in themselves distinct." But whereas he laid down general principles, he recognized that in applying them, enough flexibility had to be allowed to meet immediate situations. For example, he believed strongly in delegation of responsibility and expected the men under him to use imagination and initiative in attaining the ultimate goal.

As he once put it: "The human mind is so constituted that no two men often agree about the details of anything, and the only way to accomplish things is to let those who are charged with the responsibility take their own methods of reaching the end in view."[2] What Perkins had to say about running a railroad and his comments on strategy deserve a book of their own. Here a mere sampling must suffice.

Not long after Perkins took office, he told Peasley that he had long felt the need of "a more thorough statistical department." The railroad was growing rapidly, and he was convinced that a record of all facts and figures connected with operations and traffic should be gathered and presented "as a guide to those in charge of the company's affairs." Accordingly he set up an Auditor of Statistics, with authority to call upon any officer for facts or figures with the understanding that any officer, in turn, could call upon the auditor for whatever information he thought would enable him to conduct his department more efficiently. Perkins specified not simply that the auditor should collect data, but also that "it would be his duty to go beneath the surface . . . to judge whether we are getting all we ought to get, and spending as little as we ought to spend." The auditor should not simply wait for suggestions, but be "sufficiently intelligent and zealous and interested in his business to make suggestions and to catch rays of light which officers who are busily employed about other things would very likely never think of."[3]

The matter of administrative organization had always intrigued Perkins; in May 1882, he sent a lengthy and forceful memorandum to Thomas Potter on the subject. By way of introduction he observed that the most important decisions on the railroad related to the traffic it had been created to carry. Second in rank were the decisions relating to economical maintenance of the physical plant and equipment. He made another preliminary distinction: particularly on a new road in sparsely settled territory, the matter of securing business was of paramount importance; the level of maintenance might well be temporarily kept far below perfection. But as traffic increased, the highest possible level of scientific efficiency should be attained. As he put it, scientific methods which would be "unnecessary and extravagant" on a new line would become "necessary and economical" on an established one. Indeed, the organization of a large road was inevitably a complex matter. Here Perkins visualized a first vice-president as necessary to assist the chief executive in matters of expenditures, negotiations, reports, and, in particular, "new schemes." A second vice-president should look after accounts and finances; a third vice-president should be concerned with operations and have under him a general manager and a purchasing agent. The general manager, in turn,

[2] Perkins to Joseph W. Blythe, December 17, 1887, CB&Q/N, quoted in TCC, p. 446.
[3] Perkins to James C. Peasley, March 21, 1882, CB&Q/Sec.

should have reporting to him a general superintendent, a chief engineer, a general freight agent, and a general passenger agent. If the road was large enough, it should have several divisions, and Perkins spelled out how responsibilities should then be divided.

One matter that Perkins discussed at length was how much railroad should be entrusted to any one general manager. The appropriate mileage, he thought, might range anywhere from 250 to 2,000, depending on density of traffic; the important point was to establish adequate local responsibility. "It is obvious," he wrote, "that to hold a manager responsible for results, it is necessary to give him pretty full power over the property. . . . It is also clear that to get this kind of responsibility it is desirable that the unit of management, so to speak, shall not be too large and that it shall be homogeneous." On the other hand, he was aware that to divide the system into subdivisions that were too small would endanger the uniformity of action necessary on system-wide matters. One solution, wherever practicable, would be to group second-class or branch-line mileage separately, though in many regions the property consisted of both main line and branches. What was needed on a large system, in any event, was a genuine federal system. If that could be achieved, then the president and the three vice-presidents of the parent road could take care of an indefinite number of subsidiary units, "if they keep clearly before them the necessity of local self-government."

Again and again he stressed this matter of on-the-spot responsibility. He was convinced that the men on the line would do more work and do it better if their superior was near at hand. Furthermore, the local population could get to know the general manager in person. "This is a consideration," he emphasized, "of importance, and is alone a good reason for not making a unit too large. Personal acquaintance promotes good understanding, and the people like to see those in authority."[4]

No less important than the matter of organization, in Perkins's mind, was the question of labor relations. In this respect, he felt, two factors were essential: that proper personal influence be exerted by good officers and that a strictly business relation be maintained between the corporation and its employees. Accordingly, each employee should feel that he was receiving a reasonable return for his labor and had a chance for promotion; each man should be treated by his superiors with "that personal respect which is due from one man of proper feeling to another." The problem was to find officers who would neither take the subordinates' view of every question nor treat the men as mere tools. "The good officer," he wrote, "goes to neither extreme. He guards the interests of the corporation and teaches the men to do so, and, while insisting upon strict discipline and attention to business, he at the same time shows all possible consideration for the men and explains to them the necessity if

[4] Perkins to Thomas J. Potter, May 22, 1882, CB&Q/Sec.

sometimes rules seem too strict. He sees also that justice is done to his subordinates by those still higher than he is, and makes them feel that, while he is their superior in authority, as someone always must be, he and they are, nevertheless, all working for the same master and the same end. Such a man will make men zealous and loyal and honest and efficient. He will give a tone to the service which benefits the men as well as the company."

On the other hand, Perkins felt it essential always to remember that the relation of the employer and the employee was purely a commercial one. If this was forgotten, and the employer, through feelings of philanthropy or mistaken self-interest, gave something for nothing, then the employee simply came to look on this extra something as his right and to demand its continuance and an increased amount of it. "I think it is sound to say," he summarized, "of a railroad corporation, as of a state, that the best government is that which is the simplest, and leaves men to reap according to their desserts. I would pay necessary wages, furnish proper tools to work with, endeavor to elevate the pace and the tone by the personal example and influence of those in authority, and try to be just in rewards and punishments, thus placing men squarely on their own feet, and there [I would] stop."[5]

In hiring new men, Perkins favored a well-defined system of examination. As far as possible, he felt, new men should be taken into the service only in the lower grades; higher grades should be filled by promotion. Perhaps most basic of all, "in selecting employees, the employer should, when he can, have regard not alone to what the man can do, but also to what he is, and what he may become. In the rush and hurry of railroad business too little attention is paid to what men are."

When it came to promotion, Perkins admitted that seniority and the fact that a man was married might be considered, but he thought they were by no means the most important factors. "Character," he wrote, "is of more consequence than long service; personal habits are more important than homes. To make long service in itself a reason for better pay or better position would be unwise, if for no other reason than [that] it would tend to make men satisfied to wait instead of stimulating them to earn promotion by exceptionally good conduct. . . . Other things being equal . . . men with homes are more to be depended upon than wandering single men who have less motives to do their best. But practically other things seldom or never are equal, so that it is not wise to make any fixed rule on this point."[6] As a practical man, Perkins knew when to part company with the doctrinaire.

Like Forbes, Perkins was forever on the lookout for promising young men. But simply choosing the right employees was not enough. It was up

[5] Perkins, Memorandum, 1882?, CB&Q/Sec.
[6] Perkins, "The Selection of Employees," August 15, 1885, C–O, Set M–2, p. 109.

to every officer in a position of responsibility "to see that, in the ranks below him, men are growing up who can take the responsible places now filled by himself and others, and no officer is as good as he ought to be unless he pays attention to this duty, although it is neglected probably more than any other duty which is imposed upon railroad officials." Shrewdly enough, Perkins had observed that many young officers felt that the only ladder to promotion was within their own department. Disagreeing, Perkins wrote: "Promotion to the highest positions should be made from all branches and departments of the service, if you can find the men of the requisite mind and character."[7]

On some points Perkins was adamant. He recognized fully that any individual was entitled to his own private opinions, but he believed that "every man who works for a railroad company is nevertheless bound to carry out its policy in matters where it has a policy, and to do this in good faith and regardless of private opinions."[8] The question of outside individual investments by officers or agents of the company always had been a delicate one, and it had been highlighted by the River Roads situation. Perkins stated his views in a memorandum of 1883: "A man who is engaged in managing property for others cannot properly permit himself to have interests of his own in a business which may be directly affected by his official acts."[9]

This being so, Perkins felt that railways were bound to pay salaries sufficiently attractive to induce good men to enter their service, on the express condition that they would not expect to make money out of a directly affiliated enterprise. On the other hand, he realized that certain kinds of investments, where personal interest and official duty could not possibly come into conflict, were permissible. In cases of this sort, he specified that an employee should discuss such investments with his superior, with the right of appeal up through the hierarchy to the president if necessary. If the proposed outside investment was approved, the circumstances were to be reduced to writing, and a memorandum was to be kept on file for the information of the board of directors. Perkins's files contain numerous decisions in this area. He decided, for example, that the smallest kind of an interest in a coal mine served by the railroad would be highly objectionable. On the other hand, he felt it perfectly proper for a railway official to have interests in a townsite along the road, for although any rise in land values might be a result of railway construction or service, such increase would never be at the expense of the railway's stockholders.

As far as business on the whole was concerned, Perkins was a devout and unwavering disciple of laissez-faire. Economic life, he believed, was

[7] Perkins, "Promotion and Dismissal," May, 1883, PLB, Vol. VI, pp. 338–40.
[8] Perkins to Potter, January 1, 1885, CB&Q/N, quoted in TCC, p. 85.
[9] Perkins, Memorandum, May 11, 1883, PLB, Vol. VI, p. 340.

inevitably governed by "natural laws," and just as an individual should be left free to work out his own destiny, so business should be left strictly alone. "Railroads will," he said, "in the long run produce transportation cheaper if let alone to meet the market like all other traders than if hampered with laws fixing prices." He was well aware that charging large shippers less than small ones was regarded by some as unjust discrimination, but he stoutly disagreed, for although he admitted that the practice might occasionally work hardship on an individual, he thought it, on the whole, "beneficial to mankind."[1] To his mind this was simply wholesale transportation and therefore a matter of business expediency rather than of justice. The same reasoning applied to distance, which, in the railway field, he thought equivalent to quantity: a lower rate per mile for a long haul than for a short one was the same as a lower rate per car for a thousand cars than for ten cars. Nebraska, he argued, by way of example, could not possibly send corn to Europe at the same rate paid by shippers from Ohio and Indiana. The fact that the Nebraska rates were lower was not unjust discrimination, but simply a natural reflection of the laws of trade.

As a matter of fact, during the early 1880's what prompted a Senate inquiry was not the high level of railway rates, but alleged discrimination between persons and places. On April 10, 1885, Senator Cullom of Illinois addressed letters to the chief operating officials of all the railways in the nation, asking, in effect, what sort of federal legislation, if any, should be devised to eliminate such discrimination. In his lengthy reply, Perkins reached the unqualified conclusion that the government should leave the railways "alone commercially." He pointed out that in no other country in the world was rail transportation so cheap and that, in particular, railways had made possible the settlement of the West and given value to farm lands which otherwise would be worthless. All this, together with the steady decline in rates, had been accomplished under a system of "tolerable freedom." Consequently he urged that well enough be let alone. "Merchants, bankers, lawyers, all discriminate in the same way; and it is for the interests of society that they should do so." Any railroad, he urged, was concerned with promoting the prosperity of the country it served, and therefore would make rates just as low as possible. To substitute for the imperfect but interested agents of the railway companies the imperfect agents of the government, with no pecuniary interest at stake, would, he thought, accomplish precisely nothing.

In response to Cullom's inquiry as to whether pooling should be outlawed, Perkins responded vigorously in the negative. Pools, he believed, prevented railway agents from cutting rates to unreasonably low levels, and similar agreements were made by manufacturers and traders all over the world. Certainly, stability of rates was a great benefit to the public.

[1] Perkins, Memorandum, December 20, 1883, CB&Q/Sec.

To Cullom's suggestions that there should be uniform accounting and a commission to administer any legislation that was passed, Perkins retorted that such provisions would be class legislation of the most undesirable sort. Neither could he see any justice in having the government develop and maintain a system of water routes simply to force rail prices down; this, he felt, would simply be subsidizing competition.

Perkins admitted that the right of the government to fix railway rates had been legally established. But he stoutly maintained that it would be inexpedient to exercise the power. The free market alone, he insisted, was the best regulator, not only of rates, but of expansion as well. If the government stepped in, private capital would undoubtedly be scared away from the industry, and railways would be driven first into the hands of speculators and ultimately into those of the government. "Among the evils of government ownership and control," he concluded, "would undoubtedly be higher charges and increased taxation."[2] On another occasion in 1885 he expressed his general philosophy even more succinctly: "If experience teaches anything, it is that the individual is the best judge of his own interests."[3] It was his view that Adam Smith should be required reading for all businessmen.

Years later Perkins wrote that his letter to Cullom "did not have as much effect as a fly on a cartwheel."[4] But for all his opposition to the Granger laws and to the Interstate Commerce Act passed in 1887, Perkins insisted that once those measures were on the books, they should be obeyed unless set aside by the courts. Instinctively, he wasted no time crying over spilt milk. He never changed his mind about the dangers of government regulation, but spent his energy instead in trying to keep the Burlington prosperous despite such regulation.

In the process, both Perkins and his fellow officers inevitably exerted some measure of political influence. Perkins's continuous support of Senator Allison, whom Cochran characterizes as "the great champion of business," was well known.[5] And during the senatorial campaign in Iowa in 1881, Jacob Rich, a seasoned politician and journalist who correctly assumed that the railroads would support John H. Gear rather than his choice, James F. Wilson, for the Senate, wrote Kirkwood that "the only danger is Perkins. We must have Allison see him sometime in New York. He [Allison] can do more with him than anyone else. The C. B. & Q. mixes more in politics than any other Co. and has the most power. We must spike them."[6]

[2] "A Letter to Hon. S. M. Cullom . . . from Charles E. Perkins [September 21, 1885]" (Cambridge: University Press; 1885).

[3] Perkins, June 18, 1885, C–O, Set M–2, pp. 105–7.

[4] Perkins to Henry L. Higginson, March 20, 1907, PLB, Vol. XXII, p. 483.

[5] TCC, p. 190.

[6] Jacob Rich to Samuel J. Kirkwood, March 3, 1881, quoted in Leland Sage: *William Boyd Allison* (Iowa City: State Historical Society; 1956), p. 178.

In the very next year J. Sterling Morton, who had earlier written many an editorial on behalf of the B. & M. in Nebraska, ran for the Senate on the Democratic ticket. Asserting that the Republican Party was "as thoroughly the property of the railroads as the engines on their tracks," he went on to say that "every Republican candidate for office was freely spoken of as the Union Pacific candidate or the Burlington and Missouri candidate; the people had no candidate."[7] This, of course, was Democratic electioneering. Yet in his book *J. Sterling Morton*, Olson himself concludes: "It was generally conceded that the officers of the two large railroads serving the state, the Union Pacific and the Chicago, Burlington and [sic] Quincy, wielded much influence in the election of senators from Nebraska. The extent of this influence was never demonstrated, nor even its presence absolutely confirmed; yet it probably existed, and in a considerable degree, because all of the politicians in the state acted in senatorial matters with an eye to the two railroads."[8] In this particular case, the Burlington opposed Morton, and whether its influence was decisive or not, he dropped out of the race. Eventually, General Charles Manderson, a Republican destined to become general solicitor for the B. & M. in Nebraska after two terms as senator, won the seat. Later in the 1880's, to quote Donald L. McMurry, George W. Holdrege, general manager of the Burlington's Lines West, "built up a political machine in the interest of his road which made him one of the most potent forces in Nebraska politics. He did this by quiet management, following a policy of 'public obscurity,' keeping himself out of the public eye as much as possible."[9] Meanwhile Joseph W. Blythe, who became general solicitor for Lines East in 1890 and general counsel for the system in 1900, established a similar position for himself in Iowa. Yet Perkins, just before his death late in 1907, could write to General Palmer without any apparent reservations: "I feel much as you do about politicians. I have no confidence in any of them."[1]

Perhaps the company would have liked to keep out of politics entirely. And perhaps its influence was exerted, unofficially, only when its officers felt that something had to be done to protect vital interests. Nothing but further research—and more material—can provide definitive answers.

• On to the Rockies •

THE RECURRENT RAILWAY THEME for the nation as a whole and for the Burlington in particular during the years 1881–87 was the tremendous

[7] *Omaha Herald*, October 3, 1882, quoted in James C. Olson: *J. Sterling Morton* (Lincoln: University of Nebraska Press; 1942), p. 273.

[8] Olson: op. cit., p. 275.

[9] Donald L. McMurry: *The Great Burlington Strike of 1888: A Case Study in Labor Relations* (Cambridge: Harvard University Press; 1956), p. 24.

[1] Perkins to Palmer, October 18, 1907, C–O, RCO Notebook #16, p. 159.

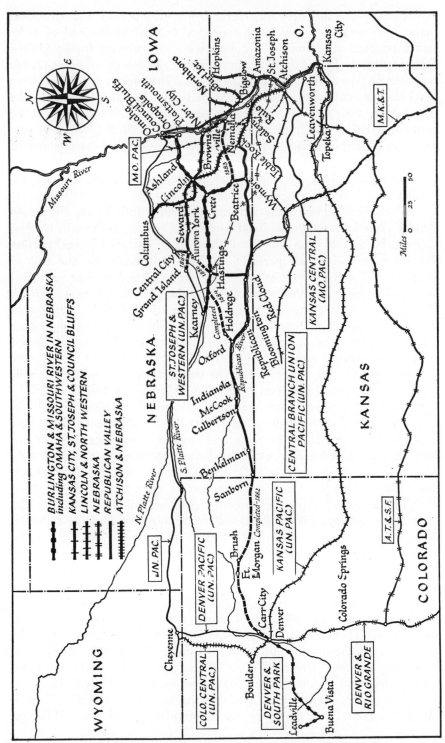

West of the Missouri River, 1881, with Extensions to 1886

expansion of the rail network. Never before or since in any seven-year period have so many new rails been spiked to ties. At the end of 1880, somewhat over 93,000 miles of railway were in operation in the United States; by the end of 1887 the figure exceeded 149,000 miles. Most of this construction was in the Middle West. On the Burlington, conditions were particularly favorable to rapid growth. As Forbes had pointed out to the stockholders early in 1881, it appeared to him that at the moment no further regulation was imminent; revenues on the C. B. & Q. for that year were the highest in history. Small wonder, then, that in the summer of 1881 the directors of the Burlington felt fully able to meet the threat of Gould's encirclement by authorizing construction of the Denver extension.

When the decision was reached, materials and forces, thanks to Perkins's foresight, were already on hand. On October 10 the rails reached Culbertson, and by the middle of November the track-layers, putting down a mile and a half per day, reached Benkelman. By the end of 1881 the railhead was across the Colorado line, and grading extended some eighty miles into that state. At that point Holdrege, who with T. E. Calvert and Alex Campbell was in charge of the project, suggested that construction might well start simultaneously from the western end; arrangements were made accordingly. Meanwhile, the C. B. & Q. acquired appropriate terminal grounds and facilities in Denver at a cost of $300,000.

Fortunately, the winter of 1881–82 was exceptionally mild. The rails from the east reached Brush on April 7, Fort Morgan on April 17. Grading over the entire line was complete by May 1, and a fortnight later track-layers working eastward from Denver put down rails made of the first steel to be turned out in the State of Colorado. Thereafter the crews at each railhead moved rapidly; at four o'clock on the afternoon of Thursday, May 24, 1882, Holdrege drove the last spike at Carr City, about eleven miles east of Denver. A few moments later a train from the East filled with Burlington officials rolled over the completed line and on into the mile-high city. The new road was opened for business on May 29, 1882, more than three months ahead of schedule. The completion of 247 miles of railroad in 229 working days was no mean accomplishment. In appreciation of that fact, the directors increased Holdrege's salary to $6,000 and boosted that of Calvert, chief engineer, to $3,600.

Meanwhile, division points were established at Red Cloud and at the brand-new town of McCook. The only trouble with the new line was that between Hastings and Oxford it went around two sides of a triangle. At Holdrege's urging, Perkins authorized building a direct sixty-two-mile line along the hypotenuse. This cut-off was opened for business on August 4, 1884, and shortened the distance between the Missouri River and Denver by twenty-eight miles. The principal new town established on it by the Lincoln Land Company was appropriately christened Holdrege, destined to become one of the principal trading centers in southwest Nebraska.

Meantime, while the railhead had been moving toward the Rockies, construction continued east from Red Cloud, and on December 5, 1881, the new line was opened to Table Rock and a connection with the former Atchison and Nebraska. This provided a through route not only to Atchison but also, by means of the Council Bluffs road, to Kansas City. Thus, when the Denver extension was completed, new through routes were open both between Chicago and Denver and between Kansas City and Denver.

The arrival of the Burlington in Denver was a blow to the Union Pacific. Until then, that road had shared all Colorado traffic only with the Santa Fe and the Rio Grande. Now, rather than touch off another ruinous rate war, the Union Pacific and its allies simply had to share business with the Burlington as well. Not only that—the U. P. also was forced to give its Omaha connections, including the C. B. & Q., more eastbound business if it hoped to secure a reasonable share of westbound traffic at that point. This, in turn, meant less traffic for the roundabout Wabash. By breaking the truce of October 1880 and thereby renewing his competitive struggle with the Burlington, Gould had injured both the Union Pacific and the Wabash.

• REGAINING THE HANNIBAL AND ST. JOSEPH •

THE "SOUTHWESTERN QUESTION" had been a problem for the Burlington ever since it had lost control of the Hannibal and St. Joseph in 1871. As a partial solution, the company had acquired the old Burlington and Southwestern, and between 1882 and 1885 extended it from Laclede to Carrollton, where, to this day, the railhead rests. It never was carried on to Kansas City because, by then, it was not needed.

Early in 1882, Duff, who held a considerable amount of Hannibal stock, offered it to Perkins, but at a price beyond all reason. By the fall of that year, Gould had secured outright control of the property and was again threatening to build to Chicago. This time Perkins would not be hurried; the C. B. & Q. had other possibilities, and while it was willing to buy back the Hannibal, it simply refused to pay a fancy price. Eventually this Fabian policy paid off. On April 18, 1883, Gould agreed to sell the Hannibal at $43.66 per share. The C. B. & Q. undertook to make payment with thirty-year, five-percent bonds at par, but only if the Gould group would also sell to the company 40,000 shares of preferred Hannibal stock. In due course the C. B. & Q. acquired 81,000 shares of common stock and enough preferred stock to go through with the contract. Thus on May 1, 1883, the Hannibal and St. Joseph at long last was again turned over to the C. B. & Q., where it was destined to remain. As Perkins told his stockholders, he believed this "the best solution of the Southwestern

Question, and it places us in a strong position at Kansas City, the great and growing commercial center of that region."[2]

From 1883 to 1886, freight carried over the Hannibal increased from 800,000 tons to over a million, and gross annual revenues averaged about $2,500,000. Results were even better in 1887, when gross reached $3,200,-000 and net earnings per mile for the 295-mile system exceeded $4,600. Apparently the Hannibal not only was healthy, but could look forward to a brilliant future. Already, however, the specter of strong competition was hovering overhead.

In 1883, Touzalin left the Burlington to become a vice-president of the Santa Fe and, among other things, promptly surveyed for that company a direct line between Chicago and Kansas City. Three years later, in 1886, Touzalin returned to the Burlington, and in September of that year warned Perkins that the Santa Fe was seriously considering building the very same short line that he had surveyed. In his opinion, the segment between Keokuk and Kansas City would most certainly be authorized. But, he continued, "the C. B. & Q. line Keokuk to Chicago is as good a line as any that can be built. If the C. B. & Q. were to take the initiative at once in building the short-cut from Keokuk to Kansas City, it might be a good thing, and at the worst lead to a trade with the Atchison later . . . under which the Burlington and Atchison would jointly own the line from Kansas City to Keokuk, and use the C. B. & Q. line from Keokuk to Chicago."[3] Touzalin pointed out that such a route would be forty-five miles shorter than the existing C. B. & Q. route, would have the easiest grades west of the Mississippi, and would not cost over $30,000 per mile.

Perkins immediately informed Forbes. It seemed to him absurd that another Boston-based road should build a new line between Chicago and Kansas City, and he seconded Touzalin's idea that the C. B. & Q. might well arrange to build a joint road between, say, Chillicothe, Missouri, and Keokuk, Iowa. The chief danger was that W. B. Strong, then president of the Santa Fe, was apparently bent upon acting both promptly and independently.

In view of that fact, Perkins persuaded Strong to travel to Burlington in October for a long conference. Strong was frank; he was determined to have his own line of about 440 miles. As an alternative Perkins suggested that the C. B. & Q. build a shortcut from Liberty, on the Cameron branch, to Bogard, Missouri, just north of Carrollton, thus cutting down total mileage to 472 miles. And if that was not enough to satisfy Strong, the Santa Fe might build a new link between Laclede and Fort Madison, and then use the C. B. & Q. from that point into Chicago. Strong promised to think all this over.

[2] CB&Q, AR 1883, p. 17.
[3] A. E. Touzalin to Perkins, September 30, 1886, PLB, Vol. VIII, p. 119.

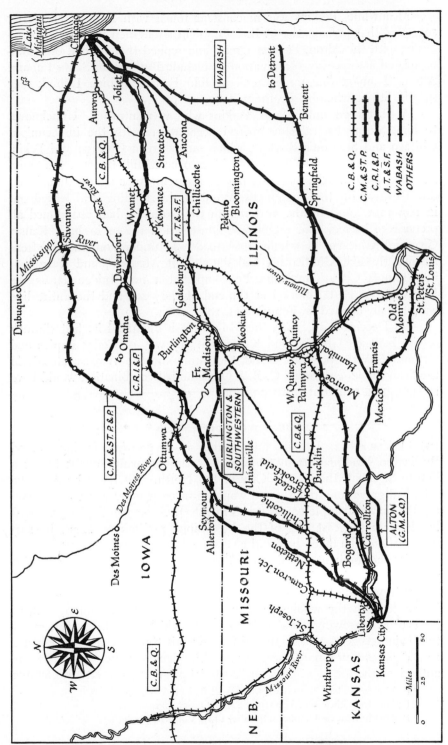

Competition between Chicago and Kansas City, 1889

Meanwhile, Perkins was in constant touch with Forbes. The latter suggested that perhaps the C. B. & Q. might strengthen its hand by combining with the Alton. Perkins agreed, and replied that he had even contemplated a three-way combination to include Burlington, Santa Fe, and Alton. "I am getting up figures," he told Forbes, "which I think may surprise Strong when he sees them."[4]

As it turned out, it was Perkins who was surprised. Unbeknown to him, Strong had already opened negotiations with the impecunious Chicago and St. Louis Railway, which ran between Chicago and Pekin, Illinois. That struggling line would have to be rebuilt to serve the Santa Fe's purpose, but the stretch from Chicago to Ancona was sufficiently direct to warrant the investment. Word of the pending deal leaked out in November, and by the next month the Santa Fe had abandoned all pretense of secrecy and established construction offices in both Kansas City and Chicago. A wholly new road was under construction from Ancona through Chillicothe, Galesburg, Fort Madison, and Carrollton into Kansas City. The Santa Fe completed a new bridge across the Mississippi at Fort Madison at the end of the year, and the entire line was officially opened on February 11, 1888.

On December 18, 1887, the Milwaukee inaugurated its first through service between Chicago and Kansas City by way of Cedar Rapids and Ottumwa. With the Rock Island, the Alton, and the Wabash already in the field, the long-standing C. B. & Q.–Hannibal combination would have to work hard to maintain its position.

• THE TWIN CITIES LINE •

IN OCTOBER 1882, Perkins told Forbes of a growing feeling around Burlington headquarters in Chicago that the company "ought to get a line to St. Paul, the Kansas City of the North."[5] St. Paul business, he said, had grown enormously and would grow even more when the Northern Pacific was completed (as it was in 1883). Consequently, he suggested building up the east side of the Mississippi; preliminary steps, he suggested, should be taken before the company's plans were suspected.

For the moment, nothing was done. But exactly a year later Perkins made an extensive trip over Hill's St. Paul, Minneapolis and Manitoba and over Villard's Northern Pacific. He told Forbes he was "a good deal impressed with the whole northern region, and with the importance of St. Paul as a growing commercial center to which the C. B. & Q. ought to obtain access."[6] As a matter of fact, by this time Perkins had taken a couple of precautionary measures on his own. On July 14, 1883, he authorized the use of $25,000 for "a special purpose," and late in October

[4] Perkins to Forbes, November 5, 1886, PLB, Vol. VIII, pp. 182–3.
[5] Perkins to Forbes, October 16, 1882, C–O, Set C–2, p. 200.
[6] Perkins to Forbes, October 20, 1883, PLB, Vol. VI, pp. 446–7.

Chicago, Burlington & Northern Railroad, 1886

a similar sum "for northern work."[7] This was for preliminary surveys along the east bank of the Mississippi north of Savanna and for acquiring rights of way. Meanwhile, on August 20, the Wisconsin Legislature incorporated a railway with an innocent-sounding name—the Winona, Alma and Northern—which would, in fact, serve the Burlington's purposes in that state. As late as November, Perkins thought that each move so far had been "successfully disguised," and jubilantly told Forbes that both Oakes of the Northern Pacific and Hill of the Manitoba, in whom he had confided, were willing to arrange for terminal facilities at the Twin Cities.[8]

By now it was fairly obvious to everyone what the Burlington had in mind. In mid-November 1883, a new railroad with appropriate authority was incorporated in Illinois, and the next month the directors authorized $300,000 for a full-fledged survey to St. Paul. Early in March 1884, the State of Minnesota granted a charter for a railway from the Wisconsin state line to St. Paul. All that remained was to determine the final route. After considering several possibilities, the company decided to extend the Chicago and Iowa forty-seven miles from Oregon to Savanna, and then build 288 miles along the east bank of the river so as to provide a through route only 435 miles in length. This would be only twenty-five miles longer than the Milwaukee and the North Western, and would have far

[7] Perkins to Peasley, July 14, 1883, CB&Q/Sec.
[8] Perkins to Forbes, November 1, 1883, PLB, Vol. VI, pp. 468–9.

better grades than either. It was estimated that the entire project could be completed for approximately $10,000,000.

For nearly a year more, however, construction was delayed while Perkins hammered out the financial and administrative details. By that time the C. B. & Q. had already spent $800,000 in making surveys and acquiring rights of way. It could, of course, complete the road itself, but this would entail an additional investment of $10,000,000. Equally important, outright ownership of the line would add substantially to the managerial responsibilities of the C. B. & Q. staff. What Perkins wanted was a controlled family line to the Twin Cities that would not put a burden on either C. B. & Q. finances or its managerial staff. Not until the summer of 1885 did he solve these problems to his satisfaction.

The key to the arrangement lay in Perkins's success in persuading Touzalin to leave his post as vice-president of the Santa Fe to become president of the new Twin Cities road. Touzalin, who had worked for the B. & M. in Nebraska from 1869 to 1882 (except for a one-year stint with the Santa Fe in 1873–74), and had then served as vice-president of the C. B. & Q. from 1882 to 1883, needed no introduction to Burlington directors or officers. He was, as Perkins told his stockholders at the time, a man of "character and energy."[9] Touzalin, in turn, was able to bring George B. Harris with him as vice-president and general manager. Harris, whose father had been land commissioner of the B. & M. in Nebraska in the early years, had started out with the Hannibal in 1866 and had spent seventeen years on various Burlington family roads before going to the Santa Fe with Touzalin in 1883. The recruitment of these two men for the Twin Cities project solved the staff problem.

The matter of finances was more complicated. It was agreed that the new enterprise should be called the Chicago, Burlington and Northern, with a capitalization of $18,000,000 equally divided between stock and bonds, the latter convertible into stock. According to long-standing practice, the C. B. & Q. promised to invest half its net profits from all business interchanged with the new company in the latter's bonds, to be accompanied by an equivalent amount of stock. In addition, S. H. Mallory and Company of Chariton, Iowa, which contracted to build the line for $25,000 per mile in stock and $25,000 in bonds, agreed to turn over 30,000 shares of its C. B. & N. stock to the Burlington for cash (at twenty cents on the dollar) and to give individual C. B. & Q. stockholders forty days in which to buy over 45,000 additional shares of stock and over 75,000 bonds. The net result of this complicated arrangement was that the C. B. & Q. wound up with a one-third stock control at the outset and the possibility of acquiring more stock through conversion of the bonds that it took in lieu of traffic balances, and with C. B. & Q. individual stockholders holding an absolute majority of stock. Thus, al-

[9] CB&Q, AR 1888, p. 23.

though the C. B. & Q. corporation technically did not control the C. B. & N., it was actually in a position to call the tune with only a minor outlay of cash.

Once these arrangements were completed, during the summer of 1885, the predecessor companies in Illinois, Wisconsin, and Minnesota all took the title of Chicago, Burlington and Northern; the Wisconsin and Minnesota companies merged in October and in the following month leased the Illinois company; thereafter there was but one C. B. & N., with Touzalin at its head.

Meanwhile there was a bustle of activity all along the line. Early in September a considerable force at La Crosse began converting a large prairie into a divisional yard. A week or so later, more than a hundred men and teams were concentrated at Oregon, and boardinghouses and tents were set up all along the line. Prevailing wages were $1.50 a day for men, $3.50 a day for man and team.

As a matter of fact, the speed and extent of these activities caused Perkins some concern. "Are you not," he asked Touzalin in October, "perhaps trying to crowd your construction too fast, to force conclusions which perhaps would be sooner reached if not forced? Of course time is important, but so is peace with your neighbors; sometimes you can make haste by going slow. Men don't like to be crowded, and of course you can't expect that the North-Western and the St. Paul people are going to welcome you with outstretched arms. They have power as well as you, and they also have more or less possession, and I should say the best general policy would be to let them take all reasonable time to talk and consult and negotiate even if it should delay you a month or two, but I don't believe it will. You can catch more Millers and Hughitts with molasses than with vinegar!" Perkins did not stop there; he advised Touzalin to organize his board of directors as soon as possible and to get its members to share responsibility with him. "You will find," said he, "[that] this will save you lots of annoyance. You can carry many things through this board if you consult it beforehand which directors might be slow to approve afterwards."[1]

But Touzalin, inclined more to energy than to restraint, plunged ahead. Track-laying began in November, and by the end of the year about forty-five miles were completed between La Crosse and Winona and on to Chippewa Crossing. About the same time other crews started laying rail from Savanna toward Fulton. But as Perkins had foreseen, such activities brought repercussions. The Illinois Central already occupied the narrow shelf of land between Portage Curve and East Dubuque, a distance of some twelve miles, which the C. B. & N. would have to share.

[1] Perkins to Touzalin, October 6, 1885, GM, 1879-92, p. 119. Roswell Miller was general manager of the Milwaukee, and Marvin Hughitt was general manager of the North Western at the time.

Fearful of losing a considerable amount of its Dubuque business, the I. C. immediately began laying unnecessary sidings in the narrowest part of the right of way and refused to operate C. B. & N. construction trains through the disputed area. A truce was finally arranged in November, and eventually a federal court granted the C. B. & N. specific authority to share the right of way. Although the I. C. gained a reversal of this decision in 1887, by which time both roads were running freely over the disputed stretch, the matter was eventually settled early in 1889 by an agreement by which the C. B. & N. turned its tracks over to the Illinois Central but retained the right to operate on equal terms upon payment of rent and a share of the expenses.

Happily, other arrangements proceeded smoothly. Before the end of 1885, an agreement was concluded with Hill's Manitoba line for use of its track between Minneapolis and St. Paul and for joint terminal facilities at those points. And in 1886 the C. B. & N. arranged by contract to use the existing bridges at Winona and Dubuque, thus avoiding the necessity of building new structures at those points.

On May 8, 1886, operations began on the C. B. & N. between Savanna and Fulton. Early in June, the line between La Crosse and Trevino opened for business, and during the summer the remaining sections were completed in rapid succession. On August 23, the entire line began accepting freight shipments though there was still a lot to do: stations and freight houses had to be completed, equipment bought, and the operating crews familiarized with the line. Not until Sunday, October 24, did the first special passenger train, filled with railway officials, newspapermen, and various prominent citizens, make the the initial run from the Twin Cities to Chicago. Ensconced in two Pullman Palace cars hauled by a 4-4-0 locomotive with 69-inch drivers, the party left Minneapolis at 6:30 a.m., pulled out of St. Paul an hour later, and reached Chicago at 6:40 p.m. Just a week later, on October 31, the road was open for passenger business. Two trains were operated daily each way on schedules of approximately twelve and a half hours. In that opening year, the C. B. & N.'s roster included twenty-nine locomotives and six switch engines, twenty passenger coaches, twelve head-end cars, and slightly over a thousand freight train cars of various sorts. Within the next two years, fifteen more locomotives, fourteen coaches, and some sixteen hundred freight cars were added.

From the very outset, the question of rates posed a thorny problem. Harris thought that the C. B. & N. should be a free-lance for a year, and then enter one of the established pools when its traffic-carrying capacity had been established. He was convinced that in order to get any business at all from the roads already in operation, it would be necessary to cut prevailing rates sharply at first. But Perkins urged caution; he thought that pooling should at least be attempted and that the Milwaukee and

North Western could be counted upon to cooperate. Potter of the Burlington was far more blunt. He told Perkins in the summer of 1886 that regardless of the technical corporate relations between the C. B. & Q. and the C. B. & N., the former would inevitably be held responsible for any rate demoralization brought about by the C. B. & N., and that consequently the latter should be restrained.

What actually happened during the first three years the railway was in operation was enough to try the patience of Job. The basic difficulty lay in the fact that although strategically the C. B. & Q. and the C. B. & N. had a strong common interest in providing a competitive through route between Chicago and the Twin Cities, they were hopelessly at loggerheads as to commercial policy and relations with other railroads. Unless the C. B. & N. could cut rates enough to attract the necessary volume of business to remain solvent, it would prove a wretched investment for those who had bought its securities. But rate-cutting on the Twin Cities line would inevitably provoke retaliation that could injure the Burlington throughout the system. To avoid this, the C. B. & Q. was willing to carry its share of C. B. & N. traffic (east of Savanna) at cost, and even to reimburse the C. B. & N. for losses it suffered by adopting any high-rate policy forced upon it by the C. B. & Q. But Touzalin, backed by a substantial number of his stockholders, persisted in following an independent course. Consequently, as early as March 1887, Perkins urged upon his board outright purchase of the C. B. & N. But Geddes and Griswold, among others, flatly opposed any such action until the new company had proved itself on its own merits. The C. B. & N. stockholders were willing enough to sell, but, fully aware of their strategic position, demanded $110 per share, a price the C. B. & Q. board thought wholly unrealistic in view of the fact that the new line had not begun to make money.

As time went on, Perkins became increasingly exasperated at Touzalin's independence. "He thinks," he wrote Forbes in August 1887, "the C. B. & Q. was made for the Northern, instead of the reverse. . . ."[2] If the property could not be acquired at a fair price, he thought, perhaps it would be necessary to change the C. B. & N. board at the next election to "make it either *more* or *less* C. B. & Q."[3] Perkins's original idea of setting up the C. B. & N. on an autonomous basis to relieve the C. B. & Q. of a financial and administrative burden had been logical enough, but it was proving impracticable. "The C. B. & N. is making C. B. & Q. lots of trouble," Perkins sighed in November 1887, "and I wish we could absorb it."[4] Meanwhile the rate situation was hopeless: the charges per hundredweight between Chicago and the Twin Cities had varied between forty cents and

[2] Perkins to Forbes, August 8, 1887, BF.
[3] Perkins to Forbes, September 1, 1887, BF. Underlining in original.
[4] Perkins to Forbes, November 17, 1887, PLB, Vol. VIII, p. 307a.

eighty cents during the first fifteen months of operation and, as Potter had correctly forecast, the North Western and the Milwaukee held the Burlington squarely responsible. The fact that the C. B. & Q. frankly admitted, early in 1888, that it could no longer restrain its volatile affiliate did little to improve matters. Neither did Perkins's earnest effort to explain both to Hughitt of the North Western and to the C. B. & Q. stockholders that the C. B. & Q. did *not* control the C. B. & N., and thus could not be held responsible, help in the least.

By the late summer of 1888 the situation was as ridiculous as it was serious. The Burlington directors still refused to purchase the C. B. & N. But because of its essential strategic value, they did agree to lend the Northern line $700,000 to keep it from receivership. This was a stop-gap at best. In September 1889, the tough-minded Touzalin, whose health had been failing steadily, died. But he left behind him the thorny problem of rates and the divided interests of individuals holding both C. B. & Q. and C. B. & N. stock. The next month Perkins had an inspiration: perhaps the Pennsylvania would be willing to join the C. B. & Q. in acquiring control of Hill's Manitoba line as well as the C. B. & N., which would then be indispensable as a connecting link. But when Perkins tried out this idea on Hill himself, he discovered that that determined empire builder was planning to build his own line to the Pacific and had no disposition whatever to sell the Manitoba. Faced with these realities, the C. B. & Q. board finally, on March 12, 1890, authorized purchase of enough additional stock of the C. B. & N. to gain outright corporate control, provided that it could be obtained at not over $40 a share. With Touzalin gone and deficits mounting, the C. B. & N. shareholders likewise recognized the realities of the situation. By the end of that year, the Burlington held 98.33 percent of the Northern's stock, though corporate consolidation was not achieved until 1899. But at least the C. B. & N. could now be run wholly in the interests of the C. B. & Q., as indeed it was from that day forward.

Meanwhile, Perkins still favored sharing the financial burden that the C. B. & N. involved. In 1891 he suggested to Hill that the latter acquire a joint interest in the line. But when Hill intimated that he might like to buy the entire property, Perkins drew back. And there, for the moment, the matter rested. Clearly, however, the traffic relations of the Twin Cities line and of the Great Northern were even then close and mutually valuable.

• System-wide Expansion •

The spectacular aspects of Burlington expansion during the 1880's were the leap to Denver, the recapture of the Hannibal and St. Joseph, and the sponsorship of the Twin Cities line. Yet they represented only mainline construction, and not even all of that. During the decade, two other important through routes were established while Nebraska, and to a lesser extent Missouri, Kansas, and Iowa, were laced with a multitude of branches.

Much if not most of this construction resulted from the resumption of unrestricted competitive warfare. The linking of the Southern Pacific and Texas Pacific, and of the Central Pacific and Rio Grande in 1882, demolished the Union Pacific's monopoly of transcontinental traffic. Early in 1884, the North Western acquired over 400 miles of line west of the Missouri River, and the Iowa Pool finally fell apart. Now each major western road would expand whenever and wherever it pleased. In May 1884, the C. B. & Q. began construction west from Holdrege; the rails reached Elwood in August 1885, and eventually continued to Cheyenne, Wyoming. A link from Aurora to Grand Island, both in Nebraska, was completed in June 1884, and thence gradually pushed northwest; the railhead reached Alliance on February 3, 1888. As a matter of fact, as the rails started westward from Grand Island, no definite idea, apparently, had been formed as to what the eventual goal might be. At the time, the Burlington was conducting extensive surveys west of the Rockies, and serious thought was given to carrying the line all the way to Salt Lake City.

From the time Perkins became president, in September 1881, until June 1, 1888, the C. B. & Q. almost doubled its mileage—from 2,838 to 4,874. More than half of this increase was in Nebraska, where the company built over 1,200 miles of line. Colorado stood second in the amount of mileage added, Kansas third, and then Missouri, Illinois, and Wyoming, in that order. To describe each branch is beyond the scope of this book, but a glance at the map will tell the story quickly. Expansion of this sort, of course, involved bridge building. A single-track structure at Rulo was erected across the Missouri so as to link the two lines merging at Table Rock (from Lincoln and from Denver, respectively) with the Council Bluffs line on the other side of the river. This particular project was completed on October 2, 1887, at a cost of approximately $1,000,000. Farther north, the high bridge at Nebraska City connected the direct line to Lincoln and York with the Council Bluffs. Built for a half a million dollars, this structure was ready for business on August 12, 1888.

Almost as important, and certainly as intriguing as what actually was done, were the countless projects seriously considered from time to time, only to be laid aside. Even before the Burlington reached Denver, for example, Touzalin was anxious to make surveys toward the Pacific. Lest the Rio Grande be offended, this was not done at the time, but by 1883 the C. B. & Q. began making line locations west of Denver toward Fraser and Hot Sulphur Springs. Activity was stepped up in 1885 and 1886, and the company acquired rights of way in Gore Canyon and in Cottonwood Canyon, near Glenwood Springs. This, along with other developments in

Colorado, so alarmed Palmer of the Rio Grande that he implored the Missouri Pacific, building westward through Kansas at the time, to make its terminus at Pueblo. If it would, said Palmer, the Rio Grande could afford to exchange business with it at a much lower rate than it was currently charging on business exchanged with the Burlington at Denver, 120 miles further north. Impressed, the Missouri Pacific brought its rails into Pueblo on December 15, 1887, thus leaving the Burlington at a distinct disadvantage as far as traffic interchange with the Rio Grande was concerned. When the Rock Island reached Colorado Springs in November 1888, the C. B. & Q. found itself at an even greater disadvantage. Although the Burlington neither then nor later built through the Rockies, the possibility of its doing so in the mid-1880's was one factor, among others, that brought rivals into the area. Not until half a century later, when the C. B. & Q. threw its weight behind the building of the Dotsero cut-off, was the Denver Gateway restored to the position the C. B. & Q. always had hoped it would hold.

The idea of consolidation with the Santa Fe has already been mentioned, but the prospect became far less inviting once the Santa Fe built its own line into Chicago. More persistent was the idea, at its height in 1887, of acquiring Hill's Manitoba and of making some firm alliance with an eastern trunk road. Hill's determination to proceed on his own eliminated all hope of acquiring his road, but for many years Perkins considered an eastward alliance. Since the Vanderbilts were already closely associated with the North Western, and there were rumors of an alliance between the Baltimore and Ohio and the Santa Fe, Perkins felt in 1887 that "it would seem pretty clearly for the interest of the C. B. & Q. to do everything it can . . . to strengthen itself as an attractive ally for the Pennsylvania, which is its natural eastern connection."[5] Perkins, in fact, conferred at length with President Roberts of the Pennsylvania early in 1888. The upshot was an agreement to establish traffic connections not only at Chicago, but also by way of the Toledo, Peoria and Western. To facilitate this, the C. B. & Q. and Pennsylvania each acquired large stock interests in the T. P. & W. in 1893.

In summary, it was apparent that the C. B. & Q. was determined to control without question the main lines linking the major cities on the periphery of its system: Chicago, St. Louis, Kansas City, Denver, and the Twin Cities. It was equally determined to hold the intervening territory by a network of branches. Beyond this, both Perkins and his board acted with considerable caution. Although they considered, often enough, major extensions and alliances, they seemed more interested in the intensive development of the territory already staked out. Growth was recognized as essential, but it was less prized than stability and solvency.

[5] Perkins, Memorandum, June 24, 1887, C–O, Set M–3, pp. 171–3.

CHAPTER 12

Machines and Men, Laws and Dollars

1881-88

• PLANT, EQUIPMENT, AND OPERATIONS •

S O SPECTACULAR was the expansion of the Burlington during the
early years of the Perkins administration that other essential
aspects of the growing enterprise tend to be overshadowed.
But the drive for internal efficiency never ceased. Beginning with 1882, for
example, steel rail was laid in all new extensions west of the Missouri. And
as traffic volume increased, a great deal of second track was laid; in 1884
alone, over $645,000 was spent for this purpose in Illinois and Iowa. Mean-
while, grade reduction continued steadily; to cite one case, grades between
Aurora and Oregon were reduced from sixty-five to forty feet per mile during the summer of 1886, in anticipation of Twin Cities traffic. And half a
million dollars went for enlarging the West Burlington shops.

There were indications, too, of technological progress. The company
spent $2,725 in 1884 for oil-testing machines for the Aurora laboratory.
Three years later, "pneumatic signals" were installed between Chicago and
Downer's Grove at a cost of $40,000; another $15,000 was spent to provide
electric lights for the general office building in Chicago.

Out on the line, the 4-4-0 American-type engine still held sway. But in 1879 the company had experimented with a heavier class when it bought two Consolidation type (2-8-0) engines from Baldwin for freight service over the heavy grades in Iowa. Between that date and 1888, more than fifty such locomotives were bought or built in company shops.[1] In January 1886, twelve Consolidations were ordered at a cost of $9,000 each. Boxcars were obtained for $425 each, passenger coaches for $5,000. The most expensive item on the shopping list was a dining car at $12,000. By 1888, all major trains between Chicago, Denver, and the Twin Cities were equipped with vestibules and electric lights.

Railway motive power and rolling stock changed little in outward appearance during the latter part of the nineteenth century. One possible exception awaits future investigation by specialists. During the spring of 1882, Forbes, planning a trip to the West Coast, asked Perkins to obtain for him, if he could, a special car particularly adapted for sightseeing. "I am sorry to say," replied Perkins, that "the bird-cage car cannot go to California. When you brought up before the doubt of its going over the Sierras, I wrote [the Southern Pacific] . . . to have the question settled, and found that it could not go through their tunnels and snow sheds. I suppose, perhaps, it could go by the southern route. . . ."[2] Who owned the car, what it looked like, and whether Forbes used it on this particular trip is a mystery. Research may some day reveal that a vista dome, or something very much like it, traveled on Burlington rails long before 1945.

Less spectacular but far more important were the improvements in air brakes, in which the Burlington played an intimate role. Although Westinghouse had tried out his first power air brake on the Pennsylvania in 1869, it was of the "straight-air" variety, in which air under pressure set the brakes directly. The trouble with that system was that if the train parted or an air line connection broke, the entire system became inoperative. Three years later, Westinghouse devised a method whereby air pressure was used to keep the brakes off rather than to put them on; the heart of the system was the triple valve which was gradually adapted to passenger trains during the early 1880's. This improvement, however, was still not practical for heavy freight trains. Consequently, exhaustive test runs were made during the summers of 1886 and 1887 by the C. B. & Q. on West Burlington hill. As a result a faster, heavy-duty triple valve was developed that met all requirements, an improvement that revolutionized train operation. Meanwhile, Janney had perfected his automatic coupler, which

[1] Railway and Locomotive Historical Society: "Locomotives of the Chicago, Burlington & Quincy Railroad, 1855–1904," Part 2 (Boston, July 1937), p. 12; Bernard G. Corbin and William F. Kerka: *Steam Locomotives of the Burlington Route* (Red Oak, Iowa: The Thos. D. Murphy Co.; 1960), pp. 37, 39.

[2] Perkins to Forbes, April 4, 1882, PLB, Vol. VI, p. 78.

quickly replaced the dangerous link-and-pin that all roads had used up to that time.

Better brakes and better couplers meant faster operation, although the speeds achieved even on regular hotshot passenger runs were only about half of what they are today. In the summer of 1888, Burlington's fastest train between Omaha and Denver covered the 538 miles in sixteen hours and forty-five minutes, an average of 32.1 miles per hour. This was more than three miles an hour faster than the Union Pacific's *Overland Flyer* made over a comparable run, and very slightly higher than the C. B. & Q.'s fastest runs from Chicago to Omaha, Kansas City, and St. Paul.

Reliability and on-time performance appear to have been as highly prized as speed, however, and in this respect the Burlington grasped a spectacular opportunity to prove itself in 1884. Early that spring the Post Office Department arranged for an expedited solid mail train between New York and Chicago, arriving in the latter city at 12:35 a.m. What the government then needed was another train that could hurry the mails to Council Bluffs in time to make a connection for California leaving at 7:59 p.m. the same day.

The first Chicago road that Postmaster General Gresham approached refused even to discuss the matter. A second was willing to attempt the assignment for a daily bonus of $1,500 and a premium of $75,000 a year. Gresham turned to Potter of the Burlington; would he, in return for the exclusive mail contract, but without any premium whatever, operate a solid mail train six days a week to Council Bluffs in fifteen hours and fifty minutes, an average of 31.5 miles an hour? Potter agreed, and as Gresham turned to sign the contract he asked when the train would be ready. Potter replied: "Tomorrow morning, General."[3] And so it was. At precisely 3 a.m. on the raw morning of March 11, Burlington's first *Fast Mail* pulled out with the mail car from New York, a baggage car full of Chicago newspapers, and a special coach bearing the Postmaster General, his party, and Potter. Taking nothing for granted, the engineer on the first lap covered the thirty-eight miles to Aurora in fifty-three minutes. At 7:40 a.m., the *Fast Mail* arrived in Burlington, having covered the 205 miles, including five stops, at an average speed of nearly forty-four miles an hour. That evening the mail was in Council Bluffs on time.

Thus began a train and a tradition that have continued to this very day. Time and again rival roads have set up competitive schedules, but the C. B. & Q. has always met the challenge. Between 1884 and 1897, for example, the schedule was reduced on ten different occasions while the load was rising to six cars. When the Burlington celebrated the train's seventy-fifth anniversary in 1959, the fifteen-car Diesel-hauled flyer was cov-

[3] David P. Morgan: *Fast Mail: the First 75 Years* (Chicago: C. B. & Q. R. R. Co.; 1959), p. 13.

ering the 493 miles to Council Bluffs every night of the year in a minute less than eight hours, an average speed of nearly sixty-two miles per hour. It was said that when Potter signed the historic pact in the spring of 1884, he knew his men and his road. Time has amply justified his confidence.

The achievement of the *Fast Mail* on its first run prompted Perkins to send off a long memorandum to Potter with suggestions for advertising "the new route from the lakes to the mountains." Specifically, he thought that the company should adopt a simple device, such as the familiar Western Union sign, which could be easily and quickly comprehended and then "*iterate and reiterate* it constantly, that is to say: place it in so many and so prominent places that the eye and mind become familiar with it, that a mere glance is sufficient to bring before the mind the fact of the road and its whereabouts." Perkins thought it of utmost importance to create the impression of stability and solidity: "Stability," he said, "carries with it the idea of safety and regularity."[4]

Touzalin heartily agreed with Perkins's idea of a standard designation and strongly urged that "The Burlington" rather than "The Q" be established as the name of the system. Perkins at once endorsed this; in fact, he quashed any alternative by observing that he was not aware that other designations were being considered. And from that moment on, all booklets, pamphlets, timetables, and maps emphasized the name that Perkins clearly considered the home base of the railroad. In 1885 the company retained Lord & Thomas, an advertising agency, to place newspaper advertisements far and wide, and in the fall of that year began ordering calendars and fans. During 1886 and 1887, the company established city passenger and freight offices in Chicago, New York, Denver, Kansas City, Omaha, and San Francisco. Meanwhile, 50,000 calendars were ordered from Rand McNally at a cost of $31 per thousand. The Burlington proposed to tell the world about the services it offered.

Apparently it succeeded. In his book *American Railroads as Investments*, published in 1893, S. F. Van Oss observed that the Burlington "excels all others in advertising. By constantly keeping its name before the public, this railway has made its attractions known from the Pacific to the Atlantic." More specifically, Van Oss alleged that the company's playing cards, on which the system name was prominently displayed, "have become the principal implements of 'poker' between the lakes and the Gulf."[5]

• REFINEMENT OF ORGANIZATION •

THROUGHOUT HIS LONG ADMINISTRATION, Perkins never abandoned his efforts to adapt the top managerial staff to the tasks confronting the rail-

[4] Perkins to Potter, June 13, 1882, covering Memorandum dated May 28, 1882, PLB, Vol. VI, p. 139. Underlining in original.

[5] S. F. Van Oss: *American Railroads as Investments* (New York: Putnam's; 1893), pp. 496-7.

road. As described above, he started out with three vice-presidents, but Touzalin, originally assigned to Boston as liaison man with the board, was restless, and in the latter part of 1883 resigned to assume the vice-presidency of the Santa Fe. His post at Boston, which because of Forbes's position really was superfluous, never was filled. In the summer of 1884, however, Potter assumed the title of first vice-president; his duties as chief operating officer remained the same. Peasley continued as second vice-president in charge of financial affairs, and the title of third vice-president was eliminated.

This organizational structure remained intact until August 1887, when, much to Perkins's chagrin, Potter resigned to become vice-president of the Union Pacific. Peasley succeeded him and acted as the only vice-president for a year until, in November 1888, Henry B. Stone was moved from the general managership of the system to the second vice-presidency. It is worth noting that, contrary to the customary practice today, the Burlington's chief legal officer did not hold vice-presidential rank. In fact, however, Wirt Dexter, who succeeded Walker as general counsel upon the latter's death in 1881, not only reported directly to the president, but also was, as Walker had been, a member of the board of directors. Furthermore, throughout the 1880's Perkins and Dexter constituted the Western Executive Committee. In practice, therefore, the general counsel exerted as much if not more influence than any of the vice-presidents.

The position of the traffic officers, however, was different in both name and fact from what it is today. They had never held vice-presidential rank, and when, in 1884, Potter was made first vice-president, the board specified that the general freight agent and the general passenger agent on both the C. B. & Q. and the B. & M. should be subordinate to the general managers of those properties.

Perkins always insisted that a good man was worth a good price. Therefore, during his administration salaries increased markedly at virtually every supervisory level. He himself was receiving $25,000 when he was elected president, but on that occasion received no increase beyond the $5,000 expense allowance previously voted to Forbes. Not until 1886 was Perkins's salary raised to $40,000; the allowance was then discontinued. When Potter and Touzalin became vice-presidents in the fall of 1881, they were paid $15,000 apiece, but when Potter took over as vice-president in 1884, his salary was raised to $20,000; it was boosted to $25,000 just two years later.

Although these raises were substantial, they were exceeded in percentage by the increases in the lower brackets. When Stone and Holdrege, for example, were promoted to assistant general managers in the summer of 1883, Holdrege's salary went from $6,000 to $7,000, and Stone's to $7,500. Early in 1885, when each became a full-fledged general manager, both were paid $9,000; they were raised to $12,000 late in 1886. Increases, in fact, were made all along the line. In the spring of 1883, for example, the general agent at Des Moines was raised from $135 to $150 a month; both the chief dispatcher at Creston and the foreman of the Burlington shops received increases from $110 to $125 a month. At the same time, William Forsyth, mechanical engineer, had his salary boosted from $1,800 to $2,400 a year.

Within the industry the Burlington already was regarded as a training ground for rail executives; the natural teaching abilities of some of its chief executives may have had a great deal to do with it. At any rate, as has already been noted, one of Perkins's former lieutenants, W. B. Strong, had become president of the Santa Fe during the 1880's, and Robert Harris was headed for the top post on the Northern Pacific. E. P. Ripley, general freight agent of the C. B. & Q. during the mid-1880's, was destined for the presidency of the Santa Fe. W. C. Brown, later on in the decade superintendent of the Iowa lines, went on to become president of the New York Central. Howard Elliott, general freight and ticket agent of the Burlington's Missouri lines in 1886, eventually became a vice-president of the Burlington, and then successively president of the Northern Pacific and of the New Haven.

• REGULATION •

IN THE LAST REPORT to the stockholders that Forbes wrote as president, early in 1881, he observed that there seemed to be "a cessation in the attempt witnessed in the West a few years ago to regulate rates by law." He went on to say that the directors had "faith to believe that the business world has reached the wise conclusion that no legislative enactment can take the place of the natural laws regulating all prices, including the price of transportation by rail."[6]

No sooner were these words spoken than events began to cast doubt on their accuracy. In the spring of 1881, the directors noted that a recently enacted law in Nebraska regulating freight rates was against the interests of the railways and of all producers in the state. Perkins moved, however, and the directors agreed, that it would be "unwise and hazardous to disregard the law." Consequently all local officers were directed "to comply with the letter and spirit of the law until either its unconstitutionality shall be decreed by the courts or the good sense of the people shall cause its repeal."[7] Similar action was taken in respect to a law in Illinois.

When Senator Cullom's Select Committee began investigating the necessity for a federal regulatory act, the Burlington and the Santa Fe jointly employed Richard Olney, distinguished Boston attorney and later Secretary of State, to oppose the adoption of any federal measure. Neither

[6] CB&Q, AR 1880, p. 19.
[7] CB&Q, ORB, April 6, 1881, Vol. II, p. 700.

his efforts nor the lengthy memorandum that Perkins himself sent off to Cullom, as mentioned above, had any appreciable effect. In February 1887, President Cleveland signed the Interstate Commerce Act.

The main provisions of this basic law can be summarized briefly. It applied only to common carriers by rail engaged in interstate or foreign commerce; all rates charged by such carriers were to be "just and reasonable"; rebates and discrimination of any sort were strictly forbidden. The famous Section Four, known then and since as the "Long-and-Short-Haul Clause," made it illegal to charge as much or more for a shorter than for a longer haul over any one line in the same direction unless, after appropriate investigation, the Interstate Commerce Commission approved an exception to the rule. Pools of any sort were forbidden, and all rates and fares had to be made public and filed with the Commission. Administration of the act was entrusted to a Commission of five members, only three of whom could be from the same political party. The findings of this body were to become effective immediately, but only if obeyed voluntarily. In practice, therefore, the carriers were free to disregard the orders of the Commission without penalty unless and until such orders were upheld by the courts after suit had been filed by an injured party.

As the events of the following decade demonstrated, the new law was feeble indeed. Its terms, for example those requiring that rates should be "just and reasonable," were vague; witnesses refused to testify for fear of retaliation; the railroads themselves were almost uniformly hostile, and the courts were notably unsympathetic. But of course none of this was apparent at the outset, and the reaction of the railroads in 1887 was one of aggrieved dismay and extreme caution. Perkins felt that the prohibition against pooling was a particularly serious mistake; interestingly enough, his vigorous arguments against that provision were revived almost word for word in the hearings leading up to the Transportation Act of 1920, which, belatedly, legalized pooling under appropriate restraints.

For the moment, the Burlington contented itself with two precautionary steps. A fortnight after the law was passed, Olney submitted to Perkins a lengthy memorandum forecasting the probable interpretation of various sections of the act, and pointing out its most vulnerable points. It was agreed that these should be submitted to court test as soon as possible. The second step was to establish new rates to conform with the act, which became effective in April.

As the effects of the new law became apparent, Perkins grew increasingly pessimistic. By the fall of 1887, he felt that the financial prospects for the C. B. & Q. looked less promising than they had for many years past. Indeed, he suggested that it might be well to reduce the dividend from the current eight percent to perhaps six percent, both as a matter of retrenchment and as a warning against further legislation. As both through and local rates fell, Perkins wrote early in 1888 that he was "inclined to think there is more cheating going on today than ever before, in the way of secret rebates of one kind or another."[8] In his *Annual Report* to the stockholders for 1887, Perkins blamed the general demoralization of rates squarely on the Interstate Commerce Act. Late in 1888 he doubted whether, in the railway world, there could be "any peace until the public wakes up to the truth & actually sees the effect of its foolish laws. When it does there will be a change, and, if not till then, may it not be best in the end for the strong roads to let *paliatives* [sic] alone & just let the disease run its course?"[9]

• THE GREAT STRIKE OF 1888 •

THE STRIKE OF 1888 was the most serious and most significant labor conflict in the history of the Burlington. On the surface it was virtually unthinkable that the engineers, known as self-respecting, reliable, and skilled men belonging to a conservative brotherhood, suddenly, and almost to a man, should walk out on one of the largest, best-managed roads in the nation, taking with them the firemen, and eventually, the switchmen. But that is precisely what happened.

Fortunately, the records of the strike are voluminous. While it was still in progress, Perkins commissioned M. L. Scudder, an economist, to compile a detailed account based on original documents and first-hand observation. The archives of the company, the records of the brotherhoods, Pinkerton reports, and a wealth of newspaper material, as well as three novels based on the affair, fill out the story. From these rich sources, Donald L. McMurry has written his authoritative account entitled *The Great Burlington Strike of 1888* (Cambridge, 1955). As this classic is readily available, it is necessary here only to summarize events; much of what is said is drawn from McMurry's full-length study.

Since the 1860's, the Burlington, like many other railroads, had paid its train crews on a trip basis; main-line runs paid better than runs on branches. In 1886, a grievance committee of the engineers demanded uniform mileage pay; furthermore, they demanded that a run of a hundred miles in either freight or passenger service should constitute a day's work, and that any excess mileage should be paid for on a pro-rata basis. If less than a hundred miles was covered in ten hours, overtime pay was to be allowed after ten hours' work.

The granting of these demands would automatically have abolished a second major grievance, the classification of engineers and firemen. According to this practice, common among the nation's railroads and adopted by the C. B. & Q. in 1876, an engineer newly promoted from the rank of fire-

---

[8] Perkins to Forbes, January 19, 1888, BF.
[9] Perkins to Forbes, November 30, 1888, PLB, Vol. VIII, p. 436. Underlining in original.

man received only two thirds as much as a "first class" engineer for his first year at the throttle, and five sixths as much during his second year; only at the beginning of the third year did he receive the full rate. A similar system applied to firemen. The men complained that the company could and did keep its expenses down by discharging first-class engineers and continually promoting lower-paid firemen, although the statistics of labor turnover on the C. B. & Q. give no evidence that this was true. However, the company did recruit almost all its engineers from the ranks of the firemen. Adoption of mileage pay would, of course, do away with classification. It would also mean, as the men realized, that the older engineers, unable to withstand the strain of main-line runs, would not suffer a cut in pay when relegated to branch-line service. These were not the only grievances presented by the engineers in 1886. They complained about such extra tasks as local switching, about long detention away from home, and about the discharge of men for no apparent reason other than activity in the brotherhood.

All these complaints were brought before Vice-President Potter in March 1886 by a grievance committee composed of two engineers from each of the Burlington system lines. Although Potter was at first reluctant to bargain on a system-wide basis, he eventually called in the general managers of the Proprietary Lines. On the matter of mileage pay and classification, however, he would not budge. But he agreed to adopt new rules in other respects, and to adjust inequitable pay wherever it could be shown to exist. On April 1, 1886, he signed an agreement to that effect.

Both sides seemed satisfied. The men were pleased by the fact that the brotherhood had in effect been recognized as the system-wide bargaining agent for the engineers, and the adjustment of pay inequalities removed immediate sources of irritation. Furthermore, specific rules governing each run were to be observed throughout the system. On the other hand, Potter felt that a major strike had been avoided without granting the two principal demands of the men.

Unfortunately, the good feelings of 1886 soon began to deteriorate for a number of reasons. Perhaps most important of all was Potter's resignation on May 15, 1887. He had been approachable and trusted by both employees and management. His duties in respect to operations and labor relations were thereupon assumed by Henry B. Stone, the general manager. In many ways this young man of thirty-six was the direct opposite of the self-made, genial Potter. A Harvard graduate, Stone had started work with the Burlington as a shop apprentice in 1877 and had been promoted rapidly until he had become general manager of the C. B. & Q. in 1885. He was, without question, extremely able, honest, and fearless. But in the opinion of many employees he was a symbol of absentee Boston control, of nepotism, and of chilly indifference to the human rights of the workingman. Unfortunately, he was extremely hard of hearing and thus gave the impression of being preoccupied and brusque. As long as Potter remained on the property, the men felt that the agreement of 1886 was being carried out in good faith. After his departure, they felt that they received little attention or cooperation from their local officers when they went to them with troubles. As the year 1887 ran out, engineers and firemen alike regarded themselves as little better off than two years before.

A second factor, in some ways intangible, was at work. For years the engineers, convinced of their indispensability, had considered themselves aristocrats among railway workers. But there were two sides to this coin: the lofty attitude of the engineers, while prompting them to bold action, also tended to isolate them from some of their fellow workers.

Certainly the shift among the personnel of the engineers' general grievance committee during 1886 and 1887 contributed to mounting tension. When that committee met in Burlington on January 23, 1888, the conservative chairman resigned. From then on, the more radical elements were in control. A few days later, the reconstituted committee joined forces with a similar committee representing the firemen; thereafter all negotiations with the company were conducted by a joint committee composed of two engineers and two firemen from each of the seven principal Burlington companies. On January 28, 1888, this joint committee telegraphed Perkins at his Boston office, asking for an interview with him in Chicago at his "earliest possible convenience."[1] When Perkins received the message in Washington, he replied immediately that he would be glad to see the men, but that they would have to meet with him in Boston, where pressing business awaited his attention. Meantime he suggested that they see Stone, and promised that the general managers from the entire system would be called to the conference.

A second communication to Perkins from the joint committee specified that what the men wanted was mileage pay. Even though this demand had been rejected in 1886, Perkins promptly wrote Stone on February 4 that "in a general way, our position ought to be, I think, that we are ready to consider any reasonable suggestions, but that we expect our men to stand by us in times of trouble, and not to ask for an increase of pay beyond what our neighbors are giving especially at a time when receipts are falling off."[2]

None of these developments suggested a crisis. The joint committee, with a specific set of complaints, was assembled in Chicago, ready to meet Stone and other system officials. Perkins not only approved negotiation on a system-wide basis, thus tacitly recognizing the union and accept-

[1] McM, p. 47. The seven companies involved were the CB&Q; the B&M in Nebraska; the Hannibal and St. Joseph; the Kansas City, St. Joseph and Council Bluffs; the St. Louis, Keokuk & Northwestern; the Chicago, Burlington and Kansas City; the Chicago and Iowa.

[2] Perkins to Henry B. Stone, February 4, 1888, quoted in McM, p. 49.

ing collective bargaining, but also showed himself willing to listen to reasonable proposals. What happened next might be termed a comedy of errors had it not had such tragic results. The points at issue did not change. Yet, because of human impatience and the failure of each side to recognize and take into account the different values and sensibilities of the other, enough misunderstanding was generated to weaken the delicate bridge of mutual confidence and to drive those who were cautiously advancing over it back to uncompromising positions.

Trivial as it may seem, the joint committeemen apparently failed to realize that the system's top officials could not easily drop what they happened to be doing at the moment and foregather in Chicago on short notice. General Manager Holdrege of the B. & M., for example, was in Boston on February 4, and Stone had had to go to New York for a few days; others were out on the line. Hence the general conference that Perkins had suggested could not be scheduled until February 15. This delay, coupled with Perkins's absence, was construed by the joint committee as a deliberate attempt to stall. When S. E. Hoge, chairman of the committee, failed to receive a prompt answer from Stone (who was away) in respect to a preliminary meeting, he telegraphed Perkins on February 6: "Wired Mr. Stone twice, received no reply. Give you three days to get here and adjust matters or we shall place the matter in the hands of our Grand Officers."[3]

This was obviously not the sort of message to put Perkins in a conciliatory frame of mind. Yet he replied courteously that Stone probably had failed to receive Hoge's telegrams; he even wired Stone to answer Hoge at once. But Perkins determined then and there that for the sake of discipline he, at any rate, would not budge from Boston as long as his doing so might be construed as complying with such a summons. A second telegram from Hoge, specifically threatening a strike if Perkins failed to arrive within three days, had precisely the same effect. So it was that the one man who might have avoided an open break did not go to Chicago until after the break had become a reality.

The delay in the anticipated conference had another significant result. During it Hoge sent a letter to every engineers' and firemen's local on the system, asking for a referendum vote by every brotherhood member as to whether the unions should demand mileage pay and the abolition of classification. The response was almost unanimously in the affirmative. Thus, without the knowledge of management, the hand of the committee was strengthened immeasurably by what was in effect a vote to strike if the demands of the men were not granted.

At practically the same moment, the C. B. & Q. directors met in Boston. Undoubtedly Perkins told them about the pending negotiations in Chicago. But the board took no official notice of the situation and went about its affairs. Business had been bad; the final quarter of 1887 revealed a

[3] S. E. Hoge to Perkins, February 6, 1888, quoted in McM, p. 49.

net deficit of nearly $1,500,000. But, as Forbes and Perkins often remarked, when times were bad, many small holders of the widely owned Q stock relied heavily on regular dividends. It was voted, therefore, to continue the regular rate and pay two percent on March 15. Apparently no one at the meeting considered, at least for the record, any possible effect of this action on the engineers and firemen, though in fact payment of the dividend made it difficult thereafter to convince the men that the company was hard up financially.

When the joint committee representing the engineers and firemen met with the Burlington officials in Chicago on February 15, they demanded adoption of mileage pay, establishment of a 100-mile run or ten hours' duty or less as a day's work in regular road service, and specific provisions for overtime and special assignments. Other demands were for investigation of discharges and suspensions by a joint labor-management committee, for promotion by seniority when ability was equal, and for the abolition of yard work for road crews except at penalty pay. Somewhat more radical were the demands that brotherhood officials be given free passes and that all tests and examinations be abolished unless approved by the general grievance committee.

The general managers could not agree among themselves quickly on either immediate tactics or long-run strategy. Consequently they decided to issue, at a second conference scheduled for February 18, a temperate reply and to print and circulate it, along with the men's demands and the agreement of 1886, so that all employees, the press, and the public could learn precisely what was at issue. In their reply, the general managers explained why they could not see their way clear to accept mileage pay, why they felt the enginemen were fairly paid as matters stood, and why classification should remain. They flatly rejected the notion of joint investigations, the issuance of passes for union officials, and the abolition of tests. They did say they were willing to pay as much as neighboring roads for similar services and to adjust any inequalities of pay which could be shown to exist. Meanwhile, they promised that all matters would be considered fully by all concerned. This last meant that everyone wanted to consult Perkins, and indeed led Hoge to send another peremptory summons to him.

On the basic issues, Perkins emphatically instructed Stone to be receptive and reasonable. "I advise conciliatory spirit and methods and do not see how you can help doing substantially the same as your neighbors," he wired on February 19.[4] Two days later he told Stone that he did not think it important whether pay was based on the trip or on mileage as long as it reflected the value of the service. "Remember," he added significantly, ". . . that it is not always wise to be too rigid even if you are right."[5]

[4] Perkins to Stone, February 19, 1888, quoted in McM, p. 56.
[5] Perkins to Stone, February 21, 1888, quoted in McM, pp. 56-7.

This was excellent advice, and no doubt Perkins would have followed it had he been on the spot. But, as he said, maintenance of discipline made it definitely inadvisable for him to go to Chicago as though obeying a summons. Furthermore, it was the responsibility of the president and the directors to determine general policy; that could best be done jointly in Boston. Finally, Perkins had clothed Stone with full authority, and to go west at the moment would imply a lack of confidence in Stone's ability to handle the negotiations. Perkins remained where he was.

That he did so was a tragedy for all concerned. When Hoge met Stone again, on February 22, the latter refused even to consider mileage pay; apparently he thought he had the situation fully under control, for he even wired Perkins not to hurry west. Still worried and still willing to accept mileage pay, Perkins asked whether some compromise could not save everybody's feelings. But Stone was adamant. A final conference on February 23 ended in a stalemate, and the next day the grand officers of the brotherhoods sanctioned a strike scheduled to become effective at 4 a.m. on Monday, February 27. When Perkins finally arrived in Chicago that morning, only forty-five out of 2,137 engineers and firemen on the Burlington were at their posts. Obviously Stone had underestimated the extent of disaffection and overestimated his ability to handle it.

If the Burlington officials were surprised, so were the men. Hastily assembled crews recruited from the ranks of the trainmen, conductors, and supervisory personnel kept most of the through and suburban passenger trains running even on the first day of the strike. New engineers, most of them former Reading Railroad employees, began filling the old places as early as March 2. Even though the company deliberately moved slowly in hiring replacements, in the hope that some of the more capable strikers would return, Stone was able to announce on March 19 that the ranks had been filled. By then, both freight and passenger service were virtually back to normal. Efforts of the brotherhoods to intimidate or buy off the hated "scabs" were fruitless. To prevent violence, several thousand loyal employees were sworn in as special officers. With them worked some five hundred Pinkerton agents, as well as local constabulary forces. Management felt sure that the strike was doomed.

The strikers, however, were far from convinced. On March 5, a secondary boycott had been invoked by the brotherhood against all C. B. & Q. cars, and officials of most of the western roads, fearing trouble on their own lines and harboring no great affection for the competing C. B. & Q., did little to force their men to handle them. Perkins was furious; he felt that the Burlington was fighting the battle of all rail managements to retain control over their own property. Furthermore, he realized that if the boycott was not checked, it could seriously retard recovery from the original walkout. Consequently the company on March 8 turned to the federal courts for injunctions against those railroads which refused to exchange cars with the Burlington, claiming that they were practicing illegal discrimination in violation of the Interstate Commerce Act. In a series of vigorous decisions, notably by Judge Dundy in Omaha and Judge Gresham in Chicago, the C. B. & Q. was upheld, and by March 22 the boycott was rescinded.

The engineers and firemen now turned to their fellow employees for help. But the conductors, long annoyed by the arrogance of the engineers, refused to quit; the brakemen were prevented from doing so by the constitution of their own brotherhood. But the switchmen, beguiled by the offer of strike payments and a pledge of future federation with the engineers, walked out without warning at midnight on March 23, despite the fact the railroad had kept all switchmen on the payroll during the height of the engineers' strike, when there was little for them to do. Replacements were quickly found, but the switchmen then invoked a boycott. Once again the Burlington turned to the courts, and when Judge Gresham issued another injunction, the boycott was rescinded as of April 4. On that day the strike of 1888 was over to all intents and purposes, although the final peace treaty was not signed until exactly nine months later.

Just as in a war, the actual battlefield was by no means the only theater of activity. The moment Perkins returned to Chicago on February 27, he began a three-week series of intensive meetings with the chiefs of the brotherhood. He offered to rectify wage inequalities, to pay as much as neighboring roads, to hold investigations in the spirit of the 1886 agreement, and to negotiate with the brotherhood on a system-wide basis. He would not, however, fire men that had been taken on in good faith, and he would not abolish classification. He was willing to deal with any Burlington men either individually or as representatives of a system union, but he would not negotiate with them as a national brotherhood. Neither would he arbitrate, for the simple reason that he did not believe the judgment of any intermediate party, no matter how wise or just, could alter the "natural laws" under which only a purchaser of services could determine how much he could and would pay, and only the seller could decide how much or how little he would accept. Because the chiefs of the brotherhood insisted on mileage pay (which would automatically abolish classification) and the rehiring of all strikers at their old wages, progress was impossible.

Actually, Perkins was pursuing a middle course. The president of the Reading, for example, urged him not to rehire a single striker, whereas the Governor of Iowa strongly urged arbitration. But Perkins stuck to his position, and his course was unanimously endorsed by the directors on March 27, and by the stockholders on May 16. At this point the national chiefs of the engineers and firemen urged the men on the C. B. & Q. to give up, but to no avail. In June, and again in July, the company renewed its offer to take back all strikers for whom places still were open; the strikers, however, interpreted this as a sign of weakness and refused to make peace.

Meanwhile, each side did its best to sway public opinion. The company issued "broadsides" and releases for the newspapers, and in general kept its case effectively before the public. The strikers' publicity was not so well handled or so effective. One reason, perhaps, lay in the public's instinctive fear and resentment of acts of violence. These, at first, were few, for the brotherhoods prided themselves on their peaceful conduct. As their hopes of victory waned, however, the union chiefs found it increasingly difficult to restrain the irresponsible elements in their organizations. Attacks upon "scabs" and the hated Pinkertons became more frequent, and more than a hundred attempts were made, many of them successful, to disable locomotives or place obstructions on the track. The climax came in May, June, and July, when seven charges of dynamite exploded in or under trains. The brotherhoods officially denounced such tactics, however much they may have sympathized with the feelings that prompted them.

During the summer of 1888, the engineers and firemen voted to continue the strike. But in the fall the national brotherhoods virtually withdrew their support, and the engineers alienated both the firemen and the switchmen by refusing federation into unified brotherhood. Meanwhile, a significant change took place in the Burlington management: general freight agent E. P. Ripley was appointed general manager in October, and Stone was transferred to the second vice-presidency, with a reduction in pay. "A man of great ability in many respects," as McMurry put it, Stone "was not at his best when dealing with personnel problems."[6] For the time being, however, and because he had attended every conference with the strikers, Perkins left him in charge of the final negotiations with the brotherhoods. On December 11, the switchmen officially called off their strike, and when the company again promised to take back such men as were needed and to recommend to other companies all those who had not participated in violence, the engineers and firemen finally laid down their arms on January 4, 1889.

The struggle had been costly to both sides. McMurry estimates that the brotherhoods spent more than $1,500,000 in benefits and for publicity, and the company probably twice that much for protection and to state its side of the case. Never again during Perkins's administration did dividends reach the pre-strike level, and Forbes frankly asserted that the conflict had retarded the expansion of the entire system. Other factors, of course, reduced C. B. & Q. earnings in 1888, but the strike was by all odds the principal cause. Even so, management felt that the financial sacrifice had been a sound investment, for to their thinking, the company had successfully reasserted its right to manage its own property.

[6] McM, p. 282.

For the striking brotherhoods, and to some extent for railway labor in general, the failure of the strike was a stinging defeat. Prestige and bargaining power were seriously compromised; union men were not hired generally on the Burlington until 1904. Furthermore, the use of the injunction in labor disputes was given a fresh lease on life. Yet the cause of the workingman was, indirectly, advanced in several ways. After stoutly opposing any form of "social security" for years on the ground that it smacked of paternalism, Perkins finally agreed to the establishment of a company Relief Department. Set up in January 1889 as a sincere attempt to strengthen the bonds between the men and their company, it paid sickness, accident, and death benefits to those who joined voluntarily and contributed to it by means of monthly payroll deductions; all administrative expenses and the entire risk were underwritten by the company. By the end of 1961, the Relief Department had paid out approximately $42,000,000 in benefits and the company had contributed more than $7,000,000 to operate the department. A less tangible though hardly less important result of the strike over the long run was the tempering effect on management, particularly on Perkins. Never for a moment did he alter his conviction that wages were and should be fixed by the laws of supply and demand, or that managers had a right to control their own property. But he doubled his efforts to make certain that his subordinate officers dealt justly with the men and that such agreements as were made were scrupulously carried out by the company.

• THE COURSE OF BUSINESS, 1881–88 •

DURING THE FIRST YEARS of the Perkins administration, from the latter part of 1881 through 1888, the most significant aspect of the company's development was the increase in average miles operated (including those of the Proprietary Lines) from 2,822 to 4,859. Because a great deal of this new construction was in partially developed regions, neither total revenues for the system nor gross revenues per mile increased with equal rapidity. As a matter of fact, Perkins was constantly aware of the danger of expanding so rapidly that earnings would be diluted to the point of jeopardizing the entire financial structure. And his views were shared by the board. As he put it in 1883: "The policy of the C. B. & Q. as a corporation up to this time has been not to speculate in railroads, but to buy them after they have shown that they were valuable, or with some definite protective objective. On the whole, this seems to me the sound corporate policy."[7]

Even though the C. B. & Q. practiced a certain measure of restraint, however, the decade of the 1880's was not a period of unqualified pros-

[7] Perkins to Forbes, October 22, 1883, PLB, Vol. VI, pp. 450–4.

perity. Business during 1881, for example, was only moderately good. Although gross earnings showed a healthy increase over the preceding year, there was a sharp decline in net income as a result of mounting prices of labor and material and because of damaging floods.

Owing principally to the poor crops of 1881 and to increasing competition, earnings east of the Missouri River took a sharp dip in 1882; corn traffic, for example, was off approximately forty percent. But as had occurred so often, earnings elsewhere on the system redressed the balance. Partly because of the building of new lines west of the Missouri and partly because of excellent crops in that area, system earnings showed a slight increase over 1881; the year 1883 witnessed an increase of more than twenty percent in operating revenues. By this time the new lines built in 1880–82 were coming into their own, and although wages kept rising, the cost of most materials used declined. Net income for 1883 exceeded $8,700,000, the highest figure for the nineteenth century, and one not to be exceeded until 1902. In that banner year the C. B. & Q., as just one of seventeen railways serving Chicago, brought into the metropolis forty-one percent of all corn received there, thirty-four percent of the rye, thirty-three percent of the wheat, and twenty-one percent of the oats; it delivered more cattle, sheep, live hogs, and wool than any of the other carriers. Westbound, the company ranked first in the shipment of salt and lumber.

On the C. B. & Q., as throughout the nation, 1884 was characterized by a dullness of trade. Compared with 1883, net income was off approximately fourteen percent. Business during 1885, 1886, and the opening months of 1887 remained remarkably stable. Gross revenues varied less than four percent, and although net income again topped the $8,000,000 mark in 1885 and 1886, dividends were held to eight percent.

From the standpoint of traffic hauled and gross earnings, 1887 turned out to be the best year up to that point in the history of the company. But elements of weakness existed: although passenger revenues increased sharply, receipts from freight declined. Furthermore, business from the newly opened Chicago, Burlington & Northern was being carried at extremely low rates. At the same time, the prohibition in the Interstate Commerce Act against pooling brought about a demoralization of rates generally while operating expenses soared upward, partly because of the heavy expenditures for steel rail and partly because much of the new mileage built in the mid-1880's still lay in undeveloped areas. Finally, with most of the best granted lands already sold, receipts from that source declined rapidly. Some of this was offset, however, by steadily mounting dividend income from the various Proprietary Lines. Thus, net income in 1887 fell only to approximately $7,500,000, and the board felt justified in continuing the established eight percent dividend rate.

As Perkins bluntly reported at the end of 1888: "After many prosperous years, the Chicago, Burlington & Quincy Company has experienced a year of serious reverses."[8] Freight revenue dropped off more than seventeen percent while operating expenses increased by the same percentage. While taxes and interest on the debt were mounting, other income disappeared entirely, and the end of the year showed a net loss of nearly a quarter of a million dollars, a result, primarily, of the prolonged strike. As already indicated, however, the financial difficulties of 1888 had other causes. Some traffic was diverted to new competing railroads, notably the Santa Fe's recently constructed line to Kansas City. And rates continued to drop alarmingly; railroaders felt that the decline was owing principally to the difficulty of self-regulation among the railways now that the right to pool had been prohibited. A final factor in the poor showing of the year was the addition of more than 600 miles to average mileage operated. Most of this was in western Nebraska and eastern Colorado, and served strictly new country where few or no crops had been raised in 1887. Thus a combination of factors brought the Burlington its worst financial year up to that time. Dividends were cut from eight to five percent, and even they were paid from surplus.

Because 1888 was such an unusual year, a comparison between 1881 and 1887 is more meaningful as an indication of what went on during the opening years of the Perkins administration. During this period, while road mileage was increasing fifty percent, operating revenues rose only thirty percent and gross earnings per mile decreased thirteen percent. Concurrently, however, operating expenses rose thirty-nine percent, so that *net* earnings per mile decreased twenty-two percent. The ultimate result, then, was that with a fifty percent increase in average miles operated, net income mounted just fifteen percent. The long-run effects of this tremendous expansion are perhaps reflected more accurately by the balance sheet, and in this respect it is proper to compare 1888 with 1881. During that interval, the value of road and equipment rose almost exactly as fast as the mileage, namely by more than forty-nine percent. Capital stock and funded debt combined increased fifty-four percent, but while stock increased somewhat less than thirty-eight percent, funded debt mounted nearly sixty-nine percent. Fortunately, interest rates on most new bonds issued were four percent; the liability of the company for bond interest increased exactly fifty percent from 1881 to 1888.

The net result was that the C. B. & Q., and indeed the entire system, was growing about as rapidly as its resources would permit. Its managers were betting heavily on the growth of the new country they were constantly opening to rail service. The relatively rapid growth of fixed debt in proportion to stock represented a departure from the balance achieved by the end of the 1870's, and was characteristic of the company's financial structure until after the close of World War I. As long as railways

[8] CB&Q, AR 1888, p. 19.

were and seemed destined always to be the backbone of overland transportation, there appeared to be nothing inherently dangerous in financing
capital improvements through funded debt. The Burlington had paid substantial sums in order to expand, and fully intended to reap the benefits
of its policy. Time alone would test the wisdom of this thinking.

CHAPTER 13

Regulation, Stringency, Strategy and Personnel

1889 - 1901

• CHANGE OF TEMPO •

WITHOUT QUESTION, the first phase of the Perkins administration (1881–1888) was characterized by explosive expansion. The C. B. & Q. built and acquired approximately 2,000 additional miles of line of its own (about 285 miles a year), regained control of the Hannibal and St. Joseph, and sponsored the road to the Twin Cities. In contrast, only 1,350 miles were added in the thirteen years between mid-1888 and mid-1901, or about 104 miles a year. It is true that the mileage operated by the C. B. & Q. increased over 3,100 miles during these thirteen years, but that was because, at the very end of the century, the company assumed operation of the Proprietary Lines that it had acquired prior to 1888.

What lay behind this change of pace? Certainly the company appeared to be as growth-minded as ever: it continued to explore with vigor the possibility of building to Salt Lake City, of acquiring a connection to Portland, Oregon, and of obtaining some control over such major lines as Hill's Manitoba, the Northern Pacific, the Union Pacific, and the Rio

Grande. Yet, for a variety of reasons, none of these ideas was translated into reality.

In the first place, passage of the Interstate Commerce Act in 1887 and the enactment of various regulatory laws, particularly in Iowa and Nebraska, made it a great deal harder to earn as much money as before and to attract new capital. As the directors resolved on February 16, 1894, for example, when the Merchants' Association of Milwaukee invited the C. B. & Q. to build into that city, "the board deems it inexpedient, on account of existing state and national legislation, to consider building any road in competition with other existing roads."[1]

A second obstacle to expansion was the recurrent difficulty of raising new capital because of the prolonged depression of the mid-1890's. Money markets were tight when the company was emerging from the sharp retrenchment forced on it by the strike of 1888, and then, just when recovery seemed near, the panic of 1893 broke upon the nation and made further caution mandatory. Not until 1897 did any real measure of prosperity return, and by that time several major strategic opportunities for expansion had passed by.

A third reason was the fact that by 1888 the Burlington system (including the Proprietary Lines) linked all the major cities on its periphery: Chicago, St. Louis, Kansas City, Denver, and St. Paul. Thus, as long as connecting lines freely exchanged business at terminal gateways, no pressing reason for expansion existed, and in view of the distances involved in reaching the West Coast, a good many reasons militated against it. So it was that the only major penetration into an unoccupied new region was the line northwest to Billings, completed in 1894. Aside from that, growth on the Burlington during the second phase of the Perkins administration was intensive rather than extensive.

Two other characteristics of the second phase of the Perkins administration deserve separate mention. At the very close of the century, in order to simplify the financial structure, the C. B. & Q. absorbed the various Proprietary Lines into the parent C. B. & Q. corporation. This development naturally involved major financing. Finally, the years from 1888 to 1901 witnessed virtually no changes in upper management, and a welcome absence of labor difficulties.

• REGULATION •

FROM THE MOMENT the Interstate Commerce Act became effective in the spring of 1887, the officials of the Burlington devoted an enormous amount of time and thought as to how best to cope with it. Basically, they were convinced that it should be repealed, and they felt the same way

[1] CB&Q, ORB, February 16, 1894, Vol. III, p. 617.

about state legislation. After all, they reasoned, these were merely "artificial regulations and limitations opposed to those natural laws of human action which, it is now universally admitted, govern individuals engaged in business."[2] But the men in charge of the Burlington were realistic enough to know that the public was hardly in the mood to heed any plea for wholesale repeal of regulatory legislation. They concentrated their fire on the most objectionable features of both national and state laws, hired the best counsel they could find to explore loopholes, and sought to devise voluntary methods to control the "chiseling" that inevitably sprang up in the wake of the Interstate Commerce Act.

The C. B. & Q. was particularly hard hit by the long-and-short-haul clause. As the company spelled it out in its *Annual Report* for 1887, the difficulty was that there was generally some one competitor between given points with little local business. Such a road could and did fix through rates at a low level, with the result that lines like the C. B. & Q. which had built up valuable local business were forced to lower local rates to the point at which profits either were minimized or vanished altogether.

Even more harmful, in Perkins's view, was the prohibition against pooling. For many years prior to the Act, Perkins pointed out, this form of self-regulation had brought about an orderly and steady decline in rates which had been beneficial alike to shippers and the railways. Rate wars were uncommon because all members of any given pool could be sure of a full share of the pool's total earnings and could thus resist pressure from shippers for special or secret advantages.

But the Act of 1887 changed all this; many different ways were found to give an advantage to a large shipper even without resorting to secret rate-cutting. A powerful customer, for example, could demand commissions or could insist on using his own cars, for which the railways had to pay rentals. By devices of this sort, established rates could be nominally maintained. Furthermore, various railways, feeling that secret concessions had been made by others, would cut rates openly in order to get their share of the traffic, thus precipitating a genuine rate war. Then, as Perkins put it, the railway agents would get together and after much argument re-establish the old rates and "all agree to be honest. . . . This would last for a little time, and then, as men are weak, somebody would fall, and the business of certain of the large shippers would begin to go over some one road. Then the whole thing would be done over again . . . and everyone would go round again in the old circle. . . . You should not make laws which put a premium on weakness and dishonesty. Is the honest railroad owner to lose all his traffic by conforming to the law, while the weak or dishonest ones make money by violating it in the spirit, if not in the letter, by giving secret advantages through evasions of the

[2] CB&Q, AR 1890, pp. 20–1.

law?"[3] The upshot, as Perkins saw it, was that certain large shippers had all the advantages and were making money while the small shippers and the railway stockholders suffered.

If pooling could not be restored legally, Perkins favored establishment of associations to maintain reasonable rates: "Without some method of effective cooperation, competing lines must become bankrupt, and in the end consolidated."[4] Throughout the early part of 1888, discussions were held among the railways along these lines, and in January 1889, J. Pierpont Morgan summoned virtually all the western railway presidents to New York in an effort to work out a viable agreement. Twenty-two lines, including the C. B. & Q. and the C. B. & N., were represented, and after vigorous discussion the Interstate Commerce Railway Association was established to enforce the provisions of the Act of 1887 and to establish public, reasonable, uniform, and stable rates in conformity with the law. But the new dispensation was short-lived. Within a year some of the leading members withdrew, and an attempt to form a more effective association failed in 1890. Once again, early in 1891, a new organization called the Western Traffic Association was formed, but the commissioners entrusted to administer it acted in such arbitrary fashion that by mid-1892, not only the C. B. & Q., but also the Missouri Pacific, the Wabash, and the Southern Pacific gave notice of withdrawal. Thereupon the Western Traffic Association virtually passed out of existence, and with it vanished the most ambitious attempt at self-regulation without benefit of pooling. From then on it was very much a case of the survival of the fittest, a situation that led to the bankruptcy of many railroads when panic burst on the nation a year later.

On April 17, 1889, Richard Olney of Boston became a director of the C. B. & Q. in place of Sidney Bartlett and was concurrently appointed counsel for the Burlington at a salary of $10,000 a year. For years Perkins and other members of the directory had sought the advice of this brilliant, shrewd lawyer. Once he became a member of the family, so to speak, he not only supplied interpretations of the Interstate Commerce Act, brought attention to amendments which should be supported or defeated, and mapped out lines of attack in order to test both that law and the state laws, but also drafted bills, lobbied in both Boston and Washington, and in a few instances argued cases in the courts and before the Interstate Commerce Commission.

Early in 1889, even before Olney's appointment as counsel, he advised Perkins that "the best mode of testing the constitutionality of the Act would be for a railroad company to violate some of its rules" and to continue such violation until the case could be carried by appeal to the

---

[3] Perkins, Memorandum, January 7, 1895, PLB, Vol. XIII, pp. 66–76.
[4] CB&Q, AR 1890, p. 18.

Supreme Court.[5] But that was not Perkins's way of doing things. Much as he detested the law, he was convinced that as long as it remained in force, it had to be obeyed. Perkins thought it would be better to press for amendments of the Act or to have practical businessmen appointed to the Commission. And he also suggested on at least two occasions that Olney try to convert the I. C. C. into a special court, thus depriving it of its non-judicial functions over such matters as rates. Olney actually drafted a bill to accomplish this purpose, but it failed to pass Congress. It is worth noting, however, that in 1910 a special Commerce Court was established to carry out the very purposes Perkins had had in mind years before.

The most famous exchange of ideas between Perkins and Olney took place at the end of 1892. In a letter dated December 22, Perkins suggested that everything possible be done to get the public to see how useless the Commission was. In his estimation, indeed, it was "of no earthly account to anybody; and as it cost a good deal of money, it ought to be abolished."[6] To this Olney replied: "The Commission, as its functions have now been limited by the Courts, is, or can be made of great use to the railroads. It satisfies the popular clamor for a government supervision of railroads, at the same time that that supervision is almost entirely nominal. Further, the older such a commission gets to be, the more inclined it will be found to take the business and railroad view of things. It thus becomes a sort of barrier between the railroad corporations and the people and a sort of protection against hasty and crude legislation hostile to railroad interests. The Commission costs something, of course. But so long as its powers are advisory merely, for the reasons just stated, it strikes me it is well worth the money. The part of wisdom is not to destroy the Commission, but to utilize it. . . ."[7]

This well-known letter has been cited frequently over the years, often irrelevantly and misleadingly. Far less well known is Perkins's reply of January 2, 1893: "My idea," he wrote, "is that the Commission, if it is not abolished, is certain to be given more power; and the power in the hands of the Commission, whether it can be constitutionally exercised or not, is exceedingly troublesome if not dangerous. . . ." To clinch his argument, Perkins pointed out that the Commission established in the State of Iowa, so far from having a business point of view as it grew older, or from serving as a barrier between the popular clamor and the railroads, had taken more and more of the Granger view of things "and has become an added weapon in the hands of the confiscators instead of a barrier of protection

---

[5] Richard Olney to Perkins, January 28, 1889, CB&Q/Sec.

[6] Perkins to Olney, December 22, 1892, Olney Papers quoted in Gerald Eggert: "Richard Olney, Corporation Lawyer and Attorney General of the United States, 1835–1895" (MS. thesis, University of Michigan, Ann Arbor; 1960), Ch. iii, p. 22.

[7] Olney to Perkins, December 28, 1892, quoted in Eggert: op. cit., Ch. iii, p. 23.

to railroad property. I think," he concluded, that "any Commission appointed for the country at large will drift the same way; certainly that has been its tendency so far."[8]

As a matter of fact, the Burlington, along with other western railways, made its most successful defense against regulation in the arena of state legislation. In 1888, the Iowa Legislature empowered its State Railway Commission to fix rates for all roads doing business within its jurisdiction. The railways of Iowa promptly secured a temporary injunction from Federal Judge David J. Brewer on the grounds that if the proposed schedule were put into effect, the companies could not earn their operating expenses and fixed charges, much less a profit. While the temporary injunction was in effect, and on the advice of Olney, Perkins decided to negotiate with the Iowa Commission for a modified tariff. He was moderately successful in that he obtained a new schedule that allowed the rails a small profit. As a result, Judge Brewer in February 1889 refused to make permanent his injunction against the Act of 1888. The Iowa Legislature then compounded difficulties in 1890 by passing a joint-rate law that allowed the State Commission to fix the rates of all shipments that passed over two or more roads.

Thereupon the C. B. & Q. decided to test the Iowa joint-rate law. The case never reached the Supreme Court, however, probably because of that court's decision in *Chicago, Milwaukee & St. Paul Railway Company v. Minnesota,* in which a Minnesota state law similar to that in Iowa was held unconstitutional because the rates prescribed constituted a deprivation of property without due process of law. This doctrine of judicial review, as it came to be called, was to prove the strongest bastion of defense the railways had against regulation. Indeed the Burlington, with the eventual support of several other railways, evoked one of the most celebrated expressions of this doctrine.

Early in 1893, the Nebraska Legislature passed the so-called Newberry Law establishing maximum rates on all freight transported in the state. It was designed to go into effect on August 1. Perkins, in June, promptly expressed himself in a memorandum. "No legislative body or government commission ever did or ever could make a freight tariff," he thundered, "because a freight tariff is of necessity the result of experience in the market. All that any legislative body or any government commission has ever done about freight rates has been to take a tariff which has been formed to fit the business conditions, and cut down the rate. This," he exploded, "is not reason, but temper."[9]

It was estimated that the Act, if put into effect, would cost the Burlington $1,000,000 each year. Perkins did not content himself with mere

[8] Perkins to Olney, January 2, 1893, Eggert: op. cit., Ch. iii, p. 24.
[9] Perkins, Memorandum, June 28, 1893, PVB, Vol. XXIV, pp. 403–9.

words. As the result of a series of conferences in Lincoln, it was determined to have the bondholders and stockholders bring a suit against the company and against the Nebraska Board of Transportation to enjoin the latter from putting the new schedule into effect. Perkins then went to Chicago, where he persuaded the Chicago and North Western and the Union Pacific to join in the contemplated legal action. Their combined efforts were successful; on July 29, Judge Dundy, on behalf of the three railways, issued a temporary order restraining the State of Nebraska from putting the law into effect.

In June 1894, Justice David J. Brewer of the United States Circuit Court reached the conclusion that the Newberry Law "deprives these property owners of all chances to make profit, which result from private control of business, and compels them to pay out of their pockets all the losses which result in the enforcement of an absolute system [of rates]."[1] Reluctant as he said he was to interfere with the deliberate judgment of the Nebraska Legislature, he felt constrained to enjoin permanently the enforcement of the Act. Decrees to that effect were entered on November 15, 1894.

As every student of constitutional law knows, the State of Nebraska appealed the decision in these three cases: the suit brought by the Union Pacific became *Smyth v. Ames*; that of the North Western, *Smyth v. Smith*; and that of the Burlington, *Smyth v. Higginson*. The three cases were argued together by J. M. Woolworth of the Burlington; counsel for the State of Nebraska was no less a person than William Jennings Bryan. Arguments before the United States Supreme Court took place in April 1897, and on March 7, 1898, the principles at stake were decided in the landmark case of *Smyth v. Ames.*

The decision was a sweeping victory for the railways. The Supreme Court held that the basis of all calculations as to the reasonableness of rates had to be the fair value of the property used for the convenience of the public. The court then attempted to ascertain what elements should be considered in arriving at fair value. The criteria set up were vague indeed, and have caused confusion and litigation ever since. From the standpoint of the Burlington, however, the important result was that the Newberry Law was permanently set aside, and a promising new avenue of defense against regulation appeared in the form of judicial review.

Perkins was jubilant. "It seems to me," he wrote, "the court has made a distinct advance in the right direction, and that the doctrine of the Munn case is now definitely abandoned."[2] It will be recalled that in *Munn v. Illinois*, the Supreme Court had permitted state legislatures to fix rates and had pointed out that the only recourse was at the polls. It now ap-

[1] U. S. District Court, District of Nebraska, "Nebraska Maximum Rate Cases," Opinion of Mr. Justice Brewer, November 1894, pp. 33–43.
[2] Perkins to J. C. Carter, March 28, 1898, PLB, Vol. XV, p. 460.

peared, as a result of *Smyth v. Ames*, that the question of reasonableness was to be reserved for judicial determination.

Yet the sense of relief on the part of the railways was somewhat offset by another finding of the Supreme Court, handed down while the rate case was being litigated. In a further attempt to stabilize western rates, eighteen railways had, prior to 1892, formed the Trans-Missouri Freight Association. By a five-to-four decision in 1897, the court held that the Association violated the Sherman Anti-trust Act and therefore was illegal. A week later, Perkins wrote to Senator Allison suggesting that the Sherman Anti-trust Law should be amended so as to prohibit only those contracts which were "in unreasonable restraint of trade. . . . It would seem as if nobody could object to that."[3] Here, interestingly enough, was a plea for the very "rule of reason" that the Supreme Court itself was to adopt a little more than a decade later.

To trace in detail the reactions of the C. B. & Q. to all the regulatory laws of the 1880's and 1890's is far beyond the scope of this book. Perhaps enough has been said to indicate that the Burlington was in the forefront in defending railways in particular and business in general against what appeared to be the most unreasonable aspects of regulation. Eventually, of course, (in 1906) the Interstate Commerce Commission itself gained effective power to prescribe maximum rates. But that is part of another story; for the remainder of Perkins's administration the railways held their ground, on both the state and national level, against further restrictive regulation.

• THE COURSE OF BUSINESS •

DURING THE EIGHT YEARS following the strike of 1888, net income for the C. B. & Q. was only about sixty percent of what it had been during the seven prosperous years 1881–87 inclusive. The several reasons were fully recognized at the time: for one thing, the prosperity of the C. B. & Q. during those earlier years had prompted others to build railways into its territory, with the result that, despite growth of population and traffic, the C. B. & Q. now had a smaller amount of business than before. A second factor that reduced income was the dullness in trade that followed the failure of Baring Brothers in 1890, and more particularly the national depression that followed the panic of 1893. Third, the impact of regulation, and particularly the prohibition of pooling and the consequent demoralization of rates, inevitably reduced net income. Other factors also were operative. Whereas fixed charges during 1881–87 ranged from three and a half to four and a half million dollars a year, they moved upward from slightly over five million in 1888 to beyond six and a half million in the middle of 1900. At the same time, tax accruals virtually doubled. The

---

[3] Perkins to W. B. Allison, April 4, 1897, PLB, Vol. XIV, pp. 457-9.

increase in both funded debt and taxes, of course, reflected expansion of the property, but the net effect, at least until the heartening recovery of business in 1897, was to depress net income throughout the period 1889–1896.

During the difficult years no one was more aware of the necessity for economy than Perkins. Early in 1889 he told Stone to cut down the hours of work in company shops and wrote to Holdrege: "It is quite evident that we have got to get down into the details of expenses and cut off everything possible, little and big; we can't begin too soon."[4] But he refused to be pessimistic about long-run prospects. "One swallow doesn't make a summer," he observed to Forbes in 1889,[5] and to the Boston financier, Henry L. Higginson, he was even more outspoken: "It seems to me somewhat singular that, after the C. B. & Q. has paid to its owners such very liberal returns for the last 25 years, there should be so much kicking because of one or two bad years now. . . . Of course it is unpleasant to lose money, but I should think any sane individual with investments in railroad stocks would realize that he might reasonably expect at least one bad year in ten or fifteen."[6] He insisted that the country as a whole was prosperous and that a better attitude on the part of the public toward the railroads minimized the chances of more adverse legislation.

As a matter of fact, hard times persisted for several years. Once the panic of 1893 broke upon the country, Perkins viewed the situation as critical. There was cause for alarm; both the mighty Union Pacific and the fast-growing Santa Fe plunged into receivership, and as the C. B. & Q. was of course exposed to the same external conditions, rumors spread in speculative circles that it soon would follow its neighbors into the hands of the courts. Yet, despite wretched corn crops during 1893–95, the Burlington managed not only to pay its fixed charges but also to keep up its sinking funds and dividends. Indeed, from 1889 to 1896 inclusive, after the payment of all expenses and dividends, the company accumulated a surplus of $10,400,000. Small wonder that Perkins refused to agree that the poor years were a measure of the future.

His forecast was correct. As he wrote Forbes in the summer of 1897, "it begins to look, I think, as if we may be on a rising tide in commercial affairs in this country." Good crops, a favorable tariff, the stimulus of the Klondike gold rush, and various other factors finally appeared "to have inspired confidence which it is to be hoped may continue. We have had a pretty long period of depression."[7] The closing years of the nineteenth century indeed brought a new prosperity that affected the entire property.

[4] Perkins to George W. Holdrege, March 27, 1889, PLB, Vol. IX, p. 20.
[5] Perkins to Forbes, March 25, 1889, PLB, Vol. IX, p. 12.
[6] Perkins to Higginson, March 26, 1889, PLB, Vol. IX, pp. 16–17.
[7] Perkins to Forbes, August 23, 1897, PLB, Vol. XV, pp. 196–7.

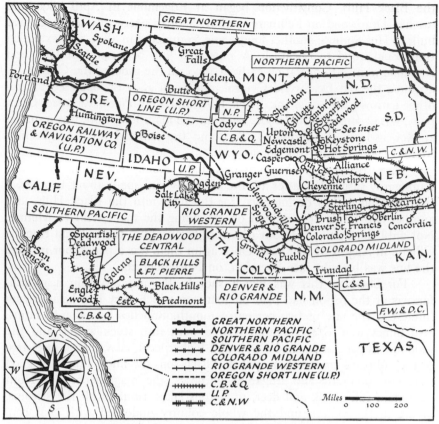

The Burlington and the Far West, 1901

• EXPANSION AND GRAND STRATEGY •

INEVITABLY the ups and downs of business and prospects for further government regulation had a great deal to do in determining to what extent
the company would expand. Even in 1889, with prospects not very good,
Perkins told the stockholders that the directors had felt justified in "making moderate expenditures and borrowing money for the purpose where
it was clear that the permanent interests of the property required it and
that it could not safely be postponed."[8] For example, it was decided on
June 13, 1889, to extend the main stem from Alliance northwest across
South Dakota and into Wyoming; among other incentives, excellent coal
was available in the region. Work progressed rapidly; the road reached
Edgemont on October 19, and Newcastle a month later. A seven-mile
branch to Cambria and the coal mines was opened December 1.

Meanwhile, the C. B. & Q. decided to tap the mineral resources of

[8] CB&Q, AR 1889, pp. 17–18.

the Black Hills. Construction began at Edgemont in April 1890 and reached Deadwood on February 1, 1891. Shortly afterwards, a branch was built to Hot Springs; another longer one, completed in 1893, was extended from Englewood to Spearfish. A nine-mile link between Hill City and Keystone went into operation early in 1900. In the process, the C. B. & Q. acquired the old Deadwood Central, and from 1893 on operated it. Another narrow-gauge line, the Black Hills and Fort Pierre Railroad Company, was absorbed in mid-1901. Back on the main line, work was resumed at Newcastle in the spring of 1890, and the railhead was brought into Merino (now Upton) on August 5.

Then, because of the extremely tight money situation, work was temporarily suspended; after all, the company had spent about two and a third million dollars during 1890 for the lines into the Black Hills, and another two thirds of a million on extending the main stem to Merino. Not until the summer of 1891 did work begin again; the railhead reached Gillette in August of that year. Once again there was a pause, but in 1892 the line was brought into Sheridan, on November 26.

For Sheridan this was like a shot in the arm. Within a month, farmers of the region had paid off loans on which they had been paying interest at the rate of two percent a month. Ranches turned into farms, coal mines were opened, more people went into stock-raising, and the economy in general reached a new and higher level. As Gillette, in charge of the railroad's construction, put it: "Rich soil, the finest supply of good water for domestic and irrigation purposes, the magnificent Big Horn Mountain full of elk and deer, numerous lakes, trout in all the streams, grouse in the valleys, and the whole country underlaid with coal convinced many in the party that this at last was what they had been looking forward to in making their permanent homes. The greatest attractions, however, were the young ladies with whom we became acquainted, and later fully half of the party returned to Sheridan, married, and made this town their permanent abiding place."[9]

For those who had been locating and building the railroad in this far-off area, Sheridan must indeed have seemed like civilization itself. The Black Hills survey party, for example, had worked when temperatures were so low that the men's hands froze on their instruments; thereafter they prudently worked only when the thermometer was above twenty degrees below zero! As there was still some chance of raids by the Sioux, the men had been supplied with rifles. As they had made their way beyond Alliance, they found several ranches deserted for fear of the Indians. But when word spread that the survey party had come, a good many settlers drifted back home; the guns stacked around the center poles in the railway tents proved to have a salutary effect.

[9] Edward Gillette: *Locating the Iron Trail* (Boston: The Christopher Publishing House; 1925), p. 78.

Perkins, of course, had no notion of letting the main-line railhead rest at Sheridan. In January 1893, he told Forbes that the road could be extended to a junction with the Northern Pacific for a mere $2,000,000, thus opening the shortest through route between the areas south and west of Chicago and the Pacific Northwest. If, he added, the Northern Pacific should be unwilling to exchange business, the C. B. & Q. could simply continue building northwest into the rich mining districts of Montana. But in May the Northern Pacific said it would be very glad to open a gateway at Billings. The Burlington resumed construction beyond Sheridan the following month.

Shortly thereafter, however, the panic of 1893 burst upon the nation, and once again the railhead paused. Not until April 10, 1894, did the board authorize further building, but construction then moved forward rapidly. The railhead reached the Montana boundary on August 1, and the 102 miles to a connection with the Northern Pacific at Huntley were completed on October 28, 1894. From Huntley the C. B. & Q. obtained trackage rights over the Northern Pacific into Billings, some thirteen miles farther west.

Once the physical connection was made, traffic immediately began to flow through the new gateway, in accord with a contract signed in Chicago the previous April. Among other things, the contract provided that all Burlington territory east of Billings should be open to Northern Pacific eastbound traffic of every kind and that the entire Northern Pacific territory west of Billings should be open to westbound Burlington traffic. In special consideration for the large market thrown open for lumber originating on the Northern Pacific, that road agreed to turn over to the Burlington all traffic of any kind destined west of the Missouri River to points on or south of a line drawn through Omaha and Burlington. All through passenger and freight rates were to be divided on a pro-rata, per mile basis west of the Missouri River, with a minimum of twenty-five percent to the line with the shorter haul. Finally, the Northern Pacific agreed to handle through passengers or sleeping cars between Billings and either Helena or Butte.

From the standpoint of the Burlington, this was an exceedingly favorable agreement. The surveys conducted by McClure in Colorado prior to 1888 made clear that the Burlington had long been thinking seriously of extending toward the West Coast. The fact that further surveys had been made from Guernsey, Wyoming, to Ogden and Salt Lake in 1886, 1887, and again in 1889 underscored this fact. Even more pertinent was the series of surveys the C. B. & Q. made during the early 90's to such points as Helena, Montana, and The Dalles in Oregon.

In this context, then, the Northern Pacific made the favorable arrangement with the C. B. & Q. in April 1894. As the 1890's wore on, traffic exchanged through the Billings Gateway increased steadily. Even so, the

C. B. & Q. for some years thereafter continued to think and plan in terms of an alternate outlet over its own rails to the Pacific Northwest. As Perkins put it to Forbes as early as May 1895: "With our Montana line in operation to Billings, we are in so strong a position for offense that I feel quite comfortable about it."[1]

One basis for this feeling was the status of the Union Pacific. During the summer of 1893, the securities of that road had fallen sharply in the market, and in August Perkins suggested to James J. Hill, president of the Great Northern, that it might be well to make up a party to buy a size-able block with the idea of putting the property on a paying basis as a strictly neutral road that would treat all its connections with absolute equality and impartiality. After consultation with Forbes, Perkins broached the idea to President Roberts of the Pennsylvania and, when the Union Pacific finally went into receivership in the fall, reiterated his thought that no matter how the property might be reorganized, it should be required to adopt a neutral attitude. Much to his dismay, no such requirement was ever made.

As far as expansion was concerned, however, the bankruptcy of the Union Pacific immediately raised the possibility that it might have to relinquish its interests in either the Oregon Short Line (from Granger, Wyoming, to Huntington, Oregon) or the Oregon Railway and Naviga-tion Company (Huntington to Portland, Oregon), or both. Over the next four years the C. B. & Q. exhibited a lively interest in these properties. The most frequent suggestion was to extend the Burlington from Chey-enne to Granger to make a direct connection with the Oregon Short Line. But some thought also was given to building from Sheridan to Hunting-ton. Meanwhile, beginning in the latter part of 1894, Perkins and Forbes, together with some of their Boston associates, bought a substantial in-terest in the Oregon Railway and Navigation Company. In the fall of 1895, Perkins suggested that Hill join this Boston group in order to bring about joint control of the O. R. & N. by the Burlington and the Great Northern. After considerable deliberation, Hill turned down the propo-sition, whereupon Perkins and Forbes did their best to persuade the C. B. & Q. directors to acquire the Oregon Short Line, which, by then, had itself obtained control of the O. R. & N. But the C. B. & Q. board declined to take the risk. As it turned out, a group of New Yorkers subse-quently bought the property and eventually turned it over to the Union Pacific. Years later, Hill told Perkins how much he regretted not having seized joint control of these Oregon lines; Harriman never could under-stand why the Burlington let the opportunity slip by. But it did, and the project remained in the category of "might-have-beens."

In view of the caution displayed by the C. B. & Q. board in respect

---

[1] Perkins to Forbes, May 24, 1895, GM, 1893–5, p. 161.

to the Oregon Lines, it was somewhat surprising when the very same board, on November 20, 1895, resolved that an attempt should be made to acquire control of the Northern Pacific itself, which was then in receivership. Forbes, somewhat skeptical of the proposition, shrewdly remarked that if the C. B. & Q. was to make any such move, it would be necessary to kill Jim Hill first. And when Perkins, on a hunting expedition in Kansas at the time, heard of the proposal, he reported that it took his breath away. His reaction was that the enormous debt of the Northern Pacific made the plan impractical; he thought that it would be more to the interest of the C. B. & Q. if Hill acquired the Northern Pacific. "So far as the C. B. & Q. is concerned," he wrote, "I do not think it has very much interest in the matter, because whoever controls the Northern Pacific will, I believe, always find it to the advantage of that property to have an outlet down into our country west of the Mississippi River, and more especially west of the Missouri River, from its lumber and mining country. I have always felt that if Mr. Hill acquired the Northern Pacific, he would take that view of it, as a broad-minded and long-headed businessman."[2] As later events proved, this prophecy was not only shrewd but accurate.

In retrospect, it seems clear enough that although the C. B. & Q. continued to consider alternate outlets to the Northwest, the opening of the Billings Gateway accomplished so many objectives sought by the Burlington that no other plan in respect to that area could secure the support of the directors. From the standpoint of the Northern Pacific, the traffic agreement of 1894 had saved the day.

While these developments were taking place in the Northwest, the Burlington was busy rounding out its network in the opposite corner of the system, and even casting its eyes beyond. Ever since the summer of 1879, one of the C. B. & Q.'s Proprietary Lines, the St. Louis, Keokuk and North Western, had provided access to St. Louis by using trackage rights over the Wabash south of St. Peters. Under that arrangement, however, the Burlington was somewhat at the mercy of the Wabash, upon which it had to depend for terminal facilities. Consequently, as early as June 1887, the C. B. & Q. began buying property in St. Louis and making plans for an independent line into the city. In the spring of 1889 these activities became public when the company started construction of a freight house and station at Franklin Avenue. These facilities and an office building were completed early in 1892. Concurrently the company acquired fifteen acres near Mound Street for a freight yard, and in one corner of it built a passenger station and train shed for use until the Union Depot, then under construction, should be completed. Farther north, the Burlington acquired an additional 500 acres between Hall Street and the

---

[2] Perkins to G. M. Lane, August 30, 1895, PLB, Vol. XIII, pp. 312–13.

river. On this land it built enough track for 3,000 cars and still had plenty of space for future expansion.

Construction on the forty-eight-mile access line to St. Louis began at Cuivre Junction (about ten miles north of St. Peters) in April 1892 and was completed twenty-four miles south to a junction with the Missouri–Kansas–Texas on July 21, 1893. From that point on, a double-track line was built another twenty-four miles into the city; this portion was completed on March 4, 1894. The most notable structure on the new line was the Bellefontaine Bridge across the Missouri River.

At West Alton, between Texas Junction and the Bellefontaine Bridge, the Burlington connected with a short railway which owned and operated its own bridge into Alton. When this bridge was opened to traffic on May 1, 1894, the C. B. & Q. immediately inaugurated fast and frequent suburban service between Alton and its temporary Mound Street Station in St. Louis. As soon as the new Union Depot in St. Louis was opened, early in September 1894, the Burlington began to use it for through trains, and a few months later, after certain track connections had been completed, suburban trains also ran into the Union Station; the Mound Street passenger depot was then closed.

Although the prime aim was to establish for the Burlington a firm foothold for traffic flowing in and out of St. Louis, that was by no means the only objective. As early as 1889, Howard Elliott had been commissioned by Perkins to make a careful investigation of the Yazoo Valley Railroad as a possible first link in an extension south toward New Orleans. Later, in 1893, both Elliott and Perkins made a detailed, first-hand inspection of the Missouri–Kansas–Texas from Galveston all the way to Kansas City and St. Louis. As it turned out, however, the only other substantial acquisition in the general area was the Keokuk and Western, purchased in 1899. This 255-mile line reached west and north from Keokuk, forming a natural link between St. Louis and the Humeston and Shenandoah, and providing also an entrance into Des Moines from the southwest by way of Osceola.

What actually happened in the "southeast corner," then, was not so much extensive expansion as internal perfection of an existing network, and improvement of terminal and gateway facilities. Once this had been accomplished, the company seemed more concerned with using what it had than with extending new lines beyond its self-imposed perimeter.

The same attitude prevailed in the "northwest corner." Business flowing through Billings grew steadily. One result was the establishment in March 1899 of through sleepers between St. Louis and Butte and between Kansas City and Seattle; a year later, a solid through train began operating daily between St. Louis, Kansas City, and Puget Sound; it was known as the *Burlington-Northern Pacific Express*. A second result was the decision to link Alliance with Denver. Construction began in June

1899 toward Sterling, Colorado, where arrangements were made to use the tracks of the Union Pacific for twenty-three miles to Union, Colorado. From that point on, a new C. B. & Q. link was built to Brush on the main line between Omaha and Denver. The entire 150-mile line was open for business on September 16, 1900, bringing Denver closer to Helena, Butte, and Spokane than by any other route. A third development in the area was construction of the 131-mile branch from Toluca, Montana, to Cody, Wyoming. Work on it began in the spring of 1900 and was completed on November 11, 1901; the branch gave the company access not only to Yellowstone Park but also, of more importance, to the productive Big Horn Basin.

While the Alliance–Denver route was being run through Northport, Nebraska, south to Brush, an extension built westward from Northport reached Guernsey, Wyoming, on June 11, 1900, thus opening up the North Platte Valley and tapping a rich mining area. As one might have suspected, there was more in this project than met the eye. In December 1900, Holdrege advised Perkins that surveys between Guernsey and Salt Lake were nearly complete. If this 461-mile major line were built, and if the company then would construct the relatively short link between Kearney and Northport, a through route between Omaha and Salt Lake could be provided which would be only 975 miles long, seventy-six miles shorter than the existing Union Pacific main line. Not only that—an extension from Guernsey would provide an excellent springboard for a line into central Oregon, whence it would be possible to build down the Pitt River to San Francisco, and northwest to Portland. Implementation of this proposal would take the place of building through the rugged Colorado mountains and would obviate the risk of antagonizing the Rio Grande. Holdrege urged that the Guernsey–Salt Lake segment be got underway at once; at the same time, he, for one, vigorously recommended that the long-considered Billings–Great Falls extension be built forthwith. He calculated that this 203-mile road would cost approximately $4,500,000.

These were by no means the only proposals that the expansion-minded Holdrege sent to Perkins's desk; if Holdrege had had his way, the C. B. & Q. would have acquired the Colorado and Southern then and there. Early in 1899, that corporation had been formed by linking together, after receivership, the main segments of the former Union Pacific, Denver and Gulf. Its lines stretched from Orin Junction in central Wyoming southward through Cheyenne, Denver, Pueblo, and Trinidad and on to the New Mexico–Texas border, where they connected with the Fort Worth and Denver City, whose rails extended to Fort Worth and there connected with various lines to the Gulf. The Colorado and Southern controlled the Fort Worth and Denver City through stock ownership.

The arguments for C. B. & Q. acquisition of the property that both Harris and Holdrege urged upon Perkins were impressive indeed. During

September 1899, Perkins gave them careful consideration and forwarded Holdrege's memoranda to the directors in Boston. Apparently they were returned without comment to Perkins and there, as far as the record goes, the matter rested for the moment.

But not for long. Early in 1900 the C. & S. bounced back into the spotlight, this time playing quite a different role.

In March of that year the C. & S. resolved to join the Rio Grande Western (running from Grand Junction, Colorado, to Salt Lake, and not to be confused with the Denver & Rio Grande, which linked Denver and Grand Junction) in purchasing joint control of the Colorado Midland, which owned a 222-mile line from Colorado Springs to New Castle, Colorado, with trackage rights into Grand Junction. This meant that the C. & S. and the R. G. W. between them would control a through route that could compete with the Denver & Rio Grande between Grand Junction and Salt Lake for transcontinental business; the situation was brought sharply to Perkins's attention when, some time in May or June 1900, General W. J. Palmer, who controlled the Rio Grande Western, offered to sell his property to the C. B. & Q.

Perkins's immediate reaction was that if the C. B. & Q. accepted this proposition, it was almost certain that the Denver and Rio Grande, to protect itself, would build its own road from Grand Junction to Salt Lake or Ogden. Therefore, he reasoned, if the C. B. & Q. bought *either* the C. & S.–Colorado Midland–Rio Grande Western combination *or* the Denver and Rio Grande, together with the extension it was certain to have built, inevitably some other major system such as the Rock Island or the Missouri Pacific would buy whatever combination the C. B. & Q. did not, thus touching off intense competition. Second, if the C. B. & Q. bought *all* these mountain roads, then one of its eastern competitors might well build an entirely new line between Denver and Salt Lake. Third, however, if the C. B. & Q. did nothing at all it might permit, as he put it, "our neighbors to step in, a little later, and do what we are in a better position than anyone else to do now."

These three possibilities, all attended with great risk and expense, prompted Perkins to urge a fourth possibility: that all existing mountain roads west of Denver be combined "so as to make one railroad, occupying that country, to be an independent and neutral concern, holding the mountain region between the Union Pacific on the north and the Atchison, Topeka & Santa Fe on the south. Such a combination," he emphasized, "if really independent, and so operated as to fairly divide business among the railroads east of Denver, could probably hold that region indefinitely." To help bring this about, Perkins thought the C. B. & Q. might share in underwriting the securities of any such consolidated company; even though the Burlington would then be only a minority owner, he felt that its influence would be sufficient to prevent any other eastern competitor from gaining absolute control.

In view of the development of the Denver and Rio Grande Western during the last generation, the logic of this plan needs no elaboration here, and it is intriguing to speculate on what might have happened had Perkins's proposal been put into effect when he made it. As it was, he laid the scheme before Palmer in July but, in describing that occasion, simply noted cryptically, "and so it was left."[2]

In retrospect, the striking feature of all construction during 1888 to 1901 was that, despite the many grandiose schemes considered, the Burlington limited itself to filling out the territory it had already earmarked as its own (by building to Billings, for example, or gaining its entry into St. Louis), to providing internal shortcuts (such as the Alliance–Brush line), or to adding short branches (as in the Black Hills).

Yet the strategic planning and occasional threats to build had served their purposes. They kept the system's gateways open and, in effect, saved the Burlington from the enormous expense and risk any major extension would have involved. In particular, so long as the Northern Pacific kept the Billings interchange freely open, and so long as the Denver and Rio Grande remained neutral, there was indeed little reason for leaping toward the Northwest or California. Internal strength, firm control of the heartland, and solvency were evidently still prized more highly than spectacular, risky expansion. And at least over the two years beginning in the midsummer of 1899, one new factor may have operated as a restraining influence on large-scale expansion: the strategically strong and financially solid Burlington could conceivably prove to be an invaluable adjunct to one of its neighboring systems. Unless and until the possibility of a formal alliance should be translated into reality, ordinary prudence suggested maintenance of the status quo.

• PLANT, EQUIPMENT, OPERATIONS, AND LABOR RELATIONS •

As MIGHT HAVE BEEN EXPECTED from the course of business, improvements to plant and rolling stock were held to a minimum during the difficult years 1889–96. For example, although the company tentatively agreed in 1889 to share the cost of an elaborate new joint terminal with the Union Pacific at Omaha, it later decided to construct an independent station, which finally was built in 1897.

One major undertaking was the construction of a new locomotive shop at Havelock, a point just outside Lincoln. The necessary facilities were built during 1890–91 and since that day have played an important

[2] Perkins, Memorandum, "The Colorado Railroad Situation," July 25, 1900, C–O, Set M–1, pp. 65–9.

role in company affairs. Another improvement was authorized when business showed a light upturn in 1892: the board authorized spending $50,000 to build sheep yards at Montgomery, near Aurora. In 1899, a similar facility was installed near Lincoln to serve Lines West. The bridge at Burlington, a serious bottleneck, was double-tracked in 1891, and during the next two years substantial sums were spent for new ballast. With better times on hand in 1897, a new station was authorized for Quincy, and the C. B. & Q. participated in elevating the St. Charles Air Line into metropolitan Chicago.

The company pursued an extremely conservative policy in purchasing motive power and cars; new acquisitions fell considerably behind the national average, and showed no marked increase until 1899. No additions to equipment whatever were made in 1895, and virtually none in the eighteen months ending in mid-1898. There were, however, some rather notable changes in the types of motive power. In 1888, the first of the 2-6-0 locomotives known as Moguls saw service on the system. Many of these were built in the company shops, and as they were extremely successful in both freight and passenger service, they soon became the standard main-line engines for all except lighter trains. The fact that the C. B. & Q. was located in fairly level country with light curvature permitted the two-wheel leading trucks to operate satisfactorily even on high-speed runs.

Perhaps the most unusual locomotive of the period was the famous No. 590, a Columbia 2-4-2 type. Designed as a high-speed engine, it had drivers 84½ inches in diameter and an unusually wide firebox carried on trailers. Because of a tendency to sway, the new locomotive was not satisfactory, but it did lead to the development and adoption of the 4-4-2 Atlantic type, which made its first appearance on the Burlington in 1899. Far more stable than the Columbia, and with drivers just as large, the Atlantics established excellent records and became known locally as the "Greyhounds" of the system. Meanwhile, in 1891, the first of many ten-wheelers (4-6-0's) made their appearance west of the Missouri River and became as popular there as the Moguls were in the East. Finally, in 1900, a new type built for freight service, the Prairie (2-6-2), made its national debut on the C. B. & Q. These engines were particularly suited to the long level stretches of the Burlington, and in time many of them were built.

Regardless of business conditions, one improvement could not be postponed. This was the installation of automatic couplers and air brakes. Even in 1890, for example, the board authorized spending $400,000 for this purpose, and in 1895, when nothing else was spent on new equipment, more than $62,000 went for brakes and couplings.

Not until the end of the century were plant improvements resumed on a large scale. During the year ending June 30, 1899, for example, the company spent more than $315,000 on elevating the four main-line tracks for two and three-quarters miles west of Western Avenue in Chicago, approximately the same amount for reducing grades in Iowa and adding second track, and about half as much for the same purpose in Illinois. Additional elevator grounds in Chicago required over $200,000; new buildings and waterworks in Nebraska accounted for $110,000 more. During the next fiscal year, the C. B. & Q. built its first tie-treating plant at Edgemont, South Dakota, and in 1900–01 spent over $2,500,000 on reducing grades in Iowa and constructing additional second track.

That even the economies put into effect during the lean years of the 1890's had in no way affected Burlington's ability to produce safe and rapid transportation was spectacularly proved by a spur-of-the-moment run from Chicago to Denver early in 1897. At eight o'clock on the morning of February 15, Henry J. Mayham, a wealthy New Yorker, telegraphed that he would arrive in Chicago from the East at 9:15 a.m. and wanted a special train to take him to Denver to the bedside of his dying son. Because time was so short, Superintendent Besler simply hooked his business car to an old 4-4-0 engine that had just arrived with a surburban train from Aurora. This was the special that left Union Depot at ten o'clock in a heavy snow storm. Thanks to nine different engines—eight of them 4-4-0's, the ninth a ten-wheeler—Mayham was whisked to Denver, a distance of 1,025 miles, in eighteen hours and fifty-three minutes, an overall average speed of fifty-four miles an hour. Deducting eighty-six minutes of dead time for necessary stops, the average actual running time was 58.74 miles an hour.

Well aware of the publicity value of this accomplishment, the company issued a pamphlet with the headline: "Breaks the World's Record— the Burlington Route Accomplishes the Greatest Feat in the History of Railroading." Even if this claim took in a good bit of territory, the fact that the run was made with ordinary motive power and without the slightest advance planning reflected not only the superb condition of roadway, track and rolling stock, but even more important the ability and discipline of the personnel involved. The *Annual Report* for 1893 had had a great deal to say about economies and the postponement of expenditures, but it had specified that all this should be done "without impairing the safety and efficiency of the service."[3] The run of the Mayham Special gave evidence that these instructions had been followed.

• LABOR RELATIONS •

HAPPILY, labor relations on the Burlington during the 1890's were essentially stable. The strike of 1888 was still a vivid memory, and presumably neither labor nor management wished to risk a repetition of it.

[3] CB&Q, AR 1893, p. 17.

Furthermore, during much of the decade, times were difficult and jobs none too plentiful. Finally, the establishment of the Relief Department may well have provided a measure of security that tended to offset minor differences.

The nearest thing to a major conflict arose early in April 1891, when eleven switchmen were discharged at Omaha, apparently for no other reason than to make room for men regarded as more capable by their superiors. Immediately their fellow switchmen at Omaha struck, and a few days later fifty more walked out in Denver. Sensing immediately how serious the situation could become, Perkins ordered Holdrege to settle the matter promptly. He reminded Holdrege that the company had shown it could fight a strike if necessary; there was no need to prove it again. "What we want is peace and quiet," he said, "and neither the railroad company nor you nor I can afford to have anything like a general strike or boycott. . . . May it not be," he inquired, "that some injustice has been done? . . . You cannot," he added, "let unions dictate, but you can do justice. . . . I care not whether men belong to unions or not; we must treat them fairly and wisely." In particular, Perkins ordered that if the discharged men had been let go simply to make places for others, and not for any dereliction on their part, they should be taken back and given further fair opportunity. "In dealing with large numbers of men," he specified, "we must not only be just, but we must appear to be just. . . . If the first act by the railroad company was a mistake, then I should be inclined to overlook the act of the men who thought so and acted on that belief. The important thing is to settle the point that men shall not be discharged to make room for others, but for cause."[4] Holdrege, thus instructed, complied speedily, and within three days the storm had blown over.

Trouble threatened again in the spring of 1894, when the Great Northern, among others, was faced with sharp labor disagreements. This time the general managers in Chicago stood firm, and even when the hard-fought Pullman strike took place during the same year, the C. B. & Q. escaped with relatively minor damage. Its passenger trains were able to make their regular runs even though freight business was suspended in Chicago for a time. The most serious damage occurred when a mob burned about a hundred and fifty freight cars at various yards in the city; outside of Chicago there was little trouble, save for brief episodes when switchmen struck in Kansas City and St. Louis. By July 19, 1894, the strike was over, and Perkins felt that the C. B. & Q. had had less difficulty than any other Chicago road because of the object lesson of 1888, when the men had found out "how serious it might be for them to give up their places."[5]

[4] Perkins to Holdrege, April 12, 1891, GM, 1879–92, pp. 209–12.
[5] Perkins to John L. Gardner, July 19, 1894, PVB, Vol. XXV, pp. 251–60.

• THE MEN AT THE TOP •

AT THE END OF OCTOBER 1888, Henry Stone had been transferred, with a reduction in pay, to the post of second vice-president. As such, he was the top operating man directly under the president and had ample scope for his talents. But the situation was not a happy one; Perkins felt that Stone failed to keep him adequately informed of what was taking place on the property and that this could probably be remedied by having more men at the top of the C. B. & Q. organization. Consequently he suggested to Stone that he become vice-president of operations, and that E. P. Ripley, then general manager of Lines East, assume the post of vice-president of traffic. Furthermore, since Perkins preferred to make Burlington his headquarters, he thought that it might be a good plan to have George Harris come over from the C. B. & N. to act as his chief general assistant and liaison man in Chicago. As Perkins explained it: "Our object must be to get the utmost efficiency by having each man do what he can do best."[6]

But neither Stone nor Ripley thought well of this scheme, and in April 1890 they both resigned. So it was that as of June 1, George B. Harris took over as second vice-president and general manager; Peasley, of course, remained as first vice-president in charge of financial affairs. "I feel confident," Perkins wrote his wife at the time, "that in Harris we have got a man of good business sense and judgment."[7] By September he was even more convinced: "Harris takes hold well," he told Forbes, "and I feel as if we had now an organization closer down to the ground and better for every day working purposes than we have had before. It is not noisy, but industrious and vigilant."[8]

Meanwhile—in mid-June—the company's able general counsel, Wirt Dexter, had died suddenly. For the moment, his post was left vacant and the system's legal duties were shared by J. W. Blythe, general solicitor for Lines East, and T. M. Marquett, who held the same position for Lines West. In 1900, Blythe was named general counsel, and Chester M. Dawes succeeded him as general solicitor. The position of Olney in respect to the company was, incidentally, a special one. His advice as a counsel and director was highly valued, and the relationship was continued when he became a member of President Cleveland's cabinet in 1893 as Attorney General. As Forbes put it: "Of course we shall lose the benefit of constant and early counsel with Olney, but I think we can get more good out of him on great points for his being at headquarters where he may have a chance to do good work for all railroads against Interstate Commerce

6 Perkins to Stone, January 10, 1890, PVB, Vol. XXIII, pp. 160–1.
7 Perkins to his wife, May 12, 1890, C–O, RCO Notebook #8, p. 158.
8 Perkins to Forbes, September 20, 1890, C–O, RCO Notebook #8, p. 175.

meddling and paternalism generally."[9] As a matter of fact, Olney continued to draw his regular railway salary through August 1894, after which
time it was suspended until, after his subsequent service as Secretary of
State, he left the cabinet. Incidentally, J. Sterling Morton, long a retained
spokesman for the Burlington, also served in Cleveland's cabinet, as Secretary of Agriculture; as both he and Olney were men of strong laissez-faire
principles, their appointments were pleasing to business.

With Peasley and Harris occupying the vice-presidential positions
throughout the 1890's, top-level management was characterized by stability. So, with two notable exceptions, were the directorate and the principal committees. With the death of Dexter, the old Western Executive
Committee on which he and Perkins had served so long was reconstituted
into the Executive and Finance Committee, composed of Gardner, Forbes,
Paine, Endicott, and Hunnewell. This group functioned without change
until the latter part of 1898, when the company lost, through death, two of
its most stalwart directors, John Murray Forbes and John L. Gardner.
Thereupon Coolidge took Gardner's place, and J. Malcolm Forbes replaced
his father. The only other change until the end of the century was the
addition of Perkins to the committee in 1900.

The death of Forbes on October 12, 1898, marked the passing of the
man who had stood very much in the same relation to the railroad as
George Washington had to his nation. An investor since 1852, a director
continuously from 1857 to his death, president of the company from 1878
to 1881, and thereafter chairman of the board, he had consistently been
the strong man in the East. No exaggeration was involved when the board,
in words framed by Perkins, resolved that to him the company owed a
large measure of its success. The death of John L. Gardner on December 10 was likewise a serious loss. A respected Bostonian like Forbes,
Gardner had lent much to the strength and solidity of the Burlington
directorate.

As might have been expected, executive salaries were not raised greatly
during the difficult years of the 1890's. The pay of the general manager of
Lines East had been $12,000 when Stone held the post during the strike
of 1888, and it was not increased until the end of 1896, when it was set at
$18,000, thus matching the salary Holdrege had been receiving as general
manager of Lines West ever since mid-1890. As superintendent of motor
power and cars for Lines East, F. A. Delano received $5,000 early in 1899,
and a year later was raised to $7,000. Meanwhile Howard Elliott, as gen-
eral manager of the Missouri Lines, was raised to $12,000 in 1896. As
general solicitor for Lines East, Blythe received $10,000, but this was in-
creased to $20,000 early in 1898. In the fall of 1898, Harris, in charge of
the actual operations of the railroad, had his pay increased from $20,000 to

[9] Forbes to Perkins, March 8, 1893, quoted in Eggert: op. cit., Ch. vi, p. 21.

$30,000. Another up-and-coming younger man who had been with the company since 1880, Charles I. Sturgis, found his salary as general auditor raised from $6,000 to $7,000 in the fall of 1899. In Perkins's estimation, the company had to give good pay to keep good men.

In the case of a man like Perkins, who was so closely identified with the Burlington as to be a symbol of it, the boundary between his business life and his personal life was hard to determine. For one thing, he spent an enormous amount of time going over the property in person. Between August 1887 and November 1893, for example, his business car No. 200 made seventy-eight trips, covering 84,000 miles, an average of thirteen trips and 16,000 miles a year. He was not on every trip the car made, of course, but on the other hand he traveled extensively by regular trains and on other business cars. Almost invariably one or more of his top officers or directors traveled with him, and local officials climbed aboard while the car was in their territory. Visitors, of whom Perkins kept a meticulous record, constituted a "Who's Who of the West." A favorite and frequent guest was Colonel W. F. Cody, better known as "Buffalo Bill." Other guests were judges, politicians, literary men, and "local characters." Perkins loved nothing so much as good conversation and an occasional game of poker. Indeed, the carefully kept logbooks of his business car are worth a volume in themselves.

Two or three specific examples of Perkins's thinking and action in the borderline area between business and private life deserve mention. The first has to do with politics. During the presidential campaign of 1896 considerable pressure was applied on the railroad to exert its influence. As a citizen of the community, the Burlington of course had always taken note of the political climate and had done its share of fence-mending. But in this case, Perkins could see no reason for involving the company. Specifically, he was opposed because the C. B. & Q. covered such an extensive territory that taking a position in one part of it might antagonize the public in another. He was perfectly aware that a good many railroads were playing an active part in this particular campaign, and he thought this might be all right for roads in the East, although, he added, "the expediency of it may, I think, be questioned. But it would be foolish for the C. B. & Q."[1]

No less interesting was Perkins's reaction to the proposal of Henry Lee Higginson and others in the spring of 1896 that a school of railroading be established at Harvard. "I think the plan you speak of is all *damm* [sic] nonsense," he told Higginson. He thought it would be a mistake to make Harvard into a technical school; it was not the purpose of colleges "to turn out young men with their opinions formed about current questions." Rather, he thought it was their job "to train the mind to think accurately.

[1] Perkins to Higginson, October 28, 1896, PLB, Vol. XIV, pp. 219–20.

. . . I think the time spent on a railroad course would be time wasted, and that the man whose time had been spent on Greek, mathematics, and history would be better able to have distinct perception of things in themselves distinct."[2] Harvard, he concluded, should concentrate on a general course and leave training for business to the hard school of experience.

Perkins, incidentally, had a strong sense of history. He kept memoranda and logbooks of key events and his travels, and in 1888–89 hired a trained economic historian to write a documentary account of the strike of 1888. In February 1900, he wrote that for a long time he had had in mind the preparation of a history of the C. B. & Q. Consequently, he promptly organized a Historical Department in Chicago, with T. S. Howland, secretary of the company, at its head, and J. C. Bartlett of the Relief Department as chief assistant. Two months later he reported that these gentlemen had "done *something* but not much as yet."[3] He thereupon authorized Holdrege to write the story of the B. & M. in Nebraska, assuring him of every necessary assistance. Unfortunately nothing, except Scudder's invaluable account of the strike, resulted. The men who knew the Burlington story so intimately simply were too busy with other duties to take the time they discovered such undertakings demanded.

One of the most colorful episodes in Perkins's career centers around the almost unbelievable action by which, singlehandedly, he saved the First National Bank of Lincoln from collapse. At the time, Perkins was a very small stockholder, with a total investment of approximately $15,000. Late in 1895 it was discovered that unless confidence could be restored in the institution, it would have to close its doors. Had this happened, the economy of the South Platte Valley would have been ruined. Consequently, in a desperate move to win public confidence, the stockholders of the bank, without Perkins's knowledge, elected him a director and promptly gave the fact wide publicity. As a result, no runs were made on the bank funds, and the institution survived the crisis.

Perkins's first reaction, of course, was to repudiate this unauthorized action, but when those on the spot pointed out the perilous condition of the bank, he consented to let his name remain. Before he was through, he not only paid all the assessments for all shareholders, but also raised over a million and a third dollars by selling securities of his own at a heavy sacrifice. Not until May 1899 was the institution on a stable basis, leaving Perkins with assorted questionable assets, which, before his death in 1907, eventually offset less than half the money he had supplied.

The point of the story is this: his personal liability as a stockholder was a matter of a few thousand dollars. And he had every right to refuse to serve as a director. But because the entire area and the railroad would

[2] Perkins to Higginson, March, 1896, C–O, RCO Notebook #12, pp. 8–10.

[3] Perkins to Morton, May 15, 1900, PLB, Vol. XVII, p. 661. Underlining in original.

have suffered had he done so, he willingly sacrificed half his life's savings. He not only refused to let others share the burden, but also flatly forbade anyone to make public what he had done. This was not an official action on Perkins's part, but it revealed as little else could his character and his sense of obligation both to the railroad and to the community.

CHAPTER 14

Integration and Sale: The End of an Era

1899-1901

• CORPORATE AND FINANCIAL STREAMLINING •

B Y THE MID-1890's, the financial and corporate structure of the Burlington was bewilderingly complex. Ever since Joy had embarked on his branch-line policy in 1869, the C. B. & Q. had frequently expanded by acquiring independent companies by either lease or stock ownership or both. As many of them had issued their own securities to the public, it had been deemed simpler to let them retain their corporate identities. Some of these companies were operated by the C. B. & Q., like the Chicago and Iowa, but many of them, such as the Kansas City, St. Joseph and Council Bluffs, the St. Louis, Keokuk & Northwestern, and the Chicago, Burlington and Kansas City—to mention only the most important—were operated separately. For administrative purposes Perkins thought this procedure sound.

But from the financial and corporate standpoint, the existence of countless independent companies required a mountain of paper work and made calculating exactly how the entire Burlington system was doing as a whole extremely difficult. Any large-scale refinancing for the system, such as would become necessary in 1903, when the seven percent Consolidated Mortgage of nearly $29,000,000 fell due, would inevitably be complicated and time-consuming. Moreover, some provision would have to be made for acquiring the Chicago, Burlington & Northern.

On various counts, then, corporate simplification was imperative. Accordingly, on March 15, 1899, the directors voted to buy the C. B. & N. through an exchange of stock and, of far greater importance, to buy all other lines then held under lease by the C. B. & Q. east of the Mississippi River, subject, of course, to the approval of the stockholders. To acquire all C. B. & N. bonds still outstanding would require over $11,000,000, and it would require even more to acquire the bonds of leased lines.

Throughout the early months of 1899, then, Perkins devoted great thought to the sort of financing that would be best suited to these various ends. He rejected the idea of a one-hundred-year mortgage to cover the entire system because it was too unwieldy and might place the road at the mercy of moneylenders when it became due. His thought, rather, was to limit an issue to the Illinois lines, including the C. B. & N., and to cover the properties farther west later. Accordingly, in a circular dated April 20, 1899, the directors proposed issuance of an Illinois Division Mortgage in the amount of $85,000,000 to be dated July 1 and to mature fifty years later, with interest at a rate not to exceed five percent. Upon payment of the seven percent bonds of the C. B. & Q. due in 1903, this mortgage would become a first lien on the C. B. & Q. and on the leased lines east of the Mississippi. It was large enough to provide for retiring the C. B. & N. bonds as well as those of various smaller companies for which the Burlington had assumed responsibility.

As a first step, the company offered $12,000,000 of its new bonds at three and a half percent to its stockholders at a price of 75, and at the same time offered $4,000,000 in capital stock at par. This offer was taken up fully by stockholders, and at a special meeting on May 20, 1899, they ratified not only issuance of the mortgage but also the purchase of the C. B. & N., the Chicago and Iowa, and other lines east of the Mississippi. In a second major step, the stockholders in November 1900 voted to purchase all the railroads in Iowa and Missouri formerly held under lease. Included among them were such properties as the Kansas City, St. Joseph and Council Bluffs, the Chicago, Burlington and Kansas City, the Humeston and Shenandoah, the St. Louis, Keokuk & Northwestern, the Keokuk and Western, and various smaller concerns.

At the turn of the century the bewildering corporate structure of the Burlington thus was greatly simplified. The company now owned and operated virtually all the major lines that have formed a part of the system ever since. Only a few smaller roads and the narrow gauge mileage were left under separate operation, and they too were brought under a single corporate roof during the following decade. With one company owning virtually all the mileage, financial management and corporate diplomacy would inevitably be far simpler.

• ELIGIBILITY •

IN MANY WAYS, the corporate and financial streamlining of the Burlington system achieved at the turn of the century was like putting the final, finishing touches on a vast house that had been under construction for years. More than half a century before, the humble one-room cabin labeled Aurora Branch had been joined to three similar structures nearby and the whole had been placed on a solid foundation accurately rechristened the Chicago, Burlington and Quincy. Over the years additions were made, first to the southwest, then to the west, and finally to the northwest. A second story and additional closet space, representing double-tracking and countless short branches, were added later, and the internal facilities and furnishings of the building were continually improved in the interests of more economical living, better communications, and more comfort for those who used it. Finally, at the turn of the century, a new corporate roof and a uniform coat of paint were applied. The structure was complete, and its owners were proud of it.

Meanwhile the occupants, like any householders, had had their hands full with their neighbors. But somehow they had managed to acquire a respectable front lawn, had staked out a good-sized back yard, and had acquired enough adjacent property to take care of all the foreseeable needs of the family. Frequently they had been tempted to buy an adjoining pasture or even a far-away woodlot. But by and large the heads of the household had concentrated on improving the grounds and making the most of what they had. Fortunately, they occupied a choice corner lot, and although all sorts of development was going on round and about that constantly improved the value of the neighborhood, they were in the fortunate position of being able to sit tight and to enjoy their property, or, if opportunity offered, to sell out at a handsome price if that should seem desirable.

Probably the Burlington's neighbors in the late 1890's never happened to think of this particular analogy, but some of them certainly looked at the system with shrewd and calculating eyes as it reached full and well-coordinated maturity. Its strategic location as a whole, and of certain of its lines in particular, could obviously lend tremendous strength to roads that terminated, say, in St. Louis, Kansas City, Omaha, or the Twin Cities and did not enjoy access to the heartland of the Middle West so neatly criss-crossed by the C. B. & Q. For years the Burlington deliberately had tried to provide such good service between these outlying cities and Chicago that none of the roads on the outer perimeter would feel compelled to build independently into Chicago. In the case of the Santa Fe, the C. B. & Q. had failed to restrain the impetuous Strong, but it had success- fully withstood Gould's threats to take his Missouri Pacific into Chicago, had shared with the Iowa Pool lines the enormous business transacted with the Union Pacific, and belatedly had joined the Milwaukee and North Western in providing adequate rail capacity between the Twin Cities and Chicago. The chances were that the Burlington could look forward to carrying this intercity bridge traffic indefinitely; in addition, an enormous amount of varied and valuable traffic originated and terminated within its own generous borders. The company might well be a tempting morsel for any of the large systems surrounding it, but it was perfectly able and content to leave things as they were. The one thing it did not wish to do was to acquire responsibility for any other major system.

As Perkins neatly put it in a letter to one of his fellow directors on May 31, 1900: "There can be no doubt, I think, about the value of C. B. & Q. to any scheme for combining roads west of Chicago. . . . I do not quite see, however, any way in which the C. B. & Q. can control any such combination without taking risks and responsibilities which I do not suppose such a body as our present stockholders want to take or ought to take. . . . In the meantime, we are in a strong position either to go it alone or to combine."[1] On February 26, 1901, he particularized: "I do not think we have anything serious to fear from the fact that while we are one of the big systems today, we may be one of the small ones ten years hence. I think our situation is so strong, and so large a proportion of our traffic is taken up and put down at points on our own lines, that we are reason- ably sure to make a good living however much our neighbors may con- solidate."[2] In view of this attitude, which was consistently shared by a majority of the directors, any proposal for combination would have to come to rather than from the Burlington. And that is precisely what happened.

Even before James J. Hill changed the name of his St. Paul, Minne- apolis and Manitoba Railway to the Great Northern and decided to extend it to the Pacific Coast, he was interested, understandably, in a reliable link to Chicago. The two older, established lines were the North Western and the Milwaukee. But their roads to the Twin Cities were only parts of much larger systems with widespread interests elsewhere. Thus, from the outset, Hill had been particularly friendly to the Chicago, Burlington & Northern. He had been prompt to allow the C. B. & N. to use his tracks between St. Paul and Minneapolis and to share certain

[1] Perkins to T. J. Coolidge, May 31, 1900, PLB, Vol. XVII, pp. 708–9.
[2] Perkins to F. W. Hunnewell, February 26, 1901, GM, 1896–1905, p. 111.

terminal facilities. In 1890 he seriously considered acquiring the property jointly with the C. B. & Q.; in the following year he suggested acquiring it alone, a proposal which did not appeal to Perkins.

Two chains of events, however, each beginning in 1893, were destined to increase Hill's interest in controlling, at least in part, a link to Chicago. Early in that year his Great Northern reached the Pacific coast, and in midsummer the Northern Pacific fell into receivership. For many months Hill had clearly foreseen the mounting difficulties of his long-established rival. More to the point, the investors in the Northern Pacific and the banking fraternity were fairly well agreed that if only the methods Hill had employed so successfully on his own road could be applied to the Northern Pacific, that company might, in time, prove equally successful. So it was that a plan of reorganization for the Northern Pacific worked out by J. P. Morgan and others in the spring of 1895 provided that the Great Northern, in exchange for guaranteeing interest on the bonds of a reorganized Northern Pacific, would acquire half its capital stock and name a majority of its directors. But this proposal aroused fears of a monopoly, and in March 1896 was enjoined by the United States Supreme Court.

Under the circumstances, the Northern Pacific was reorganized independently. But Hill and his friends acquired approximately $16,000,000 worth of stock in the new corporation, as well as large holdings of bonds, thus gaining a substantial voice in its affairs. The net effect was to make Hill more eager than ever to acquire the Chicago, Burlington & Northern, not only on behalf of his tightly controlled Great Northern, but also for the benefit of the Northern Pacific. One sure way to accomplish this, of course, would have been to acquire control of the Burlington, and indeed Hill discussed this very possibility seriously with his London bankers during 1897. His advisors, however, thought this too large an undertaking for the Great Northern alone, and the Northern Pacific, so lately reorganized, was not yet strong enough to participate in a joint purchase. There, for the moment, the matter rested.

Interestingly enough, however, apparently no one connected with the Burlington knew at the time of Hill's rather serious interest in purchasing the system. At any rate, as Perkins later wrote, the first outright suggestion to buy the C. B. & Q. was made, as far as he knew, to Harris early in the summer of 1899 by E. H. Harriman, chairman of the Union Pacific. Harris and Perkins discussed the proposal then, and again when Harriman reiterated his ideas to Harris in the autumn. These conversations were general, but in 1900 Harriman sought and obtained five conferences with Perkins during which the two got down to brass tacks.

At the first meeting, in January, Perkins made it perfectly clear that any initiative for an alliance would have to come from Harriman's New York office and that, at the moment, the C. B. & Q. was not for sale.

Furthermore, for fear that Harriman was thinking in defensive terms, Perkins assured him that Burlington had no disposition whatever to buy the Union Pacific. Before they parted, Harriman asked what Perkins thought Burlington stock was worth. At least $200 a share to anyone who would hold it for the next twenty years, Perkins replied. Harriman seemed to think this price out of the question, and on that note the first conference came to an end.

At Harriman's insistence, a second meeting was arranged for March 15 in Chicago at which both Perkins and Harris were present. There Harriman offered to pay $200 a share, but not in cash; instead he offered Union Pacific three percent bonds, with a cash alternative of $140. When Perkins flatly refused to talk at such a price, Harriman increased his offer the next day to three and a half percent Union Pacific bonds, with $150 as a cash alternative. Perkins declined to consider anything less than $200 a share in cash. Harriman still thought this an impossible figure, but said that he would discuss it with his banker, Jacob Schiff, of Kuhn, Loeb and Company in New York.

On April 21, Harriman was back again, and this time Schiff was with him. Taking a subtle tack, the New York banker observed that perhaps the time was not yet ripe for consolidation; with this Perkins emphatically agreed. Schiff then suggested that when Perkins thought the time had arrived, he should bring the matter up. To this Perkins demurred; any move would have to come from Schiff or Harriman for the simple reason that Perkins was not offering the C. B. & Q. for sale or proposing to make a trade of any kind. Perkins made clear that, notwithstanding the conversations, he was in no way bound to the Union Pacific. Thus rebuffed, Harriman promptly formed a syndicate with Schiff, James Stillman of the National City Bank, and George J. Gould to purchase Burlington stock. As a result, sales of C. B. & Q. on the market jumped sharply, and the price of the stock, which had been slightly over $124 in January, rose above $131 in June.

Perkins reported these developments to members of the board, but he did not think Harriman would be able to acquire nearly enough shares to control the company without raising the stock to $140 or $150. Perkins indicated that as a director he might advise selling at $200, or perhaps less, but in his opinion the board should take no formal action in regard to Harriman's proposal as it stood. Of the directors, only Coolidge seemed to be strongly in favor of Harriman's proposition.

By the first week in June, Harriman's syndicate had accumulated almost 70,000 shares, whereupon the market supply seemed to run short. During the next six weeks the syndicate added only 10,000 shares to their holdings, and on July 25, when they had 80,300 shares in their possession, at a cost of approximately $10,000,000, market operations were suspended. This was less than nine percent of the 984,461 shares then outstanding;

clearly, the great body of small C. B. & Q. stockholders were unwilling to sell at the prevailing market price of approximately $125.

Late in August and again in early September, Harriman visited Perkins at the latter's summer home in New Hampshire. This time he simply proposed that it might be well to have Union Pacific directors on the Burlington board and vice versa. But neither Perkins nor the Burlington directors could see that anything would be gained from such a plan and told Harriman so. Meanwhile Burlington stock remained relatively inactive; sales averaged around 150,000 shares a month, and the price actually dipped close to $120. But in October the demand stiffened. Sales in both November and December exceeded 330,000 shares, and prices topped $140. But in view of the total shares outstanding, the supply was still relatively short, and Harriman liquidated his pool at prices between $130 and $140. Thus 1900 ran out in an atmosphere of calm. But it was the calm before the storm.

That Hill and his banker, J. Pierpont Morgan, were interested in the Burlington was clear. By 1900 they had reached the definite conclusion that a railroad system would have to be acquired to give them a dependable entry into Chicago and, if possible, to the markets of the Middle West as well. Furthermore, they desired protection against the Union Pacific, whose activities in acquiring a substantial interest in the Southern Pacific were well known. The question was simply which of the three principal lines between Chicago and the Twin Cities to acquire. As 1901 opened, these stood as follows:

Railroad	Mileage	Approximate Amt. Stock	Approximate Amt. Bonds
C. & N. W.	5,576	$ 64,000,000	$145,000,000
C. M. & St. P.	6,746	100,000,000	127,000,000
C. B. & Q.	7,922	110,500,000	145,000,000

Of the three lines, the North Western would be the most difficult to obtain because of the large interests held in it by the New York Central. Between the other two, Hill strongly favored the Burlington. As he later wrote to Lord Mount Stephen: "The best traffic of the Great Northern and Northern Pacific is the cotton and provisions west and the lumber and timber eastbound. . . . The great provisions centers are Kansas City, St. Joseph, Omaha, Chicago, and St. Louis, none of which are [sic] reached directly by the Great Northern or Northern Pacific. Both companies have to divide the through rate with some other line to reach those important points. . . . The Burlington lets us into all these districts and commercial centers over better lines and with better terminals than any other road."[3]

[3] J. J. Hill to Lord Mount Stephen, April, 1901, quoted in J. G. Pyle: *The Life of James J. Hill* (New York: Doubleday, Page & Company; 1917), Vol. II, pp. 119–20.

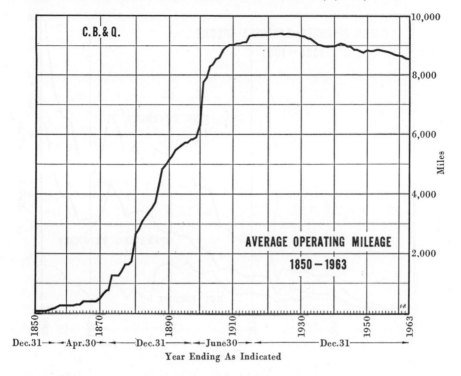

Morgan definitely preferred the Milwaukee because the financial responsibility for acquiring it would be less. The Milwaukee, however, refused even to discuss terms. Morgan therefore advised Hill to go ahead and see what could be done with the Burlington.

In January 1901, more than 700,000 shares of Burlington stock changed hands while the price per share moved inexorably forward to $148½. It was increasingly apparent that one or more serious bids for control were in the making. In this context, two momentous events took place in Burlington history. The first concerned a man.

• END OF AN ERA •

IN A NOSTALGIC LETTER to Griswold dated January 2, 1901, Perkins noted that he was entering his twentieth year as president of the C. B. & Q. and his forty-second with the company. After harking back to some of the experiences that he and Griswold had gone through together, he prophesied that the new century would see railroad combinations that would make the last half of the nineteenth century look like "the days of small things in spite of the fact that we have accomplished so much."[4] Perhaps when Perkins penned these words, he had no idea how soon his prophecy

[4] Perkins to Griswold, January 2, 1901, GM, 1896–1905, pp. 96-7.

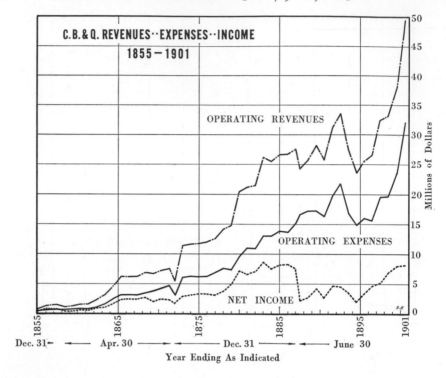

C.B.&Q. REVENUES··EXPENSES··INCOME
1855—1901

OPERATING REVENUES

OPERATING EXPENSES

NET INCOME

Millions of Dollars

Dec. 31   Apr. 30   Dec. 31   June 30

Year Ending As Indicated

would be borne out in a way that would intimately affect the Burlington. Yet, judging from his specific though abortive dealings with Harriman and his full awareness of Hill's long-standing desire for a firmly controlled link to Chicago, the chances are that Perkins well knew that for the Burlington the days of isolated splendor were inevitably numbered.

Whatever hopes he may have had to the contrary on this score were blasted by the dramatic developments on the stock market during the month of January 1901. As Perkins put it later: "The market was after us. We had 12,000 or 14,000 stockholders; prices were going up, and our small people were selling out." At the moment, as Perkins realized, nobody was in control. But it was well known that both Harriman and Hill were in the market; that being so, then, as Perkins shrewdly appraised it, "Wall Street would soon have had 51 per cent of the stock in spite of us. Then the question was, who to sell to, and I made up my mind that . . . if we could get $200 [per share] for *all* [the Burlington stock] it was better than to let the *market* get 51 per cent, even if it paid more than $200."[5]

By the end of January, then, this much was clear to Perkins: although he might continue as president of the C. B. & Q. organization, it could not be as the undisputed leader of a faithful band of long-standing stock-

[5] Perkins to ? , June 3, 1903, C–O, RCO Notebook #14, pp. 118–19.

holders. Instead—and his daughter was the source of this phraseology—
he would become "office boy" for either Harriman or Hill or, worse yet,
subject to the whims of a shifting group of Wall Street speculators.
Perkins had reigned and ruled too long to face such a prospect if he could
avoid it honorably.

As matters stood, he could. He had pointed out to Paine the previous
May that the value of both the C. B. & Q. and the Union Pacific would
be improved if they combined, and he was even more convinced that the
most natural and the best combination, if combination was inevitable,
would be with the Great Northern and Northern Pacific. The fact that
either of these alliances now appeared possible if not probable cleared
the ground and served as a catalyst for a personal decision that seemed,
on a number of other grounds as well, overwhelmingly logical and wise.

For two decades, Perkins had borne an increasingly heavy load of
responsibilities. That he liked his work was beyond doubt; it was as much
a part of him as eating and sleeping. On the other hand, he was devoted
to his headquarters and home in Burlington, and the necessity of attending
endless meetings in Chicago, as well as in Boston and New York, was
becoming more and more of a chore. As he expressed it: "I have no wish
to *leave* the C. B. & Q.—it has been too large a part of my life for too
many years. But I do think the time has come when it is best for the
company and for me to push others more to the front, and place on them
such responsibility for details as we safely can. To accomplish much in this
direction it is desirable to put someone else nominally at the head as
president, because modern railroad presidents are expected to attend to
details, by the public, by railroad commissions, and by neighboring railroads—to go to meetings, to make tariffs and time tables, and to do many
other things which *might* be done but are not done by subordinates."[6]
More specifically, Harris for some years had represented the company more
often than not at such gatherings as Perkins had in mind. Thus, as Perkins put it, it would be only fair that Harris should have the title that was
expected to go with the duties he was carrying out.

Just how much relative weight Perkins gave to those separate considerations is impossible to determine, but taken together they overwhelmingly prompted one clear course of action. On February 5, 1901, he wrote
Hunnewell, who was chairman of the board, that he wished to resign the
presidency of the C. B. & Q. in favor of George B. Harris. "I have held
the office for nearly 20 years," he told an old family friend, "and I give it
up when things are in good shape, and do it voluntarily, instead of drifting
along until I am forced out by age, or illness, or dissatisfaction."[7]

[6] Perkins to Hunnewell, February 16, 1901, C–O, RCO Notebook #13,
pp. 113–14.
[7] Perkins to Mrs. J. C. Peasley, February 25?, 1901, C–O, RCO Notebook #13,
pp. 122–3. Underlining in original.

Hunnewell took more than a week to reply to Perkins's letter of resignation. When he did so, he said the board felt obliged to accede to Perkins's wishes, but on the understanding that, regardless of title, Perkins as a director would continue at the helm. Indeed, the board urged Perkins to become chairman.

Perkins was deeply touched. "To be thought well of after long acquaintance should satisfy anyone's vanity!" he replied.[8] But he declined the offer of the chairmanship, explaining that he did not want to feel obligated to attend the frequent meetings of the directors in Boston. On the other hand, as he told Griswold, "while letting Harris be the executive officer, I intend to have more or less to do with steering the ship, [and since] . . . I remain on the Board, and as a sort of guiding director, the break is more in name than in reality."[9] As he put it succinctly to his friend Morton: "I have been too long in harness to be comfortable out of it . . ."[1]

Harris welcomed this arrangement. "My selection as president of the company," he told the press, "does not reflect any change of ownership or change of policy in the Burlington . . . . In the capacity of president I shall relieve Mr. Perkins, who desires it, of the duties he has heretofore performed. He still remains a director with a large personal interest in the company. The change, so far as I am concerned, makes little difference in my relations to Mr. Perkins or to the Burlington property."[2] Thus, with the least possible dislocation, the presidency of the C. B. & Q. fell on new shoulders.

In point of fact, Harris was only seven years younger than Perkins. Born in Brookline, Massachusetts, in 1848, he had spent his boyhood in Vermont. When his family had moved to Hannibal, Missouri, Harris, then eighteen, had taken a job as office boy with the Hannibal and St. Joseph. He later became paymaster of the road, transferred to the Burlington and Missouri River in Nebraska as clerk in the Land Department, moved up to purchasing agent for that company in Omaha, and then served as superintendent of the Atchison and Nebraska. Returning to the B. & M., he became its general freight agent, and later purchasing agent of the C. B. & Q. at Chicago. For a year he served as assistant to the general manager of the Santa Fe, but in 1884 he returned to the Chicago, Burlington and Northern, then under construction. When Touzalin died in 1889, Harris was placed in active charge of that road and remained there until he was brought to Chicago as second vice-president of the C. B. & Q. in 1890. Since that time, he had been Perkins's right-hand

8 Perkins to Hunnewell, February 16, 1901, C–O, RCO Notebook #13, pp. 113–14.

9 Perkins to Griswold, February 28, 1901, C–O, RCO Notebook #13, pp. 124–8.

1 Perkins to Morton, March 2, 1901, GM, 1896–1905, p. 115.

2 *Chicago Times Herald*, February 21, 1901.

man. There was little doubt, therefore, that the two men could and would work together harmoniously, regardless of what titles they happened to hold.

• CONSUMMATION OF THE SALE •

ALTHOUGH IT WAS NOWHERE STATED SPECIFICALLY, it was apparently understood on all sides when Perkins resigned the presidency that he, rather than Harris, would continue whatever negotiations might take place in respect to ownership of the Burlington. This was logical on two counts: Perkins was well known both to Hill and to Harriman. Furthermore, as owner of more than 13,000 shares, he was the largest stockholder of the C. B. & Q.

Between the time Perkins sent his resignation to Hunnewell on February 5 and the announcement of it a fortnight later, the pot had again begun to boil. At Harriman's urgent request, Perkins met the Union Pacific chairman in Chicago on Sunday, February 10. This time Harriman wanted to buy half the C. B. & Q. stock. But Perkins refused to recommend that sort of arrangement to his stockholders. Presumably he did so because any such scheme was intrinsically unattractive. But he may have had another reason: while this conference was in progress, a message came from Hill asking whether Perkins could see him in Chicago the following day.

When Hill arrived on February 11, he went directly to the point: he suggested combining the Burlington and the Great Northern on the basis of exchanging six Great Northern shares (then selling at $193) for seven shares of C. B. & Q. (then selling at about $140). Perkins replied that he thought the C. B. & Q. was worth every bit as much as the Great Northern, and that a cash offer of $200 a share was the least he could recommend to the stockholders. On this note, the two men parted. But they agreed to meet again before long.

The scramble for the C. B. & Q. was now at its height. On February 13, Charles F. Mellen, president of the Northern Pacific, sought out Perkins and proposed a long-term traffic contract between the two roads. Perkins shied away from any long-term commitment, but finally said that he might make a five-year arrangement with the right to terminate it on a year's notice. Mellen seemed to think that this would be satisfactory and said he would send Harris a memorandum of his ideas. Nothing ever came of this scheme.

Meanwhile, Burlington stock continued to be traded actively on the exchange, and on February 18, with his usual bluntness, Hill asked Perkins who was doing the buying. Perkins replied that none of the purchases was being made for him personally or, as far as he knew, for any of the C. B. & Q. people. "I have thought," he suggested tactfully, that "possibly your friends might be buying." He went on to comment on Hill's proposals of February 11; he could now say that the Boston directors agreed with him that not even an exchange of stock on a share-for-share basis would be acceptable. But Perkins did suggest this: "Could any scheme be devised by which, whatever might be offered in exchange, there might also be a fixed cash offer as an alternative? This would involve an underwriting, and being prepared to take all stock, preferring cash to securities, which I suppose could be arranged by you and Mr. Morgan if you thought it worth while, and it might help us to get together. I can meet you in Chicago at any time," said Perkins, "if you think we had better follow it up."[3]

Receptive as Perkins was to continuing the negotiations with Hill, he was leading from strength. As he wrote Charles F. Adams on the same day, he had no fear whatever that the Burlington would be "bottled up," for he thought it would be stupid for any of the transcontinentals to try to shut out the C. B. & Q., thus forcing it to build its own line to the Coast, which he said it could well do on an economical basis. Incidentally, he expressed some fear of combinations that might be too large, for even though they might be harmless—in fact, beneficial—from an economic standpoint, they might create public sentiment "which will bring about bad legislation and injury to property interests through increased taxation and otherwise."[4]

As the turnover in C. B. & Q. stock continued at a brisk pace on the exchange, Malcolm Forbes became worried that the Burlington had let a golden moment slip by. Perkins reassured him on February 22 that the Union Pacific people might pick up 200,000 shares or so at the market price and then offer perhaps $175 or $200 for the additional shares necessary to achieve control. But Perkins was convinced that the U. P. had its hands too full with Southern Pacific matters to act hastily. Another possibility existed. Perkins thought that the Pennsylvania might be preparing to offer to buy the Burlington at $200 a share in three and a half percent bonds. Yet this too seemed unlikely. Would the Pennsylvania take simply the Burlington, at the risk of antagonizing the Santa Fe and the Rock Island? And to take all three would be a mighty undertaking even for the powerful eastern road. The buying, Perkins thought, was more probably on the part of "miscellaneous speculators"—although Hill might conceivably be at the bottom of it.[5] If that was true, so much the better, and all the more reason to go slow.

On the evening of February 22, Harriman, at his own request, dined with Perkins, Hunnewell, and Forbes. This time he made no specific proposition. He merely expressed the hope that the U. P. and the C. B. & Q.

---

[3] Perkins to Hill, February 19, 1901, C–O, RCO Notebook #13, pp. 115–17.
[4] Perkins to C. F. Adams, February 19, 1901, PLB, Vol. XVIII, pp. 113–14.
[5] Perkins to Malcolm Forbes, February 22, 1901, PLB, Vol. XVIII, pp. 124–6.

could be put together and that the directors would empower someone to negotiate. He added that he understood Hill and Morgan to be engaged actively in buying Burlington stock. Three days later, Perkins and Hunne-well agreed that nothing was to be gained by appointing an official com-mittee of the board to carry on negotiations. In fact, it would not be wise to do so, Perkins thought, until Hill had had more time to make another move. Perkins was perfectly willing to have Hunnewell see Harriman again if the latter desired it, but with the clear understanding that no binding agreement should be made.

On Sunday, February 24, Harris and Perkins sat down with E. F. Leonard, president of the Toledo, Peoria and Western, who was a trusted friend, to weigh the relative desirability of an alliance with Harriman or one with Hill. "Either would make a strong combination in many ways," Perkins reported to Hunnewell the next day, "but our unanimous conclu-sion was that if Hill means also Morgan and the Northern Pacific, as he says it does, that would be the stronger and safer place for us to land."

The reasons, which Perkins gave in great detail, may be quickly summarized: (1) The bonded indebtedness of the Union Pacific and the Southern Pacific, taken together, was far higher than that of the two Northern roads. (2) The Great Northern–Northern Pacific occupied better country, which would sustain a larger and much more vigorous population. (3) The Northern Lines had the best supply of lumber in the United States, and the Burlington reached the best markets for it; the Northern Lines could probably carry lumber profitably at rates which the Union Pacific–Southern Pacific would find unremunerative. (4) The Northern roads had an endless supply of coal between the eastern base of the Rockies and Puget Sound, whereas on the U. P.–S. P. there was no coal west of Utah. (5) At Billings, the Northern road could turn over to the Burlington not only lumber but also miscellaneous freight, receiving in exchange agricultural produce and miscellaneous traffic of other sorts. The Union Pacific, on the other hand, could give and take little or nothing from the Burlington west of the Missouri without robbing its own line; furthermore, the Union Pacific would probably not think it expedient to utilize Burlington to the exclusion of other roads and could thus furnish little traffic beyond that already moving. (6) Politically, a merger of the parallel Union Pacific and Burlington lines west of the Missouri River might be a liability and encourage "bad legislation." This objection would not hold for an end-to-end alliance with the Northern Lines. (7) Com-bination with the Northern Lines would be safer. The U. P. could do nothing seriously to hurt the Burlington, whereas if the C. B. & Q. joined the U. P., Hill might well build roads from Sioux City to Denver and Omaha. (8) Finally, if the Burlington made a trade based on Union Pacific securities, that paper might depreciate. In any northern combina-tion, however, "there would be no conflict of interests, as there is no

[2 5 7]

duplication of lines, and therefore much less temptation to let our property depreciate."[6]

No sooner was this letter on its way to Hunnewell than Hill requested another meeting. When he and Perkins met in Chicago on March 7, Hill proposed a joint lease to the Great Northern and Northern Pacific on the basis of a guaranteed seven percent return on C. B. & Q. stock. But Perkins was not satisfied with seven percent; furthermore, he insisted on an alternative cash price and stipulated that, prior to any arrangement, the C. B. & Q. be allowed to divide some or all of its accumulated surplus in the form of bonds. When Hill agreed to such a distribution, Perkins then said that no purpose was served by talking about a deal at a price less than $200 for the stock. Hill thought this was too high, but promised to consult Morgan.

Determined to sit tight, Perkins did not have long to wait. An urgent wire from Hill on March 18 requested an early meeting. So as to attract a minimum of attention, this and subsequent gatherings were arranged for the quiet Victoria Hotel in Boston. There, beginning on March 27 and ending on April 9, Hill, sometimes accompanied by George F. Baker, met with Perkins, Paine, Forbes, Hunnewell, and Olney. Hill started out by suggesting a price of $185 a share, payable in three and a half percent bonds. But the Burlington Committee set as a minimum $200 in four percent bonds, with a cash alternative of $200 a share. Finally, on April 9, Hill, with Morgan's blessing, accepted these terms. Three additional meetings between the bankers and lawyers were required to spell out the details. These were finally concluded on Thursday afternoon, April 18. Perkins then announced to the press that the matter was practically settled.

On April 20, 1901, the Great Northern and Northern Pacific transmitted their formal offer to purchase not less than two thirds of the Burlington stock, provided that it were turned in on or before May 20. In payment, the Northern companies offered their joint four percent bonds in an amount equal to twice the par value of all the stock so deposited (that is, at the rate of $200 a share), and agreed to pay cash for deposited stock up to the amount of $50,000,000, a sum judged ample to take care of those shareholders who would prefer cash instead of the joint bonds. These joint bonds were to mature on July 1, 1921, but were subject to redemption at $105 on any coupon date after January 1, 1906. The Northern companies agreed to issue no additional bonds under this mortgage except to acquire additional C. B. & Q. stock; the C. B. & Q. agreed to deposit with the trustees of the new mortgage whatever amount of new stock it might issue as necessary to keep the ownership of the Northern Lines on the same percentage basis. As long as the joint bonds were not in default, the Northern companies could vote their C. B. & Q. stock and receive dividends on it. Naturally, the purchasing companies would undertake to maintain the Burlington property in top condition. In a letter to the stockholders dated April 29, 1901, the directors of the Burlington recommended that this offer be accepted.

The day after Perkins announced to the press that agreement had been reached with Hill and Morgan, the Burlington *Daily Hawk-Eye* reassured its readers that the Great Northern, Northern Pacific, and Burlington would retain their individuality and be operated simply as independent companies in close harmony with one another. But the rival Burlington *Gazette*, while admitting that Hill and Morgan were great men and that in their hands the Burlington might continue to prosper, viewed the proposed sale as "a calamity," not only for the city of Burlington, but for the C. B. & Q. as well. "There can be no sentiment between the new management and the people of this state," it editorialized. "The bargain was a cold-blooded one, made to increase their power and enlarge their monopoly. Everything they do will be looked upon with suspicion. There will be no memories or associations in the conduct of the new management."[7] Much the same sentiment was reflected in the *Boston Herald* of April 23 under a banner headline reading "A Big Loss for Boston." Sentiment in that city, said the paper, was "deeply stirred" as "this grand railroad property" joined the long list of companies once owned in Boston but now held by powerful syndicates elsewhere.[8]

These comments from his home town of Burlington and his adopted town of Boston made a deep impression on Perkins. Believing, as he earnestly did, that the proposed trade was for the benefit of all concerned, he sent a letter on April 24 to the editor of the Burlington *Daily Hawk-Eye* in a vigorous effort to allay the effects of these dire predictions. "It is not," said he, "by any means the 'passing away of the C. B. & Q.' as described in some of the newspapers. On the contrary, there will be no change in the C. B. & Q. in name or management, and the alliance of properties will greatly benefit all of them, and all of the people they serve. The C. B. & Q. company will continue to do business precisely as heretofore. . . . But it will be assured of what it does not now possess, a permanent connection by the shortest line with the great Northwest, rich in minerals and lumber, with its markets for agricultural and other products, and with the commerce of the Pacific Ocean. . . . On the other hand the Northern Roads will be assured of a permanent connection by the shortest line with the agriculture and manufactures of the Middle West, and the markets to be found there for the products of the North and the commerce of the Pacific. No argument is necessary to show that

[7] Burlington *Gazette*, April 20, 1901.
[8] *Boston Herald*, April 23, 1901.

this assured permanency is of the greatest importance to all of the interest concerned, the people as well as the railroads.

"As to the management, there is not only no intention to make changes in the official staff and organization, but the strongest desire on the part of those who are proposing to buy the stock to hold on to C. B. & Q. men and C. B. & Q. methods."[9] He added that he expected to return to Burlington shortly and hoped to continue for many years to occupy his office in the familiar building on the river front. This letter, which effectively quieted the fears of the good people of Burlington and of Iowa, was reprinted widely. As the *Chicago Post* said, it "created a feeling of security among the employees which they had not felt since the reports of the change were first heard."[1]

From the outset, little doubt existed that the proposal of the Northern Lines would be accepted. The hearty recommendation of the C. B. & Q. board, particularly of Perkins, was enough to assure the success of the deal. On May 20, Perkins wrote his wife: "The 'C. B. & Q. deal' is now practically settled, eno' stock having been deposited Saturday [May 18] . . . . It is a great trade all around, and future generations will say so."[2]

On May 21, official announcement was made that about ninety-one percent of all C. B. & Q. stock had been deposited under the terms of the agreement; by November the percentage amounted to 96.79 of the total authorized shares outstanding. As might have been expected, the price of C. B. & Q. stock on the exchange spurted forward from a low of 143¼ in March to a high of 199¾ in April and remained there throughout May and June. From the standpoint of the Northern Lines, the price of $200 paid was high. But, as Hill wrote his colleague Lord Mount Stephen, this could not have been avoided and he at least had no doubt of the value of the property he had acquired.

As Perkins pointed out several times subsequently, neither he nor a majority of the directors had wished to sell the C. B. & Q., but when loss of control seemed inevitable, sale to the Northern Lines at a thumping good price had seemed an ideal move. "Great Northern and Northern Pacific combined with the Burlington," Perkins wrote Higginson in November 1901, "is going to make a stronger and better property than the Union and Southern Pacific under Harriman. Hill is in many ways a wonderful man, not only a prophet and a dreamer, but he has a very unusual faculty for figures. . . . He is a great man—there is no mistake about it."[3]

"The truth is," Perkins wrote Geddes the following July, ". . . Mr. Hill has seen more clearly than any of us that the fittest to survive would

---

[9] Burlington *Daily Hawk-Eye*, April 28, 1901.

[1] *Chicago Post*, quoted in Burlington *Daily Hawk-Eye*, May 1, 1901.

[2] Perkins to his wife, May 20, 1901, C–O, RCO Notebook #13, p. 142.

[3] Perkins to Higginson, November 18, 1901, C–O, RCO Notebook #13, p. 183.

be the railroad which could work at the lowest rate per ton mile. That has been his central idea, and he has educated everybody on his road to make everything [else] subordinate to it. He has devised a most elaborate system of monthly statements, which are sent out promptly to the operating people, and watched closely at headquarters, and it is to that [system], and to his personal supervision as the owner, and to the fact that there have been no side-shows and no stealing, that the road has been so successful and has beaten everybody else in the business."[4]

The year 1901, then, was truly one of great decisions for the Burlington. It is not for the historian to say what might have happened had things been different. For good and sufficient reasons of his own, Perkins saw fit to retire as president, and for still another set of persuasive reasons, he felt the moment was ripe to sell the property to the Northern Lines.

At the annual meeting of the C. B. & Q. early in November 1901, Perkins, Hunnewell, and Malcolm Forbes were re-elected to the directorate. A majority of the members, however, including James J. Hill, represented the Northern Lines; Harriman, Schiff, George Gould, and H. M. Twombley represented interests directly connected with or friendly to the Union Pacific. How these rivals found places on the Burlington board is a story in itself.

• GIANTS AT WAR •

IT APPARENTLY had not been until March 1901 that Harriman and Schiff had realized how much progress Hill and Morgan were making toward acquiring the Burlington. When the truth finally dawned on them, they urged Hill to give the Union Pacific a one third interest in the C. B. & Q., and offered to furnish one third of the purchase money. Hill refused, not only because it would defeat his own ends, but also because he thought it contrary to the laws of several of the states in which the Burlington and the Union Pacific each had extensive mileage, much of it more or less parallel. Stung by this rebuff, Harriman simply decided to go after the Northern Pacific itself, and with it a one half interest in the Burlington.

At this point a word of explanation is in order: ever since its reorganization, the Northern Pacific had had $80,000,000 outstanding in common stock, and $75,000,000 in preferred stock. The articles of reorganization provided, however, that on the first of January of any given year, the common stockholders could vote to retire the preferred shares. Consequently, the frantic struggle on the stock exchange which reached its climax during the first week of May 1901 was centered about control of the strategic common stock.

By Tuesday evening, May 7, the battle was over. Although Harriman

---

[4] Perkins to Geddes, July 2, 1902, C–O, RCO Notebook #14, pp. 21–2.

held a majority of the total stock (i.e., common plus preferred) outstanding, Morgan and Hill had secured more than half of the vital common. In the process, the price of that issue skyrocketed to $1,000 a share for the simple reason that speculating brokers had sold stock they did not possess and had been caught short. To the credit of the bankers involved, incidentally, both Schiff and Morgan agreed to allow the "shorts" to settle with their firms at $150 a share. The "Northern Pacific panic" subsided as rapidly as it had started.

When the excitement was over, Morgan and Hill planned to retire the preferred shares of Northern Pacific on the first of the following January, thus leaving Harriman with only a minority of the common. Yet a question existed as to whether or not this could be done. There would be a meeting of Northern Pacific stockholders in October at which all classes of shareholders could vote. It was entirely possible that Harriman could elect enough directors to control the board and thus indefinitely postpone retirement of the preferred shares. To avoid a resumption of costly hostilities, therefore, a compromise seemed best, and Morgan arranged one of his famous conferences. By the terms of an agreement signed on May 31, Morgan was empowered to fill any vacancies on the Northern Pacific board, but Harriman, together with some of his associates, were to be assured places on the directory of both the Northern Pacific and the Burlington. This, then, accounted for the fact that Harriman and Schiff, as well as Gould and Twombley, found places on the Burlington board elected in November 1901.

The sequel to Harriman's attempt to capture the Northern Pacific was the formation by Hill of the Northern Securities Company. His purpose, in effect, was to provide a single holding company for the Great Northern and the Northern Pacific and, through them, the Burlington, in such a way that future attacks would be unable to split control. A holding company would also provide a medium whereby Harriman could be represented without holding directly the stocks of either of the Northern Lines or of the Burlington. The Northern Securities Company therefore was incorporated in New Jersey on April 12, 1901, with a capitalization of $400,000,000. On its board of fifteen directors were six representatives of the Northern Pacific, four of the Great Northern, three (including Harriman) of the Union Pacific, and two of no particular affiliation. Hill was unanimously chosen president, and all holders of Great Northern and Northern Pacific stock were invited to exchange their shares for shares of the Northern Securities Company. Eventually, about seventy-six percent of the Great Northern stockholders and ninety-six percent of the Northern Pacific stockholders (including Harriman) surrendered their railway shares for those of the new corporation.

The well-known story of the Northern Securities Corporation need not be repeated here. Suffice it to say that Theodore Roosevelt, eager to re-establish the virility of the Sherman Anti-trust Act, directed his attorney general to file suit under that law against the corporation. On March 14, 1904, the United States Supreme Court, in a five-to-four decision, upheld the government, and the Northern Securities Corporation was dissolved forthwith.

The Burlington, of course, was little more than an interested spectator in all these developments, even though it had been the sought-after prize which had brought them about. But the dissolution of the Northern Securities Corporation might have had a lasting effect on the C. B. & Q. if Harriman had had his way. When the corporation was dissolved, Harriman demanded that he be given back the Northern Pacific stock that he had exchanged for Northern Securities shares. On March 6, 1905, however, the Supreme Court of the United States supported Hill's contention that Harriman was entitled only to a pro-rata distribution of the assets of the Northern Securities Company, namely stock representing a minority interest in both the Great Northern and the Northern Pacific. Had the court decided otherwise, and had Harriman received his original Northern Pacific stock, he would, of course, have had a large, if not a controlling, voice in the management of the Burlington. As it was, he and his associates gave up their places on the C. B. & Q. board during 1905 and were replaced by unquestioned friends of Hill.

The war of the giants was over, and the C. B. & Q. became identified, then and thereafter, with the Northern Lines. A new era began.

PART III

Steady Development

1 9 0 1 - 2 9

CHAPTER 15

Integration into the
Hill Empire

1901-15

ROM THE TIME the Northern Lines purchased the C. B. & Q. until the beginning of World War I, a dominant theme in Burlington history was the integration of the property into the larger complex of which it had become a member. This process took place on both a quantitative and a qualitative level. Even though the C. B. & Q. fitted amazingly well into the existing Great Northern–Northern Pacific pattern, some lines remained to be built either to complete the logical extensive shape of the Hill system as a whole or to provide internal links. On the qualitative level, steady and cumulatively important improvements were made in plant, motive power, and, especially, methods of operation. Finally, the added infusion of Hill's energy and imagination led to intensification of the colonization and agricultural development programs in various respects.

Fortunately, the economic and political climate was such that the entire program of integration could be carried out with a minimum of difficulty and distraction. The country remained at peace, and, except for the so-called panic of 1907, the economic waters were relatively untroubled. Activity took place on the regulatory front, notably in 1906, when the Hepburn Act was passed to give the Interstate Commerce Commission effective power to prescribe maximum rates. Not until the eve of World War I, however, did the cumulative effect of the new act become a major item in railway thinking and performance. More pertinent to the Burlington were passage of the Panama Canal Tolls Act in 1912 and, two years later, the opening of the canal itself; henceforth, all carriers participating in transcontinental business felt the competition afforded by the new shortcut by water. That, however, was at the very end of the prewar period; throughout most of the years 1901–15, Hill had virtually ideal conditions to carry out the policies he had in mind for the C. B. & Q.

From the standpoint of personnel, relatively few changes were made on the C. B. & Q. under the new regime. Hill had a great deal of faith in George B. Harris, and the men that Hill brought into the system were as congenial to Harris and his successors as they were to Hill himself. On the whole, therefore, the process of integration was carried through with a minimum of dislocation. At the end of the period the C. B. & Q. found itself a smoothly operating member of a highly efficient rail family. And, as has been the case ever since, the Burlington, for the benefit of all concerned, was given a wide measure of autonomy.

• FILLING OUT THE SYSTEM •

THE YEARS 1901–15 mark the last great period of expansion in Burlington history. Between June 30, 1901, and June 30, 1915, mileage operated increased 1,373 miles—17.2 percent—to bring the total to 9,366, just about eight miles short of the all-time peak achieved in 1916.

One project of long standing was the improvement of the old Hannibal and St. Joseph across northern Missouri. Ever since the Santa Fe had completed its through line between Chicago and Kansas City in 1888, the service between those two points over the Burlington's longer route had been at a growing disadvantage. As one step to improve this situation, the directors of the Burlington in 1897 had authorized rebuilding of the Quincy Bridge. Work began that summer, and by the fall of 1902 the new central drawspan was put in place. But that was only one step in correcting the unsatisfactory situation in northern Missouri. Two other steps were authorized early in the new regime. Since 1881, a railroad had operated between Quincy and Trenton, Missouri. In 1896–97 it had been extended under a separate organization to Pattonsburg, Missouri, and in the following year, still another company had pushed the line to the outskirts of Kansas City. In 1897, the Quincy, Omaha and Kansas City Railroad Company had been formed to acquire and operate this entire 254-mile system. On January 22, 1902, the directors of the Burlington authorized Harris to buy the company at not more than $13,000 per mile.

Whatever role was contemplated for the Q. O. & K. C., it was obviously necessary to improve the old Hannibal and St. Joseph. Accordingly, work began in 1902 between Hannibal and Brookfield on the reduction of grades to a basis of .66 percent; that is, they were to be limited to a rise of about six and a half inches in every hundred feet. No sooner had the segment between Macon and Bevier been completed, however, than the program was halted. This abrupt change apparently came about after Hill had made an inspection trip over the line. For one thing, he thought attention should have been concentrated between St. Joseph and Cameron Junction, and in addition, he was not convinced that the reductions being made were sufficient to warrant the expenditure involved; if existing grades were not to be reduced by the largest amount possible, he said, it was probably better to do nothing.

Meanwhile, Hill's restless mind was formulating a new far-reaching scheme which, if carried out, would intimately affect northern Missouri. The plan he devised sometime between 1902 and 1905 was to link Billings, Montana, by way of St. Joseph or Kansas City, St. Louis, and the Paducah Gateway with a port on the Gulf. This bold idea was squarely in line with Hill's long-standing policy of seeking balanced traffic for his system as a whole. As he conceived it, goods from the Orient and lumber gathered up in the Pacific Northwest could be shipped cross-country to the Gulf and could continue thence to the eastern seaboard by water. On the return journey, manufactures from the East could flow over this route into the Pacific Northwest.

In this connection, and to open up the Big Horn Basin, an entirely new line from Billings was put underway. Construction began southward from Frannie Junction on October 3, 1905, and was carried through to Kirby, 110 miles, on September 3, 1907. There, for the moment, the railhead rested, but activity continued on various other parts of the proposed through route. On the assumption that the new extension through Kirby would eventually join the existing C. B. & Q. line at or near Guernsey, a survey was run from Northport along the valley of the Platte River directly to Kearney. From there trains could proceed over the main line through Lincoln to Napier, Missouri, and thence to St. Joseph. In 1907–08, another new line was surveyed in a southeasterly direction from a point on the old Brookfield division at Saxton along a line north of Plattsburg and Lathrop, past Bogard, thence to Brunswick, and finally to the small town of Clark, where the survey ended within striking distance of Francis, a town lately become important in C. B. & Q. affairs.

As matters stood before 1903, the Burlington's wholly owned line between St. Louis and Kansas City was extremely circuitous: it ran north from St. Louis to Hannibal, then west to Cameron Junction, and finally southward to Kansas City, a total of 348 miles for passenger trains and only slightly less for freight trains. In order to remedy this situation, in the spring of 1903 the directors resolved to construct a branch line from a point near Old Monroe (fifty-two miles north of St. Louis on the line

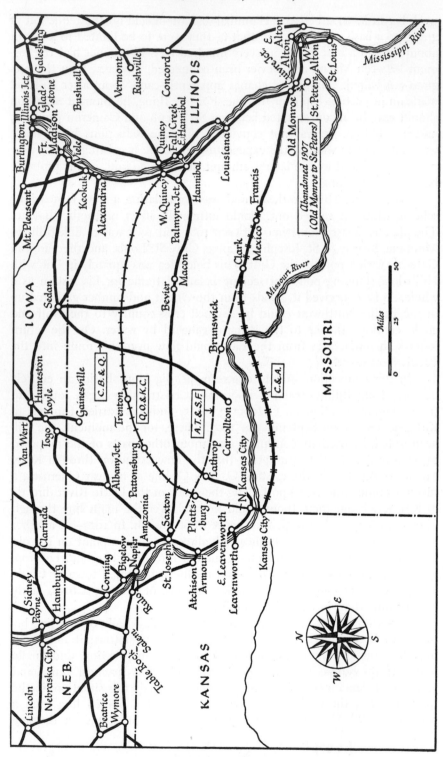

Missouri, 1901–15

to Hannibal) to a connection with the Chicago and Alton Railroad at Francis, just east of Mexico, Missouri. The use of the Alton from that point to Kansas City would save approximately sixty miles over the existing route. Accordingly, construction on the Old Monroe–Francis cut-off was begun during the summer of 1903 and completed in August 1904. On September 1 of that year, service over the new route went into effect.

By the latter part of 1908, the progress that had been made in piecing together a new through line between Billings and St. Louis and beyond consisted of a new railway constructed between Frannie and Kirby, Wyoming, a survey between Northport and Kearney, a second survey from St. Joseph to Clark, and a newly constructed line between Francis and Old Monroe. Thereupon the entire situation changed with the entry of the Colorado and Southern into the Burlington picture.

• Acquisition of the Colorado and Southern •

It was logical that as the Colorado and Southern, after the turn of the century, developed as a carrier of goods and people between the Gulf and the Rockies, Hill and his associates would look upon it as one means of fulfilling their dream of access to the Gulf. Indeed, the interest of the C. B. & Q. in the Colorado and Southern was not new; both Holdrege and Harris had urged its purchase upon Perkins in 1899, only to see the project laid aside.

Meanwhile the Colorado and Southern had begun to expand under its energetic president, Frank Trumbull. One step, taken early in 1900, was to join with the Rio Grande Western Railway Company in buying the stock of the Colorado Midland. The C. & S. thus acquired joint control of more than three hundred miles of standard-gauge mountain railroad extending due westward from Colorado Springs through Leadville to a junction with the Rio Grande Western at Grand Junction. Internal development of the C. & S. kept pace with its extensive growth. At the turn of the century, the C. & S. spent $350,000 to construct its own shops at Denver and, with the growth of the sugar-beet industry, invested additional funds in providing facilities to move this promising new crop. At the same time, the company invested more than $600,000 in special equipment to handle the growing tonnage in coal, coke, and ore moving to and from the Colorado Fuel and Iron Company at Pueblo. As Trumbull observed in the *Annual Report* for 1901, "it was good policy to stimulate in every reasonable way the steel business of Colorado."[1]

Before the company could undertake further major expansion in accord with long-term plans, however, sufficient funds had to be made available. The C. & S. had issued a $20,000,000 four-percent General Mortgage in 1899, but by the spring of 1905 only $450,000 of unsold bonds were still

---

[1] C&S, AR 1901, p. 4.

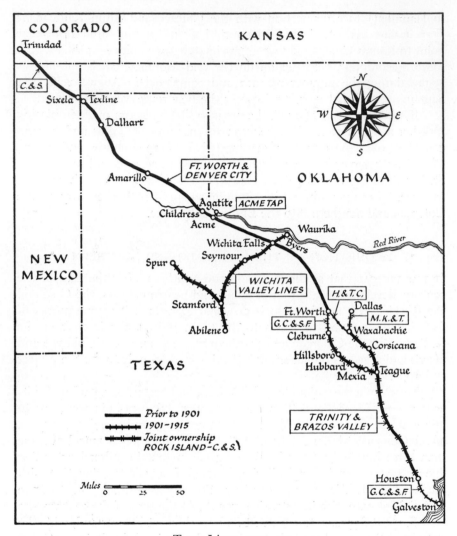

Texas Lines, 1901–15

available for sale to the public. A new issue was thereupon authorized, consisting of $100,000,000 in Refunding and Extension bonds. They were to mature on May 1, 1935, and to pay four and a half percent interest.

With the proceeds of this issue available, the C. & S. turned its attention to the completion of through lines between Fort Worth and Dallas on the one hand, and Galveston and Houston on the other. An independent start had already been made with the chartering of the Trinity and Brazos Valley late in 1902, and the first part of that line, from Hillsboro to Hubbard City, had been opened in 1903. By January 1904, it extended seventy-nine miles between Cleburne and Mexia. Between 1905 and 1907, the 157 miles from Mexia to a point near Houston, and north from Teague to Waxahachie, were finished. Trackage rights over Santa Fe subsidiaries were secured between Fort Worth and Cleburne, and between Houston and Galveston; trackage rights over the Katy from Waxahachie north gave access to Dallas. At the same time the T. & B. V. acquired a quarter interest in the Houston Belt and Terminal Railway.

Through service between Fort Worth and Houston was inaugurated on February 10, 1907, between Dallas and Houston in July, and between Houston and Galveston in 1908. The new railroad offered the shortest route to Galveston from both Fort Worth and Dallas, and was thus in an excellent position not only to compete with the railways already in existence, but also to provide an efficient southern link for the long-sought through line between the Northwest and the Gulf. Incidentally, while the Trinity and Brazos Valley was under construction, Colorado and Southern kept purchasing its securities, and early in 1906 made a contract with the Rock Island by which that company shared on an equal basis the ownership of the new Texas line. This move laid the basis for the joint ownership and operation that has continued, under varying arrangements, to the present.

This major acquisition, by which the C. & S. added joint control of 317 miles of rail (including trackage rights), was only part of a comprehensive program of expansion. In the summer of 1906, the C. & S. purchased from Morgan Jones and Grenville Dodge the Wichita Valley Railway Company and the Wichita Falls and Oklahoma Railway Company, which together had built seventy-five miles of line from Byers, Texas, through Wichita Falls to Seymour. Furthermore, the C. & S. agreed to purchase a sixty-mile extension of the Wichita Valley between Seymour and Stamford, as well as the thirty-eight-mile Abilene and Northern between Stamford and Abilene, then under construction. Thus, apart from the jointly owned Colorado Midland, but including the Fort Worth and Denver, the Trinity and Brazos Valley, and the other railroads purchased and under construction, the company looked forward to operating some 2,250 miles of road.

The potential value of the C. & S. to the Burlington was obvious: it was already connected from Hartville Junction (near its northern terminus of Orin Junction) with the C. B. & Q. at Guernsey, and another link could readily be built to some point on the Alliance–Billings line. The range of possibilities was extended farther by the fact that with the completion of the Western Pacific, the Colorado and Southern—by virtue of its joint control of the Colorado Midland and its working alliance with the Rio Grande Western—would form another through railroad from San Francisco to the Gulf, thus becoming a worthy competitor of the Harriman-held Southern Pacific.

Just how many of these considerations entered into Hill's mind can hardly be known, but the fact is that he and Harris opened negotiations with Hawley and Trumbull some time late in 1907 with a view to purchasing the Colorado and Southern Lines for the C. B. & Q. Certainly the C. & S. fitted into the balanced traffic program so prominent in Hill's thinking. If the Billings–Kirby line could be extended south to Orin Junction, or if a connection could be made from Orin Junction to the existing Alliance–Billings line, then it would be entirely possible to move the cattle, cotton, and farm produce of Texas, as well as the coal, ore, and steel of Colorado northward, while the lumber, fish, fruit, and Oriental imports of the Northwest could flow in the opposite direction.

By this time the C. & S. was indeed an imposing property. On June 30, 1908, it included the following:

Colorado and Southern Railway Company	1,249.64 miles
Colorado Springs and Cripple Creek District Railway	74.30 miles
Fort Worth and Denver City Railway	454.14 miles
Wichita Valley Lines	174.40 miles
	1,952.48 miles

In addition, the C. & S. owned a half interest in the Colorado Midland, 337.64 miles, and in the Trinity and Brazos Valley, 421.72 miles. Excluding these two jointly owned properties, the consolidated system reported gross revenues in excess of $14,000,000 and net income of over $2,000,000 for the fiscal year 1907–8. The combined system owned 297 locomotives, 266 passenger cars, and 10,302 freight cars. In 1907–8, it produced over a billion ton miles of freight service and 140,000,000 passenger miles.

Negotiations between Hill and Harris on the one hand and Hawley and Trumbull on the other continued throughout most of 1908, but not until December 19 did Hawley announce officially that the purchase had been completed. The price paid was $16,416,337.50 for $30,876,200 worth of preferred and common stock of C. & S., representing 64.3 percent of the total issue outstanding. For this sum the Burlington acquired 1,952.48 miles of railroad, together with the company's half interest in the Colorado Midland and in the Trinity and Brazos Valley.

On February 11, 1909, the new board elected for the C. & S. reflected the change of ownership. Of the old board, four members were re-elected: former chairman Grenville M. Dodge, his close associate Henry Bronner, Edwin Hawley, and former president Frank Trumbull. The new members represented the leading figures in the Hill empire and, more particularly, in the C. B. & Q. administration. George B. Harris was elected president of the C. & S. and chairman of the board. Serving with him were James J. Hill and his son James N. Hill, William P. Clough, and Edward T. Nichols—both of whom were or had been on the C. B. & Q. directorate— George F. Baker of the First National Bank of New York, and James W. Blythe. The thirteen-man board was completed by Darius Miller and Daniel Willard, vice-presidents of C. B. & Q. who then became vice-

Colorado, Wyoming, and vicinity, 1901–15

presidents of the C. & S. A neat blending of holdover and new talent was
accomplished by naming Bronner, Hawley, and Trumbull, along with
Harris and Willard, to the Executive Committee.

Logically, an immediate task of the new ownership was to fill out the expansion of the Colorado and Southern and integrate the property fully with the Hill system. Probably in line with earlier commitments, the C. & S. advanced funds for the Stamford and Northwestern, which completed an eighty-two mile line between Stamford and Spur, Texas, in the late fall of 1909. In June 1910, the directors voted to build the thirty-four miles of railroad necessary to connect Wellington, Colorado, with Cheyenne, Wyoming, thus regaining the independent access to that city which the old Colorado Central had enjoyed years before. At the same time, they determined to eliminate the one remaining gap covered by trackage agreement on the main line by laying a new railroad between Southern Junction, just south of Pueblo, and Walsenburg, Colorado.

Furthermore, an agreement was made between the Colorado and Southern and the Denver and Rio Grande whereby the new line of the former and the old line of the latter would be used as paired double-track. These two major improvements, one in the north and one midway in the system, were completed within a few days of each other in October 1911. Meanwhile, beginning in 1909, the company adopted a program for laying heavier rail and installing more permanent bridges. In Texas, new and modern shops were constructed at Childress to replace those destroyed by fire in the spring of 1902.

Finally, acquisition of the Colorado and Southern immediately sparked further construction on the part of the C. B. & Q. itself. In July 1909, work was resumed at Kirby southward through the Wind River Canyon and by way of Casper to a meeting with the northern end of the Colorado and Southern at Orin Junction. This stretch of heavily constructed railroad with easy grades was completed and open for service on October 18, 1914. Still another link was improved between the C. B. & Q. and the Colorado and Southern when the former opened a short eight-mile stretch between Guernsey and Wendover on December 15, 1915; this line was on a better grade than the older Guernsey–Hartville Junction road. Meanwhile, the Great Northern extended its rails from Great Falls southward to Billings, finishing that job in 1909. The net result was to bring into existence the direct heavy-duty railroad between the Gulf and the Pacific Northwest that Hill so ardently desired. As one byproduct, Denver was now closer to such cities as Spokane, Portland, and Seattle than ever before.

While construction on this through route was underway, two changes were made at the northern end of it. To provide the new line with a short-cut to the Northern Pacific, the C. B. & Q. constructed thirty miles of line from Warren (north of Frannie) to Fromberg, a point on the Northern Pacific a few miles southwest of Billings; this stretch was completed and open for business on April 24, 1911. Once this line was in service, no need remained to maintain the portion of the Toluca Branch between Warren and Toluca, which accordingly was abandoned in May 1911.

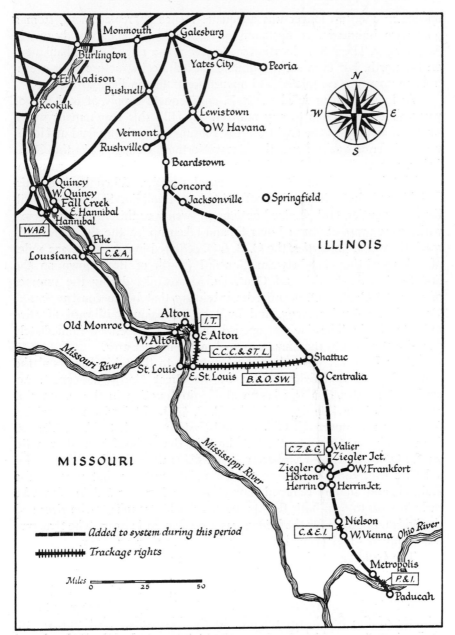

Southern Illinois, 1901–17

In a quite different area, a major improvement of the routes leading into Kansas City was accomplished just in the nick of time to handle growing traffic during World War I. The one-track iron bridge at Kansas City that had changed the entire economy of the region when it had been opened in 1869 no longer was adequate. Hence its replacement, from a point two hundred feet upstream on the northern end, was begun in August 1915. The shift in location made necessary a 1,400-foot embankment on the north, but even so, the double-tracked steel structure with a central drawspan was completed and opened for traffic on February 1, 1917.

As long as steam ruled the rails, an adequate supply of coal was of paramount importance to any railroad. To Hill, this requirement was a source of anxiety, as the coal from the Burlington's existing field at Herrin was of inferior quality, and the Great Northern's supply, via the Great Lakes, was undependable. Hill therefore sent the Great Northern's coal specialist into southern Illinois for several months. When he had satisfied himself that high-grade coal existed in Franklin, Saline, and Williamson counties, Hill obtained options on twenty or thirty thousand acres, which were promptly turned over to, and taken up by, the Burlington. To reach these coal properties, the C. B. & Q. acquired in 1904 some 122 miles of a long-existing line between Concord (south of Beardstown on the line to East St. Louis) and Centralia. Meanwhile, during the summer of 1904 the C. B. & Q. organized a subsidiary that began construction at Centralia on April 1, 1905, and built an extension southward fifty-five miles to Herrin. The line was opened on April 1, 1906, and immediately gave direct access to the numerous coal mines in that area.

From Herrin it was only a short distance to the Ohio River and the new high-grade coal fields located by the Great Northern's expert. Accordingly, construction was begun at Herrin Junction in the summer of 1909, to Neilson, Illinois, where the C. B. & Q. obtained trackage rights for sixteen miles over the Chicago and Eastern Illinois to West Vienna, from which town new construction brought the railhead into Metropolis, on the Ohio River, on October 15, 1910. Plans were already underway for a bridge over the Ohio River at that point, and for that purpose the Paducah and Illinois Railroad Company was incorporated in Kentucky early in 1910 to own both the approach from Metropolis to the river and the bridge. Location for the bridge was agreed upon in 1912. The structure was completed and opened for service on December 15, 1917.

The building of this line and bridge accomplished two major purposes: it made available a fine grade of locomotive coal which could be hauled by a virtually water-level line into Burlington territory and directly to the Twin Cities, over 600 miles north. It also opened a gateway to the railways of the Southeast, notably to the Nashville, Chattanooga and St. Louis Railway, which shortly acquired joint control of the Paducah and Illinois Railroad. The N. C. & St. L. also entered into contracts with the Burlington in 1914–15, providing for the interchange of passenger, freight, and other traffic over their jointly controlled line and bridge. Thus a link was forged between the Northern Lines and the Southeast by way of the Twin Cities, Savanna, Beardstown, and Centralia. This heavy-duty route was destined to play an important part not only in the movement of coal but also in the interchange of general traffic with the entire South and Southeast.

The extensions so far described under the new regime were at opposite ends of the Burlington system: the line from Fromberg to Orin Junction in Montana and Wyoming, and the southern Illinois lines terminating at Paducah. The third major acquisition and new construction took place squarely in the center of the system, the objective being to create closer links among the Twin Cities, the Omaha–Lincoln area on the C. B. & Q., and a western extension of the North Western.

Back in 1889–90, a local company, the Nebraska and Western Railway, had built a line from Covington (South Sioux City), Nebraska, 128 miles due west to a connection with the Chicago and North Western at O'Neill. After a series of reorganizations and changes of name, this line emerged in 1899 as the Sioux City and Western Railway, was subsequently operated by the Great Northern, then leased to the Burlington in November 1907 and deeded to the C. B. & Q. in December 1908. Meanwhile, in 1915–16, the Sioux City and Western built an important 103-mile branch south from Laketon (just below Sioux City) to Ashland on the C. B. & Q. main line between Omaha and Lincoln. Since the Great Northern served Sioux City, this 231-mile "system" provided a valuable internal connection linking the North Western, Great Northern, and Burlington. For example, cars carrying Nebraska grain could move to the Twin Cities, exchange grain for flour destined for Chicago, and bring back merchandise to western Nebraska, a most profitable triangular trade.

One other development of note took place at the turn of the century. In the 90's, local interests at Davenport, Iowa, and Rock Island, Illinois, had obtained authority for a bridge over the Mississippi between those cities, and for a railroad connecting East Moline, Moline, and Rock Island on the east bank with Davenport and Clinton on the west side. Christened the Davenport, Rock Island and Northwestern in 1898, this forty-one-mile road completed its bridge early in 1899, and on February 27, 1901, leased itself jointly to the Burlington and the Milwaukee. From that day to this, this important facility has given the C. B. & Q. excellent access to the many industries in the area.

So it was that during the first fifteen years after the sale of the C. B. & Q. to the Northern Lines, the company achieved its greatest physical expansion. As of December 31, 1916, the C. B. & Q. operated 9,373.65 miles, the all-time high in its history. In that same year the national network of the United States reached its peak of 254,251 miles.

• THE DRIVE FOR GREATER EFFICIENCY •

As THROUGHOUT BURLINGTON HISTORY, extensive expansion of the system was accomplished by continual development of the internal plant: road-

way, structures, motive power, and rolling stock. The most notable characteristic of the period between 1901 and 1915 was the persistent drive,
sparked by Hill himself, for greater operating efficiency.

No one appreciated better than Hill the inherent strength of the Burlington, with its strategic location and gateways, its varied sources of traffic,
its demonstrated earning power, and its conservative capitalization and
heavy sinking funds. These were all factors that had prompted him to purchase it. On the other hand, the Empire Builder's eagle eye recognized at
once that it would take several years of hard work to put the property into
the top-flight physical condition that would enable it to contribute maximum benefits to his whole system. Grades and the sharpness of curves
would have to be reduced, new rail and ties installed, passing tracks lengthened, and new terminal facilities built. In fact, the task was to develop the
centralization process that had begun in 1900–1 with corporate simplification and to systematize the tighter control that Harris had already begun
to exert. This was the "new order" that Hill brought to the Burlington.

Apparently one of the very first things to which Hill turned his attention was the length and tonnage of freight trains. He observed, for example,
that the four daily freights operating between Savanna and St. Paul averaged only 400 tons a train, whereas the engines were capable of handling
2,000 tons. He immediately gave orders that all over the system trains
should be filled out to the maximum tonnage rating of the motive power,
and that each car should be loaded more heavily. The results of this campaign quickly bore fruit. During the four years ending in the middle of 1905,
ton-miles produced on the C. B. & Q. increased 35.4 percent while freight-
train miles *decreased* 24.6 percent. Furthermore, in 1906 average train
load had climbed to 376 tons a train, as compared with 200 tons in 1901.

The team of officers primarily responsible for this initial spurt was
composed of President George B. Harris, Howard Elliott, appointed in
1902 as second vice-president in charge of operations, and Darius Miller,
named at the same time first vice-president with particular responsibility
for traffic.

Harris, of course, had long been identified with the C. B. & Q. and in
1901 at the age of fifty-three enjoyed the full confidence of both Perkins
and Hill. Howard Elliott, born in 1860 and a Harvard graduate, had
worked his way up through the Burlington ranks for twenty years, proving
his ability principally on the Missouri lines, where he had held increasingly
important posts in both the Operating and the Traffic departments. Unlike
Harris and Elliott, Darius Miller was new to the C. B. & Q., but his railway
experience, which began at the age of eighteen in 1877, was extensive. Late
in 1898, Hill brought him from the Michigan Central into the Great
Northern as vice-president, promoting him to a similar position on the
C. B. & Q. at the beginning of 1902.

Effective as this team was, Hill was determined to improve it. Consequently, when Elliott left in 1904 to assume the presidency of the Northern Pacific, Hill brought in Daniel Willard, then vice-president of operations on the Erie. At the time Willard was just forty-three and in the prime of his long and active career; perhaps the best indication of his ability is that so hard-headed a businessman as Hill was prepared to pay him $50,000 a year.

Willard's job was to put the Burlington at the highest possible level of operating excellence. As Hill had fully expected, Harris, Willard, and Miller made a smoothly working, congenial team that got results. Willard strongly championed the acquisition of the Prairie-type locomotive (oOOOo, with a two-wheel pilot truck, six drivers, and a two-wheel trailer truck) and carried through an extensive program of well-drilling to provide the best possible water for engine use. He was also behind the establishment of new tie-treating plants at Sheridan and Galesburg and in charge of the program for laying new rail and lengthening passing tracks.

When Willard was offered the presidency of the Baltimore and Ohio in 1910, Hill did his best to retain him. As Harris desired to retire, Hill offered Willard the presidency of the Burlington, but Willard's early ties to the B. & O. proved more attractive, and he began his long and distinguished career as president of that railroad. So it was that as of January 31, 1910, Darius Miller was chosen chief executive of the Burlington; Claude G. Burnham and H. E. Byram were elected to the posts on both the C. B. & Q. and the C. & S. previously held by Miller and Willard, respectively.

As chief executive, Miller was known as "Darius the Silent." He said very little in a conference, but listened carefully and then gave his opinion. A man of the old school, he was tactful and genial, a prodigious worker, and possessed of both courage and administrative sagacity. Enjoying Hill's complete confidence, Miller's key assignments on the Burlington were to create more traffic and to see to it that it moved with maximum efficiency.

A fourth member of the team made his appearance at about this time. During the summer of 1907 a promising thirty-eight-year-old lawyer, a native Kansas Cityan and graduate of Williams and of Harvard Law School named Hale Holden, became general attorney for the C. B. & Q. in Chicago. He did so well that at the beginning of 1910 he was named assistant to the president. His major responsibility during the next two years was the handling of the crucial Minnesota Rate cases, which, when finally decided by the Supreme Court in 1913, proved to be a landmark in railway regulation. Although not an operating man, Holden was a born diplomat, and as a result of his superb performance before the courts, as well as his constant assistance to Miller, he was appointed a vice-president in 1913. When Darius Miller died suddenly in Glacier Park late in August 1914, Holden was elected president of the C. B. & Q., a post he was destined to fill with distinction during most of the next fifteen years. Byram and Burnham continued in their respective posts as operating and traffic vice-presidents, so that the team so carefully assembled by Hill underwent a minimum of change.

A major project started in 1909 was the virtually complete rebuilding of the Twin Cities line. This was particularly essential to accommodate traffic flowing between Chicago and St. Paul and also to provide easy grades and curves for the extremely heavy coal traffic that was beginning to move from the southern Illinois coal fields over the long 648-mile water-level stretch between the Ohio River and the Falls of St. Anthony. The project was not completed until twenty years later, but a good start was made in 1909–15. As a matter of fact, of the 238 miles that eventually were relocated and rebuilt between Savanna and St. Paul, 138 were reconditioned by the end of 1915.

Meanwhile a number of new stations were built on the system, some of them at such key points as Alliance (1907), Galesburg and Sheridan (1912), and Casper (1915). The Burlington also participated in construction of the Kansas City Union terminal, which opened for service in 1914, and the new Great Northern depot at Minneapolis, opened in 1916. Foremost among new structures, however, was the company's sixteen-story, general office building completed in Chicago in 1913. Located at the corner of West Jackson Boulevard and Clinton Street, the imposing U-shaped structure was faced with glazed terra-cotta on the sides that gave on the two principal boulevards and had the advantage of being directly across the street from the Union Station used by the trains of the system.

Among other notable projects of these years was the installation in 1910 of the Morkrum Printing Telegraph between Chicago and Galesburg. This was the forerunner of the modern teletype, and the first such installation on any American railroad. Subsequently it was extended to link Chicago with Omaha, Denver, Alliance, and St. Paul. At the same time the dispatching of trains by phone was stepped up, so that by the middle of 1912, 2,589 miles of road were equipped for this sort of modern communication.

Although the locomotive fleet was augmented principally between 1901 and 1909, additions continued to be made down to the beginning of the war. Between 1901 and 1916, while mileage was increasing 17.4 percent, the number of engines went up 51.8 percent. At the same time the supply of freight-carrying cars rose 52.4 percent. Meanwhile, on the Colorado and Southern Lines the motive-power roster remained essentially the same in 1916 as when the C. B. & Q. had taken control in 1908, but the supply of freight-carrying cars showed a substantial increase, 24.8 percent. Thus the capacity of the Burlington to produce transportation was vastly increased, and none too soon. In 1916, under pressure of events in Europe, war traffic was already mounting, and the C. B. & Q. in that year was able to produce 60.6 percent more ton miles than in 1901. Meanwhile, at the beginning of 1912, the Burlington had established a separate Department of Safety, one of the first in the country.

So far as operating efficiency went, C. B. & Q. freight-train miles decreased between 1901 and 1915 by 13.9 percent. At the same time, however, ton-miles shot up 120.3 percent while freight revenue increased 85.6 percent. To no small degree this was a result of increasing average train-loads from 200 tons in 1901 to 484 tons by 1914. The same general trends, while not so spectacular, were clearly evident in passenger operations. Over the same period, passenger-train miles increased 26.8 percent, but passenger-miles increased 102.4 percent while corresponding revenues moved ahead 73.7 percent. The same trends, so sharply discernible on the C. B. & Q. itself, were reflected to a lesser degree over the Gulf-to-Rockies route.

Statistics are dry at best, but the lesson is clear: Hill had purchased a strong railroad in 1901, but by 1915 he had increased its efficiency enormously and made it an even more valuable property. Indeed, the *Annual Reports* reflected the emphasis of the new regime. The *Report* for 1901 devoted no less than seven and a half of its fifty-four pages to "Length of Road" and seventeen to a description of the company's mortgages. The 1915 thirty-seven page *Report* tersely summarized the length of the road in half a page and covered the simplified mortgages in ten and a half. But the later edition carried four pages of statistics with 121 separate entries, as against 42 entries on two pages in 1901. Furthermore, an innovation made in 1912 was emphasized: the composition and division of traffic by commodities. In 1915 C. B. & Q. traffic was divided as follows:

Products of Agriculture	23.77%
Products of Animals	7.18%
Products of Mines	39.11%
Products of Forests	5.76%
Manufactures	15.46%
Merchandise	6.84%
Miscellany	1.88%
	100.00%

This close attention to detail was characteristic of Hill's way of doing business, and characteristic also of the lasting changes that took place on the Burlington during the years 1901–15.

• COLONIZATION AND AGRICULTURAL DEVELOPMENT •

JUST AS THE PERIOD 1901–15 witnessed the last great surge of expansion on the Burlington, it likewise embraced the last concentrated effort within the company's territory to colonize a broad region that had hitherto been too remote for systematic settlement. The area in question was an imperial domain indeed. As Perkins described it in the fall of 1901, it was "a great, big country lying west of the north-and-south line of the C. B. & Q. [namely] at the base of the Rocky Mountains and between the Northern Pacific and Union Pacific." And, he added prophetically, this was a region "which the C. B. & Q. must be built to sooner or later."[2]

No full-fledged colonization campaign really got underway until it was certain that the company would build south from Frannie to Kirby. As this possibility approached realization in 1904, an Immigration Bureau was established within the Passenger Department under the leadership of D. Clem Deaver, former Registrar of United States lands at O'Neill. Deaver's office was set up in Omaha, and as the railhead started south from Frannie in the fall of 1905, he established a Land Seekers' Information Bureau designed to promote settlement everywhere along the company's western lands, but concentrating particularly on the broad new acres being made accessible in central Wyoming.

The results of his efforts were prompt and gratifying. By the end of 1906, Deaver had received more than 4,000 inquiries about lands in the Shoshone area, and two years later he reported no less than 5,000 inquiries concerning the Garland–Powell region. The flood of mail continued, and in 1910 the company brought out an elaborate folder extolling the prospects of the Big Horn Basin. As Homeseekers' Excursions continued, the new region began to grow; through July 1, 1913, Deaver reported, approximately 8,000 families had settled in the area as a direct result of the railroad's efforts.

Indeed, it seemed that Deaver and his assistant, S. L. Fee, were connected with every important development in the Valley. Deaver particularly worked long and hard for liberalization of the land laws and eventually was instrumental in having the stock-raising Homestead Law of 1916 passed, which provided up to 640 acres for each head of family. All told, it was estimated that the company paid out well over half a million dollars for special folders, bulletins, newspaper and magazine advertising, product exhibits at fairs, and the operation of special exhibit cars throughout the Missouri and Mississippi river basins. In addition to Deaver and Fee, agents of the Burlington throughout the country were supplied with material on the new area and lent their aid in directing intending colonists to the regions open for settlement.

Essential as colonization was, it was also by its very nature a transient phenomenon. Not so agricultural development, work that commenced the moment the first settlers occupied a farming region and continued year after year, bringing to the people the latest advances in agricultural techniques. On the Burlington, agricultural development, like colonization, was nothing new. But as settlers moved farther west in Burlington territory, they inevitably ran into a problem universal to the Great Plains: lack of

[2] Perkins to Higginson, November 18, 1901, C–O, RCO Notebook #13, p. 184.

adequate moisture. That is why in 1903 Holdrege turned over to Hardy W. Campbell, an authority on dry farming, a 300-acre tract of C. B. & Q. land near the town of Holdrege to be used as an experimental farm. During the next half dozen years the Burlington not only supported Campbell and his dry farming, but also donated funds for the establishment of additional experimental farms near New Castle and Cheyenne, Wyoming, and Akron, Colorado. Meanwhile, beginning in 1907, the company lent financial support to the Dry Farming Congress, in whose activities both Deaver and Campbell were active from the start.

While Campbell was devoting his energies to the spread and development of dry farming, Deaver devoted particular attention to the improvement of corn and its culture. In 1904 he organized a Seed Corn Lecture Train which traveled the rails for two weeks in Nebraska, attracting thousands of interested farmers. To spread the gospel as to the proper storage of corn, Deaver in 1911 put out 10,000 pamphlets urging the construction of silos and in 1913 conducted a special Silo Train which made stops in forty-two towns in Iowa, thirty-six in Nebraska, and twenty-two in Colorado; all told, some 16,000 farmers heard lectures on the subject. Meantime, in 1912 and again in 1913 a Seed Corn Instruction Special toured no less than 171 towns attracting over 35,000 farmers.

As the pace of these activities was stepped up, it was logical that in 1913 the Burlington should form a separate Agricultural Department. John B. Lamson, a specialist from the University of Minnesota, was engaged to take charge, and in the first year all types of activity were greatly intensified. In addition to promoting the Seed Corn Instruction Special of that year, the company embarked on a campaign to encourage the culture of alfalfa. Joining forces with the International Harvester Company and the agricultural colleges in Iowa and Missouri, the company sent a special train into southwest Iowa and northwestern Missouri for a ten-day period in midsummer. In the latter part of September, the company operated a Dairy Special through thirty-six Nebraska towns in cooperation with the University of Nebraska, the State Dairymen's Association, and the Chicago and North Western Railway. Some 12,000 people turned out to hear the lectures, and so successful was the trip that another one was operated through twenty-four towns in Iowa in the latter part of February 1914. Encouraged, Lamson took a Livestock and Better Farming Special to sixty-five towns in Montana, Wyoming, South Dakota, Nebraska, and Colorado. Last but not least, the C. B. & Q. undertook important developments in farm demonstration.

Along a broad front and throughout its far western territory, the Burlington thus carried on its earlier tradition of giving all possible assistance and encouragement to better farming. The onset of World War I brought a pause in these activities, but the groundwork had been laid for the far-reaching program of the 1920's.

• THE HUMAN SIDE •

THE YEARS 1901–15 were marked by the absence of any serious labor disturbances; both the number of employees and the wages paid increased rather steadily through 1910. Thereafter, as the plant stabilized and more efficient machinery was made available, the trend of wages tended to flatten out. The number of employees reached a peak on the C. B. & Q. in 1913 and declined sharply thereafter. In essence, the period was one of relative stability and steady growth, one reason, perhaps, why labor relations were so harmonious.

In 1904, the Burlington signed its first agreement with a national brotherhood. Although the negotiations leading up to this event were handled by F. A. Delano, Daniel Willard had to operate successfully under the new dispensation. This he did, and part of his success was doubtless a result of his elimination of the old practice of laying men off for minor offenses and stopping their pay as a disciplinary measure. Instead, he introduced the demerit system for such cases: an entry was made in a man's record for infractions of the rules; the man kept on working and thus had an opportunity, through good conduct, to clear his record. Employees were discharged only for major offenses.

A third factor contributing to harmonious relations was the growing importance of the Relief Department. At various times, as small roads were purchased and operated as part of the C. B. & Q., they were brought within the scope of this organization.

• REGULATION •

BY THE TURN OF THE CENTURY, it was clear that the original Interstate Commerce Act of 1887 fell short of providing a comprehensive regulatory structure. For one thing, the Commission lacked the power to fix rates; all it could do was to declare, upon complaint, that a given rate was not just and reasonable, leaving it to the carrier to establish a new rate which might or might not be reasonable. Furthermore, the Commission had virtually no way to act against special rebates, drawbacks, or other concessions which powerful industries forced upon the hapless carriers. Primarily to stop this latter evil, the railways themselves took the initiative in sponsoring what eventually became the Elkins Act of February 19, 1903. In brief, the law prohibited any departure whatever from the published tariffs of a railroad and invoked severe penalities for all infractions. Furthermore, not only the agent who granted rebates, but also the railway corporation itself and the shippers were made equally liable.

The Hepburn Act of June 29, 1906, however, really rounded out the strength and effectiveness of the Commission. Its most important provision was the explicit delegation of rate-making power to the Commission;

from that day forth, upon complaint and after full hearing, the I. C. C. was empowered not only to condemn existing rates but also to determine and prescribe what it considered just and reasonable maximum rates for the future. Furthermore, all orders of the Commission were to become effective as determined by that body and were to remain in operation unless suspended or set aside by a court of competent jurisdiction. For the first time the burden of proof was thrown upon the carriers; they now had to obey an order or take the necessary steps for testing its validity. At the same time, the Commission was given the authority to prescribe uniform accounts, putting all railway reports on a standard basis.

Despite its far-reaching provisions, from the standpoint of the Commission the Hepburn Act left some things to be desired. The original long-and-short-haul clause was still weak; the Commission was able to act only upon complaint and not on its own initiative; carriers could adopt new rates without public interference, and the burden was still on the shipper to show that such rates were unreasonable. Finally, the Commission could prescribe only maximum and not minimum rates.

The Mann-Elkins Act of June 18, 1910, sought to remedy some of these regulatory defects. Its most significant provision revitalized the long-and-short-haul clause by removing the phrase "under substantially similar circumstances and conditions" from the original Fourth Section. In other words, except upon authority of the Commission, the carriers were denied absolutely the right to charge a higher rate for a shorter than for a longer haul over the same line or route; no longer could competitive conditions be cited as an excuse for departure from the rule. Furthermore, the Commission was authorized, either upon complaint or on its own initiative, to suspend changes in rates or classification pending an investigation. After passage of the Mann-Elkins Act, feeling was general that a reasonably comprehensive and effective system of railroad regulation had been enacted.

But it had one serious weakness: both the basic 1887 legislation and the amendments of 1903–06–10 were predominantly negative in approach and restrictive in character. Their primary aim was to eliminate abuses and to protect the public; they made no attempt to strengthen the transportation economy as a whole. Although the railroads might object to rates so low as to take property without due process of law, there was a vast difference between rates that were simply non-confiscatory and rates that were adequate to attract necessary capital into the industry and to serve as an incentive for efficient and progressive management. Indeed, the enforcement of competition between carriers appeared to stimulate some of the very evils which the act sought to eliminate, while the growing activities of state regulatory bodies led to conflicts between federal and local authority, a conflict which caught the railroads in the middle. Consequently, from the standpoint of the railroads and the public, the various "improvements" in the regulatory structure were to a considerable degree matched by defects and handicaps which, unless corrected, promised prolonged difficulties in the years ahead.

Despite these emerging difficulties, no comprehensive revision of federal railway regulation was made during the decade between the passage of the Mann-Elkins Act and the adoption of the Transportation Act of 1920. Indeed, only the stringencies of the war situation brought forth legislation that for the first time called for a positive approach toward the railway industry. During this decade, however, some piecemeal legislation affected the railways either directly or indirectly.

The Panama Canal Act, though designed primarily to provide for the operation of the Canal, made it illegal, after July 1, 1914, for a railway to have any direct or indirect interest in any water carrier using the Panama Canal or, for that matter, in any water carrier anywhere else if the railroad competed with it for traffic. The net result of this provision was that numerous railroads were required to divest themselves of subsidiary water-carrier operations. As the Burlington had none, it was not affected directly by this Act, although of course the opening of the Panama Canal was a blow to the plans Hill had for carrying traffic from the Gulf to the Pacific Northwest.

The Valuation Act of March 1, 1913, was an attempt to translate into statute the precepts set forth in *Smyth v. Ames*. In other words, Congress tried to provide an official federal valuation of all railroad property. The theory, of course, was that once a particular value had been established, it could be used as a yardstick for the measurement of rates appropriate to the needs of each and every particular carrier.

The Clayton Anti-trust Act of October 15, 1914, made it clear once again that railroads in particular were subject to anti-trust laws despite the fact that they were already closely regulated under the Interstate Commerce Act. A section of the Act specifically provided that no common carrier should have dealings in securities, supplies, or other commodities or make any contracts for construction or maintenance in excess of $50,000 in any one year with any concern in which a railway official might be interested in any capacity, except under conditions of competitive bidding.

To a very considerable extent, the progressivism so ardently championed by Theodore Roosevelt in the White House found its echoes locally in Burlington territory, notably in Nebraska. There the progressives in the Republican Party conceived it necessary to break what they called the railroad domination of affairs, and by the fall of 1906 the politicians of that persuasion announced dramatically that "there never will be a square deal in this state until the railroad machine is overthrown."[3] Their

[3] James C. Olson: *History of Nebraska* (Lincoln: University of Nebraska Press; 1955), pp. 250–2.

campaign was effective, and during 1907 Nebraska enacted, among other things, an Anti-free-pass Act and a two-cent passenger-fare law. The legislature also established a State Railway Commission with increased powers.

That the Burlington and the Union Pacific between them had long exerted strong influence in the politics of Nebraska seems well established. And it also seems certain that the years 1906–07 marked a climax of the anti-corporation movement. Unfortunately it is impossible to determine the exact nature and extent of such political influence as the railroads exerted in Nebraska: the correspondence which would reveal such matters apparently has been destroyed long since. Even if it were possible to reconstruct the facts, it is not the province of this history to attempt any judgment as to whether such influence was benign, malignant, or (more probably) a human mixture of the two. The scanty official files of the railway for this period say nothing on this subject or on regulation in general.

• Finance and Performance, 1901–15 •

THE LAST MAJOR FINANCING of the nineteenth century on the C. B. & Q. had occurred when the company, on July 1, 1899, issued the Illinois Division Mortgage, authorized for a total of $85,000,000 at not more than five percent interest; by 1906 the full $85,000,000 authorized had been sold. As of 1906 no further unissued bonds were available for financing new acquisitions or extensions or for additional refunding.

Accordingly, the first entirely new indenture of the twentieth century was the C. B. & Q. General Mortgage authorized on March 2, 1908, for a total of $300,000,000 at not more than five percent interest. This issue was to run for fifty years and was to be a first lien on 8,494 miles after prior bonds constituting liens on 5,528 miles were retired. In due course the controlling stock interest in the Colorado and Southern also was pledged under this indenture.

This large issue had three major purposes: (1) to reimburse the C. B. & Q. treasury to the extent of $45,000,000 for capital expenditures previously charged off to operating expenses; (2) to provide for additions and improvements up to an amount of $78,000,000; and (3) to retire all outstanding bond issues, a step that would require $177,000,000.

The net bonded indebtedness of the company actually outstanding in the hands of the public in mid-1915 was $181,690,000. This represented an increase of only 10.4 percent in the outstanding debt since June 30, 1908, and an actual decline of 2.6 percent in the amount of interest payable because the average rate of interest was reduced from 4.24 to 3.92 percent. Despite all the construction that had taken place since 1901, the debt outstanding in the hands of the public had increased only 37 percent between 1901 and 1915; the amount of interest paid *decreased* 4.2 percent, reflecting, of course, the drop in the average interest rate from 5.62 percent in 1901 to 3.92 percent in 1915.

In 1912, Roger Babson, the well-known security analyst, wrote that "all bond issues of this company may be regarded as 'ultraconservative.'" Observing that total net revenue before taxes for the year ending June 30, 1911, was 46.3 percent ahead of the equivalent figure for 1901, he emphasized that there had been an increase of only 2.7 percent in total capitalization per mile, and that over the same period the ratio of fixed charges to total gross had declined from 14.9 percent to 9.8 percent. He concluded that the Burlington's bonds were "of the most conservative character, suitable for the most careful institution's trustees, and individuals."[4]

Between 1909, the first full year under C. B. & Q. ownership, and 1915, the funded debt of the Colorado and Southern increased 9.4 percent, or at about the same rate as on the C. B. & Q. In contrast, however, interest charges also increased by 5.9 percent over the same period. It was natural, therefore, that Babson's comments about the C. & S. in 1912 were somewhat more restrained than his remarks concerning the Burlington. He said frankly that earnings of the C. & S. were "somewhat subject to severe fluctuations," but that even so the bonds were considered "safe, suitable." It was, he added, "remarkable how rapidly this railroad has come to the front, and it seems strange to be recommending stocks of a company the value of whose bonds was questioned only a few years ago." He was, of course, referring to the two issues of preferred stock; he observed that the common stock was "somewhat of a speculation."[5]

Indeed, the operating and financing performances of the C. B. & Q. and the C. & S. were in considerable contrast during the period under discussion. Generally speaking, the trends in both traffic and earnings on the C. B. & Q. were prolonged and steady in contrast to the rather erratic results on the western subsidiary.

In respect to revenue ton-miles, the period 1901–15 represented steady growth on the C. B. & Q. A marked downswing had resulted from the panic of 1907, of course, and after 1913 chronic car shortages temporarily slowed the upward trend, but it was resumed by 1916 under the impetus of growing traffic incident to the European war. Revenue ton-miles on the C. B. & Q. increased 71.9 percent between 1901 and 1908, and growth was nearly as marked in the latter half of the period, with a rise of 120.3 percent between 1901 and 1915. Although fluctuations were far more severe on the C. & S., the same general trends were apparent over the comparable period.

Through 1910, the number of passengers transported over both the

4 Moody's *Steam Railroads* (New York: The Publishers Printing Co.; 1912), pp. 286-7.
5 Ibid., pp. 295-6.

C. B. & Q. and the C. & S. increased sharply and then tended to level off. Revenue passenger-miles on the C. B. & Q. in 1908 had advanced 90.6 percent over 1901, but by 1915 the total advance over 1901 was only 102.5 percent. On the C. B. & Q., freight rates and passenger fares declined rather steadily, whereas the fluctuations in average revenue per ton-mile were more characteristic of the C. & S.; on that line, average revenue per passenger-mile actually tended to increase.

Both freight and passenger revenue on the C. B. & Q. tended upward during the 1901–15 period, but more sharply in the earlier than in the later years. Freight revenues of 1908 were 57.7 percent over 1901, and by 1915 they had increased 86 percent over 1901. C. B. & Q. passenger revenues shot upward 62 percent between 1901 and 1908, but then leveled off, so that the 1915 figure was only 73.2 percent over 1901. On the Colorado and Southern, on the other hand, both freight and passenger revenues declined over the 1908–15 period, although each reached a high point in 1910. The respective trends in total revenues logically followed the trend of its principal components. On the C. B. & Q., 1908 showed a rise of 56.8 percent over 1901, after which time the increase was more moderate, amounting to 82.2 percent for 1915 over 1901. Total revenue for the C. & S. line in 1915 was slightly under the 1908 figure, although an intermediate peak had been reached in 1910.

Total operating expenses on the C. B. & Q. mounted swiftly in the earlier part of the period; in 1908 they increased 72.5 percent over the 1901 figures. Thereafter the program of more efficient operation and tighter control of expense apparently took hold: by 1915 the increase over 1901 had been held to 86.4 percent. Meanwhile, total expenses on the C. & S. increased only 4.3 percent between 1908 and 1915. Both parent and subsidiary felt the sharply mounting burden of taxes. Whereas they increased 53.1 percent on the C. B. & Q. between 1901 and 1908, by 1915 taxes were 151.8 percent higher than in 1901. Between 1908 and 1915 taxes mounted 51.3 percent on the Colorado and Southern Lines. On the C. B. & Q., interest charges fell 6.2 percent between 1901 and 1908 and for the whole period 1901–15 showed a decline of 4.2 percent. In contrast, interest charges on the Colorado and Southern between 1908 and 1915 increased 27.3 percent, a discouraging omen.

During 1901–7, net income on the C. B. & Q. stabilized at around $13,000,000 a year. The next two years showed the effects of the panic of 1907, but thereafter net income showed a steady and gratifying rise, so that by 1915 it had increased to 134.5 percent of the 1901 figure. In contrast, the Colorado and Southern showed fairly steady gains until 1910, but thereafter, except for 1913 and 1915, the decline was sharp and steady. Net income on the C. & S. in 1915 was 74.5 percent under that of 1908. Certainly part of the difficulties of the C. & S. resulted from the fact that on December 13, 1912, the Colorado Midland went into receivership and that on June 16, 1914, the Trinity and Brazos Valley sought protection of the courts. Thus important sources of other income were cut off completely so far as the Colorado and Southern was concerned.

The performances of the two systems were reflected in dividends paid. On the C. B. & Q., dividends remained on a modest plateau during the first part of the Hill period and then were increased. The rate of 6.5 percent for 1901 was increased to 6.75 percent the next year and in 1903 to 7 percent, where it remained through 1907. In 1908 a dividend of 8 percent was declared out of income, and this rate prevailed through 1916; in 1908, however, a distribution of 6 percent out of surplus—the first since 1880—was made upon acquisition of the C. & S. By contrast, dividends on the Colorado and Southern followed a highly irregular course. Payments of $1,300,000 were made in 1908–12, inclusive, but they fell to $990,000 the next year, to $340,000 in 1914, and were eliminated entirely in 1915.

Dull as they are, these statistics—and they represent only the highlights—tell a story. They reflect, on the part of the C. B. & Q., a steady growth both in volume of business and in the efficiency with which it was handled. The Colorado and Southern Lines, on the other hand, reflected more of a feast-or-famine regime, owing primarily to the facts that its welfare was dependent on more restricted types of traffic and that it was heavily committed on behalf of its subsidiaries. As the years ahead were to demonstrate, these divergent characteristics of the two properties were to become even more marked.

Fortunately these developments took place during a period of economic and political stability. But the rumblings of the European war that broke out in the summer of 1914 suggested that the years immediately ahead would be anything but normal and peaceful. If the system was to be tried under more difficult conditions, it was fortunate indeed that there had been an opportunity for the C. B. & Q. to integrate itself with the Northern Lines and to digest the Colorado and Southern. The strength of the resulting combination was soon to be tested.

CHAPTER 16

World War I and the New Dispensation

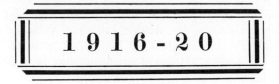

1916-20

• CONFLICT QUICKENS THE TEMPO, 1915–16 •

I N COMMON with the nation's other railways, the C. B. & Q. performed less freight service and earned less revenue in 1914 than in
1913 and witnessed further declines in 1915. In contrast, 1916
brought an upsurge of both traffic and revenues, as well as of operating
expenses, as the influence of the European war made itself felt. Principal
traffic increases were in grain, livestock, bituminous coal, and petroleum,
all basic raw materials. The twenty percent rise in coal traffic could be
traced to the demands of the conflict as well as to the fact that western
consumers, unable to obtain eastern coal because of the car shortage and
the congestion already becoming apparent there, had begun buying from
nearby sources. The stimulus to business was likewise reflected on the
Colorado and Southern Lines; the directors, in fact, duly noting an almost
threefold increase in net income, declared a modest two percent dividend
on the preferred stock.

System officials soberly realized, however, that costs, already on
the upgrade, could be expected to rise even more rapidly than revenues,

chiefly because of the wage situation. As a result of the general disappointment among employees of the western roads over their failure to achieve higher wages in the spring of 1915, the four train-service brotherhoods met in Chicago in December of that year to inaugurate a national movement for the so-called eight-hour day. The intention was not, of course, to limit the working day to eight hours, but to use eight hours, rather than the established ten hours, as the basis for computing one day's work. Early in 1916, the railways formed a committee to negotiate with the brotherhoods, but every plan of compromise, mediation, or arbitration failed, and in consequence the unions called a nationwide strike for Labor Day, September 4.

As the date drew near, neither side showed the slightest disposition to yield. On August 29, President Wilson dispatched to Congress a special message urging that an act be passed at once, establishing the eight-hour day, in order to safeguard "the life and interests of the nation."[1] A bill to this effect passed the House on September 1, the Senate on the following day, and was signed by the President on September 3, to become effective January 1, 1917. The threat of a paralyzing strike was averted, though unfortunately Congress, despite President Wilson's recommendations, solved only the immediate crisis and failed to provide any orderly machinery for the future settlement of disputes as to wages, hours, and working conditions.

The expected impact of this new wage act, known as the Adamson Law, was specifically mentioned by Hale Holden in both the C. B. & Q. and the C. & S. annual reports as one of the principal causes of the additional expenses that could be expected. "The 1917 figures," he added, "will also reflect the more recent increases in cost of locomotive fuel and materials and supplies, accruing on account of economic and other conditions affecting the country as a result of the European War and conditions relating thereto. Pending revenue measures likewise indicate a substantial increase in taxes payable during the coming year."[2]

Even more pertinent than finances to the probable performance of the Burlington during the oncoming crisis was the state of its physical plant. In this respect, the system was in a peculiarly happy position because it was just bringing to completion major improvements that would speed traffic and increase transportation capacity. The heavy-duty line between Laurel, Montana, and Orin Junction, Wyoming, had been completed late in 1914; the essential eight-mile link between Guernsey and Wendover went into service in December 1915. The new Kansas City bridge was opened for traffic on February 1, 1917, and at the end of the

[1] Quoted in I. L. Sharfman: *The Interstate Commerce Commission* (New York: The Commonwealth Fund; 1931), Vol. I, p. 101, footnote 40.

[2] CB&Q, AR December, 1916, p. 18; C&S, AR 1916, p. 14. The wording of this paragraph was identical in both reports.

same year the new bridge across the Ohio River connected the southern end of the Beardstown–Centralia–Metropolis line with the railways from the South that converged at Paducah. Thus in the crucial period when traffic was rapidly mounting, the system opened entirely new gateways to the Northwest and to the South and removed a potential bottleneck at Kansas City. At the same time extensive remodeling of the Denver Union Terminal, carried on during 1915–16, modernized facilities at that point, and construction of nearly a hundred miles of double track, particularly on the Beardstown and LaCrosse divisions, facilitated operation where traffic was particularly dense. In 1916 alone, nearly $1,500,000 was expended on double-tracking.

Important as these improvements were in expanding the traffic capacity of the Q, they were matched in significance by extensive rebuilding of the locomotive-repair machine shops at West Burlington. The old facilities, constructed in 1880, were not equipped to repair the heavier types of locomotive then coming into use. Another outlay of $1,500,000 was devoted to the modernization of these facilities, a task that was completed in the spring of 1917. Two additional changes, less essential to efficient operation but highly desirable from the standpoint of the public, were destined to alter radically the visible aspect of the plant. Late in 1914, the Pennsylvania Lines, the Milwaukee, and the Burlington organized the Chicago Union Station Company to carry out the long-planned rebuilding of their common passenger terminal in the metropolis. A few months later, action by the authorities of Aurora compelled the Burlington to elevate its tracks through that city, requiring the purchase of large amounts of property and relocation of the line at a cost of over $3,000,000. Satisfactory progress on both projects was made through 1915 and 1916. Thus, so far as the physical plant was concerned, the company was in an excellent position to handle an increased load.

One episode during 1916 underlined the fact that the company was specifically bracing itself for possible wartime conditions. On June 20, 1916, Holden directed that all employees who were or might become members of the National Guard in the various states, and who might therefore be called for army service, should be granted leaves of absence "with the understanding that their regular positions will be held for them while absent and will be available for them upon return from service."[3] On July 6, when J. N. Redfern, Superintendent of Employment, reported to Holden that 126 employees were already in the National Guard, Holden responded that he wanted a complete list kept in all cases where enlistment caused "distress or privation resulting from lack of support of dependent relatives during enlistment period."[4] The management was

[3] Hale Holden to H. E. Byram, et al., June 20, 1916, CB&Q/Emp.
[4] J. N. Redfern to Holden, July 6, 1916; Holden to Redfern, July 7, 1916, CB&Q/Emp.

determined to see that not only its employees, but their families as well, should not be placed at a disadvantage as a result of responding to the needs of the country. On August 3, Vice-President Bracken reported to the general superintendents that, in line with the policy adopted by the management, the general chairmen of the operating brotherhoods had agreed without qualification to protect the seniority of all employees called into the army.

These signs of the times had their ominous counterparts in Washington. The Army Appropriation Act of August 29, 1916, carried two provisions of prime importance to the railways. Certain members of the President's cabinet were named as a Council for National Defense and given the power to nominate to the President a seven-man advisory commission composed of persons having some special knowledge of the nation's industries and natural resources. Among the seven appointed was Daniel Willard, president of the Baltimore and Ohio, who less than a decade before had served as vice-president of the C. B. & Q. lines. As Transportation Commissioner, he was in a position to act as key liaison man between the government and the railways, and his first-hand knowledge of the Burlington gave him added insight into the particular status of that system.

The second pertinent provision of the Act provided that "the President in time of war is empowered, through the Secretary of War, to take possession and assume control of any system or systems of transportation, or any part thereof, and to utilize the same, to the exclusion, as far as may be necessary, of all other traffic thereon, for the transfer or transportation of troops, war material and equipment, and for such other purposes connected with the emergency as may be needful or desirable."[5] As long as the nation remained at peace, this provision would remain inoperative, but if war became a reality, it would have laid the legal basis for federal control, should conditions warrant it.

Late in 1916, it became increasingly apparent that conditions were indeed growing worse. Allied purchases reached new peaks each month, laying a particularly heavy burden on the lines serving the Atlantic seaboard. The situation was aggravated by a failure to coordinate either railway or port facilities, and reached critical proportions when the western grain crop and the fuel supply for the winter began moving into the Northeast. Congestion of terminals and the widespread use of cars for storage purposes virtually choked the eastern lines while draining the western and southern carriers of their cars. As Holden noted in his report for 1916, "the car situation and serious congestion in the East [have] militated against free movement [of cars] to western territory."[6]

In desperation, shippers turned to the I. C. C., praying for an order

[5] Army Appropriation Act of 1916, 39 *Statutes-at-Large*, Ch. 436, August 29, 1916.
[6] CB&Q, AR December, 1916, p. 15.

that would require the prompt return of cars to the lines that owned them. At a hearing of the Commission on December 28, 1916, the carriers were directed to show cause "why certain rules intended to effect a relocation and more efficient use of equipment should not be prescribed."[7] Three weeks later the Commission published a report on car supply and issued specific rules, to become effective April 15, in respect to open-top coal and coke cars, and cars with regulated heating or ventilation. Rules respecting other types of equipment—including ordinary boxcars—were held in abeyance, pending expected action by the carriers themselves, but unfortunately certain roads refused to subscribe to a voluntary agreement dated February 2, 1917, which would have laid the basis for uniform action. As the United States came closer to entering the war, the Commission reached the reluctant conclusion that "none of the several carriers' committees . . . was vested with full power by all carriers to deal with the urgent transportation requirements of the country."[8] Unless the situation could be improved, federal control appeared ever more likely.

Early on the morning of Good Friday, April 6, 1917, Congress declared war on the Central Powers. To discover what was expected of the Burlington and all the nation's railroads in respect to overall mobilization and strategy, all eyes turned to Washington.

In a very preliminary way, the groundwork for concerted action had already been laid. At the suggestion of Daniel Willard, the American Railway Association had named an eighteen-man committee on National Defense, and early in March 1917 this group had met with the Secretary of War and others to sketch out in general terms a basis for railway-government cooperation in case of war. After the actual declaration, the administration's concern over the transport situation crystallized rapidly. President Wilson expressed his anxiety to the Secretary of War, Newton D. Baker, and said he feared that it might be necessary for the government to take over the control and operation of the railroads, as had already been done in England. Baker passed this information along to Willard, who, feeling that federal intervention was "neither necessary nor desirable at that time," immediately suggested that if the Council of National Defense would request him, as Chairman of its Advisory Commission, to take the matter up with the railroad executives, he believed "that they would take such immediate steps as might be thought necessary to meet the situation."[9] To this proposal the administration agreed, and on April 11, 1917, at Willard's invitation, fifty railroad presidents convened in an epoch-making session at Washington. The president of the Burlington, Hale Holden, was elected chairman of the gathering.

[7] ICC, AR 1917, pp. 62–3. Cf. Sharfman: *ICC*, op. cit., Vol. I, pp. 140–1.
[8] ICC, AR 1917, pp. 63–4, quoted extensively in Sharfman, *ICC*, op. cit.
[9] Daniel Willard, speech at Washington, April 11, 1917, reprinted by AAR in a pamphlet entitled "Lest We Forget" (Washington, 1940), p. 7.

The first and basic step was adoption of a pledge on the part of all the nation's railroads to "coordinate their operations in a continental railway system, merging during such period [of crisis] all their merely individual and competitive activities in the effort to produce a maximum of national transportation efficiency."[1] To implement this pledge, the A. R. A.'s Committee on National Defense was enlarged, and a special five-man executive committee, generally known as the Railroads' War Board, was chosen from its membership. To this Board, responsibility for formulating an operating policy for "all or any of the railways" was voluntarily delegated, the said policy to be "accepted and earnestly made effective by the several managements of the individual railroad companies."[2] Fairfax Harrison, president of the Southern, was appointed chairman. Elected to serve with him were Julius Kruttschnitt, chairman of the Southern Pacific; Samuel Rea, president of the Pennsylvania; Howard Elliott, president of the New Haven; and Hale Holden of the Burlington. To provide effective liaison with the government, Daniel Willard and E. E. Clark of the Interstate Commerce Commission were named ex-officio members. It was a significant commentary on the reputation of the Burlington as a training school for railroad executives that three of the seven men constituting the Board either were or had been officials of the system.

Spurred by the sobering realization that the United States was at war, and possessing at last the pledged cooperation of all the nation's railroads, the War Board sprang into immediate action. Because traffic congestion and the resulting car shortage presented the most immediate problems, its first step was to set up a special Commission on Car Service. Throughout the rest of 1917, therefore, while the Railroads' War Board was functioning, the I. C. C. virtually held its own Car Service Bureau (authorized by the Esch Car Service Act of May 29, 1917) in abeyance, on the sound theory that as long as the carriers had their own organization at work, and as long as net results were satisfactory, nothing would be gained by duplicated effort.

A somewhat similar situation existed in respect to the Priorities Act of August 10, 1917, under which a Director of Priority was authorized to centralize all orders requiring preferential handling of essential traffic. Up to December 1917, only two orders emanated from this source. This apparent restraint did not spring solely from a desire to leave the matter of priority in the hands of the carriers; the War and Navy departments, the Shipping Board, and the Fuel Administration each possessed separate authorities for insisting on preferential treatment. All of them exercised these functions to an increasing extent, and apparently the desire of the Director of Priority not to confuse matters further, rather than his will-

[1] Ibid., p. 27.
[2] The resolution is quoted in full in ICC, AR 1917, p. 64.

[298]

ingness to leave the situation to the railroads, accounted for his lack of activity. Yet in a sense his authority, like that of the I. C. C.'s Car Service Bureau, was a weapon in the War Board's closet. It is perhaps fair to say that insofar as the I. C. C. and the Commissioner of Transportation were concerned, the Railroads' War Board and the carriers as a whole were left virtually free during 1917 to work out the rail transportation problem as they thought best.

• THE BURLINGTON GOES TO WAR, 1917 •

WHEN HALE HOLDEN returned to Chicago from the Washington meeting of April 11, 1917, one of the first things he did was to call a special session of the board of directors for April 20. Present on that occasion, among others, were former president George B. Harris, future president Ralph Budd (then chief engineer and assistant to the president of the Great Northern), and Charles E. Perkins, Jr. The direct experience of these men on the Burlington, past and future, was to span the period from 1866 to 1949; such a tradition of continuity of management meant that at times of crisis particular decisions could be made with a full understanding of the capabilities and policies of the road. As far as the future was concerned, it meant that those who would some day be charged with executive responsibility had an early opportunity to see policy in the making.

Holden presented to the directors the pledge of cooperation adopted in Washington on April 11, and secured its acceptance on behalf of the company. He also obtained authority to act on the Railroads' War Board. Turning then to the immediate necessities, the directors authorized purchase of fifty-five freight engines and ten passenger locomotives. Less than a month later, Vice-President Byram advised all superintendents that recruiting of several regiments of railway men for service in France was underway; the Burlington had been asked to supply a captain as engineer of maintenance of way, several lieutenants to act as roadmasters or supervisors of track, sergeants as extra gang foremen, and corporals as bridge and section foremen. Ten days later came a call for twenty-four telegraphers. By mid-July, more than 400 employees had enlisted, and on August 1, 449 others were called up in the first draft. These developments—random samples from the complex life of a vast institution—meant one thing: war was a reality on the Burlington, and there was a colossal job to be done.

In Chicago and Childress, Burlington and Billings, Denver and Deadwood—wherever the system penetrated—wheels moved a turn faster, cars carried an extra ton or two, and men and women worked harder and longer. Immediate objectives were to speed to completion those additions and betterments already authorized and to put underway construction of special facilities specifically required for military purposes. The former category included rebuilding the freight terminals in Chicago. Temporary facilities adjacent to Canal Street were completed, and the foundation was laid for the freight houses at the southeast corner of Harrison and Canal streets. At Clyde, beyond the city limits, twenty-nine miles of additional yard trackage, coal and water facilities, a new roundhouse and shop, and miscellaneous other buildings were finished in rapid succession. More than $1,250,000 was spent during the year on these metropolitan facilities alone. Meanwhile, the Burlington, South Chicago Terminal Railroad Company was incorporated and acquired a considerable tract of land near the mouth of the Calumet River in South Chicago, with trackage and docks adjacent to the Belt Railway of Chicago. Although there was no need at the moment for these facilities, it was felt that they would soon be necessary to handle expanding traffic. Similar potential bottlenecks were eliminated by widespread terminal improvements throughout the Burlington Route, priority being given to work vital to the war effort. Among special facilities rushed to completion were those at Camp Grant, where a large amount of trackage, as well as passenger and freight stations, was constructed in connection with the army cantonment established there in July 1917.

The company's Agricultural Department, backed by long experience, launched an extensive program to increase agricultural production. By demonstrations and circulars, the Department taught improved methods of farming, with especial reference to such staple foods as beans and potatoes. Improved techniques in dry farming were advertised with great success throughout southern Kansas, Nebraska, Wyoming, and Colorado. In addition, an equally successful campaign on the preparation of silage averted the feed shortage that threatened the livestock and hog industries. Similar programs in plant improvements and agricultural propaganda were undertaken by the Colorado and Southern.

Inevitably these special efforts, combined with the national increase in all lines of activity, resulted in establishing new records for transportation service performed. Ton-miles on the Burlington in 1917, for example, increased twenty percent over 1916, and total operating revenues, for both the C. B. & Q. and the C. & S. Lines, reached new all-time highs. Operating expenses also reached new peaks, principally because of increases in rates of pay, the rise in the number of employees, and the mounting cost of fuel and other supplies. Taxes shot sky high: on the C. B. & Q. federal levies increased 364 percent, to reach a combined total of $8,400,000; on the Colorado and Southern Lines, taxes exceeded one million dollars, representing an increase of approximately fifty percent. There were indications, however, of increased efficiency. On the C. B. & Q., for example, the twenty percent increase in ton-miles of revenue freight was handled with an increase of only ten percent in freight-train miles run; total average tons per freight-train mile rose from 670 to 726. This showing was partly a result of the addition of fifty new freight-train locomotives and nearly 5,000 freight cars. Nevertheless, the system could not provide as many cars as were demanded, largely, according to Holden, because of the "general heavy traffic conditions throughout the country and the absence from home of large numbers of cars . . . on other lines throughout the country."[3]

In respect to financial results, the experience of the C. B. & Q. in 1917 mirrored national conditions: total operating revenues increased approximately thirteen percent over 1916; expenses rose about twenty percent; net income, some ten percent. It is noteworthy, however, that the Q's net income per share equaled the national average, despite the fact that its taxes mounted twice as fast as the average of all roads. The disparity between the C. B. & Q.'s transportation job and that of the nation's roads in general was even more striking; its twenty percent increase in ton-miles was far above the nine percent rise recorded by all roads. From both a financial and an operating standpoint, then, the company was carrying its part of the war burden successfully. Yet, as the summer of 1917 gave way to fall, the national railway situation was deteriorating rapidly. Despite heroic efforts by the Railroads' War Board, only emergency measures could forestall a serious breakdown.

• THE GOVERNMENT STEPS IN •

IN RECAPITULATING THE FACTORS that eventually led to federal control late in 1917, it is essential to point out that some causes were of long standing and of a chronic nature; the war emergency simply made them acute. As Perkins had never wearied of pointing out, for example, the prohibition of pooling in the original Interstate Commerce Act of 1887 had taken away the principal and most effective means the roads had to eliminate rate wars, prevent discrimination, and stabilize railway income. And as Howard Elliott made clear in his book *The Truth about the Railroads*, published in 1913, after more than a quarter century's experience with the Interstate Commerce Act, there were many indications that the degree of competition enforced by the regulatory structure as it then stood was a deterrent to the normal expansion of trade.

"All the legislation," Walker D. Hines later wrote in referring to the period, "both Federal and State, proceeded on the principle that the sole concern of the public was to see that the railroads did not impose upon the public. The possibility that the laws might be so strict as to prevent the railroads from adequately serving the public had not become a substantial motive in legislation."[4] Specifically, the railroads during the years

---

[3] CB&Q, AR 1917, p. 19.

[4] Walker D. Hines: *War History of American Railroads* (New Haven: Yale University Press; 1928). Hines had been Assistant Director-General of the United States Railroad Administration under McAdoo in 1918, and succeeded McAdoo early in 1919. I. L. Sharfman: *The American Railroad Problem: A Study in War and Reconstruction* (New York: The Century Co.; 1921), pp. 105, 123–5.

immediately preceding the war crisis had not been permitted to earn sufficient revenue to maintain their plants and equipment properly or to attract into the industry the new capital essential to keep the plant at peak efficiency and to finance improvements. On the whole, and particularly after the passage in 1910 of the Mann-Elkins Act, which authorized suspension of contemplated rate increases, the Interstate Commerce Commission had adopted a consistently restrictive rate-making policy.

Like other roads, the Burlington had inevitably been affected by this situation. In 1912, for example, despite a substantial increase in freight and passenger traffic over the previous year, a decrease occurred both in gross earnings and in unit revenue for the service rendered; the average rate per ton-mile of 7.52 mills was the lowest in the history of the road. The decreases in freight earnings were partly the result of a larger movement of low-grade traffic, but they also stemmed from rate reductions ordered by both the I. C. C. and state commissions. Even a relatively prosperous line like the C. B. & Q. most definitely felt the pinch.

The confusion that resulted from the conflict between state and federal regulation had imposed still another burden on the railways during the prewar years. Because the Constitution of the United States, as well as the Interstate Commerce Act and its various amendments, limited the authority of the federal government to interstate commerce, a great mass of state laws, variously interpreted and enforced by forty-eight different authorities, applied to the carriers. Different regulations were in effect regarding safety devices, operating practices, service, and finance. But particularly in the field of rates the situation was chaotic. Although a large majority of all railroads were, as they are now, interstate carriers, much of their business, both passenger and freight, was conducted within the territorial limits of one state. Strict and concurrent application of both local and federal rates was not merely difficult and expensive; it was often impossible.

This situation had led the Great Northern and Northern Pacific to play a prominent part in the Minnesota Rate cases (1913), and though that litigation led to a validation of the specific state rates in question, the Supreme Court recognized clearly the discriminatory effect state rates could have upon interstate commerce. Consequently in the Shreveport case of the following year, the Court specifically sustained an I. C. C. rate order that in effect replaced and rendered void a local rate deemed discriminatory. Thus the Burlington's owners lent their weight to the movement toward the centralization of rate-making which eventually bore fruit in the provisions of the Transportation Act of 1920. This relief, however, was obviously too late to ameliorate the situation just before World War I.

Other weaknesses in the prewar railroad situation stemmed partly, and in some cases wholly, from practices within the industry. There were just enough cases of unsound over-expansion and financial manipulation to suggest that the hard times so loudly proclaimed by the roads were not caused entirely by the depressed level of rates or the confusion between federal and state regulation. Pressed by the exigencies of competition, some roads were inclined to heed the importunities of shippers who demand special services detrimental to the public as a whole; demurrage charges, for example, were laxly enforced, and the reconsignment privilege was grossly abused. Then, too, there was some duplication of service and facilities, circuitous routing, and consequent unnecessary expense. As far as labor was concerned, the absence of legal safeguards against certain forms of exploitation, in terms of either wages or working conditions, created a situation that might become explosive if, as actually occurred in 1916, labor was suddenly put in a dominant bargaining position. Furthermore, there was no effective machinery to adjust labor disputes when they arose.

In respect to these particular elements of weakness, it is difficult to assess the extent to which the Burlington was typical of, or different from, the industry as a whole. Financially, the C. B. & Q. proper had kept its house in extraordinarily good order; on the other hand, the Colorado and Southern was still suffering from the over-ambitious plans of the Hawley regime. But at least the system was definitely free from the twin bugbears of "manipulation" and "banker control." Whether, or to what extent, the management catered to influential shippers or provided unnecessary service is simply not a matter of record. Then, as now, business over the Chicago–Omaha and Chicago–Twin Cities routes was among the most competitive in the nation, and the company probably followed whatever lawful practices had proved most effective in getting the largest possible share of available traffic. As to labor, the meager records reveal a situation neither better nor worse than throughout the country generally.

Inevitably, however, the Burlington was but one link, albeit an important one, in the national railway chain, and that chain was no stronger than its weakest link, particularly in respect to plant capacity. Physical breakdown or congestion in any strategic area could—apart from all other factors—slow down the nation's wheels; in such a situation, whatever other comparative advantages the Burlington might possess would avail it nothing. As 1917 drew to a close, the company found itself individually in better than average shape, but inescapably involved in a fundamentally unsound national situation.

Actually, the approaching crisis was somewhat ironic in view of the fact that from April to September 1917 the situation had seemed under control. Acting principally through its Car Service Commission, the War Board had put into immediate effect regulations affecting the use of equipment and the movement of freight. Embargoes were placed on congested areas, equipment was shifted to points of heaviest traffic density, successful campaigns were launched for heavier loading of cars, and to some extent both traffic and equipment were pooled. As a result, accumulation of cars at eastern terminals was cut from 145,000 in February to about 60,000 in July, and car shortages were reduced from more than 148,000 on May 1 to less than 35,000 on September 1. The voluntary reduction in non-essential passenger service not only conserved an enormous amount of coal but also saved 25 million train miles.

Yet new and alarming elements of weakness tended to offset these gains. When the grain harvest of 1917 began moving east in the late summer, congestion on the seaboard increased abruptly. Even more serious, however, was the coal situation—the worst in history. Normally a good deal of this traffic moved northeast by sea, but the scarcity of vessels threw an unusual burden on the rails, whose prevailing system of distribution was poor at best. Matters were complicated further by the onset of an abnormally severe winter. As car shortage increased, so did the conflicting orders of the half-dozen government agencies authorized to issue priority orders and insist on preferential handling of freight. By November 1, car shortages exceeded the May peak; cars waiting to be unloaded on eastern lines reached 180,000 above normal.

Fully alive to the gravity of the situation, the War Board met with Harry Garfield, Fuel Administrator, on November 24, 1917, and agreed "that all available facilities on all railroads east of Chicago be pooled to the extent necessary to furnish maximum freight movement";[5] the operating vice-presidents of the lines involved constituted a Committee of Seven to manage the properties as a unit. On December 5, with the situation still precarious, the Interstate Commerce Commission sent Congress a special report urging immediate and outright unification of the railway plant. Two alternatives were suggested: (1) leave the roads under private management, but suspend both the anti-pooling clause of the Interstate Commerce Act and the Sherman Anti-trust Act as applicable to railways for the duration and extend government financial aid to the carriers; (2) put the roads in the hands of the President of the United States and guarantee to the carriers a specific return for the use of their property.

In response to this report, Hale Holden, speaking for the Railroads' War Board, issued a public statement on December 8, 1917. The railways, he declared, were hauling all supplies for seventy-two military cantonments, representing the movement of some 2,500 cars daily, in addition to handling essential coal and foodstuffs. "It can," he said, "be truthfully stated that the measures taken under the direction of the Board have adequately met the transportation requirements of the country up to the present time." As to the immediate crisis, he felt that the Committee of

[5] Fairfax Harrison to T. W. Gregory, Attorney-General of the United States, November 27, 1917, CB&Q/Pres File #1045; quoted portion from Sharfman: *The American Railroad Problem*, p. 81.

Seven at Pittsburgh would succeed in its efforts and predicted that "in the near future traffic will be moving in much better manner than heretofore."[6] His suggestion that some order should be introduced promptly into the existing priority muddle was seconded the following day (Sunday) by Harrison at an emergency closed meeting of railway executives in New York. At that family gathering, a large part of the blame for the existing situation was laid on the government's failure to "coordinate their own activities and take off our backs all these quartermasters, who are giving preference orders to the extent that on the Pittsburgh division of the Pennsylvania, 85 percent of their traffic is moving on preference order," and, he continued, "if they will . . . sit with us and tell us what the Government wants as to questions of policy, we will do what is necessary to move the traffic."[7] It was true, he said, that the roads could use $600,000,000 for equipment and facilities, but he doubted both the wisdom and the necessity of repealing the anti-trust and anti-pooling laws. He was convinced that the railroads were getting as much service out of the plant as was possible under any form of management.

But time was running out. The vigorous and presumably exhaustive report of the I. C. C. to Congress on December 5 not only foreshadowed a drastic change in government policy designed to meet the emergency, but also forced the railway executives, still eager to keep the rails under private management, back to their last line of defense. While the outcome still hung in the balance, Harrison on December 24 forwarded to Senator Newlands a set of proposals prepared by Kruttschnitt—and presumably representing the views of the War Board—designed to give the necessary legal basis for effective unification under private control.

But neither recapitulations of past performance nor promises and plans for the future forestalled federal control. Electing to follow the second alternative suggested by the Interstate Commerce Commission, President Wilson issued a proclamation on December 26 whereby, through the Secretary of War, he took possession and assumed control of the railways as of noon, December 28. William G. McAdoo, given the title of Director General of the Railroads, was to act for the President, and to enter at once into negotiations with the several companies with the purpose of concluding agreements under which, in exchange for revenues from their properties and the use of these properties, the government would undertake to guarantee to each road annually the equivalent of its average net operating income for the three-year period ending June 30, 1917.

Accordingly, the Railroads' War Board met for the last time on December 31. In tendering their resignations to McAdoo, its members offered the services of their various sub-committees. The Director General,

---

[6] Statement by Hale Holden, December 8, 1917, CB&Q/Pres File #1045.
[7] Statement by Fairfax Harrison, December 9, 1917, CB&Q/Pres File #1045.

on accepting the resignations, asked that one of the five regular members of the War Board be assigned as a member pro-tem of his own Advisory Committee, to take over, until further notice, immediate supervision of these sub-committees, and to act as custodian of the voluminous information and special reports accumulated by the Board. Hale Holden was named for this key assignment during the period of transition; telegrams were dispatched to the nation's railway executives so advising them on the same day. Some years later, Holden had this to say of the War Board's efforts during 1917: "We were so serenely unprepared for the whole situation that I feel certain that the career of the War Board and its experience would, in case of another emergency, be utilized as the basis for a substantial improvement in method. . . ."[8]

· WINNING THE WAR ON THE RAILS, 1918 ·

IN VIEW OF THE ENORMOUS TASK AHEAD, the organization set up by the government and the railroads at the close of 1917 was surprisingly simple. A central administrative agency at Washington included divisions of Finance and Purchases, Capital Expenses, Operation, Public Service and Accounting, Law and Labor. For purposes of operation, the country was divided into seven regions, each in charge of a regional director with his own operating staff. Each region was divided into districts, each of which included a number of individual railroads presided over by federal managers. Without exception, all the operating directors and managers were experienced railroad men, and as a rule the former president of each railroad became its federal manager. Disturbance of administrative organization was kept to a minimum; the actual operating head of each railroad simply reported to a representative of the Director General instead of to his own board of directors. Affairs of a strictly corporate nature were carried on by the railroad companies in their private capacity.

On the Burlington, Hale Holden, president of the C. B. & Q., was appointed regional director of the Central Western Region. Consequently the executive vice-president, Claude G. Burnham, became the ranking official on the C. B. & Q. and the logical choice for federal manager. At the same time, Charles E. Perkins, Jr., son of the former president, and a director of the C. B. & Q., stepped in as president of the private corporation for the duration. The corporate and federal administrative organizations then were completed by selecting certain former officers for each. For example, Vice-Presidents Howland and Howard remained with the corporate organization, whereas Vice-President Baldwin became treasurer for the federal manager. There were two sets of officials, but their work was complementary rather than overlapping, and no confusion resulted. Similar reassignment of officials took place on the Colorado and Southern

[8] Holden to Hines, January 26, 1926, CB&Q/Pres File #1045.

Lines; Robert Rice became federal manager, but as he reported to Hale Holden, regional director of the Central Western Region, matters were much the same as before.

The matter of compensation to railroads under federal control was likewise worked out on a simple basis. As finally authorized in the act of March 21, 1918, the government guaranteed to each carrier an annual compensation equal to its average annual railway operating income for the three years ending June 30, 1917. Provision was made for adjusting this compensation if for any reason a carrier's earnings during the base period were abnormal. For the Burlington this meant that the C. B. & Q. was to receive a standard annual return of $33,360,683.11; the Colorado and Southern Railway Company, $2,481,211.88; the Fort Worth and Denver City Railway, $1,891,386.40; and the Wichita Valley, $352,367.05. Operating revenues, operating expenses, taxes (other than war taxes), equipment rents, and joint facility rents were assumed by the federal government. On the other hand, revenues from non-operating income were to accrue to the private companies, who were responsible for paying out, from the "standard return" and non-operating income, their corporate expenses, rents, miscellaneous and war taxes, interest, miscellaneous charges, and dividends, if any. As part of standard contracts between the companies and the government, the Director General undertook to return each railroad property at the end of federal control in "substantially as good repair and in substantially as complete equipment" as it was on January 1, 1918.[9] Various minor provisions took care of unusual circumstances, but the general theory of the underlying settlement was to guarantee sufficient earnings to the carriers to enable continuation of dividend payments and the maintenance of current security values. It was recognized that under war conditions deferred maintenance could hardly be avoided and that the diversion of traffic in the interests of unification would inevitably upset the long-established traffic relations of many railroads. For this reason, the standard return, based on an unusually prosperous test period, was deliberately designed to be on the generous side.

During 1918 the C. B. & Q. and C. & S. Lines set new records for transportation service as measured by revenue ton-miles. As a matter of fact, the increases were far above the 1.9 percent rise for the nation as a whole. On the C. B. & Q., the movement of livestock and animal products increased more than twenty percent, that of agricultural products over ten percent. Soft coal constituted more than one third of the entire tonnage handled by the railroad, thus setting an all-time record. That the company carried nearly two million more tons of revenue freight with practically no increase in the number of cars revealed the true character of the wartime performance. The management frankly stated that this

[9] C&S, AR 1918, pp. 7, 9–11.

achievement was "largely due to the hearty cooperation of shippers . . . in securing a maximum load."[1] On the Colorado and Southern Lines there were substantial increases in the products of agriculture, animals, and in manufactured products. Owing partly to a marked increase in traffic and partly to rate increases, averaging approximately twenty percent, which became effective on June 25, 1918, system freight revenues rose to new heights. Throughout the system the number of passengers carried during 1918 decreased, but passenger revenues mounted slightly, owing to the establishment in June 1918 of a basic rate of three cents per mile.

Expenses, however, mounted even more rapidly than revenues. One reason lay in the rapid rise of labor costs. During the first year of American participation in the conflict, the high wages paid by war industries had consistently placed the railways at a competitive disadvantage in the labor market. Consequently, in April 1918, McAdoo, in General Order No. 27, authorized a general wage increase. The basis of calculation used, however, completely upset the long-established system of differentials that had existed among various types of work. Furthermore, in a laudable but overzealous attempt to eliminate certain wage discrepancies, the new order created a new set of inequalities. As a result, both management and labor protested vigorously; McAdoo thereupon named a new Board of Railroad Wages and Working Conditions to reconsider the situation. The conclusions of this Board affected not only immediate labor costs, but also labor-management relations for years to come. Supplement No. 4 to General Order No. 27, issued on July 25, 1918, provided that overtime beyond eight hours should be paid for at time and a half. Of equal if not greater importance, it spelled out a minute classification of jobs which meant that each man would perform but one restricted function; for any other task, no matter how closely allied or how near by, someone else had to be called in or the first man—should he do it—would receive extra pay while the "someone else" would be paid as well for doing nothing. This was the beginning of the now-famous featherbedding.

Other labor-management rulings of the Director General contributed both to rising costs and to future problems. General Order No. 8, dated February 21, 1918, had provided that no discrimination would be made against employees for membership or non-membership in labor organizations, a condition which at once cleared the way for the organization of those employees not already affiliated with some union. Shortly afterwards, General Orders Nos. 8 and 13, taken together, inaugurated a system of three Railway Boards of Adjustment to settle wage disputes. These boards had no jurisdiction over wage levels or hours; they were empowered to interpret agreements establishing wages and hours and relating to discipline and grievances. Each board consisted of four representatives of management and four representatives of labor. If any board was unable

[1] CB&Q, AR 1918, p. 16.

to reach a majority decision, provision was made for final appeal to the Director General. So effective was this system during the war that of some five thousand cases submitted to the boards, only ten were carried to the Director General. Later on, however, under the New Deal, the role and performance of these adjustment boards led to new complications in labor-management relations.

These changes, together with an expansion of the working force to more than 50,000, led to an increase of C. B. & Q. payroll costs in 1918 of over fifty percent compared with the preceding year. Nor was this all. The cost of materials and supplies mounted with alarming rapidity. The price of fuel for the C. B. & Q. increased forty-one percent over that of the preceding year; much of the coal used on the road was bought at prices fixed by the Fuel Administration because operators generally refused to make contracts on a lower basis in view of the demands from other industries and the increased cost of production. Materials other than fuel rose only some twelve percent, primarily because most of them had been contracted for in previous years.

It is difficult to judge by normal standards the efficiency of an entire plant under wartime conditions. As a matter of cold statistics, the operating ratio of the C. B. & Q. increased thirteen percent; that of the Colorado and Southern, eleven percent; and that of the Fort Worth, fourteen percent. The average for the system mounted from approximately sixty-four percent in 1917 to seventy-seven percent in 1918. In wartime, however, the objective was to move essential materials and troops; efficiency of handling necessarily took second place. What counted most, as far as the individual property was concerned, was the nature and extent of maintenance and long-run improvements. Naturally enough, these were confined primarily to projects immediately essential for moving the burden of war traffic. Total expenditures for road on the C. B. & Q. in 1918 were almost exactly the same as in 1917, whereas expenditures for equipment were cut almost seventy-five percent. Heavier rail, additional passing tracks, and miscellaneous servicing facilities were added at points of heaviest density, and the usual program of permanent bridge construction continued practically unabated. On the other hand, the rebuilding of the Chicago freight terminals, construction on the new Union Station, and the elevation of Canal Street either were stopped entirely or were reduced to a minimum. Relatively speaking, improvements of the Colorado and Southern Lines were far more extensive, for the capacity of the parent company was far greater at the outbreak of war than that of the subsidiary. All along the line from Cheyenne to Fort Worth, facilities were added to carry the war load. Coal chutes and turntables, stock and hog pens, industrial spurs, and in particular equipment for handling the mounting oil traffic were constructed, and the program of removing track from abandoned lines was speeded up.

As early as February 1918, more than 1,800 employees of the C. B. & Q. were serving in the army and navy, and two months later the total exceeded 2,000. At the end of the year the company pointed with pride to the fact that 5,511 employees were in service. Apparently no separate records were kept of the women who came to work on the system, though in the nation as a whole, the number of women railway employees rose from about 30,000 at the beginning of the year to over 100,000 on October 1, 1918. The Burlington Lines reflected this trend.

On November 11, 1918, the signing of the Armistice marked the end of hostilities. In line with the company's pledge of May 31, 1917, that as far as possible, every employee in military service would be reinstated in his old job, without loss of seniority, and in accord with the Director General's order No. 51 of November 1, 1918, Burnham as federal manager issued instructions on December 3 that every effort should be made to restore men in military service to their old positions, or to similar positions, as rapidly as possible. It took time, of course, to carry out demobilization, but by the end of 1919, 4,891, or nearly ninety percent of former Burlington employees in military service, had returned to the C. B. & Q.

• THE YEAR OF UNCERTAINTY: 1919 •

ALTHOUGH THE WAR ENDED LATE IN 1918, federal control continued till the end of February 1920. The reasons were several: the nation's economy was operating at a maximum level demanded by war requirements, and it was impossible to slow down the machine except in gradual fashion. The railways were geared to the economy as a whole, so they too remained on something of a war footing until their return to private management. But the temper of the nation underwent a change that can perhaps be most succinctly described as a let-down. This state of mind was apparent in many quarters. Many of the able railroad men who had served in the United States Railroad Administration resigned and returned to their own properties. The public at large, weary of wartime controls, was clamoring for the return of the carriers to private hands. Even Congress, called upon to appropriate funds to meet the deficit incurred by the Director General in operating the railways, failed to respond until the middle of the year, and then responded inadequately. Realizing the difficulty of enforcing many of the regulations put into effect during the war months, Walker D. Hines, who had succeeded McAdoo in 1919, gradually permitted separate railroads greater discretion in both operating and traffic policies.

During 1918, when the prime operating problem had been the elimination of freight-car congestion, car shortages had been reduced from more than 144,000 in January to less than 40,000 by November. The year 1919 witnessed a marked decline in business; by March, there was an unprecedented surplus of nearly half a million cars. Partly because of this decline in traffic and partly because of the nation-wide coal strike in November 1919, the volume of freight traffic dropped considerably on both the C. B. & Q. and the Colorado and Southern, though there were some increases on the Fort Worth and the Wichita Valley. On the other hand, the job of demobilizing military personnel was as difficult as the mobilization had been in 1918. Each constituent company of the system carried a much heavier passenger load than ever before. On the C. B. & Q., both freight and passenger revenues, thanks to the rate and fare increases of 1918, rose to new highs, though, as in 1918, expenses rose proportionately. But, as had so often occurred in the past, the C. & S. and the Fort Worth reported contrasting results; net revenue from railway operations dropped thirty-five percent on the former and rose seventy-eight percent on the latter, compared with 1918. The difference lay partly in the growing movement of agricultural and petroleum products from Texas and partly in the necessity of making large outlays for maintenance on the Colorado and Southern.

The failure of Congress to pay promptly what the government owed the railways and the prevailing high interest rate on funds borrowed privately meant that no new construction of any magnitude was undertaken on the Burlington in 1919. Progress was made, however, on projects already underway at Chicago and Aurora, while normal maintenance went ahead much as usual. Furthermore, and of long-range importance, the company focused its attention during the year on the undeveloped acres of public domain in the western parts of its territory.

Some six thousand inquiries about land came to the railroad during 1919, and a number of specialized farm problems called for immediate attention and assistance. This was a familiar challenge to the Burlington, and despite the uncertainties characteristic of other phases of the railroad situation, the company's Agricultural Department, operating on a system-wide basis, doubled its activities. Although advertising for settlers was restricted under government control, some twenty thousand booklets had been distributed, and the United States Railroad Administration published three new books about Colorado, Wyoming, and Nebraska. No less than 1,451 cars of immigrants' effects moved over the C. B. & Q.'s four western divisions, and 4,800 families were located. In addition, more than 2,000,000 acres were homesteaded in Wyoming, pointing to a further influx of some 2,500 families. Much of the demand, which the company largely ascribed to previous advertising, was from recently discharged military personnel; in one instance 3,300 soldiers applied for eighty farms available near Fort Laramie. As a result (and an unhappy one, as it turned out), land values increased from fifty to a hundred percent throughout the territory affected. The C. & S. experienced the same sort of boom on a smaller scale.

Looking toward the future, the company in 1919 assisted in securing

181 head of high-grade purebred dairy cows for farmers in Wyoming, Colorado, and New Mexico; held thirteen silo meetings and demonstrations; and recorded, as a result, the construction of 290 silos in the territory. In March, a potato-exhibit car was operated on the system's western lines. Through its agency, about 4,000 farmers were instructed in improved methods, 2,700 pounds of certified seed were distributed free, and special bulletins were circulated; as a result, other farmers in the region bought 120,000 pounds of good seed. Meanwhile the company purchased three cars of Minnesota seed potatoes; two were sent to various parts of the system, but one was reserved for the dry-land farmers along the Falcon line of the C. & S., who thus were given an excellent start in the production of seed potatoes for the Texas growers. The same themes ran through the reports of the Agricultural Department for the year: better livestock, planting of only the best seed, improved cultural methods, rotation and diversification, maintenance of soil fertility, increased production per acre, and greater returns per acre for the unit of labor expended. This last, after all was said and done, was the key objective of the company, for it alone could bring the higher farm incomes that would spell prosperity for the community and the railroad alike. Whatever might transpire in respect to labor-management relations or in Washington, the Burlington knew instinctively that the problem of efficient agricultural production and marketing would require continuous attention and prompt action.

With the signing of the Armistice, the psychological let-down that permeated the entire nation inevitably affected the labor-management situation on the railways. The patriotic stimulus that had prompted both sides to accept specific arrangements not altogether to their liking diminished noticeably. Labor naturally sought to gain as much as possible before the roads were returned to private control; management was equally eager to avoid further concessions that might later pose serious administrative and financial problems. Director General Hines unhappily found himself in the middle of these diverging viewpoints, a position complicated by the fact that even he was uncertain how long federal control would last. He was reluctant therefore to initiate additional basic changes in labor-management relations which might retard the inevitable readjustment to more normal conditions.

The early months of 1919 saw a rapid decline in overtime which caused hardship to the individual employee who found it increasingly difficult to meet the rising cost of living. Supplementary orders from the Director General brought certain categories of work into line. Such changes were minor in comparison with the sweeping changes made the previous year; they merely whetted labor's appetite for more adjustments. A strike begun during the first week of August 1919 by the Burlington shop crafts was settled by arbitration on the part of the Director General, who took a middle road in the dispute and authorized an increase of four cents an hour. As in other strikes that year, however, a return to work was demanded as a prerequisite to negotiation. The reluctance of labor to accept this stipulation was a characteristic that boded ill for peaceful settlement of future disputes.

The status of labor was not, however, the only factor militating against long-range planning and affirmative progress in the industry during 1919. Throughout the year, Washington was the focal point of a full-fledged debate of critical significance to all railways. On what basis and under what sort of regulatory system, if at all, should the roads be returned to their private owners and managers?

The defects of regulation as it had existed prior to the war were, on the whole, widely recognized, and it was generally agreed that the entire structure needed revising. The fundamental weakness was the negative character of the complex and often conflicting statutes and procedures that had been built up in a rather haphazard fashion over more than a generation. Public policy-makers had seemed more concerned with correcting specific abuses than with laying down a system which, while functioning as a safeguard against malpractices, would encourage the industry to serve the public interest best.

Rate-making, by and large, was anything but scientific. Indeed, it had been so restrictive, particularly in the decade before the war, that it had been impossible to coax an adequate amount of new capital into the industry, a fact that endangered both service and solvency. No clear guide existed as to what standards should be used in establishing a rate-base value for the roads or what might constitute a fair return on such value. So well established was the tradition of rate uniformity for competing lines that to take into account the varying and contrasting needs of strong and weak carriers had been virtually impossible.

Other defects in the regulatory structure had arisen not so much from the existence of legal obstacles as from the absence of adequate regulation in areas where the railroads themselves seemed either unwilling or unable to take appropriate action. Securities, for example, had always been issued with complete freedom from supervision, thereby not only complicating the task of determining the intrinsic worth of any given company's capitalization and the returns to which it was fairly entitled, but also leaving the door open to financial mismanagement and a certain amount of public skepticism concerning railroad credit. Unification of facilities, or even of entire companies, was frequently shunned by individual railroads more concerned with short-run advantages than with the prospect of eventual gains and improvement of service. Neither construction nor abandonment was controlled, despite the risk to railroad solvency represented by the building of duplicate and unnecessary facilities and the danger of such dislocation of trade as might follow cessation of operations.

Finally, no readily available machinery had existed which was capable of dealing with labor questions in such a way as to guard against sudden interruptions of service.

As early as December 1915, President Wilson had called the attention of Congress to the need for a general revision of the regulatory structure. In response, a joint Congressional sub-committee held hearings from November 1916 through December 1917. The immediate demands of war diverted attention from the long-range legislation that it had in mind, however, and not until December 11, 1918, when McAdoo proposed extension of government operation for five years, was the matter officially reopened. Vigorous and widely unfavorable reaction to McAdoo's suggestion led to the prompt submission of a wide variety of possible schemes.

The problem at hand was acute—no one denied that—but recognition of the situation was only the first step toward its solution. The barest outline of the principal proposals made reveals the range of the suggestions put forth. McAdoo felt that a five-year transitional period under federal tutelage would provide a test for some of the measures he had taken in the interests of efficiency and would afford an opportunity to rehabilitate railroad credit, thus rendering more sound any permanent adjustment that might be made. The four train-service brotherhoods, supporting the so-called Plumb Plan, advocated outright purchase of the railways by the United States in exchange for government bonds and lease of the properties to a single operating corporation whose stock would belong to all employees and whose directorate would represent equally the government, the "appointed" officials, and the "classified" employees.

On behalf of the railways, Howard Elliott and Daniel Willard, who naturally were strongly in favor of private ownership, asked first for the clear establishment of federal supremacy in the field of regulation; they suggested also that the authority of the I. C. C. be limited to quasi-judicial matters (such as the reasonableness of rates, discrimination, valuation, and the like), and that a Secretary of Transportation in the President's cabinet assume the Commission's executive and administrative functions. Like the I. C. C., the railroaders favored regulation of securities and construction and legal sanction for consolidation found to be in the public interest. They desired also greater freedom, subject to the Secretary's approval, for railways to cooperate with each other in respect to such matters as rate agreements, pooling, and service. The Commission was to be required to authorize rates adequate to maintain good service, attract new capital, and, specifically, cover wage costs and other transportation expenses. Such labor controversies as could not be solved by collective bargaining were to be referred to a board under the Secretary's jurisdiction, composed equally of representatives of the public, the employees, and the employers. Neither lockouts nor strikes were to take place pending the findings of the board or for a reasonable time thereafter.

These were by no means the only plans proposed. As the summer of 1919 wore on, however, it was apparent that the trend of opinion was definitely away from any form of government operation, whether of a temporary or a permanent nature. Two bills, each reflecting ideas presented in the long series of hearings, were accordingly introduced in Congress: the Esch bill in the House, the Cummins bill in the Senate. After full debate, they were passed in November and December, respectively, and were immediately referred to a joint Conference Committee, which held its first session on December 22. Two days later, President Wilson announced by proclamation that the railroads would be returned to their private owners on March 1, 1920. Congress therefore had to agree on a single measure that would gain presidential approval before that date.

Thus, not until the end of 1919 was it known precisely when federal control would cease, and even then only the broad outlines of the eventual legislative adjustment were discernible. The uncertainty over this situation and the prevailing labor unrest made it hardly surprising that the nation's railways were clearly reluctant to commit themselves to long-range plans.

• THE TRANSPORTATION ACT OF 1920 •

THE MEMBERS of the joint Conference Committee to which the Esch and Cummins bills were referred on December 22, 1919, were well aware that they had barely two months in which to iron out the differences between the two measures if legislative action was to be taken before the termination of federal control. On the advice of this committee, then, the compromise Esch–Cummins bill was accepted without amendment by the House on February 21 and by the Senate two days later. On February 28, 1920, the day before the carriers were to return to private hands, President Wilson signed what has become known as the Transportation Act of 1920. A landmark in the formulation of public policy, this law remains today the fundamental basis of the railway regulatory system.

In many ways the most striking innovation of the new measure was the sharp modification of the long-established policy of enforced competition. The Act provided that one railroad might acquire another through lease, stock ownership, or complete consolidation, provided that the I. C. C. found such acquisition to be in the public interest. The pooling of traffic or revenues was likewise legalized, and the carriers were specifically exempted from the operation of the anti-trust laws to the extent necessary to permit such combinations or cooperative arrangements as the Commission might sanction. One further requirement had to be met in cases involving any complete merger of two or more companies: no permanent consolidations could be authorized unless they were in accordance with a plan to be drawn up by the Commission under which the railways of the continental United States were to be grouped into a limited number of systems. In drawing up such a plan, the Commission was required insofar as possible to preserve competition and existing channels of trade and so to group the individual companies that the resulting systems could employ uniform rates and earn substantially the same rate of return on the value of the respective properties. This last proviso was a definite attempt to solve the weak-road situation; the general thought was that the peculiar problems of independent weak roads might be solved if they were parceled out among the stronger carriers and merged with them into systems of approximately equal size and strength.

As widely recommended during the hearings of 1919, the new Act gave the Commission virtually plenary authority over railway securities. It was made illegal for any railroad to issue any stocks or bonds or other evidences of indebtedness or to assume any obligations (as lessor, lessee, and so on) unless and until the Commission, after thorough investigation, granted its permission.

There were a number of fundamental changes in respect to rate-making. For the first time, the Commission was given authority to prescribe minimum as well as maximum rates. The obvious purpose was to prevent unrestrained reductions that might inflict serious loss on the carrier involved, demoralize the rate structure, and seriously alter the character and flow of traffic. In addition, minor modifications were made in respect to the power of the Commission to suspend rates and in regard to the long-and-short-haul clause. More fundamental was the substantial change in the rule of rate-making itself. The Act specified that the Commission, when prescribing just and reasonable rates, should fix them so that the carriers as a whole might earn a net railway operating income "equal as nearly as may be to a fair return upon the aggregate value of the property of such carriers held for and used in the service of transportation."[2] This rule, of course, would involve use of the valuation figures that were being laboriously compiled in accordance with the Act of 1913, and was a distinctly new departure in that the Commission, in effect, was to assume an affirmative responsibility for seeing to it that such roads as were honestly, efficiently, and economically managed should receive a "fair" return. For the two-year period beginning March 1, 1920, the Act itself specified that this rate of return should be fixed at not less than five and a half percent.

[2] Transportation Act of 1920, 41 *Statutes-at-Large*, Ch. 456, Title IV, Sec. 422, paragraph (2). February 28, 1920.

Quite as revolutionary as the new rule of rate-making was the famous recapture clause, which provided for the disposition of all railway operating income in excess of the specified fair return. Any funds recaptured under its provisions were to be divided equally between a reserve fund maintained by the carrier and a contingent fund to be held and administered by the Commission. From this latter, loans were to be made to deserving railroads for meeting capital expenditures or purchasing equipment and other facilities. A final provision in respect to rates contemplated further cooperation between the I. C. C. and state rate-making bodies and specifically recognized the dominance of the federal tribunal in situations in which state ruling might bear upon interstate commerce.

The powers granted the Commission in respect to service were sweeping. Although the railways were left to initiate their own policies in regard to the supply, control, and use of locomotives, cars, and entire trains, the Commission was authorized to require any changes it saw fit in car-service rules. In times of emergency, the I. C. C. was given unlimited discretion as to both the use of facilities and the movement of traffic. A logical counterpart of this extended control over service was the authority given the Commission for the first time not only to control construction and abandonment, but also to force railroads to acquire new facilities and to extend their lines.

Finally, the Transportation Act established the Railroad Labor Board, and permitted, but did not require, the organization of adjustment boards. If any dispute arose between labor and management, every effort was to be made to solve the difficulty by direct conference between the parties involved. If this procedure failed to produce agreement, the dispute might be referred to an adjustment board. If such a board failed to solve the problem, the matter could then be referred to the Railroad Labor Board, which was specifically authorized to establish just and reasonable wages, salaries, and working conditions. No provision was made for the enforcement of the Board's orders; the assumption was that pressure of public opinion would compel acceptance of its findings.

Viewed in its entirety, the Transportation Act of 1920 marked a turning point in public regulatory policy. It reflected a frank recognition of the fact that if regulation was to be as thoroughgoing as that embraced in the provisions of this law, the government must assume positive responsibility for the maintenance of adequate transportation service. If this end, in turn, was to be achieved under private ownership and management of the carriers, the Commission would be obliged to exercise its powers so as to assure the roads a fair return as a reward for safe, efficient, and economical management. The Act, in short, contemplated a sort of working partnership whereby the initiation of policy, by and large, was left to the carriers, but its adoption and execution were subjected at virtually every step to the approval of the Commission. In many respects, of course, the

Commission itself could initiate policy, and in any number of situations it could, in effect, substitute its judgment for that of railway executives. The Act unquestionably signalized the deepest penetration of government into business up to that time. How successful it would be in serving the public interest and improving the general health of the industry would inevitably depend in part on the way in which the Commission saw fit to use its newly found powers and in part on the response of the carriers to the new dispensation. Whatever the outcome, a new era had dawned for the railroads.

CHAPTER 17

Grand Strategy in the Twenties

1920 - 29

IN RETROSPECT, the 1920's marked a plateau period in Burlington history. Road mileage, for example, remained virtually constant at about 9,300. Total train miles, ton-miles of freight transported, total operating revenues and expenses, and net income varied only slightly during the nine years from 1921 to 1929, inclusive. The only marked alteration was the decline of about one third in passenger traffic as the result of the spectacular growth of the use of the private automobile. Naturally, the individual components that made up these trends fluctuated somewhat more widely. Traffic in mineral and forest products, for example, increased nearly fifty percent, whereas less-than-carload shipments dropped off about twenty-five percent as intercity trucks began to coax business away from the rails. On the one hand, operating expenses were consistently reduced in relation to revenues, but, on the other, both federal and state taxes increased while other income fell off. As a result, net income moved upward only modestly.

The apparent stability of these trends, however, is far more evident in retrospect than it was at the time. Early in 1923, Hale Holden referred to "recurring economic disturbances" during the preceding three years, and went on to say that "sharp changes in the volume of traffic, increases in rates of wages, decreases in freight rates, unfortunate strikes by railroad labor and the coal mining industry seriously affecting expenses of operation, and continued high cost of materials and supplies have all contributed to a confused and variable set of conditions which made the problem of management perhaps more difficult than ever before in the history of the railroads."[1] In other words, what the current generation may fondly look back on as "the good old days" was hardly regarded as such by the persons then managing the Burlington.

A closer look at Holden's remarks reveals a rather significant fact: most of the "disturbances" he cited were the result of national economic trends or conditions affecting the entire railroad industry rather than problems that originated or were particularly acute on the home property. As a matter of fact, in Claude Burnham and Edward T. Bracken, vice-presidents in charge of traffic and operations, respectively, Holden had two excellent and trusted lieutenants to whom he could and did entrust the internal affairs of the Burlington. Thus, partly because he was free to do so, but more important because he thought the times required it, Holden— especially during the early 1920's—devoted the major part of his attention to questions involving the relations of the Burlington with other roads and to matters affecting the industry as a whole, in which, of course, the Burlington had an important stake.

Not since the days of James F. Joy had a chief executive of the company been better equipped to deal with such broad problems than Holden. Perkins, of course, had been a past master at negotiations with other railways, but his pronounced laissez-faire views on the role of government had made it extremely difficult, if not painful, for him to deal as effectively with public agencies. Holden, on the other hand, was as much at home before a court or public tribunal as when dealing across the table with other railroaders. An advocate and diplomat of the highest order, he was able to grasp and appraise external forces at work and to exert both weight and leadership in directing them along channels that he hoped would best serve the interests he represented.

Unquestionably, the railway industry as a whole was in dire need of statesmanlike leadership in the years immediately following World War I. It had just emerged from a period of federal control to face the twin problems of undermaintenance and dissatisfaction of shippers. Now that the roads were back in private hands, would they, on their own initiative, rehabilitate their properties so that, if faced by another crisis, they could meet it without government intervention?

The companies themselves were as one in their desire to resolve any possible doubts on this score. On the other hand, a considerable segment of the public, including many prominent labor leaders, numerous Con-

[1] CB&Q, AR 1922, p. 27.

gressmen, and a goodly number of editors and self-styled experts on the subject, were frankly in favor of government ownership. As had been true during the debates over the Transportation Act, so throughout the 1920's the subject was widely and often warmly discussed. The proponents of federal ownership were in the minority, but they were extremely articulate, and the statesmen of the railway industry saw that unless the roads took full advantage of the new spirit and provisions of the Transportation Act of 1920 and put their own houses in order, the advocates of government control might well have their way. Consequently, Holden urged publicly that the Transportation Act be given a thorough trial without substantial amendment, on the ground that the railways were overcoming the problems produced by the war and were earnestly endeavoring to return as soon as possible to a lower scale of charges and normal conditions of service.

This could be done in a number of ways. One was to improve the physical plant, not only to make up for such undermaintenance as had occurred during federal control but, more important, to enable it to handle whatever foreseeable burden might be put upon it in either peace or war. A second way was to coordinate freight car supply and demand so as to reduce car shortages to a minimum and thus improve both car utilization and freight service. A third way was to rationalize the plant by working out combinations—through merger, stock control, or lease—that would take full advantage of the most efficient routes, clear out "deadwood," and bring about the many economies of consolidation.

All three of these possibilities received formal attention throughout the industry. Beginning in 1921, a series of meetings under the sponsorship of the American Railway Association led, two years later, to a collective pledge on the part of the roads to inaugurate a far-reaching improvement program. Annual expenditures by the industry, divided about equally between roadway and equipment, averaged $734,000,000 during the five years 1921–25, and increased to $812,000,000 a year during 1926–30. While this program was getting underway, the A. R. A. also sponsored a series of conferences between shippers and rail carriers designed to work out a more accurate reporting of car needs. From these meetings emerged, in March 1923, the Northwest Shippers' Advisory Board. Before the year was out, six more regional groups were organized; by 1926 the number reached thirteen, blanketing the nation.

In both these developments the Burlington was concerned primarily from a domestic point of view. In contrast, implementation of the third major industry-wide objective—plant rationalization through consolidation—inevitably involved aggressive relations with other railways. For the Burlington this was nothing new. During its first half century it had undergone three definite phases of rapid growth by acquisition and consolidation: the mid-1850's, the late 1860's, and during the Perkins administration. In 1901 the Burlington had, as it were, married into an

expansion-minded family, thus perpetuating and reinforcing its own in-
herited characteristics. Now that the law of the land specifically encouraged combinations, it was logical, if not inevitable, that expansionist
policies—"grand strategy"—in the 1920's would constitute a separate and
colorful chapter in Burlington history.

Among the larger problems in which the Burlington was intimately
interested, perhaps the central one was, as it had been since 1901, its relations with its two proprietary companies, the Great Northern and the
Northern Pacific. As it turned out, 1921 was a most difficult year for the
Northern Lines, primarily because the "Joint 4's" each road had issued
in the amount of $115,000,000 in 1901 to pay for the Burlington fell due.
This would have been a huge amount to refinance under ideal conditions,
and in 1921 they were anything but that. Owing to the sharp recession of
that year, interest rates were high, rail traffic fell sharply, and many roads
felt that the settlement made by the government to compensate for lack
of proper maintenance during federal control fell short of what would
actually be required to put rolling stock and roadbed back in shape.

Consequently it was apparent—and during the year borne out in fact
—that the Northern Lines would have to refund the Joint 4's with bonds
bearing a much higher interest rate, and underwriting costs would be high.
Thus it was logical that the Burlington should offer such timely assistance
as it could.

At the beginning of 1921, as for many years, 1,108,391 shares of
C. B. & Q. stock were outstanding. On this amount the company paid a
two percent dividend from income on March 25, thus channeling over
$1,000,000 to each of the Northern companies. Next, to all stockholders of
record on March 31, 1921, the C. B. & Q. declared a stock dividend of
54.1325 percent, payable out of surplus accumulated prior to July 1, 1909.
This increased the holdings of each Northern company by nearly 300,000
shares, and raised the total amount of C. B. & Q. stock outstanding to
1,708,391 shares.

On this broader base the Burlington on June 25, 1921, declared a
dividend from income of five percent, amounting in all to over $8,500,000;
another dividend of like amount was paid on December 27. Finally, on the
same date, the C. B. & Q. authorized an additional fifteen percent dividend from surplus accumulated prior to 1921. This amounted to over
$25,000,000, and brought total cash disbursements for the calendar year
1921 to the substantial figure of $44,925,917. As the Northern roads held
equally more than ninety-eight percent of C. B. & Q. stock, each received
approximately $22,000,000.

Of this operation, Ralph Budd later observed: "The large dividends
paid by the Burlington at this time were on the basis of making use of the
asset which the Northern Lines had in Burlington ownership and the assumption that it was the proper thing to do. The fact that the Burlington

was able to assist as it did was considered to be in large part because of the conservative dividend policies through the twenty years of ownership by the Northern Lines."[2]

Refinancing of the Joint 4's, however, was but one task that faced the three roads in common. Even while they were working out a solution, the Interstate Commerce Commission tossed a bombshell into the camp which threatened the survival of the alliance itself. As part of the plan for grouping the nation's railroads into a limited number of systems— drawn up largely by Professor William Z. Ripley of Harvard and made public on August 3, 1921—the Commission suggested, among other things, that the Great Northern be divorced from the Northern Pacific and Burlington and combined with the Milwaukee, and that the Colorado and Southern Lines be assigned to the Santa Fe. The additional proposal that the Burlington–Northern Pacific acquire the Chicago Great Western, Minneapolis & St. Louis, and possibly the Spokane, Portland and Seattle, did little if anything to offset the shock to the Hill Lines. Furthermore, the I. C. C. proposal to give direct entrances into Chicago to the Missouri–Kansas–Texas, the St. Louis–San Francisco, the Missouri Pacific, and the Kansas City Southern by consolidating them with various competitors of the C. B. & Q. threatened severe losses of interchange business with the Southwest.

There was one mitigating factor, however. The Act of 1920 did not give the Commission the right to impose its plan upon the railroads. The Commission was simply empowered to suggest an arrangement and to use its best offices in securing the voluntary adherence of the various companies. Nevertheless, however tentative these proposals might be, they were enough to galvanize the Hill roads into instant action. Without a moment's delay, they mounted the strongest possible defense at their command and began preparing a counter-offensive, on the theory that if they were going to attack what someone else had proposed, they had better have a demonstrably better alternative to take its place. By common consent, Holden, of the Burlington, was named spokesman for the Hill forces, with Howard Elliott, senior statesman and chairman of the Northern Pacific, as his chief aide.

The choice of Holden was logical, for his ability as an advocate was already legendary. One thing, however, he could not do: being but fifty-three at the time, and having been associated with the Burlington for only fifteen years, he could not present as first-hand information many of the facts and policy decisions of an earlier day which might be of crucial importance in the case. But Howard Elliott, who had begun his railway service with the C. B. & Q. in 1880, could. During the twenty-three years he had spent with the C. B. & Q., he had been intimately associated with Charles E. Perkins, Sr. As president of the Northern Pacific between 1903

[2] Ralph Budd to Overton, October 16, 1957.

and 1913, he had had a top policy-making position in the Hill Lines, and since his return to the Northern Pacific as chairman of the board in 1917, after a four-year stint as head of the New Haven, he had been continuously active in the formulation of system policies. His personal experience, therefore, neatly complemented Holden's and provided a broad foundation for mounting a strong defense. Working smoothly in tandem, Holden and Elliott presented their carefully dovetailed statements to the Commission on November 17, 1922.

Fundamentally, of course, both men, although using different lines of argument, were trying to prove one cardinal point: that preservation of the Hill system as it then stood would, in preference to any other arrangement, best fulfill the requirement imposed on the Interstate Commerce Commission by the consolidation provisions of the Transportation Act of 1920. The two chief prerequisites, and the ones at issue in this proceeding, were (1) that competition should be preserved as fully as possible and (2) that "wherever practicable the existing routes and channels of trade and commerce" should be maintained.[3]

Of the two propositions, the first was by far the more difficult to handle, and the less valuable if proved. In respect to it, the Northern Lines were on the defensive: in the broad framework of the West, and in the opinion of much of the public, they served more or less the same territory. Consequently, one task of the Hill forces was not so much to prove that maintenance of their alliance would create competition not then existing as it was to prove that it would not destroy such competition as there was between the Great Northern and Northern Pacific.

In respect to the second proposition, the two Northern Lines were in a far better position. In fact, they had a double-barreled case: they had extremely strong grounds for asserting that the Hill Lines *did* in themselves constitute "existing routes and channels of trade" which should be maintained, and equally solid grounds for asserting that the alternatives proposed by the Commission would, in a very substantial and tangible way, disrupt such routes and channels. These general strategic considerations guided the presentations by both men.

The nub of Elliott's argument pictured the arrangement of 1901 as perfectly meeting the long-range plans of all three partners: "The Burlington has retained and increased its financial strength, because it did not have to spend, as the St. Paul [Milwaukee] did, the large sums necessary for a new line to the Coast. Nor did the N. P. or G. N. have to spend money to build other lines to Kansas City, or St. Louis, or Chicago." Purchase of the Colorado and Southern, development of coal roads in southern Illinois, and completion of the Big Horn Basin line were, to be sure, all carried out with C. B. & Q. money, "but who can say that these large

[3] Transportation Act of 1920, 41 *Statutes-at-Large*, Ch. 456, Title IV, Sec. 407. February 28, 1920.

expenditures were justified if it was to have its connection either with Northern Pacific or Great Northern weakened in any way?" To pull this system apart would not only disrupt these routes, but would also retard the growth of the country served by them. "The next twenty-five years," Elliott said confidently, "will show a much greater development in the United States and in the western country than the last twenty. The country needs big tools of every kind for its development, particularly big transportation machines that can furnish the service needed. . . . Size," he asserted flatly, "should not be disturbing."[4]

Holden carefully selected the grounds on which to open his testimony. Prefacing his remarks with his definition of the sort of competition the Act of 1920 had envisaged, he asserted that the competition the framers of the law had in mind was not that between separate lines, but that among such groups or systems as might be created or, by implication, were already in existence. Since the Hill Lines were as large as many of the systems contemplated by the 1921 plan, Holden took occasion to comment that the several systems to be set up under the new law might vary in mileage or density of traffic "within any limits that may be practicable" as long as they could operate at essentially the same costs and under the same rates and earn substantially the same return as each other.

Of course, what he was trying to do was to define the terms of the Act so that he could blunt the edge of any charge that might be made as to lack of competition between the two Northern Lines, and at the same time ward off attacks that might be leveled at the mere size of the Hill system. To this end he concentrated his attention on the intimate relations between the Burlington and the Northern Lines and more particularly on those improvements paid for by the C. B. & Q. specifically to strengthen joint routes developed since the alliance of 1901 had been concluded. "The loss to the Burlington of either of the Northern Lines," said he, "will not only impair the support of these investments but seriously weaken the Burlington strength and capacity to grow."

He went on to produce similar evidence concerning the Colorado and Southern, which, he asserted, had been progressively developed since its acquisition by the C. B. & Q. in 1908, in order to handle interchange not only with Burlington but with the two northern companies as well. As evidence he cited a half dozen regions in which new roads or additional tracks had been created for this specific purpose.

But joint planning on the part of the Hill system had not been confined merely to new lines and double-tracking. Each partner, Holden pointed out, had vigorously supported experiments in dry farming in cooperation with federal and state agencies and had lent assistance to irrigation and reclamation projects. Each had helped develop the lumber industry, mining, and manufacture on the fundamental premise that

[4] Howard Elliott, ICC Docket No. 12964, November 17, 1922, p. 40.

"these companies . . . recognized fully that their interests were bound up with the interest of the country they served; upon the success of one depended the success of the other. . . ." As a result, and "very naturally," Holden said, routes and channels of trade had been established by reason of this system traffic developed since 1901. Consequently—and this was the crux of his argument—it was clear to Holden "that the separation of Great Northern from the present association by the inclusion of it in a different system with an important competitor of Burlington would not only constitute a discontinuance of existing routes and channels of trade and commerce of the most serious character, but would be a serious impairment to Burlington present and future earning power and financial strength."

Turning next to the particular problem of competition, Holden dismissed at once the notion that the C. B. & Q. competed with either of the Northern Lines, stressing the fact that it was, rather, complementary to them. And he devoted more attention to dispelling the notion that the Great Northern and the Northern Pacific were not truly competitive. There was, he said, a comparatively small population in communities reached exclusively by those two companies, amounting in fact to 4.8 percent of the total served by both lines. Thus, he concluded, competition existed and would continue to exist.

Just as the three major companies were tightly bound by traffic and interchange arrangements, they were even more closely linked financially. He pointed out that bonds of the Northern Lines to the amount of $215,227,000 were secured by the deposit of Burlington stock, and that the Northern Lines depended upon Burlington dividends to pay interest on their joint obligations. He took pains, however, to point out that this was not a one-way street: "Burlington under its present relations with the Northern Lines not only benefits greatly from this association but is in large measure *thereby* enabled to pay this return."

Holden reserved what was in many ways his most telling argument for the last: the precise effect on the Burlington of loss of interchange traffic. Here he was not so much a representative of the three Hill Lines as the president of the C. B. & Q.; his bill of particulars was impressive.

Under the contemplated I. C. C. plan, he asked, what was to happen to the existing interchange traffic between the Burlington and the Frisco, and the Katy, which totaled more than $3,500,000 annually? Similarly, how much of the annual $3 million business between the Burlington and the Missouri Pacific and the Kansas City Southern would be diverted from the C. B. & Q. if the proposed changes were made? The only possible result of the I. C. C. plan, in Holden's view, was that the Burlington "stubs" at St. Louis, Kansas City, and Denver would simply "dry up." "This plan," he asserted bluntly, "threatens isolation of the Burlington for which no similar parallel is found in the whole plan."[5]

[5] Holden in ICC Docket No. 12964, pp. 6–56.

The cross-questioning that followed Holden's presentation was searching. By far the most persistent examiner was Professor Ripley. His questioning was not unfriendly, but he was well aware that Holden's prime purpose was to preserve the Hill alliance, and for the sake of the record he was determined to have that admitted.

Holden did so frankly. But like Patrick Henry, he proposed to make the most of it, whether it was treasonable or not. "What we want to do here," he asserted, "is to accomplish something. We have a practical situation. We have a system here that has been signally successful and, as I have had very little to do in making that success, I have no hesitation in boasting of it. . . . We want," he insisted, "to try to participate in a practical demonstration of the wisdom of this law, but we must build from what we have, instead of retrograding and starting all over again. . . ."

But Ripley was not done. "Would it be your contention," he asked, "that the prohibition of the Northern Securities decision was intended to be considered here?" Holden met the inquiry head on. He would not go so far as to say that that decision should not be considered, but rather would say that two new elements merited attention: the Act of 1920 itself threw "a new and a broader aspect on the whole situation" by contemplating creation of the very sort of systems the Northern Securities decision struck down. Second, the fact that the Milwaukee had since built through almost all the territory occupied by the Hill Lines introduced a new factor that had radically altered the situation.

Ripley was not entirely satisfied. He suggested that another basis of Holden's argument was that "certain existing relationships which have grown up since 1901 are the defense for the existing conditions." He asked whether Holden thought these new conditions were in compliance with the prohibition of the Supreme Court in the Northern Securities case. Holden replied that in his opinion the Northern Lines had assiduously obeyed the Court's instructions. The Burlington's status, he hastened to add, "was not involved in the decision." In fact, because control by the Northern Lines of the Burlington had existed and continued, Holden felt that he had "the right to say that it now had the status of an approved relationship, if it ever was in doubt, but I assert that it never was in doubt. It was not dealt with or exploded in the Northern Securites case. The opportunity was there for the Supreme Court . . . to have commented upon it if they felt the law was in any way being violated."

Ripley persisted. Granted that the Burlington's position in the alliance was not in question, might it not be questioned as to whether "there was an essential difference between combining two roads through their common ownership from above or combining those same two roads through their common ownership of a road, so to speak, below?" Holden admitted that the question might be discussed, but repeated that if such an arrangement was in violation of the Sherman Act, that fact would have developed sooner, and that consequently "after all these years of acquiescence in the building up of these three roads in this manner . . . with the broad latitude which this Transportation Act now gives the Interstate Commerce Commission, and the evident change in the policy of the law that consolidations are now to be promoted . . . the Sherman Act situation, so far as these properties are concerned, is obsolete." And there, for the duration of the hearings, the matter rested.

In another line of argument, however, Ripley appeared even more difficult to convince. He agreed that under the Commission's proposed plan there would be a limitation of free interchange for the Burlington at various gateways. But, he went on, was it not equally true that a similar drying up of interchange with non-Hill roads had been taking place at St. Paul ever since the 1901 alliance went into effect? If that were true, was not such a drying-up process an inevitable consequence of any consolidation, and should not the balance be redressed? Holden disagreed with Ripley's basic assumption. The St. Paul Gateway, he asserted, was wide open, as evidenced by the fact that forty percent of the traffic on the Northern Lines went to connections other than the C. B. & Q. simply because the interests of the Northern Pacific and the Great Northern required them to exchange business with such other roads as the North Western and the Chicago Great Western. Holden admitted, of course, that the three Hill roads worked "preferentially together," but argued that that fact did not mean exclusion of the others.[6]

Carrying on the questioning, Commissioner Hall reminded Holden and Elliott that they had referred to the existing Hill combination as being the logical outcome of seventy-five years of sustained effort. Was it not true, he asked, that the existing alliance was rather the outcome of twenty-one years of development? Holden replied that he had been speaking in broader terms: each of the three properties in its own way and over its long growth, "by the careful direction of its several managements contributed in 1901 the accumulated energy in the joint alliance that was then made. So, broadly speaking, the story of the three parts of this line runs back seventy-five years." But Hall knew his history too. "If the cat had jumped a little differently twenty-odd years ago," he persisted, "this combination might not have been in existence." Holden had to agree that if the matter were put in that fashion, the Commissioner's views were correct. Yet here again he was prepared to make the most of the ground that had been left to him. The long-accumulated development of each, he maintained, was an asset in common when they joined forces in 1901. "But even if it were not," said Holden, "twenty years is a long time, and a great deal of right, it seems to me, has developed over that period which we think should be protected." He recalled that the three roads had spent

6 Ibid., pp. 63–71.

$900,000,000 during those two decades in the development of their joint properties. "Twenty years of studious effort to make this combination what it is," he repeated, "is a long time when it has cost a lot of money, and we are very anxious to safeguard it."

Hall turned to another sensitive point. He wanted to know whether the Burlington had had "any independent thought or plan as distinct from the thought and plan of its owners during the last odd-twenty years." Holden did not answer that one directly. "I think," he said, "we have lived in harmony and peace, and we have all thought along the same lines except when we were locally competing up there in the Northwest, but that is so far away I never heard of the row from Chicago. But seriously," he continued, "the plans have been made and the development has gone on by mutual, joint effort."

But the Commissioner was not constrained to mercy. "Isn't it straining the term 'mutual' a little bit when ninety-eight percent of the stock of one road has been acquired by two others, to leave that first road in the position of a road having a choice?" Again Holden avoided a direct answer, but replied in personal terms that probably lent more conviction than anything else he could have said. "Well," he answered good-naturedly, "Mr. Perkins started it and Mr. Hill made good with it, and the Burlington independence of management has never been interfered with, and we have gone on in our own way as an equal partner in a very large and fine sense." That, the Commissioner commented, was what one might call personal relations between the officials of one carrier and others. But, he insisted, were not the owners of the road still in the position to control policy at any time? Holden had perforce to agree.[7]

The distinction made was fine, yet real. The Northern Lines could dictate policy if they so desired, but in effect, because the various managements shared strongly similar ideas, joint policies had been agreed on harmoniously and without friction.

Hearings on the Commission's 1921 plan were completed in December 1923. By then the record concerning the plan consisted of some fifty-four volumes of testimony and exhibits, most of it conflicting in nature. On the whole, the weight of opinion appeared to be against consolidation according to any formal plan. Genuine skepticism prevailed as to whether wholesale consolidation of all the nation's roads into a limited number of systems was either necessary or desirable, and considerable fear existed that a single fixed plan would prove too rigid. Finally, nearly everyone had what he considered a better solution for various specific suggestions made by Ripley and the Commission.

Yet this widespread opposition to a fixed, comprehensive plan by no means implied any lessening of interest in consolidation as such on the

[7] Ibid., pp. 72–3.

part of individual roads whenever it seemed to afford possibilities of further economies, strategic advantages, or other benefits. Nowhere was consolidation more actively supported and urged than in the councils of the Northern Lines at St. Paul. In fact, as early as February 1923, a joint report of committees composed of representatives from the Great Northern, the Northern Pacific, and the Burlington made to their superiors stated that the union of those companies would result in an annual net saving of over $9,000,000. These findings were, at this stage, solely for the information of the companies concerned; the Northern Lines were fully aware of the necessity of creating favorable public opinion well in advance of whatever fresh public proposal they might make.

A long step toward this goal was achieved by the publication in the influential *Harvard Business Review* for July 1923 of an article entitled "The Relationship of the Burlington–Great Northern–Northern Pacific to the Federal Railway Consolidation Law," by Walker D. Hines, former Director General and an acknowledged rail expert. He drew greatly on the testimony given by Holden and Elliott at the I. C. C. hearings, marshaled the pertinent facts, and presented forcefully the benefits that could accrue from a Burlington–Great Northern–Northern Pacific union.

The existence of such a "grand design," however, did not prevent the C. B. & Q. from contemplating and actively exploring expansion in other regions, especially the Southwest. Among the various lines seriously investigated between 1923 and 1926 were the Chicago Great Western, the Denver and Rio Grande Western, the Missouri–Kansas–Texas, the Kansas City Southern, the Minneapolis & St. Louis, the Chicago and Eastern Illinois, and the St. Louis–San Francisco. But such possibilities as presented themselves, however intriguing (indeed, they deserve a chapter in themselves), were overshadowed as indications multiplied that the Northern Lines were again clearing the decks for action.

In April 1925, the reconvened committees of the G. N.–N. P.–C. B. & Q. reported a new estimate of possible savings from merger as at least $10,140,000 annually. For a year, little was done. Then, on June 19, 1926, Hines, acting as counsel for the Great Northern in respect to consolidation, wrote Holden that a few days earlier he had had a lengthy discussion with Louis Hill about consolidation which "indicated a disposition to revive as far as practicable our plan for the three-company unification."[8]

In February 1927, the Northern Lines made public their proposal. It contemplated formation of a new corporation, the Great Northern Pacific Railway Company, which was to exchange its stock, share for share, for the stock of the two Northern Lines and to lease these companies as well as the Spokane, Portland and Seattle. No change was suggested in the status of the Burlington Lines except that, of course, they were to be under a

[8] Hines to Holden, June 19, 1926, CB&Q/Pres File #1027.

single owner instead of under two as formerly. The new corporation did not propose to acquire the various minor railways listed in the I. C. C. plan of 1921, but did include (through the Burlington) control of the Colorado and Southern, the Fort Worth and Denver City, and the Trinity and Brazos Valley.

Many of the arguments on behalf of the Great Northern Pacific were the familiar ones outlined by Holden in 1922–23. New emphasis, however, was placed on the operating economies, estimated at $10,143,000 annually; these savings, it was argued, would enable the companies to undertake extensions and improvements, step up agricultural and industrial development, increase colonization work, improve the companies' credit ratings, and further safeguard the stockholders' investment. Furthermore, as Ralph Budd pointed out in *Railway Age* on February 26, 1927, unless operating economies such as those suggested could be made, rate increases might well become necessary, especially in view of the fact that since 1913 the rate level in the Northwest had risen only forty percent as against fifty-three percent for the nation as a whole. Budd stressed another consideration of particular significance to the Burlington: the fact that it would have one rather than two owners.

During the spring of 1927, the Great Northern Pacific proposal was approved by a majority of the stockholders of the Northern Lines. On July 8, 1927, application was filed with the I. C. C., and argument before the Commission was scheduled for the fall. The intervening months were to be busy ones for the Burlington.

It will be recalled that in making their application, the Northern Lines did not include as part of the proposed system the short roads and minor companies which had been assigned to the Northern Pacific–Burlington or to the Great Northern–St. Paul groups in the 1921 plans. They were well aware, however, that as a prerequisite for approval, the Commission might well insist upon inclusion of some, if not all, of these smaller companies. Consequently, the two Northerns immediately undertook a study of the short lines in their territories in order to have a basis for the offers they might make if compelled to do so. They also called on the Burlington to undertake similar studies of some thirty minor roads in its territory which might conceivably be involved.

T. J. Thomas, assistant to the president of the C. B. & Q., was placed in charge of this latter assignment. He submitted his report to Hale Holden on September 13, 1927. Of the thirty railroads considered, Thomas felt for various reasons that twenty-three would probably not be assigned to the Burlington. The remaining seven roads operated a total of 198 miles, reported a net income of $156,016 in 1926, and brought a total revenue to the Burlington on interchange business of slightly more than $1,000,000. Thomas's report was transmitted to St. Paul promptly. In acknowledging its receipt on October 3, 1927, Messrs. Dorety and Lyons, general counsel for the Great Northern and the Northern Pacific, respectively, observed: "The plan is that the Burlington will be mentioned as little as possible at the hearing."[9] This policy was scrupulously carried out; later on at the hearings, when Thomas was prepared to testify, he was assured by Dorety that if he should be questioned on Burlington policy as such, Dorety would promptly object, the Burlington not being "a party to the application or cause under consideration."[1] It was clear that neither Northern Line wished the relative position of the Burlington to be brought in question.

Arguments for and against the Great Northern Pacific proposal were heard by the Commission on October 3-4, 1927. As might have been expected, the principal opposition came from the Milwaukee, whose general counsel, F. H. Wood, claimed that the size and resources of the proposed corporation—embracing one fifth of all railway mileage west of the Mississippi—not only would overwhelm the Milwaukee, but also would eliminate competition and lead to the establishment of systems in the Northwest which would not earn substantially the same rate of return at uniform rates in the movement of competitive traffic. Further, in his view the G. N. P. proposal served merely "to confirm the suspicion that the real purpose of this application is to convert their present divided control of the Burlington into a single and unified control and that but for this purpose they would not themselves be seeking to unite the two strongest railroads and the two most competing [sic] railroads in the Northwest and thus bring about a situation so repugnant to the policy of the law as declared in the Transportation Act."[2]

This statement tended to shift the spotlight back to the Burlington, something which the Northern Lines specifically sought to avoid. Wood's move was a clever one, as subsequent events amply demonstrated. There were, of course, many other arguments for and against the Northern Lines' proposal, and eventually some 178 intervening petitions were entered, most of them favorable to the application. With all the arguments for and against on the table, there was nothing to do but await the Commission's decision.

Meanwhile, the Burlington's attention was drawn to new developments in two areas that had long figured in its strategic planning: improvement of the St. Louis–Kansas City and Chicago–Kansas City routes in northern Missouri, and the possibility of acquiring a direct link to the Southwest. The two prospects were not unrelated. If the C. B. & Q. was to

[9] F. G. Dorety and D. F. Lyons to T. J. Thomas, October 3, 1927, CB&Q/Pres File #1027.

[1] Thomas to Holden and Claude G. Burnham, March 23, 1928, CB&Q/Pres File #1027.

[2] 162 ICC 42; Argument of F. H. Wood in *Traffic World*, Vol. XLII, No. 14 (October 6, 1928), pp. 768–70.

increase its handling of the growing traffic to and from the Southwest via the Kansas City Gateway, improvements in northern Missouri were highly desirable, for the Burlington service in this region trailed far behind that of its chief competitor, the Santa Fe. If it should acquire a line of its own beyond Kansas City, then improvements were not merely desirable, but imperative.

With regard to the St. Louis–Kansas City and Chicago–Kansas City routes, several possibilities were considered only to be shelved again. As R. T. Scholes of the Engineering Department stated in one of the reports, the key to the unsatisfactory situation was that the Burlington operated into a dead end at Kansas City; yet feelers put out to investigate the possible acquisition of the Frisco or the Katy were abruptly withdrawn on each occasion when control seemed within reach. In this whole question of additions and improvements in northern Missouri on the one hand and outlets to the Southwest from Kansas City on the other, the factors involved were extremely complex. Inevitably, the negotiations, which constitute a fascinating insight into rail diplomacy, were complex also. At one point, for example, it seemed that the Burlington's hand would be forced by the avowed intention of the Santa Fe to enter St. Louis. Inclined at first to oppose such a move, the C. B. & Q. later leaned in its favor even though other lines serving St. Louis voiced strenuous objections. Accordingly the stage was set for a battle royal in northern Missouri just when the Great Depression struck. In the light of the economic situation, the conflict was postponed: each company realized the impossibility of carrying out its program. Similarly, the Burlington's plan for more direct Kansas City–St. Louis and Kansas City–Chicago routes was shelved once more until such time as prosperity might reappear.

Meanwhile, in December 1929, the Interstate Commerce Commission finally published its revised consolidation plan. The reason for the delay had been the conviction on the part of the Commissioners that it was not feasible to work out a limited number of systems for the nation to which all the railroads would voluntarily agree. Testimony taken in 1922 and 1923 on the original plan had convinced them of this, and as early as February 1925 they had asked Congress to be relieved of the assignment. The Commission felt that results would be as good and perhaps better if consolidation was permitted to develop, under their guidance, "in a more normal way." Consequently, they proposed various amendments to the Interstate Commerce Act which, in effect, were designed to broaden and simplify the necessary procedures. Their recommendations were repeated in 1926 and mentioned with approval in their reports to Congress for 1927 and 1928. By the summer of 1928, however, it was clear that Congress was not inclined to amend the consolidation provisions of the Act. Therefore the Commission reluctantly published its own plan on December 9, 1929. Obviously this "final" plan was a hybrid that sought to find a middle ground among the suggestions of individual railways and the ideas of the individual commissioners. As the members of I. C. C. candidly said: "Not all of us have agreed as to all its parts, but all concur in the result."[3]

Among the twenty-one systems proposed by the Commission, Number 12 grouped the Great Northern, the Northern Pacific, the S. P. & S., and a score of shorter lines in a single system. The Burlington, however, was grouped separately in System Number 14, which included the Colorado and Southern Lines, the Green Bay and Western, the Missouri–Kansas–Texas, and an imposing list of short but relatively unimportant companies.

The proposal to divorce the Burlington from the Northern Lines was directly contrary to the hopes of all three Hill Lines. And it was not, by any means, the result of a unanimous view on the part of the I. C. C. Even though Commissioner Eastman opposed unification of the Northerns, he nevertheless characterized "the divorce of the Burlington as an impracticable and undesirable undertaking. The situation," he went on, "is satisfactory as it now stands. Because of the competition of the Northern Lines, which are joint and equal partners in the control of the Burlington, it has the effect of making that road practically an independent system, so far as management is concerned. Yet the advantages of direct intercourse between each of the Northern Lines and the Burlington, which is naturally tributary to both, are preserved."[4] Eastman consequently suggested that the Burlington be left with the Northern Lines rather than with the Katy, and that as an alternative the Katy should be merged with the Chicago Great Western and the Kansas City Southern. But Eastman was in the minority. The majority favored separation. Understandably, the Burlington was dismayed by the proposed I. C. C. plan. Ralph Budd was outspoken in protest, pointing in support of his arguments to the reports issued by the various combined committees on the economic advantages to accrue from a Great Northern–Northern Pacific–Burlington merger, and also to the record of the way in which these same companies had operated since 1901.

The Commission handed down its decision in the Great Northern Pacific case on February 11, 1930. It authorized the proposed G. N. P. to acquire control of the two Northerns and of the Spokane, Portland and Seattle, but *only* on condition that (1) the Burlington be divorced from control by the Northern companies within a reasonable period of time, (2) the Great Northern Pacific acquire all the short lines named in System 12 of the 1929 plan except those the I. C. C. might specifically exempt,

---

[3] 159 ICC 524.

[4] 159 ICC 567. In respect to Eastman's dissent, Ralph Budd later wrote: "In my opinion Mr. Eastman was not justified in presuming that equal ownership by the two Northern Lines in Burlington meant that there was no effective control over the Burlington management. That was not true. . . ." (Budd to Overton, October 27, 1957).

(3) a comprehensive program be adopted for unified terminal operations, and (4) assurance be given to the Milwaukee that it might have access to Spokane and Portland over the S. P. & S.

One fact was now clear: for a variety of reasons, unification of the Northerns *together with* continued control of the Burlington was out of the question, at least for the time being. The decision was put squarely up to the Northerns as to whether they wished to combine and lose the Burlington in the process, or to remain as they were and retain their divided control of the C. B. & Q.

During the spring of 1930, the executives of the Great Northern and the Northern Pacific discussed this thorny problem at length with J. P. Morgan & Company, their long-standing financial advisors. While the matter was under discussion, a resolution was introduced in Congress to suspend the authority of the Commission to approve railroad consolidations, and members of the House of Representatives from the northwestern states filed a protest with the I. C. C. against the G. N.–N. P. merger. What effect, if any, these developments had on the conferences of the Northern Lines with Morgan is not a matter of record. Congress, in fact, adjourned without acting on the resolution concerning consolidations. But in July the Great Northern and the Northern Pacific announced that their proposed merger would be deferred.

In October 1930, the Commission granted a petition filed by several state commissions to reopen the case, the implication being that even if the Northerns elected to proceed with unification under the conditions laid down by the Commission, public opinion would by no means be uniformly favorable. Furthermore, the inescapable fact that Burlington stock was pledged as collateral for some $215,000,000 of Northern Lines bonds posed exceedingly complex legal and financial problems if divorce were to be undertaken. Finally, would merger—without the C. B. & Q.—leave the Northerns better off than before?

In January 1931, the application for creation of the Great Northern Pacific Railway was formally withdrawn. In a joint statement published in *Railway Age* on January 17, 1931, Budd and Donnelly made public their reasons for the decision. A great deal of time had been spent, they said, in trying to devise an effective and acceptable way to segregate the Burlington and at the same time grant full protection to the stockholders of the Northern Lines as well as to secure an entry for those lines into Chicago. But, they concluded, "It has become apparent that under present conditions a segregation of the Burlington could not be carried out so as to promote the welfare of the carriers involved or appeal to their stockholders as being in their interest or the public interest." Yet they added significantly, "we have been reluctant to withdraw our application because it cannot be too strongly emphasized that the problem is one of deep concern, not merely to the transportation industry but to all business and agricultural interests as well of the Northwest."[5] This much was perfectly clear: the desire of the three principal Hill Lines to unite was undiminished. And the implication was that the proposal might well be made again when conditions seemed more propitious.

Thus ended, in a period of growing economic depression, the most important episode in the "grand strategy" so characteristic of the 1920's. For a full decade—1921 to 1931—deep thought and untold labor had been devoted to the possibilities of combination, expansion, and plant rationalization. For the moment it had come to naught; the relationship among the Hill Lines, as well as the situation in northern Missouri and the Southwest, remained unchanged. Yet the effort and thought were hardly wasted. Information had been gathered and ideas hammered out that might well bring rich returns later on. In any case, for the moment, other tasks closer to home were demanding attention, problems whose roots lay in the domestic developments on the Burlington during the 1920's.

[5] *Railway Age*, Vol. XC, No. 3 (January 17, 1931), pp. 199–200.

CHAPTER 18

Internal Development

---

1 9 2 0 - 2 9

S O LONG AS BUSINESS WAS PROSPEROUS, as it was until the chilly
fall of 1929, few persons indeed concerned themselves about
politics during the 20's. The nation, business, and the railways
in general were relatively free from outside restraints and interference.
With the confidence born of seventy years of successful operation, the
Burlington in particular wanted nothing more than the opportunity to
put its plant in order, bring its equipment and operations to the peak of
efficiency, and develop as much new traffic as possible in order to do
the most effective overland transportation job possible. The apparent stability of the economy led to long-range programs, particularly in respect
to the plant, which brought the physical face of the railroad to look much
as it does today.

• PLANT •

FOR THE FIRST TIME in the company's history, an entire decade came and
went without any net growth in system road mileage. Improvements were
intensive rather than extensive; among them were—to take random examples—the building of several spurs to collect beet sugar in western Nebraska
and the double-tracking and straightening of the water-level line along
the Mississippi between Savanna and St. Paul. Work on this latter
major project started at Savanna in 1909; 138 miles had been com-

pleted by the end of 1915, and another fifteen miles were added in 1919. Not until 1926, however, was the final phase undertaken between Lytle and East Winona. Thereafter, work continued without interruption until the entire 238-mile project was completed in 1929. This undertaking cost $12,000,000 over the twenty years. But the ruling grade was reduced to 0.2 percent, and sixty-five miles of the original line were completely relocated to save 2,432 degrees of curvature, the equivalent of more than six and a half circles.

Closer to home, and as an indication of the density of traffic on the main stem east of Aurora, a fourth track was laid down over the twelve miles between Downers Grove and Eola in 1929–30. As a matter of fact, the 20's witnessed a complete face-lifting in Chicago and the suburban area. At Aurora, elevation of the main line, begun in 1915, finally was completed in November 1922; a year later, a new passenger depot and freight station were opened. The same year saw the Burlington put into operation a huge scrap-reclamation plant at Eola as well as up-to-date improvements in the shop area at Aurora.

In Chicago, the core of activity was construction of the massive new Union Station, in which the Burlington held a one-fourth proprietary interest. By the end of 1920, the surrounding viaducts were virtually completed. The next year saw the beginning of the large Railway Mail Building, which was ready for use on December 1, 1922. Early in 1923, the new inbound freight house at Harrison and Canal streets was finished, and late in 1924 the outbound facilities were put into service. Finally, on May 15, 1925, with appropriate ceremony, the station itself was formally opened for public use. The foundations were so constructed that an additional twelve stories for office space could be added when, as was confidently expected, the area around the new depot might become a center of civic development.

Further heavy expenditures on behalf of passenger service in the Chicago area had to be made before the decade ended. When the city decided to straighten the Chicago River between Polk and Fifteenth streets in 1926, it was necessary to enlarge the Fourteenth Street passenger yard and to move the passenger-engine terminal to Western Avenue. This in turn required extensive replacement of other facilities, such as the power plant, and construction of a new commissary building, storeroom, yard offices, and the like. Soon thereafter, the various companies concerned organized the separation of the complicated grade crossings of their lines at Canal and Sixteenth streets. This job was completed during 1931 at the cost of over a million dollars to the C. B. & Q. In the same year, the company completed a spanking new $600,000 terminal express building at Roosevelt Road and Canal Street, which it thereupon leased to the Railway Express Agency. These were the major improvements in the metropolitan area. Taken together, they constituted a revolutionary change both in the efficiency and in the outward aspect of the company's Chicago property.

One major setback to this vast program occurred. Just after midnight on March 14, 1922, a fire broke out in a small shop on Jackson Boulevard near the old Austin Building. Fanned by a strong northeast wind, the flames quickly spread through the whole block bounded by Jackson, Van Buren, Canal, and Clinton streets and including the elevated station and tracks. Across Clinton Street the intense heat broke the windows and ignited the frames in the new Burlington building. Fortunately, the fire did not spread upward or downward once it entered the building because the floors were of concrete, but each of the seven top floors had a fire by itself. When the embers were finally snuffed out, Chicagoans heaved a sigh of relief, for the rugged Burlington building had acted as a screen to prevent the spread of the flames across the wooden tenement buildings to the west. As for the company, the loss of vital records and correspondence was well-nigh irreparable. Fortunately the corporate archives were housed, then as now, in a lower floor and therefore escaped harm. But for months, even years, the ordinary day-to-day business of the company was hampered by the lack of essential records.

Out along its lines, the Burlington built a dozen and more new stations. The most important structures were at Lincoln and Omaha. The former, dedicated on October 8, 1927, replaced the old passenger station and office building that had been constructed in 1881. The latter, opened with appropriate ceremony on September 4, 1930, was, strictly speaking, a matter of reconstruction to keep pace with the extensive new terminal being built directly opposite by the Union Pacific.

Humans and mail, however, were by no means the only "commodities" that required stations and shelter. The C. B. & Q. spent a third of a million dollars building feeding-yards for sheep and cattle at Lincoln in 1926, a special yard for hogs at Hastings in 1928, and a sheep and cattle barn at Lincoln in 1929. In addition, expanding grain shipments prompted substantial enlargement of the elevators at Kansas City and St. Joseph in 1925, the purchase of two large elevators in Council Bluffs two years later, and the investment of well over a million and a half dollars in 1928–30 in elevators at St. Louis and at Gibson, Nebraska.

A whole series of improvements was made at Galesburg, the operating hub of the system east of the Missouri River. In 1924, a steel-car repair shop was completed, and two years later the venerable freight house in use since 1865 was replaced by an up-to-date structure. Out on the west end of the system a new large locomotive repair shop was built at Denver in 1922–23 at a cost of nearly two and a half million dollars. These shops were designed to serve the Colorado and Southern as well as the C. B. & Q. and to provide much-needed relief for the heavily burdened shops at Havelock, Nebraska.

The size and extent of these separate improvements, however, should not be allowed to overshadow the major continuous programs carried on year in and year out to keep the plant at top operating efficiency. In the ten years from 1920 to 1929 inclusive, for example, an average of 273.1 miles of 90-pound, 100-pound, and 110-pound rail was laid each year in main tracks. Over the same period, an average of approximately $450,000 was spent annually for replacing temporary pile-trestle bridges with permanent structures. Major bridge projects, such as the half-million dollar structure built at Western Avenue in 1926, the bridges built over the Platte River at Fremont and over the Illinois at Beardstown in the same year, and the major strengthening of the main-line bridge at Burlington in 1928 were all above and beyond this regular annual expenditure.

So it was with automatic block signals; in the decade 1920–29, an annual average of 112 miles of main-line track were so protected. In addition, the company installed automatic train control over the seventy-two miles between Creston and Pacific Junction in 1924, and in 1925–26 extended it through Omaha to Lincoln. Later in the decade, in 1928, the Burlington installed its first system of centralized traffic control over three and a half miles of single-track line with extremely heavy traffic between Arenzville and Concord, Illinois. An additional eight miles of centralized control was installed near Flag Center the next year, and over twenty-four miles more on single track west of Red Oak, Iowa, in 1930.

With the Iron Horse in its heyday, scarcely a year passed in the 20's without new locomotive stalls being added at one point or another. Starting off with a sixteen-stall roundhouse at Galesburg in 1920 and another for six locomotives at Pacific Junction, additions were subsequently made at Centralia, Rock Island, Mendota, Beardstown, Casper, Edgemont, Lincoln, Hannibal, Gibson, Peoria, and Chicago. Because the efficiency of steam engines depended so largely on pure water, sixteen new water-treating plants were completed during the decade; to slake the thirst of the hungry beasts, a 900,000,000-gallon reservoir was constructed at Galesburg at a cost of a quarter of a million dollars.

• MOTIVE POWER •

THE MOST STRIKING FACTS about motive power on the Burlington during the 20's were the sharp decrease in the number of units, the spectacular rise in average tractive effort, the introduction of gas motorcars in the last half of the decade, and the purchase, at the end of the 20's, of the most efficient high-speed steam locomotives ever to run on the line. Meanwhile, and typical of the steam age, improvements were constantly made in the existing fleet of locomotives.

At the beginning of 1920, the C. B. & Q. owned 1,879 locomotives with an average tractive effort of 34,398 pounds. At the end of 1929 there were only 1,575 locomotives on the system, a decrease of more than six-teen percent. Average tractive effort had risen, however, to 41,928 pounds, an increase of over twenty-three percent. As a result, *total* tractive effort available actually increased more than 2,000,000 pounds.

Undoubtedly the most colorful event of the decade, and indeed in all Burlington history, in respect to steam power was the ordering of eight 4-8-4 dual-type passenger and freight high-speed locomotives in December 1929, for delivery the following year. These "o-5's" or "Northerns" (so-called because they were first used on the Northern Pacific), had a trac-tive effort of 67,500 pounds, but it was their versatility that made them so effective and popular on the road. Along with the o-5's in 1930 came an even dozen 4-6-4 "Hudsons" (named for the famous River Division of the New York Central, on which they first appeared). With a tractive effort of 47,700 pounds, these "S-4's" were designed for hauling heavy passenger trains at high speeds. Delivery of these twenty engines in 1930, along with the scrapping of 171 old locomotives, gave another abrupt boost to the fleet's average tractive effort.

Meanwhile, existing motive power was constantly being overhauled, improved, and reclassified. In 1923, for example, general repairs were given to no less than 896 engines. Among other things, feedwater heaters to preheat water supplied to boilers were installed under a regular program beginning in 1920. In 1925, the company added boosters to produce smoother starting power and to help tonnage trains up grades; as it turned out, this particular innovation proved temporary, for with the introduc-tion of roller bearings and other improvements, boosters were eventually eliminated. Back pressure gauges were installed to help engineers operate at maximum efficiency, and grates were made increasingly efficient. In 1926, combustion chambers were added to fire boxes; in 1927, an imposing list of improvements was introduced: front-end throttles to furnish steam immediately from superheaters rather than by way of the boilers, steam driers to reduce the moisture in steam, prime washout and Huron arch tube plugs to assure tight boilers, force-feed lubricators, and Alemite lubrication for valve motion as well as for main and side rods. In 1928, cab curtains and side-window windshields became standard equipment; 1930 witnessed introduction of one-piece cast-steel locomotive frames, integral water bottoms for tenders to eliminate rivets and bolts, and con-stant curve-resistant devices on engine trucks and trailers to ease the nosing of the locomotive on track while taking curves at high speeds.

One innovation of the decade that for a time successfully met a spe-cific problem was the gasoline-powered rail motorcar. The first one, a combination passenger-baggage affair, made its appearance in 1924. As Holden explained to his directors, the car was bought for light branch-line service "in a rather experimental way."[1] By mid-July 1927, twenty-six

[1] PLD, January 3, 1925.

motorcars and nine trailers were in operation on the system; all were placed in service on branch lines, where they performed satisfactorily. A year later, Holden reported that motorcars were logging approximately 120,000 train miles a month and saving more than $300,000 a year in operating expenses; he looked forward to an additional saving of $275,000 a year as soon as twenty-six additional units were delivered. Meanwhile, the Aurora shop was busy converting coaches into motorcar trailers. Through the rest of the decade these motorcars and trailers carried most of the light branch-line passenger business. By 1930 the C. B. & Q. was operating sixty-five such cars and forty-two trailers.

• EQUIPMENT •

AS IN THE CASE OF MOTIVE POWER, though not so markedly, there was a decrease during the decade in the number of cars (both freight and passenger) on the Burlington, but a gradual increase in their carrying capacity, accompanied by a definite change toward all-steel construction. The year 1921 witnessed the launching of one of the largest equipment programs in the company's history, which, during the following year, boosted total freight car ownership to an all-time peak of 71,365. Meanwhile, the company's car shops at Aurora, West Burlington, and Plattsmouth went to work on a substantial rebuilding program. As a result, Holden could report at the end of 1923 that the company's cars were generally in better condition than for many years.

Completion of the Galesburg car-repair shop in 1924 measurably increased the company's capacity to handle its own car supply. After 1925, the Aurora shops, which until then had produced box, stock, auto, and way cars, began to concentrate almost entirely on passenger cars. West Burlington concentrated on flatcars and refrigerator cars; Plattsmouth contributed gravel cars. As the decade wore on, Galesburg took over most of the company's new freight car building and repairing.

With new equipment being delivered in sizable amounts in every year from 1924 through 1930, retirement of old cars was accelerated. By the end of 1930, total freight-train car ownership had declined to 61,198, a decrease of more than 10,000 units since the end of 1922. At the same time, average capacity increased from 42.16 to 43.25 tons. As in the case of motive power, the decrease in units did not imply a decrease in service; quite the reverse. Although freight-train miles were almost identical in 1921 and 1929, the company produced nearly twenty-eight percent more revenue ton-miles of service.

New additions to passenger-train car supply rose sharply in 1921 and again in 1925–29, inclusive. As part of the postwar program, sixty passenger-carrying cars, along with thirty-five mail and baggage cars, were ordered in 1921 and delivered the next year. In the last half of the decade, the company undertook to rebuild virtually the entire suburban car fleet. Older all-steel coaches were reconstructed to seat a hundred persons. Deliveries began late in 1926 and continued through the succeeding four years. Eventually 128 modernized cars were put into service. After the large order placed in 1921, no new passenger equipment for long runs was ordered until 1926; in that year ten coaches and eight chair cars were authorized. When they arrived in June, they were assigned to Trains Number 1 and Number 6 between Chicago and Denver. Before they went into service, however, they were exhibited in the Union stations both at Chicago and Denver, and in both cities the mayors participated; as Holden put it, there was "quite a little ceremony in both places."[2] Early in 1928, new lounge cars arrived for the Chicago–Twin Cities and Chicago–Lincoln runs; they too were exhibited at Chicago before going into service.

• THE LABOR FORCE •

ONE REASON for investing more money in fixed plant and more efficient power and rolling stock was to reduce the number of men and man-hours necessary to operate them in proportion to the service performed. During the 20's, as both plant and equipment became more efficient while traffic remained fairly steady, there was, as might have been expected, a steady decrease in the number of employees. At the end of 1921, employment on the C. B. & Q. alone stood at 46,558; average employment throughout 1929 was 43,961. Thus, as in the case of motive power and cars, it took fewer human units to provide an ever increasing amount of transportation. There were other reasons, too, for the added efficiency of labor; thanks to the unremitting efforts of the Safety Department, men took precautions to avoid personal mishaps. As a result, reportable injuries as well as fatalities decreased consistently throughout the decade.

Interruption of service because of labor disputes was rare. The most serious strike was that of the shopmen in the summer of 1922; for some weeks thereafter, economical operation was difficult. Otherwise, however, the decade was happily free from interruption on this score.

This is not to say that there was not the usual quota of negotiations over increased pay and changes in working conditions. In 1923–24, both train and engine-service employees won increases that added approximately $3,000,000 to the payroll. In 1926, shopmen gained a one cent an hour increase. In the next year, there were advances in the wages of yardmen, telegraphers, clerks, signalmen, maintenance-of-way men, and mechanics. In the spring of 1928, both locomotive engineers and firemen received boosts of approximately 6.4 percent. As Holden put it in a letter of July 3, 1928, to the directors, conditions with reference to wages were

[2] PLD, September 3, 1926; CB&Q, AR's 1925–30, *passim.*

relatively quiet from the fall of 1924 to the fall of 1926. Thereafter, he said, an upward movement had started which, since November 1, 1926, had added approximately $1,740,000 a year to the payroll. Later in the same year, the trainmen won a 6.5 percent boost in pay, and in 1929 both the signalmen and the shopmen obtained increases. Yet operating expenses declined steadily in each successive year from 1923 through 1929 (except for a temporary increase in 1928); in other words, the cost of increased wages was more than offset by improvements in plant and operation and by reductions in manpower.

On January 1, 1922, the company established a pension system. During its first full year of operation, the management received many expressions of loyalty and appreciation, and by the end of the year, 579 retired employees were carried on the rolls, and disbursements had exceeded $300,000. By the end of 1929, the pension roll had risen to 1,166. Disbursments for that year brought the cumulative cost of operation of the plan since its establishment to more than $4,620,000. Meanwhile, of course, the long-established Relief Department continued to provide insurance for sickness, accident, and death. At the end of 1929, more than seventy-two percent of the employees were contributing members; total disbursements for death benefits, disability, and surgical attention in the year exceeded $712,000.

One significant development that affected all employees took place at the beginning of the decade. On September 26, 1920, thirty-eight men, each with at least twenty years of service, formed the Veterans' Association at Havelock, Nebraska. Chapters sprang up rapidly from one end of the system to the other, and on January 26, 1925, the Ladies' Auxiliary was organized.

• SERVICE •

MIDWAY IN THE DECADE, a new and formidable challenge to rail service arose. Already the passenger automobile was eating away at travel by train. Far more important were the trucks, which by 1925, using the growing network of paved intercity highways and equipped with heavy pneumatic tires, were beginning to compete with the railways for line-haul freight. The diversion started as a local phenomenon, but spread with alarming rapidity. "We are continually meeting increased motor truck competition in the territory affecting our LCL business out of the large cities," Holden advised his directors in mid-1925.[3] In 1929, he cited truck competition as the principal reason for the lightest movement of animals and animal products in several years.

The Burlington lost no time in meeting this challenge. In the spring

[3] PLD, June 4, 1925.

of 1925, it shortened freight schedules from Chicago to the Twin Cities and to Omaha so as to provide for second- rather than third-morning delivery. A few months later, twenty-four hours were lopped off the Kansas City–Denver schedule, and the next month a new, fast, joint freight train was operated with the Alton between Kansas City and St. Louis for perishable freight and livestock. So it was down the line: on March 21, 1928, the Burlington established a twenty-four-hour freight train between Chicago and Omaha and, a week later, between Chicago and the Twin Cities. Both left in the morning so as to save a full day on traffic received too late for the evening trains.

Little or no attempt was made to speed up passenger trains with the hope of holding or gaining traffic. In fact, the tendency seemed quite the reverse. When, in June 1926, the Milwaukee and the North Western shortened some of their passenger schedules between Chicago and the Twin Cities, Holden told his directors that "this disturbance . . . was vigorously protested by the executives of all the other lines, and finally the North Western and Milwaukee agreed to restore the old schedules."[4] Indeed, in 1925, the Burlington's crack *Aristocrat* took twenty-seven and a half hours from Chicago to Denver; running time to the Twin Cities was ten hours. Speed took the spotlight when it came to mail, however. When, in May 1925, the Post Office Department requested an improvement of the eastbound transcontinental mail schedules through Omaha, the Burlington lopped twenty-five minutes off the running time of Train Number 8 and was able not only to maintain the new schedule regularly but also to add some express cars to the train.

Other measures were introduced to improve efficiency of operation, some of which reflected better service for the customer, others a saving in expense to the company, still others both. Shippers, for example, gained immeasurably when the average miles per car-day on the system rose from 25.9 in 1922 to 34.8 in 1929; they also benefited from the fact that net ton-miles per train hour increased from 7,894 to 11,194 during the same period. This meant more revenue for the railway, too, as did the fact that net tons per train mile rose from 617 in 1922 to 827 in 1929. At the same time, the number of pounds of coal necessary to move a thousand gross ton-miles declined from 148 to 117.

During August 1924, the operating ratio, which had averaged seventy-six percent in 1921, dipped to 67.03, the lowest in any month for four years, while the transportation ratio went to 31.83, the lowest since early 1917. In February 1929, the operating ratio dipped to 58.8 percent, the lowest since December 1916. At the same time, loss and damage payments struck a new low, with a ratio to freight revenue of .803 percent, the lowest since 1904 and an indication of the organized effort in claim

---

[4] PLD, July 3, 1926.

prevention. Small wonder that *Moody's* commented laconically in 1929 that the C. B. & Q. was characterized by "liberal maintenance expense and low operating costs."[5]

It is worth noting that in all but one of the nine annual reports from 1921 to 1929, the phrase "rigid economy" was used to characterize operating expenditures. Running as close seconds were the phrases "increased efficiency," "improved facilities," and "increased maintenance expenses."[6] Yet this was in a decade popularly known for the speculative nature of investments and for a high, wide, and handsome way of doing things. That state of affairs simply did not exist either in the minds or in the performance of the men in charge of the Burlington. Times were relatively stable, to be sure, and freight traffic held up with remarkable consistency. But rising costs could not be immediately offset by raising the price of transportation; there was arduous competition from other railways and growing competition from trucks, buses, and automobiles. The Burlington brought down its transportation ratio (the relation of transportation expenses to total railway operating revenues) from 37.68 in 1921 to 32.07 in 1929 by careful planning and sheer hard work. However conventional the problems may have been, the operating people still had to keep on their toes.

• THE SOURCES OF TRAFFIC •

BUT SMART OPERATION was not enough. The Burlington was not and never had been a specialized carrier. It could not rely, as some railroads could, on one or two constant sources of traffic. It carried a wide assortment of goods and travelers bent on all sorts of business. Consequently, its traffic officers had learned long since that unless they were constantly on the lookout for new sources of business, they might be caught unprepared as one or another type of cargo or traveler petered out or chose other forms of transportation.

One way to get new business, of course, was to open up new channels of trade. This the company sought to do in the spring of 1926 by establishing a new perishable-freight service to and from the Southeast by way of the Paducah Gateway. Negotiations with the Gulf, Mobile and Northern and with the Nashville, Chattanooga and St. Louis were undertaken to secure a share of the business moving to and from the Southeast. Arrangements were successfully completed, and carload traffic through the gateway began to increase immediately. Furthermore, in the summer of 1926, the G. M. & N. acquired trackage rights from its northern terminal at Jackson, Tennessee, to Paducah over the N. C. & St. L.

The Paducah Gateway gained another boost in July 1927, when the

[5] *Moody's Steam Railroads* (New York, 1929), p. 940.
[6] CB&Q, AR's 1921–9.

G. M. & N. extended its line from Union to Jackson, Mississippi, thus forming a new through route to New Orleans in connection with the New Orleans Great Northern. The Burlington immediately began soliciting New Orleans business. By the end of 1927, business over this new route was firmly established and growing.

The best way to understand the overall traffic situation of the 20's is to consider the six principal commodity groups carried. The most notable change, destined to be a continuing one, was the marked growth of manufactures and miscellaneous goods. In 1921, these accounted for slightly over one fifth of all freight revenue; in 1929, for nearly a third. In 1921, products of mines and products of agriculture—traditional sources of Burlington revenue—were neck-and-neck in the lead as revenue producers, with manufactures and miscellaneous goods a close third. Among them, these three commodity groups accounted for about seventy percent of the company's freight revenue. But manufactures and miscellaneous goods began to pull ahead in the next year, and by the end of the decade had established the wide lead that has not been challenged since.

In the broadest sense, this was a reflection of the industrialization of the Midwest, a trend indicated, for example, by the large relative increase in gondola and automobile cars purchased and built by the company. This trend also was logically reflected by the activities of traffic solicitors and, in particular, those of the Industrial Development Department. Another aspect of commodity movement perhaps even more important to the formulation of traffic policy than the quantities moved was the fact that the most erratic year-by-year changes occurred in respect to the products of agriculture. Providing roughly a fifth of the company's freight revenue, this category was, even under "normal" economic conditions, the least predictable source of traffic. It therefore required, and received, as much if not more attention than any other group.

• AGRICULTURAL DEVELOPMENT •

IN THE 1920's, the farmer was beset by problems. Production had risen astronomically during the war years while money poured into land and capital investments. Farm prices rose to new peaks. In 1919–20, however, the inevitable collapse came; the American farmer never entirely recovered from the setback. Even in 1925, a good farm year, the ratio of prices received to prices paid by farmers stood only at ninety-two percent of the 1910–14 ratio. The basic cause of the difficulty, of course, was overproduction, but restriction of output, however logical, was an unpopular solution. Voluntary controls could hardly achieve it. Other remedies were tried: easier farm credit, higher import duties, and price supports, but none was successful or sufficient.

At least two other correctives were possible: more efficient production and diversification to foster regional stability. Toward these goals the

Burlington's Agricultural Department turned its attention. In contrast to the war period, the company's objective now was not simply to encourage increased output (which would have been reflected immediately in more freight to haul), but rather to make farming more profitable and to increase the income of the individual farmer. If that could be accomplished, tonnage would presumably take care of itself.

The most spectacular and probably the most effective feature of the Burlington's program was the operation of special educational trains. The idea was not new: a Burlington seed-corn special had operated as early as 1904. It was during the 20's, however, that the educational trains fully came into their own as the best means of solving the special problems of the decade. In almost every case, representatives of various state colleges cooperated, helping to plan the routes so that particular demonstrations would reach those most interested and participating in the tours themselves. The usual program consisted of lectures, exhibits, and demonstrations held both on the trains and in the field. Moreover, the company followed up each campaign, to keep the new ideas alive and also to determine as precisely as possible the tangible results of each venture. All this, it should be noted, took place on a system-wide basis; many of the trains ran over both the C. B. & Q. and the Colorado and Southern Lines.

As a harbinger of this program, a number of individual demonstration cars were taken to various spots on the system in 1919, 1920, and 1922. In 1923 the program got fully underway. From then until the end of the decade, no less than twenty-five educational trains went on the road. Among them they covered virtually the whole range of agricultural production, but the spotlight fell on the Purebred Sires Specials that toured Colorado in 1923 and Nebraska in 1924, the Poultry Specials of 1926–27, and the Sugar Beet Trains of 1925–29. The collective story of these educational trips is a saga in itself and richly deserves the telling in book form: over the years the impact of these tours markedly altered the social and economic life of the areas affected. A single example must suffice here.

In October 1923, a Purebred Sires Special stopped at twenty-nine towns in Colorado and Nebraska. The central feature of the tour was the exchange, at each town, of a purebred bull and a purebred boar—supplied by the breeders' associations—for scrubs. These trades, made on an even basis, were all prearranged with great care; in each town, agents for the tour located in advance a leading farmer who agreed to act as recipient and demonstrator of the purebred sire idea for each community. He was obligated financially in no way, but bound himself by written agreement properly to care for and develop his sire for at least two years.

The train left Denver with fifty-eight purebred sires, conservatively valued at $10,000. Nearly every town greeted the train with a band concert. Newspapers overflowed with publicity. A month after the trip, clippings were pouring in not only from the area visited but also from as far away as Indiana, Montana, and Texas. Altogether, 25,407 people attended the demonstrations and visited the exhibits (picking up 90,000 pieces of literature as they did so); probably several hundred thousand more heard about the tour.

In large measure the success of the campaign was the result of the thoroughness of the advance work. By the same token, it was realized that permanent results would depend on meticulous follow-up. Accordingly, in August 1924, representatives of all the interests who had cooperated on the train visited twenty-eight of the twenty-nine bulls and twenty-five of the twenty-nine boars that had been exchanged for scrubs. When the inspection was completed, it was found that the twenty-five boars had gained an average of 255 pounds, had been bred to 406 sows, and had produced 1,283 pigs that were farrowed and saved. Results from the pure-bred bulls were similar. They had gained an average of 340 pounds apiece, and although it was too soon to count the calves, they had been bred to 330 cows.

So much for the primary results of the trip; from the secondary angle, public relations, it had unquestionably been a rousing success. The follow-up party was received courteously and enthusiastically in each community by businessmen and farmers alike. When the final survey was made in 1926, it revealed a net increase of 12.6 percent in the number of purebred hog sires, a 20.5 percent increase in the number of dairy cattle sires, and an 11.5 percent increase in the number of beef cattle sires.

The story was much the same with the other tours that followed in rapid succession during the 20's; each year the trains concentrated on what seemed to be the pressing problem of the moment. The Nebraska Purebred Sires Train of 1924 was much like its Colorado predecessor, but its emphasis was on diversification and long-run dairy development to offset the uncertainties of wheat-growing. In 1925, and again in 1927, when wheat was seriously threatened by smut, the Burlington ran two demonstration trains on how to control it. In the next few years similar specials were run, dealing with problems in poultry, swine, sanitation, and the production of sugar beets.

These special trains were the most colorful aspect of the Burlington's work in agricultural development, but they were by no means all of it. As colonization agent at Omaha, Val Kuska began in 1922 to put together basic information that prompted the federal government to take a more active interest in irrigation projects; federal activity in this field reached a peak in the 30's. Kuska cooperated too with the 4-H Clubs and, as his title implied, served as a one-man information bureau and escort service for those desiring to make their homes in Burlington farm territory. And in the 20's the company continued a policy that reached back to the 1870's: the planting of trees of various varieties along its right of way.

· Industrial Development ·

As BUSINESS WORKED OUT of the short-lived depression of 1920–21, mercantile concerns throughout Burlington territory began to expand, and by 1924 home-building showed a marked increase which reached boom proportions in 1925, particularly, but not exclusively, in and around Chicago. The second half of the decade was characterized by steady and prolonged industrial expansion. Several indices reflected the extent and continuity of this movement: new plants located along the line, industrial leases executed, and industrial spurs built. There were two general surges, one reaching a peak in 1923, the second in 1928. The industrial complex that was Chicago led the way. In 1926, for example, the C. B. & Q. was serving no less than 571 industries on its own rails; in the next year, twenty-seven new plants were built on Burlington rails in Chicago alone. But industrialization was spreading west also. New industry tracks on Lines West accounted for more than a third of those installed during the decade.

Like so many other things about the railroad, the special activities of the Burlington's industrial agent could fill a book. In North Kansas City, where the C. B. & Q. owned considerable land, a partly owned subsidiary, the North Kansas City Development Company, was particularly busy during the 20's. In Chicago, a six and a half acre tract in the Twenty-second Street industrial district was bought jointly by the Western Electric and the Illinois Bell Telephone Company; the newcomers would be served by C. B. & Q. rails. The summer of 1928 witnessed erection of a new International Harvester Company plant at Rock Island and new grain elevators at countless points along the line. A year later, Galesburg, Peoria, St. Joseph, and Omaha as well as North Kansas City were the scene of ever increasing industrial expansion. Boom times indeed!

· Problems ·

PLENTY OF HEADACHES REMAINED, however, even in respect to freight traffic. For one thing, coal movements were irregular, owing principally to unsettled labor conditions in the industry and, later on, to the increased use of fuel oil. There were other disquieting factors. As if competition from trucks was not enough, in the summer of 1927 the I. C. C. required the railways to establish joint rates with the barge line on the Upper Mississippi River between Dubuque and the Twin Cities. When the municipal barge terminal was formally dedicated at Burlington, Iowa, on October 11, 1928, another potentially powerful competitor appeared to have gained a foothold in the very heart of the system. Furthermore, the increasing use of the Panama Canal was placing an ever-growing handicap on rail traffic. Because rates through the Canal were so low, manufacturers and merchants in territory east of Chicago were rapidly absorbing markets in the territory west of the Rockies.

The Hoch–Smith Resolution that Congress passed on January 30, 1925, posed even more of a threat to the Burlington. The resolution provided that "in view of the existing depression in agriculture, the commission is hereby directed to effect with the least practicable delay such lawful changes in the rate structure of the country as will promote the freedom of movement by common carriers of the products of agriculture."[7] As Holden aptly put it, this represented a tendency "to brush aside the patient and expert processes of the Interstate Commerce Commission and substitute direct legislation by Congress upon matters of intricate rate adjustments."[8] The principle of direct Congressional intervention in an effort to favor a particular class of shippers was, from the standpoint of the railways, a dangerous one.

One rate decision to which the Burlington was a party not only benefited the railways; it was a landmark in constitutional history. In a series of decisions in 1920, and notably in the *Wisconsin Passenger Fares* case of that year, the Interstate Commerce Commission found that state-prescribed rates, fares, and charges lower than the level of the corresponding interstate rates were unjustly discriminatory against interstate commerce and therefore invalid. The Wisconsin Railroad Commission appealed this decision and, citing the C. B. & Q. as defendant, took the case to the Supreme Court. That tribunal, in 1922, fully sustained the I. C. C. order.

One problem that touched all railways during the 1920's, and the Burlington in particular because of Hale Holden's position as chairman of the Association of Railway Executives, was that of railway labor legislation. As noted earlier, the Transportation Act of 1920 had established a Railroad Labor Board consisting of nine members appointed by the president, three representing labor, three management, and three the public. The Board was empowered to hear any dispute involving wages, rules, or working conditions. In an effort to ease the shock of the immediate postwar inflation, the Railroad Labor Board granted wage increases in 1920 of approximately twenty-two percent. In the following year, however, it authorized, except for operating employees, a reduction of about twelve percent, and in 1922 another reduction, which very nearly wiped out the increases of 1920. This second reduction, along with other grievances, had caused the serious strike of shopmen during the summer of 1922.

From that time on, railway labor in general became increasingly skeptical of the Board. There was another complaint: the Act of 1920 permitted, by agreement between management and labor, the establishment of the sort of adjustment boards which had existed during the period of federal control. But the carriers were firmly opposed to such

[7] Sharfman: *ICC*, op. cit., Vol. I, pp. 227–8.

[8] Hale Holden: "The Burlington in Nebraska," an address delivered in Omaha on January 29, 1925, p. 14, CB&Q/Pres.

boards on a national basis and would agree only to their establishment on individual systems or in localized areas. Meanwhile, the Labor Board, by failing to settle disputes as effectively as management and labor felt they were able to on a system basis, became increasingly unpopular with both the carriers and the labor organizations. As early as 1922, President Harding suggested a revision of the labor provisions of the Interstate Commerce Act; President Coolidge twice made the same suggestion.

Eventually, labor and management agreed on a bill that was enacted into law as the Railway Labor Act of 1926. According to its provisions, which are still in effect, a National Board of Mediation appointed by the president was established with power to mediate any dispute between carriers and their employees at the request of either party or on the Board's own motion. Should the Board prove unable to settle any controversy, it could use its influence to persuade the parties to submit to voluntary arbitration. If the parties at issue could not agree to arbitrate, then the Board of Mediation could so notify the president, who was empowered to create an Emergency Board to investigate the facts and report back within thirty days. No strike could be called during this period or for an additional period of thirty days after the report of the Emergency (or "Fact Finding") Board. The 1926 Act also provided that boards of adjustment might be created by agreement on a national, regional, or local basis, but their creation was not obligatory.

All things considered, probably the most persistent, separately identified problem of the 20's was the decline in passenger traffic as autos became increasingly popular. The Burlington tried "everything in the book" to stem the tide. The company in 1925 considered, for example, a plan of selling vacation tickets on a weekly installment basis. Meanwhile, it introduced weekend excursions at reduced rates and continued the emphasis on escorted tours. In 1926, the company added an additional overnight train, the *Commercial Limited*, between Chicago and the Twin Cities; travel on that route was the most encouraging feature of passenger traffic that year.

Hope was short-lived, however. By the summer of 1927, passenger revenues had fallen ten percent from the previous year, owing to the growth of bus lines and the fact that people were taking longer vacation trips by automobile. By fall the company was actively reducing passenger-train miles. Two of the St. Louis–Denver trains were consolidated with Kansas City–Billings trains between St. Joseph and Table Rock, and with Denver–Alliance trains between Brush and Denver. At the same time, six diners were taken out of service.

On the other hand, the Burlington improved what service remained by, for example, putting individual-bedroom cars on the night trains between St. Louis and Kansas City and shortening the running time of the day trains. But by the end of the year, traffic on virtually all main-line

Locomotive No. 903 lifting a freight over Crawford Hill, Nebraska, 1945

Vista-Dome *Twin Cities* Zephyr along the Mississippi

Station at Burlington, Iowa

Station at Quincy, Illinois

Call board listing assignability of crews, Ottumwa, Iowa

Collector checking tickets, double-deck commuters' gallery car

46-seat, double-deck Chicago suburban-service commuter car

Vista-Dome chair car "Silver Brand," 1956 Denver Zephyr

56-seat chair car "Silver Halter," 1956 Denver Zephyr

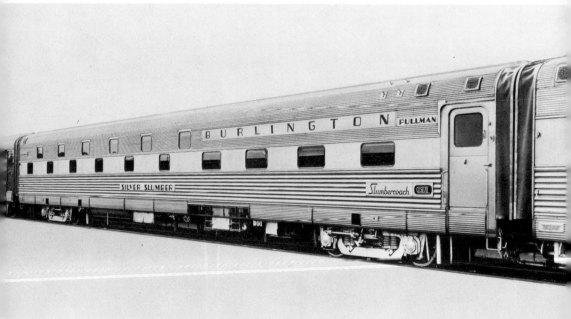

Budd Slumbercoach "Silver Slumber," introduced on 1956 Denver Zephyr

Railway postal car "Silver Post"

Dome-observation car "Silver Chateau," 1956 Denver Zephyr

48-seat dining car "Silver Manor"

10-roomette, 6-double-bedroom sleeper "Silver Bay," 1949 *California Zephyr*

Double-deck commuters' gallery car at suburban station, as introduced in 1950

The *Nebraska Zephyr* pausing at Aurora, Illinois, 1961

trains had decreased as much as twenty-three percent in comparison with the preceding year. Nor did the situation improve the following spring. In March 1928, passenger revenues were off 14.62 percent as compared with the previous year. Once again, various local trains were discontinued. But this was, at best, a stop-loss policy.

A positive major step was taken in the fall of 1928, when plans were laid for a bus subsidiary. The Burlington Transportation Company was incorporated in Illinois with $500,000 capital stock on February 14, 1929. Even though immediate plans contemplated only bus operations, the Articles of Incorporation were deliberately drawn so as to authorize truck operations as well when and if it should prove desirable to establish them. Implicit in this action was the Burlington's belief that rail-highway coordination could be achieved more successfully through a wholly owned subsidiary than by negotiating with independent bus and truck companies. Actually, bus operations began with a single vehicle shuttling along U. S. Highway 34 between Galesburg and Burlington; soon thereafter, short runs were set up in Nebraska, with a view to provide substitute service for unprofitable local passenger trains. A little later the B. T. Company acquired (a) the Cannon Ball Motor Transportation Company, which had established bus routes between Peoria and Galesburg and between Burlington and Kewanee by way of Galesburg, (b) Crandic Stages, running between Chicago and the Tri-Cities (Rock Island, Davenport, and Moline), and (c) a portion of the Black Hawk Bus Line providing a connection between the Chicago–Tri-Cities Line and Kewanee. These acquisitions had the approval of the state regulatory authorities; as yet no federal certificate was required for interstate operations. By the end of 1929, Burlington buses were covering 858 route miles, and although these operations were conducted at a loss, it was estimated that the loss was more than offset by savings (estimated at about $45,000) for the railroad in substituting buses for unprofitable passenger service.

As 1929 wore on, the Burlington's rail passenger situation improved slightly. Summer travel brought in more business, and a growing number of persons availed themselves of escorted tours. During the winter, earnings increased on both the Twin Cities and the Omaha lines, owing, in the company's opinion, to better service and new equipment. Despite these isolated bright spots, however, the long-run outlook was none too promising.

• THE FINANCIAL PICTURE •

THE BURLINGTON made money consistently through the 20's. Aside from the steady decline in passenger revenues (happily matched by decreasing operating expenses), income remained steady, and even on the broader stock base established in 1921, earnings per share exceeded by a wide margin the ten percent dividend paid in each of the years 1922–1929 inclusive.

At the beginning of 1921, funded debt outstanding in the hands of the public amounted to $174,038,300 and stock (mostly held by G. N.– N. P.) to $110,839,100. Total fixed charges amounted to $6,807,134.36. Average rate of interest was 3.94 percent on the entire debt.

In 1921, new financing was imperative: the vast improvements to plant and equipment then planned clearly would require more funds than could be raised under existing mortgages. But the laws of various states, where savings banks and trust companies were permitted to invest in rail bonds, required a larger proportion of stocks to bonds than would exist if the C. B. & Q. issued additional bonds without at the same time broadening the stock base. As Holden said, the directors "were practically under compulsion to increase the stock" to provide the necessary market for the bonds.[9] So it was that the Interstate Commerce Commission approved the issue of the 600,000 additional shares of stock mentioned in the preceding chapter. Both before and after this transaction, and for the reasons noted earlier, cash dividends were paid as well, $12 from earnings (which had amounted to $16.43 per share that year), and $69.1325 from surplus ($54.1325 from that accumulated prior to 1909, and $15 from that accumulated between 1909 and 1921).

As might have been expected, questions were raised publicly about the payment of dividends from surplus. But as Holden explained it, "this surplus was not in cash, but in double tracks, renewed bridges, and other improvements to the property, the cost of which had been paid for out of savings that might have been distributed in dividends on the stock. The public, during all these years, has had the use of these improvements which, otherwise, would have had to be paid for out of borrowed money. . . . What the Burlington did," he summarized ". . . was to take a part of its savings invested in the property in previous years and distribute them to its stockholders, to whom they honestly belonged."[1]

Once this broader stock base, now $170,839,100, was established, the management authorized the initial issue of a new series known as the First and Refunding Mortgage Bonds. The purposes of this new issue, in addition to providing funds for improvements, were to retire any prior debt outstanding and to reimburse the treasury for funds expended during the previous five years for construction. Under this indenture, $70,000,000 in bonds were sold between 1921 and 1927; in the latter year the old Nebraska Extension Mortgage was retired. By 1929, therefore, debt outstanding in the hands of the public consisted of the three major mortgages due in 1949, 1958, and 1971–77, respectively. During the decade, however, total interest-bearing debt increased twenty-seven percent and interest charges rose thirty-one percent, to a total of $9,084,635 a year. Average rate of interest

9 Hale Holden to Editor, *Sioux City Tribune*, 1922?, CB&Q/Sec.
1 Holden: ibid.

paid on the entire debt rose more moderately from 3.94 percent to 4.14 percent.

Meanwhile, operating expenses steadily declined. Taxes rose, but only from $1,035 to $1,283 per mile of road operated. Income from other sources, notably from the Colorado and Southern Lines, held steady, and rentals and other charges were reduced substantially. In view of these factors, the increase in debt interest was more than offset, so that net income, which at no time went below $19,290,530 during the decade, moved gradually forward, to reach an all-time high of $29,576,538 for 1929. Based purely on the actual earnings and expenses of the company, therefore, the increase in fixed debt hardly appeared out of line. With earnings at $17.31 per share for 1929, there seemed indeed little cause for worry.

• SYSTEM LINES WEST •

BY AND LARGE the experience of the three western members of the Burlington Lines family during the 20's paralleled that of the C. B. & Q. In contrast to the preceding and succeeding decades, this was most definitely a period of "normalcy" and of rather unaccustomed stability, for during the ten years ending in 1929, freight revenues varied less than ten percent. As on the C. B. & Q., passenger revenues declined steadily but net income held firm. The only "weak sister" was the half-owned Trinity and Brazos Valley, which remained in receivership throughout the decade.

As on the C. B. & Q., investment in both plant and rolling stock was heavy. Throughout the whole Burlington system, the only expansion of the decade took place in Texas. First of all, the line from Wichita Falls north to Byers was carried across the river into Waurika, Oklahoma, in 1925. Then, on June 1, freight and passenger service on the Fort Worth and Denver City was extended into Dallas over the tracks of the Rock Island. Daily manifest freight trains were established on a sixty-three-hour schedule between Dallas and Denver, and a fruit and vegetable special between the two cities was advertised on a fifty-nine-hour schedule. Double daily, through passenger service went into effect at the same time. All trains carried through sleepers between Denver and New Orleans via Dallas; trains Number 1 and Number 2 also handled a Denver–San Antonio sleeper; Number 7 and Number 8 handled several additional local sleepers between points in Texas. The fastest running time between Dallas and Denver, that of Number 1 northbound, was twenty-eight and a third hours.

Almost immediately thereafter, work began on the Fort Worth and Denver South Plains Railway, running west from Estelline through Sterley and Plainview to Dimmitt, 132 miles away. A seventy-two-mile north-south line crossed the main stem at Sterley and linked Silverton on the north with Lubbock on the south. The entire line was opened for service with appropriate fanfare on November 23, 1928. For the 8,500 square miles

Texas Lines, 1925–35

served, the South Plains Extension, as the new line was called, brought promise of unlimited expansion. Attention was drawn particularly to the superior service that would be available to the Pacific Northwest; in fact, the only freight schedules specifically given were those which provided ninth-morning delivery from Seattle to Fort Worth, and third-morning delivery from Denver to Fort Worth on the one hand and to both Plainview and Lubbock on the other.

On May 20, 1929, a third major extension in Texas, and the last for many a long year on the entire Burlington system, was incorporated as the Fort Worth and Denver Northern Railway, to build from Childress north through Wellington and Shamrock to Pampa, a distance of approximately 110 miles. Despite the depression that soon engulfed the country, the road was completed in the summer of 1932.

[356]

From the standpoint of traffic, by all odds the outstanding development in the 1920's for the combined Colorado and Southern–Fort Worth and Denver City was the diversification and increased output of agricultural products. Throughout the decade, the Agricultural departments conducted exhibits, demonstrations, and meetings over the length and breadth of the property and in respect to every conceivable agricultural undertaking appropriate to the area. As in Wyoming and Nebraska, an important byproduct of this activity was stimulation of colonization, both into the older, established regions and into areas made accessible by new construction.

Even the prosperous 20's demonstrated how important diversification was. In 1922 a slump in oil prices, and in 1923 destructive floods, had an adverse effect on revenues on the C. & S.–F. W. & D. C. But the next year saw better business in such diverse commodities as petroleum, sugar beets, and metals. Revenues continued to increase in 1925–26 as a result of good wheat and cotton crops. Despite a marked decline in the products of mines as well as in wheat and other grains, there were more than compensating increases in cotton, animals, and animal products in 1927. The following year, owing partly to weather conditions, was not so good on either the C. & S. or the F. W. & D. C., and a further modest decline occurred on both roads in 1929. Had it not been for the marked increase of shipments by the Colorado Fuel and Iron Company of Pueblo, the "boom year" of 1929 might have been discouraging indeed. Trends on the Wichita Valley, included in the Colorado and Southern Lines, faithfully followed those on the C. & S. and F. W. & D. C.

On the Trinity and Brazos Valley, feast and famine alternated. The bringing-in of the Mexia Oil Field resulted in a substantial operating profit in 1921, but the slump in production the following year led to a deficit. The cycle was repeated in the next two years as a new oil field was brought in near Navarro in 1923, resulting in an increase of half a million dollars in net railway operating income. This was followed by a deficit in the next year, when the field passed its peak. So it went until 1928, after which deficits became increasingly heavy.

As was true of all the nation's railways, passenger revenues on the western subsidiaries declined steadily in the 20's. The inroads of the automobile were most noticeable on the Colorado and Southern. The Denver and Interurban was finally placed in receivership in the summer of 1926 and discontinued operations entirely on December 16. Over a period of years, the total loss to the Colorado and Southern had amounted to more than a million and a half dollars. The Denver and Interurban Motor Company that replaced it, however, turned in a profit for 1926, and in order to protect passenger traffic between Denver and Pueblo, a new bus company in which the C. & S. took a quarter interest was organized to operate between those points and others in Colorado.

[3 5 7]

Dividends on the Colorado and Southern first and second preferred stock at the stipulated rate of four percent were paid every year from 1921 to 1930, inclusive, and on the common stock at the rate of three percent every year except 1923–25, inclusive. Payments were omitted in those three years to conserve funds for increased maintenance, to improve the general credit of the company, and in order to conserve cash for retirement of the First Mortgage.

The First Mortgage four percent bonds authorized in 1899 matured on February 1, 1929. To pay them, the C. & S. obtained temporary loans of $9,000,000 from the C. B. & Q. and $3,000,000 from the F. W. & D. C., and on May 1, 1930, issued $20,000,000 General Mortgage four and a half percent bonds due May 1, 1980. Funds derived from their sale were used to repay the C. B. & Q. and F. W. & D. C. advances and to reimburse the C. & S. treasury for approximately $7,500,000 advanced for construction of the line of the Fort Worth and Denver South Plains Railway Company.

On completion of this financing, the C. & S. bonded indebtedness outstanding in the hands of the public was $28,978,900 in four and a half percent Refunding and Extension Mortgage bonds due May 1, 1935, and $20,000,000 in four and a half percent General Mortgage bonds due May 1, 1980. The Fort Worth and Denver City Railway Company had outstanding with the public $8,157,000 of its First Mortgage five and a half percent bonds due on December 1, 1961, and the Fort Worth and Denver Terminal Railway Company had $300,000 principal amount of its First Mortgage six percent bonds outstanding with the public. The total bonded debt of the system in public hands amounted to $57,435,900; total interest came to $2,670,685 annually. Intra-system dividends paid by the Fort Worth to the C. & S. slightly exceeded an even million dollars in 1921–22, were increased to nearly a million and a half over the next three years, moved up to a peak of $4,621,900 in 1927, and tapered off to $2,773,140 in 1929.

As the "prosperous 20's" drew to a close, the problems in sight on the west end included the extension of the highway network and of long-distance pipelines. But the plant had been put in excellent shape and extended, traffic had become more diversified, and, except for the faltering Trinity and Brazos Valley, the western subsidiaries seemed fully able to take care of themselves.

• THE MEN IN CHARGE •

IN 1926, the C. B. & Q. ran a full-page advertisement in various magazines and newspapers, highlighting the fact that ten presidents or chairmen of United States railroads had had their training on the Burlington. These were William G. Besler of the Central Railroad of New Jersey, Harry Byram of the Milwaukee, Howard Elliott of the Northern Pacific, James

Gorman of the Rock Island, Howard Hetzler of the Western Indiana, N. L. Howard of the Chicago Great Western, Charles M. Levey of the Western Pacific, Henry Miller of the Terminal Railroad of St. Louis, Henry Nutt of the Monongahela, and Daniel Willard of the Baltimore and Ohio. "Gently boastful though these advertisements were," commented *Time*, "yet they revealed a quaint modesty. They might well have told of the eleventh Burlington-trained railroad president. He is Hale Holden, 57, president of the Burlington itself."[2]

Without doubt, Holden was one of the ablest men ever to occupy the Burlington's presidency. His standing in the industry as a lawyer and advocate enabled him throughout his administration to play a leading role in national railway affairs; he was at his best in expounding lucidly and forcefully whatever idea he thought important for the company or industry he served.

Late in 1928, Holden was offered the chairmanship of the executive committee of the Southern Pacific. After due deliberation, he accepted the position, effective January 1, 1929. Finding a successor for him was, of course, the responsibility of the Northern Lines, and in particular of Charles Donnelly and Ralph Budd, then presidents of the Northern Pacific and the Great Northern, respectively. Their choice was Frederick Ely Williamson, an Easterner who had been trained on the New York Central and who in a little over three years had made a brilliant record as operating vice-president of the Northern Pacific.

Upon graduating from Yale in 1898, Williamson had joined the New York Central. In 1925 he was serving as general superintendent of the New York Terminal District when Howard Elliott, on the lookout for a vice-president of operations for the Northern Pacific, brought him to St. Paul. In September 1928, at the age of fifty-two, Williamson became executive vice-president of the Burlington, with the understanding that he would succeed to the presidency when Holden left at the end of the year.

The prospects before the new chief executive on New Year's Day 1929 were bright indeed. During 1928 the company had carried more manufactured products than ever in its history; the industrial boom was at full peak. Certainly, 1929 seemed destined to be a year of unsurpassed prosperity. The Q and its vigorous new president, backed by a seasoned team, faced the future with confidence.

[2] *Time*, Vol. VIII, No. 9 (August 30, 1926), p. 28.

PART IV

New Challenges

1929 - 49

CHAPTER 19

Depression

1929-33

• 1930: DARK CLOUDS •

WHEN THE STOCK MARKET CRASHED in October, 1929, it was difficult at first to believe that the general health of the economy, and with it the prospects for railway earnings, were seriously threatened. Consequently, even though the shock from Wall Street was almost immediately reflected in declining traffic on the Burlington, a persistent note of hopefulness ran through Williamson's monthly reports to his directors for the next eight or nine months. This was not simply whistling in the dark; there was some concrete evidence that things were not quite so bad as they seemed. Net railway operating income for 1929 increased almost two and a half million dollars over the 1928 figure, and was the largest in any year since 1916. Net income increased to an all-time high of $17.31 a share. Could such favorable returns be entirely discounted?

In March 1930, however, total gross revenue was less than it had been in any comparable month since 1919. Williamson reported reductions in maintenance and transportation expenses; most of the forces in the Mechanical Department, he indicated, were working on a five-day-a-week basis. Except for heavy grain movement, traffic in July continued to fall alarmingly; in sharp contrast to the previous year, the drop in building materials, automobiles, iron and steel products, and practically all manufactures boded ill for the future. Passenger revenues plummeted as travel dropped off on both long- and short-distance runs. Not even low rates, vigorous advertising, or solicitation seemed to have any effect. When the returns for 1930 were all in, they reflected a drop in business of something over twelve percent. Freight revenues, to be precise, were off 12.32 percent; total operating revenues, off 12.95 percent; and carloadings, off 12.48 percent. It was significant and by no means purely coincidental that even though the precise extent of this decline was not known until well into 1931, both the labor force and operating expenditures had been reduced in almost the same proportion: 12.23 percent and 11.37 percent, respectively.

Outlays for improvement of plant and equipment were therefore confined, as Williamson said, to "the most important and necessary work."[1] Nevertheless, the major grade separation at Canal and Sixteenth streets, started in 1929, was continued, as was construction of the new $600,000 railway express terminal at Roosevelt Road and the nearly completed renovation of the Omaha Station. By all odds the most important major project launched in 1930 was the three-year program for complete reconstruction of the Galesburg classification yards, at an estimated cost of $5,000,000. Originally put into operation in 1906, the yard was still using the old manually operated humps and short receiving and departure tracks. The new program called for enough tracks to permit classification without reswitching and a lengthening of all track so as to hold full-length trains. In addition, there were to be electrically controlled car-retarders, modern icing and coaling facilities, an interlocking plant, and a new repair yard. Approximately twenty percent of the total program was completed during 1930.

There was some reduction in the normal maintenance programs: new rail installed dropped to 271 miles from the 339 of 1929, and expenses for work on permanent bridges were cut by almost two thirds in 1930. Although 171 locomotives were retired from service, the company took delivery of 1,755 new freight cars, more than in any year since 1927. During 1930, the Burlington received its first dozen Hudson-type high-speed passenger locomotives and its first eight Northern-type 4-8-4 dual-purpose freight and passenger engines.

Even though agricultural production declined generally, the farmers in Burlington territory, particularly on Lines West, raised normal crops in 1930. Some shipments were withheld to resist low prices, but it was mainly truck competition that caused the reduction in agricultural tonnage. Significantly, industrial unemployment stimulated a renewed interest in western farm land. As a result, the company had some three thousand inquiries for land and carried 220 carloads of immigrant movables into western Nebraska and Wyoming. The Agricultural Department doubled its effort,

---

[1] CB&Q, AR 1930, p. 22.

with tangible results: it put on demonstrations of better seed, more productive livestock, soil improvement, efficient marketing, and management. As before, efforts were made to encourage specialization where soil and climate warranted it. Even in the face of a twelve percent loss in business, results in 1930 did not seem to warrant undue pessimism. Earnings of $12.87 per share exceeded those for the years 1922–25 inclusive, and for 1927. Not until 1942 did total operating revenues or earnings per share again equal those of 1930.

Thus there was nothing unusual about the fact that the Burlington continued to purchase Gulf, Mobile and Northern stock throughout 1930. By November 11, the company had acquired 25,800 shares of preferred and 27,601 shares of common stock. Rumors had already been published that the Burlington was on the point of acquiring the G. M. & N., and late in November the press reported that the C. B. & Q. would probably lease the road, guaranteeing about $6 on the preferred and at least $2 on the common stock. At a meeting of Burlington's executive committee in New York on December 4, 1930, the possibility of a lease rather than purchase found strong favor, and it was agreed that the C. B. & Q. should have two representatives on the G. M. & N. board. A more tangible indication of the company's faith in the future was the payment of a five percent dividend on June 25, and one of ten percent on December 26.

• 1931: THE STORM THICKENS •

SO DARK WAS THE OUTLOOK in 1931 that no one dared guess, officially at least, when a turn for the better might be expected. For the first time since anyone could remember, there were not even the usual seasonal upturns in traditional standby traffic. As might have been expected, therefore, the all-absorbing objective of management during the year was to cut costs to the bone whenever and wherever it could without compromising safety and the long-run health of the property and organization.

As early as January 1931, Williamson reported that all forces had been kept "at just about the minimum possible," but in April further reductions were made.[2] By fall, not only each department but every position on the railroad was examined with the thought either of consolidation or elimination wherever possible without loss of business. Shop and maintenance forces were pared even farther toward the end of the year. The car shop at Plattsmouth was discontinued entirely, but most of its facilities and employees were taken over by the Burlington Refrigerator Express Company. At the same time, the locomotive shop at Havelock was converted into a freight-car repair shop, and work that previously had been carried on at various points was consolidated there. Locomotive work formerly done at

[2] PLD, June 2, 1931.

Havelock was transferred to West Burlington and Denver. Both passenger-and freight-train miles were reduced by changing schedules and consolidation. Furthermore, a vigorous fuel-conservation campaign was launched; along with the falling price of coal, it brought about considerable savings.

Major projects that had been started in better times, of course, had to be continued. Such were the grade separation in Chicago at Canal and Sixteenth streets and construction of the Railway Express terminal at Roosevelt Road, both of which were completed during the year. So was the eastbound unit of the large new classification yard at Galesburg. In addition, regular programs such as the conversion of wooden-trestle bridges into permanent form and the laying of new rail had to be continued; both of these, however, were put on a restricted basis.

When the figures for 1931 were in, they reflected a decrease in revenues and in carloadings of approximately twenty-one percent. Average employment on the C. B. & Q. dropped from over 38,000 to just over 31,000, and quite naturally employees became uneasy as to whether the company could continue its liberal pension plan. On the request of various brotherhoods, the railways of the nation appointed a committee to confer with union executives on the subject of a uniform railroad pension plan.

In terms of dollars and cents, annual revenues were off about $30,000,000. By dint of rigorous economy, the operating ratio for the year was held to 69.65 percent, and expenses were cut more than $21,000,000. Taxes declined substantially, as did hire of equipment, so that net railway operating income was held within $7,500,000 of the 1930 figure. On the other hand, dividends the company received declined while interest on the funded debt remained fixed; these were the chief factors that brought about a drop of more than $8,600,000 in net income, which in 1931 amounted to $13,319,735.11. Of this amount, $8,541,935 was dispersed as a five percent dividend on June 25; no further payments were made during the year, so that the balance of net income was transferred to profit and loss.

· THE WESTERN SUBSIDIARIES, 1930-31 ·

PARADOXICALLY, at least two developments in Texas during 1930-31 gave promise—and some evidence—of better times ahead. On April 30, 1930, the Trinity and Brazos Valley Railway finally emerged from its sixteen-year receivership. During this long period it had been forced to relinquish many of the joint facilities it had previously enjoyed, such as access to Dallas and to Galveston. One prime objective, therefore, upon emergence from receivership was to restore efficient main-line operations. The first move, symbolic of a fresh start, was to change the name of the company on July 7, 1930, to Burlington–Rock Island Railroad Company. This at once identified the line with its joint proprietors and did away with the title associated in most people's minds with the longest receivership in Texas history.

On June 1, 1931, the Burlington–Rock Island entered into a number of agreements which radically changed both its operation and its prospects. The long-standing arrangement by which its freight trains had run between Waxahachie and Fort Worth over the Texas and New Orleans was replaced by an agreement to use the rails of the Missouri–Kansas–Texas from Waxahachie to Dallas. This contract was then taken over by the Fort Worth and Denver City and the Chicago, Rock Island and Gulf, which also leased the line of the B.–R. I. itself between Waxahachie and Teague. Finally, on the same date the Burlington–Rock Island extended its freight service from Houston to Galveston and to Texas City by a joint track arrangement with the T. & N. O., thus entering southern terminals it had not used since 1914. The capstone of the new dispensation was that the B.–R. I. should be operated alternately by the Rock Island and the Fort Worth. Effective June 1, 1931, the Rock Island took over management to last until the end of 1935. Thereafter, management would rotate in five-year periods.

For the Burlington–Rock Island, 1930 was a year of adjustment. The net railway operating deficit amounted to $795,925. During 1931, this was cut to $453,414, and indications were that even under depressed conditions the loss would be further reduced the following year.

As has already been indicated, while the economy was still booming in the spring of 1929, the Fort Worth and the Denver Northern Railway had been incorporated to build from Childress to Pampa, Texas. When the I. C. C. granted permission to do so on August 5, 1930, work began at once; the road was completed in time to handle the 1932 crops. Construction costs, as in the case of the Fort Worth and Denver South Plains Railway, were met by advances from the Colorado and Southern in return for all stock of the new corporation and a six percent note. For its first sixty-odd miles, between Childress and Shamrock, the new line ran through well-developed agricultural country; beyond Shamrock it lay in the center of the Panhandle oil and gas region. Thus it looked forward to well-diversified traffic.

Because the Colorado and Southern Railway financed the Texas extensions, and in turn relied on dividends from the Fort Worth and Denver City for the major portion of its other income, results in Texas inevitably affected the financial results of the C. & S. Thus, the necessity of advancing funds for construction of the South Plains Line to the extent of $7,634,509, together with the necessity for meeting the maturity of $19,402,000 of First Mortgage bonds on February 1, 1929, led to the issuance of a new $20,000,000 four and a half percent General Mortgage due on May 1, 1980. Long-term debt of the C. & S. was thus increased to $58,869,800 by the end of 1930.

Operating revenues on the C. & S. during 1930 declined approximately sixteen percent from the previous year, more sharply than on the C. B. & Q., but less than on the Texas Lines. The drought and short crops in Texas that year and a marked reduction in mining and shipping of coal and iron ore in Colorado and Wyoming meant, among other things, a reduction of more than eleven percent in interchange between the C. & S. and the Denver roads. Net railway operating income, as good an indication as any of results in the local territory, amounted to $1,384,364 on the C. & S. in 1930, a decrease of approximately twenty-two percent under 1929. Other income, however, in which the biggest item was the dividend from the Fort Worth, contributed to a gross income only eleven percent under that for 1929, and after payment of interest on the funded debt, net income was nearly two and a half million dollars, sufficient to pay four percent dividends on both first and second preferred stock and three percent on the common, a total disbursement of $1,609,571.

Operating revenues of the C. & S. in 1931 continued to decline at approximately the same rate. The principal cause, of course, was the general decline in business throughout the country, but there were special reasons, too: increasing truck and automobile competition, increased use of gas and fuel oil instead of coal, and unfavorable agricultural conditions.

These factors combined to cut net operating income on the Colorado and Southern Railway in 1931 forty-eight percent under 1930. Once again, dividends from the Fort Worth and Denver, though less than in 1930, and interest on construction advances, provided much-needed other income, so that the company's gross income fell off only twenty-one percent as compared with the previous year. After payment of all interest charges, there was still sufficient to pay four percent on the first and second preferred stock, payments aggregating $679,982. Because this left a balance of only $643,936, however, no disbursement was made on the common stock. Employment on both the Colorado and Southern and Texas Lines was reduced approximately thirty percent between 1929 and 1931.

• A Change at the Top •

Late in 1931, Burlington's president, Frederick E. Williamson, was elected to the presidency of the New York Central, and to the regret of those who worked with him on the Q, he resigned at the end of the year. Although Williamson's tenure on the Burlington was the shortest since John Murray Forbes's "regency" in 1878–81, he had made a distinctive place for himself in its development, and had amply proved himself to be the right man at the right time. An operating man to the core, he had acted quickly and decisively in tightening the Burlington's belt as the recession of 1930 deepened into crisis. Despite his constant concern over such matters as transportation ratios, on-time performance, and condition of the track, he always had considered himself a committee of one to support the efforts of the Traffic Department to bring in more business.

Because Williamson talked railroad language and was easily accessible, the men on the line instinctively regarded him as "one of the boys." He abhorred procrastination, made his decisions quickly and clearly, and as one of his subordinates recalled, "he never forgot to compliment an associate over a good job . . . morale under his administration was excellent."[3]

The man elected by the directors on December 8, 1931, to take Williamson's place was no stranger to the Burlington. Ever since the latter part of 1916, Ralph Budd, at that time assistant to the president of the Great Northern, had been a director of the C. B. & Q. As president of the Great Northern from 1919 on, he had shared, with his opposite number on the Northern Pacific, chief responsibility for the formulation of all Northern Lines policy in respect to the Burlington. If only because of this vantage point, which he had occupied for fifteen years, Budd was singularly well fitted to assume the Burlington presidency. Even more important were the professional and personal qualifications he brought with him.

Born on a farm near Waterloo, Iowa, in 1879, he completed high school and college in six years, graduating from Highland Park College in Des Moines with the degree of civil engineer in 1899. Thereupon he went to work as a draftsman for the Chicago Great Western Railway. The next year found him out on the line as an assistant engineer. So skillful was he in applying new techniques that his superiors recommended him to the Rock Island engineers, who were then building their line between St. Louis and Kansas City. They offered him a job in 1902, and the next year he became their division engineer.

The vice-president of the Rock Island at that time was John F. Stevens, who liked what he saw of Budd's work; consequently, in 1906, when Stevens became chief engineer of the Panama Canal and needed a man to take charge of the engineering for the railroad across the Isthmus, he sent for Budd. The assignment was a tough one, but despite the fact that a new line had to be pushed through tangled jungles, it was completed well in advance of the projected date. Meanwhile, Stevens returned to the United States to carry out various engineering assignments for James J. Hill in the Northwest. Once again, in 1909, he called on Budd, this time to undertake reconnaissance work on the Oregon Trunk. Budd, his line finished in Panama, hastened to rejoin his old chief.

Early in 1910, Budd became chief engineer of the Oregon Trunk, and shortly afterward chief engineer of the Spokane, Portland and Seattle as well. As such, he came under the direct and constant scrutiny of Hill, who, like Stevens, instantly recognized the versatile abilities of the young engineer. Late in 1912 he invited Budd, then thirty-three, to come to

[3] J. W. Cooper to Overton, November 30, 1955.

St. Paul as assistant to the president of the Great Northern. At first in charge of capital expenditures and contracts, Budd shortly became chief engineer of the system as well and, in 1918, its executive vice-president. To this responsibility he added, during the period of federal control, the assistant regional directorship of the Central Western District. In 1919, at the age of forty he was elected president of the Great Northern.

Perhaps Budd's most spectacular achievement in that post was construction of the new Cascade Tunnel in central Washington. Of specific future importance to the Burlington was the fact that during construction of the tunnel Budd installed several stationary Diesel engines to provide standby power for air pumped to the workers far underground. He was tremendously impressed by the dependability and economy of these engines. Even though the metal of which they were then made was so heavy in relation to horsepower that such engines were impractical for mounting on a locomotive frame, Budd made careful note of their performance and stored the information away in his mind for possible future use.

No sooner had the Cascade Tunnel been completed, in January 1929, than the Great Northern, in partnership with the Western Pacific, proceeded to build a line Budd had surveyed years before between Klamath Falls and Keddie. When it was opened in 1931, it brought rail service to a huge, previously inaccessible area and provided an alternate through route between California and the Northwest.

Ralph Budd's intense interest in the proposed merger of the Hill Lines in 1927–30 has already been noted, but this was only one of many projects he put in motion. Among other things, he was responsible for enlarging the capacity of the standard ore-carrying cars from fifty to seventy tons and for inaugurating the Great Northern's up-to-the-minute *Empire Builder* on a schedule that saved an entire business day on its run to the Coast.

To the Burlington, then, on January 1, 1932, Ralph Budd brought an extraordinary combination of ability, experience, and imagination. Even more pertinent at the moment, he brought courage and patience. It was clear that he would need all these qualities in full measure to cope with the bleak situation that confronted him as he took up his duties as the fourteenth president of the Chicago, Burlington & Quincy Railroad Company, and seventeenth of the Burlington.

• 1932: Low Tide •

ON FEBRUARY 16, 1932, barely six weeks after he had taken office, Budd addressed the Inland Daily Press Association in Chicago. Until the depression, he began, it had been assumed that railways had a virtual monopoly of transportation and that therefore the various regulatory bodies would be able to prescribe such rates as would enable them to earn a fair return on their property and thus maintain sufficient credit for improvements and expansion. Under this assumption of ever increasing traffic, the railroads had undertaken a record-breaking program of improvements during the 1920's; capital expenditures during that decade had equaled the amount spent during their entire history prior to 1920. As a result, the roads had achieved their highest degree of efficiency and had the greatest capacity in all their history. Yet, said Budd, what was not commonly understood at the time was that a great deal of this activity was incidental to the building of new and improved highways and the development of the automotive industry. The net result was what Budd termed "an elemental change"; railways no longer possessed a monopoly of overland transportation.

Under such circumstances, said he, "it should be very clear that the controlling ideas and policies of regulation which may have been entirely appropriate when railways enjoyed a practical monopoly of overland transportation have now become obsolete and should be modified." Budd's second suggestion was one he had made many times before: the consolidation of a large number of railway companies into a limited number of systems that would permit effective competition among strong companies rather than ineffective competition among many small companies; small companies would be so weakened that they would be incapable of giving adequate service. Budd's third point was that because railway taxes had increased out of all proportion to earnings, remedial action was in order. Finally, he emphasized that other transportation agencies would of course continue to grow, as they should, but he cautioned that "in comparing the charges for their services with those of the railways, care should be taken to include the whole cost in every instance. . . . The most desirable outcome, of course, would be that whatever agency is best adapted to rendering a given type of transportation under given circumstances should be employed."

With this simple analysis of the situation and his program of concrete suggestions on the record, Budd had a firm factual basis for his considered conclusions. No one knew, he observed, when the current depression was going to end, but of one thing he was certain. The depression, he said, "will end sooner if we all apply ourselves to earnest thinking and constructive action, according to sound and proved rules and laws of economics and business. . . . A return," he concluded, "may and probably will begin before we realize it. Let us prepare now to take full advantage of it and be careful to make it endure."[4] Circumstances might force him to concentrate on daily economy, but Budd clearly had no intention of overlooking the entirely new opportunities he was certain the future would offer.

[4] Budd, luncheon talk at Inland Daily Press Association, Annual Meeting, Chicago, February 16, 1932, CB&Q/Pres.

The first thing Ralph Budd did when he took office was to dig out every conceivable fact that would illuminate not only the immediate critical situation but also trends that might be developing. This information he subjected to rigorous analysis, comparing it not only with similar data for past periods and for other railroads, but with general financial and business reports. He saw to it that his findings, lucidly arranged and accompanied by such interpretative comments as he thought appropriate, went to the directors each month; he saw to it also that management in depth was brought fully up to date so that it could understand precisely what the problems were and what it was expected to do about them.

The picture was black indeed; for the month of January 1932, net railway operating income on the C. B. & Q. had fallen seventy-two percent in comparison with the previous year; and on the C. & S. Lines, twenty-five percent. Total carloadings had been barely half of what they had been in January 1929, and had fallen nearly twenty-eight percent even since January 1931. Some relief for the company, although not for the individuals working for it, became effective on February 1, 1932, when the organized employees, through their representatives, accepted a deduction of ten percent from their pay checks. The agreement provided that full rates would be restored a year later, unless otherwise arranged by negotiation. Equally notable, though less publicized in the press, was the fact that similar deductions were applied to the wages and salaries of all other employees from top to bottom. Budd estimated that in 1932 these steps would mean a saving of $4,675,000 on the C. B. & Q., and of $613,000 on the C. & S. Lines.

One thing that disturbed Budd was mounting truck competition and, more particularly, the apparent lack of a concerted policy to meet it. Determined to delve farther into this situation, he asked Horace Holcomb, his traffic vice-president, to let him have a statement of every important instance in which reduced rates had been put into effect during the previous six months to meet truck competition, and to indicate anything else that had been done to retain traffic that might be lost to trucks. He asked also whether any efforts had been made to increase railway rates on traffic that was least vulnerable to truck competition.

Holcomb replied that certain specific reductions had been made, the theory being that the company should proceed cautiously, particularly where the railroad thought the truck rates were below truck costs and consequently temporary. Holcomb reported that committees had been appointed for the various regional railway groups to make a study of the traffic situation in general. Budd, pencil in hand, underscored Holcomb's statement that the C. B. & Q. had been "perhaps too conservative." At the top of the letter he wrote: "Follow up rate reduction."[5]

In May 1931, Williamson had reduced the five general superintend-

[5] Budd notation on: H. H. Holcomb to Budd, March 17, 1932, CB&Q/Pres.

ents' districts to three. One of the first things Budd did was to carry this move several steps farther, so that by April 1 the seventeen operating divisions were reduced to eleven. The general situation in April, however, showed little improvement. With the Illinois mines shut, coal movement was extremely light, and the outlook for grain was bleak indeed. News from Texas was more encouraging. Rail on the new Pampa line had moved through Wellington and Shamrock, and it was expected that regular operation would commence on the completed portions about June 15, in time to participate in the grain movement. Closer to home, Budd announced that the Burlington had earmarked an exhibit track at the Century of Progress Exposition in Chicago, to be held during the summer of 1933. The company, he said, planned to display a typical modern passenger train.

As it turned out, C. B. & Q. managed to cover its fixed charges for the first six months of 1932, but only by a margin of slightly over $400,000, an equivalent of twenty-four cents per share of stock, as compared with earnings of $3.90 per share during the first half of 1931. Consequently, the dividend of one and a half percent paid in June was charged wholly to profit and loss. The C. & S. Lines were even worse off: they failed to earn one half of the year's fixed charges by more than a million dollars; this deficit was more than $400,000 greater than for the first six months of 1931.

Passenger traffic continued to drop precipitously, and in June several local passenger trains were withdrawn and two pairs of main-line trains between Chicago and Lincoln were consolidated. Total employees on the C. B. & Q. averaged only 23,135 in June, a drop of more than 7,000 since the same month of the previous year; total payroll for June was less than $3,000,000, compared with a payroll of nearly $4,500,000 in June, 1931.

The opening of the Denver Northern to Pampa on July 15, 1932, was celebrated in true Texas fashion and evoked from the citizenry along the line much the same sense of participation and satisfaction that had been so noticeable when the Burlington, as a pioneer road, had moved west in Illinois and Nebraska. In contrast, the truth that independence of a community from its railway means certain death for the latter became evident on another part of the system. When the C. B. & Q. acquired the Colorado and Southern late in 1908, it received, as part of the transaction, 412 miles of narrow-gauge mountain railroad that had originally formed the fabled South Park Lines. With the decline of mining and the substitution of electrical power for rail-borne coal at such mines as remained, business had already begun to decline. Service west of Hancock through Gunnison and beyond had been discontinued by the C. & S. in 1911. The increase in paved roads and in trucking during the 1920's added the final blow. Between 1922 and 1926 the rails on all but eighteen miles of the eighty-one and a half mile main line between Garos and Gunnison

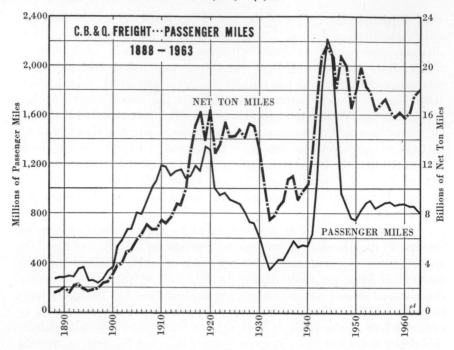

were removed; the remaining portion, between Quartz and Parlins, was operated by the Rio Grande, which made a connection with it at the latter point.

In September 1928, with more and more traffic going to the trucks, the management of the Colorado and Southern applied to the Interstate Commerce Commission for authority to abandon all the main-line trackage west of Waterton (near Denver), including the historic line through Como and over Boreas Pass to Climax and Leadville, as well as the Como–Garos line and the branches to Alma and Leavick. The Commission, thinking that business might improve, withheld permission. But conditions deteriorated farther, and the C. & S. renewed its petition for abandonment on August 16, 1935, except in respect to that portion of the line between the valuable molybdenum mines at Climax and the Junction with the Rio Grande at Leadville, a distance of 14.64 miles. The hearings and the Commission's consideration of the case occupied more than a year, but in the fall of 1936 permission for abandonment was granted. The effective date was set at April 10, 1937. On that day, to the dismay and despair of rail fans the country over, the last picturesque train chugged over the scenic line from Leadville into Denver. A year later, track was taken up. Similarly, the C. & S. narrow-gauge system formerly known as the Colorado Central which had served Denver–Georgetown, Central City–Blackhawk was also abandoned and the rails removed between 1931 and 1941.

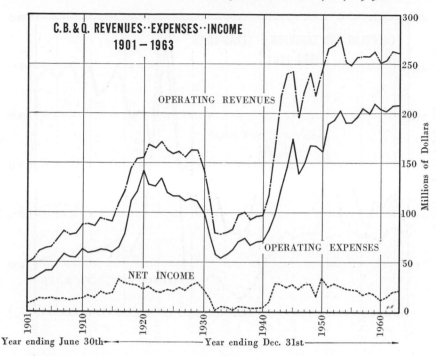

C.B.&Q. REVENUES··EXPENSES··INCOME
1901 – 1963

OPERATING REVENUES

OPERATING EXPENSES

NET INCOME

Millions of Dollars

Year ending June 30th — Year ending Dec. 31st

Whereas the Burlington could abandon its narrow-gauge lines in the mountains, no such relatively easy solution could even be entertained in respect to the C. B. & Q. itself. In retrospect, 1932 could well lay claim to being the blackest year in the history of the company. Carloadings were off twenty-five percent; the largest decreases were in forest products (36.57 percent) and agricultural products (31.94 percent). The causes of the declines were closely related: the price of grain was so low that it did not repay the farmer for the cost of production, while the lack of purchasing power in agricultural communities particularly affected forest products. Passenger revenues, despite the long decline over preceding years, were 34.75 percent below those of 1931; even bus revenues on the Burlington Transportation Company fell 21.6 percent.

Small wonder, then, that average employment on the C. B. & Q. declined nearly twenty-one percent, to 22,963, and that capital expenditures during the year were confined largely to improvements of existing facilities with a view to increasing safety and economy of operation. At Galesburg Yard, work on the westbound unit was deferred. Instead, tracks were so arranged that classification of both eastbound and westbound traffic could be handled over the eastbound unit.

As revenues on the Burlington clearly revealed, no segment of the population was harder hit than the farmer. In self-defense the farmer returned to many practices that, for convenience, had long since been

[3 7 5]

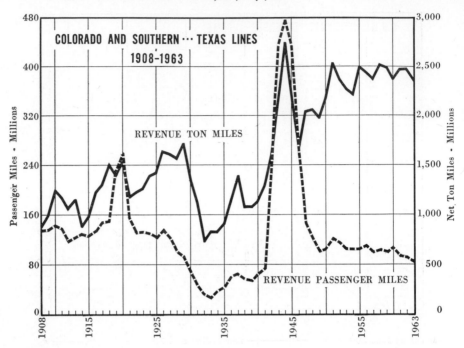

abandoned. For example, bartering was reintroduced, local gristmills were reactivated; home slaughtering and curing of meat and home canning were increased; similar economies were made throughout the whole area of farming. Meanwhile the company's Agricultural Department continued working with groups and individuals to cut production costs. Newcomers among the groups assisted were life insurance and mortgage companies who found themselves in possession of large acreages; the C. B. & Q. helped them expand their legume crops to maintain soil fertility and encourage diversification. The company also introduced improved strains of spring wheat, clover, soybeans, and potatoes into areas having natural advantages of soil and climate. Eventually these efforts could be counted on to show tangible results in both traffic and revenue. But there was precious little to talk about when the returns for 1932 were added up.

Net income on the C. B. & Q. for 1932 fell to $1,502,816, the equivalent of eighty-eight cents a share, in contrast to $13,319,735, or $7.80 a share, in 1931. Fortunately, the C. & S. Lines, taken as a whole, showed some improvement during the last quarter, so that their combined deficit was reduced to $733,888, as compared with the net income of more than half a million in the previous year.

In view of the sharply reduced net income for the year, the C. B. & Q. disbursed a total of only $3 a share in 1932, in contrast to $15 paid in 1930 and $10 in 1931. The entire amount, $5,125,161, was charged against surplus. This, incidentally, was the lowest rate paid since the formation

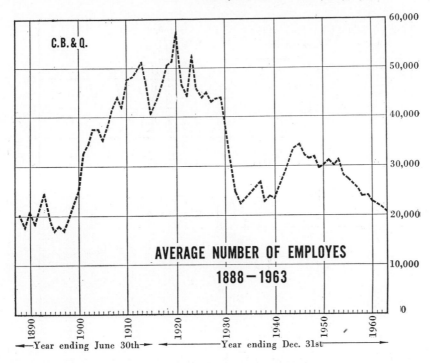

C.B. & Q.

AVERAGE NUMBER OF EMPLOYES
1888 — 1963

◄—Year ending June 30th—► ◄———Year ending Dec. 31st———►

of the company in 1864, but it was enough to maintain the C. B. & Q.'s proud record of never having failed to declare a dividend.

On January 22, 1932, President Hoover signed the Reconstruction Finance Corporation Act, which provided, among other things, for loans "to aid in the temporary financing of railroads and railways engaged in interstate commerce," provided that such loans were approved by the Interstate Commerce Commission, and when, in the opinion of the directors of the R. F. C., applicant railways were unable to obtain funds on reasonable terms through banking channels or from the general public.[6] Under this Act, several carriers applied for so-called "work loans" to undertake construction or repairs on roadways and equipment. The clear purpose of these loans, as stated in the applications, was to aid employment. Budd was opposed to borrowing money for this purpose. Consequently, and in particular because work loans from the R. F. C. bore five percent interest, the C. B. & Q. did not apply for funds from this quarter.

"The most important matter affecting the railroads and their prospects for recovery of earning power," Budd told his directors in October, "is that of wages."[7] The agreement under which organized labor had accepted a ten percent reduction on February 1, 1932, was scheduled to expire exactly a year later. Accordingly, on December 22, 1932, the carriers

[6] ICC, AR 1932, p. 12.
[7] PLD, October 8, 1932.

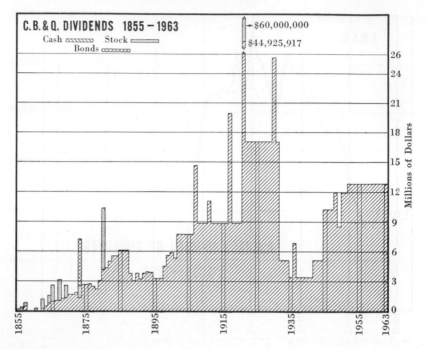

C.B.&Q. DIVIDENDS 1855 – 1963
Cash ▨▨▨▨ Stock ▭▭▭▭
Bonds ▨▨▨▨

◂ $60,000,000
$44,925,917

Millions of Dollars

and labor executives signed an agreement to extend the existing ten per-cent temporary reduction in basic rates of pay from February 1, 1933 to October 31, 1933. Among other things, the new agreement established without any question the right of the carriers to serve notices of further changes in basic rates on June 15, 1933. Thus, through the age-old process of negotiation and compromise, the vital matter of wages was stabilized for a sufficient period to enable all concerned to join hands in combatting the ever-deepening financial crisis.

Another major development of 1932—the authorization of the Dotsero cut-off—was destined to have a permanent and beneficial effect on the Burlington. Ever since 1882, the Burlington had been the most direct route between Chicago and Denver and, as today, the only one run-ning over its own rails for the entire distance. This splendid main line of over a thousand miles was clearly one of the greatest potentials on the system. Yet, when Budd came to the presidency, the company's share of through traffic moving between Chicago and the West Coast by way of Denver was pitifully small. The reason was obvious: the essential link between Denver and Salt Lake City was the Denver and Rio Grande Western, which ran from Denver southward via Colorado Springs to Pueblo, 120 miles away, before turning west. And because the Rio Grande received the same rate on through traffic to and from Salt Lake whether it exchanged it with the C. B. & Q. at Denver, with the Rock Island at Colorado Springs, or with the Missouri Pacific at Pueblo, the Rio Grande naturally favored business which it had to haul the shortest distance; thus traffic to and from the Burlington at Denver was the least attractive.

At first glance this situation seemed hopeless for the C. B. & Q. But a simple solution was possible if only the parties concerned could be induced to agree to it. In 1928, the Denver and Salt Lake Railway, running directly west from Denver, completed the Moffat Tunnel, and on the other side of the mountain continued due west to Orestod before veering northwest. The significant fact was that Orestod was only thirty-eight miles from the Denver and Rio Grande's main line at Dotsero (Orestod spelled backwards). If that short gap could be bridged, it would shorten the distance between Denver and Salt Lake by 175 miles, provide easier grades, and, above all, make Denver, rather than Colorado Springs or Pueblo, the most attractive point of interchange for the Rio Grande.

But how could the Rio Grande be persuaded to construct this cut-off? At the time it was controlled equally by the Western Pacific and the Missouri Pacific; there seemed little likelihood that these two owners would permit the Rio Grande to short-circuit their established transcontinental route via Salt Lake and Pueblo. As it happened, however, the man who effectively controlled policy on the Western Pacific was Arthur Curtiss James, long a close friend of Ralph Budd, and then a director of the C. B. & Q. Consequently, he shared Budd's earnest desire to develop Denver as a gateway for Rio Grande–Burlington transcontinental traffic.

So it was that Budd sought James's aid in forcing construction of the cut-off. James was willing enough, but could hardly find fault with the perfectly reasonable improvements the Rio Grande was making on its existing main line. It was Budd who finally provided the answer: "You could stop this work that is going on for the sole benefit of the Pueblo Gateway until such time as you get fair consideration for the building of the Dotsero Cut-off which would be equally good for the Denver and Rio Grande."[8]

James immediately grasped the point. Without criticizing what the Rio Grande was doing on its line west of the Pueblo, he simply insisted that equal consideration be given to the cut-off. Shortly afterwards, the decision was made to go ahead if the necessary funds could be found. The Denver and Rio Grande, unable to finance the project on reasonable terms through the usual banking channels or from the general public, turned to the Reconstruction Finance Corporation. Once it secured its loan of $3,850,000, grading was put underway. The dream of having Denver on a direct transcontinental route came closer to reality.

The creation of the *Pioneer Zephyr*, which was to revolutionize American railroading, was an even more spectacular example of harnessing

[8] Budd, interview with Overton, May 6, 1954.

a vision to the crying need of the moment. During Budd's first month on the Burlington, he became convinced, from the avalanche of statistics that crossed his desk and from persistent inquiries, that not much more freight traffic was to be had. The only other source of major revenue was passenger traffic, and he logically turned his thoughts to it despite the fact that it had been declining so steadily since the mid-1920's that many railroaders had ceased to regard it as possessing any possibilities for growth.

But Budd was convinced that the demand curve for passenger travel was anything but fixed. Indeed, it might prove surprisingly elastic if only the railroads could supply trains that were fast, clean, and cheap. If a train fulfilling these requirements could be produced, it might not only coax more travelers to the rails, but also replace costly steam trains. But what sort of a train should it be? The company's long experience with gas-electric cars indicated that a single internal combustion engine mounted over the forward truck would insure economy. Yet the proposed train would have to accommodate more people than any gas-electric car if it were to increase passenger revenue; it would have to be capable of much higher speeds if it were to appeal to the public, and it would have to be ultra-modern in riding qualities, interior decoration, and air-conditioning, features conspicuously absent in the "doodlebugs." These combined demands would necessitate the lightest possible weight consistent with absolute safety, and the least possible wind resistance, so that the smallest possible plant could handle the maximum of train capacity measured in seating and floor space.

With these specifications in mind, Budd went to Philadelphia on September 29, 1932, for a demonstration ride on a stainless-steel, gas-electric car that E. G. Budd Manufacturing Company had turned out the previous January. What impressed Budd most was the new process of fabrication, shot-welding, which preserved the great strength and rustlessness of stainless steel that was so easily destroyed by ordinary electric welding. As Budd subsequently said, the demonstration ride on this train "proved to be the specific factor that led to the first Burlington Zephyr."[9]

Immediately after that visit to Philadelphia, in September 1932, the Burlington ordered from the Budd Company a three-car ultra-smart day train. The fact that the train was ordered from a manufacturer who had specialized in auto bodies was a departure in itself; as yet the established railway-car builders were too wedded to the theory of massive weight and traditional design.

Incidentally, Edward G. Budd and Ralph Budd were not related in any way, although in the years immediately ahead they were to work closely together in the development of Diesel-powered streamlined trains and were to become close friends. Because of this business relationship,

[9] Budd: "Light-weight Diesel-Electric Trains," reprinted from *Civil Engineering*, Vol. VIII, No. 9 (September, 1938), pp. 592–5.

however, both press and public persisted for years in believing them to be kinsmen of varying degrees.

So it was that, during the discouraging fall of 1932, with revenues approaching the point at which they would not even cover fixed charges, Budd and his associates turned their backs on the past and reached courageously into the future as the only possible salvation for a very uncomfortable present. Even then, a key problem remained unsolved: what kind of motive power would be put into this experimental train? The resolution of that problem did not come until after the turn of the year.

· 1933: THE TURN OF THE TIDE ·

THE OLD SAYING that it is darkest just before dawn was never truer than in the opening months of 1933. In January, Budd made an extensive trip through Texas, California, Oregon, and Washington. "Everywhere in this territory," he told his directors, "there is the same serious situation, namely, the lack of demand for the things produced and a consequent surplus, a demoralization of prices, and distress among producers."

But Budd did not think the remedy lay either in bewailing a cruel fate or in looking to others for assistance. Rather, he concluded, it was "a situation which certainly challenges railway management to find some way of reducing operating expenses rather than relying on the hope that despite high transportation costs and charges, there will be a return of normal traffic and revenues." Logic then led him to note that wages and salaries represented sixty-four percent of total operating expenses. More specifically, average hourly wages were two and a quarter times what they had been in 1915. To make matters worse, a special study made in 1931 had revealed that "time paid for but not worked, overtime, and constructive allowances" had cost the railways no less than $191,186,000 in that year.[1]

Certainly the traffic picture was dismal. At the end of the first quarter, C. B. & Q. had failed to meet its fixed charges by $1,506,424; the deficit on the C. & S. Lines amounted to $495,374. Not since 1888, when the strike of engineers and firemen had caused the operating ratio to jump twenty-one percent and cut revenue from railway operations by fifty-seven percent, had the C. B. & Q. experienced such a disastrous year.

Even so, there were some very small signs of hope. The continuing efforts of the railways to coax traffic back from the trucks by granting rate reductions on specific commodities were showing some signs of success, even though the lower rate meant that as yet there was no increase in revenues. More encouraging was the fact that once the bank moratorium of March was over, commodity prices advanced, with a consequent pick-up in freight traffic. Prospects improved materially during April, especially in

[1] PLD, February 11, 1933.

eastern Wyoming, northern Colorado, western Nebraska, and Kansas. Could it be that the long-awaited corner had been turned?

By the midpoint of the year, it seemed that it had. C. B. & Q. earned $323,097 more than its fixed charges in May; more significantly, it was the first month in almost four years to show an increase in gross revenue over the corresponding month of the preceding year. Furthermore, it looked as though charges would be cleared by some $900,000 in June, which would reduce the deficit in net income for the first six months to approximately $600,000. If traffic continued to improve, there was every indication that the entire deficit would be wiped out with July earnings. Prospects were better on the C. & S. Lines too, although no black ink was in sight as yet. The western companies failed to earn their fixed charges in May, and for the first five months their combined deficit amounted to $892,196.

Fortunately, June turned out better than expected. Even passenger traffic increased materially, primarily on account of the opening of the Century of Progress Exposition on Chicago's lake front, partly because of the very considerable movement to the Civilian Conservation Camps located in the territory. During the forty days between the opening of the Century of Progress on May 27 and July 5, no less than 544,959 persons— a daily average of 13,624—went through the Burlington's exhibition train.

Welcome news came from two other quarters. Under the agreement of December 22, 1932, railroad managers and railway labor executives had agreed to extend the ten percent temporary reduction in wages to October 31, 1933. In June, the agreement was extended to June 30, 1934; the date on which either party could submit notice of any change in basic rates was extended from June 15, 1933, to February 15, 1934. Extension of this agreement stabilized the wage situation for another full year.

In retrospect, then, the six weeks between late March and early May marked the turning point in the company's fortunes. This by no means meant that the depression, or even the acute crisis, was over. Not until business became stimulated by the threat of World War II did revenues approach the 1931 level, and in the meantime some of the proposed remedies for the depression proved worse than the disease. But there had been a change of direction and a revival of confidence—for which, perhaps, the contagiously hopeful words of the new President of the United States were at least partly responsible. For better or worse, the day of the New Deal was dawning.

CHAPTER 20

Novel Ideas and Gradual Recovery in Granger Country

1933-40

• THE NEW DEAL •

THE YEARS 1933–40 constitute a clearly distinguishable period in the fortunes of the Burlington and, to a considerable extent, in the lives of the nation's railways as a whole. In one respect—and in one respect only—it resembled the lush 1920's: statistically speaking, it represented a plateau, though at a far lower level than that of the 20's. During all but one of those eight years (1935), net income on the C. B. & Q. ranged between the relatively narrow limits of 3.6 and 5.5 million dollars, with income per share ranging from $2.13 to $3.28. This was a far better showing than that of its nearest neighbors, the North Western, the Milwaukee, and the Rock Island, all of which were forced to seek the protection of the courts during the decade. At least the C. B. & Q. was "in the black," but with little to spare.

The contrast these eight years provided with the period from 1921 to 1930, when each year earnings per share were in double figures, is clear enough in terms of dollars and cents. But the contrast went deeper. In the earlier period the feeling of normalcy had led people to think that the volume of traffic as well as operating techniques had become more or less stable, that with ordinary prudence and attention to details, business would go along indefinitely "as usual." The sobering experience from the days of the stock-market crash in the fall of 1929 to the closing of the banks in March 1933 however, had effectively exploded any lingering notion that stability had come to stay. When, about May 1933, the tide finally turned, it was reasonably clear that for the next several years recovery was going to be inch by inch.

The most distinctive new element was the all-pervasive hand of the federal government in virtually every phase of the economy. As might have been expected, the immediate results of the "First Hundred Days" of the New Deal and of the recovery measures that followed were mixed. Vast government support for the farmer restored a measure of confidence and lightened the burden of indebtedness on many a hard-pressed farm family. But the sharp increase in agricultural products moved in 1933 was really a reflection of a national rise in non-farm income which led to a demand for farm products. Similarly, government building projects resulted in an upswing of some types of manufactured and miscellaneous goods, as well as of forest products. In the field of labor, the unions, encouraged by the government, steadily gained more power. As a result, labor costs increased, as did the costs of government pension and unemployment insurance plans; taxes, necessary to support the entire program, also went up. Regulation by the federal government was extended to common and contract carriers by highway, and to a lesser extent to carriers by waterway and air; the railways themselves were further regulated, particularly in the sensitive fields of labor and finance.

While these government experiments—many of them short-lived—were underway, Dame Nature, with a fine disregard for the planners in Washington, inflicted disastrous floods on the Republican River Valley in 1935 and visited a devastating drought on the greater part of Burlington territory in 1936. Thus, combined, the contrivances of man and the vagaries of nature called for continuous adaptation and improvisation on the part of management.

During the early years of the New Deal—1933 through 1935—neither traffic nor revenues moved much above 1932 levels; Burlington operating revenues ranged between seventy-eight and eighty-three million dollars a year. In the last five years of the decade, 1935–40 inclusive, they stepped up to between 93 and 100 million dollars. In view of what had gone before, this was encouraging. Yet, even so, both traffic and revenues were at only two thirds the levels of the 1920's; not until the end of 1940, under the tragic stimulus of a European war, did business move forward in high gear.

• THE CHARACTER OF TRAFFIC: AGRICULTURE •

DURING THE 1930's, measured by weight alone, the Burlington as usual hauled more tons of mine products than anything else; the largest share of its freight revenues came from miscellaneous goods and manufactures. Nevertheless, the company considered itself, as always, primarily a granger road. More than half of the entire system mileage lay in Nebraska, Illinois, Missouri, and Iowa, in that order; branch lines made up between a third and a half of the typical operating division. This meant, and has always meant, that the road has been closely and characteristically identified with the farm. This correlation was nowhere better exemplified than in the way the Burlington's balance sheet reflected the decline in national farm income, during the period 1920–32, from 15½ billion dollars to 5½ billion.

In March 1933, President Roosevelt declared that "an unprecendented condition calls for the trial of new means to rescue agriculture," and urged Congress to enter "a new and untrod path."[1] In response, the special session on May 12, 1933, passed the Agricultural Adjustment Act, the first of several New Deal laws designed to re-establish equality of the prices the farmer would receive for his produce and those he had to pay for what he needed. Central to the plan were the provisions authorizing the Secretary of Agriculture to grant government subsidies to growers of certain stable commodities—including wheat, corn, hogs, and tobacco—who would agree to take a part of their land out of production.

The impact on the Burlington of this "stupendous recovery plan," as Budd put it, was startling, to say the least.[2] Over forty-four percent of the benefits paid to wheat, cotton, and tobacco farmers, or $58,274,478, went directly to farmers in Burlington territory. More than half of the 550,000 wheat growers who signed allotment contracts lived in states served by the company; by the end of the year, they alone had received over $13,000,000, a sum that seemed large in the aggregate, but averaged out to only $40 to $45 per farmer. As part of the corn-hog reduction program, Burlington states contributed more than three fourths of the sows and little pigs purchased for slaughter; the farmers received more than $23,000,000 for them.

In addition, as an emergency measure the Secretary of Agriculture lent $150,000,000 on stored corn. By the end of the year, farmers in Burlington territory had availed themselves of $51,000,000 of this corn loan money. Meanwhile, under the Federal Farm Loan Act of May 1933, credit up to a total of two billion dollars was made available for the refinancing of

[1] Samuel E. Morrison and Henry S. Commager: *The Growth of the American Republic* (New York: Oxford University Press; 1942), Vol. II, p. 597.
[2] CB&Q, AR 1933, p. 15.

farm loans. By the close of 1933, farmers and ranchers in Burlington territory had received more than $200,000,000 of such credit.

So far, so good. But, to add to the effect of crop reductions, 1933 turned out to be one of the poorest growing years in many seasons, a fact which the railroad regarded as far more important in raising prices than the various policies of the government dedicated to that end. Corn yield in the Burlington states was twenty-five percent below that of 1932, and wheat production was off forty-two percent. On the other hand, the sugar-beet harvest, though far less important than corn or wheat, was a third larger than in the preceding year. Livestock production, except for sheep, was about normal.

These developments had an understandably erratic effect on Burlington traffic. Despite the sharp drop in both wheat and corn production, wheat movement declined only 7.6 percent, and corn loadings shot up 69.5 percent, primarily because the rise in prices of those commodities led to brisk shipment of old grain that had been in storage. For more normal reasons, beet movement increased twenty-nine percent, so that the total increase in revenues from agricultural produce went up a comforting 16.7 percent over 1932. Despite the normal production of livestock, however, the amount carried on Burlington rails declined 8.7 percent, primarily because of the increasingly heavy movement by truck.

As 1934 got underway, Budd reported to his directors that "farmers generally are co-operating with the government in its corn-hog reduction program; in some of the leading corn producing counties, 90 percent have signed up for curtailment."[3] Another portent of what lay in store was the signing in April of an agreement between the sugar-beet growers in Burlington territory and the processors, whereby growers were guaranteed a parity price of about $6.50 a ton for their 1934 crops. As a result, beet planting took a spurt forward.

By May, however, there were signs of trouble from another quarter. Territory west of the Missouri was already suffering from drought, and by June, crop conditions were critical. Not only that; an onslaught of chinch bugs, a normal accompaniment of drought, threatened devastation of whatever corn plants survived. In northeastern Nebraska and parts of Colorado and Wyoming, grasshoppers added to the woes of the farmers.

As in the past, the Burlington, along with other railways, took action at once. Effective June 4, emergency rates were authorized which slashed a third from rates on whole grain and livestock feed and cut the tariff on hay in half. The situation in July was even more critical. In the corn belt, temperatures ranging from 100 to 115 degrees, with no rainfall, indicated that corn in Iowa would be an almost total loss. The shortage of feed and water was so great in Nebraska that stock to the extent of two million head was

[3] PLD, March 17, 1934.

shipped out of the state; even forage crops, supposed to resist drought, were failing. Nor were crops and animals the only sufferers. The city of Creston depended entirely on water hauled by the C. B. & Q.—at no charge—from Council Bluffs, a distance of ninety-nine miles, and the railroad itself had to take emergency measures to maintain its own supply at way points.

The drought continued through August; not until September did Burlington territory receive good rains. On September 4, the company's emergency rates expired, but on the earnest request of the Department of Agriculture, they were restored on October 1 and extended to the end of the year on livestock and until April 30, 1935, on feed shipments. So completely did the drought envelop the Middle West that of 289 counties served by Burlington Lines, only five were not indicated by the government as emergency or secondary drought-relief areas sometime during the year. Feed shortage, resulting from the drought, necessitated the slaughter of more than five and a half million cattle and more than three million sheep, all of which were paid for by the government. Swine population in Burlington states fell forty-two percent. Nevertheless, the movement of livestock increased twenty-five percent, most of it because such cattle and sheep as were not slaughtered were moved out of the drought area to regions that had adequate feed.

The combined disasters of drought and insects reduced the yields of most farm crops in Burlington states to the lowest level in many years. Indeed, as Budd told the stockholders, the efforts of planners in reducing production were made to appear puny and futile in the face of such a phenomenon of nature. Small wonder that revenue from agricultural products declined more than eleven percent in comparison with 1933. However, reduced yields brought increased prices and these, along with various government aids, raised farm income thirty-three percent above that of 1933.

Toward the end of 1934, another problem began to assume distressing proportions. Such traffic as existed was diverted by truckers, who hauled piecemeal into Burlington territory the small, less-than-carload lots of feed grains required to supply the immediate needs of the livestock that remained. This was a popular move with farmers who at the time were buying feed on a hand-to-mouth basis. Then, on the back haul, truckers would pick up small loads of distressed cattle destined for points at which more feed was available. As if this was not bad enough for the railways, the truckers also picked up coal from strip mines or wood for movement at low rates on their return trips. This kind of competition was exceedingly difficult to meet because truck rates at the time were completely unregulated. Quite apart from the monetary loss to the railways, this development had serious implications for the future.

In most ways, 1935 was better than 1934 for agriculture in Burlington territory. Yet ample rains and better crops did not necessarily mean more traffic for the railway. Because of liquidation of young swine and shortage of corn, the pig crop that spring was the smallest for many years, fewer cattle were readied for market, and breeding herds of all kinds were greatly reduced. Consequently revenues from agriculture decreased by more than seven percent.

More encouraging than the traffic moved was the improved lot of the farmer in 1935. Livestock prices increased materially and more than offset a slump in grain prices, so that the combined farm income from crops and livestock—including over $200,000,000 in federal benefit payments—was substantially higher than during the previous few years. Furthermore, farmers in Burlington states were able to borrow over $290,000,000 from the government to finance their capital accounts, and another $160,000,000 or more to maintain current operations. As a result, they purchased more farm machinery and consumer goods than they had for some years, paid some past-due debts, and renewed soil conservation and fertilizing activities.

Even though these developments did not mean more traffic for the railroad immediately, they were of prime importance, as the company had learned during the long years when it had shared the problems of the farmer. Only if the farmer stayed on his land and remained solvent could the railroad look forward to better times. An increase in carloadings was always welcome, but in the long run it was less important than a basic improvement in farm income.

The year 1935 is still remembered on the C. B. & Q. for the cloudbursts and tornadoes that wrought such ravages in western Nebraska at the end of May and in early June. Long stretches of the main line and a number of bridges were completely washed out. The principal damage occurred to the main line adjacent to the Republican River from Superior west for a distance of approximately 200 miles. There were washouts also on the line between Brush and Union, Colorado. When the line was rebuilt, it was raised above the flood plain of the Republican River and was decidedly stronger than the old line had been, and more secure against flood damage than ever before. Total cost, however, amounted to over $2,400,000, or approximately thirty percent more than the company's net income for 1935.

The alternate droughts and severe floods in southwest Nebraska had one collateral effect of considerable significance. In Nebraska and Wyoming, the federal government promptly launched in 1935 a broad series of irrigation projects designed not only to provide water for nearly 600,000 acres, but also to generate, from the North Platte River, nearly a quarter of a billion kilowatt hours of electrical energy. These activities were continued and expanded throughout the decade, not only in Nebraska and Wyoming, but in Montana and Colorado as well.

In 1936, a severe midsummer drought, similar in many ways to that of

1934, greatly reduced production of most farm crops in C. B. & Q. territory. Again drought relief rates were established on all livestock and feed. Shortages in livestock feed were so acute that the federal government designated 169 counties served by Burlington as drought areas. A seeming paradox, however, was an increase in movement of both agricultural and livestock products in 1936. For one thing, prospects of decreased production during 1936 raised farm prices, which attracted into the channels of trade the heavy feed holdover from the previous year, as well as the livestock to which it was being fed. This, together with government benefit payments, increased by twelve percent the total farm income in the states served by the company. Loans from the Federal Land Banks and other grants pumped additional millions of dollars into the area. Burlington's revenues from agricultural products went up twenty-four percent over 1935, whereas revenues from livestock increased 13.5 percent.

Favorable weather, favorable prices, and less drastic government restrictions on planting contributed to increased production during 1937 in most of the states served by the Burlington, and all major crops showed marked increases. Three key states, however, were exceptions to the general situation: Nebraska, Wyoming, and Colorado, in which the Burlington then operated 3,897 miles of track. Once again, these states suffered from exceptional midsummer drought and from a scourge of grasshoppers that curtailed the production of feed grains and forage, thus preventing the rehabilitation of the breeding herds of livestock. Partly as a result of large government benefit payments, total farm income in the states served by the Burlington increased another four percent, and once again many farmers were able to keep their property by negotiating loans with the federal Farm Credit Administration. Revenues from agricultural products during 1937 increased a scant two percent; returns from livestock movements decreased by more than eighteen percent.

The year 1938 witnessed the end of the acute crop failures in Burlington territory. Farm production in most of the states served by the company was satisfactory that year, even though the movement of grain by rail, largely because of low prices, was disappointing; because of the government's novel storage program, more grain than usual remained on the farm or in local bins. Despite a rise in government benefit payments during the year, farm income declined ten percent because of low prices partly associated with the recession of that year.

In 1939 there was a slight recovery in farm income in Burlington states and, thanks in part to a substantial increase in government payments, cash farm receipts rose almost eight percent. Of direct importance to the railway was the fact that increased storage of grain as a result of government loans meant fewer rail shipments. Thus, 1939 was not so favorable for the rail shipment of agricultural products as the preceding year. Revenues from agriculture in 1938 had increased nineteen percent over

1937; in 1939 they fell fifteen percent behind the relatively good year of 1938. On the other hand, livestock movements that went up 2.5 percent in 1938 over 1937 did somewhat better in 1939, registering an increase of 4.8 percent over the previous year.

In retrospect, 1933–40 witnessed a virtual revolution in agriculture in the states served by the Burlington. Federal control of production, introduced in the first Agricultural Adjustment Act of 1933, had been continued after that law was declared unconstitutional in 1936, first by a Soil Conservation Act which provided for direct subsidies to farmers conforming to Soil Conservation Crop Control standards, and, after 1938, under the provisions of a new Agricultural Adjustment Act that not only revived direct allotment of acreage but also provided for parity payments and standardized the conditions under which commodity loans were offered. Another feature of the 1938 Act was crop insurance of wheat.

As the 1930's wore on, farmers increasingly participated in the successive soil conservation and crop restriction programs. Commodity loans, of course, were available on stored crops, and this system tended to stabilize prices. In Nebraska alone, for example, during the years 1933–40 inclusive, farmers received nearly $200,000,000 in government payments of one kind or another. Thus, even though farm income, whether measured by dollars or by purchasing power, failed to attain the level of the middle and late 20's, the condition of farmers in general was improved. By the end of the decade it was fair to say that the acute distress from drought was over.

• THE CHARACTER OF TRAFFIC: NON-FARM PRODUCTS •

As MIGHT HAVE BEEN EXPECTED, coal movements decreased during 1933, then showed a gradual recovery for the rest of the decade except during the recession year 1938. Interestingly enough, tonnage of manufactures and miscellaneous (which have long been the major source of Burlington freight revenues) rose steadily throughout the 30's except for a modest and temporary dip in 1938. Forest products, principally building lumber, were hard hit by the financial crisis, but recovered substantially, partly because the New Deal poured funds into construction projects. The level of less-than-carload lot shipments remained virtually stationary during 1933–40 despite the increase in economic activity. Presumably, more and more of this high-rated traffic was moving by truck.

A new category that gained official recognition near the end of the decade deserves special mention. During the 30's, various freight-forwarding companies sprang up which accepted less-than-carload freight from shippers and consolidated it into carload lots for shipment as such over the railways. These companies could not and did not attempt to handle L.C.L. freight for all smaller stations, but concentrated their efforts between larger centers. As this type of service became increasingly popular with shippers, a new category called Forwarder Traffic was added in 1939 to the traditional six categories.[4] At the end of the 1930's, such traffic was in a developmental stage on the Burlington, but it gave promise of assuming larger proportions as time went on.

Throughout the decade, of course, the Industrial Department spared no efforts to lease company land for industrial purposes along the lines and to attract new industries into Burlington territory. But progress in both directions was painfully slow.

In summary, during the first three years of the New Deal—1933–35 inclusive—freight revenues on the C. B. & Q. averaged approximately $65,000,000, slightly more than half the average of the prosperous 1920's. During the last five years of the decade—1936–40 inclusive—revenues improved measurably, but still remained in a narrow range averaging about $77,000,000. In other words, there was approximately a twenty percent improvement during the latter part of the so-called "depressed 30's."

One reason why C. B. & Q. revenues did not improve more rapidly was the decline in revenue per ton-mile, partly because of the character of the traffic carried, but more largely because of reduced rates. In 1933, average revenue per ton-mile was 96 mills; this declined steadily to a low point of 84.9 mills in 1937, recovered to 94.1 in 1938, and then fell to a level of 87.2 mills in 1940. Not until 1948 did the Burlington earn as much as a penny for carrying the average ton one mile on its railroad.

There was nothing surprising about this pattern in a period of depression. Not until September 1934, did the railways feel warranted in asking for an increase in freight rates. After seven months of deliberation, the I. C. C. refused to grant the ten percent requested, but did approve certain "emergency charges," effective April 18, 1935, to remain in effect through June 30, 1936. The C. B. & Q. estimated that the increase granted would mean additional annual revenue of $2,250,000, but even this would be $1,500,000 short of offsetting the restoration of wages to the level that had been in effect before the ten percent cut of February 1, 1932.

Eventually the railways were able to secure extension of the emergency freight increases to the end of 1936 (with some exceptions), but on December 18, 1936, the I. C. C. refused to extend them beyond that year. Finally, on November 15, 1937, the Commission granted certain advances on such basic items as iron, steel, coal, coke, petroleum, and cement. Meanwhile, the railways requested a fifteen percent increase on all items except coal, coke, lumber, fruits, and vegetables. By the following March, the Commission approved about half this request. The C. B. & Q. estimated that this would bring in about $5,000,000 more in revenues, whereas

---

[4] These six were, and are: Products of Agriculture, Animals and Products, Products of Mines, Products of Forests, Manufactures and Miscellaneous, Less-than-Carload (commonly referred to as L.C.L.).

the rises in basic commodities granted the previous November would account for an additional $1,500,000.

The Transportation Act of 1940, which became law on September 18 of that year, promised some rate relief by repealing the long-standing land-grant rates and fares, except as they related to military or naval property or for military or naval forces when traveling on official duty. The restoration of all other government rates to the commercial level, however, did not become valid until each company affected thereby released whatever claims it had against the government arising out of the land grants. The C. B. & Q. filed such a release on October 24, 1940; it was approved by the Secretary of the Interior on November 22. Thereupon, the company's land-grant rates were technically canceled, but through its equalization agreement with the government, it was compelled to continue such rates on all transportation moving in competition with other land-grant railroads which did not see fit to release claims that they had against the government. Thus the relief theoretically granted by the Act of 1940 was, for the time being, of little practical consequence.

On the Burlington during the eight years 1933–40, inclusive, freight accounted for 80.35 percent of all operating revenues; passenger receipts brought in only 9.10 percent; the rest was accounted for by mail, express, and miscellaneous. Yet not only were returns from passenger trains (carrying as they did and do, the bulk of mail and express) intrinsically important. These trains were the railroad's show window, the basis on which most of the public formed its opinion of service; there was, the management believed, a close if intangible relation between a satisfied traveler and a potential shipper. These were some of the considerations that led Budd and his associates to order, in the very depths of the depression, a streamlined, stainless-steel train. With that fact in mind, a second look at the percentage figures for revenues during 1933–40 reveals some fascinating implications. During the four years 1933–36, freight revenues averaged 80.82 of the total, then edged off to 79.89 percent for 1937–40, a negligible decline of 1.02 percent. In contrast, passenger revenues averaged 8.44 percent during 1933–36, and then swelled to 9.76 percent for 1937–40, a solid increase of over 15.5 percent. Therein lay a story.

CHAPTER 21

The Revolution in Passenger Service

1933-41

· THE FIRST *Zephyr* ·

THE MOST SPECTACULAR as well as the most important development in railroading within the memory of persons now living has been the advent of the Diesel-electric locomotive. The first complete Diesel-electric streamlined train in the United States was conceived, tested, and put into regular service on the Burlington on November 11, 1934.

Diesel engines had been used for stationary and marine purposes ever since the turn of the century, but their weight per horsepower was too great for a lightweight train. As early as 1925, the Central Railroad of New Jersey had a switcher whose Diesel engine generated electricity which, in turn, provided tractive power. This combination of the Diesel as a source of power and an electric motor was of prime importance. By 1933, several score Diesel-electrics were proving their worth as switchers; their ability to develop maximum power at starting and slow speeds and to work around the clock with a minimum of servicing made them particularly adaptable to this service. But these switchers were heavy and slow.

In the fall of 1932, Charles F. Kettering, vice-president in charge of

[393]

research for General Motors, perfected a two-cycle eight-cylinder Diesel. Of crucial importance, the metallurgists working with him had developed new alloys possessing a relationship of weight to strength that made such an engine light enough to mount on a locomotive frame and powerful enough to pull a train.

H. L. Hamilton, the energetic president of the Electro-Motive Division of General Motors, was aware that the Burlington had recently ordered from the E. G. Budd Manufacturing Company a lightweight streamlined train, but had not yet decided upon the appropriate motive power. He therefore took the news of Kettering's achievement to Ralph Budd. The effect was electric. As Budd put it later: "*Immediately* I was set *afire* because I *knew* that that was something *completely* revolutionary and better—so much better—than anything we had ever had." He asked Hamilton how long it would take to build an engine of this type for the Burlington's new train.

"Well," replied Hamilton, "there are some bugs in it yet, but I think we could get it out so that we wouldn't delay the bringing out of your train very much; not more than a month or six weeks."

"I'd gladly wait a month or six weeks," said Budd, ". . . rather than to come out with a distillate engine that much earlier. . . . Hamilton," he told him, "we'll put that Diesel in there, because then we'll have a brand new motive power unit for this train and for the railroads."[1]

On June 17, 1933, the Burlington sent along the formal purchasing order for a 600-horsepower Model 201A Diesel for the sleek new train being built in Philadelphia. As Kettering himself put it years later: "The rest is history. . . . The Diesel smashed the old roadblock of steam, and revolutionized rail transportation, giving it new life for a long period. This is the sort of thing I have in mind when I use the word 'break-through.' "[2]

Yet the historic decision to put the Diesel on rails was but one of many decisions that had to be made before service could begin. Consequently, during the anxious months while Burlington's new train and engine were under construction, the company's top officers most intimately concerned frequently put their heads together to work out in advance as many details as possible.

A meeting of these men in Ralph Budd's office on a hot afternoon in the late spring of 1933 was typical. Present besides Budd were Edward Flynn, Fred Gurley, and Albert Cotsworth, Jr., all of them long seasoned in the art of railroading and all destined to play essential roles in writing a new chapter in the annals of the rails. On that particular day, Budd had just returned from watching the two 600-hp Diesels that were powering the General Motors exhibit at the Century of Progress. He told his colleagues

[1] Budd, interviews with Overton, May 6, 1954, April 30, 1959.
[2] Charles F. Kettering: "Future Unlimited," *Saturday Evening Post*, Vol. CCXXX, No. 46 (May 17, 1958).

of his hopes for the new train. The first question was: where should it run? It seemed clear that (1) it should replace an existing train that was not making money but could not be discontinued, (2) it would have to make a round trip each day so that the experimental investment would be confined to one train and all servicing could be done in one spot, and (3) it could not handle extra cars because it was articulated and had no standard couplers. Cotsworth suggested the 195-mile run between Kansas City and Omaha. This was chosen, with the run extended 55 miles to Lincoln.

As this gathering broke up, Cotsworth remarked that the new train should have a good name because of the publicity it would undoubtedly receive. When Budd asked whether he had any suggestion, Cotsworth replied that nothing suitable had occurred to him yet, but that he had been meaning to look up the last word in the dictionary because without any question this would certainly be the "last word" in passenger trains. Budd reached for the dictionary and soon began to laugh. The last word was "zymurgy: the practice or art of fermentation, as in wine-making, brewing, distilling, etc." Whatever the merits of fermentation, they could hardly be related to a high-speed railroad train. Nor did Cotsworth's search in another dictionary produce any better results; he turned up the word "zyzzle: to sputter," which, if anything, was less appropriate than "zymurgy." But Cotsworth's suggestion set Budd to thinking. It so happened that he had recently been rereading Chaucer's *Canterbury Tales* in which the god of the west wind, Zephyrus, typifies renaissance. That was it. He reached for the phone and told Cotsworth that he had a name to suggest which commenced with the last letter of the alphabet even if it was not exactly the final word in the dictionary; his suggestion: Zephyr. Thus a name was born, and the new train still in the early stages of construction in Philadelphia became known as the Burlington *Zephyr*.[3]

Budd's letter of July 11, 1933, to his directors summarized concisely developments up to that moment: "Order has been placed for a Diesel-driven stainless steel train capable of traveling at a speed of 120 miles per hour. The train will comprise three cars built as an articulated unit along aerodynamic lines, will weigh about 169,000 pounds, and have a total seating capacity of 70. The first car will contain the motor, baggage and mail compartment; second car, baggage and express, with a buffet and smoking compartment in the rear to seat 19 passengers; third car will be entirely devoted to seating space with a capacity of 51, which includes 12 parlor chairs. The overall length of the train will be approximately 196 feet, and the estimated cost $200,000. The train will be used in a daylight run such as between Omaha and Kansas City, where it will take the place of steam trains and release locomotives of the type to be used elsewhere. The esti-

[3] Budd to Overton, February 27, 1952; Budd, interview with Overton, November 17, 1958.

mates of cost of operation indicate that there will be savings equal to a return of about 15 percent on the investment."[4]

On April 7, 1934, the Burlington *Zephyr* rolled out of the E. G. Budd shops. Two days later, on its trial run between Philadelphia and Perkiomen Junction, it reached a speed of 104 miles an hour. On April 17, the spanking-new train was turned over to the C. B. & Q. The christening on the following day brought together a galaxy of top industrialists whose companies had had a hand in ushering the revolutionary new train into existence: Edward G. and Ralph Budd; General Atterbury, president of the Pennsylvania; William Irwin, president of U. S. Steel; Alfred Sloan, president of General Motors; and Gerard Swope, president of General Electric. When the great moment came, Albert Cotsworth's daughter Marguerite smashed a bottle on the head end in traditional style. The Burlington *Zephyr* was a fact as well as a name.

After the ceremonies, the little train was placed on exhibition in Philadelphia. During the one day it was there, more than 24,000 visitors went through it. But this was only the beginning; in the next three weeks it toured thirty eastern cities, covered 2,900 miles, and attracted 379,857 people. Finally, on May 11, it reached Chicago, where in two days another 33,565 visitors had a chance to see what a radically new train had hit the rails. During the next fortnight the *Zephyr* visited sixteen cities in Burlington territory and played host to 105,054 more enthusiastic people.

The event that proved beyond all doubt what a Diesel-powered streamliner could do was this little train's non-stop run from Denver to Chicago on May 26, 1934. Probably no comparable performance in modern times has had more advance publicity and at the same time less experience on which to predicate a successful outcome. Up to then, no locomotive had ever traveled more than 775 miles non-stop. Furthermore, the regular Denver–Chicago run then took twenty-six hours. To promise a dawn-to-dusk run meant that the trip had to be made in fourteen hours. When one considers that Budd was proposing to do all this with a virtually untried type of motive power and that he had committed himself to split-second timing at the finish, one marvels at his temerity. But Budd was so confident that he arranged with Century of Progress officials Rufus Dawes and Lenox Lohr to have the *Zephyr* leave Denver at dawn and arrive on the stage of the World's Fair on the shore of Lake Michigan at dusk, as the grand climax of Edward Hungerford's transportation pageant, "Wings of a Century."

At 5:05 a.m. on May 26, the *Zephyr* rolled out of Denver on its way east. As the little train roared through villages and towns—and even out in the open country—it seemed as though the entire population had turned out to watch it glide by. Meanwhile, Budd, straight razor in hand, calmly grasped the first chance he had had that day to shave. Here indeed was one

[4] PLD, July 11, 1933.

way to find out whether the train was running smoothly. It was. But, just when everything seemed to be in order, someone inadvertently slammed a steel door on an electric cable, setting up a short-circuit that burned out the starting mechanism. Instinctively, the engineer shut off the engine when the short-circuit occurred. The question was how, with the cable cut, it could be started again. As luck would have it, the train was coasting down a forty-two-mile grade, and as it slowly lost momentum the crew made a frantic search for a piece of wire to splice the break. Some was found and the cable was built up until Roy Baer, an engineer from Electro-Motive, could hold a bare end in each hand. Flynn thought the train had better stop. But Baer jammed the two ends together and a brilliant spark leaped across the gap—burning Baer's hands. The engine roared into life. By the narrowest of margins, with the train drifting along at fifteen miles an hour, a stop had been avoided.

At 7:10 p.m., thirteen hours and five minutes after leaving Denver, the *Zephyr* broke a ribbon stretched across the track at Halstead Street, Chicago. Still without a pause, but at greatly reduced speed, it continued over the tracks of the St. Charles Air Line and the Illinois Central to the lake front. At exactly 8:09 p.m., it rolled onto the stage of the "Wings of a Century." Bedlam broke loose, as well it might, for throughout the day bulletins had been broadcast of the train's fleeting run across the plains and prairies. Now the crowd watching the pageant poured down from the grandstands onto the stage, much like the spectators at the end of a championship football game.

A new age had dawned for the railroads.

In reporting the dawn-to-dusk run to his directors, Budd emphasized two facts: on the trip, the train had averaged 2.77 miles per gallon of fuel oil. At a cost of four cents a gallon, this meant that fuel for the trip cost exactly $14.64. The highest speed attained on the run was 112.5 miles an hour. "The train has demonstrated by this performance," Budd concluded, "its capacity to maintain for a long period a high average speed, and higher speeds for shorter distances, as well as low cost of operation at high speeds."[5] There, in a nutshell, was the revolution in railroading.

Naturally, the West had to have a glimpse of the train, so after a brief stay at the Fair the Burlington *Zephyr* started on another tour. Its journey westward preceded by one day the formal inauguration of regular service on the Dotsero cut-off, just west of the Moffat Tunnel in Colorado, scheduled for June 17, 1934. Consequently the *Zephyr* participated in a special ceremony at Bond (Orestod) and then continued westward over the Rio Grande and Western Pacific to the Coast, thus achieving the distinction of being the first train to cover the new transcontinental route from Chicago to the Pacific by way of the Moffat Tunnel.

While the *Zephyr* was playing host to admiring crowds on the West

[5] PLD, June 7, 1934.

Coast, the directors in Chicago were taking steps to put the Burlington in the forefront of the Diesel revolution. A pair of similar trains was ordered for the Twin Cities run. The *Zephyr* itself returned to Chicago in mid-July and spent another two weeks at the Fair grounds, where 708,964 visitors gave it a thorough inspection. On July 30, it was put to work to see what sort of schedule could be established on the Twin Cities route. It made the run from Chicago to St. Paul in six hours flat, averaging better than seventy-one miles an hour, thereby demonstrating beyond question the feasibility of the six-and-a-half hour schedule (seven hours to Minneapolis) which it was proposed to establish when the two new trains were ready.

The *Zephyr* returned to the Fair for August and the Labor Day week-end, and then started west again, this time as the principal actor in a feature motion picture, "The Silver Streak," produced by RKO. The *Zephyr* was indeed more than a new, fast train, more even than the herald of renaissance on the rails: it was a symbol of hope in a nation scourged by doubt and depression. In a way, it seemed as though it could go on forever, giving inspiration and serving as a museum train.

But there was work to do, hard work, and on November 11, 1934, the Burlington *Zephyr* became the first Diesel-electric streamlined train in America to enter regular railway service. Leaving Lincoln early in the morning, it went through Omaha to Kansas City and back the same day, a round trip of exactly 500 miles.

After it had completed two full months of service, a survey revealed that passenger miles on the Burlington as a whole during the months of December and January (except for commutation) had increased twenty-six percent over the same two months of the previous year, but that the mileage made by travelers on the *Zephyr* was 193 percent more than during the same two months of the previous year on the steam trains the *Zephyr* had displaced; meanwhile, the two remaining steam trains between Omaha and Kansas City experienced the same increase as the system as a whole. So encouraging was this overwhelming acceptance that the company ordered a fourth car to add to the little *Zephyr*.

• EXPANDING THE ZEPHYR FLEET •

EARLY IN APRIL, 1935, the first of the two new *Twin Cities Zephyrs* arrived, and in a test run on April 6, 1935, covered the 431 miles to St. Paul in five hours and thirty-two minutes, at an average speed of 77.6 miles an hour. Both new trains went into service on April 21, and as spring wore on, the *Twin Cities Zephyrs* became ever more popular. On June 2, each train began making a daily round trip of 882 miles between Chicago and Minneapolis. During August, total passengers carried averaged 316 per day, almost double the number in May, when the trains had been making a single trip each. Meanwhile, on June 23, 1935, another car was added to the original *Zephyr*, now running between Lincoln and Kansas City. On

October 25, 1935, a fourth train joined the Burlington's streamlined fleet. Appropriately christened the *Mark Twain Zephyr* at Hannibal by the humorist's granddaughter, Nina Gabrilowitsch, it was placed in daily round-trip service between St. Louis and Burlington on October 28.

Shortly thereafter, on November 10, 1935, the original *Zephyr*, which was officially renamed the *Pioneer Zephyr* to distinguish it among the growing fleet, completed its first year of continuous operation. Of the 365 days, it had been out of service (and replaced by a conventional train) only eleven days: four to renew its wheels, three to add the fourth car and for general inspection, and four days on account of motor trouble. This added up to an availability record of ninety-seven percent, an amazing feat in view of the fact that the train had covered 177,000 miles. Altogether, the *Pioneer* had carried an average of 204 passengers a day for an average distance of 114 miles. This represented not only an increase of fifty percent in the number of passengers carried, compared with the steam trains replaced, but also an increase of 113 percent in passenger miles. Obviously, travelers were using the *Zephyr* for longer trips than they had taken before. Furthermore, operating and maintenance costs of the *Pioneer* during its first year averaged thirty-five cents per train mile, as compared with fifty-nine cents for the steam trains it had replaced.

The year 1936 started off with some of the worst weather the Midwest had seen in twenty years. From January 22 through February 22 blizzards and abnormal cold persisted. Truck and bus operations were seriously hampered, but the trains kept running, and in particular the various *Zephyrs* gave an excellent account of themselves in on-time performance. Early in the spring the company decided to order two new six-car trains for the Twin Cities run (at a cost of $578,000 each) and two ten-car trains (at $1,109,000 each) for the Chicago–Denver service. These new Zephyr trains were, of course, air-conditioned throughout. Meanwhile, beginning in 1934, air-conditioning was being applied to conventional first-class trains throughout the system. Thus, the *Zephyrs* resulted in an upgrading of all passenger service offered by the Burlington.

May 1936 marked something of a milestone in Zephyr history. On the twenty-seventh of that month, the cumulative mileage of the four Zephyr trains in scheduled service topped the million mark. And on the last day of the month two of them, the little *Pioneer* and the *Mark Twain*, were shifted from their original runs and placed in service over the 1,034 miles between Chicago and Denver (via Omaha) on a sixteen-hour schedule that called for an average speed of approximately sixty-five miles an hour. Known officially as Trains Number 1 and Number 10, they were given the names of *Advance Denver Zephyrs*, to advertise the fact that the two much larger trains being built in Philadelphia would soon take over the job of offering the stiffest possible competition to the U. P.'s *City of Denver*, which entered service on June 18, 1936.

Neither the *Pioneer* nor the *Mark Twain* had sleeping accommodations, though both made the trip overnight. Nevertheless, from the first
day, they were sold to capacity and proceeded to chalk up an unheard-of
record for on-time performance. By October, just before the two *Advance
Denver Zephyrs* were replaced by their bigger brothers, the little trains had
turned in a total 271,563 miles, and in 264 trips had been late just five
times; only three delays had been the result of mechanical failures. In view
of the fact that each train was making a daily run of over a thousand
miles, this on-time performance of 98.1 percent was as revolutionary as the
trains themselves.

When the first six cars of one of the new *Denver Zephyrs* were delivered, along with an 1,800-horsepower Diesel-electric engine owned by
the Electro-Motive Corporation, they were assigned to one of the Chicago–
Twin Cities runs to test their performance. The three-car train they replaced was transferred to Texas, where, as the *Sam Houston Zephyr*, it
entered service between Fort Worth, Dallas, and Houston over the
Burlington–Rock Island. It was the first Diesel-electric streamliner to operate not just in Texas, but in the entire Southwest.

In October 1936, one of the completely new *Denver Zephyrs* was delivered. To see what it would do on the "uphill" run from Chicago to
Denver, it made a test trip on October 23 and succeeded in covering the
1,017 miles (via Oreapolis rather than Omaha) in twelve hours, twelve
minutes, and twenty-seven seconds at an average speed of 83.33 miles an
hour (top speed, between Akron and Brush, Colorado, was 116 mph). On
November 8, 1936, the two new *Denver Zephyrs* went into service. The
Pioneer returned to its original run between Lincoln and Kansas City,
while the *Mark Twain Zephyr* temporarily took over one of the trips
between Chicago and the Twin Cities.

On December 18, 1936, two new *Twin Cities Zephyrs*, each with six
cars and a single-unit 1,800-horsepower Diesel-electric locomotive of the
same type as the *Denver Zephyr*, entered service between Chicago and the
Twin Cities. Thereupon, the *Mark Twain* returned to the run between
St. Louis and Burlington; the other original twin was re-christened the
Ozark State Zephyr and put into service between St. Louis and Kansas
City over the Alton–Burlington joint line, where it made a daily round trip
of 558 miles.

By the end of 1936, Diesel streamlined service was firmly established
on the main lines of the Burlington, and no new routes were "Zephyrized"
until the summer of 1940. A number of individual trains were shifted
about, however, and on April 30, 1939, the newly built *General Pershing
Zephyr* was assigned to the St. Louis–Kansas City run. This particular
member of the fleet was notable for introducing disc brakes and fluorescent
lighting, two more Burlington "firsts."

On August 23, 1940, two new trains specifically designed for the

Denver–Fort Worth–Dallas run went into service with appropriate ceremonies. And on January 7, 1941, the *Zephyr Rocket,* jointly operated by
the Burlington and the Rock Island, began providing overnight service
between St. Louis and Minneapolis. The C. B. & Q. portion of the run
between St. Louis and Burlington already had been traversed by the
Mark Twain, but the new service greatly speeded travel over a joint route
that had been popular since the late 1870's.

The last prewar addition to the Zephyr fleet came with the christening
of the *Silver Streak Zephyr* on April 15, 1941, to take over the Lincoln–
Omaha–Kansas City run that was still being handled by the original *Pioneer.* Indeed, the *Pioneer* had done so well that it had literally crowded
itself out of a job. Replacement of the *Pioneer* did not, however, imply its
retirement. It was assigned to daily round-trip service between Lincoln and
McCook, where its ability to keep hustling despite local stops resulted in
infinitely better service for the numerous small towns along the main line
between the two major division points.

As other railroads followed the Burlington's lead by purchasing Diesel
streamliners, the trend was away from the articulated train with the forward car carrying the engine to a train made up of interchangeable cars
and a separate locomotive. The small early trains, such as the *Pioneer,* the
Mark Twain, and the first *Twin Cities Zephyrs,* saved a great deal of
weight and guaranteed riding stability by having the adjacent ends of car
bodies on a common truck, but in doing so they sacrificed flexibility.

The first Diesel-electric trains with separate power and detachable cars
were the *Rebels,* which went into service on the Gulf, Mobile and Northern in the spring of 1935. The *Denver Zephyrs* that went into service the
next year on the Burlington were a transitional type: some cars were individual, some in pairs, others in series of three. Meanwhile, such lines as
the Baltimore and Ohio, the Rock Island, and the Santa Fe, as well as the
Burlington, began ordering separate Diesel units for high-speed passenger
service. By the end of 1936, then, the Diesel age was a reality.

The appeal of the Diesel streamliner was unmistakable. In August
1937, for example, the number of through revenue passengers carried between Chicago and Denver and between Chicago and the Twin Cities exceeded the number carried in any previous August since the Passenger Department had started keeping records in 1925. The number of passengers
carried, however, represented only one component of passenger revenues.
Throughout the 1920's and until December 1, 1933, the basic authorized
fare had remained 3.6 cents a mile, with an additional surcharge of fifty
percent collected by the Pullman Company on parlor and sleeping-car
space, but turned over to the railroads. On December 1, 1933, the western
railways voluntarily made a reduction to three cents a mile for one-way and
two cents a mile for round-trip travel in parlor and sleeping cars, with a
reduction to two cents a mile for one-way and 1.8 cents a mile for round-

trip travel in coaches. The fifty percent surcharge on the parlor and sleeping-car space was canceled. Not until the summer of 1937 did the western railways venture to put an extremely modest increase in effect: as of October 16, 1937, round-trip first-class thirty-day fares rose from two to two and a quarter cents a mile. With this minor exception, therefore, fares throughout the 30's remained at bargain-basement levels.

The experience of the *Pioneer Zephyr* in nosing a truckload of scrap iron off the rails on one of its trial trips, and the light damage suffered by one of the new *Denver Zephyrs* when it was sideswiped, suggested early in the game that these new stainless-steel trains were even safer than the heavier conventional equipment. A disastrous, yet revealing accident befell the *Pioneer Zephyr* on October 2, 1939. At Napier, Missouri, a southbound local way freight was standing in the clear on a track adjacent to the main line while its engine took water. For some unaccountable reason, one of the brakemen on the freight train became confused and threw a switch which plunged the northbound *Pioneer* into the standing freight locomotive at a speed of approximately fifty miles an hour. Tragically, the engineer of the *Zephyr* was killed instantly, and subsequently the roadmaster who was riding in the cab with him died from injuries. Several other members of the crew were injured, but none seriously. Not a single passenger was seriously hurt, however, and all resumed their journey at once. "Operating officials are certain," Budd commented, "that had the train consisted of conventional equipment, a number of deaths and more serious injuries would have occurred to passengers."[6] Unfortunate as this accident was, it revealed better than any number of laboratory tests the ruggedness of stainless-steel construction.

In the fall of 1937, Ralph Budd summarized Diesel performance up to that time on the Burlington. The new trains, he pointed out, required far less servicing en route and accelerated more quickly. On the Chicago–Denver run, for example, the *Zephyrs* stood still about forty minutes less than a conventional train. This decrease in servicing time was by no means the only advantage of the Diesels. Because their tractive power was applied through electric motors—that is, by rotating rather than by reciprocal movement—they caused less wear on track. Furthermore, the load that had to be transported in the locomotive itself—including fuel and water—was reduced by forty percent or more. On the *Denver Zephyrs* alone, that meant the elimination of 300,000 ton-miles daily. And it cost a great deal less to operate these trains. At the time, cost per train-mile for locomotive maintenance, fuel, and lubricating oil on the four small *Zephyrs* was averaging 4.84 cents, in contrast to the cost of 28.98 cents per locomotive-mile for steam-drawn trains of the same carrying capacity.

The first cost of the Diesel, of course, as Budd pointed out, was far

[6] PLD, October 9, 1939.

more than that of a steam locomotive of corresponding power, but he regarded it as conservative to say that one Diesel could make as many service-miles, year in and year out, as two steam locomotives. Furthermore, the "percent of availability" of Diesels was approximately ninety-five, as against about seventy for all steam locomotives. This high degree of availability for Diesels resulted largely from their not requiring "back shopping" in the ordinary sense. Moving parts, such as wheels, pistons, cylinder liners, rods, and shafts, could be replaced on mileage schedules and removed one at a time before excessive wear or failure. Major jobs, such as changing a crankshaft, would (at that time) probably require a week in the shop, but careful calibration after more than a year of service indicated that such changes would be necessary only about once every million miles, and even in the case of the *Denver Zephyr* that would mean shopping only about once every two and a half years.

In the fall of 1937, Diesel locomotives were doing two widely contrasting jobs on the Burlington. About thirty were in high-speed passenger service, and a great many more, about 230, were engaged in switching. Yet these engines had one characteristic in common: continuity of use. Diesels in switching service were used around the clock; investment cost per service-hour was thus reduced to a parity with, and possibly below that of steam.

Without any question, the Zephyrs were headline news on the Burlington during the 1930's. Just how much difference did they make? Passenger revenues on the C. B. & Q. in 1933 reached an all-time low of $6,722,104. This was only sixty percent of the amount realized in 1931 and a mere thirty-five percent of the revenues for 1929. Despite the deepening depression, there were small but encouraging upturns in 1934 and 1935, and in 1935, revenues reached $6,978,101. In 1936, however, there was an increase of approximately eighteen percent; 1937 witnessed the same relative increase over the better figures of 1936. The return of $9,717,844 for 1937 was the best of the decade; revenues for the rest of the 30's remained well above the pre-1937 mark. The Zephyrs were the key factor in this heartening revival.

However much developments on the Zephyr deserved the headlines they got in the 1930's, these were by no means the only activities with respect to passenger service on the system. The company's program to air-condition conventional equipment, which began in the spring of 1934, was expanded in 1935, and in a relatively few years all regularly scheduled equipment on main-line trains was air-conditioned.

Despite the Burlington's leadership in the operation of Diesel streamliners, it did not have enough Diesel power even in the late 1930's to handle all main-line trains. Consequently, there was constant improvement in the steam locomotives that were still hauling most of the passenger trains as well as performing all freight service, except, of course, some of the switching. In 1933, the company began replacing the traditional spoke wheels with Double-Disc Boxpok wheels, primarily to achieve better balancing, that would reduce hammer blow on the rails and thus permit an increase in the allowable speed limit of freight locomotives. In the next year, the company began applying roller bearings to the heavy 2-10-4 locomotives, not only to raise permissible speeds but also to reduce friction and cut down servicing requirements.

In 1936, Burlington completed the program, initiated in 1924, of installing Franklin spring-type radial buffers between locomotives and tenders in main-line service so as to maintain constant contact and eliminate jolting, an improvement that meant a smoother ride for passengers and less jostling of freight loads. In the same year, installation of air-operated power reverse gears, begun in 1929, was completed on all heavy locomotives; this led to even smoother operation and a better control of steam distribution. In 1937, roller bearings were installed on valve motions as well as on side and main roads, particularly on the 4-6-4 Hudsons used in fast service. And for the first time chime whistles made themselves heard.

The next year a multitude of innovations was put into effect. With speed requirements constantly mounting, the company conducted an extensive series of slipping tests, a matter of greasing the rails and recording by motion picture the action of wheels on rails at high speeds. As a result of the findings, the company installed Timken light-weight reciprocating parts both to lessen hammer blow on the rails and to reduce fore-and-aft and shaking strains during fast running. Thereafter freight locomotives that had formerly damaged rail at speeds of from forty-five to fifty miles an hour could travel up to 85 mph without adverse effect, and passenger locomotives could exceed 125 mph without damage to rail.

Although the company had been using some locomotives equipped with automatic stokers ever since 1915, these were applied to all larger 2-8-2 and 4-6-2 types in 1938; the monster 4-8-4 Northerns were equipped with vestibule cabs as well. The next year security circulators were installed around the fireboxes of a dozen of the heavier locomotives to obtain better circulation of water. And these were only the most outstanding of countless improvements being made continuously to keep the steam-engine fleet at maximum efficiency.

As it had from its earliest days, the Burlington continued to run special passenger excursions even during the depression of the 1930's. For example, on August 8, 1937, an eleven-car special carried more than 325 model-railroad builders and camera fans from Chicago to the company's shops at West Burlington and Galesburg. The next spring, another fan tour visited the yards at Galesburg and a strip coal mine at Fulton County; later that summer, the C. B. & Q. joined the Great Northern in operating a 4,000-mile camera tour sponsored by *Popular Photography*. Perhaps the flashiest of these specials was the train of seventeen stainless-steel cars that carried a party of Kiwanians from Chicago to Minneapolis on June 16, 1940. Here was a show window on wheels that was bound to impress not only every traveler, but also everyone along the line who chanced to see the silvery train speed by. And so it went. Because times were difficult, it was all the more important that the public and the railways should keep in close touch with each other; little likelihood existed that the Burlington, which grew up with the community, would ever forget that cardinal fact.

One innovation made in the early summer of 1939 was intended as temporary but became a permanent and important fixture in the service offered by the system. As Budd explained to his directors in March 1939, the C. B. & Q., Rio Grande, and Western Pacific proposed to inaugurate on June 10 a new daily through train between Chicago and San Francisco, to be known as the *Exposition Flyer*. By today's standards, it was to have a fairly leisurely schedule: sixty hours in each direction. But it was to pass through the heart of the Rockies and also the breathtaking Feather River Canyon in broad daylight. Had the nation stayed at peace, this train would have been replaced by a stainless-steel Zephyr. As it was, this "temporary train" carried on in much the same fashion for a full decade, although its schedule in both directions was speeded up markedly in the winter of 1940–41; from then on, it made the Chicago–Omaha portion of the run in eight hours flat. Most important of all, the train established the popularity of the route and paved the way for the introduction—in 1949—of the *California Zephyr*.

Meanwhile, other changes to add to the passenger's convenience came thick and fast. Traditionally, all members of the train crew were men. No matter how conscientious and efficient they were, however, they were bound to overlook some details that a woman's eye would catch immediately. So it was that Velma McPeek, with long experience in managing department-store tearooms in Kansas and Oklahoma, came to work in time to make the first trip on the new *Denver Zephyr* in December 1936. From that day on, the spick-and-span supervisor of travel became an institution on the Burlington. Allowed to make her own schedules, she practically lived on the rails. Although she gave most of her attention to the Zephyrs, she rode every train on the line as often as she could. As she frequently put it, her job was to "look after small details, things that ordinarily might be passed up."[7] She made it her business to chat with travelers, who would invariably come forward with all sorts of worthwhile ideas. In due course, when Zephyrettes—all college graduates—were put on the Zephyr trains, Miss McPeek was given responsibility for hiring and supervising them. Her housekeeping on wheels, starting with the advent of the *Denver Zephyrs*, made an enormous "little difference" in service.

On New Year's Day 1940, the C. B. & Q., along with ten other west-

---

[7] Velma McPeek, interview with Overton, Chicago, January 30, 1953.

ern railroads made auto-rental service available for passengers at all principal points, in the hope of attracting commercial passenger traffic then moving by automobile. Initial arrangements provided for the placement of 2,000 autos in 150 key cities of the West. With the exception of wartime, this service has continued to this day.

As times improved, so did facilities. On January 27, 1940, the company opened its modern gray fieldstone station with large picture windows at La Crosse. The new building was not only a tremendous convenience and local showplace, but also, of more significance, it was located on a bypass that eliminated operation in city streets and avoided twenty-nine grade crossings. On the next day the schedules of the *Twin Cities Zephyrs* were shortened by fifteen minutes—most of it saved in La Crosse. The northbound morning *Zephyr* made the 426-mile run to St. Paul in six hours flat—this became the fastest run in the country for that distance.

While these developments were taking place on the railway, the wholly owned Burlington Transportation Company was growing rapidly and undergoing a series of major changes. Bus operations expanded gradually in the early 30's, then leaped forward, first in 1934, when through service was inaugurated between Chicago, Omaha, and Denver, and again in the next year, when service was extended from Chicago to San Francisco and Los Angeles, from Omaha to Kansas City, and between Denver and Billings. By the end of 1935, Burlington Transportation buses were covering 6,214 route miles and accounted for an average of 735,000 bus miles a month. Deficits continued, but during 1934, for example, the $58,347 loss was offset several times over by the estimated $175,000 the railroad was able to save by substituting buses for unprofitable local passenger trains.

During the later 30's, bus service increased both quantitatively and qualitatively. An Omaha–Sioux City line was acquired in 1936; three years later a fleet of air-conditioned Diesel-powered buses was assigned to the Chicago–California and Chicago–Kansas City runs. Depots were improved all over the system. By the end of 1941, Burlington buses were covering 8,035 route miles and accounted for an average of 1,225,000 bus miles a month. In that year, for the first time, these operations returned a profit ($122,232).

In a nutshell, during the difficult 1930's the Burlington made more significant changes in the carrying of passengers throughout its territory than in any similar span of years in its history. Not only did these changes pay off in increased revenues; they also provided hope, both for the community and for the railway, that times would improve. And they demonstrated beyond cavil that when imagination and will were at work, a way could be found to lick even the deepest depression and to confound the prophets of gloom.

CHAPTER 22

Competition

---

1 9 3 3 - 4 0

RECOVERY OF THE RAILWAYS from the acute crash of 1929 and the desperate years that followed was made doubly difficult by one specific factor unique to the industry: the days of a virtual monopoly of overland transport were disappearing, never to return. Competition among railways would remain, not only because it was as instinctive in the heart of every railroader as the urge to survive, but also because, in a nation dedicated to free enterprise, it was the law of the land. Now, unlike the years following 1873 and 1893, the railways had to compete against pipeline, truck and bus, private automobile, and even airplane.

Almost overnight the railway plant, from a technological standpoint, became overbuilt. Yet the cost of a great deal of it was represented by fixed debt on which interest had to be paid to avoid bankruptcy. Furthermore, an entirely new managerial approach was essential to secure and hold business. This was not simply a question of doing the same thing better, but of doing a lot of things entirely differently. To cite one example: in times past, towns and villages local to one road had traditionally been a sure and safe source of traffic. That was no longer true. Trucks and autos went anywhere. The buyer's competitive market for transportation, once restricted primarily to rail centers, had suddenly become a universal one.

• Trimming the Plant •

UNDER THE CIRCUMSTANCES, one of the obvious things every railroad could and did do was cut down on its fixed plant. For the Burlington, the 1930's were a period of quantitative contraction all along the line. From early in 1932 through 1940, the C. B. & Q. abandoned 599.61 miles, mostly cross-country branch lines that had long since outlived their usefulness and whose traffic had been taken over almost wholly by trucks.

The rate of abandonment on the Burlington, however, was higher than that for the nation at large. In 1940 the C. B. & Q., with 8,973 miles of road, operated 3.86 percent of the total Class I mileage. Abandonments for the nine years 1932–40 represented 5.39 percent of all those authorized. The rate of abandonment on the C. B. & Q., in other words, was 39.64 percent above the rate for Class I railways as a whole. The fact that the company served a region primarily agricultural that was particularly vulnerable to highway competition went a long way toward explaining this higher incidence of abandonments on the C. B. & Q.

During the 1930's, public opposition to abandonment was not strenuous. For its part, between the effective date of the Transportation Act of 1920 and the end of 1942, the Interstate Commerce Commission denied only one application of the C. B. & Q., involving seven miles of line in 1934. This high "batting average" was certainly due in part to the care with which the company prepared its abandonment applications. Constant check was kept of business on all branch lines, and only from "steady losers" did the company seek relief.

The logic of this process was inevitable: during the 1880's and 1890's, when most of the Burlington's secondary mileage was constructed, the rule of thumb was that a farmer with his wagon could not be expected to travel more than ten miles to a railroad depot. Consequently, lines were located like a grid approximately fourteen miles apart. With the coming of paved roads and trucks, the premises on which this construction had been based became meaningless. Sometimes it took time to sell the idea, but on the whole the program of abandonment progressed with a minimum of dislocation and hard feeling throughout the 1930's.

Trimming the plant, of course, involved more than abandonment or "rationalization" of existing lines. It was necessary also throughout the decade to keep operating expenses at an absolute minimum. Yet there could be no compromise with safety, and while the company frankly admitted that the physical reserves that had been established in preceding years were drawn upon to some extent, track and equipment were well maintained. As a matter of fact, the C. B. & Q. in 1934 won the coveted Harriman Medal for Safety.

But in cases where safety was assured, cutbacks were logically in order. Whereas during the ten years 1920–29, inclusive, an average of 273.1 miles of new rail was laid, the average for the eight depression years of 1933–40, inclusive, fell to 117.39 miles. There was, however, a notable change in both rail weight and quality. In 1933, the company adopted as standard for important main lines the 112-pound (to the yard) rail recommended by the American Railway Engineering Association. The Burlington, true to its pioneering traditions, was the first railroad to lay any of this rail, which soon was adopted almost universally for important main lines in the West. And in 1938, the company installed the first sections of 131-pound rail.

As in the case of rail, so in the case of bridges. Expenditures during the 30's necessarily were restricted to such individual projects as could not wait, and to the usual program of replacing temporary bridges with permanent structures. For the last eight years of the decade, average annual expenditures on this account were $205,503; as the number of temporary bridges decreased, so did the costs of replacement. Despite these cutbacks, Budd could report in the spring of 1941 that track and roadway were "in splendid condition to meet the demands of high-speed freight and passenger service."[1] Indeed, the Zephyrs could not have performed as they had if track conditions had not been superb. High speed brought another corollary: a sharp reduction in grade crossings. During 1939 alone, eight public and 148 private grade crossings were eliminated to reduce the danger of accidents. Even in the depths of depression, one improvement destined to become a major factor in increasing the speed and economy of operations was made when remote signaling control—the forerunner of centralized traffic control—was extended to five and a half miles of main line at Albia, Iowa. Although financial conditions precluded very much expansion during the 30's, CTC, as it became known, was to revolutionize the handling of fast trains in the 1940's.

Investment in terminals, yards, and other structures was at a minimum during the difficult years. As long as the level of traffic remained light, the reconstructed yard at Galesburg, with its 114 miles of track and its capacity for 7,634 cars, proved ample even though the yard was only half the size originally contemplated. The tie- and timber-treating plant at Sheridan was extensively improved in 1933, and in 1937 the company spent more than a third of a million dollars to install new coal chutes and connected facilities at Lincoln and Hastings, Nebraska.

Apart from the Zephyr trains, purchases of equipment during the mid-30's were pared to the bone. After the lean years of 1933 and 1934, the company slightly increased production of various types of rolling stock in 1935, with a substantial upturn the following year. Only with the recovery of revenues during 1936 did the company resume, for the first time in the decade, anything like a major equipment program. Orders placed outside the company increased considerably, but far more impor-

[1] CB&Q, AR 1940, p. 9.

tant to the Burlington economy as a whole was the renewed activity in the home shops. In 1937 and 1938, nearly four thousand freight cars of various types were completed, two thirds of them in 1937. During the same period the company also produced fifteen more 4-8-4 locomotives of the Northern type.

Sensitive as the equipment program was to the budget, the recession of 1938 was reflected in deliveries during the following year. Revenues recovered moderately in 1939 and inched slightly ahead in 1940, and once again the equipment program moved accordingly. Four more Diesel-electric switchers, fourteen stainless-steel passenger coaches, and three 4,000-horsepower Diesel-electric passenger locomotives were purchased. These locomotives were the first main-line Diesel-electric power units ordered separately from Zephyr trains. The company shops in 1940 produced ten more hefty 4-8-4's; in that year the car shops turned out more than 700 assorted freight cars. Notably, fifty of the regular boxcars were equipped with steel rather than cast-iron wheels and signal and air lines so that they could be used in either freight or passenger service; a hundred of the hopper cars, weighing seventy tons, had steel covers that fitted them particularly for transporting cement. The newer cars clearly were placing increasing emphasis on special purposes and speed.

One item without which the company could not long exist was its accumulated store of community goodwill. In this direction there was no thought of economy. When, for example, a devastating flood on the Ohio River rendered thousands of families destitute and homeless, the Burlington joined neighboring railroads in transporting refugees to safe districts and in hauling in at no charge materials and supplies for the building of temporary shelters and facilities.

Of long-run significance was the Burlington's purchase in 1937 of a Drinker Respirator, or "iron lung," to help fight infantile paralysis throughout its territory. Centrally located at Omaha, it was held in constant readiness for service to employees or anyone else in need of emergency treatment. During the first ten years it was available, fifty-seven requests were made for its services; except when the lung was already in use, these were instantly met, free of charge. The iron lung was used in the treatment of thirty patients, none of whom happened to be an employee of the Burlington. During epidemics it frequently performed stand-by service in various communities at the request of local health authorities, and on two occasions it was used for demonstration purposes. Thus, in addition to saving a score of lives, the respirator influenced several communities to acquire iron lungs of their own.

• Inter-railway Competition •

That competition during the thin 30's would be strong and tough was axiomatic. And as the Burlington's neighboring railroads would testify, the Q touched off plenty of it itself. The Diesel-electric train was perhaps the most spectacular example, but by no means the only one. The more subtle and continuing fact that the C. B. & Q. managed to convert more of its gross revenue into net income than its three most closely comparable neighbors—the North Western, the Rock Island, and the Milwaukee— was a major competitive factor in itself.

In 1940, the average mileage of the North Western, the Rock Island, and the Milwaukee combined was 8,997, or just forty-three miles less than the average operated mileage of the Burlington; in physical size the four companies were properly comparable. Furthermore, the gross revenues of the three neighbors averaged only five percent less than those of the Burlington. The disparity came in the carrying through of revenues to net income. Not one of the three had any net income at all. In sharp contrast to this dismal showing, the C. B. & Q. earned some net income each year, and a total over the eight years of 33.2 million dollars.

These figures, coldly reflecting the situation through the depression decade, were the basic facts of life as far as one important aspect of inter-railroad competition was concerned. But a reverse twist to the re-grettable difficulties that afflicted the Burlington's closest neighbors must be taken into account. On June 7, 1933, the Rock Island sought pro-tection of the courts in voluntary bankruptcy. A little more than two years later, on June 28, 1935, the North Western followed suit, as did the Milwaukee the next day. For the balance of the decade and well into the next, these companies remained in receivership. Whereas for each road this meant a long and painful process of reorganization, it had the immediate effect of relieving them from the payment of various fixed obligations, including interest on their funded debt. Thus, with available cash released for improvements to plant and operations, the three dis-tressed roads offered the Burlington livelier competition than would other-wise have been possible. Furthermore, with fewer obligations to meet, they could afford to be less concerned about the maintenance of rate levels. The financially difficult situation of its three closest neighbors, then, was a burden for the Burlington as well; the fact that the C. B. & Q. kept solvent was a tribute to generations of good management and care-ful planning.

Schedules represented another phase of competition. In 1932, for example, the Burlington had joined the Rio Grande and the Western Pacific in establishing freight service between California and Chicago in both directions on the basis of seventh-morning delivery. Because at the time the route west of Denver was roundabout (before the opening of the Dotsero cut-off), the C. B. & Q. had been required to set up a speedy thirty-six-hour schedule between Denver and Chicago. This service was incidental to the through schedule, but it provided better service than any then in existence for business originating in Denver destined for the

East. Consequently, the Union Pacific not only met the C. B. & Q. schedule, but also reduced its own sufficiently to move livestock between Denver and Chicago without feeding, that is, in about thirty-three hours, in order to allow for switching into the stockyards and unloading within the thirty-six-hour time limit for leaving stock on cars. For more than a year the Burlington made no move, hoping that the U. P. would revert to a thirty-six-hour schedule. When this did not happen, the Q reduced its own eastbound run to thirty-three hours. This, though more expensive, was not very difficult since the Burlington had more favorable switching arrangements at both Denver and Chicago, had the advantage of a one-line haul (thus saving transfer time at the Missouri River), and, finally, had a route that was shorter.

An entirely different facet of competition lay in the realm of terminals, and in this theater sharp, expensive warfare took place on several fronts at once at the end of the decade. As so often in the past, the Burlington's major rival was the mighty Union Pacific.

Before 1939, Denver had had no produce terminal served by any railway, but only a city market to and from which produce had to be trucked. Consequently, when this market was torn down to make way for a boulevard, the Burlington, the Colorado and Southern, the Rio Grande, the Santa Fe, and the Rock Island—which among them handled seventy percent of the perishable carload freight at Denver—joined together in constructing a produce terminal on a site favored by a majority of the shipping interests, by the mayor, and by the City Planning Commission. The new terminal, costing approximately $1,000,000 and jointly owned and operated by the five participating railroads, was scheduled for completion about August 1, 1939. At the outset the Union Pacific was invited to join in the project but declined; instead it began building a separate produce terminal on the outskirts of the city and, in turn, invited the other five roads to join it there. They declined because the Union Pacific site was neither convenient from the standpoint of the public nor favorably situated for use by any railroads other than the Union Pacific.

When the Union Pacific sought to employ the same tactics at Kansas City, it precipitated a major railroad war. For many years the fruit and vegetable business in the greater Kansas City area had been centered in the municipal market district of Kansas City, Missouri, where practically all the wholesale and car-lot dealers were located. The city itself improved the market in 1931, at public expense, and toward the end of the decade several new buildings were added and occupied by wholesale produce dealers. Although no railroad made any expenditure in connection with the terminal area, all of them afforded service to the market.

Nevertheless, the Union Pacific, acting through the city of Kansas City, Kansas, began construction of a fruit and vegetable market in the Fairfax district on the Kansas side of the river; funds for construction were provided by a $1,700,000 FWA grant and by the sale of $3 million revenue bonds of the city of Kansas City, Kansas, to the Union Pacific. As Budd pointed out to his directors in January 1940, this action of the Union Pacific was similar to what had taken place in Denver, and was a "traffic raid" pure and simple.[2]

This time reaction was prompt and decisive. The dealers in Kansas City, Missouri, promptly organized to defend their market property and requested the railroads to improve their team track and inspection and reconsignment yards in Kansas City, Missouri, by joining to establish a common terminal. The Burlington, the Rock Island, the Santa Fe, and the Missouri Pacific immediately agreed to put up a million-dollar common yard to serve the long-established municipal market. At the same time, on the request of the Interstate Commerce Commission, the Attorney General of the United States brought suit in the federal courts against the Union Pacific, the City of Kansas City, Kansas, and a number of individuals for an injunction restraining the defendants from giving bonuses and free rentals to induce shippers at the Kansas City, Missouri, market to move to the new Union Pacific market across the river, alleging that such payments constituted rebates under the Elkins Act. The abortive affair was ended by a federal judge on July 8, 1940, when he issued a permanent injunction against the Union Pacific and the Kansas City, Kansas, food terminal. Occupants were ordered to pay a rent that would constitute a reasonable return on the value of the property. That was enough; the dealers moved back to the new city market in Kansas City, Missouri. On May 1, 1941, the new yard to serve the Kansas City, Missouri, produce terminal was put into service by the Burlington, the Rock Island, the Santa Fe, and the Missouri Pacific.

Just as the struggle over the produce terminal at Kansas City was reaching a climax, the Burlington won a significant victory in nearby North Kansas City. Directly across the Missouri River from Kansas City, two main lines of the C. B. & Q. diverge, one running parallel with Murray Yards and thence north to St. Joseph, the other swinging northeast to Quincy and Chicago. In the angle formed by these two main lines lay industrial property and lead tracks in which the Burlington owned a one-third interest; the balance was originally held by the Armour and Swift packing firms. For years the C. B. & Q. had performed all switching in the area, but when the Van Sweringens bought the Armour–Swift two-thirds interest, the Missouri Pacific (which they then controlled) sought to take over most or all of this service. To forestall this, the Burlington claimed that the title to the lead tracks which the Missouri Pacific's owners controlled was defective, and that the C. B. & Q., having provided the service over the years, should be allowed to condemn and acquire certain lands adjacent to them. On March 30, 1940, the

[2] PLD, January 10, 1940.

United States District Court held that the Missouri Pacific lead tracks in question had indeed been built without proper charter authority, that they really constituted a part of the Burlington system, which had operated over them for many years, and that it was the right and duty of the Burlington to continue to operate over these tracks, to which they might acquire title by condemnation. Settlement of the suit gave Burlington clear and exclusive title to the lead tracks and paved the way for its participation in the development of the industrial area. From that day to this, the region has experienced continuous growth and improvement.

• Truck and Bus Competition •

In 1925, the 2,400,000 trucks registered in the nation were regarded mainly as feeders to the railways; they were still employed primarily in local operations because no adequately paved intercity highway system existed, and heavy-duty pneumatic tires were not yet fully developed. Trucks carried only about 2.6 percent of the combined rail-truck traffic. Small wonder that Secretary of Agriculture W. M. Jardine, whose department administered the Federal Highway Act, said in 1925 that he could see little likelihood of competition with railways over distances exceeding thirty miles, except for household goods and in a few other exceptional cases. In 1932, however, despite the acute depression, trucks accounted for 30 billion ton-miles and 9.4 percent of total intercity traffic. Meanwhile, the mileage of hard-surface roads suitable for truck traffic had grown enormously; a little over 25,000 miles in 1921, it exceeded 92,000 in 1930.

Furthermore, certain characteristics of the traffic most susceptible to motor truck competition were already becoming apparent. Even in the early stages, trucks first sought high-grade traffic which, when handled by rail, contributed substantially to net revenues. Second, the relatively slight overhead costs of trucks in contrast to railways, and their ability to select traffic, enabled them to concentrate on through movements between large cities and thus realize more economy per ton-mile than the railways, which were obliged to serve intermediate and branch-line points as well. Third, in order to fill a truck for a back haul, motor carriers were able to offer bargain rates that forced the railways to follow suit or face the possibility of losing the traffic entirely. The problem was just how to cope with this growing threat.

One line of attack was on the regulatory front. Generally speaking, railway management, with the firm support of rail labor, state regulatory bodies, and the Interstate Commerce Commission, was in favor of federal regulation. Opposed, in the main, were farmers, a great many shippers, and most motor carriers, including, particularly, small operators of trucks. By 1932, the I. C. C. reported definitely in favor of regulation of motor carriers, citing as one reason for its position the fact that the losses imposed by highway competition might so impair the ability of the railways to serve the public as to result in serious consequences. The public interest, it said, required coordination, and that could be brought about only by comprehensive regulation. As a matter of fact, from 1925 to 1935, no less than thirty-four separate bills were introduced in Congress for regulating motor carriers. But not until the opposition of auto manufacturers, organized shippers, and truck operators had been overcome—indeed, by 1935 the American Trucking Association publicly favored federal regulation—was the Motor Carrier Act of 1935 passed.

Control by the Commission was extended rather generally over common carriers, to a more limited extent over contract carriers, and to private carriers only when the owners used their trucks or buses in furtherance of a commercial enterprise. On the other hand, a considerable group of motor carriers was exempted from the operation of the Act, notably those transporting livestock, fish, and agricultural products. In these "exemptions" lay the seeds of future difficulties for the railways.

As had been true in the case of railroads since 1920, no common carrier by motor vehicle was to be permitted to begin interstate or foreign operations without a certificate of convenience and necessity. Yet here again there was a proviso: under the so-called "Grandfather Clauses," operations of common carriers in existence on June 1, 1935, and of contract carriers on July 1, 1935, could be continued; thus the Commission's power to control the supply of motor-carrier service was sharply restricted. As in the case of railways, combinations between motor carriers were provided for, with the Commission's approval, and the Act specifically permitted carriers by rail or water to consolidate with or acquire motor carriers. Here again, however, provisos were attached which could conceivably work to the disadvantage of the railways. If consolidation or control were sought by a carrier other than a motor carrier (such as a railroad), then the Commission was directed not to approve the request *unless* it specifically found that the proposed transaction would be in the public interest and would not unduly restrain competition.

By the Act, the Commission was given rather broad powers over the issuance of securities by both common and contract carriers, and over rates. Finally, and in sharp contrast to the situation in respect to railways, the Commission was expressly denied the right to prescribe or regulate in any manner rates, fares, or charges for intrastate transportation in respect to common-carrier motor vehicles. Not only that, but in respect to interstate contract carriers, the Commission was authorized to regulate only minimum rather than both minimum and maximum charges. Thus, the Motor Carrier Act of 1935 was by no means as comprehensive as the law applicable to the railroads. As in the matter of service and rates, so in the matter of regulation: the struggle between railroads and trucks for freight traffic had merely begun.

On April 1, 1935, Burlington made a defensive move when it inaugurated pick-up and delivery service on L.C.L. freight shipped in quantities of 6,000 pounds or more at Chicago and twelve other major points, including Omaha, Council Bluffs, Des Moines, and the Twin Cities. As of the end of that month, all western truck-line carriers agreed to the establishment of free pick-up and store-door delivery throughout western territory.

This, however, was only a partial measure. Fortunately the Burlington, fully aware of the broader aspects of the situation and already involved in highway transportation through its bus operations, took the major positive step early in 1935 of establishing a truck division of the Burlington Transportation Company. Since this was done prior to June 1, the B. T. Company, thanks to the "Grandfather Rights" clause of the Motor Carrier Act, was able to acquire rights to approximately 1,500 interstate route miles without obtaining the federal approval that would have been required after that date. It thus gained a type of authority far superior to that of any other rail-affiliated truck line in the country.

Starting with a Chicago–Omaha run and some associated feeder operations in 1935, Burlington truck service expanded steadily from 1,306 route miles in 1936 to 3,998 miles by the end of 1941; over the same period, truck miles rose from an average of 166,000 to 433,000 a month, and service was extended to include Des Moines, St. Louis, the Tri-Cities, Kansas City, and the Twin Cities. A modern truck terminal was built at Galesburg in 1937, and new highway units were added each year. Financially, the truck division proved modestly profitable from the start.

Speaking before the Western Society of Engineers in the spring of 1939, Harry C. Murphy (then assistant vice-president of C. B. & Q. operations, and designated by Ralph Budd to supervise the B. T. Company highway services) spelled out just how these truck operations, quite apart from furnishing through all-highway service, were closely coordinated with rail movements. In respect to less-than-carload shipments, Murphy explained how, for example, goods shipped from Chicago to a consignee on a branch line would move, by frequent and speedy rail service, to a division point where they would be transferred to a B. T. Company trailer and promptly delivered by truck, thus reaching the consignee from twenty-four to forty-eight hours sooner than if they had had to await the infrequent way freight train. Comparable savings of time were, of course, obtained on the reverse movement, thus placing the branch line customer in virtually the same competitive position as one located on the main line. This arrangement also speeded the handling of carload freight, since way trains could concentrate on this traffic and not suffer delays necessitated at terminals or intermediate stations by loading and unloading less-than-carload shipments.

Nor was this the only saving of time and money: common ownership and operation of trains and trucks permitted a better balancing of traffic. At the time, for example, rail refrigerator cars came eastward heavily laden but moved back west virtually empty, whereas the trucks, which carried their heaviest traffic westbound, often returned empty or only partially loaded. By loading eastbound trucks with rail freight, and westbound cars with truck cargoes, therefore, a far better utilization of capacity was achieved. As Murphy accurately prophesied: "It is probable that so far as the law will permit, the railroads will improve their highway operations, and the Burlington is convinced that this will react favorably upon the railroads themselves and will provide a service to the public which neither the railroad nor the highway carrier acting independently of one another could provide."[3]

In the light of these views, it is not surprising that Murphy established experimental piggyback operations on the C. B. & Q. as early as 1939. This was not a Burlington "first." The Chicago, North Shore and Milwaukee, an electric interurban line, had offered such service since 1926. Just a decade later, the Chicago Great Western became the first Class I road to enter the field, followed in 1937 by the New Haven. Such service was still a rarity, however, when, in the late summer of 1940, the C. B. & Q. began handling truck trailers on flatcars on a regular basis between Chicago and Kansas City. A group of truckers agreed to provide ramps for loading and unloading and to furnish all devices necessary to fasten trailers to flatcars. They also agreed to perform the loading, fastening, unfastening, and unloading themselves; the only service provided by the railroad was the actual movement of loaded cars on its regular trains. The plan was to load two trailers on each flatcar, and at the outset, expectations were that there would be about twenty flatcars a day, producing a gross revenue of approximately $3,850.

Certainly no doubt existed by 1940 that the Burlington, along with all other railways, would have to take drastic measures in respect to service, rates, and solicitation to meet truck competition. In that year, nearly five million trucks were on the road, an increase of approximately 400 percent since 1920, and they were carrying ten percent of all intercity traffic. This was a threat of major proportions.

Roughly speaking, and without going into detail, it may be said that bus traffic grew just as rapidly as did that by motor truck. Passenger-miles for buses almost doubled, from 11.2 billion in 1930 to 21 billion in 1940, while truck ton-miles were increasing from 20 to 38 billion. The bus, however, made a larger dent in rail passenger business than the truck made in freight traffic. In 1940, buses were carrying 26.5 percent of all intercity passenger traffic moving by public transportation, as against 67.1 percent for the railways; as yet, motor trucks were carrying only ten percent of the

[3] H. C. Murphy: "Coordination of Rail and Highway Services," address before Western Society of Engineers, April 1939, quoted in Russell B. James: "Birth and Infancy of Burlington Highway Operations," memorandum to Overton, October 19, 1960.

freight, in contrast to 61.3 percent for the rails. However the figures were viewed as between buses and trucks, the competition of highway carriers, taken together, was sharp and was growing. The railroads had to act, and act quickly, against over-the-road public transportation.

• WATER CARRIER COMPETITION •

THE ORIGINAL Interstate Commerce Act of 1887 placed under control of the I. C. C. common carriers that transported people or goods partly by railroad and partly by water. This was in no sense a move to regulate inland water carriers, however, but rather one to prevent the railways from using controlled boat lines to manipulate rates. The Hepburn Act of 1906 gave the Commission the power to require establishment of rail-water routes and to prescribe maximum rates, but a much more onerous provision as far as the railways were concerned was that part of the Mann-Elkins Act of 1910 which specified that if a railway in competition with a water route reduced a rate, it could not subsequently raise it simply by showing that water competition had been eliminated.

The Transportation Act of 1920, for all its pious declaration of intention to promote in full vigor both rail and water transportation, contained two provisions that extended special benefits to the latter: the Commission was authorized to require establishment of through rail-water routes *even though* a particular railway could haul the traffic the entire distance, and, more important, the Commission was given the power to fix minimum rail rates, thus removing the railways' chief weapon for fighting water competition.

But this was only half the story. Ever since 1819, the Corps of Engineers has been responsible for investigating and, to a large extent, for carrying out river improvements. Curiously enough, this army agency never was required to submit its proposals to the Interstate Commerce Commission. Small wonder, then, that billions in federal funds derived from the general taxpayer were spent for improvements in inland waterways even before the onset of the depression in the 1930's. As a matter of fact, in 1924 the national government incorporated the Inland Waterways Corporation to own and operate a federal-government barge line on the Mississippi and Warrior rivers.

Under the Denison Act of 1928, the I. C. C. was required to issue certificates of necessity and convenience to any common carrier that desired to establish service on those rivers, and it then became the duty of the Commission to *compel* all connecting railroads to establish through routes and joint rates with such certified water carriers. Yet, in contrast to the "convenience and necessity" provisions of the Act of 1920 respecting railways, the Commission under the Denison Act was given no authority to determine whether or not additional common carrier service by water was either convenient or necessary as far as the public was concerned. "On the contrary," commented two experts of the Brookings Institution, "the single purpose was to overcome the natural geographic limitations of water transportation by forcing the railroads to make available their facilities to feed traffic into the government-supported water transport system."[4]

From a quantitative standpoint, intercity traffic moving by water was by no means inconsiderable. In 1930, Great Lakes vessels were carrying twenty percent as much as the railways, and inland waterways 2.3 percent, a total of 22.3. By 1936, the comparable percentages were 22.3 and 4.4, for a total of 26.7 percent of the rail traffic. This was not only substantial but also growing competition, particularly in respect to the inland waterways, whose relative share almost doubled between 1930 and 1936.

Such regulation as existed varied widely in degree, with jurisdiction divided between two different agencies. By 1938, for example, the United Maritime Commission had authority to fix maximum rates for common carriers on the Great Lakes. But the Commission exercised no control whatever over carriers on river or canal, or over private carriers anywhere. Congress eventually recognized the inequitable nature of this situation and in Title III of the Transportation Act of 1940 made interstate commerce by water subject to the jurisdiction of the Interstate Commerce Commission. Yet the Act of 1940 by no means regulated inland water carriers as the parent Interstate Commerce Act regulated railroads. To begin with, the I. C. C. was specifically prohibited from any control over intrastate activities of water carriers even when such control would be essential to remove discrimination against interstate commerce. Both common and contract carriers by water had to obtain certificates of convenience and necessity to engage in business, but, as in the case of motor carriers, all *bona fide* operations prior to January 1, 1940, were protected by a "Grandfather Clause." More to the point, and in sharp contrast to the regulation over railways, the Commission was given no authority whatever to prevent abandonment of service. Whereas the Commission could prescribe both maximum and minimum rates and fares for common carriers by water, it could prescribe only minimum charges for contract carriers. Furthermore, common carriers were required to establish through routes and charges for persons or property traveling partly by rail and partly by water, but they were not compelled to do so with motor carriers. Nor was the Commission—again in contrast to rail regulation—given any control over water-carrier service or over the issuance of securities.

Perhaps most important of all, the Act of 1940 exempted from all regulation whatever the transportation of commodities in bulk when the cargo space of any vessel or barge was not used for carrying more than three such commodities. This provision had the effect of exempting from

[4] Charles L. Dearing and Wilfred Owen: *National Transportation Policy* (Washington: The Brookings Institution; 1949), pp. 238–9.

regulation practically all the traffic handled by barge on the Mississippi River system. Numerous other conditional exemptions were specified, but the net effect of the law was that only a small percentage of total domestic water traffic was subject to control by the Interstate Commerce Commission. The railways had hoped, in 1940, that passage of the so-called "Water Carrier Act" in that year would restrict what they considered unfair subsidized competition, particularly on the part of the water carriers in the Mississippi Valley area. As subsequent events were to demonstrate, however, that hope was illusory.

• AIR CARRIER COMPETITION •

BEFORE 1926, no regularly scheduled air passenger lines were in service in the United States. But passage of the Contract Air Mail Act of 1925 gave the carriers a backlog of revenue that encouraged them to offer passenger service on a limited basis. At the same time, in addition to the airmail subsidies, the federal government began spending huge sums on the improvement of airways by providing beacons, weather information, and the like. One result was a fantastic increase in commercial air travel. The one million passenger-miles flown in 1926 increased to 95 million in 1930, leaped to 439 million by 1936, and crossed the billion mark (compared to 23 billion by rail) in 1940.

The Board of Investigation and Research set up by the Transportation Act of 1940 concluded that for the period 1925 to 1941, the federal government had spent over $111,000,000 for airways improvements and estimated that 31.1 percent of this amount was chargeable to domestic scheduled airlines, 36.8 percent to government functions, and 32.1 percent to other flying. By the end of 1940, no less than $352,000,000 had been spent on publicly owned airports; of this amount, more than $270,000,000 was spent on airports used by domestic scheduled airlines.

Even before World War II, when public aid to air carriers was trivial compared with later expenditures, there was considerable discussion as to whether such aid should be given, and if so, what form it should take. By and large, it was justified as part of the government's long-established policy of providing assistance to promising forms of business enterprise during their early stages. This had always constituted one argument for protective tariffs and for land grants and other aids to highways, canals, and railroads. A further justification was the role of the airplane in national defense: aircraft manufacturers ready to meet the demands of war could be encouraged only if commercial aviation itself was constantly expanding. On the other hand, critics pointed out that public aid inevitably built up vested interests which, once established, were hard to dislodge; government policy, they felt, should be aimed toward putting the commercial airline industry on a self-supporting basis as rapidly as possible.

Whatever the merits or demerits of government promotion of commercial air transportation, however, it was apparent to the railways, even by 1940, that such assistance played a major role in enabling the airlines to compete with the railways for the carriage of both mail and passengers. Furthermore, this competitive threat was strengthened rather than limited by the passage of the Civil Aeronautics Act of 1938. Those who favored regulation by the I. C. C. argued that this would be the only possible way of achieving a national transportation policy whereby regulation of each type of carrier would always be undertaken with the entire transportation plan in mind. On the other hand, those favoring a separate agency felt that the problem of air transportation, involving special safety regulations and completely different operating conditions than those of surface carriers, required special treatment, particularly if it were to be deemed desirable in the national interest to promote as well as to regulate aviation. President Roosevelt favored regulation by a separate agency, and on this basis the Civil Aeronautics Act was passed and signed on June 23, 1938. Except for minor organizational changes in 1940 (as a result of the Reorganization Act of 1939), this basic legislation has remained in effect ever since.

Under it, the Civil Aeronautics Board exerts economic regulation over the industry, and functions, generally speaking, in a way similar to the I. C. C. in respect to railroads. It has control over rates, competition, and safety. The basic difference between this Act and those applying to all other carriers is that the C. A. B. is directed to consider the welfare of air transportation *alone*, whereas the I. C. C. is specifically charged with considering the effect of its decisions on *all forms* of transportation, whether by rail, water, highway, or by "other means," presumably including airlines. The contradictions in such a system and the difficulty of achieving a truly national transportation policy under it are obvious.

Although the specific powers granted to the C. A. B. in 1938 were somewhat similar to those of the I. C. C. in respect to the carriers under its control, the differences were significant. For one thing, the C. A. B. was authorized to exempt any air carrier or any class of air carriers from economic regulation if it decided such regulation was not necessary. As a result, the C. A. B. decided at the outset to exempt non-scheduled air carriers, although, it should be noted, it retained the right to extend regulation over them if and when it so desired. As in the case of rail, motor, and water carriers, air carriers had to obtain a certificate of public convenience and necessity from the C. A. B., but the law contained a "Grandfather Clause" similar to that applied to highway and water carriers.

More specifically, the Act provided that the C. A. B. could fix mail rates at a level sufficient to insure performance of the service and to maintain and continue the development of air transportation to the extent, and of the character and quality, required for the commerce of the United States, the postal service, and the national defense. This particular provision made possible the use of airmail service to subsidize the operation of airmail carriers. The 1938 Act provided that air carriers might consolidate with other types of carriers. Incidentally, the Act did not give the C. A. B. jurisdiction over contract carriers or over airline security issues, which were subjected to the Securities Exchange Commission rather than to the C. A. B.

• THE EFFECT OF NON-RAIL COMPETITION •

DESPITE THE VERY CONSIDERABLE, and sometimes complex, legislation of 1935–1938–1940, the railways, as fully regulated carriers, were still in the position of competing directly with either unregulated or partially regulated competitors. What made the situation increasingly difficult was the rapid growth of these competing carriers during the 1930's and the prospect that they would continue to grow thereafter. True enough, in 1940 the railways hauled 61.3 percent of all intercity freight, measured in ton-miles, while trucks handled but 10.0 percent and inland waterways only 3.6 percent. On the other hand, from 1931 to 1940, while railway tonnage was increasing twenty percent, the tonnage moving by trucks went up ninety percent and that by inland waterways, 200 percent.

Similarly, the railroads in 1940 accounted for 67.1 percent of all public-transportation passenger-miles, the buses 26.5 percent, and the airlines only 2.8 percent. But the growth figures since 1931 told an entirely different story. During the 30's, passenger-miles by rail increased only eight percent; those by bus, 100 percent; and those by air, 711 percent. Although the competitive problem in absolute terms was not yet critical, it promised to become so if the relative rates of growth of the various carriers during the 1930's were any indication of what the future might hold.

During the spring of 1938, the Burlington's Traffic Department initiated the practice on Lines West of holding, on successive Sundays, a series of agents' meetings for the purpose of sponsoring what was known as "cross-country solicitation." From Chicago and division headquarters came a delegation of traffic officials and general officers who would spend the morning outlining up-to-the-minute developments on the national scene and in respect to system policy for the benefit of the agents of all the stations in the area. After luncheon, to which all the agents and their wives were invited and at which a guest speaker usually made brief remarks, the meetings were thrown open for specific questions and suggestions from the agents on the firing line, the men who spent their days in immediate contact with shippers and receivers in an effort to get every possible pound of freight on Burlington rails. So successful were these gatherings west of the Missouri River that in the spring of 1939 they were extended to Lines East.

During the calendar year 1939, it was estimated that increased business resulting directly from information gathered and policies adopted at these meetings amounted to approximately $400,000. In 1940 these so-called "cross-country meetings" were repeated with enthusiasm throughout the system. By means of them, the more than 900 agents of the Burlington were brought up to date, encouraged to step up their solicitation efforts, and—most important of all—were given ample opportunity to make known their problems. The informal give-and-take of the discussions not only led to specific readjustment of certain rate policies, but also provided an excellent means of direct communication and for improving morale on all sides.

The meeting called to order in Aurora, Illinois, on April 14, 1940, by Superintendent Wade Haist was typical. Present from Chicago were thirty-three men headed by Harry Murphy, then assistant vice-president. From division headquarters came the chief dispatcher, train master, and auditor, as well as the traffic men. Val Kuska came from Omaha; J. V. Wolfe, then traveling auditor, from La Crosse; and P. R. Nicholson, superintendent of the stockyards, from Montgomery. Most important of all were the forty-one agents from all towns, large and small, on the division.

The first speaker, once the introductions were over, was Warren Fuller, assistant to the vice-president, Traffic, and his main point was a simple one: "We have no non-competitive territory now." That meant working a little harder, plowing a little deeper, and taking advantage of every opportunity to make the most of the excellent equipment at hand. "We have more in the show window now than we ever had before," he said; "the Burlington has led the procession in so far as passenger development is concerned. We are leading or equal to any other railroad in so far as fast freight schedules are concerned. We are jointly trying to get the best out of the tools we have to do with, and the object of this meeting is to give you men an opportunity to express your views and give us such suggestions as you may have in mind that will help us increase our revenue."[5] He concluded with a plea for candid discussion so that everyone present would learn from the others.

Albert Cotsworth, general passenger traffic manager, followed with a quick rundown of the latest developments in passenger service, stressing the low-cost round-trip fares to the Coast, explaining the advantages of the newly introduced auto-rental plan available throughout the system, and putting in a strong plug for the enormously successful *Exposition Flyer.* Turning to an activity that had long been distinctive with the Burlington, he told how the company was constantly using available equipment for excursions. The *Silver Streak Zephyr,* for example, had been received ahead of schedule. Consequently, it had been used for short excursion trips simply on the theory that lots of people liked to take a ride; it had carried no

[5] "Proceedings of Agents' Meeting in the Matter of Cross-Country Solicitation," Aurora, Illinois, April 14, 1940, pp. 3–4, CB&Q/Traffic.

Zephyr Routes, December 1941

less than 1,500 people in a single day on six round trips between Chicago and Aurora and had repeated the experience wherever it went on the system. An important value of these excursions, he said, was that they particularly attracted children. "Whether the children bring the parents, or the parents the children, I am not so sure, but the fact is they are together and to the extent we can interest children in our service we are going to be better off in years to come."[6]

George Hoffelder, assistant general freight traffic manager from Chicago, spoke next. Because of highway and barge competition, he said, the

[6] Ibid., pp. 6–7.

Burlington was losing both corn and livestock business. As a result of suggestions made at the cross-country meeting the previous year, various rates had been reduced, and it seemed abundantly clear that continuous minor adjustments made on the basis of specific situations could, in the aggregate, make a tremendous difference. Following Hoffelder, others from the main office explained specific system-wide policies.

In the afternoon it was the agents' turn. A score of them presented specific problems from their areas; if solutions could not be hammered out on the spot, the problems were carefully noted for future investigation. But in one respect everyone agreed with Warren Fuller: "We have no non-competitive territory now!"

CHAPTER 23

Revamping the Railway
Regulatory Structure

1 9 3 3 - 4 1

I N THE FIRST QUARTER OF 1933 the net loss for all Class I railways was
$94,000,000, almost double that for the corresponding period of the
previous year. The causes were obvious: the depression and growth
of competition from other transport agencies.

The Hoover administration had attempted to deal with these problems, but it was left to the New Deal of Franklin D. Roosevelt to attack
them in a comprehensive manner. Indeed, soon after the inauguration,
Congress studied various proposals for changing the Interstate Commerce
Act. The labor organizations strove for the adoption of legislation limiting
employee dismissal in any program of coordination. For their part, the railways sought the repeal of the 1920 recapture clause and the existing rate-
making rule. What actually emerged first from Congress was the Emergency Transportation Act, approved by the President on June 16, 1933.
Title I was designed to apply temporarily during the emergency; Title II
included permanent amendments to the Interstate Commerce Act.

The specific objectives of the first part of the Act were (1) to eliminate unnecessary duplication of railway services and facilities whenever this
could be done without decreasing employment below the level of May
1933 (except by the normal rate owing to death, retirement, and the like);

(2) to promote financial reorganization of the carriers, primarily by reducing fixed charges; and (3) to initiate studies designed to improve transportation in all forms.

To carry out these mandates, the president was authorized to appoint a Federal Coordinator of Transportation; President Roosevelt forthwith named Joseph B. Eastman of the Interstate Commerce Commission for a one-year term, subject to renewal. Meanwhile both the carriers and the railway labor organizations were authorized to create three regional coordinating committees. The particular task of the carrier committees was to eliminate duplicating facilities and services, preferably on a voluntary basis, and in any event in consultation with the coordinator. If any such proposals might affect the interests of workers, then conferences were to be held with the regional labor committees as well. In the event that voluntary action on the part of the roads should fail to accomplish the objectives of the Act, the coordinator was empowered to issue appropriate orders on his own initiative. This provision, of course, lodged substantial authority in the coordinator, but a safeguard was provided: any interested party could petition the Interstate Commerce Commission to suspend and review any order of the coordinator.

To bring about financial reorganization of the carriers, the Commission was directed not to approve any loans to them under the Reconstruction Finance Corporation Act if it felt that any carrier requesting such a loan was in need of financial reorganization rather than simply temporary support. Finally, to improve transportation generally, the coordinator was directed "forthwith" to launch a series of comprehensive investigations and to submit his findings to the Commission, which was directed to forward them, along with its own comments, to Congress and to the President.

Several conditions under which these various powers were to be exercised are particularly worthy of note. First, in complying with any order of the coordinator or of the Commission under the emergency provisions of the Act, carriers were to be relieved from the operation of the anti-trust laws and of any similar federal or state laws except those enacted for the protection of public health and safety. This provision was parallel to that of the National Industrial Recovery Act, which permitted businesses in general to develop codes through cooperative action despite the fact that such activity might normally be construed as "combination in restraint of trade." Second, a proviso sponsored by labor unions specified that no action under the Act should reduce the number of employees below the level of those in service during the month of May 1933, save for those who would normally drop off the payrolls because of death, retirement, or resignation. But in no case was the number of employees in any one year to be reduced more than five percent below the number in service during May 1933; neither was any employee to be in a worse position with respect to compensation than during that particular month. Not only that, but the coordinator also was directed to require the carriers to compensate employees for any property losses or expenses imposed on them because of transfer from one locality to another if that should prove necessary to achieve some form of coordination or elimination of waste.

Title II of the Act of 1933 included numerous significant amendments of the basic Interstate Commerce Act. In the first place, the consolidation provisions were streamlined and expanded. The 1933 Act, in effect, gave the Commission authority over combinations regardless of how they were achieved, and brought holding companies expressly within the scope of the Commission's jurisdiction. But the new law left undisturbed the 1920 requirement that any permanent consolidations should conform with a fixed national plan.

A second far-reaching change was the retroactive repeal of the recapture clause. In fact, not only was it repealed; funds previously collected by the government were returned to the carriers who had paid them in. As this recapture clause had itself been based on the 1920 rule of rate-making whereby the I. C. C. was to authorize only such rates and fares as would bring a "fair return" on actual property value, amendment of this basic, but unworkable, premise was only logical. Accordingly, the Act of 1933 simply provided that the Commission should prescribe just and reasonable rates based on the effect such rates would have on the movement of traffic, on the provision of adequate and efficient railway transportation service at the lowest cost consistent with the furnishing of such service, and on the need of revenues sufficient to enable the carriers under honest, efficient, and economical management to provide such service. In other words, explicit reference to the value of the properties and to a fixed return thereon was eliminated. Henceforth, the Commission would be able to adjust rate levels on a flexible basis that would take into account, among other things, fluctuating economic conditions.

Clearly, it would be years before some effects of the Act of 1933 would make themselves felt in the industry and on the Burlington. In some other respects, however, the legislation had immediate results. Budd told his directors in July 1933, for example, that, in accord with the Act, the carriers' coordinating committees had already been established in the three major divisions of the country, and that for the Western District the five members were S. T. Bledsoe, president of the Santa Fe; Carl Gray of the Union Pacific; Hale Holden, then of the Southern Pacific; H. A. Scandrett of the Milwaukee; and Ralph Budd. This assignment promised extra work for all concerned. Shortly afterwards, the Burlington began the long chore of assembling vast quantities of statistical data for the surveys of transportation needs undertaken by the coordinator.

The coordinator's term of office eventually was extended to June 1936. His expenses, incidentally, were charged against the railways on a mileage basis; over his three-year term the Burlington was assessed $63,368 on this account, and during his first two years of office it spent an additional $140,000 in replying to questionnaires. Onerous as these charges were during the depression, they did contribute to the assembling and distribution of a wealth of information on the railway situation.

The coordinator issued four major reports, the first of which was published on January 20, 1934. Its main conclusion was that in view of the obvious impracticability of the government's assuming control of all railways, similar objectives should be reached by voluntary or compulsory coordination, consolidation, pooling, and a certain amount of administrative reorganization. The clause in the Emergency Transportation Act prohibiting reduction of employment below the May 1933 level should, he recommended, be repealed, whereas further government credit should be extended to the railways, but only for the duration of the emergency. The coordinator opposed retention of a rigid consolidation plan, but favored consolidation wherever it was in the public interest, and by compulsion if necessary. On this *First Report* the I. C. C. made no comment, but merely forwarded it to Congress. The *Second Report*, issued later in 1934, illustrated clearly the instability inherent in the rate structures and finances of road and water carriers and urged that these be appropriately regulated by the Commission. Eastman also recommended the early repeal of the Hoch-Smith Resolution. With these proposals the I. C. C. concurred enthusiastically. In the *Third Report*, published in January 1935, the coordinator expressed the opinion that railway costs could be considerably reduced if the companies would cooperate in the consolidation of terminal facilities and expand their programs in trucking, air-conditioning, and the adoption of Diesel power. Once again he called for regulation of trucks, water carriers, and possibly airplanes. He also recommended reorganization of the Commission, establishment of a permanent coordinator's office, substitution of a dismissal compensation bill for the rigid provisions for the maintenance of railway employment, expediting of bankruptcy proceedings, and encouragement of consolidation wherever and whenever it seemed wise rather than according to a fixed plan. The I. C. C. endorsed all these proposals except that calling for its own reorganization. And on August 9, 1935, as indicated earlier, the President approved those amendments to the Interstate Commerce Act known as the Motor Carrier Act. The coordinator's *Fourth Report* was issued on January 21, 1936. Its first and most important proposal again was a water-carrier bill. Eastman also recommended a system of dismissal compensation for employees displaced by any form of coordination.

As it turned out, this *Fourth Report* was the coordinator's last, for on June 17, 1936, without objection from railroads, shippers, labor, or the I. C. C., Congress allowed the office of coordinator to lapse. This is not the place to attempt an appraisal of the coordinator's efforts. His reports certainly brought to the nation's attention a mass of pertinent information and suggested the growing complexity of the transportation situation. But apart from the Motor Carrier Act, which extended limited federal regulation in one area, no specific steps to meet existing problems were taken at the national policy-making level. On the other hand, successive groups and boards continued to make studies and issue reports.

After an encouraging rise in railway revenues during the years 1934-37, the recession of late 1937-38 aggravated the old problems. President Roosevelt, early in 1938, suggested to Congress that it might be well to concentrate all federal executive functions relating to transportation in a new department of cabinet rank and to place all quasi-judicial and quasi-legislative matters in a single independent commission, possibly a reorganized I. C. C. These suggestions were later spelled out in a report compiled by a presidential Committee of Three, but the railways, speaking through the Association of American Railroads, insisted that it was more important that the carriers be given greater freedom in respect to rates and labor relations. In other words, a sharp difference in opinion arose as to which problems deserved priority. Nor did a series of conferences among representatives of management, labor, and the government prove more fruitful. Discussed were such possibilities as (1) federal loans of $300,000,000 to finance equipment, (2) liberalization of R. F. C. lending policies, (3) provision of work through the W. P. A. for furloughed employees, (4) regulation of water carriers, and (5) elimination of land-grant rates. But for the moment nothing was done in any of these specific directions.

In March 1939, Budd reported to his directors that the situation in Washington was "extremely confused and enactment of a general transportation bill seems unlikely at this session of Congress."[1] A month later, however, he observed that a bill introduced by Senator (later President) Truman for repealing land-grant rates would be helpful. And he spoke favorably of a much more comprehensive measure proposed by Senator Wheeler, providing for (1) a declaration of transportation policy, (2) regulation by the I. C. C. of water carriers and airlines, (3) revision of the Interstate Commerce Act concerning combinations and consolidations, (4) subjection of all modes of transportation to the long-and-short-haul clause, and (5) a mandate to the Interstate Commerce Commission to make a study of competitive subsidies granted to different forms of transportation.

After much discussion, complicated by varied and conflicting interests, the Transportation Act of 1940 became law on September 18 of that year. Broadly speaking, its objective was twofold: (1) adoption of a policy which would recognize the transportation revolution that was taking place, and (2) enactment of specific clauses to implement this new policy.

The policy statement in the Act which constituted, and still consti-

[1] PLD, March 8, 1939.

[430]

tutes, the official position of the government began thus: "It is hereby declared to be the national transportation policy of the Congress to provide for fair and impartial regulation of *all* modes of transportation subject to the provisions of this Act, so administered as to recognize and preserve the inherent advantages of each. . . ."[2] This statement, said Budd, in his opinion represented "the first major shift in governmental transportation policy since 1920, and commits Congress to a program for promoting a financially sound and well-coordinated transportation system."[3] On the other hand, it was apparent that the Commission could translate this declaration into reality only to the extent that Congress implemented it by specific provisions, and only if the Commission itself so interpreted the Act as to bring about the stated objectives.

Of prime importance among the specific provisions of the Act was Title III, which amended the basic Interstate Commerce Act to bring coastwise, intercoastal, and inland waterway carriers under the jurisdiction of the Commission. But even though the 1940 declaration of policy referred to "all" modes of transportation and also to "a national transportation system by water, highway, and rail, *as well as other means,*" no provision was included to bring the airways under the Interstate Commerce Commission; they were left under the separate supervision of the Civil Aeronautics Board in accord with the Act of 1938. Thus, despite the declaration of policy, the 1940 Act failed to provide for an integrated national transportation system.

The Act did, however, amend the consolidation provisions of the basic Interstate Commerce Act by finally dropping the requirement of a fixed plan. Instead, carriers were permitted to combine according to their own plans, provided that the I. C. C. found these plans consistent with the public interest. As a condition of approval, the commission could still require inclusion of one or more railroads in the area concerned, and, of course, it retained complete control over financial transactions involved in any combination. More novel, and an indication of the strength of organized labor, was the provision by the so-called "Harrington Amendment" that, during a period of four years following a consolidation, no employee's position could be worsened, except that such guarantee should not be valid for a period longer than that for which the employee had been in service.

A potentially significant change in the rate-making rule was made. Since 1933, the Commission had been obliged to give due consideration to the effect of rates on the movement of traffic; in 1940, it was made clear that the traffic in question was only that moved by the carrier or carriers for which the rates were prescribed. In other words, Congress sought to prevent the Commission from fixing rates for one type of carrier on the

[2] Transportation Act of 1940, 54 *Statutes-at-Large*, p. 899, September 18, 1940. Italics supplied.

[3] PLD, October 11, 1940.

basis of protecting the traffic of another. Still in the category of rates, the Act of 1940 embraced Senator Truman's proposals to the extent that the railways were authorized to charge the government full rates, fares, and costs for transportation of persons and property *except* for military or naval property and for personnel when on official duty. As it turned out during World War II, the exception proved far more important than the relief granted, yet the provision was significant in revealing the temper of Congress in respect to land-grant rates and as providing something of a precedent for eventual complete repeal.

Of immediate interest to the railroads, as Budd pointed out, were the broader powers that the Act conferred on the Reconstruction Finance Corporation in respect to helping carriers buy in their own bonds in order to reduce fixed interest charges. This was to have a prompt and beneficial effect for the Burlington, particularly so far as the Fort Worth and Denver City was concerned.

Finally, the Act of 1940 provided for a three-member Board of Investigation and Research, to be appointed by the President with the advice and consent of the Senate, to study (1) the relative economy and fitness of the various types of carriers, (2) the extent of public aids and subsidies both past and present, direct or indirect, and (3) taxation. In addition, the Board was authorized to investigate any other matters it might deem important for the improvement of transportation. Its term of office was limited to two years, but it could be, and eventually was, extended for an additional two years by the President.

When the Act was passed, no one could tell, of course, that during the active life of this Board the attention and energies of the country would be mobilized in a war effort, nor could anyone foresee that for primarily political reasons much of the Board's efforts would be drained away by a long and controversial study of interterritorial freight rates. Certainly the idea that the facts of transportation and its plans for the future should be thoroughly examined was a sound one, and it is notable that when the Transportation Act of 1958 was passed, a somewhat similar provision was included. How effective the rest of the 1940 Act would be in practice would depend largely on the interpretations placed upon it by the Interstate Commerce Commission.

• WAGES AND LABOR RELATIONS •

IN A BROAD SENSE the early New Deal legislation relating to railways during the 1930's was designed, directly or indirectly, to enable the roads to earn more revenue. Repeal of the recapture clause, liberalization of the consolidation provisions, increased regulation of motor vehicles and water carriers, and changes in the rate-making procedure—including the limited relief granted in respect to land-grant rates—were all expected to increase the railways' potential earning capacity.

This was only half of the picture. If expenses were not subject to effective control, it was entirely possible that even though revenues increased, costs might mount even more rapidly. The appointment of the federal coordinator in 1934 was a tacit recognition of this fact: insofar as he was charged with eliminating wasteful duplication of facilities, his objective was the control of expense. But the ironic, though obvious, fact of railroad operation as a whole was that the largest single item of railway expense was and always had been wages, and it was precisely at this point that the New Deal philosophy and legislation ran headlong into a dilemma.

One of the avowed objectives of the New Deal was to increase employment. Other objectives were to provide added security for labor, guarantee and enlarge its bargaining power, and provide what became known collectively as "fair labor standards." Each of these would clearly involve added expense, and although a relatively small portion of some of the costs, such as for Social Security, was to be borne by the ultimate beneficiaries, the vast bulk of the added expense would inevitably fall on the employers in the form of increased wages and of taxes not shared by employees. Thus, while the administration and Congress sought to rationalize and improve the regulatory structure during the years 1933–40 inclusive, they simultaneously followed a policy in respect to labor, particularly in the last five years of the decade, which tended to reduce net benefits to the railways, sometimes to and beyond the vanishing point.

On February 1, 1932, as indicated earlier, organized railway labor had accepted, in view of the hard realities of the depression, a deduction of ten percent from pay checks for a period of one year, and later acquiesced in the extension of the cut to June 30, 1934. On February 15, 1934, President Roosevelt suggested that the ten percent deduction be extended for at least six months. On the next day the railroads served notice of their intention to reduce, by fifteen percent, basic (that is, pre-deduction) rates of pay for a period of one year beginning on July 1, 1934, thus superseding the ten percent deduction scheduled to expire on June 30. This proposal was later modified to the extent of suggesting that the existing ten percent cut be continued in effect until April 30, 1935. Labor rejected this compromise proposal. It not only insisted on the elimination of the ten percent deduction, but also demanded a ten percent increase in basic rates of pay, to become effective July 1, 1934. Finally, on April 26, 1934, labor and management arrived at a mutually acceptable compromise under which one fourth of the ten percent deduction would be restored on July 1, 1934; a similar amount on January 1, 1935; and the remaining half on April 1, 1935, by which time wage rates would be back at the prosperity levels of 1929. Burlington figured that this piecemeal restoration would mean an addition of over $3,800,000 to the payroll.

June 1934 was something of a landmark in the history of railway labor legislation. On June 21, the President signed a bill amending the Railway

Labor Act of 1926 by substituting the National Mediation Board for the United States Board of Mediation and by establishing an entirely new National Railroad Board of Adjustment. Broadly speaking, the reconstituted Mediation Board possessed all the powers of its predecessor under the 1926 Act in that, by invitation or on its own initiative, it could intervene in railway labor disputes in an effort to settle them by mediation. Should this fail, it could propose arbitration. But if either party rejected this course, then the National Mediation Board could certify to the President that an emergency existed, whereupon the latter could name an Emergency Board to determine the facts of the case, with the presumption that public opinion would compel settlement of the dispute along the lines of the Emergency Board's recommendations. The various "cooling off periods" provided in the 1926 Act were left intact.

By far the most important innovation of the 1934 amendments was the establishment of the National Railroad Board of Adjustment, a notable victory for labor in that the new Board was on a national basis. It was to consist of thirty-six members, eighteen selected by the carriers and eighteen by the labor organizations.

The duty of this Board, acting through four divisions set up according to categories of employees, was to settle disputes over the long-standing working contracts in respect to rates of pay, rules, or working conditions. According to the law, it was up to labor and management in the first instance to try to work out a solution through conference; if they were unsuccessful, either party could refer the matter to the appropriate division of N. R. A. B. As membership of each division (and of the Board itself) was divided equally between management and labor, however, and the possibility of a deadlock was obvious, provision was made for appointment of a referee. If the members of a division could not agree on a mutually acceptable referee, one was to be appointed by the National Mediation Board. During the rest of the decade, at least one third of the cases before the Adjustment Board were decided by referees; all awards were binding on the parties involved, though the original petitioner (but not the defendant) was given the right of judicial appeal.

On June 27, 1934, six days after President Roosevelt had approved these 1934 amendments to the Railway Labor Act, he signed the Railroad Retirement Act, to become effective August 1. It provided for the retirement of railway employees at the age of sixty-five, except that upon mutual agreement between the employee and the carrier, retirement could be postponed from year to year but not beyond the age of seventy; for the first five years, compulsory retirement was not to apply to officers. Funds to pay the annuities outlined in the Act were to be secured through employee contributions of two percent on wages up to $300 monthly, with twice that amount to be contributed by the carriers. On the basis of the 1933 payroll, it was estimated that Burlington's contribution to the pension fund would amount to approximately $1,345,000 a year, as compared with the pension costs of about $1,200,000 then in effect. The law also provided that the Railroad Retirement Board of three members, appointed by the President, should have the power to substitute provisions of the Act for pension plans then in existence on the railways.

The railroads decided to contest the constitutionality of this Act, and won the first round when the Supreme Court of the District of Columbia declared the law unconstitutional. On May 6, 1935, by a five to four decision in *Railroad Retirement Board et al. v. Alton Railroad Co. et al.*, the Supreme Court of the United States did likewise, holding that the Act not only was contrary to the due process provisions of the Fifth Amendment but also was beyond the power of Congress under the commerce clause.

The point relevant to railway history and to the story of the Burlington in particular is this: the Railroad Retirement Act of 1934 was struck down by a margin of one vote in the opening phases of a tense national struggle that was to determine whether the experiment-minded administration and Congress or a conservative-minded court was to have the upper hand. As a practical matter, it was apparent as early as 1935 that railroad management had to take into account the very strong possibility that the slim majority of the Supreme Court that invalidated the Railroad Retirement Act might become a minority at any moment. It was therefore in the interests of the carriers to scrutinize not only the majority opinion in this particular case, but also the views of the minority, with the thought of working out some new measure which, if upheld, would be less onerous than the one struck down.

In the meantime, a far more concrete problem had arisen on the Burlington. The Brotherhood of Locomotive Firemen and Enginemen announced, on December 3, 1935, that on the basis of a poll among its 15,000 members on the system, it would strike on December 9 because the railroad had not placed a fireman on its four streamlined Diesel-electric trains and on three switchers. "There are no manual duties for a fireman to perform on this Diesel-electric equipment, and the request of the Brotherhood was presented solely under the guise that it is necessary for the safety of the employees and the traveling public," Budd explained to his directors.[4] On this issue alone the union took its stand, and the strike date was set in complete disregard of the contractual and legal requirements under which thirty days' notice was required to negotiate a desired change in existing agreements. The National Mediation Board assumed jurisdiction on December 6, and both sides accepted mediation.

In the opinion of the Burlington, it was entirely safe to operate the Zephyrs with the crew provided, and it was clear that if the company acceded to the demands of the firemen, a new principle would be established

[4] Budd to Overton, December 9 and 26, 1958.

that might, in time, constitute a heavy and, so far as safety was concerned, an unnecessary burden. The Burlington was prepared to fight to the last ditch. On the other hand, management realized that to insist on operation of a passenger train as novel and speedy as the *Pioneer Zephyr* with only one man in the cab would offend public opinion; this might appear to be a disregard of safety. Equally pertinent at the moment was the fact that it seemed impracticable for the Burlington to stand alone against the indifference or the opposition of other railways, who thought, then, that they had no interest in the controversy. As Budd put it later, "Burlington could not carry the contest with the firemen single-handed any farther than it did."[5]

In a conference in the President's office which lasted until midnight on December 8, 1935, just ahead of the strike deadline, Budd and Flynn finally agreed with D. B. Robertson, national chief of the firemen, to place an additional man on the four *Zephyrs* then in operation. By the closest possible margin, service was uninterrupted.

As matters then stood, the new settlement meant that about twenty additional men would be required to cover the runs of the four *Zephyrs*, at an added cost of approximately $50,000 a year. The precedent established, however, was of crucial importance. If the Burlington, and indeed other roads, continued to dieselize their operations on a substantial scale, the employment of a man they regarded as unnecessary for the safety of the train's operation might well present a problem of enormous proportions. Significantly, under a nationwide agreement between the Brotherhood of Locomotive Firemen and Enginemen and the railroads, effective March 15, 1937, all the railways agreed to employ a fireman on Diesel-electric and other internal-combustion engines. The immediate effect was to require the C. B. & Q. to place firemen on three Diesel-electric and two gas-electric locomotives used in yard service, at an estimated cost of $23,000 a year. This, as it turned out, was only the beginning.

Meanwhile, and indeed from the moment the Supreme Court declared the 1934 Railroad Retirement Act unconstitutional, representatives of labor and the carriers began to formulate a new act on which both could agree. As a result of their efforts, a second Railroad Retirement Act was approved on August 29, 1935, along with a companion measure called the Railroad Pension Tax Act of 1935, which was designed to raise funds for the payment of the annuities prescribed.

On June 26, 1936, the Supreme Court of the District of Columbia upheld the 1935 Railroad Retirement Act, but declared invalid the companion tax law that was to raise funds for it. To be on the safe side, the Burlington accrued the sums for which it might be liable until the issue was further clarified; both the railways and the unions continued their ear-

[5] Ibid.

nest negotiations to work out a satisfactory measure and settle the issue without further litigation. By the spring of 1937, agreement was reached; contributions from both labor and the carriers were reduced to two and three-quarters percent on salaries not in excess of $300 a month, to become effective retroactively from January 1, 1937; contributions were to increase gradually to three and three-quarters percent by 1949. Congress promptly incorporated these new provisions as an amendment to the 1935 Act, and they were approved on June 24, 1937.

For the Burlington the estimated 1937 cost of the new Act, which was to replace the company's own long-standing pension arrangements, was $1,444,050. All pensions previously granted under the voluntary plan in force on the system were discontinued, but in any case where the maximum annuity under the federal law was less than the monthly pension allowance that would have been paid under the company plan, the Burlington undertook to pay the difference each month until further notice.

The invalidation of the N. R. A. in 1935 had removed federal control over hours and wages generally, so a new law—the Fair Labor Standards Act—was enacted in June 1938 and became effective on October 24. Although railroad employees were expressly excepted from the maximum-hour provisions, they were subject to a minimum-wage clause which provided that the minimum should rise in graduated steps during the next seven years. The company estimated that in the first year, this would add $30,000 to the Burlington payroll. Infinitely more burdensome was the Unemployment Insurance Act, approved June 25, 1938, to become effective June 15, 1939. Under its provisions the railways, but *not* the employees, were called upon to pay a tax of three percent on all wages not in excess of $300 a month, this money to go into a fund from which employees would receive benefits during periods of unemployment. It should be noted carefully that these "unemployment benefits" would be paid to employees on strike. As the editor of *Railway Age* subsequently pointed out: "The railways are the one industry in the country which have to finance strikes against themselves."[6] This indeed was—and is—an ironic state of affairs. Total accruals for unemployment-insurance taxes on the Burlington were $1,330,575 during 1939 and slightly more in 1940.

As indicated above, wages for all classes of railroad employees were restored, on April 1, 1935, to the levels prevailing in 1929. With some improvement of business evident in 1936, railroad labor promptly presented demands for wage increases in the spring of 1937. On March 4, the fourteen non-operating organizations asked for increases of twenty cents an hour, along with a guarantee of full-time employment for all regularly assigned forces and a guarantee of two-thirds full time for all so-called "standby" forces. On March 22, the operating brotherhoods (locomotive

[6] *Railway Age*, Vol. CLV, No. 3 (July 15, 1963), p. 46.

engineers, locomotive firemen and helpers, conductors, and train and yard men) requested a twenty percent increase in all existing rates of pay, to become effective May 1. These demands by the national organizations were passed along to the individual roads in due course; by the end of the first week in April 1937, the C. B. & Q. had received notices from all organized employees on the Burlington except the dispatchers, whose national representatives were busy sponsoring a six-hour-day bill in Congress.

Carrier-labor negotiations on a national level were carried on separately with the operating and non-operating organizations. Agreement was reached with the latter group first, through the mediating efforts of the National Mediation Board. A settlement on August 5 provided for an increase of five cents an hour effective August 1 and withdrawal by the unions of a request for the stabilization of employment. On the basis of the 1936 payroll, the Class I railroads estimated that the increase would boost annual payroll costs after August 1, 1937, by approximately $100,-000,000; increased costs to the Burlington were estimated at $2,926,000.

Meanwhile, representatives of the five transportation brotherhoods met in Chicago on August 11 to discuss their requests. To strengthen their hand, the unions took a vote that authorized their executives to call a strike in case negotiations failed to produce a satisfactory solution. In this context, direct negotiations failed, and on August 25, the National Mediation Board offered its services. Agreement was finally reached on October 3, 1937, effective as of the first of that month, providing for an increase of forty-four cents, or six and a half percent, in all basic daily rates of engine and train service employees, and for an increase of $13.20 in the monthly rates of dining-car stewards and yardmasters. On the basis of the 1936 payroll, this represented an added cost of about $36,000,000 for all Class I railroads, and an increase of $1,109,000 for the Burlington. Taking into account a revised estimate of $2,681,000 as the increased cost of non-operating increases, this meant that the total increase for all classes of Burlington employees, beginning in October 1937, would amount to $3,790,000 a year, or 7.9 percent of the payroll based on 1936 employment.

The recession of 1937–38 naturally increased the "squeeze" experienced by the railroads as a result of declining revenues and mounting costs. Accordingly, on March 24, 1938, representatives of railway labor and management held a conference in Washington at which the carriers proposed a wage reduction. Labor flatly refused even to consider such a reduction on a voluntary basis. Under the circumstances, the member roads of the Association of American Railroads voted on April 29 to serve notice on the twenty-one rail labor unions of a fifteen percent wage reduction to become effective July 1, 1938. Based on 1937 payrolls, such a reduction would save the Burlington $8,156,940. Notice was officially served on the unions on May 12, whereupon negotiations were resumed, this time with the assistance of the National Mediation Board. But mediation failed completely, and the unions rejected arbitration, even though the railroads were agreeable to such a procedure. Consequently, on August 31, the Board formally notified the parties that its services were at an end. The unions, refusing to budge an inch, announced on September 26 that unless the wage-reduction proposals were withdrawn, a nationwide strike would be called. Thereupon, the President named an Emergency Board which began hearings on the last day of the month.

The railways' case rested on the grounds that they were in desperate financial condition, that no immediate improvement was in sight, and that only a reduction of wages could control expenditures and deficits. The unions did not question the serious financial condition of the roads, but maintained that this was a result of overcapitalization, improper financial practices, and other preventable wastes, and that therefore it was unfair to require labor to assume any of the burden arising from existing conditions. Furthermore, the employees alleged that railway wages had not increased as rapidly as those in other industries and that, in addition, they should receive higher wages because of the increased volume of tonnage handled per employee. To these contentions the carriers replied by denying that their situation was the result of either overcapitalization or financial malpractice. Further, they produced evidence designed to show that the increased operating efficiency of the roads was due primarily to better management and the heavy investment of additional capital rather than any increase in the efficiency or productivity of the employees.

When the Emergency Board filed its report on October 29, 1938, it found the chief reason for the condition of the railroads to be the rapid development of competitive carriers, such as buses, trucks, pipelines, and inland waterways. That competition, the Board said, had forced the railways between 1921 and 1937 to reduce rates to such a degree that a decline of approximately thirty percent in freight ton-mile revenue and a decline of forty percent in revenue per passenger-mile had resulted. Nevertheless, the Board took the view that the roads would have to solve their problem "by means more heroic than wage reduction," and flatly rejected the railroad's proposal for a fifteen percent cut.[7]

To their considerable chagrin, the carriers had to accept the finding, but it was felt in many a board-room that the decision boded ill for the future. Such fears were well founded, and as the 1930's drew to a close, the railways became increasingly alarmed by the awards of the Railway Adjustment Board, particularly in the extremely important cases decided by referees. This dissatisfaction found expression in the brief which the carriers filed during the summer of 1940 before the Attorney General's Committee on Administrative Procedure. Among their complaints were these:

Despite usual railway practice, and quite independently of agreements

[7] Harry E. Jones: *Railroad Wages and Labor Relations, 1900–1952* (New York: Bureau of Information of the Eastern Railways; 1953), pp. 106–9.

in force, the Board was applying the principle that certain operations had to be performed exclusively by a particular type of employee, even though the amount of work involved was small, and even if other employees were already being paid for doing it. Not only that, but if the specialized employee was not on hand to do his specific task, then the man who did do it (as part of his own work, for which he was already paid) should be paid additional wages. Furthermore, the Board was applying the novel principle that once a working agreement was made, the carrier was prevented from altering, without the consent of the employees, any particular method of operation that had been in effect at the time the contract had been signed, even though the contract itself did not preclude changes of methods as technology advanced. Again, the Board was ruling that positions could not be abolished if any of the work whatever attaching to specific jobs remained to be performed, and that those who had held positions abolished under these circumstances could collect back pay for the period of time during which they had not worked after the abolition of their jobs.

Finally, the Board was ignoring the provisions of the so-called starting-time rule in such a way as to compel employment and payment of crews during hours when they were not needed and to require payment on a penalty basis beyond all reason. Thus, if a rule prescribed that starting time should be 8:00 a.m. and the crew was to work eight hours, the Board held, in one particular case, that if that crew began at 7:30 a.m., its members were entitled to pay for twenty hours. The reasoning of the Board in this case was typical of the approach used in many other instances: the half hour from 7:30 to 8:00 was part of a different day, and because an eight-hour day was guaranteed, eight hours' pay was due for that one half hour. Furthermore, as the succeeding seven and a half hours fell within a twenty-four-hour period, this separate working day beginning at 8:00 a.m. had to be paid for at the rate of time-and-a-half, or on the basis of twelve hours. Thus, although the crew worked only eight hours, the Board ordered that they be paid for a total of twenty. That decisions of this sort—and these were by no means isolated examples—made railroad operation far more expensive than either necessity or equity warranted was painfully obvious.

An equally serious problem, already clearly apparent by the end of the 30's, was the fact that the procedures outlined in the 1934 amendments actually discouraged collective bargaining in the true sense. Because the unions came to feel that they could count on the kind of findings outlined above from a presumably neutral referee, who could assume the role of judge and jury and hand down binding decisions in accord with his particular ideas of justice, the advantage of settling differences by direct bargaining with the carriers was largely lost.

To observe the new dispensation at first hand was to court respectful disbelief, but the new rules meant just what they said. For example, on

Wednesday, October 11, 1939, when C. B. & Q. Number 6, the *Aristo-crat*, arrived in Galesburg from the West, it included among its passengers two elderly but very spry ladies who decided to make some purchases and write some postcards in the station while the train paused for servicing. Unfortunately, they became so engrossed that they failed to heed the train call. When they finally emerged on the platform, Number 6 was in sight, but far out of reach on its way to Chicago. Rushing back to the ticket window, they explained their plight. In a matter of minutes, orders were given to stop Number 6 by signal about three miles from the station, a mile or two beyond the yard limits. Meanwhile, the station master escorted his bewildered but relieved travelers to an empty coach standing at the platform and helped them aboard. A yard engine on duty nearby was coupled to the car, and off they went to catch up to the waiting Number 6, which they reached in five or six minutes. The grateful ladies, quite under-standably singing the praises of Burlington service, were carefully escorted from their special car to the regular train, and after a total delay of not more than fifteen or twenty minutes were on their way to Chicago. The yard engine and coach immediately returned to Galesburg, having spent something less than half an hour on its special errand.

It happened, however, that the company's top officials were aboard: Messrs. Budd and Flynn; James H. Aydelott, then general manager of Lines East; F. R. Mullen, general manager of Lines West; and Harry C. Murphy, then assistant to the executive vice-president. They discussed just what claims would be presented as a result of this bit of extra service. The yard engine crew, who performed the entire operation within their regular working trick, would be entitled to an additional day's pay as a road crew because they had traveled a mile or two beyond the yard limits to catch up with Number 6. A yard conductor and two switchmen on the special car carrying the two ladies would likewise obtain a full day's pay as a road crew. Furthermore, the next five men on the road-crew extra list, who, of course, were not called to duty and who performed no service whatever, would also be paid a full day's wages each for the simple reason that tech-nically they were the men who would have been the road crew (beyond the yard limits), had there been time to call them. Thus, even though the five crew members who actually performed the service were already being paid as yardmen, a full day's additional wages were payable to them and to five other men who did nothing at all.

This particular affair, of course, was relatively minor. It was handled on the basis of the agreement the Burlington had made on February 4, 1939, and in conformity with fundamental principles on the subject that had been agreed upon between the unions and the railroads effective March 1, 1939. But even this agreement received short shrift from the brotherhoods; their representatives continued to press cases that went be-yond the recently concluded arrangements, and in December 1940, a referee sitting with the First Division of the National Railroad Adjustment Board decided nineteen deadlocked Burlington cases in a manner that completely nullified the agreement of March 1, 1939. The rules in question described certain switching that could, presumably, be required of roadmen at terminal and intermediate yards where yard engines had been established, and provided what was thought to be an acceptable basis for compensating employees. Now, however, nullification of these rules by the referee would have, as Budd put it, serious results at points where traffic did not require continuous yard service. To rearrange or increase yard forces to conform with this decision would increase expenses about $800,000 a year, in addition to the awards themselves for additional pay claims. To make matters worse, seven other cases were also decided adversely to the railway by the same referee and contained "new principles" which promised to be equally expensive. Finally, eighty-four additional cases were pending before the same referee, many of them including claims for additional wages. "No appeal or court review," said Budd, "has been found to be available to railroads under the present law."[8]

In theory the company could refuse to pay the award, thus forcing the matter into court, but refusal to accept agreed arbitration would have affected public relations adversely. More to the point, however, as a practical matter the company did not feel it could afford to withhold payment, because of the strike threat. Under the circumstances, Budd entered into direct negotiations with the Grand Lodge Officers of the four train-service organizations in an effort to find a reasonable solution. The company agreed that the C. B. & Q. would pay the twenty-six disputed awards, at a cost of approximately $250,000. In an effort to afford relief from the undue burden of such awards in the future, however, it was agreed that representatives of labor and management would meet promptly for the purpose of negotiating modifications in the basic agreements themselves.

For the nation's railways as a whole, 1939 brought an increase of about twelve percent in total operating revenues; with the beginning of the defense program in 1940, revenues rose another eight percent over the 1939 total. Recovery on the Burlington, however, was far less marked than on the nation's railways as a whole. On the C. B. & Q. in 1939 there was an increase of about three percent over the previous year, but the gain of 1940 over 1939 was less than two percent. Nevertheless, the greater improvement on a national basis set the stage for a new set of wage demands from the brotherhoods.

Within a year the demands of labor and the rejections and counterproposals of management had achieved a tangle surpassing anything previously experienced. In May 1940, the fourteen non-operating railway labor unions demanded two weeks' vacation with pay; a similar demand was

8 PLD, December 9, 1940.

expected from the operating unions at any moment. In response, the western railroads, because their earning power was much less than that of roads in the East and Southeast, gave notice that unless the demand for vacations with pay was withdrawn, they would make a ten percent wage reduction. Divergence of opinion on this issue led to a split in the management camp, a factor certain to redound to the advantage of the unions.

As the spring of 1941 approached, it became obvious that employees in all branches of service planned to demand substantial wage increases in addition to vacations with pay; this led the roads by June 2 to announce their intention of eliminating featherbed rules. Eight days later, on June 10, the operating brotherhoods demanded a thirty percent increase in pay, and fourteen of the sixteen non-operating unions asked for an increase of thirty cents an hour. It was estimated that meeting the demands of the operating brotherhoods alone would entail an annual increase in Burlington expenses of $4,350,000.

Inevitably, negotiation failed, and the brotherhoods refused arbitration, which the carriers were prepared to accept. With a strike scheduled for September 11, President Roosevelt thereupon created an Emergency Fact-finding Board. Because the Railway Labor Act specified that no interruption of service could legally take place until thirty days after such a board had published its findings, the strike was temporarily averted.

The Board's report, submitted to the President on November 5, granted the demands of labor in degrees varying from twenty-five to fifty percent, such increases being temporary additions retroactive to September 1, 1941, and expiring on December 31, 1942, unless amended by agreement. The Board also recommended a six-day vacation with pay for non-operating employees. The railroad demands were not discussed, but were remanded for further negotiation between the parties concerned. In an *obiter dictum*, the Board commented on the financial state of the railways and recommended either increased rates or government subsidies to cover the additional costs involved. The railways accepted these findings with reluctance. The labor unions, however, flatly rejected them, and the operating brotherhoods issued notice that they would strike on December 7, 1941, unless greater and permanent increases were assured.

All the official machinery having failed, President Roosevelt attempted first to solve the problem with a series of informal conferences. When these proved fruitless, the Emergency Board was reconvened, but after two days, and in the absence of any new evidence, it announced that it could merely reiterate its previous recommendations. At the President's behest, the Board then met a third time to act as mediator. After two more days of almost uninterrupted conferences, the carriers agreed on December 2 to make even further concessions on every major issue. According to the settlement reached that day, the original increases recommended by the Board were to be applied retroactively to all wages paid between September 1 and November 30, 1941. Effective December 1, permanent advances in the basic rates of pay were to be made as follows: an increase of nine and a half cents an hour for operating employees and ten cents an hour for non-operating employees. The original recommendation in regard to vacations was retained but expanded so that clerical and telegraph groups would receive nine days' vacation after two years of service and twelve days after three years. The only *quid pro quo* that the railways received, if indeed it could be called that, was an undertaking by both parties to forego all changes in service rules for a period of eighteen months after December 1, 1941. As most of the changes were originally desired by the carriers, this was scant comfort.

On the C. B. & Q. alone, the annual payroll increase as a result of this settlement was calculated at $8,043,000. Small wonder that the railways promptly announced that they would file petitions with the Interstate Commerce Commission for an increase in both passenger fares and freight rates of approximately ten percent; these, for the most part, were granted about three months later.

Thus, the Burlington, in common with other railways, found that costs on account of wage adjustments and taxes for social security increased far more rapidly than revenues. As long as volume of business moved gradually upward, the railroads could to some extent absorb these increased expenses. But what took place in the last half of the 30's appeared to be largely lost on the policy-makers in Washington. There was, to be sure, an upswing in operating revenues; for the railways as a whole the 1931–35 annual average of less than three and a half billion dollars rose to an average of slightly over four billion for the 1936–40 period. The C. B. & Q. followed this national trend; its total annual operating revenues averaged approximately $86,000,000 during the five years 1931–35 inclusive, slightly less than $97,000,000 during 1936–40, inclusive.

But this modest revival in operating revenues—and this was the crux of the matter—did not mean that the financial problem of the rails was solved. During 1936–40, for the nation as a whole the roads took in about two thirds as much per year as they did during 1926–30. Their average net income for the later period, however, was less than one eighth of what it had been in 1926–30. On the Burlington, a railroad financially stronger than the average, operating revenues between the two periods followed the national trend, dropping during the 1936–40 period to approximately two thirds of the amounts realized during 1926–30. Net income, at the same time, averaged one sixth of what it had been before—better than the national average, but still far lower than the drop in total revenues would seem to warrant. Why?

The simple answer, and railway management was fully aware of it, was that recovery of earnings—as distinct from revenues—could not take place because it was impossible to control expenses, notably taxes and labor costs. Of course, as doubtless the planners in Washington knew, these expenses were rising for all business. In fact, raising the income of the average worker was an avowed objective of the administration, and the imposition of new taxes was certainly an inevitable result, if not a deliberate feature, of the new dispensation. But most businesses, unlike the railways, were free to raise the prices they charged, and even the regulated utilities other than railways were normally permitted to earn a rate of return that was approximately twice the 2.51 percent average the Class I roads earned during 1936–40, inclusive.

In respect to railway labor-management relations between 1934 and 1941 as a whole, and quite apart from rapidly mounting labor costs, several significant trends stood out among the welter of detail. Labor clearly won its long struggle for bargaining on a national basis. Thanks to the procedures and philosophy of the National Railroad Adjustment Board, labor also succeeded in enforcing the classification of jobs to the point at which the ordinary dictates of efficient operation entailed penalty payment of substantial proportions; this, in brief, was the basis of the featherbed issue. Finally, labor's refusal to accept the Emergency Fact-finding Board's recommendations in 1941 suggested, in rather alarming fashion, that the unions were not averse to interrupting service in order to gain their demands, despite the pressure of public opinion or the exigencies of national defense.

The railways, though resisting extreme demands, had seemed inclined to compromise rather than to fight to the last ditch, and in at least one case had suffered from divided counsels within the industry. If, as seemed likely in 1941, defense activities were to create more traffic, revenues might be in sight which would enable the roads to meet the mounting demands of labor. But whether the companies would unite to eliminate the basic inequities of onerous working rules and stand together when demands did not seem warranted remained to be seen. Certain it is that the years 1933–41 witnessed more drastic changes in the railway labor situation than had occurred in any other similar period. And, as it turned out, the precedents then established have served as a pattern ever since.

CHAPTER 24

Trouble in the West

1932-41

WHY DID THE Colorado and Southern–Fort Worth and Denver
City suffer more acutely from the depression of the 30's than
the parent company? Basic, of course, was the fact that the
Colorado and Southern system as a whole was located in more sparsely
settled territory. As a result, traffic movement was lighter. For example,
in 1934 freight density (revenue tons moved one mile per mile of road)
stood at 400,813 for the C. & S. Lines, in contrast to 786,151 for the
C. B. & Q. Average haul per ton on the C. & S. Lines for that year was
199.75 miles, as against 284.05 for the C. B. & Q.; average revenue train
load was 433.75 tons on the C. & S. Lines and 506.60 tons on the
C. B. & Q.

Another difference between the parent and its subsidiaries lay in the
greater diversity of traffic of the former. Of the traditional fixed commodity groups, the three that contributed the most traffic for the Colorado and Southern during the thirteen years between 1939 and 1941,
inclusive, accounted for 86.8 percent of all freight revenues, while the
top three on the Fort Worth and Denver City (including the Wichita
Valley) accounted for 84.9 percent. This was in sharp contrast with the
seventy-four percent contribution of the top three commodities on the
C. B. & Q. In other words, the C. B. & Q. was less dependent on particular commodity groups than the western lines were. Not only that, but
items within each group on the C. B. & Q. originated in a greater number

of places. For example, whereas the products of mines carried by that line came from many sources, the Colorado and Southern had become increasingly dependent on the soft coal and iron ore moved to the Colorado Fuel and Iron Corporation in Pueblo. When that traffic all but disappeared during the worst years of the depression, the C. & S. was hard hit.

On the other hand, movement on the Fort Worth and Denver City was not only heavier than that on the C. & S. in normal years, but also more varied. Wheat, cotton, refined petroleum, sugar, and lumber gave the Texas road a broader base of traffic that moved at higher rates. This was one important reason why the F. W. & D. C. enjoyed a consistently lower operating ratio than its northern counterpart. Furthermore, F. W. & D. C. was in a flat country and therefore had low grades, low maintenance-of-way costs, and easier and cheaper "transportation." Thus, for a variety of reasons, the Texas line could operate on a much more economical basis. During the thirteen years between 1929 and 1941, inclusive, it had an average operating ratio of 66.01 percent, in contrast to 78.83 percent for the Colorado and Southern.

Nor was this the full extent of the difference between the two principal members of the Gulf-to-Rockies route. During the same thirteen years, 1929–41 inclusive, total capitalization per mile on the F. W. & D. C. averaged approximately $38,000, the amount for 1941 being $40,492, or approximately four tenths of one percent more than it had been in 1929. The average figure, incidentally, was approximately $5,000 per mile less than the outstandingly conservative capitalization of the parent C. B. & Q. In sharp contrast, indeed, was the average total capitalization of the C. & S. for the 1929–41 period: nearly $104,000 per mile. Even more significant was the fact that total capitalization per mile on the C. & S. increased from $89,293 in 1929 to $125,726 in 1941.

In summary, then, the C. & S. Lines together served a more sparsely settled area than the parent C. B. & Q. and had a much lighter traffic density. They were more dependent on fewer commodities. And as between the C. & S. and F. W. & D. C., the latter was substantially stronger, both because of its traffic pattern and because of its far more modest capitalization. With these inherent strengths and weaknesses, the two principal western subsidiaries faced one of the most difficult periods of their existence.

This is not, however, the whole story. It will be recalled that between 1898 and 1908, the Colorado and Southern Railway acquired all the capital stock and bonds of the Wichita Valley Railway Company, the Wichita Valley Railroad Company, the Stamford and Northwestern Railway Company, and the Abilene and Northern Railway Company. Together, these roads owned the lines between Wichita Falls and Abilene, and between Stamford and Spur; all were operated by the Wichita Valley Railway Company, which paid rental on them to the C. & S. amounting, in 1931, to slightly over a quarter of a million dollars. Furthermore, in 1905, the Colorado and Southern had arranged to acquire control of the Trinity and Brazos Valley Railway. When completed in 1908, this road owned 303 miles of line, but, by virtue of its trackage arrangements, actually operated 455 miles. Meanwhile, in 1906, the C. & S. had agreed to sell one half of the capital stock and of the First Mortgage bonds of the T. & B. V. to the Chicago, Rock Island and Pacific Railroad upon completion of the former, with the understanding that the Rock Island should deliver to the T. & B. V. such through traffic as it could control or direct. A significant part of this agreement was that the C. & S. and the Rock Island should each advance one half of any deficits incurred by the T. & B. V. Despite the fact that both co-owners routed as much traffic over the "Valley Line" as possible, the results of this operation were not successful, and both the C. & S. and the Rock Island were called upon to advance large sums to cover operating deficits between 1908 and 1914. Even these measures were to no avail, and the property went into receivership on June 16, 1914.

When the Trinity and Brazos Valley emerged from receivership in 1930 and acquired, on July 7, the new name of Burlington–Rock Island Railroad Company, it was apparent that the new corporation could not hope to reimburse its co-owners for interest on its defaulted mortgage bonds or for advances made to it both before and during the receivership. Consequently, on June 1, 1931, the C. & S. and the Rock Island entered into a new agreement superseding that of 1906. Both proprietary companies again agreed not only to route such traffic as possible between the North and South Texas gateways over the Valley Line but also, of more immediate importance financially, to forgive all accumulated interest as well as certain outright debts. The amounts so purged from the Valley Line's accounts exceeded eleven and a half million dollars. The effect of this arrangement was to cut the accumulated deficit of the Valley Line from over ten million dollars at the end of 1930 to the relatively insignificant sum of $118,164 at the end of 1931 and to convert its net current deficit of over nine and a half million dollars to a net current asset figure of $509,510.

Moreover, the Burlington–Rock Island was not the only investment of the Colorado and Southern in that region. When the C. & S. had originally bought the Trinity and Brazos Valley, it had also acquired the Galveston Terminal Railway Company. As in the case of the T. & B. V., it eventually sold a half interest in the G. T. R. C. to the Rock Island. Both companies guaranteed payment of interest and principal of the bonds of the terminal railway. This too proved to be a financial burden to the C. & S., partly because of the receivership of the Rock Island in 1915, partly because the property itself was largely destroyed by the Galveston flood of that year. Not until June 1, 1931, were arrangements made to rehabilitate the Terminal property and to incorporate it into the system.

In summary, then, the half ownership of the Brazos Valley Line and the Galveston Terminal Railway had proved a trial and tribulation for the C. & S., and a distinct financial drain. In 1931, however, the new arrangement with the Rock Island for forgiveness of B.–R. I. debt, and rehabilitation of the Galveston Terminal lent hope that the properties in southern Texas might at last fulfill the aims of their original promoters.

Three other pieces of property complete the story. Both the Fort Worth and Denver South Plains Railway and the Fort Worth and Denver Northern Railway had been constructed by advances from the Colorado and Southern Railway which in total approximated eleven and three-quarter million dollars. Both, however, were operated by the Fort Worth and Denver City under leases by which it maintained the properties, paid the taxes, and paid a rental of six percent on the indebtedness to the C. & S. As of 1931, the F. W. & D. C. also owned the Fort Worth and Denver Terminal Railway Company and operated it under a lease.

The pertinent point as of 1931 was this: the Colorado and Southern and the Wichita Valley Railway were the only sources from which advances could be made from time to time to the companies they owned or operated. As a matter of fact, at the end of 1931, investment by the Colorado and Southern in affiliated companies amounted to twenty percent of the total capital assets of the corporation; advances to affiliated companies of the Wichita Valley amounted to thirty-seven percent of its total capital assets. In contrast, only three and a half percent of the total capital assets of the Fort Worth and Denver City were invested in affiliates. In 1931, interest on the funded debt of the Colorado and Southern was the equivalent of 170 percent of that company's net income, whereas on the Fort Worth and Denver City, interest amounted to only thirty-nine percent of net income. On the Wichita Valley, interest represented eleven and a half percent of that company's deficit. In general terms, then, the C. & S. was particularly vulnerable to the ups and downs of business. In this respect, the Fort Worth and Denver City was in a far more favorable position.

• THE COURSE OF THE DEPRESSION •

AT THE END OF 1931, the C. & S. surplus stood at a record high of well over 15 million dollars while that of the Fort Worth and Denver City exceeded 10 million. It should be clearly understood, however, that "surplus" represented largely retained income that had been plowed back into the plant rather than kept as cash. Its existence therefore had little relation to the company's ability to withstand depression. Even though, for the first time, the Wichita Valley Line showed a small net deficit, that of itself was hardly disconcerting. The cash position of all three roads at the end of 1931 appeared sound: the C. & S. had a record-breaking amount of nearly three and a half million dollars, the F. W. & D. C. nearly two and a half million, and even the Wichita Valley had over eight hundred thousand. As far as the Burlington–Rock Island was concerned, the "clean slate" resulting from the agreements concluded in June 1931 seemed to have paved the way for better times. Under the circumstances, therefore, payment of a four percent dividend on the first and second preferred stocks of the C. & S., with no payment on the common, and a substantial payment on Fort Worth stock (though reduced from 1930) appeared to be entirely in line with available resources.

Unfortunately, the actual results of operations during the rest of the 30's fell far short even of the cautious hope existing at the end of 1931. All the operating companies suffered abrupt losses in 1932 when the vital freight revenues of the C. & S., F. W. & D. C., and B.–R. I. dropped to approximately two thirds of 1931 levels. Total operating revenues remained in a trough through 1935. A modest revival followed in 1936 and a somewhat better one in 1937, only to be succeeded by a discouraging decline which persisted until it was reversed by the stimulus of defense traffic generated by World War II.

Basically, of course, the underlying cause of distress was the national business depression. But special factors operated all along the western lines of the Burlington system and compounded the difficulties. Generally speaking, the succession of unusually dry years between 1932 and 1937, coupled with the diversion of grain and cotton to trucks and the decline in rates, added to the woes of all lines in Texas. A brief revival took place in 1937, when crops were good, but the next three years were again unusually dry. Farther north, on the Colorado and Southern, drought in the early years of the decade and again in 1939, as well as serious diversion of traffic by trucks, took their toll too, but the most serious blow was the fact that not a ton of iron ore was handled in 1932, and business from the mines remained light for the next two years and fell off again in 1938–39.

Despite these discouragements, the companies in their several ways tried their best to find new business and to cut costs. On October 1, 1936, Burlington *Zephyr* Number 9901—one of the original Twin Cities trains— was put on the Houston–Dallas–Fort Worth run, inaugurating the first streamlined passenger service in the entire Southwest. Christened the *Sam Houston Zephyr* and covering the run from Dallas to Houston in four hours, it immediately gained immense popularity. On August 29, 1937, the Rock Island established a companion service over the line with the *Texas Rocket*. As a result, passenger revenues of the Burlington–Rock Island in 1937 showed an increase of 116 percent. Here was evidence that the roadbed and track of the Burlington–Rock Island had been vastly improved since the days of the receivership, and that the company intended to fight for business despite the depression. The financial results of the Burlington–Rock Island over the decade, however, were not only discouraging but serious in their effect on the Colorado and Southern Lines as a whole. Although total operating revenues revived in the later 30's, net railway operating income was in the black only once—and then to the amount of $355—during the entire decade. Not once did the company even come close to covering its fixed charges; net losses for the decade of 1932–41 averaged in excess of three quarters of a million dollars a year. By the end of 1941, the debit profit and loss balance exceeded $11,000,000. Since the Colorado and Southern was obligated to meet half these losses, the impact on the parent company was obvious.

The record of the Wichita Valley Railway was somewhat better. It was able to earn some net railway operating income each year, but, even so, reported net deficits consistently throughout the decade. One immediate result of this situation was that neither the Wichita Valley Railway Company itself nor the subsidiaries it operated could pay interest on their bonds to the Colorado and Southern. Some partial payments were made in 1933, and one was made in 1938; otherwise, all bonds were technically in default, and by the fall of 1931 the Wichita Valley Lines owed the Colorado and Southern nearly two million dollars on account of unpaid interest. This, to be sure, was a smaller burden than that incurred on account of the Burlington–Rock Island, but the two together represented a loss to the C. & S. of approximately seven million dollars. It should be emphasized that this burden was above and beyond the troubles the C. & S. was having in its own territory. As the 30's wore on, the question increasingly became whether the Colorado and Southern, with such assistance as the Fort Worth and Denver City might be able to provide, could weather the storm.

• THE MOBILIZATION OF INTRA-SYSTEM RESOURCES, 1932–38 •

A CLOSER LOOK at the revenue figures of the C. & S. reveals that, standing on its own feet, the company was earning about what could be expected. In only two years (1932 and 1938) during the decade 1932–41, inclusive, did total operating revenues fail to improve over those of the previous year, and in only one year (1932) did the company fail to show a net railway operating income. With its obligation to pay its own fixed charges and to support all Texas lines except the Fort Worth and Denver City, the company found it exceedingly difficult, and much of the time impossible, to carry net railway operating income over into net income, particularly in years when the C. & S. itself received little or nothing as dividend income from the Fort Worth and Denver City. Indeed, it was precisely on this point—the extent to which the Fort Worth and Denver City could and should pay dividends to the Colorado and Southern—that the situation seemed to focus.

The problem facing top management was tough. From a strictly short-run financial point of view, the C. B. & Q. itself was, by the force of circumstances, almost in the position of a disinterested party, for it could survive without dividends from the Colorado and Southern, as indeed it did for twenty-one years after 1931. On the other hand, the book value of the C. B. & Q. investment in Colorado and Southern stock stood at $21,398,460, and the obvious risk was that this would be wiped out if the company should fall into receivership. Another intangible but no less powerful factor was at work: the Colorado and Southern and all its affiliated companies were, both in fact and in the eyes of the public, a part of the Burlington Lines. No member of the Burlington family had ever defaulted on its obligations or gone into bankruptcy while under control of the C. B. & Q. Thus, even though the C. B. & Q. had, for example, no responsibility whatever for paying interest on C. & S. bonds, it nevertheless felt a strong moral obligation beyond its financial investment to keep that company and its affiliates solvent.

The question resolved itself into what help, if any, the Fort Worth and Denver City could and should give the Colorado and Southern. The problem posed a familiar dilemma. If the Colorado and Southern became insolvent, it could no longer support the lines it owned in Texas either by making up deficits or by foregoing interest owed to it. And unless it did one or both, the Texas branch lines, and particularly the B.–R. I., would inevitably go bankrupt. On the other hand, if the Fort Worth and Denver City should be unduly weakened by the payment of dividends, particularly from surplus, it might itself become a burden and be unable to discharge its prime obligation to serve its own territory adequately.

In 1932, net income of the Fort Worth was but slightly more than half what it had been in 1931; in 1933 it was less than a third of the 1931 figure. Consequently, in neither of those years did the F. W. & D. C. pay anything in dividends to the Colorado and Southern. In 1932 the C. & S. reported the highest net deficit in its history: $1,269,824.28. Although C. & S. traffic revenues improved modestly in 1933, and expenses were controlled better, the company's deficit that year was still $943,389.56. Clearly, any help available from the Fort Worth and Denver City would be more than welcome in 1934.

Under the circumstances, the directors of the F. W. & D. C. authorized a payment of eight percent on the F. W. & D. C. stamped stock, amounting to just over $200,000.[1] As all but a few shares of this stock belonged to the C. & S., the net effect was to reduce the C. & S. deficit by the amount of this payment. Even so, when the year had ended, that company reported a loss of $854,157.55.

[1] For a description of this stamped stock, see Overton: *Gulf to Rockies*, pp. 341–51.

The deficit of the B.–R. I. exceeded one million dollars in 1935. But the net loss of the Wichita Valley was somewhat reduced, and other features on the main line were encouraging. Agricultural production inched ahead on the C. & S., and later in the year abundant rains in Texas put ranges into splendid condition. Nothing approaching a general recovery occurred, however, and the prime financial necessity of the year was to meet the maturity of the Colorado and Southern's four percent Refunding and Extension Mortgage bonds, due May 1, 1935, in the amount of $28,978,900. With the approval of the I. C. C. and of the General Mortgage bondholders, arrangements were made to extend the maturity date of the R. and E. bonds to May 1, 1945. More important, the Reconstruction Finance Corporation agreed to purchase at par all such bonds presented through September 30, 1935. By the end of the year, the total amount of extended bonds in the hands of the R. F. C. amounted to $27,925,300; the rest were purchased by the company and canceled.

The net effects of this refinancing were to relieve the C. & S. of the need to pay off any substantial amount on the principal of these bonds and to ease the burden of interest. On the other hand, to effect these desirable ends the C. & S. had required $1,053,600 cash. Accordingly, during 1935 the F. W. & D. C. made dividend payments totalling $1,941,198. This dividend disbursement enabled the C. & S. to carry out its refinancing and other obligations; despite this substantial outlay, the net deficit of the Fort Worth and Denver amounted to only slightly over $38,000, considerably less than in the preceding year. On the other hand, the C. & S. was able to show a substantial net income and to build its cash position back to over one million dollars. Thus, in one of the most difficult years of the decade, the financial equilibrium of the system was maintained.

Traffic was more hopeful in 1936, and the C. & S. Lines as a whole enjoyed a fourteen percent increase in total operating revenues, although operating expenses increased almost ten percent, largely because of the restoration (as of April 1, 1935) of the deductions that had been made in 1932 from all basic wages. As had been true throughout the decade, net railway operating income of the Fort Worth and Denver City in 1936 was more than twice that of the Colorado and Southern. Under the circumstances, the Texas road made a dividend disbursement of $739,504. After these transactions, the Colorado and Southern showed an extremely modest net income of slightly over $22,000, and the Fort Worth and Denver City reported just over $25,000. In terms of net income, equilibrium had again been achieved.

During 1936, one piece of significant refinancing took place on the Fort Worth and Denver City. All the company's five and a half percent First Mortgage bonds, due in 1961, and amounting to $8,176,000, were called and retired at a premium of five percent. To provide funds for the

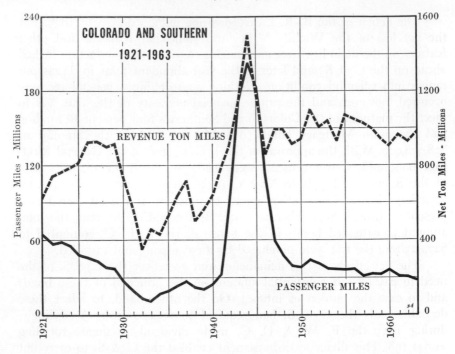

purpose, a new First Mortgage of like amount was issued, but at the lower rate of four and a half percent. These bonds in turn were pledged with the R. F. C. as collateral for a loan of $8,176,000 bearing interest at four percent and maturing in 1946.

The best news of 1937 was the exceptionally good yield of crops in Texas; the F. W. & D. C. handled almost three times the number of tons of wheat shipped the previous year. Largely as a result of this factor, total operating revenues for the Colorado and Southern Lines increased nearly thirteen percent over 1936; operating expenses went up a little over eight and a half percent, owing partly to the increase of wages, partly to rising prices of fuel and other materials. Even so, the F. W. & D. C. earned a net income of almost three quarters of a million dollars, the C. & S. slightly over a quarter of a million.

Although in 1938 both the Burlington–Rock Island and the Wichita Valley enjoyed modest increases in total operating revenues, the combined net loss on the two properties was approximately $850,000. But the most discouraging feature of the year was the sharp decline in C. & S. revenues and in those of the F. W. & D. C. A combination of the so-called "Roosevelt Recession" and continued bad weather accounted for a net decrease of nearly fourteen percent in operating revenues of the C. & S. Lines. Net railway operating income of the C. & S. for 1938 was only little over $100,000; furthermore, as the Rock Island was in reorganization under Section 77a of the Bankruptcy Act, the C. & S. was forced to assume

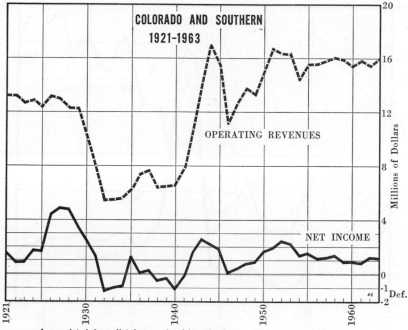

Appropriated from Net Income for debt reduction:
1942–$1,303,184; 1943 - 1951–All; 1952–$571,049.

sole responsibility for refinancing $1,072,000 bonds of the jointly owned Galveston Terminal Railway Company, which matured on March 1, 1938. By borrowing $525,500 from the Reconstruction Finance Corporation on a note maturing March 1, 1944, the C. & S. was able to purchase $526,000 par value of these bonds; it then arranged for the R. F. C. to take up the remaining $546,000 bonds and extend them to March 1, 1948.

Once again it was apparent that dividend income from the Fort Worth and Denver City could play an essential part in supporting the hard-pressed Colorado and Southern. With net railway operating income of slightly over $900,000, the Texas company was again, as usual, in a stronger position than its northern neighbor. Accordingly, even though it reported a net deficit of slightly over $120,000, its directors declared a dividend of five percent, amounting to $462,190, all of which was drawn from surplus. As a result, the C. & S. wound up the year with a deficit of slightly over $450,000, an amount that would have been approximately doubled had it not been for dividends received from the Texas company.

• The Lease Proposal, 1939–41 •

ALTHOUGH BUSINESS IMPROVED SLIGHTLY on the C. & S. as 1939 wore on, extreme dryness persisted in Texas, and it was soon apparent that revenues for the year would be substantially lower than those for 1938. The time

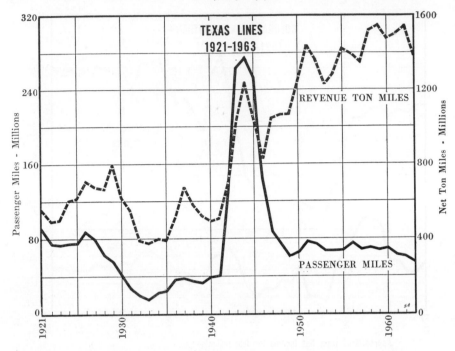

for drastic, positive action was clearly at hand, and in the opinion of management the simplest and most effective way to make substantial and lasting economies would be to combine the Colorado and Southern and the Fort Worth and Denver City in such a way as to eliminate duplicate forces, particularly in the general offices and shops. Such a combination, in whatever way achieved, would also greatly simplify all accounting procedures. Since, because of charter restrictions, the Fort Worth and Denver City had less freedom of action than the C. & S., and since all the system's extensions and subsidiaries in Texas had been financed by the Colorado and Southern, it appeared simpler to let that company play the dominant role, even though, as something of a *quid pro quo*, the Burlington was perfectly willing to change the name of the combined property to Fort Worth and Denver Railway. On June 28, 1939, the Colorado and Southern applied to the Interstate Commerce Commission for authority to lease the properties owned and operated by the Fort Worth and Denver City and by the Wichita Valley Lines, and to assume liability for the former's note of $8,176,000 held by the Reconstruction Finance Corporation.

The details of the proposed lease were simple enough. It was to run for twenty-five years, except that it would be terminated at once if the C. & S. became bankrupt. During its term, the Colorado company would lease all the properties and assets of the Texas roads, and assume their obligations. The significance of the arrangement and the crux of all subsequent controversy lay in the fact that there would be a net decrease

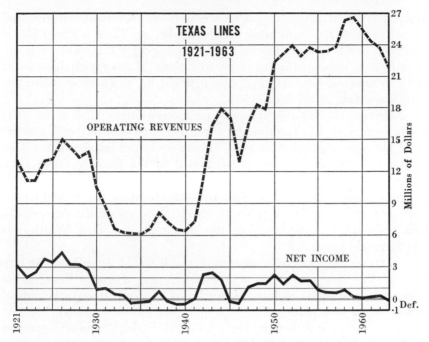

of 184 positions. In functional terms, the plan contemplated moving the top management of the Texas Lines, along with the Accounting Department, to Denver and transferring the heavy repair work done at Childress to shops on the Burlington system, although light repairs would continue to be made at Childress. No change was contemplated in the size or disposition of traffic forces or in the quality and quantity of service to be rendered to the public. The latter, it was confidently expected, would actually be vastly improved, and it was estimated that beginning with the sixth year after the lease became effective, net saving under the new plan would amount to at least $323,538 a year.

Announcement of this plan in Fort Worth had the effect of a bombshell. The fact that it had not been publicly discussed prior to its submission to the Interstate Commerce Commission led one journalist to characterize the whole scheme as a "Burlington Blitzkrieg against Texas."[2] Opposition was strong, swift to mobilize, and grimly determined. Opponents of the plan admitted that the railroad had to economize to meet changed conditions. What stirred their passions to the boiling point was the conviction that the plan would produce results quite opposite to those intended, that it was grossly unjust in view of the unwavering support Texans had accorded to the "Denver Road" for more than sixty

[2] This was the title of a publication issued in 1940 in Fort Worth by a group formed by Amon Carter and others called "The Committee Organized to Oppose the Removal of the Fort Worth & Denver Headquarters from Fort Worth and the Closing of the Shops at Childress."

years, and that it constituted a mortal blow to that most sensitive and vital element of all, Texas pride. On November 25, Texas interests filed a brief with the I. C. C. examiner, vigorously opposing the entire proposal. Thus matters stood as the year drew to a close. The company felt that it had a strong case, however unpopular it might be, and a good chance for gaining approval of the lease.

Although the net railway operating income of the C. & S. for 1939 was between four and five times as great as it had been in 1938, another net deficit was in sight. As the net railway operating income of the Fort Worth and Denver was almost twice that of the C. & S., logic again pointed to the disbursement of another five percent dividend of exactly the same amount as in 1938—$462,190—which, as in the previous year, was taken from surplus. As a result, the C. & S. ended the year with a deficit of slightly over $275,000; the deficit on the Fort Worth was approximately $225,000.

As far as the future was concerned, much would depend on the outcome of the lease application. On July 31, 1940, Division Four of the Interstate Commerce Commission concluded that even though the annual savings under the proposed plan would probably not exceed $250,000 beginning with the fifth year, the plan would indeed eliminate needless duplication. The proposal, they held, was fully consistent with prevailing transportation policy and should therefore be granted. The Division took careful note of the vigorous opposition so vocal in Texas, but expressed the hope "that antagonism will not be as serious as suggested on oral argument."[3] As might have been expected, those opposing the lease were unwilling to let matters rest, and promptly petitioned for a rehearing and postponement of the order of July 31. This request was granted by Division Four on August 29; the case was thereupon docketed for consideration by the entire Commission.

Meanwhile, despite the storm swirling around the lease and the still serious financial situation, the C. & S. Lines offered striking evidence of their determination to improve service. The first step was the inauguration, on June 2, of the *Advance Texas Zephyrs*, Diesel-powered conventional trains between Denver and Fort Worth–Dallas which, by means of close connections with the *Sam Houston Zephyr* and the *Texas Rocket* of the B.–R.I., chopped over eight hours from the Houston–Denver trip. These were harbingers of the two new *Texas Zephyrs* that went into regular service on August 22-23. Pulled by 4,000-hp Diesels, each train included stainless-steel baggage, mail, and express cars, two chair cars of the latest design, three specially converted sleepers, and a gleaming diner–observation–lounge.

On September 18, President Roosevelt signed the Transportation Act of 1940. Among other things, and as indicated previously, this new law

[3] 240 ICC 654–7.

amended Section 5 of the Interstate Commerce Act by incorporating in it the so-called Harrington Amendments specifically designed to protect labor displaced by consolidation or by the lease of one railroad by another. The new provisions superseded the informal Washington Agreement, and therefore changed the criteria by which the Colorado and Southern had reckoned its estimated savings. Under the circumstances, the I. C. C. ordered the C. & S. to file an amended application. This the railroad did on November 1, and new hearings were held in Washington on December 2 and 3, 1940.

One point to consider was the fact that the net deficit of the C. & S. Lines for the first nine months of 1940 exceeded a million and a quarter dollars, as compared with a net deficit of $981,000 for the comparable period in 1939. Presumably, then, if the system had needed relief in mid-1940, it needed it even more in the spring of 1941. A second point to consider was the probable effect of the Harrington Amendments. The railroad contended that even under their provisions, savings under the proposed plan would eventually exceed $300,000 annually. A majority of the Commission, however, was concerned by the fact that the skilled railway labor which would be released might have difficulty in finding other employment and that future savings under the plan were uncertain and problematical. Furthermore, they stressed the fact that the Texas road was stronger than the C. & S., "with the greater probability of survival if not encumbered by consolidation with the applicant." Indeed, they went further, inferring that one purpose of the lease was to prevent or delay financial reorganization of the Colorado and Southern. They were not so sure that the public interest would be served by such delay; if the lease were approved, bankruptcy of the Colorado and Southern would then "probably have the effect of disabling the Fort Worth and Denver City from continuing as a separate property."[4] Accordingly, by a vote of six to four, the application of the C. & S. was denied by the full Commission on June 9, 1941. Under the circumstances, the entire plan was dropped, and in its stead management determined to embark upon a thorough-going long-run voluntary debt adjustment.

• VOLUNTARY DEBT ADJUSTMENT, 1941–43 •

THE FINANCIAL CONDITION of the Colorado and Southern Lines as a whole had been steadily worsening. Income available for fixed charges during the preceding decade had been sufficient to cover them only in 1931 and in 1937, and the combined deficit for the C. & S. Lines had reached a peak of $1,246,168 in 1940. Furthermore, during the years 1934–39, inclusive, the Fort Worth and Denver had withdrawn nearly $4,000,000 from surplus to make payments on stamped stock or to declare dividends. By the end of 1940, its total surplus had been reduced to approximately five and

[4] ICC, Docket #12460, June 9, 1941, pp. 13–15.

three-quarter million dollars, just over half of what it had been in 1931. Its cash position was at the lowest point in more than a decade. Even though no dividends had been paid since 1939, the Texas road plainly could not be counted on for further aid to its northern sister. The position of the Colorado and Southern was even more discouraging; its cash position was clearly inadequate.

Accordingly, in mid-September 1941, the company announced a plan for the voluntary extension of maturities and the adjustment of interest on Colorado and Southern bonds, designed to reduce fixed charges from over $2,000,000 a year to slightly less than $1,000,000. The plan did not change the capital structure of the company, shrink invested principal of bondholders, disturb liens or collateral, or change any of the several classes of capital stock. In brief, the details of the proposal were as follows:

(1) The Reconstruction Finance Corporation, as owner of the entire issue then outstanding of the C. & S. four and a half percent, Refunding and Extension bonds of 1945 in the amount of $27,443,200, was asked to accept fixed interest at the rate of two and a half percent and contingent interest (that is, payable only if earned) at the rate of one and a half percent, making a total of four percent, a rate which the R. F. C. agreed to accept.

(2) Holders of the $20,000,000 four and a half percent General Mortgage bonds due in 1980, most of which were publicly held, were asked to reduce the total interest rate to four percent and to accept fixed interest at the rate of one and a half percent and contingent interest at the rate of two and a half percent.

(3) All bondholders, including the R. F. C., were asked to consent to an extension of maturities for ten years or more (but in no event beyond January 1, 1955) on all obligations maturing between 1944 and 1948, including notably the Refunding and Extension bonds of 1945 and various other notes.

To be made effective, the plan required the assent of the Reconstruction Finance Corporation and of the holders of eighty-five percent of the General Mortgage bonds, and, of course, approval by the Interstate Commerce Commission. No provision was made for payment of any dividends by the C. & S. during the life of the plan. Thus, the C. B. & Q., as controlling stockholder, agreed in advance to forego any dividends, even if earned, while the plan was in effect.

Reaction to the plan in Wall Street was mixed, though generally favorable. The attitude of institutional bondholders, notably the large insurance companies, was one of cautious cooperation, and during the fall J. C. James, vice-president and general counsel of the Burlington and chief architect of the plan, and his assistants held several meetings designed to answer various detailed questions and to secure active cooperation. Meanwhile, half a dozen representatives of the Colorado and Southern combed virtually every state of the union in an effort to secure assents to the plan from the individual holders of the General Mortgage bonds. By mid-November, however, the situation had become something of a stalemate. Although a substantial majority of the General Mortgage bondholders, the R. F. C., and the insurance companies had given their assent, those favoring the proposal did not yet constitute eighty-five percent of all holders. Those who withheld assent appeared unwilling to commit them-selves definitely until the plan had been passed on by the Interstate Commerce Commission. The company accordingly withdrew its soliciting forces from the field and set to work on a formal application to present to the Commission. Thus matters stood as the year closed.

A quick survey of the four operating companies in western territory indicated some hope for the future, but still a most serious situation. During 1941, total revenues on the Burlington–Rock Island had declined slightly while those of the much smaller Wichita Valley had made a modest increase; combined operating deficits of the two systems, however, amounted to almost $975,000. The two major companies were faring better. Total revenues on the C. & S. rose from approximately six and a half million to almost eight million dollars, while the Fort Worth and Denver City enjoyed a more modest increase from approximately 5.9 million to over 6.7 million. As a result, net loss on the C. & S. for the year was but slightly over $50,000 while the F. W. & D. C., for the first time in four years, was in the black, to the extent of approximately $160,000. On a combined basis, the net loss of the C. & S. Lines of $1,246,168.18 in 1940 had been converted to a net income for the two roads in 1941 of $63,950.89. Of basic importance, weather conditions were most favorable throughout the system and excellent crops were harvested. On the other hand, at the end of the year a special Board of Mediation granted sub-stantial wage increases which, based on 1941 payrolls, would mean in-creased costs in 1942 of approximately $925,000. Although some of this added burden might be offset by increased rates, the higher tariffs were not scheduled to become effective until March 1942. Thus there were grounds for caution as well as for hope in the months lying ahead.

In an order dated August 31, 1942, the Interstate Commerce Com-mission approved the company's voluntary debt reorganization plan, and solicitation of bondholders to accept it was put underway immediately. Very shortly thereafter, on October 16, 1942, President Roosevelt approved the McLaughlin Act, which, among other things, permitted a railroad in the position of the Colorado and Southern to file its plan in a competent federal court when two thirds of the holders of all its outstanding bonds and fifty percent of the holders of any one issue had assented to such a plan. When sixty percent of the holders of each issue had indicated their assent, the court could pass on the merits of the plan and, if so inclined, issue an order declaring it effective.

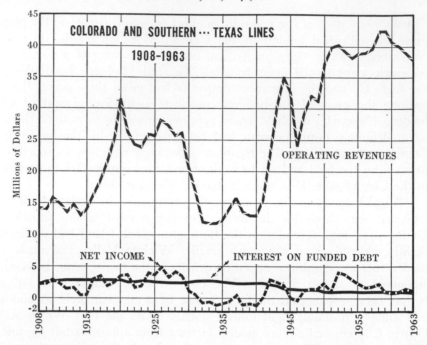

On November 9, 1942, therefore, the C. & S. filed a petition pursuant to the McLaughlin Act, in the District Court of the United States at Denver. By this time earnings for September and for the first nine months of 1942 were available and reflected the phenomenal rise in freight and passenger traffic incident to requirements of the war. As it eventually turned out, the company earned not only all fixed, but also all contingent, interest under the plan throughout the calendar year 1942. Thus the only sacrifice made by any bondholder was in accepting total interest at the rate of four percent rather than four and a half percent. By early 1943, more than seventy-five percent of all bondholders of the C. & S. and more than sixty percent of each class had assented to the plan. Consequently, the court at Denver on March 8, 1943, approved the plan and declared it in effect as of November 1, 1941.

At long last substantial grounds existed for hoping and believing that the financial troubles of the Burlington's western lines were coming to an end. As had been the original objective, fixed charges for the C. & S. system were now reduced from over two million to under one million dollars, and the steadily rising revenues resulting from war traffic gave hope that a substantial amount of earnings above and beyond that required for interest could be applied toward retirement of C. & S. system debt. The extent to which this could be accomplished would depend, of course, on the degree to which the war effort would stimulate business.

CHAPTER 25

The Financial Challenge

1 9 3 1 - 4 1

· THE PARTIES AT INTEREST ·

THE ENTIRE C. & S.–F. W. & D. C. situation during the 30's was important to the C. B. & Q. because the inability of the combined roads to pay any dividends after 1931 substantially reduced "other income" of the parent company. Furthermore, that period witnessed drastic reorganizations and reduction of fixed charges on the part of the competitors of the Burlington. The vast Missouri Pacific, the Rock Island, the North Western, and the Milwaukee all sought the protection of the courts. The fact that these roads while in receivership had to pay no interest or dividends allowed them to spend money for improvements. In contrast, such solvent roads as the Burlington, the Great Northern, the Northern Pacific, the Union Pacific, and the Santa Fe in varying degrees did two things which, under the circumstances, were not easy: (1) made improvements and betterments to their physical plants in order to keep up with technological advances and at the same time maintain credit by paying interest and some dividends, and (2) reduced debt and fixed charges so as to be at as little disadvantage as possible after their competitors emerged from reorganization proceedings.

As far as the C. B. & Q. was concerned, a third and equally binding obligation existed: its principal owners were two railways that had been particularly hard hit during the depressed 30's. Great Northern showed a net loss of more than $13,000,000 in 1932, more than $3,000,000 in 1933, and slightly over $1,000,000 in 1934. In none of these years did the company cover its fixed charges. The Northern Pacific seemed better able to withstand the initial onslaught, and although it suffered a deficit of nearly $2,000,000 in 1932 and failed to cover fixed charges, it made a modest recovery the next year and barely managed to earn net income through the middle of the decade. The recession of 1938, however, affected the Northern Pacific more seriously than the Great Northern; the former reported a deficit of over $4,000,000 in 1938 and again failed to meet fixed charges, whereas its northern neighbor had substantial net income.

In view of these facts, the dividends received by each of the Northern companies from the C. B. & Q. were of paramount importance. In each of the years 1930 to 1933 inclusive, non-operating income on the Northern Pacific exceeded its net railway operating income. The same thing was true of the Great Northern in 1932. Even though both Northern Lines (and especially the Northern Pacific) had sources of non-operating income besides the C. B. & Q., in 1933 C. B. & Q. dividends accounted for exactly one third of the Northern Pacific's total dividend income, and over seventy-four percent of the Great Northern's.

But what of the other side of the coin? How did the perfectly normal obligations of the C. B. & Q. to its principal owners affect its own welfare, particularly during the crucial 30's? As Budd made clear, the mere fact that the two principal stockholders were railway corporations rather than individuals seemed to keep alive a recurrent uneasiness based on emotion rather than fact. "What I thought was a singular thing when I went to the Burlington as president," he observed a quarter of a century later, "was that the great benefits accruing to the Burlington from its association with the Northern Lines never seemed to be understood or explained to the public. On several occasions I went to considerable pains to point this out. If, for example, the Milwaukee or North Western road had been taken over instead of the Burlington, I am sure that that road would have benefited."[1]

Suppose, indeed, that either the Milwaukee or the North Western had been acquired by the Northern Lines. In 1899, before Hill began his active efforts to secure a controlled link to Chicago, the C. B. & Q. was first in mileage and gross revenues, followed by the Milwaukee and the North Western; in respect to gross earnings per mile, however, the order was exactly reversed. The operating ratios in that year were almost identical as was interest on the funded debt and net income.

In physical and operating respects, the situation in 1933 was much the same. The Milwaukee had by then outstripped the Burlington in mileage, with the North Western still in third place. By a lesser margin

[1] Budd to Overton, November 14, 1957.

the Milwaukee led the three in gross revenues, followed by C. B. & Q. and C. & N. W., while the North Western's gross earnings per mile still ranked at the top, as they had in 1899, followed now by the C. B. & Q. and then the Milwaukee. In these three respects, therefore, the three roads were still closely comparable.

The changes that had come about between 1899 and 1933 were evident, however, in the trend of operating ratios. The North Western's was still the poorest of the lot; its rise of over sixteen percentage points had been closely paralleled by that of the Milwaukee. In contrast, C. B. & Q.'s operating ratio rose only eight percentage points—just half as much as the others—and in 1933 was the only operating ratio under seventy percent. But the sharpest contrast among the three roads lay in the changes in financial strength that had occurred between 1899 and 1933. While the Milwaukee's interest on funded debt had tripled and that of the North Western had doubled, interest requirements on the Burlington had gone up only eleven percent. The result as reflected in net income was what might have been expected: that of the Milwaukee plummeted 300 percent, that of the North Western 200 percent, whereas that of the Burlington decreased less than eighteen percent.

It may at least be suggested that the alliance with the Northern Lines was basically if not largely responsible for this showing. For one thing, Hill's constant and primary objective in railway operation was to drive incessantly for lower costs in freight handling. Every major improvement he made on his own Great Northern was to that end, and it is necessary only to point to the C. B. & Q.'s easy-grade line between Billings and Orin Junction or to the efficient extension into southern Illinois to indicate that he followed the same policy in respect to the Burlington. Another facet of Hill's policy was the deliberate and frequent interchange of operating officers among the three Hill Lines.

Another salient fact in quite a different realm was a direct result of the Burlington's alliance with the Northern Lines. The sale of the property in 1901 had meant that the Burlington, without having to build any extensions itself, had the benefit of two superb outlets to the rich markets and raw materials of the Pacific Northwest. What is more, the C. B. & Q. immediately became an increasingly important channel, through both St. Paul and Billings, for Northern Lines traffic flowing in both directions. Thereupon, both the North Western and the Milwaukee were faced with a challenge. The former, possibly because of its already established close relations with the Union Pacific, decided to stand pat. In so doing, it conserved its financial resources but on the other hand was forced to take a subordinate position in respect to traffic from the Northwest. The Milwaukee, on the other hand, took the plunge of building its own line, suffering bankruptcy as a result and, even after reorganization, finding itself in an inferior competitive position.

On these counts, it would seem no exaggeration to assert that the C. B. & Q. alliance with the Northern Lines turned out precisely as Perkins and Hill thought it would. It would be exceedingly difficult otherwise to explain the markedly stronger financial position of the Burlington in 1933 as compared to the North Western and the Milwaukee. Whatever the emotional reaction of stockholders in 1901 or in the 1930's, the hard facts certainly appeared to support amply Ralph Budd's laconic but unqualified observation in 1957 that "the Hill Line association has been good for the Burlington."[2]

Even from the standpoint of the Northern Lines, however, it would have been short-sighted in the extreme for them to compel the C. B. & Q. to pay dividends that might have threatened either its physical strength or its credit. This, of course, was clearly understood throughout this difficult period.

• The Debt Structure and Dividend Policy •

For a road as large as the Burlington, the debt structure during the 1930's was extremely simple. As had been true since 1921, only three mortgages existed on the entire property. Of these the oldest and largest was the Illinois Division Mortgage of 1899, with more than $84,000,000 outstanding at rates of three and a half and four percent interest. The second largest was the First and Refunding Mortgage, with $70,000,000 outstanding at the beginning of the decade at four and a half and five percent. The third was the General Mortgage of 1908, with slightly over $65,000,000 outstanding at four percent. From the beginning of 1928 through 1937, bonds outstanding in the hands of the public remained unmoved at $219,672,000. Total interest requirements were $9,084,635.

In respect to maturity dates and call provisions, however, significant differences existed among these mortgages which would assume greater importance as the decade of the 30's wore on. The large Illinois Division Mortgage would become due on July 1, 1949, before which time it could be redeemed only as a whole, on seven months' advance notice at a price of 105 and accrued interest. The General Mortgage would mature on March 1, 1958, and could not be redeemed before that date under any circumstances. On the other hand, Series A of the First and Refunding Mortgage would not become payable until 1971 or Series B until 1977. Series A was redeemable on sixty days' notice on any interest date after February 1, 1942; Series B could be redeemed on the same notice at any interest date after February 1, 1952. But, like the Illinois Division Mortgage, each series under the F. & R. mortgage could be redeemed only as a whole. Their redemption figures varied from 103 to 107½, plus accrued interest.

[2] Budd to Overton, October 27, 1957.

The relatively small size of the Burlington's fixed debt, the maturity dates of the three mortgages, and the restrictive call provisions all suggested that, under the adverse economic conditions in the early 1930's it was neither desirable nor necessary to attempt any substantial reduction or modification of the debt structure at that time. Interest charges as they stood were not oppressive, and no bonds would fall due until nearly the end of the following decade. Until economic conditions should improve, it was logical that the problem of the funded debt should remain quiescent. Attention was directed rather toward the disposition of net income, with one eye on working-capital requirements, the other on the situation facing the two Northern companies.

In view of the value of the Burlington's investment in road and equipment and its demonstrated earning power, its fixed debt was modest indeed; in 1933 it amounted to only $23,781 per mile in contrast to $41,233 for the North Western and $42,536 for the Milwaukee. As a matter of fact, at the end of 1932 Budd pointed out in the *Annual Report* that the company was "greatly undercapitalized"; its ratio of debt to property investment stood at 36.1 percent. This was in sharp contrast to the 58.3 percent ratio for all Class I railroads and to the ratios of the Rock Island, the Milwaukee, and the North Western, all of which stood over sixty percent.

Although gross revenues on the C. B. & Q. in 1933 were slightly lower even than in 1932, operating expenses were cut sharply, and there was a notable drop in taxes, so that the company was able to report a net income of more than five and a half million dollars, an increase of more than four million dollars over the previous year. The Northern Lines, however, were still experiencing difficulties. Although the Great Northern had chopped $10,000,000 from its 1932 deficit, it still reported a net loss of more than $3,000,000; net income for the Northern Pacific was only slightly over $300,000. Consequently, as Budd reported, "it was considered practicable and desirable under the circumstances to declare a $3 dividend."[3] This action was taken on December 6, 1933. Payment at this rate meant a disbursement of $5,125,161. Even so, net income exceeded the amount paid out (for the first time since 1929) by $472,862.61.

Total operating revenues of the C. B. & Q. in 1934 showed only a modest increase over those of the previous year, slightly more than one and a half million dollars; expenses increased over three and a half million. Taxes again declined and revenues from other sources moved upward, however, so that whereas net income was off more than a million dollars, the C. B. & Q. still earned $2.61 per share. At the time, the Northern Lines were still in need of a larger share of Burlington income. Whereas the Northern Pacific reported a net income of almost $900,000, net loss on the Great Northern exceeded $1,000,000. Accordingly, as in 1933, a

[3] PLD, December 11, 1933.

dividend of $3 was paid by the C. B. & Q. and charged to surplus. If any doubts lingered in the minds of the banking community as to the wisdom of this move, they certainly were not reflected in bond prices. Whereas all issues had straddled par during 1934, all of them sold well above par throughout 1935.

The financial performance of the Burlington in 1935 was the least promising since 1932. Total operating revenues moved upward encouragingly by more than $2,500,000, but expenses went up $4,500,000, reflecting the restoration of wage cuts and the rising costs of materials as well as the cost of the Republican River flood (over $2,400,000). Furthermore, for the first time since 1929, taxes showed an increase, although a very slight one, over the previous year. Thus, even though other income showed a substantial gain, net income fell below $2,000,000, to reflect earnings per share of $1.08. During December, the decision was reached to pay a dividend of $2 per share, the smallest made by the C. B. & Q. since the formation of the company in 1864.

The reasons for this were not far to seek. The most obvious was that earnings per share had dropped from $2.61 in 1934 to $1.08 in 1935. At the same time, the needs of the Northern roads were far less pressing. Whereas the Northern Pacific reported a net income of only $431,782, the Great Northern, recovering sharply from the three previous deficit years, earned over $7,000,000. Neither of the Northern companies had paid a dividend since 1931, and neither did so in 1935; they, in other words, were matching the Burlington's conservatism. Once again, if the bond market was any index, the financial community reflected no lessening of faith in the Burlington's financial and dividend policy. Prices on all C. B. & Q. issues throughout 1936 were higher than in 1935.

• Modest Revival, 1936–37 •

By 1936 it seemed as if the Burlington was catching a second breath. It was apparent, while the year was still young, that business was going to be better, and it was equally clear that if the Burlington expected to remain in the forefront in its ability to provide top-flight freight service and distinctive passenger service, heavy investments would be necessary. Early in the spring, the company applied to the I. C. C. for authority to issue $3,950,000 of two and a half percent serial trust certificates (to be paid off in equal installments over ten years), to be sold at competitive bidding to help pay for new equipment, estimated to cost $5,279,000; the balance required was to be provided from treasury cash. Only about a third of this amount was for freight equipment; the rest was to pay for two new *Twin-Cities Zephyrs* and the two new ten-car *Denver Zephyrs*. These last cost just over $1,100,000 apiece.

These obligations, which were duly authorized by the I. C. C. and issued on May 1, 1936, represented the first addition to fixed debt since the sale of the First and Refunding Series B bonds in February 1927. The equipment obligations, however, differed materially from the long-term mortgages in that the entire issue was for a relatively short term, specific provision was made for their retirement in annual installments, and the security consisted of equipment which, under ordinary circumstances, would have a far longer life than the term of indebtedness. These features accounted for the fact that the certificates could be successfully marketed at as low a rate as two and a half percent. Before the year was out, the company took an even longer step in the same direction. In December it sought, and eventually obtained, authority to issue $7,000,000 in ten-year collateral serial notes at two and a quarter percent interest to purchase freight cars and steam locomotives. By the close of the year, therefore, total fixed obligations of the Burlington had mounted from the 1928–35 level of $219,672,000 to $230,622,000.

Essentially, 1936 was an encouraging year for the Burlington. Whereas gross revenues between 1932 and 1935, inclusive, had remained within the very narrow range of from 78.4 to 82.9 million dollars, they forged ahead in 1936 to exceed 98 million, a gain of more than eighteen percent over those of the preceding year. Expenses increased too, but not nearly so much, and although the increase of taxes was an uncomfortable forty-three percent, other income paralleled revenues with a rise of eighteen percent, so that net income again topped the five-million mark, with earnings at $3.02 per share. Business was good on the Northerns too; net income of the Great Northern increased almost forty percent, while that of the Northern Pacific doubled, though neither declared dividends for the year. For its part, the Burlington board authorized a $4 disbursement.

Business on the Burlington showed a modest improvement in 1937; gross revenues increased slightly over two million dollars, to bring the total over 100 million for the first time since 1931. But expenses were up over three million, and whereas taxes fell off slightly, net income fell a quarter of a million, so that earnings per share went down from $3.02 to $2.87. More to the point, so far as month-to-month financing was concerned, cash available for working capital decreased steadily during the year while the need of funds for new equipment mounted. Consequently, the company obtained from the I. C. C. on October 28, 1937, approval to issue $3,650,000 of two and a half percent equipment trust certificates to provide seventy-five percent of the necessary funds. This raised total interest requirements to a new high of $9,318,894.69 for 1937. Thus, net income was down and fixed interest up, two elements that certainly would affect dividend policy.

The situation on the Northern Lines was mixed. Net income of the Northern Pacific fell to only $118,000, but on the Great Northern it exceeded $10,000,000, so that that company declared a dividend of $2 per share in December, 1937, its first disbursement since February 1932. On the Burlington the decline in net income, the rise in fixed charges, and the decline in available cash to the lowest level of the decade (slightly over $5,500,000) prompted the directors to authorize a dividend on December 8 of only $2 per share, just half that of the previous year. This was eighty-eight cents per share less than the amount earned; it permitted a carry over to surplus of nearly $1,500,000.

• ADJUSTING TO THE RECESSION, 1938 •

THE YEAR 1938 saw a marked slackening in all phases of the economy. As the Burlington had usually withstood recessionary effects better than railroads in general, its gross was not likely to fall as rapidly as that of railways as a whole. But the year was not far advanced when emergency measures became necessary to strengthen working capital. On January 29, the company arranged to borrow in installments $6,000,000 at two and a half percent from the First National Bank of New York, and on May 2 it applied to the I. C. C. for authority to issue $15,000,000 in First and Refunding five percent bonds to be dated February 1, 1938, and to mature in ten years. One purpose of the bond issue was to provide repayment for the bank loan. Fortunately, the C. B. & Q. was able to pay off half its bank loan from earnings on July 20, and revival of business during the third quarter of the year permitted repayment of the outstanding balance on September 15.

The mere fact that the company had found itself so short of working capital that it had had to resort to the banks was not only a danger signal but raised serious doubts among the investment and financial fraternity as to the credit of the Burlington. As *Barron's*, the financial weekly, reported as early as May 15, 1939: "Financial status of the Burlington undoubtedly would be far stronger than it is at present had not Northern Pacific and Great Northern drained it of a large part of its liquid resources to bolster their own reported earnings. Possibility of further such drains is the principal adverse factor for the road. . . ."[4] The reaction of the bond market was immediate: by the middle of 1938, every Burlington issue had dropped sharply below par.

In view of earnings, the overall debt structure of the Burlington was conservative, and it is ironic that during the six years 1932–37, inclusive, net withdrawals from surplus to pay dividends to the Northern Lines had been nearly $2,000,000 less than the total withdrawn in 1930–31. Undoubtedly the symbolic impact of the loan rather than its intrinsic implications made it seem so important. As a matter of fact, the market for Burlington bonds recovered approximately half its lost ground before the

---

[4] *Barron's* (Boston: H. Bancroft), May 15, 1939, p. 19; quoted in John T. O'Neil: *Policy Formation in Railroad Finance: Refinancing the Burlington, 1936–1945* (Cambridge: Harvard University Press; 1956), pp. 44–5.

year was out, presumably reflecting the recovery of earnings and repayment of the loan to the First National Bank of New York. Furthermore, by the end of the year, cash available for working capital had mounted from $5.7 million to $8.2 million, and although gross operating revenues declined, they were off only seven percent from 1937. Net income, as always, dropped more sharply in percentage, but the company earned $2.13 per share. With this result in the offing, a dividend of only $2 per share was declared on December 2, leaving a balance of approximately $225,000 for credit to the profit and loss account.

The decision as to the dividend rate underscored the constant realization that the Burlington's financial strength had to be kept unimpaired. The Northern Pacific reported a net loss of over $4,300,000, the worst showing of the decade; net income of the Great Northern fell from over $10,000,000 in 1937 to just over $2,700,000 in 1938. Under the circumstances, neither road declared a dividend. Nevertheless, the Burlington kept its rate at $2, reflecting an apparent determination not to make further withdrawals from surplus.

It is notable that during 1938 only one new obligation on account of equipment was assumed. On October 15, a conditional sales contract was arranged with the First National Bank of Chicago to provide $360,000 payable in monthly installments over nine years at a rate of two and three-quarters percent. The interesting thing about this contract, the first of several of a similar nature used by the Burlington, was that the equipment involved actually cost $409,574; the difference, $49,574, was paid from treasury cash upon delivery, leaving the amount of deferred payments outstanding at $360,000. Over the next years it was the rule, rather than the exception, for a substantial down payment to be made on this kind of equipment purchase.

As far as earnings were concerned, 1939 proved to be a twin of 1938. Although gross revenues increased slightly over three million, operating expenses mounted almost as rapidly so that net income rose less than $20,000, producing earnings per share of $2.14, just one penny more than in the previous year. The status of the underlying bonds remained unchanged, and the market for them, which had started to recover in the middle of 1938 and continued to improve through the first half of 1939, dropped off sharply thereafter. At the end of the year trading prices for the Generals and First and Refundings had receded to the approximate low points of 1938; only the Illinois Division Bonds, with their early maturity, remained well above the 90 mark.

· Emphasis on Equipment Financing, 1939–40 ·

In respect to overall financial policy, the outstanding development of 1939 pertained to equipment obligations. The dieselization and streamlined-train program was now in full swing, and money was required for it. Between May 15 and December 22, equipment costing $3,825,689 was acquired, for which $353,543 was paid upon delivery. The balance, $3,472,146, was financed by means of four separate conditional sales contracts with the First National Bank of Chicago, repayment to be made over periods varying from six to eleven years.

As the end of the year and the necessity for determining the size of the dividend approached, as always both favorable and unfavorable factors had to be considered. Total interest requirements of the company had declined over $35,000 from the previous year, but cash available for working capital had decreased nearly $1,000,000, owing, in part, to the substantial down payments on new equipment. The situation of the Northern roads, however, was vastly improved. The Northern Pacific, recovering strongly from disastrous 1938, reported a small, encouraging net income; the Great Northern more than tripled its net income of the previous year, to earn over $8,500,000. Neither of the Northern companies, however, declared a dividend. Accordingly, the Burlington directors again declared a dividend of only $2 per share, thus leaving nearly a quarter of a million dollars as a credit to profit and loss.

If 1940 was not identical with 1938 and 1939, it was certainly close to it. Gross revenue inched up a million and a half dollars, but increased expenses and taxes nearly closed the gap. Only the fact that other income rose faster than other charges accounted for the fact that the company could report better than half a million increase in net income and earnings per share of $2.57. Once again no change was made in the underlying mortgages, and as in 1939, so in 1940 the principal financial moves were in respect to equipment obligations. All told, the company acquired equipment costing $6,669,220, paid $378,042—or slightly over five percent —on delivery, leaving a net increase of $6,291,178 in conditional sales contracts for 1940. Thus, although interest requirements on account of the collateral trust notes and the equipment obligations of 1936 and 1937 were decreasing because of repayments of principal, interest on account of conditional sales contracts rose over $70,000, to bring total interest requirements to a new all-time high of $9,413,698.40.

This, however, was the price of progress. With competition increasing and the matter of national defense assuming greater and greater priority, could the Burlington follow any other course than to strengthen to the utmost its ability to provide transportation power and capacity? Furthermore, the market was extremely favorable for equipment obligations, as was evident from the steadily decreasing cost of the money obtained. These were loans for which the equipment itself provided the collateral, and in most cases the company had been able to "sweeten" that collateral by making substantial down payments. Thus the fact that the total fixed obligations of the Burlington had risen from the static figure of $219,672,000 during the 1930–35 period to $234,794,000 by the end of 1940 did not, in itself, represent a problem at all; the *added* amount was invested in equipment that was obviously more than paying its way.

The central problem in 1940, as it had been in 1936 prior to the assumption of any equipment obligations, was what to do about refinancing the Illinois Division bonds, scheduled to mature in 1949. The fact that bonds outstanding in the hands of the public amounted to almost $85,000,000 made it a large problem; the fact that the issue had to be called as a whole and only after seven months' notice made it an extremely complex and delicate operation. Consequently, on November 26, 1940, the directors appointed a committee consisting of Ralph Budd, F. J. Gavin, and Charles E. Denney, the three presidents of the Hill Lines, to launch a full-fledged offensive to reduce and revise the Burlington's underlying debt structure.

Meanwhile, a decision had to be reached as to a dividend payment for 1940. Burlington cash available for working capital had risen approximately two and a quarter million dollars in comparison with the end of 1939 and stood at nearly nine and a half million. The situation on the Northern Lines had vastly improved: Northern Pacific would show a reported net income of over two million and that of the Great Northern exceeded ten million by a comfortable margin, reaching the highest level since 1930 and amply justifying disbursement of a modest dividend of fifty cents a share, the first paid since 1937. Thus, and with the approaching debt problem obviously in mind, there seemed little reason to increase the rate of Burlington dividend payments. Accordingly a disbursement of $2 per share was declared, leaving a balance of over $975,000 to be credited to the profit and loss account.

• EQUIPMENT AND DEBT, 1941 •

DURING 1941, the C. B. & Q. expanded its equipment program and, as an inevitable concomitant, worked out a financial program to accommodate it. With national defense requirements increasing daily, the company took delivery of twenty-five Diesel-electric switchers, four Diesel-electric passenger locomotives, five passenger cars, and no less than 2,918 freight cars of various types, the last being built in the company shops. By the end of the year, conditional sale contracts outstanding had reached a total of $15,309,377; interest charges on them for the year 1941 amounted to $230,178.69. And this was by no means the total involved in purchase of equipment. By the end of 1941, the equipment trusts of 1936 and 1937, which together had originally totaled $7,600,000, had been reduced by annual payments of principal to $4,165,000, requiring a combined interest payment of $114,260.41. On August 1, 1941, however, the company floated another equipment trust, to be paid off in annual installments over seven years, in the amount of $9,387,000, with interest at one and a half percent.

During 1936–41, then, mortgage debt actually decreased, or, if the serial collateral trust notes are taken into account, rose very conservatively. On the other hand, fixed debt assumed on account of equipment within this relatively brief period amounted to $28,861,377. Consequently, interest payments which had remained stable at $9,084,635 over the 1928–35 period rose in 1941 to an all-time high in company history of $9,564,643.45.

It should be stressed again that the added increment of interest resulting from equipment purchases was an essential investment amply secured. Nonetheless, from a purely financial standpoint, interest charges, for whatever reason assumed, had to be paid. This fact, coupled with the absence of any plan to meet the 1949 maturity, doubtless accounted for the ever weakening market for Burlington bonds throughout 1941. Only the Illinois Division issues remained above 80 while the Generals dropped to 71¼ and the First and Refunding Series A to 70. The low point for Series B was 63¼. Perhaps the most discouraging factor was that these lows reflected the situation at the end of the year. It was apparent that the financial community would remain skeptical until the company devised a refunding plan that would restore confidence.

Certainly the business and the earning capacity of the company during 1941 left little to be desired. Gross revenues increased almost twenty million dollars, to reach the highest level since 1930, whereas increases in operating expenses were held to a little over eleven million. Even an increase in taxes of more than three million was more than offset when other income rose twenty million while other charges rose only fourteen million. Against the background of these figures, the increase in total fixed charges of $150,000 appeared trivial, and cash resources available for working capital shot up from under nine and a half million dollars to over thirteen and a half million. Net income, for the first time since 1931, reached double figures, to total $10,419,142, representing earnings of $6.10 per share.

As might have been expected, the situation on the Northern Lines also improved markedly. The Northern Pacific reported net income of over seven and three-quarter million dollars, the best since 1931, but still not enough, in the judgment of its directors, to warrant a dividend. Great Northern, on the other hand, earned a net income of over sixteen and three-quarter millions, and under the circumstances paid a dividend of $2 per share.

From the standpoint of the Northern roads, therefore, no reason existed to make a large dividend disbursement, though the satisfactory level of the Burlington's cash position might have warranted it. The basic problem was still that of accumulating cash to implement whatever plan might be adopted for meeting the 1949 maturities and the increasingly heavy annual installments due on equipment obligations. Consequently, the C. B. & Q. again held its rate of dividend to $2 per share, declared by the directors on December 18, 1941. This meant that more than $7,000,000 was available as a credit to the profit and loss account, thus reducing the net balance of withdrawals from that account for the entire period 1930–41, inclusive, to just over four and a half million dollars.

Much more to the point was the fact that for the years 1932–41, inclusive, the profit and loss account actually received $2,868,294.54 more than was withdrawn from it. Furthermore, if the 1941 upsurge in railway business continued, it might eventually provide the solution for the approaching maturity of 1949.

When Japanese bombs fell on Pearl Harbor on Sunday morning, December 7, 1941, not only the financial planning, but also every other aspect of Burlington policy called for immediate revision and adaptation to the war crisis.

CHAPTER 26

World War II

1940-45

• PERSPECTIVE •

ROM THE SPRING OF 1940 until V-J day, August 15, 1945, the all-absorbing task of the nation's railways was the strengthening of the country's defenses and the successful prosecution of the war. Their specific job was to transport the vast military traffic and personnel over the lines, and to do it quickly and safely. Everything, everybody, top to bottom, was dedicated to that end; everything else had to be done on a "when, as, and if" basis.

Conversion of a railway from a peacetime to a wartime footing did not involve so much of a change as in some industries whose production was, for a time, either diverted wholly to different products or discontinued altogether. After all, railways existed solely to move things and people, and that is precisely what they were called upon to do. The major change lay in the staggering size of the load to be carried, the greatest up to that time. Hardly less exacting was the constant and often frustrating task of finding enough men and materials to do the job at hand.

That the Burlington—and all railways—under private ownership and management accomplished far more than the most sanguine expectations was one of the most brilliant achievements in the nation's wartime history. It was a performance in sharp and happy contrast to the experience during World War I, and as such was an accurate measure of the tremendous strides the industry had taken since then to improve its plant, operating techniques, finances, administration, and shipper relations.

In retrospect, the entire period 1932–49, which coincided exactly with Ralph Budd's presidency of the Burlington, was one of sharp and sudden change. The toughest depression of history was followed, without pause for recuperation, by the most destructive of all global conflicts; small wonder that the years 1945–49 inevitably posed unfamiliar and difficult problems of adjustment. In some respects, however, the order of events over the seventeen-year period was fortunate. Had the depression followed the war instead of preceding it, for example, the shock might well have been far more disastrous than the painful constriction of the economy in 1929–32. As it was, the lean 30's had forced the railroads to trim off all their dispensable fat and strengthen their essential sinews. As a matter of fact, as rail management was well aware, by 1939 there was a large surplus of transportation facilities capable of far greater utilization. A further favorable factor in 1939–40 was the fact that the more experienced railroaders at every level had been through World War I; they were well aware of the pitfalls to be avoided.

Very shortly after Hitler's troops poured into Poland in September 1939, and again early the following spring, Ralph Budd was called to the White House. The all-important question discussed was how best to mobilize the nation's transport facilities—especially the railways—for defense and, if necessary, war. The President, it should be said, really "liked" railroads. He was fully aware of the situation that had led to government control during World War I, but he was also mindful of the enormous improvements the industry had made since then, and despite his already established record for creating new federal agencies, he appeared receptive to the idea of leaving the roads under private management *if* he could be convinced that they could do their job.

On this point Budd took a firm stand, both against immediate seizure should a crisis come and against piecemeal accomplishment of the same end by such means as having the government provide new equipment. Why not, he suggested, work through existing organizations—notably the Interstate Commerce Commission, the Association of American Railroads, the Shippers' Advisory Boards, and the like? Such a procedure, he argued, would avoid creation of duplicate and, to some extent, conflicting and rival organizations. Of utmost importance, it would leave the carriers free to devote their full energies to meeting whatever specific requirements were put before them. He was confident that the best possible results could be obtained under such conditions. Ralph Budd's advice prevailed, despite pressure from influential circles. The importance of Mr. Roosevelt's stand, crystallized during the winter of 1939–40, can hardly be overemphasized, for it thereupon became the official policy of the administration.

It was not long before the railways were given a chance to prove themselves, for when the "Phony War" on the Western Front burst into flame in May 1940, the speed of the German onslaught forced immediate recasting of military thinking and planning in the United States. On May 16, the President asked Congress for huge appropriations for guns, tanks, motorized equipment, and no less than 50,000 planes.

Inevitable results of this sudden development were a scramble for manpower and materials and the realization in Washington that the economy would have to be placed, without delay, on a war footing. To achieve this, President Roosevelt, invoking a law passed in 1916 under somewhat similar circumstances, revived, on May 28, 1940, the Council of National Defense, consisting of the six secretaries of War, Navy, Interior, Agriculture, Commerce, and Labor. The same law provided for an Advisory Commission to the Council, to be composed of seven experts whose collective duty was specifically to coordinate and supervise defense production in their respective fields. To this Advisory Commission *to* the Council of National Defense (generally referred to as N. D. A. C.) Ralph Budd was appointed as Commissioner of Transportation. Not attached to any official department, the N. D. A. C. was not limited by departmental protocol. Budd reported directly to the Commander-in-Chief, who alone had the responsibility for visualizing the defense effort as a whole. His duties did not supersede or conflict with those of the Interstate Commerce Commission, the state commissions, traffic bureaus, or labor-relations board. His job was simply to guarantee adequate service.

Budd's immediate aim when he reached Washington was to determine transportation requirements as far in advance as possible. To accomplish this, he took what he always regarded as the most important step of his administration. Rather than set up an elaborate agency to do the job from scratch, he arranged, on his first day in office, to have existing organizations, chiefly national in scope, undertake this vital task; they were asked at once to make studies by commodities and by regions so that each type of carrier would know what traffic it would be expected to handle, where that traffic would be, and, in addition, what means were available for moving it.

To keep his office posted on railway requirements and facilities, Budd enlisted the aid of the Car Service Division and Bureau of Railway Economics of the Association of American Railroads, and the Bureau of Service of the Interstate Commerce Commission. These agencies reported directly to Budd and to his Deputy Commissioner, Karl W. Fischer, borrowed from the C. B. & Q. to serve as Budd's adjutant in Washington. To keep abreast of the needs of the other essential carriers, Budd named as consultants on his staff the presidents of the various road, water, and air transport organizations, together with officers of the American Petroleum Institute and of the American Transit Association.

The crucial question for all carriers, of course, was not only the size of the load to be hauled, but also its distribution over the year. For railroads, the usual freight traffic pattern had always been characterized by a gradual rise in carloadings through the first six months of the year, then a steady increase, with a sharp peak in the autumn, followed by a sudden drop after October. The steady, if increased, flow of defense production altered this pattern to one showing a flatter outline, with a relatively lower peak.

This change in the traffic pattern, which Budd emphasized over and over again, was of prime importance, for it meant that with the load more evenly distributed than ever before, the railways could move it with less equipment and motive power. The fact that they carried the peaks of 1940 and 1941 without difficulty led Budd to observe that "we may face the future with greater confidence."[1]

Meanwhile, frequent and lucid public statements made by Budd throughout his administration kept the nation informed and highlighted specific needs as they arose. In the spring of 1941, for example, he directed attention to the absolute necessity for the railways to obtain new cars, locomotives, and other essential materials as needed. As the summer of 1941 gave way to fall, the growing difficulty of getting enough steel for railway maintenance and additions led him to rivet attention on that situation. In fact, Budd had continually to fight for adequate supplies. One of the difficulties was that priorities were being established by government agents with no first-hand knowledge of the problems involved.

On another front, the Commissioner urged the railways to keep reducing their bad-order motive power and equipment, to adopt standard specifications, and, if necessary, to use substitute materials for those desperately needed in defense work. To these pleas the railways responded vigorously; by November 1, 1941, for example, the bad-order car ratio was reduced to 4.1 percent of ownership, the lowest figure on record. Budd's office also worked out a far-reaching storage system so that freight cars could always be unloaded at centrally located distribution points promptly upon arrival. Coal users were urged to build up their stocks during the summer (thus helping to whittle down the traditional traffic peaks), and all railroads were requested to discontinue unnecessary passenger trains, combine others, and discourage unnecessary travel. Budd's efforts were not confined to the rails: he gathered more detailed data on bus and truck availability than ever had been assembled before; he suggested plans—later carried out—for access highways to relieve congestion, especially around defense plants, and he made a survey of inland water facilities. On the Great Lakes he brought about additional ice-breaking service that resulted, in 1941, in the longest navigation season in history.

Essential as these varied activities were, the fact remained that the railways were carrying approximately sixty-two percent of the nation's inter-

[1] Budd: "Some Experiences in Washington," address before the Commercial Club, Chicago, January 31, 1942, CB&Q/Pres.

city freight; hence the nation's transportation effort still depended primarily on the availability of the humble freight car. This is why Budd spent so much time urging that the railways be given sufficient steel and other materials to do their job.

As time went on, Budd realized that the Commissioner's responsibilities deserved full time; this he could not give in view of his concurrent heavy duties as president of the Burlington. Accordingly, on February 28, 1941, he asked the President to be relieved. "The major movements of the coming season," he explained, "like iron ore and grain, are being carefully planned, and every carrier will take pride in carrying its part of the load."[2] The President understood, but asked Budd to remain at his post until a successor could be named; he also asked him for suggestions as to who should be appointed in his place. Thus, as it turned out, Budd continued his work in Washington until the end of 1941; on January 1, 1942, his good friend Joseph B. Eastman, the distinguished chairman of the Interstate Commerce Commission, and former Federal Coordinator, became chairman of the newly constituted Office of Defense Transportation, an organization set up to continue the work Budd had put in motion.

Eastman, like the President, was fully mindful of the essential groundwork the Transportation Commissioner had laid. With characteristic fairness, he referred to it more than once in discussing the origin and tasks of O. D. T. The Burlington, indeed, could well be proud of the contribution of its "first citizen." The example of accomplishment, patience, and confidence that he set, both in Washington and in Chicago, was a direct contribution to the war effort.

· The Nation's Railways in World War II ·

THE PROBLEMS AND PERFORMANCE of the Burlington Lines during wartime can be understood only in the context of the total railway effort; that is why attention must be directed to the national scene. The emergency, in effect, caused all individual systems to subordinate their normal competition for traffic in order to play whatever part seemed appropriate in the one great drama that engulfed them all. Thus the primary objectives of the Burlington were shaped by and merged with those of the railways as a whole. The common aim—in contrast to the years immediately preceding —was not where to find traffic, but how to handle it.

The load was increased not only because of expanding production, but also because some other transportation media had to be curtailed. Road transport was restricted to save gasoline and rubber. The activities of U-boats off the Florida coast forced the closing of the Panama Canal to transcontinental intercoastal traffic, so that its 27 million tons of annual

2 Budd to Franklin D. Roosevelt, February 28, 1941. File in possession of R. C. Overton.

commerce, plus much of that normally carried by the severely restricted Atlantic coast shipping, fell on the rails. In terms of figures, traffic on coastwise and intercoastal steamships declined seventy-seven percent between 1941 and 1944 while truck traffic decreased thirty percent. Consequently, the railways were called upon to handle eighty-three percent of the increase of *all* traffic between 1941 and 1944.

Regional variations in the traditional traffic bulge posed additional problems. The impact of World War II on the roads in the eastern district (which normally enjoyed heavy traffic density) was far less sharp than on those in the western and southern districts. This fact, combined with the change in the timing of the load, presented new challenges for railways like the Burlington in the West.

As everyone expected, freight traffic—measured in ton-miles—skyrocketed in 1942, smashing all previous records and registering a thirty-four percent increase over the previous year. Thanks to the vital planning and policies of the Transportation Commissioner's office and the unstinting cooperation of individual railways, shippers, and the armed services, the freight-car crisis normally associated with such an increase failed to materialize. Incredibly, in 1942 carloadings increased only one percent! This performance was bettered in 1943; while ton-miles moved up fourteen percent over 1942, carloadings actually decreased one percent. And this was not the end of a performance that astounded even those with the greatest confidence in the railways. The peak wartime traffic load came in 1944, when ton-miles exceeded the 1943 record by one percent. Yet carloadings inched up only two percent. By the following year, with the fighting over on both fronts, the freight load diminished and the potential crisis was over.

The bulge in passenger traffic occurred in the same years as the bulge in freight, but it was even sharper; revenue passenger-miles in 1944 exceeded those in 1939 by 322 percent! Nor did the peak subside as rapidly as that in freight traffic; as a matter of fact, the task of getting the servicemen home at the end of hostilities strained passenger-carrying facilities to the limit throughout 1945. But this burden, more than twice as heavy as the previous all-time peak in 1920, was successfully carried. How did the railways manage to carry these oversize loads of goods and people?

Without any question, the basic reason was that between 1921 and 1940 the railroads had spent nearly 11 billion dollars for equipment, roadway, and structures, and these improvements were definitely qualitative rather than quantitative. In 1944, for example, there were over thirty percent fewer locomotives than in 1918, nearly twenty-four percent fewer freight cars, over thirty-seven percent fewer passenger-carrying cars, and some twenty-three percent fewer employees. Nonetheless, in 1944 the nation's railways accounted for eighty-two percent more revenue ton-miles and over 124 percent more passenger-miles.

The secret of this astounding performance lay primarily in technological improvement. Average rail weight, for example, increased more than nineteen percent. This in turn permitted operation of heavier locomotives and larger freight cars. Between 1918 and 1944, the average tractive effort of steam locomotives alone increased over fifty percent; average freight-car capacity rose more than twenty-two percent; and freight-train net tonnage was stepped up by sixty-five percent. Stronger and more efficient locomotives averaged fifty-six percent more miles per day, though the average number of freight cars per train increased more than fifty percent. The combined result of these factors—and this was what counted—was a phenomenal rise of 115 percent in ton-miles per car day. Stronger and speedier locomotives moving over sturdier rails led to an even more spectacular performance in respect to passengers. Compared with 1918, the average number of passenger cars per train increased sixty-seven percent by 1944; average passengers per train increased more than 150 percent; and average length of trip per passenger, nearly 170 percent.

The advent of the Diesel-electric locomotive and the introduction of centralized traffic control were perhaps the outstanding individual technical improvements between the two wars that contributed most to the successful handling of the enormous traffic of the second conflict. The great efficiency of the Diesel was important, but the feature that made it priceless during the war was that, unlike a steam locomotive, it was available virtually around the clock, day in and day out. On this score alone, it took only half as many Diesel as steam units to move a given tonnage over the same distance in the same time; this represented an enormous saving in on-line maintenance and materials. Adaptation of the Diesel-electric to freight service did not occur until 1941, on the very eve of America's active participation in the war, and throughout the conflict many roads (including the Burlington) could have used more units than they were able to obtain. But the boost that the units in service were able to give the total effort, though impossible to measure, was great.

Centralized traffic control, which had been inaugurated in 1927, and in which the Burlington was a consistent leader, was a godsend in wartime. Under normal traffic conditions, a single-track line equipped with C. T. C. could handle about eighty percent as many trains as a double-track line. Through 1940, 1,838 miles of railway in the United States had been equipped with C. T. C. During the years 1941–44 inclusive, 3,503 more miles were added, bringing the total to 5,341, and another 1,658 miles were converted in 1945 alone.

Typical of the response of the railroads to wartime problems was the way in which they met the demands made by the massive mobilization program. To carry the mounting tide of military personnel, the O. D. T. called for and obtained voluntary revisions in passenger schedules which released both motive power and cars. As a basis for doing this, the Office of Defense Transportation continued to obtain estimates of future traffic from all the carrier organizations that had served Budd as consultants, as well as from government agencies.

In respect to one major problem, the O. D. T. was no more successful than Budd had been: its efforts to secure essential supplies and equipment for the railways fell far short. During the three years 1942–44, the O. D. T. asked the War Production Board for 311,500 freight cars and received 130,826; it requested 4,159 locomotives and received 2,500; it asked for 5,150 passenger-train cars and obtained 1,977, which included 1,600 troop sleepers and kitchen cars; it sought 5,410,000 tons of steel rail and received 4,701,850. Perhaps this response was a calculated risk on the part of the War Production Board; however justified it may have been, it made the task of the railways just that much harder.

Another problem that mounted in intensity as the war progressed was how to keep and hold enough manpower to run the plant at top capacity. To help solve it, Eastman created a Division of Transport Personnel in his Office of Defense Transportation. The major efforts of this division were directed to holding enough skilled men in transportation to maintain the flow of traffic and to developing new sources of manpower and maintaining harmonious relationships between employers and employees. The greatest service of this division to the railways was its work in mitigating the effects of the draft and of recruiting desperately needed replacements. Even though enough skilled personnel to do the job never seemed to be at hand, railway employment actually rose from 1,308,600 in July 1941 to 1,630,300 in July 1944. It must be borne in mind, however, that replacements and additions were largely inexperienced. This was what made the situation so difficult throughout the war period.

Nevertheless, during World War II the nation's railways handled ninety-one percent of all military freight within the country and ninety-eight percent of military personnel movements. By common consent this was termed a "magnificent performance."[3] The big job was successfully done, and in time of war that fact outweighed everything else.

The collateral effects of the war effort, however, inevitably meant a great deal to the railways. As business corporations, they naturally were concerned with returns from their service, the extent and character of expenses, the net effects on their financial health, and, perhaps most important of all, the condition in which they would find themselves, both internally and competitively, when the hostilities were over.

Inevitably, wartime traffic brought a marked rise in total operating revenues. It gained momentum in 1940 and moved sharply upward in 1941, reaching a peak in 1944. This was brought about by the tremendous increase in the volume of transportation carried. And, amazingly enough, when the war ended, rates and fares were no higher, and in some instances

[3] *Moody's Steam Railroads* (New York, 1946), p. a–7.

were less, than when it began. After the very substantial wage increases granted at the close of 1941, the roads had requested a ten percent rise in passenger fares (except for military personnel) and a ten percent increase in freight rates except for coal, coke, and ore. The Interstate Commerce Commission granted the passenger-fare increase, effective February 10, 1942, and permitted a six percent increase in freight rates effective March 15, 1942 (except for agriculture, livestock, coal and coke, for which the increase was three percent, with none at all on iron ore). Late in 1942, however, both the Office of Price Administration and the Department of Agriculture entered strong objections to these increases, and as a result the Commission suspended all increased freight rates as of May 15, 1943, and revoked the ten percent rise in commutation fares. There the rates and fares remained until after the close of the war; in fact, early in 1944 the western railways, including the Burlington, agreed to reduce westbound freight rates on government traffic retroactive to January 1, 1942, and for the duration of the conflict.

Another factor in the wartime revenue situation is worth special attention. As indicated above, both commodities and people were diverted to the rails from other means of transport, but the diversion was relatively greater for passengers than for freight. In 1938, returns from passenger service had been just over seventeen percent of total operating revenues; in 1945 they accounted for more than twenty-four percent of the total. Consequently, in 1942, the net railway operating deficit that had plagued passenger-train service since 1929 was converted for the first time in thirteen years into a healthy income; in the three years 1943–45 inclusive, net railway income from passenger-train service, which showed more than a quarter-billion deficit in 1939–41, inclusive, and a small profit in 1942, averaged nearly a quarter of a billion dollars, thus giving a welcome boost to total net railway operating income.

The total net railway income of the nation's Class I railways, however, started declining in 1943, and by 1945 was lower than during any year since 1940, and forty-two percent less than in the peak year of 1942. The reason lay in the increased costs of doing business, particularly in two respects. During the four years 1938–41, inclusive, taxes (other than payroll) had absorbed an average of about 6.8 cents for every dollar of the railways' gross revenue. In the three years 1942–44, these taxes reached a peak of 18.1 cents per revenue dollar and averaged 16.3 cents. In 1945, with taxable income sharply reduced, the proportion paid in taxes other than payroll returned pretty much to normal. In that year, however, the railways charged off over 825 million dollars against depreciation to amortize defense projects; this, added to normal depreciation and retirements, meant that in 1945, 13.3 cents out of each revenue dollar (in contrast to an average of just over five cents per dollar during the seven years 1938–44, inclusive) was spent for these purposes. Furthermore, the relatively modest increase in the amount spent for maintenance of equipment in 1944 over 1943 was followed by the abrupt upturn in 1945, when more than twenty-four percent of total operating revenues went for this purpose.

The combined effect of these factors was to raise the number of cents per dollar of gross revenue spent for expenses and taxes from 80.1 in 1942 to 90.4 in 1945, the highest since World War I. By the same token, the total operating ratio for the nation's railways rose from a low point of 61.63 percent in 1942 to 79.21 percent in 1945, the highest figure since 1922. Net income followed very much the same pattern. Starting with a deficit in 1938 for all Class I railways, it was modestly in the black the next year, then shot upward to a high point of more than $900 million in 1942. It declined slightly the next year and more sharply the two following years, so that in 1945 net income was almost exactly one half what it had been in 1942. By far the greater share of these net earnings was plowed back into the property or used for the reduction of debt; total property investment (road and equipment, material and supplies, and cash) was more than $1.2 billion higher in 1945 than in 1942, whereas fixed and contingent interest charges were reduced $148 million during the same period. As *Moody's* put it in 1946, "Many railroads took advantage of the high earnings to reduce their funded debt."[4] This was indeed fortunate, if not essential, for it was overwhelmingly apparent, even during the war years, that once the conflict ended, the railways might well face tough sledding financially.

For one thing, such competition as had been restricted by wartime shortages would most certainly return with a vengeance. Deprived of new cars and strictly rationed in respect to gasoline and tires, the average American car owner could hardly wait to turn in his faithful jalopy for something new, tell the gas-station attendant to "fill 'er up," and hit the road. Whereas rail management hoped to retain some of the increased patronage handled so faithfully during the war years, and was willing to invest in new equipment to that end, it certainly did not expect that passenger-train service would contribute as much to net railway operating income as it had during the years of conflict. Furthermore, even though passenger-miles by air had never amounted to more than three percent of those by rail in the prewar years, fantastic advances in air technology had occurred during the conflict, and a whole generation of young men had become accustomed to travel by air as a matter of course rather than as a stunt or a special privilege. Certainly competition from this direction might assume major proportions with the return of peace.

Increased competition for freight was equally certain. In the last full year before direct American participation in the war, the trucks had carried 10.5 percent of all intercity freight. Tire and gas rationing caused this to dip to 5.4 percent in 1944, but it had already recovered to 6.5 percent be-

[4] Ibid., p. a–21.

fore the end of 1945 and was clearly pointed upward. Without doubt there would also be stronger competition than ever from the pipelines, which in 1941 carried 8.9 percent of total intercity freight traffic. Unlike any other type of carrier, these had been expanded rapidly during the actual war years to take the place of unavailable coastwise shipping, so that by 1945 they were carrying 12.3 percent of the total load.

Quite apart from competitive prospects, certain inescapable railway costs inevitably would rise also. Taxes, particularly those based on income and excess profits, might be expected to decline. But any such relief would surely be more than offset by increased costs of material and labor. This was not a matter of mere guesswork. Despite the efforts of the government to hold prices down throughout the war, the wholesale price index (with (1939 equal to 100) rose from 113.4 in 1941 to 137.3 in 1945; at the same time, the consumers' price index rose from 105.9 to 129.5. More specifically, the charge-out prices of fuel, materials, and supplies used by the railways rose from an index figure of 55.2 (with the 1947–49 average as 100) in 1941 to 69.3. Wage rates for all railway employees followed the same pattern: the index (based on the 1947–49 average) moved from 58.7 in 1941 to 71.2 in 1945.

Perhaps the most accurate forecast of what was in store lay in the wage pattern of the railways during the war years. It will be recalled that the pay increases won by the unions at the end of 1941 added approximately $315,000,000 to the labor bill of the Class I railways. Nevertheless, in the closing months of 1942 and early in 1943, demands from both operating and non-operating unions led to a series of reports from successive Emergency boards. None of the proposed solutions was acceptable to labor, however, and a nationwide strike was called for December 30, 1943.

A stoppage of railway service at this critical juncture of the war would, of course, have been unthinkable. Consequently, President Roosevelt immediately called representatives of the carriers, all the unions, and the stabilization authorities to the White House. When his attempts to mediate directly failed, he offered to be sole arbitrator. This proposition was accepted by the carriers and by the engineers and trainmen; the non-operating unions promised to "consider," but the conductors, firemen, and switchmen flatly rejected the arbitration proposal. Thereupon Mr. Roosevelt took two steps: to the engineers and trainmen who had withdrawn their strike order, he offered a four cents per hour increase effective retroactive to April 1, 1943, an additional five cents per hour in lieu of overtime and expenses while away from home, and one week's paid vacation. The Director of Economic Stabilization promptly approved this proposition, and it thereupon went into effect. On the other hand, since none of the other unions had accepted his arbitration, the President on December 27, 1943, took over the railways and directed that they be operated through the War Department.

One effect of this move was to prompt the non-operating unions to accept, as far as wages were concerned, the increases of from four to ten cents suggested the previous November by one of the emergency boards. They were still dissatisfied with overtime arrangements, however; consequently their Emergency Board was reconvened. On January 17, 1944, it proposed not only a wage increase of from four to ten cents per hour, effective retroactive to February 1, 1943, but also an increase of one to five cents an hour for overtime. This the non-operating unions accepted. Meanwhile, on January 14, 1944, the firemen, switchmen, and conductors accepted for themselves the same arrangement the President had worked out for the engineers and trainmen. When, on January 18, 1944, the Economic Stabilization Director approved all these advances, the railways were returned to the owners. It was estimated that the awards would add approximately $374,000,000 to their payrolls.

A parallel development during the hectic year 1943 became important not so much for the dollars and cents involved as for the procedure. For some time the engineers and firemen had been pressing for increased wages and also for the placing of an extra man on Diesel engines. Their requests, known at the time as the "Diesel Cases" were eventually presented to an Emergency Board, which on May 24, 1943, recommended against any wage increase and against an extra man on Diesels, but in favor of slightly higher rates on newer and larger engines. Unsatisfied with this outcome, the president of the Brotherhood of Locomotive Engineers promptly asked for and obtained a conference at the White House. As a result, Mr. Roosevelt on May 29 requested the head of the Association of American Railroads to persuade the carriers to resume conferences. In due course, new agreements were worked out which, among other things, equalized the rates of pay in all portions of the nation and granted some slight increases beyond those recommended by the Emergency Board. The point was that, as in 1941, labor had found that by going to the White House and exerting pressure, it could gain more than could be obtained through the regular processes of the Railway Labor Act. For the future, this boded little comfort for the railways.

In contrast to 1943, 1944 was relatively peaceful on the wage front until the very end of the year, when the engineers and trainmen presented to the carriers requests for thirty-seven changes in working rules. Conferences continued from March 1945 through July, to no avail. Finally, on July 24, 1945, the engineers and trainmen formally demanded forty-five rule changes, including a twenty-five percent wage increase, with a minimum raise of $2.50 a day. Concurrently, the firemen, conductors, and switchmen asked for forty-seven changes in their working rules and an increase of $2.50 in wages. The next month, the carriers countered with a request for twenty-nine changes in these rules, designed to eliminate a certain amount of featherbedding. In September, the non-operating unions, which had also been considering requests for changes in rules, converted their demand to a straight increase of thirty cents an hour. When no progress was made in any of these disputes through the medium of conferences, mediation was invoked toward the end of the year. There matters stood as 1945 ran out. As a postscript, it should perhaps be repeated that except for the period March 15, 1942, to May 15, 1943, there had been no increase whatever in freight rates, and only a slight increase in civilian passenger fares. The only bright spot on that horizon appeared on December 12, 1945, when Presi- dent Truman signed the Boren Bill to eliminate reductions in land-grant rates, effective October 1, 1946.

In summary, the railways of the United States performed a herculean task during World War II. So far as the war effort was concerned, this was the all-important fact. As a result of the volume of traffic carried, their operating revenues surged forward despite the fact that average rates and fares declined. Owing to heavy taxes, increased costs of maintenance, and rising wages, both net railway operating income and net income increased far more modestly than revenue; the larger part of net earnings was de- voted to plant improvement and debt retirement because, from all indica- tions, competition and rising costs were certain to present major problems in the postwar period.

One intangible ingredient, however, deserves mention. Despite crowded conditions and occasional delays, the railways had done such a magnificent job of carrying the load during the war that they gained the solid respect of the public. There was perhaps another reason for this: dur- ing World War I, government operation of the railways *cost* the taxpayers of the United States nearly two million dollars a day, whereas during World War II the railways *paid* to the federal government more than three million dollars a day in taxes, a total difference of five million dollars daily. At any rate, when the conflict was over, the railways had certainly increased their prestige. More to the point, no considerable body of opin- ion anywhere in the nation favored government ownership and operation of the railroads.

In this context the Burlington went to war. More than at any other time in its existence, its objectives, techniques, and problems were merged with those of the railways as a whole. But it also faced problems and solu- tions peculiar to, and distinctive of, the Burlington.

CHAPTER 27

The Burlington at War

1941 - 45

· HIGHLIGHTS ·

URING THE SIX YEARS from 1934 to 1939, inclusive, the C. B. & Q.
produced nearly 49½ billion ton-miles and 3 billion passenger-
miles of transportation. In the six years—1940 to 1945, inclusive—it accounted for more than 93 billion ton-miles and nearly 8½
billion passenger-miles of transportation, increases of 88 and 179 percent,
respectively. As Budd succinctly put it afterwards: "During the war years
we at the Burlington did twice as well as we thought we could."[1]

The ingredients of this spectacular achievement were many and
varied. For example, during the four years 1942 through 1945, plants
located directly on the C. B. & Q. originated 370,685 cars of shells and
bombs. During the same years, the C. B. & Q. alone handled 446,521 cars
of petroleum; the C. & S. and Fort Worth and Denver City boosted the
system load of this commodity to 620,419 cars. At the same time, Burlington participated in moving the largest grain crops ever produced up to
that time. Performance in the passenger field was even more spectacular.
From Pearl Harbor through the end of 1945, the Burlington operated
10,117 special trains carrying 3,075,643 men and handled 1,479,698 additional military personnel in extra cars on regular trains, a total of over

[1] Budd: "93 Billion Ton-Miles," *Army Transportation Journal*, Vol. II, No. 3
(April, 1946).

4½ million for an average of nearly 3,000 a day. And this did not include other millions of servicemen traveling individually or in small groups on regular trains, nor did it include skyrocketing loads of civilians who took to the rails as gasoline and tires were rationed.

Indeed, every type of rail transportation smashed records. During September and October 1944, for example, the C. B. & Q. handled 1,800 carloads of Christmas packages destined for fighting men overseas. At the peak of the movement, 103 cars were dispatched on October 15; the largest single trainload was probably the ninety-seven-car, solid mail train that ran from Chicago to Galesburg on October 18, 1944.

The best way to obtain a complete and comprehensive view of the Burlington's wartime performance is to analyze, or observe in graph form, the detailed and often complex statistics relating to traffic, operations, and finance. In a general treatment of this sort, however, certain highlights must suffice:

The full impact of the war effort was felt first by the railways in the northeastern quadrant of the United States. For the Burlington, the peak, both in freight and passenger traffic, came in 1944.

As in the case of the nation's railways as a whole, the Burlington Lines were able to carry the wartime torrent of business primarily because of (a) the vast improvement the system had made in plant and equipment between the two world wars, and (b) the economies that could be realized under conditions of heavy traffic volume. As to improvements, between 1918 and 1944 the various segments of the Burlington (i.e., C. B. & Q., C. & S., and the Texas Lines) experienced the following typical increases:

50 to 65 percent in average locomotive-tractive effort
10 to 33 percent in average freight-car capacity
43 to 73 percent in freight cars per train
45 to 95 percent in net tons per train
153 to 236 percent in length of average trip per passenger
115 to 258 percent in average number of passengers per train

Gains in efficiency, in themselves a reflection both of improved plant and of increased volume, showed up particularly in comparisons between the prewar year 1938 and the peak traffic year 1944:

Bad-order freight cars, which in 1938 exceeded seven percent of ownership on the C. B. & Q. and on the Texas Lines, and over four and a half percent on the C. & S., were reduced, by 1944, to 3.3 percent on the C. B. & Q. and to less than two percent on the C. & S.–Texas Lines.

Gross ton-miles per train hour, a revealing index of efficiency, rose from just over 30,000 to more than 40,000 on the C. B. & Q. between 1938 and 1944, while the comparable figures of the C. & S.–Texas Lines mounted from 21,000 to over 26,000 in the same period.

The transportation ratio (the relation of maintenance and op-

erating expenses to revenues) declined from just over thirty-six percent to slightly over twenty-six percent for the C. B. & Q., and in a
similar fashion on the C. & S.–Texas Lines.

In respect to both revenues and expenses, the C. B. & Q., as well
as it western subsidiaries, followed pretty much the general trend of
railways during World War II. When it came to net railway operating
income, however, and more particularly to net income, the C. B. & Q.
again displayed the distinctive quality that had characterized it from the
earliest days: steadiness and an ability to earn a profit under rapidly
changing conditions. Coming out of the depression, the C. B. & Q. in
1938 and 1939 reported far more net railway operating income than its
near neighbors. As the war progressed, the Milwaukee, the Rock Island,
and the North Western all experienced a wave of sharp and welcome
prosperity; in 1943, the C. B. & Q. trailed them all as to net railway
operating income and fell behind both the North Western and the Milwaukee in net income. In 1944, however, the staying power of the C. B.
& Q. began to reassert itself; it stood a close second to the Milwaukee
in net railway operating income and outstripped it in respect to net income; by the end of the next year it had a comfortable lead in both
respects.

The contrast between the C. B. & Q. and its western lines was even
more marked. Like the C. B. & Q.'s own neighbors, the western subsidiaries benefited from the sudden surge of traffic, and in 1943 especially
were able to carry through substantial sums to net railway operating income and on to net income. But expenses, particularly on the Texas Lines,
increased more rapidly than revenue, and in 1945 the F. W. & D. C.
reported a net deficit.

Most of C. B. & Q.'s net income during the war years was retained
in the business for future improvements or was used to reduce funded
debt. Dividends on the C. B. & Q. were held at the two-dollar annual
rate through 1941, increased modestly to three dollars during 1942–44, and
only in 1945 boosted to six dollars. Of course, no dividends were paid by
either the C. & S. or the F. W. & D. C. Interest charges on debts of the
system taken together were sharply reduced; from a high point of nearly
$12,000,000 a year in 1941, they were brought below $9,000,000 by the
end of 1945, a reduction of one fourth.

So much for statistics. They are cold in themselves and fail to dramatize the human planning and effort that went into the Burlington's
achievement. During World War II everyone on the system, from top
to bottom, was busy, sometimes doing the work formerly done by others
as well as by himself. And in many situations women took over jobs formerly held by men. There simply was no time to lose; trains had to be got
over the road and through the yards. Behind that ultimate objective of
every railroader lay added effort for muscle and mind.

· Plant and Equipment ·

The appointment of Ralph Budd as Transportation Commissioner on May 28, 1940, brought the European war home to the Burlington in a dramatic and personal fashion. Yet, as he reported to his directors a month later, the Middle West was at the moment suffering a decline in traffic. As already indicated, the great impact of war traffic was slow to reach all parts of the Burlington system.

By the spring of 1941, however, no less than seven major armament plants and camps were under construction in C. B. & Q. territory. At Burlington, Iowa, for example, a shell-loading plant local to the C. B. & Q. would soon engage 6,000 workers, require 3,500 cars of construction materials, and offer 200 cars of traffic a day. On the Twin Cities line at Savanna, enormous proving grounds were being built local to the C. B. & Q.; annual carload business was estimated at 3,600 cars once the operations went on full schedule. Camp Grant, Illinois, was located so as to be served by the C. B. & Q. and the Milwaukee, but reached over tracks of the former; it was estimated that approximately 5,000 men a week would be moved in and out. Small wonder that the *Annual Report* for 1941 carried the terse comment: "Burlington continued to cooperate to the fullest extent in furthering the national defense and war effort."[2]

The Burlington Lines did not grow in road mileage during the war; in fact, the system abandoned 383 miles, thus contributing, incidentally, much-needed steel to the war effort. Among others, the colorful narrow-gauge line to Black Hawk, Colorado, was relinquished in 1941. On the other hand, the vital thirteen and a half mile link between the molybdenum mines at Climax and the Rio Grande's main line at Leadville was widened to standard gauge in 1943 so that the essential rare mineral could be speeded to destination without transfer.

One abandonment, that of the lightly used, twenty-two mile branch between Mt. Ayr, Iowa, and Grant City, Missouri, in 1944, led the Interstate Commerce Commission to enunciate what has since become known as the "Burlington Formula." According to it, any employee who, as a result of the abandonment, found himself in a worsened position in respect to his pay or to working rules affecting his pay was to receive a displacement allowance. If he had to move to a new job on the system, he was to be reimbursed for his moving and traveling expenses and for any losses he might sustain in selling his old home and buying a new one. Finally, if he lost employment altogether, he was to receive compensation for the next four years. This formula has been invoked ever since by the I. C. C. in all comparable abandonment cases.

One of the most striking technical advances during the war was the

[2] CB&Q, AR 1941, p. 12.

rapid extension of centralized traffic control. By the end of 1945, CTC had been installed on 131 miles of C. B. & Q. main line between Hastings and McCook, Nebraska, and work was being carried on between McCook and Akron, Colorado, a distance of 142 miles, as well as on the fifty-seven mile stretch between Flag Center and Savanna, Illinois. These major improvements on the company's two main lines were completed in the fall of 1946, whereupon the Burlington had either multiple-track or centralized traffic control over the entire 1,034-mile route between Chicago and Denver, as well as on the 437-mile line between Chicago and Minneapolis.

Equally spectacular were the advances made in communication. In 1944 the Burlington began extensive experiments with high frequency radio communication between yard offices and switch engines, and between locomotives and cabooses of freight trains. On the basis of these tests, the company asked for and received from the Federal Communications Commission construction permits and a frequency assignment which, effective December 31, 1945, allowed two-way radio telephone communication on a broad, permanent basis.

As the demands of World War II traffic rose, the company on June 15, 1942, authorized completion of the westbound unit of its freight-classification yard at Galesburg. Work progressed at a furious pace, so that on November 3, 1942, the thirty-five-track yard with retarders, together with an eleven-track receiving yard and twelve departure tracks, was put into operation. At the same time, radio communication was established among various parts of the yard and a teletype system was installed for the "consist lists" which gave the name of each car owner, its origin, destination, contents, and weight. Thus the capacity of the yard was doubled, and this fact, together with the increased speed of handling, saved 100,000 car-days annually. Despite the steady increase in the tonnage of freight trains, twenty percent more trains were cleared through Galesburg in October 1943 than in the same month of 1941. Indeed, when all modernization was completed, the Galesburg yard (renamed Willis Yard in 1946) had no less than 114 miles of track and a total freight-car capacity of 7,634. It was the largest facility of its kind then on the railroad. Reconstruction of the yard at Lincoln during 1944 was almost as big a project as that at Galesburg. When that job was done, it was estimated that 175,000 car-days could be saved annually; put otherwise, each freight train saved one and three-quarter hours going through Lincoln.

Although the extensive modernizations at Galesburg and Lincoln were the outstanding accomplishments of their sort during the war period, they were by no means the only ones. The capacity of the freight yards at Denver, for example, was increased from 862 to 1,535 cars during 1944. Improvement at that point continued, until by the end of 1947 freight-car capacity had been increased to 3,234 cars, four times what it had been just three years previously.

The building of new passenger stations during wartime was deferred, except in cases of emergency, such as occurred at Burlington, Iowa. At one minute past midnight on January 20, 1943, an overheated or exploding temporary oil heater in the waiting-room put the torch to the rambling historic structure that had been built in 1882 and was, ironically enough, in the process of being rebuilt. Tragically, four employees lost their lives in the blaze. Application was immediately filed with the War Production Board for authority to construct a new depot on the site at a cost exceeding a quarter of a million dollars. On March 28, 1944, the completely new, fieldstone edifice was dedicated by Governor Hickenlooper, Mayor Conrad of the city of Burlington, and Ralph Budd. In honor of Charles E. Perkins, an entire panel on the west wall recited his countless contributions to the Burlington and drew attention to the fact that throughout his long career the city had been the base of his operations.

The singling out of specific improvements should not obscure the importance of the system's regular maintenance program; roadbed was widened and drainage improved; on high-speed lines specially prepared ballast consisting of crushed rock, blast-furnace slag, or "chatt" (a by-product of lead and zinc mining) was applied. And what happened on top of such ballast? In 1944, for example, exactly 2,229,085 new creosoted cross-ties were placed in track, over fifty-three miles of track were relaid with new 131-pound (per yard) rail, and over 160 more miles were relaid with new 112-pound rail.

War demands required not only strong, fast track, but also sufficient cars and locomotives. During 1940, the C. B. & Q. stepped up its car-building program for 1941, and in the latter year turned out 2,918 freight cars from its own shops, in comparison with 746 the previous year. Furthermore, it purchased twenty-five Diesel-electric switchers (in contrast to ten the previous year) and added four more road passenger Diesels to the five it had acquired in 1940.

In compliance with recommendations of the Association of American Railroads, Burlington in 1941 agreed to undertake a construction program which would represent a fair contribution to the national freight-car supply for handling wartime traffic; plans called for the building of 3,925 additional cars in its own shops during 1942. Of these, 2,875 were to be closed and the others open-top cars. Since this program involved the expenditure of more than eleven million dollars, the company issued and sold, on August 15, 1941, $9,387,000 of one and a half percent equipment trust notes to cover eighty-five percent of the estimated outlay. The program was put underway with all possible speed, and 1,878 cars had been completed when, on April 30, 1942, the War Production Board ordered construction to cease even though all materials for 172 more cars were on hand and ready for assembly in the Havelock shops. Not until October 30, 1942, after a delay of six full months, did the Burlington receive permission to complete those 172 boxcars. By November 18 they were ready for service, but the delay caused by governmental red tape had cost the nation's railways exactly 31,648 car-days.

Meanwhile the Office of Defense Transportation was attempting to bring about the greatest possible use of freight-carrying equipment. After having issued preliminary orders, the O. D. T. on October 15, 1942, prohibited railroads from accepting for shipment, with certain exceptions, any freight cars not loaded to their marked load limit or to their visible capacity. Only tank cars, flatcars, and cars containing less-than-carload freight were excluded from the provisions of the order.

When 1942 came to an end, Burlington had constructed in its own shops a total of 2,228 cars, acquired a hundred refrigerator cars, and converted twenty-four other cars of various types. By then, as Budd told his directors, of even greater importance than cars was the supply of locomotives to handle the steadily rising traffic. Ever since early 1942 the company had had on order fifteen Diesel road engines and fifteen switchers, but not until 1943 were any delivered, and then only a dozen switchers. During 1943, the company constructed 170 special-type boxcars for the United States Navy, but was permitted to build only 900 sorely needed freight cars for its own use.

In 1944, the freight-car supply situation eased considerably. The company was able to build in its own shops 2,023 new freight cars of various kinds, as well as a hundred steel-sheathed mail, baggage, and express cars. As 1944 closed, 1,105 additional freight cars for delivery the following year were under construction. Of equal importance, C. B. & Q. received delivery of sixteen 5,400-horsepower road freight locomotives, at a cost of $500,000 each. The first unit went into operation on January 3, 1944, inaugurating freight Diesel service on the Burlington. In the course of that year, twenty-seven more Diesel switchers of 1,000-horsepower each joined the roster.

Not until 1945, however, was Burlington "over the hump" as far as equipment and motive power were concerned. During that year, the company built 1,225 freight cars of various types and acquired ten 4,000-horsepower passenger locomotives. This last delivery enabled the company, in December 1945, to complete dieselization of all passenger-train service between Chicago, Omaha, and Denver, and to assign Diesels to several other important runs on the system.

The most spectacular development in passenger equipment during the World War II period, and indeed for some time to come, was the introduction of the Vista-Dome, another Burlington "first." The idea first occurred to C. R. Osborn of General Motors, who, in July 1944, was studying the movement of wartime freight through the Rockies. Riding one day in the fireman's seat of a Denver and Rio Grande Western freight locomotive, he suddenly realized that if only passengers could have the same sort of unobstructed view of the magnificent scenery, they would, when conditions permitted, do a lot more traveling. Back in La Grange, Osborn put his designers to work, and in due course built a model passenger car with a glass-covered compartment in the roof. The question then was whether the railway industry, traditionally conservative, would adopt anything so radical and so expensive to build. "We'll show it to Budd," Osborn is reported to have said. "If he doesn't like it, we'll take an axe and chop the thing to bits."[3]

But Ralph Budd liked what he saw and asked Osborn if there was any objection to the Burlington taking one of its stainless-steel coaches, cutting a hole through the roof, and building a dome on it. Osborn was delighted. So it was that the C. B. & Q.'s "Silver Dome" made its debut on July 23, 1945, on one of the northbound *Twin Cities Zephyrs* and returned to Chicago the next day. During the next fortnight it made a round trip from Chicago to Lincoln and then to San Francisco and back. Public reaction to the Vista-Dome amounted to an ovation. Within less than six months, the Vista-Dome idea became so popular that forty more such specially constructed cars were ordered for service on trains operating over the Burlington.

· MANPOWER ·

As THE WAR PROGRESSED, the manpower situation on the Burlington, as on other railroads, became increasingly acute. The pinch began to be felt in 1942. Men in increasing numbers were entering the armed services and to a lesser extent leaving the railroad for the extraordinarily high wages in construction and in war plants. Equally important was a growing shortage of experienced help. Other sources of labor clearly would have to be tapped. Accordingly, toward the end of 1943, 798 Mexicans, recruited for the most part by John Williamson, director of personnel, from the Querétaro mining district, were brought in to help with essential work on track. Even so, continued shortages, along with the lack of materials, prevented the system from carrying out as much maintenance work as the heavy traffic demanded.

In February 1944, Budd reported that the manpower situation on the Burlington was serious and would be critical except for the mild weather. System lines, he said, were short 3,000 men, especially brakemen, switchmen, firemen, telegraph operators, skilled mechanics, linemen, bridge and building crews, and water-service employees. Furthermore, the Selective Service authorities were proposing to add 2,150 Burlington employees within the next six months to the 6,100 already in service.

[3] Lucia Lewis: "This Is Ralph Budd," *Chicago Daily News*, March 6, 1954.

Because the Burlington's problem was typical of that across the nation, the Office of Defense Transportation, the Railroad Retirement Board, the War Manpower Commission, and the Association of American Railroads joined the carriers in March 1944 in a nationwide effort to recruit railroad workers. By November, the situation had eased somewhat. Not only had volunteers stepped forward from the C. B. & Q. offices and other departments; also, the importation of Mexican nationals was resumed at increased tempo. During 1944, the Burlington brought in 2,983 more, of whom 2,736 went to work on the C. B. & Q., and the rest on the C. & S. and Texas Lines. Furthermore, many girls just out of high school were recruited for office jobs, in which, despite their youth and inexperience, they filled many an important gap.

As of December 1, 1944, 7,740 Burlington-system men and women had entered military service. Of these, 72 were reported deceased, 465 had been released and returned to their former positions, and 132 had been released but had not returned to work on the railroad. This left a balance in the services of 7,071.

One result of the increasing participation of women in railway work was the formation, in the spring of 1944, of the National Association of Railroad Women. Velma McPeek, supervisor of travel on the Burlington, was one of its organizers and served as its second president. As more women stayed on in the industry and assumed greater responsibilities, the need for a permanent organization soon became evident. In due course, the Association changed its name to the American Council of Railroad Women. Mrs. Edith Alden, who had become secretary and assistant treasurer of the C. B. & Q. in October 1938, was the highest-ranking railroad officer in the organization, and subsequently served as its president.

Because the manpower situation remained acute well into 1945, another detachment of 3,449 Mexicans was brought in during the year. As Budd told his stockholders, "these neighbors from south of the border have proved themselves efficient workers."[4] By November 1, 1945, the total number of Burlington employees who had entered military service since the beginning of the conflict was 8,343. At the end of that year, as demobilization progressed, 1,801 had been released and had re-entered company service. Meanwhile, the toll of those who had lost their lives for their country mounted to 166. In their honor a plaque bearing each name was placed in the lobby of the General Office Building in Chicago, where it remains as a reminder of their sacrifice.

Although Burlington men and women served in every branch of the armed forces, the contribution of the C. B. & Q. was highlighted by its sponsorship of the 745th Operating Battalion for the United States Army's

4 CB&Q, AR 1944, p. 8.

Military Railway Service. On May 19, 1943, the Battalion was activated at Camp Harrahan and began its basic training.

The stage on which the 745th was destined to play its dramatic role was an unfamiliar one indeed: the far northeastern reaches of India. The Battalion's assignment was to help operate the Bengal and Assam Railway, specifically the vital 658-mile stretch, all of it of meter gauge, from Katihar Junction (some 250 miles due north of Calcutta) east to Ledo, near the Burma border. The facilities of this line were badly strained, and operations were severely handicapped because of the need to use inadequate ferry service across the Brahmaputra River. In May 1943, only 15,000 tons of American supplies went over it; in the following months, not enough freight was handled to fill the cargo planes that were flying over the "hump" into China.

When the British regained control of the Bay of Bengal and reopened the port of Calcutta in May 1943, the Bengal and Assam assumed new and pressing importance. Some of its roadbed was excellent, but all equipment was in a woeful state of disrepair, most of the line was single-track, and sidings were so short they could handle hardly more than forty "goods wagons." Dispatching was poor, and there was the bottleneck where the road crossed the Brahmaputra River. Major improvements were called for immediately. Six months went by, however, and the Bengal and Assam was carrying little more freight at the end of the period than at the beginning. But in October 1943, General Brehon Somervell, in command of U. S. Army Service Forces, arrived in India, and with General W. A. Wheeler, soon to become Deputy Commander for Southeast Asia, conferred with Admiral Lord Louis Mountbatten, Supreme Allied Commander in the area. From this discussion emerged the decision, in November 1943, for the U. S. Military Railway Service to take over and operate the essential 658 miles of east-west line between Katihar Junction and Ledo; including branches, total trackage under American control would amount to 804 miles.

Once this decision was made, events moved rapidly. The main body of M. R. S. troops started to arrive at Bombay on January 11, 1944, and officially assumed control of the Katihar–Ledo portion of the Bengal and Assam Railway on March 1. Each of five operating battalions, including the 745th, was given a section of the vital main lines. The C. B. & Q.'s battalion established its headquarters and assumed responsibility for the 108 miles from Lumding to Mariana, including several branch lines.

The task facing the Americans was far from simple. The meter-gauge railway was laid on wooden ties with sixty-pound rail; ballast was hand-crushed rock from six to twelve inches in depth. This had been sufficient for prewar civilian operations, but the heavier power, longer trains, and higher speeds the M. R. S. knew to be necessary required the installation of rail anchors. Furthermore, the railway was subject to constant washouts of the bridge over the Beki River. Not until men from all five battalions had dug a channel to divert the river was that particular bridge free from trouble; for the first time in nearly thirty years, the railroad was kept in service throughout the monsoon period. Nor were the forces of nature the only handicaps. In the spring of 1944, the Japanese penetrated to within four and a half miles of the yards at Mariana, where the 745th was on duty. British and American troops were rushed to the danger spot and the Japanese were driven back, although wandering bands of snipers continued to harass railway operations. Indeed, it became necessary during this period to run rail motorcars with mounted machine guns ahead of trains to watch for damage to track and structures and to clear the area of snipers.

But there were amusing incidents too. From time to time it became necessary to transfer elephants, who, when motive power was short, performed yeoman service, switching cars in the yards. On one occasion, however, while elephants were being moved, the engineer, despite frequent stops for water, found it impossible to keep enough in his tank. Upon investigation, it developed that an elephant riding in the first car of the train was placidly sucking the water out of the tank and giving himself a continuous shower bath.

Despite these various vexations of greater or lesser degree, the 745th and its colleagues kept the Bengal and Assam in operation and made extensive improvements. The net result was that the line, which had handled only 109,000 tons in March 1944, carried more than 506,000 tons in May 1945. This meant that enormous stores of critically needed supplies were set down in Ledo, whence they were flown by air-lift to China or hauled by trucks over the Ledo and Burma roads, later relocated and ultimately called the Stilwell Road.

With the collapse of the Japanese forces, the M. R. S. troops were ordered to turn over operation of the Bengal and Assam to its owners and to leave for home. The last detachment of the 745th arrived in New York on October 28, 1945. Thus ended a chapter in World War II history in which the men of the C. B. & Q. played a distinctive and heroic part.

Even before the United States officially entered the conflict, the Burlington was making plans on behalf of those who had already joined the armed services or who would do so later on. A circular issued by Executive Vice-President Flynn on November 25, 1941, elaborated Burlington additions to what was required of the company by law. The company indicated that if any discharged man, because of sickness or temporary disability, was unable to resume his position within the statutory limit of forty days, he would still be entitled to re-employment upon his recovery. Furthermore, the courtesy of free and reduced rate transportation would be continued during any period of active training or service.

During the early years of the war, very few men were released, and the company's attention was directed primarily toward those in active service. Late in the fall of 1943, money belts were dispatched as Christmas gifts to every Burlington employee. A year later, a compact Christmas gift box was sent to each man and woman in service for whom an address was available. Apart from the provisions to protect the positions and seniority of returning veterans, every effort was made to take care of special cases. For example, to facilitate placement of injured war veterans, a survey was undertaken of positions available to men with certain handicaps. And if a veteran had acquired more education or a particular new skill while in service, arrangements were made to place him in a position in which his particular talent could best be utilized.

One major innovation adopted during wartime in respect to the health and welfare of all Burlington employees became immediately available to returning veterans. On June 1, 1943, the C. B. & Q., at the request of representatives of the non-operating employees, established a Group Hospital Expense and Surgical Benefits Insurance Plan, open on a monthly contributory basis to all non-operating employees. Train, engine, and yard-service employees did not participate in the formal request for the insurance, but a considerable number of them elected to join the Plan. Indeed, so great was the response to the Plan that it was made available to all departments on July 1, 1943; three months later, coverage was extended to wives and dependent children.

Since modern warfare requires a total effort, it was inevitable that the people of the Burlington should undertake a wide range of special activities during the conflict. For example, the company encouraged and facilitated the purchase of war bonds. Early in 1943, approximately eighty-five percent of all employees were regularly purchasing and paying for them through payroll deductions. A campaign also was waged for the collection of scrap, and the company became, in effect, a collecting agent for the government. In addition, along the right of way and in the back-yards of employees, victory gardens sprang up over the length and breadth of the system. The Burlington name acquired new associations abroad too. Early in 1944, word reached the company that Lieutenant Don Weiss, a former fireman on the La Crosse division, was flying a B-17 bomber on missions over German-occupied Europe. The name of his plane: The Twin Zephyr.

• WARTIME OPERATION—USUAL AND UNUSUAL •

THE AMOUNT OF FREIGHT and passenger service produced by the Burlington during wartime has already been discussed in quantitative terms. But the way in which the job was done was as remarkable as its size.

In view of the shortage of critical materials and skilled manpower, the safety performance on the system was little short of miraculous. In 1941, for example, the C. & S. had the best safety performance in its history. With no fatalities and only thirteen reportable employee injuries, it achieved a casualty rate of only 3.85 per million man-hours. This splendid performance won for the C. & S. the 1941 award of the National Safety Council for railways of its size. Again in 1944, the C. & S. won the award, its casualty rate then being 6.46 per million man-hours worked, as compared with an average of 16.61 for railways of comparable size. So far as the system as a whole was concerned, the potentially greater hazard of operating so many more and heavier trains during wartime was offset by increased vigilance. For the twenty-year period from 1927 to 1946, inclusive, Burlington ranked first sixteen times and second four times in the lowest number of accidents per million locomotive-miles. In the war period itself, from December 7, 1941, through December 31, 1945, the system handled 3,101,790 military personnel in 10,165 special trains and another 1,479,922 men in 44,536 special cars on regular trains—without the loss of a life in a train accident.

Wartime conditions often called for ingenious improvisation. Early in 1945, the C. B. & Q. leased a chicken ranch near Lincoln so that, despite the shortage of meat, passengers on Burlington diners would be well fed. The ranch provided 30,000 birds a year, thus helping to preserve the company's reputation for providing good fare on the rails. Still another facet of unlisted service continued to be provided; when the *American Royal*, enroute from Kansas City, reached Quincy in the middle of an early spring night of 1944, it had one passenger aboard with no ticket: a baby born enroute. Mother and child were taken to a Quincy hospital, where both were promptly reported as doing well. As Charles Kettering of General Motors put it at the *Pioneer Zephyr's* tenth birthday party held at about the same time, "so long as we do what has to be done today, there is no limit to what can be done."[5] A railroad, by its very nature, had always to be ready for emergencies as a normal part of its existence.

But it also had to keep looking ahead. During 1942, an exhaustive study was made as to the extent, if any, to which the Burlington should participate in air transport. The research, completed in September, indicated a distinct place for feeder service between major points on the C. B. & Q. main lines and outlying cities within or close to the system's territory. Thus in the early summer of 1943, the Burlington Transportation Company, the C. B. & Q.'s bus and truck subsidiary, filed an application with the Civil Aeronautics Board for permission to offer helicopter service between such points as Des Moines and Ottumwa, and Peoria and Galesburg, so that passengers could be brought to and from the Zephyrs.

Later on, in June 1945, the B. T. Company made a more compre-

5 Burlington *Zephyr*, Vol. VII, No. 2 (March–April, 1944).

hensive application: it sought authority to transport passengers, mail, and express by helicopter over six routes along which there would be a total of sixty-seven stops. Although every one of the communities involved was already served by either the C. B. & Q. or the B. T. Company or both, most of the towns or cities were on branches. More to the point, only thirteen of the sixty-seven communities were then served by air. The company's proposal would serve not only to funnel business to the existing main lines, but also to offer to some fifty-four localities far quicker service than they then had. Nevertheless, some of the airlines added their opposition to that of those (including the counsel for the federal government) who feared that the company's proposal was a step toward restoring to the railroads a monopoly of public transportation. On February 28, 1946, the examiner in charge of the case recommended to the Civil Aeronautics Board that the application be denied. In effect, the company was told to restrict its operations to the ground.

This still left room for the Burlington Transportation Company, which, like its parent railroad, shouldered a mounting traffic burden during the war. Whereas route miles covered by buses rose modestly from 8,035 in 1941 to 8,415 in 1945, bus miles over the same period soared from 14.7 to 20.9 million, and net income jumped from $122,232 to $715,586. At the same time, truck route-miles increased from 3,998 to 4,952, and truck miles from 5.2 to 6.3 million; the modest net income of $51,265 in 1941, however, declined steadily in 1942–43, went into the red in the next year, and resulted in a net loss of $209,572 in 1945, primarily because of rising wages and taxes.

• Wages, Labor Relations, and Material Costs •

Despite the efforts of the New Deal to modify, postpone, or offset the inexorable workings of the law of supply and demand in respect to the economy as a whole, human nature clung to it tenaciously. As the demand for skilled workers increased and the supply steadily fell off, it was inevitable that the brotherhoods should take full advantage of their vastly improved bargaining position to demand more favorable wages and working conditions.

The course and disposition of these demands have been traced in the previous chapter. Particularly relevant to the Burlington was the fact that when the federal government, to avoid a strike, took possession of the railroads on December 27, 1943, and divided the nation into seven operating regions, Ralph Budd was appointed colonel in charge of the Central Western District, and in that capacity served in uniform until January 18, 1944, when, after settlement of the disputes, the roads were returned to their owners. Suffice it to say, further, that the increases applicable to 1943 added approximately $5,600,000 to C. B. & Q. payroll costs, $595,000 to those of the Colorado and Southern Lines. It was estimated that for 1944, the new pay scales would add over ten and a half million dollars to system payrolls.

Although peace reigned on the labor front throughout most of 1944, new demands between November of that year and the end of 1945 would, if granted, have cost the Burlington Lines more than $46,000,000. Not a single one of the disputes was settled in conference between the unions and the company, and toward the end of 1945, mediation was invoked. There matters stood as the year ran out.

Meanwhile, material costs were rising at a time when more than usual had to be spent throughout the system for maintenance and improvements. That prices for materials rose more than twenty-five percent between the end of 1941 and the end of 1945 suggests the importance of this factor. The sharp increase in 1945 on all system lines was particularly notable, although the C. B. & Q., C. & S., and F. W. & D. C. all elected, pursuant to a Presidential Proclamation of September 29, 1945, to charge to operating expenses in that year the unamortized portion of the cost of facilities acquired or constructed to further the war effort. This increased expenses both for maintenance of way and structures and for maintenance of equipment over what they would otherwise have been. At the same time and as a consequence, however, federal taxes were substantially reduced for 1945.

• RATES, FARES, AND TAXES •

THE EFFORTS of the Burlington, and of the other railways, to offset any substantial portion of the wartime wage increases and the rising costs of materials by higher rates and fares were, on the whole, unsuccessful. As was true for all business and individuals, taxes leaped upward during the war years. In comparison with 1941, the C. B. & Q. paid over four and a half times more in 1943. Both in 1943 and in 1944, taxes were approximately twice the net income earned in those years, owing principally to the impact of excess profits taxes, which, of themselves, exceeded net income. Some relief came in 1945, when, as a result of the President's proclamation of September 29, railways were permitted to charge to operating expenses the unamortized portion of the cost of facilities acquired or constructed to help the war effort. This resulted in a tax credit in that year of slightly more than $20,000,000 for the system.

During the war, everyone expected to pay higher taxes to help meet the crushing expenses of the conflict. What all businesses wondered, looking to the future, was how long wartime rates would remain in effect. The railways in particular had a special concern: in 1941, a five percent tax had been laid on all passengers traveling by common carrier. This levy was raised to ten percent in 1942 and, specifically in order to discourage travel, to fifteen percent in 1944. It was still in effect at the end of 1945. Meanwhile, in 1942, Congress had laid a tax of three percent on all freight (except coal, which paid four cents a ton) moved by common carriers by rail, air, highway, or waterway (the tax on pipelines was four and a half percent). These taxes, too, were on the books as 1945 drew to a close.

The potential problem was clear: such taxes, paid by the traveler or shipper (but collected for the government at the expense of the carriers), discriminated against for-hire carriers and favored private transportation, such as the private automobile and the company-owned truck or barge, all of which were exempt from the levy. So long as private carriage was sharply curtailed, as it was during the war, the problem was not pressing, but as the economy returned to normal, these "wartime taxes," if left in effect, might become a major competitive handicap to all common carriers. This is precisely what happened.

• Financial Results •

Of course, the fundamental offset to constantly rising wages, material costs, taxes, and "frozen rates" was the revenue from the huge volume of traffic the Burlington carried throughout the war period. Net income on the C. B. & Q. for the four years 1942–45 inclusive, was ninety-eight percent of total net income for the thirteen years 1929–41, inclusive, though this calculation does not take into account the decline in the purchasing power of the dollar. The effect of the war was even more spectacular on the C. & S. Net income for 1942–45, inclusive, amounted to 218 percent of that during the previous thirteen years. The comparable figure on the Texas Lines was 139 percent. Although the western subsidiaries outstripped their parent in the extent to which net income during the war exceeded that of the previous lean years, this was, in one sense, simply an indication of how much worse off the western lines had been during the depression.

During 1941, net income of the C. B. & Q. exceeded ten million dollars for the first time since 1931. With this nation serving as the "Arsenal of Democracy," it was clear that traffic would continue to grow, and that is the principal reason why so much thought during the first half of 1941 was devoted to the possibility of reducing funded debt, notably the Illinois Division Mortgage that would mature in 1949. But the uncertainties of the times and differences of opinion as to what course to follow had simply resulted, in June 1941, in the adoption of a "watch-and-wait policy" and the determination to build up cash resources. In accord with this latter objective, the dividend declared on December 18, 1941, was only $2 a share, compared with earnings of $6.10 a share.

As business continued to mount through the opening months of

1942, Budd took the initiative in exploring, once more, specific methods for handling the maturity of 1949. Business was better, and if the extremely modest size of the 1941 dividend was any indication, the Northern Lines—in contrast to what happened in the decade ending in 1940— might be willing to leave the dividend rate at a conservative level in relation to earnings, thus greatly increasing the prospect that C. B. & Q. would have substantial amounts of excess cash on hand by the end of each year.

Budd sought, then, on May 7, 1942, the approval of the presidents of the Northern Lines to spend five million dollars of Burlington cash to acquire Illinois Division bonds in the open market. He pointed out that there would be an actual gain in money in so doing because, at the current market, the bonds were yielding 5.7 percent. Even more important, such purchases would improve Burlington credit both by sustaining the market for its bonds and by reducing the amount to be paid on maturity. Furthermore, if the total amount outstanding were to be reduced substantially, then the interest rate on the portion to be extended could be materially lower. Budd suggested a specific program of yearly purchases over the seven-year interval prior to maturity, to diminish the total debt to $60,000,000; then a twenty-five percent payment on this balance, to bring the amount to be refunded, by extension or otherwise, to $45,000,000. This program would require the use or accumulation of an average of about five million dollars a year beginning in 1942 and running through 1949.

So it was that in May and June 1942 the Burlington was authorized to spend five million dollars to purchase Illinois Division bonds. By mid-October, nearly all of this amount had been expended. The board then authorized use of another ten million for the same purpose.

This action, it should be noted, had been made possible by a combination of high earnings and an extremely conservative dividend policy. Net income for 1942 amounted to $28,646,920, equivalent to $16.70 per share. Nevertheless, the dividend was held to $3 per share, thus leaving $23,521,759 as surplus. The greater part of this was used for the retirement of debt.

During the early months of 1943, Burlington temporarily suspended its program of bond purchases, but on May 7, 1943, an additional five million dollars was authorized for that purpose. By the end of the month, another $1,500,000 was similarly earmarked, and in early July, five million more. Thus, within fourteen months the Burlington spent $26,500,000 to retire bonds with a par value of $27,377,000. As Dr. John T. O'Neil states in his monograph on the subject: "Surely this represented a creditable attack upon the $85,000,000 maturity in that short period of time."[6] The company stood to save over $950,000 per year in interest charges as well.

[6] O'Neil: *Policy Formation in Railroad Finance*, p. 89; see also pp. 81–9.

During 1943, the Burlington also reduced its equipment obligations by $3,924,312, a step made possible by a conservative dividend policy; although net income amounted to $16.53 a share in 1943, only $3 was paid out as dividend. In short, funded debt and equipment obligations together were reduced $41,120,391 in 1942 and 1943. As a result, Burlington's senior securities rose to par and beyond on the market, and the credit position of the company was greatly improved.

Under the circumstances, the company's officers began, during the summer of 1943, to consider seriously the possibility of calling the $56,773,000 in Illinois Division bonds still outstanding before maturity and replacing them with equivalent or lower coupon issues. On the assumption that sufficient treasury cash would be available to retire outstanding bonds in excess of $40,000,000, the major question was how to retire this remaining balance and when to put the plan in operation. The problem was complicated by a curious fact: the Illinois Division Mortgage provided that if these bonds were to be called, it was necessary to give bondholders six months' notice, and to publish such notice daily for four consecutive weeks in advance of this six-month period. In other words, definite refunding plans would have to be completed some seven months before the date chosen for the redemption of the bonds. What might happen to the bond market during that interval would be problematical, to say the least. The company concluded that the best way to make sure of a market for its new bonds would be to place them privately at an agreed-upon price rather than to offer them for public subscription and take a chance on the price they might fetch. Furthermore, to simplify the operation it was decided to let a single investment banker, rather than a group of bankers, work out the details of the new issue and find the purchasers for it. The problem was placed in the hands of Morgan, Stanley and Company, investment bankers already fully familiar with the objectives sought.

On April 5, 1944, Budd recommended to the presidents of the Northern Lines the following plan: all outstanding Illinois Division bonds were to be called for redemption. To provide for their retirement, the company proposed to sell $10,000,000 one and a half percent Serial Collateral Trust notes and $30,000,000 three and a half percent Collateral Trust bonds; the other funds necessary were to be provided from treasury cash. The Serial notes were to be repayable at the rate of $2,000,000 annually over a five-year period and were to be secured by $15,000,000 of First and Refunding Mortgage four and a half percent bonds, Series of 1970. The Collateral Trust bonds were to mature in twenty-five years and be secured by $55,000,000 of First and Refunding Mortgage four and a half percent bonds, Series of 1970. Furthermore, after the fifth year, the Collateral Trust bonds would be subject to a sinking fund of $1,000,000 a year. This plan was accepted by the Executive Committee of the

C. B. & Q. on April 18, and approved by the Interstate Commerce Commission on May 22.

Meanwhile, five large life insurance companies had agreed, subject to I. C. C. approval (which was subsequently granted), to purchase at par the $30,000,000 Collateral Trust bonds as of December 1, 1944. Only the problem of marketing the $10,000,000 Serial Collateral Trust notes remained. Like the bonds, the notes were to be dated December 1, 1944; the last of them would be paid off December 1, 1949. Responses to advertisements for bids were gratifying, and eventually the notes were sold to a group headed by the First National Bank of New York and J. P. Morgan and Company at a price representing an interest cost to the Burlington of approximately 1.7 percent, a notable saving under the two percent that had been originally contemplated.

The resounding success of the plan to refund the Illinois Division Mortgage bonds led to a prompt and substantial improvement of Burlington's credit position in the financial community. The company immediately sought to translate the favorable climate into a specific advantage by refunding other issues outstanding.

Logically, the first issue to replace was the First and Refunding Series A five percent bonds due in 1971, amounting to $40,000,000. Accordingly, these were called for redemption on December 1, 1944, and replaced by bonds in the same amount carrying three and three-quarters percent interest due in 1974. This transaction required a premium payment of three million dollars, which was supplied by treasury cash, but as the Burlington was in the excess profit bracket, the net cost was considerably less; furthermore, the operation resulted in the saving of $500,000 in interest charges per year. Here matters stood at the end of 1944; the company had achieved a net decrease in capital liabilities of well over $12,000,000 during the year. Furthermore, the conservative dividend policy was continued. Net income in 1944 amounted to $14.33 per share of capital stock, but the dividend was again held to three dollars a share, permitting transfer of $19,521,961 to surplus.

Developments in 1945 have been neatly summarized by O'Neil in the table reproduced here.[7] Step I describes the Illinois Division refunding already explained, Step II the refunding of the F. & R. five percent bonds outlined immediately above. Step III, originated in 1945, simply converted the three and a half percent Collateral Trust bonds that played such an important role in the Illinois Division refunding, as well as the three and three-quarters percent F. & R.'s so lately issued, into a new series of First and Refunding bonds due in 1985 at the lower coupon rate of three and one-eighth percent. This operation, conducted through competitive bidding in accord with the I. C. C.'s *Ex Parte* Number 158 ruling, resulted in a saving of interest charges of more than half a million

[7] Ibid., Table 25, p. 181.

Chicago, Burlington & Quincy Railroad Company, steps in 1944–45 refinancing

Step	Call date	Issue affected	Maturity date	Price called	Yield at call	Cost including premium (millions of dollars)	Principal amount (millions of dollars)	New issue	Price received	Interest cost	Principal amount (millions of dollars)	Treasury cash provided (millions of dollars)	Principal banker
I.	(December 4, 1944)[a] January 1, 1945	Illinois Division 3½'s and 4's	1949	105	2.5	59,612	56,773	Collateral Trust 3½'s	100.000	3.50	30.00		Morgan Stanley
								Serial Note 1½'s	99.399	1.70 / 3.05	10.00	19.612	
II.	(October 23, 1944)[a] February 1, 1945	F & R 5's Series A	1971	107½	4.5	43,000	40,000	F & R 3¼'s, Series '74	99.137	3.79	40.00	3.300	Morgan Stanley
III.	(October 26, 1945)[a] January 15, 1946	Collateral Trust 3½'s	1969	105	3.20	31,500	30,000	F & R 3⅛'s, Series '85	100.0399	3.13	65.00	7.51[c]	Morgan Stanley
	February 1, 1946	F & R 3¾'s	1974	103⅝	3.545	40,925 / 72,429	39,493						
IV.	(December 12, 1945)[a]	General Mortgage 4's	1958	120	2.27	39,072	32,568	F & R 2⅞, Series '70	100.1399	2.87	49.765	10.77[c]	Halsey Stuart
	November 26–December 10[b]	F & R 4½'s Series B	1977	123	3.33 / 2.74	21,327 / 60,399	17,340 / 49,908						

[a] Date new issue awarded.
[b] Period for submitting tenders of acceptance of exchange offer.
[c] As reported in CBQ Annual Report, 1945, p. 13.

dollars. Treasury cash amounting to slightly more than seven and a half million dollars was used to complete the exchange.

When this transaction had been carried out, the only two remaining issues that had been outstanding in 1940 were the four percent General Mortgage bonds due in 1958, outstanding in the amount of $65,247,000, and $29,800,000 in four and a half percent F. & R. bonds Series B due in 1977. As Step IV, therefore, the company on November 26, 1945, on invitations for tenders, purchased $32,568,000 of General Mortgage bonds at the call price of 120, and $17,339,900 of the F. & R. four and a half percent bonds were replaced by bonds carrying a two and seven-eighths percent coupon.

To accomplish Steps III and IV together had required $18,272,314 in treasury cash, but of this substantial amount, $13,541,795 (including certain other expenses) was deductible from taxable income for the year 1945. The burden of paying premiums to call the bonds therefore was materially diminished.

The net effect of all four steps on the capital structure of the Burlington was spectacular. When the Illinois Division Mortgage was officially released on June 13, 1945, the General Mortgage of 1958 became a first lien on substantially the entire railroad, and as a result of Step IV that mortgage had been cut approximately in half. By Step II, the F. & R. five percent bonds of 1971 had been eliminated entirely, and by Step IV the F. & R., four and a half percent bonds of 1977 had been reduced sixty percent. The two new obligations issued in the process bore lower coupon rates. And at the close of 1945, the C. B. & Q. had over $42,500,000 in cash and cash assets.

Thus, between the end of 1940 and the end of 1945, long-term debt was reduced $45,620,000, or 19.4 percent, while the interest on this debt declined $3,550,000, or 37.6 percent. And the total of all fixed charges, including equipment obligations, declined from 9.66 million to 6.11 million dollars, or nearly thirty-seven percent. As a result, outstanding funded debt at the end of 1945 was smaller than at any time since 1922, whereas fixed charges were at a lower rate than at any time since the Illinois Division bonds had been originally issued in 1899.

From the very beginning, the Burlington's debt-reduction program had two main objectives: to improve the company's credit position and to bring the Burlington's debt structure into line with those of its three principal competitors, the Milwaukee, the North Western, and the Rock Island, all of which were under reorganization when the Burlington program began. Both objectives were achieved. Furthermore, the new bond issues all contained flexible call provisions that would give the company far greater freedom of action if circumstances warranted revision of the capital structure in the future.

Meanwhile, the major debt adjustment on the Colorado and Southern that had been so successfully carried through in 1943 was making itself increasingly felt. As a result of a vigorously applied program, the C. & S. Refunding and Extension Mortgage, which had stood at $27,015,700 at the end of 1942, was reduced to $21,400,000 at the end of 1945, and of the latter amount, $3,900,000 was held by the Fort Worth and Denver City and was subject to retirement as soon as the Texas company paid its note to R. F. C. At the same time, the C. & S. General Mortgage in the hands of the public was cut by nearly thirty-seven percent, and the F. W. & D. C. note to the R. F. C. was reduced by more than eight percent. Meanwhile, the C. & S., under its debt-adjustment plan, paid all fixed and contingent interest on both its Refunding and Extension and General Mortgage bonds. All this boded well for the financial stability of the western subsidiaries as they faced the inevitable adjustments of the postwar period.

· The Outlook ·

As the hectic war period drew to a close, more thought was inevitably devoted to the years that lay ahead. The direction in which developments were likely to move was suggested in a radio broadcast over the Mutual Network on June 18, 1944, when Budd participated in a panel with representatives of the airlines, the automobile industry, and the truckers to discuss "The Future of Transportation." It was agreed that swift technological progress undoubtedly would follow, as would changes in the traffic pattern and, if the war years were any indication, rising taxes and wages. One thing was certain: competition would be stiffer than ever.

Perhaps the best indication of how that—and other—challenges would be met can be found in what Budd wrote in the spring of 1945 under the heading "Outlook" in the *Annual Report* for 1944: "During its history of nearly a hundred years, the company has met its financial obligations and has provided dependable service, in spite of wars, panics, and depressions. Burlington will endeavor to maintain its position as an essential carrier in the years that lie ahead. . . . Unless Burlington, in common with other railroads, suffers severe loss of traffic through the subsidizing of competitors, it should be able to progress and to offer better and still better service."[8] In this spirit the company faced the postwar years.

[8] CB&Q, AR 1944, p. 15.

CHAPTER 28

The Postwar Period: Plant and Operations

1945-49

• THE POSTWAR SCENE •

WHEN WORLD WAR II came to an end in the summer of 1945, many a leader of government, industry, and labor feared that, after the war boom, the nation could reasonably expect a period of unemployment, hard times, and even depression. After all, men at the decision-making level could remember only too well the shock the economy had suffered in 1921; the farmers, indeed, never really recovered from it until the onset of the second world conflict.

But the innumerable people who had expected a postwar depression were happily surprised, for no such thing took place. On the contrary, the high rate of industrial productivity that had characterized the war years continued at full speed, albeit in new directions. The replacement needs in industry, continuing exports for relief and reconstruction abroad, and, more importantly, the pent-up demand for consumer goods that had been scarce or unobtainable for four years stimulated production all along the line. This was the first notable "attendant circumstance" of the immediate postwar period.

Prosperity of this sort, however, had potential hazards, which, unfortunately, promptly materialized. Whereas industry welcomed the almost immediate removal of controls by the War Production Board and the reduction of taxes, the removal of price controls by the Office of Price Administration very shortly thereafter contributed to a dangerous and progressive inflation far more severe than any that had occurred during wartime. The consumer's price index, which had risen from its 1939 base point of 100 to about 130 by V-J day, shot up to approximately 175 by mid-1948 before the appearance of any sign of stabilization. The second important characteristic of the postwar scene was rampant inflation.

The inevitable result was an immediate, prolonged and determined drive on the part of organized labor for higher wages. But more was at stake: the unions were determined to consolidate the gains they had achieved under the New Deal. Despite the fact that many satisfactory agreements were worked out through collective bargaining, labor historian Foster Rhea Dulles soberly commented upon the trend thus: "The tremendous economic power of the unions, and the constant danger of national strikes threatening public health and safety, increasingly alarmed the public. A feeling grew that some way had to be found to prevent arbitrary domination over the country's economic life by any organized minority, even as representative as labor. The government was called upon to meet the challenge of big labor as it had once been called upon to assert its authority over big business."[1] The third cardinal factor at work in the postwar years was organized labor's determined drive for higher wages. How well it succeeded is suggested by the fact that during the four years 1946–49, inclusive, the total number of civilian employees across the nation increased 7.6 percent; civilian wages and salaries increased 36.9 percent.

How did these three elements—prosperity, rising prices, and increased labor costs—affect the railway industry? A general answer may be suggested immediately by making two assumptions: if the railways had been able to retain the share of the transportation business which they had had during the war years, and if they had been free (from both a competitive and a regulatory standpoint) to adjust their rates and fares to meet increased costs, they would have floated on top of the wave of prosperity, as did most businesses that could maintain their competitive status and enjoy freedom of pricing. But as neither of these assumptions was true, the railways found themselves, despite the prosperity that stimulated the rest of the nation, in severely straitened circumstances. Indeed, if the railways had not drastically reduced their fixed charges during wartime, and had they not invested heavily in labor-saving and cost-cutting devices in the postwar years, they might well have experienced a plague of bankruptcies similar to that of the mid-1930's.

Consider first how radically the competitive traffic pattern changed in

[1] Foster Rhea Dulles: *The United States Since 1865* (Ann Arbor: University of Michigan Press; 1959), p. 473.

Grain elevator along the C. B. & Q.

Containers to be transloaded to and from ships, carrying Hawaiian pineapples

All-welded double-door, 50-foot boxcar No. 47790, built February 1964

B.R.M.X. mechanical refrigerator car No. 5100, built July–August 1963

Double-door, 50-foot boxcar No. 47100, built April 1963

Conventional covered hopper car No. 85544, built June 1963

Center-flow covered hopper car No. 85407, built May 1963

Double-deck stock car No. 50596, built December 1962

Jumbo-size open-top hopper car No. 160006, built July–August 1963

Steel caboose No. 13595, built February–March 1964

Burlington's two remaining steam locomotives (coal-burning No. 4960, built 1923; oil-burning No. 5632, out-shopped 1940), at Galesburg, Illinois, 1963

Postal clerks aboard the *Fast Mail*, operated since March 11, 1884, between Chicago and Council Bluffs-Omaha

Automatic classification yard, Cicero, Illinois, completed 1958

A century of locomotive evolution on the Burlington: diamond-stack No. 35, wood-and-coal-burner of the type used from 1850 well into the twentieth century; mikado-type coal-burner No. 1960, built 1923; Diesel-powered Zephyr locomotive, introduced 1934; E-9 passenger unit built for Zephyrs by General Motors; turbo-charged GP-30 locomotive No. 974 for fast freight, built December 1963 by General Motors the immediate postwar years: substantial amounts of freight business were lost to trucks, while buses, airplanes, and, above all, the private automobile made great inroads on passenger traffic. Business was also lost to water transport and pipelines. In absolute terms, the picture, thanks to the "general prosperity," was far less bleak. Each of the four postwar years saw more freight moved by rail than in any prewar year. Even in 1949, when traffic was at the lowest level since World War II, the railways produced 17.8 percent more ton-miles than in the booming year 1929. And even though passenger traffic dropped very sharply after the war years, revenue passenger-miles in 1949 were higher than in any prewar year since 1926. Despite the deteriorating competitive condition of the railways in relation to other carriers, they still had a substantial amount of business to move.

What effect did all this have on earnings? During the postwar years, the Interstate Commerce Commission granted a number of freight-rate and passenger-fare increases; the net result for Class I railroads was that total operating revenues for the four years 1946–49 were only 3.6 percent less than those of the four war years.

The operation of the other two factors so characteristic of the postwar scene—price inflation and wage increases—bore down heavily on the railway industry. In the period 1946–49, materials cost 41.7 percent more than during the war, and wage rates went up 40.5 percent. Although these rising costs were, to a certain extent, offset by related freight and passenger-rate increases, the railways were obliged, during the postwar years, to spend much more than under normal conditions (1) to rehabilitate their plant and equipment after the extraordinarily hard usage of the war years, and (2) to undertake a crash program of entirely new improvements in a dual effort to bolster their competitive situation and to take advantage, insofar as possible, of labor-saving and cost-cutting devices. Inflation meant that for these enormous new expenditures the railways obtained far less than they would have in earlier years for the same amount of money.

These, then, were the broad outlines of the situation that faced the nation's railways in the postwar years. What could the Burlington do to meet this situation? It could and did determine policy as to changes in fixed plant, the equipment program, the drive for more traffic, and efficiency of operation. But the success of these policies, as measured by net income, was largely dependent on the rate and regulatory structure, the extent of competition, material costs, and the wage level. These matters were all essentially beyond the control of management.

• FIXED PLANT VS. FLEXIBLE STRATEGY •

TESTIFYING before the Interstate Commerce Commission on November 30, 1948, Ralph Budd emphasized a few homely truths about railroads.

Their physical plant, he said, was the result of an evolution extending over more than a hundred years, and consisted essentially of fixed property such as roadways, structures, and equipment that represented an investment of well over 20 billion dollars. Consequently, it was simply "out of the question to have any immediate or exceedingly rapid revision and reconstruction of the physical properties. There would be no economic justification, and the country could not afford, to scrap billions of dollars of property which is usefully employed. . . simply because somewhat better results could be achieved if, by magic, an entirely new plant could be substituted which would embrace all the most recent developments of science and industry. . . . The only feasible method of providing adequate and efficient transportation and of adapting the railroad plant to the growing and changing needs of the country is to do so gradually but continuously. . . ."[2]

There was food for thought in these comments; implicit in them was a program for action. Clearly, the railways' major competitors for business—the motor truck and bus, the private auto, and the airplane—possessed an increasing degree of adaptability as new highways, more airports, and better motors permitted them to serve more and more communities. In contrast, the railways appeared more rigid than ever before. But, as Budd emphasized, the main railway routes were as essential as ever, in peace and in war. The imperative necessity was for the railroads to bring their principal lines, connecting large population centers, to the highest possible level of efficiency and to weed out the lightly patronized branches which could no longer compete effectively with the newer modes of transportation and which simply drained the resources of their owners.

One way for the Burlington to achieve the first objective was simply to follow its long-established policy of concentrating its efforts in any given year on what seemed to be the weakest portion of its main-line system. There was no question, as World War II ended, where this was; for a generation at least, successive C. B. & Q. administrations had sought to rectify and improve the situation in northern Missouri. Specifically, they wanted to improve St. Louis–Kansas City service and to shorten the through route between Chicago and Kansas City. As a matter of fact, just before World War II, Budd had drawn up a plan to do just that, only to have it turned down by the Northern Lines. Nothing could have been more logical than for him to attack the problem again as the end of the war drew near. Fortunately a combination of circumstances opened the way for a feasible and relatively inexpensive solution.

Ever since 1904, the C. B. & Q. had intermittently operated both freight and passenger trains over the joint route consisting of its own line between St. Louis and Francis (near Mexico) and the Alton between

2 Budd: statement in ICC, *Ex Parte* 168, November 30, 1948, pp. 3–5.

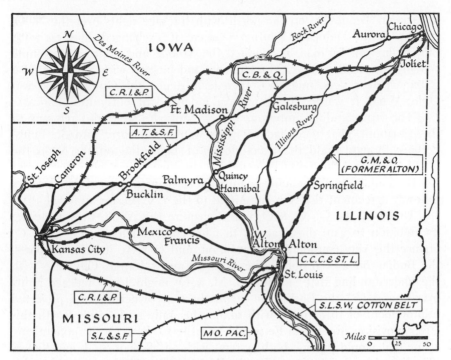

Northern Missouri and vicinity, 1945–52

Francis and Kansas City. Since May, 1937, however, freight service over this route had been discontinued, partly because each participant was naturally disposed to solicit the full line haul over its own tracks, and partly because of the difficulty of coordinating the schedules of the two roads; as a result, Burlington freight trains in 1945 were using the company's wholly owned, roundabout rails through Hannibal, Palmyra, and Cameron Junction. On the other hand, both the daylight *General Pershing Zephyr* (then hauled by steam power) and the *Night Hawk* were making daily round trips over the joint line. The future of the Alton, however, with its main lines linking Chicago to both St. Louis and Kansas City, was uncertain. Controlled by the Baltimore and Ohio from 1931 to 1942, the Alton had gone into receivership in the latter year, and although it had regained its independent status in the spring of 1943, plans for its reorganization had still not crystallized by 1945.

In contrast to the long-established Alton, the Gulf, Mobile and Ohio was a relative newcomer among the nation's major systems. It had started as a forty-nine-mile local road under another name in 1917, and had gradually expanded under the guidance of its extraordinary president, I. B. Tigrett, until, at the end of 1929 (as the Gulf, Mobile and Northern) its main line stretched from both New Orleans and Mobile on the south to Jackson, Tennessee, on the north, with trackage rights over the N. C. and St. L. to Paducah, Kentucky, where it exchanged business with the Burlington. In 1940, it acquired the Mobile and Ohio, a 1,000-mile system connecting Mobile, Montgomery, and Jackson with St. Louis. The system of over 2,000 miles was then rechristened the Gulf, Mobile and Ohio. What it wanted most was an independent entry into Chicago.

The long-standing ambitions of the Santa Fe were also relevant to this situation. That road had for years wanted an entry into St. Louis. Perhaps, thought Budd, the several desires of the Burlington, the Alton, the G. M. & O., and the Santa Fe could be coordinated in a plan that would suit them all. Thus the scheme he initiated early in 1945 eventually led to a four-way agreement that was submitted to the I. C. C. for approval.

Under it, the G. M. & O. was to acquire the Alton, thus achieving its ambition to gain direct access to Chicago. To help the G. M. & O. finance this very considerable acquisition, and to serve its own purposes, the Burlington was to obtain the Alton's Francis–Kansas City line, with the understanding that (a) the G. M. & O. might have trackage rights over it, and (b) the Burlington might share its ownership and projected improvement of this stretch with some other railway. In accord with this latter provision, the Santa Fe would join the C. B. & Q. in modernizing a line that would provide both systems with an efficient St. Louis–Kansas City link. As a *quid pro quo* for the Burlington's willingness to share this line, the Santa Fe would permit the C. B. & Q. to use, under a trackage arrangement, its direct main stem between Kansas City (or Camden Junction) and Bucklin, a point on the Hannibal and St. Joseph ten miles east of Brookfield. This would create, as far as Burlington was concerned, a fast Chicago–Kansas City through route.

A more logical plan could hardly have been devised. Without building one foot of new railroad, all the lines involved could achieve their objectives; the shipping public would be provided with a second high-speed service between Chicago and Kansas City, a direct link under single management between St. Louis and the vast territory served by the Santa Fe, and an additional through line between the Great Lakes and the Gulf.

The first step, G. M. & O. acquisition of the Alton, was approved by the Interstate Commerce Commission in 1945. The rest of the plan, however, was rejected by the Commission in July 1948 on the grounds that there was no pressing need for additional St. Louis–Kansas City service, and that entry of the Santa Fe into St. Louis would divert much traffic from those roads which stoutly opposed the scheme, namely the Missouri Pacific, the Frisco, the Rock Island, and the Cotton Belt (all of which were then in receivership), and the Texas and Pacific. Three members of the Commission dissented vigorously from this finding; Commissioner Mahaffie, speaking for them, said plainly that "competition, unless clearly shown to be destructive, still has advantages as a spur to progress. I would approve the applications and permit improvement to continue."[3]

But the Commission had spoken, and the ingenious plan first devised early in 1945 was dead. Yet it appeared that a less ambitious proposal designed simply to improve service might win approval. As far as Burlington's passenger service between St. Louis and Kansas City was concerned, the outlook was not promising. The *General Pershing Zephyr*, therefore, was discontinued in September 1948, the *Night Hawk* a year later. But the company had no intention whatever of giving up the substantial freight movement it had built up over the years between the two major cities of Missouri. In December 1948, it sought, and on July 12, 1949, obtained, from the I. C. C. authority to establish through freight service over its own rails from St. Louis to Francis and thence by trackage rights over the Gulf, Mobile and Ohio into Kansas City. In contrast to the arrangement in force before 1937, the new operation was to be Burlington all the way. That is, Burlington's equipment and crews would move through from one terminal to another, thus eliminating any delay at Mexico. Service was inaugurated on September 26, 1949, and promptly justified current expectations.

Notable as this achievement was, it was overshadowed by the successful resolution of the chief problem in northern Missouri. Hardly had the dust settled after the Commission's rejection in 1948 of the 1945 plan when the Burlington took definite action. At a meeting on December 15, 1948, the directors authorized the construction of an entirely new railroad between Missouri Junction, Missouri (a point on the Wabash Railroad twelve miles east of Birmingham), and a junction near Tina on the C. B. & Q.'s Carrollton branch, forty-five miles away, and improvement of that twenty-six-mile branch. This would provide the essential high-speed link for an efficient through route between Chicago and Kansas City. Interestingly enough, the proposed line was not far different from one that had been suggested by Perkins more than sixty years before.

For various reasons, the directors decided that the new road should be built by a subsidiary company and leased to the C. B. & Q. Accordingly, with approval from the I. C. C., the newly formed Kansas City and Brookfield Railroad Company (all of whose capital stock had been purchased by the Burlington) began construction in mid-1949. As work progressed, minor changes were made, and inevitably, in days of inflation, costs increased from the estimated $14,000,000 to $16,000,000. In addition, the completion date was eventually extended from mid-1951 to the fall of 1952 because of extremely severe weather conditions. In all essentials, however, the plan was carried on as first envisaged; the entire

[3] ICC, Docket #15365, July 6, 1948, p. 86.

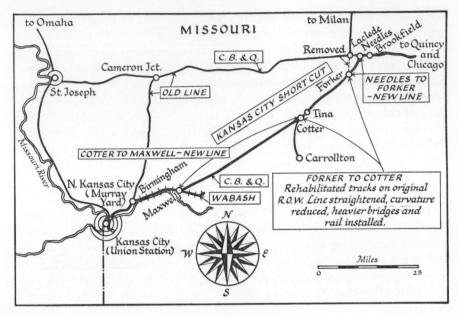

Kansas City Cut-off, 1953

seventy-one-mile cut-off was laid with 112-pound torsion-resistant rail; grades were limited to .8 percent, curves to one degree.

A lesser, though not inconsiderable project completed directly after the war was Burlington's acquisition of the single-track bridge across the Mississippi River between Alton, Illinois, and West Alton, Missouri, owned by the Missouri & Illinois Bridge & Belt Railroad Company. The Burlington accounted for about ninety percent of the business over the Alton Bridge; the rest came from local traffic at Alton and from interchange between the Missouri–Kansas–Texas and the railways on the east side of the river. This, then, was an essential facility, but one in which the C. B. & Q. held no proprietary interest. Accordingly, during 1946 and 1947 the C. B. & Q. bought the Bridge stock of all the proprietary railroads and of the individual owners except for a two-elevenths interest of the Missouri Pacific. Thus the company gained control of a vital link and insured the continued prompt movement of its trains back and forth across the river in the St. Louis district.

A somewhat similar precautionary investment was made in the Illinois Northern, a switching carrier in Chicago operating approximately nineteen miles of road connecting with twenty-one carriers, including the C. B. & Q. The Illinois Northern was owned by the International Harvester Company, although a large part of its trackage was operated under lease from the Santa Fe, and a smaller portion under lease from the Burlington. Consequently, when the Harvester Company decided in

[518]

1947 to sell the line, it approached the Santa Fe and Burlington, and eventually the Pennsylvania and New York Central. These four railways agreed to a joint transaction whereby, when carried out on February 7, 1950, with I. C. C. approval, the Santa Fe would own fifty-one percent of the Illinois Northern's stock; the Burlington, twenty-five percent; and the Pennsylvania and New York Central, twelve percent each. Although in this case the Burlington did not acquire a controlling interest, it made sure that it could participate in the management of this strategically located property.

• POSTWAR IMPROVEMENTS •

ONE ESSENTIAL INGREDIENT in improving traffic capacity was the modernization of key freight yards around the system. As already indicated, the strategic yards at Galesburg and Lincoln had been substantially enlarged during the war. In 1946 the much smaller yard at North La Crosse was expanded to accommodate 971 cars, and in the next year construction at West Quincy provided room for 694 cars. The most notable achievement in this respect was at Denver, where, in 1947, enough additional miles of track were built to increase freight-car capacity from 1,535 to 3,234 cars. In the following year, Murray Yard at Kansas City was expanded so as to accommodate 3,937 cars. Other improvements ranged all the way from construction of a brick locker and washroom at Fort Worth for shop employees to the acquisition of an electric snowplow and installation of mechanical passenger-car washers at Chicago and Denver.

A recital of quantitative improvements should not obscure advances in quality. To eliminate water pockets in roadbed, for example, the company began injecting grout under high pressure. There was vast improvement in rail also. The torsion-resistant rail, designed by Burlington engineers during the war, provided more uniform distribution of stress under all conditions of use than did standard rail. The new rail reduced the possibility of split heads, web failures, and broken bases, and considerably increased the normal life of rail.

The cumulative effect of major improvements to roadway was impressive indeed. During 1946–49, inclusive, the C. B. & Q. placed enough new creosoted cross-ties in track to stretch from Chicago to Billings by way of Lincoln, and enough new rail to reach from Chicago to Alliance over the same route. If all the ballast that was applied in those four years had been stacked up so as to cover a regulation football field completely, it would have made a pile 1,750 feet high, more than the combined height of the Empire State Building and the Golden Gate Bridge. Net capital expenditures on roadway alone were actually more than the average C. B. & Q. net income of the three years 1946–48. Nor were the cumulative statistics for the Colorado and Southern Lines (with eighteen and

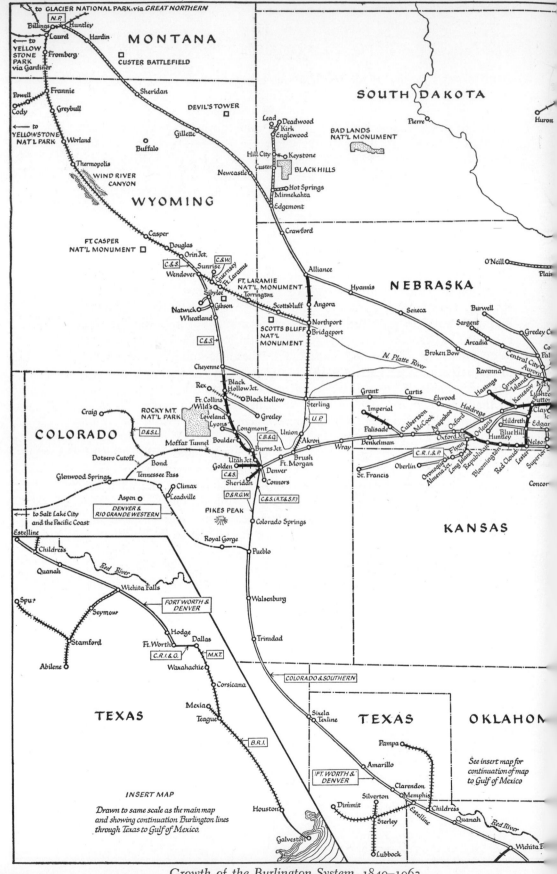

Growth of the Burlington System, 1849–1963

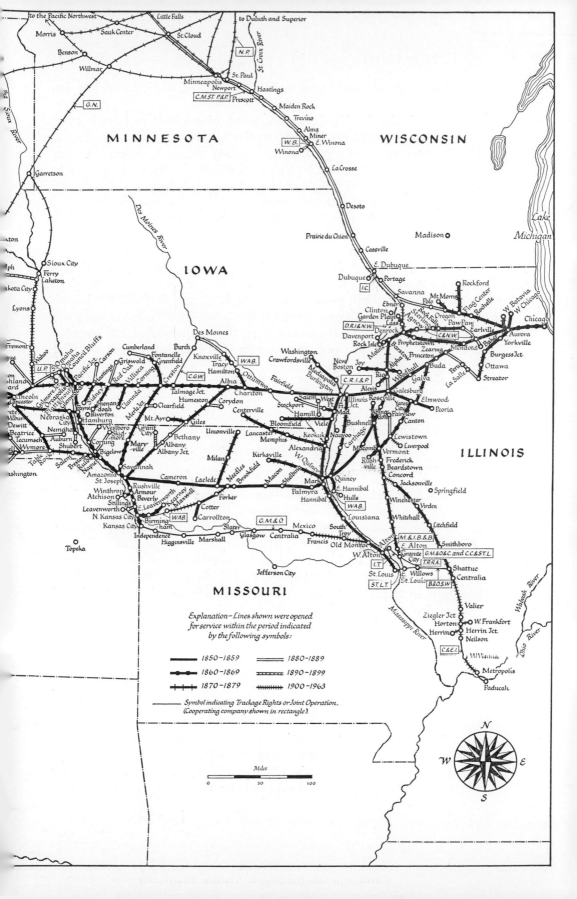

Explanation—Lines shown were opened
for service within the period indicated
by the following symbols:

1850–1859		1880–1889	
1860–1869		1890–1899	
1870–1879		1900–1963	

Symbol indicating Trackage Rights or Joint Operation.
(Cooperating company shown in rectangle).

Miles
0   50   100

a half percent as much road mileage as C. B. & Q.) any less impressive.

Hand in hand with the development of roadway and track came further improvements in signaling, particularly in respect to the centralized traffic control program that had meant so much during wartime. Advances in communication kept pace with those in signaling. In January 1947, for example, all freight trains operating between McCook and Denver were equipped with cab-to-caboose radio intercommunication, and in the spring of 1949, radio communication between switching engines and yard offices was established at Galesburg and Kansas City. In respect to communication between division points and terminals, the teletype was largely replacing the traditional railway telegraph system. By the spring of 1948, ninety-two percent of the 50,000,000 messages sent each year went by teletype; only eight percent by telegraph, these principally on branch lines. The Burlington's own plant for the handling of such messages was impressive indeed: as of the end of 1947, the company used and operated 8,520 miles of pole line, over 26,000 miles of telegraph wire, and a similar amount of telephone wire.

The cumulative effect of these substantial improvements simply meant that heavier trains could be operated at faster speeds both over the line and through yards and terminals. This factor certainly helped to offset mounting truck competition and rising labor costs.

• Equipment and Service Tailored to the Times •

The burlington had always felt that, quite apart from what the best-patronized passenger trains contributed in the way of revenues, passenger service as a whole constituted a show window by which the public, shippers as well as travelers, were likely to judge the spirit and efficiency of the road. Thus it was both logical and inevitable that as quickly as possible after the end of the war, the Burlington should embark on a "crash program" in respect to equipment, with major emphasis on an enlarged fleet of Zephyrs. As a matter of fact, hostilities had not ended before the directors took action that, because of its timing, was positively dramatic.

In his letter to the directors dated August 9, 1945, Budd announced that orders would be placed for two new seven-car *Twin Cities Zephyr* trains, twelve cars to represent Burlington's proportion of five new Great Northern *Empire Builders*, two mail-baggage-express cars, ten 4,000-hp Diesel switchers. Although the company well knew that the passenger equipment could not be delivered until the latter part of 1946 or early in 1947, it further committed itself to purchase its share not only of five new Northern Pacific *North Coast Limited* trains, but also of six 10-car Zephyr trains to replace the *Exposition Flyer* in Chicago–San Francisco service offered jointly with the Rio Grande and the Western Pacific.

Negotiations were also underway through which the railway companies as a group might buy the Pullman sleeping-car business; simultaneous operation of car construction and service by Pullman Incorporated had been declared illegal under anti-trust proceedings. Change of ownership was finally effected on July 1, 1947, by which time the C. B. & Q. was one of fifty-seven roads comprising the buying group. In due course the C. B. & Q. acquired forty-five sleepers; the Colorado and Southern, nine.

At the same time, Burlington stepped up its regular equipment program. In the summer of 1946, the directors authorized expenditure of no less than $23,213,000 to cover seventeen new freight Diesels, twenty-five passenger cars for which the company had already committed itself, and other passenger and freight cars, the last to be constructed in the company's shops. In the fall of 1947 another $13,000,000, was authorized for the purchase of thirty new Diesels, fourteen for passenger service, one for freight, and the rest for switching purposes. It was estimated that when these locomotives could be put in service late in 1948, they would provide enough additional power on the C. B. & Q. to dieselize fifty-five percent of all freight-train miles, eighty-five percent of regularly scheduled freight-train miles, sixty-five percent of passenger-train miles, and seventy-five percent of switch-engine hours. These lump-sum authorizations, which by no means covered all outlays for equipment and motive power, suggest the magnitude of the postwar program. The best way to comprehend it is to summarize the results.

Headline news in respect to motive power during the postwar years (1946–49, inclusive) was the accelerated dieselization of C. B. & Q.'s freight service, brought about by the acquisition of 159 new Diesel units that could be used in combinations producing anywhere from 1,350 to 6,000 horsepower. Meanwhile the company enlarged its passenger Diesel locomotive fleet 125 percent and added sixty-four percent to the substantial number of switchers in its service. Measured in terms of tractive effort, the C. B. & Q. was still predominantly a steam-powered railroad at the close of 1949. But in terms of train miles and switching hours, Diesels already accounted for a major share of the work performed.

From the standpoint of units owned, the Colorado and Southern and the Texas Lines were still in the preliminary stages of dieselization, although their inclusion in the system power pool meant that as conditions on the parent road permitted, their through freights were hauled from time to time by C. B. & Q. Diesels. One example will indicate what the Diesel meant: purchase by the C. & S. of four Diesel switchers during the postwar years permitted the retirement of fourteen steamers. As was true across the nation, steam was on the way out.

During 1946–49, inclusive, the C. B. & Q. constructed in its own shops 4,200 boxcars, 2,100 hopper cars, 500 stock cars, and 200 tank cars, making a total of 7,000. The trend toward more specialized service was indicated by the fact that 600 of the boxcars were equipped with special loading devices, and 615 of the hopper cars were covered so that they could be used for the transportation of cement and other commodities that could not be exposed to the weather.

To gain added information on the basic problem of transporting perishables, the Burlington built two test refrigerator cars, one equipped with ice bunkers at the ends and air-circulating fans using portable heaters, the other with overhead ice bunkers and underslung heaters in which air circulation was maintained by natural convection. On the basis of these test cars, the company's wholly owned subsidiary, the Burlington Refrigerator Express Company, constructed 290 additional cars, boosting total system output in the four years to some 7,300 freight-carrying cars. Meantime, the company purchased such special equipment as air dump cars, ballast spreaders, and clam shells.

The net effect of this program was twofold: it permitted retirement across the system of the oldest and least efficient cars, and it boosted the average capacity of those that were kept. As a matter of fact, freight car ownership (exclusive of cabooses) by the C. B. & Q. actually increased slightly less than 1,000 cars during the four postwar years, and declined on both the C. & S. and Texas Lines. Yet average freight-carrying capacity per car moved up steadily on all parts of the system, reflecting the impact of more up-to-date equipment.

The most dramatic developments were in the field of passenger equipment. During the postwar years, the Burlington participated in launching a veritable fleet of new streamlined trains, "Zephyrized" several new runs, and took the first steps toward revolutionizing its suburban service.

Because the car builders needed time to produce the new trains, even those ordered in 1945, none went into service in 1946. But as a harbinger of things to come for the rail passenger, Burlington participated in the earliest handling of through sleeping cars between the two coasts. When the *Exposition Flyer* pulled out of San Francisco on March 31, 1946, it carried a sleeper for New York; the first through car from the east coast was attached to the *Flyer* leaving Chicago on April 4. Daily service in each direction was thereupon established; east of Chicago the transcontinental sleeper was handled on alternate days by New York Central's *Commodore Vanderbilt* and Pennsylvania's *General*. During the first six days this service was in operation, the average number of passengers through Chicago averaged nine eastbound and thirteen westbound.

The first of the entirely new postwar fleet to become available, early in 1947, were Great Northern's five *Empire Builders*. Because the C. B. & Q. operated approximately one fifth of the mileage between Chicago and Seattle, it owned one of the five trains that on February 23 went into regular service on a forty-five-hour schedule between Chicago and Seattle–

Portland. This new running time cut previous schedules by thirteen hours and forty-five minutes westbound and by eleven hours and forty minutes eastbound.

Before another new train could be delivered, the Burlington inaugurated, during the summer of 1947, a new Zephyr run that in effect extended daily commuter service to Chicago to residents of Hannibal, Quincy, Keokuk, Fort Madison, and Burlington. Scheduled to leave Hannibal at 5:50 a.m., it picked up passengers along the Mississippi River, reached Burlington at 8:01 a.m., Chicago at 11:40 a.m. Returning, it left the Windy City each evening at 6:15 p.m. and arrived in Burlington at 10:25 p.m. and in Hannibal at 12:40 a.m. This, to be sure, made a long day of it for the good citizens of the river towns, but the little *Zephyr* had all the comforts of home: a parlor-coffee-shop car and a reclining-chair coach, as well as a full-size diner for the evening meal out of Chicago. The train was popular and profitable from the start, for it brought one-day service to and from Chicago to a sizeable group of towns whose citizens previously would have had to spend at least one night on the road or in Chicago.

During the fall of 1947, enough cars for the new Vista-Dome *Twin Cities Zephyrs* had been delivered to permit moving the second *Twins* (which had each covered more than 3,000,000 miles during their eleven-year assignment) to a new location. Refurbished and rechristened, they entered fast daylight service as the *Nebraska Zephyrs* between Chicago, Omaha, and Lincoln. Leaving each terminal in midmorning, they permitted businessmen to dispose of their early mail before departing, and still brought them to their destinations early in the evening.

By the end of 1947, sixteen streamlined trains in operation on Burlington system lines were covering 10,630 miles daily. On February 24, 1948, the C. B. & Q. was given the Passenger Service Award for 1947 by the Federation for Railway Progress, in recognition of outstanding achievement in progressive railroad passenger service. On hand to receive the plaque was Donald Ashton, executive assistant to Budd, whose imaginative publicity had done so much to make friends for the Zephyrs. Commenting on the award, the Federation's publication cited not only the overall excellence of Burlington's streamlined passenger service, but also the company's several new stations, "outstanding for their architecture and appointments," and the fact that the company was making wide use of centralized traffic control.[4]

Headline news in 1948 was introduction of the entirely new twelve-car *North Coast Limited*. In September, this up-to-the-minute train began its colorful run over C. B. & Q.'s Twin Cities line and Northern Pacific's "Mainstreet of North America." As in the case of the *Empire Builders*, the C. B. & Q. owned one of the five new trains.

[4] *Railway Progress*, Vol. II, No. 2 (April, 1948), p. 28.

The climax in passenger service during the immediate postwar years occurred on March 20, 1949, when the six 10-car *California Zephyrs* went into service over the Burlington–Rio Grande–Western Pacific between Chicago and San Francisco. Everything the Burlington had learned in the fifteen years that it had operated high-speed stainless-steel streamliners was brought to bear in the construction and appointments of these magnificent trains.

The *California Zephyr* was, in short, a cruise ship on rails. It was not meant to compete with planes, or even with the fastest trains connecting Chicago and the West Coast. Rather, it was designed for the most comfortable travel that could be offered over a route unparalleled in scenic beauty. To take full advantage of the spectacular countryside, the train was scheduled, in each direction, to pass through the heart of the Colorado Rockies and the breathtaking Feather River Canyon in California by daylight. The trip was made in fifty-one hours twenty minutes westbound, fifty hours thirty minutes eastbound. C. B. & Q. ownership of the new trains was pro-rated with the Rio Grande and Western Pacific on a mileage basis.

From the moment the *California Zephyr* went into service, it began establishing new records for occupancy. After ten years, its recorded average daily occupancy over the central portion of the run was 89.4 percent of capacity, a record unexcelled by any of its competitors. Not only was the train, as the Rio Grande pointed out in 1959, "an ally of site-seekers and sightseers," but also "a good freight solicitor . . . a monument in itself to the modern role of railroad passenger service."[5]

With the *California Zephyr* setting a new standard for Burlington service between Chicago and Denver, both *Denver Zephyrs* were in turn shopped, completely renovated, and returned to service in May 1949. These trains had not been given a major overhauling since they had entered the run in November 1936. Each train had traveled over four and one half million miles, but thorough inspection of the underframe and basic parts of the cars showed no noticeable deterioration, thus confirming the stability of stainless-steel construction.

Long-distance service was not the Burlington's only concern. When the C. B. & Q. celebrated the hundredth anniversary of its charter at Aurora on February 12, 1949, Ralph Budd brought great cheer to the commuting community when he announced that the company intended to invest $8 million or more to revamp completely its suburban service. As a first step, seventy-nine all-steel coaches were to be modernized and air-conditioned in the Aurora Shops. Next, and most striking of all, thirty completely new stainless-steel gallery cars were to be ordered for delivery in 1950. Finally, the service was to be dieselized as rapidly as possible. By

[5] D&RGW, AR 1959, p. 26.

the end of 1949, thirty-nine of the reconditioned coaches were in service. The philosophy behind these suburban improvements was simple and realistic: the company had been carrying commuters ever since the 1870's, and although suburban passenger service was not a money-making proposition, there was not the slightest prospect that it could be dropped. The logical thing to do was to provide a service that would at least produce contented instead of irritated patrons—including some important shippers—and perhaps attract enough new traffic to change red ink into black.

At first glance it may seem paradoxical that the years 1947–49, notable for the introduction of the most luxurious Zephyrs ever and for the dawn of a new day for commuters, should also mark a high point in the curtailment of another type of passenger-train service. But as Budd told his stockholders early in 1949 "dwindling traffic since the end of the war and excessive costs of operation on secondary main and branch lines [have] necessitated discontinuance of some passenger trains which . . . [have] not even been paying out-of-pocket costs."[6] Actually, of course, this was no paradox at all, but merely a reflection of the fact that the best if not the only profitable market for rail passenger traffic was on high-speed main lines with fairly long runs; the branch-line locals and secondary trains on main lines were fast becoming costly anachronisms. Late in 1947, and particularly in 1948 and 1949, the Burlington stepped up its efforts to eliminate as many of these "passenger-abandoned" runs as possible.

The reactions of the state commissions varied considerably, not merely between different states but also with regard to separate but similar cases within the same state. The Burlington had frequently to appeal to the appropriate state supreme court of a federal district court. One notable judgment was handed down on January 6, 1949, in the company's case against the Illinois Commerce Commission: the federal district court found that enforced continuation of a train that consistently lost money constituted dissipation of the company's assets and was a deprivation of property without due process of law. Furthermore, the court held that the prolonged continuance of cases on the part of the Commission contravened the Fourteenth Amendment.

Not every application for the reduction of service required appeal to the courts. For example, on August 27, 1949, the Public Utilities Commission of South Dakota authorized discontinuance of trains Number 141 and Number 142 between Edgemont and Deadwood, South Dakota; on September 9, 1949, the Public Service Commission of Missouri permitted the company to cease operating the last gasoline motor passenger trains anywhere on the system, Number 7 and Number 8 between Cincinnati,

---

[6] CB&Q, AR 1948, p. 13.

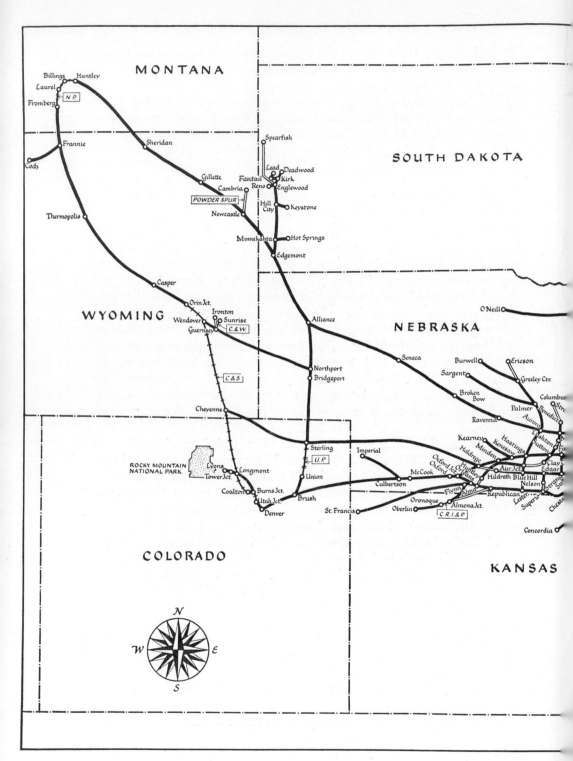

Main Line Abandonments, 1917–63

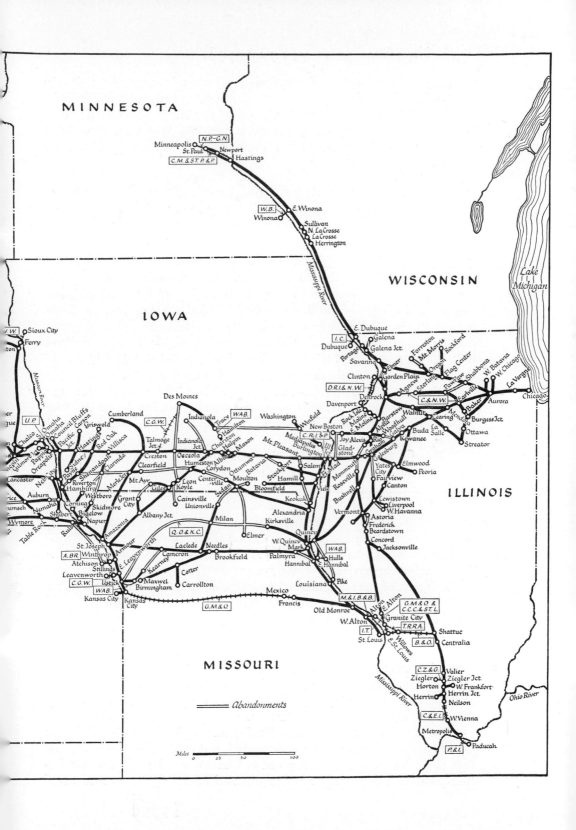

Iowa, and Laclede, Missouri. Similarly, on January 5, 1950, the Colorado Commission authorized the company to stop operating the portion of the Sterling–Holdrege run that lay in Colorado. The Burlington was, in effect, systematically weeding out the services that had long been abandoned by the public and that constituted a serious drain on the resources of the system.

• The Pattern of Traffic and Efficiency of Operation •

Although, as everyone expected, railway traffic during the postwar years was lighter than during the conflict, the general prosperity of the nation restricted the decline in freight moving by rail to minor proportions, particularly on the C. B. & Q. Whereas revenue ton-miles for all the nation's railways declined 13.3 percent during 1946–49 in comparison with 1942–45, they were off only 5.8 percent on the C. B. & Q., and for the Burlington system as a whole the decline was limited to 6.3 percent. Interestingly enough, the relative ranking of commodities hauled according to tonnage remained the same during the postwar years as during the war itself on both the C. B. & Q. and the Colorado and Southern Lines. Except during the two-month coal strike in 1946 and the prolonged work stoppage in the mines in 1949, the Burlington had plenty of business to carry during the postwar years, and so was in a position to make fruitful use of the vast improvements in roadway, structures, and equipment in which it had invested so heavily.

One notable contrast with the war period deserves consideration. During the conflict, business poured in on the railways without solicitation; the problem was not finding traffic, but handling it. When peace returned, however, so did competition, not only among the railways but, more importantly, with other forms of transportation, notably trucks. Not only Burlington's regular traffic forces, but also its Industrial and Agricultural Development agents again turned their efforts to active sales promotion as well as to service.

Industry, of course, continued to locate in midwestern territory, but a good deal of the expansion and new plant building planned for 1947 was postponed because of high building costs and shortages of material. Nevertheless, substantial though decreasing development took place in the three postwar years 1947–49. As at other points on the system, the railway's Industrial Development Department participated actively in civic programs of the sort undertaken in Burlington, Iowa, where the Chamber of Commerce sought to attract new industries to fill the vacuum left by the closing of large-scale war industries.

During the war period, the Burlington's agricultural campaigns, as might have been expected, were suspended. But even before the war came to a close, Val Kuska, operating out of Omaha, was laying plans for further promotion of irrigation in the Missouri River Valley. As a result of his efforts, the company published in January 1945 a sixteen-page booklet entitled *Irrigation: A National Asset*. Profusely illustrated, the publication was designed principally to convince eastern labor, industry, and big busi-- ness in general that irrigation was a sound investment. This pamphlet was widely distributed in both the United States and Canada. Requests for it poured in from all sides; the National Reclamation Association, for example, requested 3,000, and by 1950 the brochure had gone through three printings and had been adopted as a classic in the field.

Indeed, irrigation was the principal concern of the Agricultural Development Department throughout the postwar years. In 1946, for example, Kuska collected reams of material to support revival of the Oregon Basin (Wyoming) project and, by writing to each Congressman, helped secure the desired allocation of federal funds. Two years later he was active in reviving the La Prele Dam project in Converse County, Wyoming.

The Agricultural Development Department, indeed, undertook a wide variety of activities. In 1947 the company gave active encouragement to the spreading of over three million tons of agricultural lime in Iowa, and helped to promote terracing, contour farming, and other soil-conserving practices. In November 1947, Burlington operated a seventeen-car special train carrying bankers, industrial men, and rail executives through Texas on a "Soil Conservation Tour" which featured Louis Bromfield, scientific farmer and author, as lecturer. The sponsors, in addition to the Burlington, were the Second National Bank of Houston and the Texas A. & M. Extension Service. Every one of these undertakings, of course, was designed to increase farm income and thus, eventually, to bring more freight to Burlington rails.

Before World War II, one of the most effective means of sparking the drive for more business was the series of cross-country meetings inaugurated under the leadership of L. R. Capron, vice-president of traffic, in 1938. Early in 1942 these meetings had been discontinued: the problem then was how to handle the traffic rather than how to find it. In 1949, however, they were resumed, although on a somewhat different theme. More and more, the problem had become one of competition from other modes of transportation. The principal objective now was to develop more and better ways of increasing the volume of traffic handled by rail. Discussion was centered on new techniques and changes in the physical property designed toward this end. As before the war, hundreds of officers, agents, and other employees participated. The net result was to reinvigorate the constant drive to bring more business to C. B. & Q. rails.

One way to do this was to coordinate the company's highway operations in the most appropriate fashion. Even though the Burlington Transportation Company's bus division had greatly increased its patronage and its profits during the war years, its services were no longer needed to protect the system's territory. The Interstate Bus Lines (a jointly owned subsidiary of the Union Pacific and the Chicago and North Western) was merging with Greyhound, which in effect meant that two of Burlington's principal rail competitors were withdrawing from the bus business. Consequently in 1945, when All American, which was establishing a system to compete with Greyhound to the Coast, offered a good price for the Burlington Transportation Company buses, it was deemed best to take advantage of the opportunity. Accordingly the B. T. Co. sold fifty-one percent of its stock (representing its bus division) to All American for $1,500,000, subject to I. C. C. approval. At the same time, permission was requested to transfer B. T. Co.'s truck franchises and operations to Burlington Truck Lines, Inc., a newly formed, wholly owned subsidiary of the C. B. & Q. On March 28, 1946, the I. C. C. approved these arrangements, and on June 1 the Burlington Truck Lines started business under its own name. The remaining forty-nine percent of the old B. T. Co. stock was then sold to All American in December 1946. The only buses the C. B. & Q. retained—which it still owns—were those that provided short train connections at points such as East Dubuque and Winona Junction.

The role of the newly established Burlington Truck Lines corporation was all-inclusive. Fulfilling its original purposes, it not only served as a traffic feeder in territory adjacent to the system's rail lines, but also provided intermediate service for less-than-carload lots along both main and branch lines, thus immeasurably speeding service and avoiding the necessity of running very expensive way freights. Finally, and of increasing importance, the Truck Lines conducted a general business in competition with independent trucking companies.

Throughout this period, B. T. L. operated 4,952 route-miles and averaged something over five million truck-miles a year. When the new company began operations under its own name on June 1, 1946, it had no new equipment, but purchases were gradually stepped up during the next three years. At the same time the net deficit from operations, which reached a high point in 1947, was quickly brought under control, and in 1949 the company was in the black, albeit by a tiny margin. Furthermore, with more of the nation's traffic moving by highway and with the definite possibility that the transportation of trailers on flatcars would grow as the years went by, Burlington Truck Lines held promise of a major development on their own account.

In summary, railway freight traffic during the postwar years held up remarkably well in respect to volume, but vigorous efforts had to be made on many fronts to hold traffic to the rails and to develop new sources of business. So it was that both the Industrial and Agricultural Development departments renewed their traditional efforts, and truck operations were put on a new basis. There was plenty of freight to be hauled; it was simply a question of attracting it to the rails and handling it in the most efficient manner possible.

In contrast to the situation in respect to freight, passenger traffic was undergoing a major change. The Burlington system experienced steady decline in revenue passenger-miles, which, in the four postwar years 1946–49, inclusive, decreased 46.3 percent, as compared with 1942–45. It is worth noting, however, that even in 1949, the low point of the postwar period, both the C. B. & Q. and the C. & S. accounted for more passenger-miles than in any prewar year since 1927, while the record of Texas Lines was better than for any prewar year since 1928.

Efficient railway operation reflects the skill with which the assets at hand are put to work and the obstacles to their full utilization are overcome. But a factor that can never be overlooked is the weather. Something must be said on that score before looking into the Burlington's operating record during the postwar years.

Except for hot dry periods during the growing season in the Southwest, the weather in 1946 was favorable along the Burlington system. In 1947, however, widespread floods following unceasing downpours cost the Burlington more than two million dollars in repair and restoration, without taking into account loss of revenue caused by reduced shipments. In 1948, the 1946 conditions were repeated almost exactly, but in January and February 1949, blizzards, sleet storms, and gales hit the Burlington region with a prolonged ferocity that cost the company a million dollars to maintain operations and five million more in lost revenues. These facts must be borne in mind in considering the operational results on the system during the postwar years.

Since railroading is essentially a mass-production industry, it is axiomatic to say that, given an adequate plant and equipment, operating efficiency, and hence earnings, are more directly dependent on volume of business than on any other single factor. Except for the pipelines, this is far less true of all transportation agencies competing with the railways. If a railway is to operate a line at all, it must maintain it constantly and under all conditions. Furthermore, in view of motive power and equipment costs, no railroad can afford to have an appreciable amount of its rolling stock standing idle. In the 1947–49 era, for example, Burlington freight Diesels cost $161,000 for A units, and $145,000 for B units; passenger units came to $231,000 each. Vista-Dome coaches bore a price tag of $145,000; observation cars, considerably more. The cost of even an ordinary boxcar exceeded $5,000. Thus the Burlington, like any railway, was and is peculiarly dependent upon volume for profitable survival.

This point, of course, was amply demonstrated during World War II, when it was possible to fill both freight and passenger trains to the fully rated capacity of motive power, cars, and track. The inherent advantage of the railway was demonstrated in most striking fashion then; no other overland carrier could approach it in operating efficiency either in ton-miles or in passenger-miles.

One index of the direct relationship between volume and earnings lies in a comparison, for freight service, of revenue ton-miles with freight-train miles and, for passenger service, of revenue passenger-miles with passenger-train miles. If ton-miles or passenger-miles increase faster than train miles, potential earnings increase in almost exact proportion.

In the difficult transition year 1946, neither the C. B. & Q. nor the C. & S. nor the Texas Lines was able to reduce freight-train miles as fast as ton-miles decreased. During the next two years, however, all three portions of the system achieved a favorable balance, and the C. & S. and the Texas Lines did so in 1949 as well. Only the bad weather and interruptions in coal loadings (factors beyond control of the railway) prevented the C. B. & Q. from matching the performance of its subsidiaries in that year. So far as freight traffic was concerned, then, the system as a whole was able to adjust to new conditions with considerable success.

The inability of any part of the system to repeat this performance in respect to passenger traffic graphically highlighted the seriousness of the situation. In every one of the four postwar years and on all parts of the system, reduction in passenger-train miles did not even come close to matching the decline in passenger-miles. Here was proof positive, if any was needed, of the essential importance of discontinuing lightly patronized trains operating either on branch lines or in secondary service on main lines.

The adjustment of train miles to volume of traffic is probably the basic and most importance prerequisite to efficiency and earnings, but it is by no means the only one. On a number of counts, speed of movement is important too. For one thing, it is important to any shipper, and a factor in competition both with other railways and other forms of transportation. Furthermore, the faster the freight trains move, the greater the capacity of any given line. In this respect, the performance of the C. B. & Q. during the postwar years was outstanding, and among other things reflected the impact of the progressive dieselization of freight-train movement. The company steadily widened the gap between its performance and that of all Class I roads. The improvement on the C. & S. was even more marked; in 1949 it outstripped even the Texas Lines, which had had a consistently good performance.

Perhaps the best single all-inclusive index of physical operating efficiency is gross ton-miles per freight-train hour, combining as it does volume and speed. In this respect the C. B. & Q. had surpassed the national average in every year since 1940 and increased its lead through 1948; despite the unforeseen difficulties of 1949, the index still rose in that year. Whereas, owing to their much lighter density, the C. & S. and the Texas Lines could offer no comparable performance, their vast improvement in 1949 was auspicious for the future.

Measuring the efficiency of a service with as many imponderables as affect passenger traffic, particularly in a period of sharp decline, is difficult at best. What the Burlington was trying to produce was a quality product more appropriately measured in terms of satisfaction to patrons than in dollars, although the cost of producing such a service could never be out of mind. One simple index of the quality of that service was its speed, and in this respect all portions of the system turned in a creditable perform-ance in the postwar period. In 1949 all of them had attained a faster average speed than that of the railways as a whole.

One hallmark of good operation is the maintenance of safety, and in this respect the Burlington Lines kept their enviable record throughout the postwar years. In 1946, the Colorado and Southern again won the National Safety Council Award for having the lowest employee casualty rate among railroads of its group. Yet that same year there was a tragic accident at Naperville, Illinois, in which thirty-nine passengers and six employees were killed, 110 passengers and nineteen employees injured. This disaster was the result of a regrettable human failure; after thorough investigation, the Interstate Commerce Commission stated that the cause was "failure to operate following train in accordance with signal indica-tions."[7] No blame was attached to the C. B. & Q. operating rules or to the functioning of its signal system.

That the C. B. & Q. was in no way relaxing its eternal vigilance in the matter of safety was evident when in 1948 the company won the Harriman Medal for Group A railroads. This award was based on Inter-state Commerce Commission records, which showed, among other achieve-ments, that Burlington hauled more than eleven million passengers in 1948 without a single fatality or reportable injury caused by a train acci-dent. In 1949, at its Centennial Anniversary, Burlington received a special award from the National Safety Council for conspicuous achievement in preventing accidents to passengers and to employees.

So much, then, for plant, equipment, traffic policy, and operations during the postwar years. In dealing with each, Burlington had made vigorous efforts to adjust to the realities of a highly competitive prosperity, a period of rising costs, and one that put a premium on labor-saving devices. At the same time, it sought to keep long-run considerations in mind: such major changes as took place obviously were not, by their very nature, designed simply for the moment; the company would have to "live with them" for a long time to come.

To what extent were these postwar efforts of the Burlington successful? Or, to rephrase the question, how well equipped was the company to survive and prosper during the difficult years of transition—despite the fact that such vital matters as rates and regulation, competition, material costs, and wages were largely beyond its control?

[7] PLD, August 8, 1946.

CHAPTER 29

Performance and Promise

1945 - 49

A PROMISING VOLUME of freight traffic to be carried in the postwar years and the fact that the Burlington was well equipped to handle it were not enough to insure profitable operation; net income was inevitably affected also by the rate level and operating expenses. Other factors like taxes, interest, and such intangibles as public relations were important too. But, basically, financial success (and therefore the ability to provide low-cost service to the public) depended not only on (1) volume of business and efficiency, but also on (2) rates and costs *and* (3) the interplay of all these factors. That is, if rates increased without seriously affecting volume, say, or mounted when wages went up, the effect of growing payrolls could be offset. But if either volume or rate levels lagged behind rising expenses, net income inevitably suffered.

The degree of control any railway possessed over these various factors differed markedly. Volume and efficiency were perhaps the most responsive to the carrier efforts. By increasing capacity, improving service, and vigorously soliciting business, a company like the Burlington could attract more traffic. By investing heavily in plant, by installing labor-saving devices, and by using manpower and equipment as economically as possible, efficiency could be increased. But the matter of rates, as to both amount and timing, depended ultimately on government sanction; though the railroads could propose revisions upward or downward with a view to maximizing earnings, the Interstate Commerce Commission, and to a lesser degree the state commissions, disposed of each and every request. Costs, too, especially for materials and wages, were less subject to the control of the carriers. Producers of steel and fuel, for example, could raise their prices at will. Wages, in most cases, were determined by government boards on a national basis.

Further complications existed. So far as traffic volume was concerned, the railways were compelled to fight for their share of the market against non-rail competitors whose plant, equipment, and services were provided wholly or in part by public funds, which enabled them to solicit and obtain business at rates below true total cost. Furthermore, as far as railways were concerned, rate and wage levels were determined by different tribunals which did not necessarily give the same weight to the complex factors involved in their decisions. To prosper under such conditions was a challenge indeed for any railroad.

So much for generalities. What actually happened on the Burlington in respect to traffic, costs, and rates? The volume of business and the means for handling it have been discussed in the preceding chapter. Logically, the next point to examine is costs, for costs determined whether or not the company, along with other railways, felt compelled—despite competition from other forms of transportation—to ask for rate increases.

• WAGES, THE LABOR MOVEMENT, AND PRODUCTIVITY •

THE POSTWAR YEARS witnessed the sharpest rise in wages since World War I. For example, although the average number of employees on the C. B. & Q. dropped from 34,407 in 1945 to 29,643 in 1949, a decline of nearly thirteen percent, the payroll rose from about $89½ million to more than $104 million, up over sixteen percent. The reason for this apparent anomaly lay in the substantial wage increases granted in each of the postwar years. Average annual compensation on the C. B. & Q. increased nearly thirty-five percent from 1945 to 1949.

Important as the dollars and cents were, the deeper issue was whether the nation possessed adequate safeguards against the tremendous economic strength of the railway unions and their ability, as a strictly disciplined minority, to call national strikes that threatened public health and safety. Between 1926, when it was passed, and World War II, the Railway Labor Act, with its elaborate provisions for conferences, mediation, arbitration, and fact-finding, as well as for various cooling-off periods, had been generally regarded as such a safeguard. But during the war years the brotherhoods had seemingly paid scant heed either to the provisions of the law or to its spirit; instead, they had repeatedly, and not unsuccessfully, exerted pressure on the White House for settlements more favorable to them than those gained through the orderly processes of the Act. Should they continue this policy, it was inevitable that the federal government, sooner or later, would be called upon to meet what in effect was a continued challenge not only to the Railway Labor Act, but to the public welfare as well.

Wages, in contrast to rail rates, went up during the war years, first late in 1941, and again during 1943. Nevertheless, at the end of 1944 the operating brotherhoods drafted a long series of proposals for rules changes which were discussed with the carriers intermittently during the spring of 1945. When no agreement was forthcoming, the five operating unions served formal demands on July 24, 1945, not only for many rule changes, but also for minimum pay increases of $2.50 a day. Shortly thereafter, the non-operating unions asked for an increase of thirty cents an hour, and when the usual round of conferences failed, the services of the National Mediation Board were invoked in December 1945.

Early in January 1946, all unions except those of the engineers and trainmen agreed to arbitration; Ralph Budd served as one of the carrier representatives in the non-operating case. On April 3, the arbitration boards awarded an increase of sixteen cents an hour, effective January 1, 1946. Even though the Emergency Fact-finding Board that had been convened to consider the requests of the engineers and trainmen had not yet reported, it was apparent that they too would be granted advances. So it was that on April 15 the railways asked the Interstate Commerce Commission to advance freight rates from twenty to twenty-five percent (depending on the commodities affected), making clear at the time that this request was specifically to offset the rise in wages which had been granted retroactive to the first of the year.

On the very day that the railways made their request, however, the fifteen non-operating unions announced that the sixteen cent an hour increase awarded by the Arbitration Board was grossly inadequate and served demands on the railways for a further advance of fourteen cents an hour. Three days later, the Emergency Board handling the request of the engineers and trainmen recommended (as had the Arbitration boards) an increase of sixteen cents per hour; but, like the non-operating employees, the engineers and trainmen declined to accept the recommendation and called a strike for May 18. On May 3, 1946, the firemen, conductors, and switchmen, also dissatisfied with the award of their Arbitration Board, served notices demanding an additional fifteen cents per hour. Thus every one of the railway unions expressed its dissatisfaction with the April awards, and two of them threatened a strike.

In an effort to avert this calamity, President Truman intervened in the negotiations, but to no avail. Accordingly, on May 17 he took possession of the railroads and placed them under the control of the Office of Defense Transportation. The events of the next few days were dramatic indeed. Conferences proved fruitless, and on May 23, 1946, the engineers and trainmen struck, bringing the nation's railways to a virtual standstill.

On the evening of May 24, President Truman, in a nationwide radio address, called on all employees to return to service by four o'clock on the following afternoon and announced that at that time he would appear in person before a joint session of Congress to deliver a message on the subject. A few moments before he was scheduled to speak, the carriers reached a settlement with the striking unions, later extended to all the others. It provided for an additional increase of two and a half cents an hour, effective May 22, and, in the case of the five operating unions, for a moratorium on rules changes for a period of a year. Even so, the President spoke before Congress, asking specifically for authority to draft the engineers and trainmen into the armed forces, and presenting a program of legislation to prevent such crises in the future. Because the immediate dispute was settled, however, no legislative action was taken, and the railroads were returned to their owners on the afternoon of May 26.

These developments of 1945–46 were typical of the immediate postwar years; to recount in detail the negotiations and compromises of 1946–49 would serve no new purpose, for the issues were similar, the arguments much the same, and the results—as before—a steady rise in labor costs. In the parlance of the day, three successive "rounds" of wage increases took place, accompanied by parallel requests by the carriers for upward rate adjustments. These requests were heeded tardily by the I. C. C. and only partly offset mounting costs. The railroads did succeed in warding off demands for an additional fireman on multiple-unit Diesels. On the other hand, the non-operating unions gained a five-day working week, and it was merely a question of time before the same dispensation would apply throughout the industry. Sharp disputes over wages and working rules led to a two-month period of federal seizure in the spring of 1948; once again it was apparent that the steps provided by the Railway Labor Act were insufficient to preserve peace between labor and management.

During the postwar period, wage increases granted railway employees may be summarized as follows:

INCREASE PER HOUR (CENTS)[1]

Effective date	Non-operating employees	Operating employees
Jan. 1, 1946	16	16
May 22, 1946	2½	2½
Sept. 1, 1947	15½	—
Nov. 1, 1947	—	15½
Oct. 1, 1948	7	—
Oct. 16, 1948	—	10
Sept. 1, 1949	5-day week with no loss in pay— 23½¢ increase	

The effect of these adjustments was to raise the average straight time rate of pay per hour on the C. B. & Q. from 90.5 cents during 1945 to

[1] Figures from ICC, Bureau of Transport Economics and Statistics, quoted in J. H. Parmelee: "Rebuttal and Supplemental Statements of the Association of American Railroads, No. 2," p. 47, Washington, 1950.

$1.43 during 1949. Because wages were such a large item of railway expense, these advances made a vital difference in the distribution of the railroad revenue dollar. In 1945, for example, 35.4 cents out of each dollar the C. B. & Q. earned from transportation was paid out in wages; in 1949, 45.8 cents went for this purpose, an increase of over twenty-nine percent. The situation on the C. & S. and on the Texas Lines was similar. They were paying only slightly more than twenty-nine cents out of each revenue dollar for wages in 1945, but the figure had risen to more than thirty-eight cents in 1949. This represented an increase of over thirty percent for the C. & S. and over thirty-two percent for the Texas Lines.

But the financial effect of increased wages tells only part of the story. Were the railways getting better value for their investment? One way to find out was to relate total production to the average number of employees. Total production was calculated by adding net ton-miles to twice passenger-miles; this figure was then divided by the average number of employees. The result was the total production per average employee. During the four war years, the quotient of this calculation on the C. B. & Q. averaged 681, but in the four postwar years it dropped to 621, a decrease of almost nine percent. Meanwhile, the average straight time rate rose from 87.1 cents for 1942–45 to $1.247 for 1946–49, an increase of over forty-three percent. In other words, although each man working received on the average forty-three percent more, he was turning out approximately nine percent less transportation.

The conclusion was inescapable; the C. B. & Q. was not only paying a higher labor bill, but also getting less in return. The wage situation on the Burlington, both quantitatively and qualitatively, entered a critical period during the postwar years.

• MATERIAL COSTS AND TAXES •

THE STORY OF MATERIAL COSTS may be briefly told. With 1939 as the base point, they rose, for Class I railroads, about thirty percent during the war years and then turned sharply upward, so that toward the end of 1949 they had approximately doubled in a decade. The only saving grace was that, unlike average wage rates, material prices began to recede in 1949, though not to any great extent. In sum, the postwar period witnessed the beginning of the wide divergence of wages and material costs both from the cost of living and from revenues earned by the railroads. This was perhaps the most significant single development of 1946–49.

Broadly speaking, the total taxes paid by the system during the postwar years remained relatively steady, although individual taxes underwent significant changes. For one thing, as might be expected, the income tax varied considerably, and especially on the C. & S. and Texas Lines. On the other hand, there was a marked rise in payroll taxes; on the C. B. & Q. in 1947, for example, they exceeded fixed charges by over thirty-four percent.

Potentially the most dangerous development in respect to taxes on the Burlington system during the postwar years occurred when, on September 17, 1946, an agent of the Bureau of Internal Revenue served a Report on the Colorado and Southern Railway, claiming that additional income and excess profits taxes of over $3,000,000 were due for 1942 and 1943. If the position of the Bureau were to be upheld for those two years, there was the possibility that additional taxes of from $2,000,000 to $4,000,000 might be due for 1944 and 1945. Because these claims, if allowed, might so undermine the C. & S. Plan of Adjustment approved in 1943 as to render it ineffective and futile, the company immediately mobilized its defenses and determined to enter a protest.

The central issue was simple enough. Excess profits taxes were levied on that portion of income that exceeded a certain percentage of return on the invested and accumulated capital of any given company. In this instance, the government simply maintained that the invested-capital figure used by the Colorado and Southern was over four times as high as it should have been, and that consequently substantial earnings which the railway had thought exempt from excess profits taxes were, in fact, subject to them. There were other aspects of the government's case, but the dispute over invested capital was the heart of the matter. The background, however, was highly complex, and the full story belongs in a history of the Colorado and Southern.

Fortunately for the Colorado and Southern, for the R. F. C., and for the bondholders whose cooperation had made possible the Plan of Adjustment, the Federal District Court in Denver, on April 29, 1949, upheld the position of the railroad in respect to taxes for 1940–43, inclusive. No findings were made concerning taxes for 1944–46, inclusive, because the Bureau had not yet completed its audit and had not entered any specific claims for those years. The government promptly appealed this decision to the Supreme Court of the United States, but on October 17, 1949, that body refused to review the matter. This disposed of the original Report, and though no specific judgment had been made in respect to 1944–46, little likelihood existed of further difficulty. It was clear that the reasoning on which the revenue agent based his findings for 1942 and 1943 would not be upheld in the courts.

So much, then, for taxes, which, along with wages and material costs, comprised the principal elements of expense in running a railroad. In view of these rising costs, the railways were compelled to seek increases in rates and fares. To what extent, and with what success, did they do so?

• RATES AND REVENUES •

AT THE END OF WORLD WAR II, and indeed until July 1946, railroad freight rates were no higher than they had been at the beginning of the conflict.

On April 15, 1946, the carriers asked the I. C. C. for an increase of approximately twenty-five percent. That body granted an interim advance of 6.5 percent on July 1 and authorized a permanent rise of 17.6 percent effective January 1, 1947. Burlington's management calculated that this advance would boost system revenues slightly less than $18 million. At the same time, the temporary ten percent passenger-fare increase that had been granted in 1942 was made permanent. And it should be added, parenthetically, that as of October 1, 1946, land-grant rates were discontinued.

Helpful as all this was in its effect on revenues, it was more than offset by the fact that during 1946 (that is, before the major freight-rate advances became effective) the rise in payrolls as a result of awards during that year (eighty-six percent of which were retroactive to January 1, 1946) amounted to $14,700,000 for the system. Added material costs approximated $4,000,000.

Between January 1, 1946, and January 1, 1947, working capital of Class I railroads declined 23.5 percent while their net income slumped 36.2 percent. On the relatively strong C. B. & Q., net income fell 15.7 percent; a substantial amount of this reduction was attributable to the distorted relationship between rates and costs which resulted from the Commission's slow handling of the 1946 rate requests. Nor did the prospects for the following year appear better. On July 13, 1946, President Truman approved the Crosser amendments to the Railroad Retirement and Unemployment Insurance acts which vastly broadened the scope of old age and disability annuities, established annuities for survivors of railroad employees, increased unemployment benefits, and expanded the unemployment insurance system to include benefits for unemployment resulting from sickness and maternity, which had not previously been included. To finance this liberalized system, tax rates were increased for both carriers and employees, effective January 1, 1947, from three and a half percent to five and three-quarters percent on compensation paid up to $300 per month. A further increase to six percent was scheduled for January 1, 1949, and a rise to six and a half percent for January 1, 1952.

Offsetting factors were, in contrast, minor. At the end of February 1947, the Western railroads canceled the furlough rates for servicemen they had voluntarily granted in 1940, and effective June 1, 1947, the I. C. C. authorized these same roads to raise coach and first-class fares six and a half and fifteen percent, respectively. On the other side of the ledger, the United States filed a complaint with the I. C. C. seeking reparation for allegedly excessive and unreasonable charges on certain military traffic during the war. The amounts of these claims were not stated, although government attorneys indicated that the aggregate for all railroads would approximate two billion dollars. Referring to this huge claim, Budd told his stockholders that in no case did the government pay the Burlington more than the tariff available to other shippers, and in most cases paid less.

In view of these developments, the railways in July 1947 sought authority from the I. C. C. to make further freight-rate increases of from thirty-one to forty-one percent, depending on the territorial movement of traffic. The I. C. C. moved with extreme deliberation and authorized a series of interim increases, only one of which was granted in 1947. As in the case of wages, so in respect to rates, this pattern was typical of the immediate postwar years. Repeatedly the carriers saw their requests to the Commission for increases delayed and whittled down while successive wage hikes compelled them to make renewed appeals. Freight-rate advances sought in September 1947, for example, became effective only in the following May; meanwhile the railroads obtained their first upward adjustment of mail rates since 1928. Again, when wages rose further in 1948, the roads petitioned for additional freight-rate increases. More than ten months later, approximately seventy percent of the requested advance was granted. This was a perfect illustration of the inflationary spiral and of the well-nigh hopeless task of trying to keep rates abreast of mounting costs.

Because various states were slow to allow increases on intrastate traffic corresponding to those granted by the I. C. C. on interstate business, and because the railways made downward adjustments in various instances to meet subsidized competition, the exact percentages of freight-rate increases either nationally or for the Burlington are difficult to calculate. The following table, however, indicates the approximate extent of the rises authorized during the postwar years:

CLASS I RAILROADS
AUTHORIZED PERCENT INCREASE IN FREIGHT RATES[2]

Effective Date	Increase over prior rates		Cumulative percentage increases over rates in effect June 30, 1946
July 1, 1946	Interim	6.5	6.5
Jan. 1, 1947	Final	10.4	17.6
Oct. 13, 1947	Interim	8.9	28.1
Jan. 5, 1948	Interim	7.6	37.8
May 6, 1948	Interim	3.6	42.8
Aug. 21, 1948	Final	1.0	44.2
Jan. 11, 1949	Interim	5.2	51.7
Sept. 1, 1949	Final	3.7	57.3

No precise data are available for the Burlington, but in the spring of 1949 the president pointed out that after the increases of January 11 of that year, system freight rates were approximately 47.4 percent higher than they had been on June 30, 1946. This suggests that, presumably because of the character of traffic and local adjustments, the increase on Burlington Lines was about 4.3 percent under the national average.

One fact should be kept in mind, however: the only source of earnings

[2] Ibid., p. 55.

from railway operations was revenue derived from transporting traffic. Consequently the rate level, multiplied by volume, accounted for all gross revenues. On the other hand, operating expenses were many and varied. In the preceding paragraphs, rates have been related almost wholly to wages, but the point to remember is that revenues produced by those rates had to cover not only wages, but also material costs, as well as traffic solicitation and general expense. Furthermore, taxes, hire of equipment, and joint facility rents had to be deducted from what was left if one was to arrive at net railway operating income. Simply to have rates increased to meet wage advances never was enough; they had to produce sufficient revenue to cover many other items as well.

How, then, did gross revenues perform during the immediate postwar years? The C. B. & Q. and its immediate neighbors followed the national pattern in experiencing a sharp decline in 1946; the decline on both the Colorado and Southern and the Texas Lines was sharper than on the parent company. The C. B. & Q. and the Texas Lines made a substantial recovery in the next two years; the C. & S. underwent a more gradual rise. In 1949, both the C. B. & Q. and the C. & S. suffered sharp declines; only the Texas roads reported an encouraging upswing.

In sum, total system operating revenues during 1946–49 were almost exactly what they had been during the war years; in fact, they decreased less than four tenths of one percent. Put otherwise, rate increases were just about sufficient to offset the decrease in volume and to keep total revenues at about the same level as during the war years.

On the face of it, this was encouraging. But, in fact, there were two reasons why it was not. In the first place, the index of railway revenues as a whole was rapidly losing ground in relation to the index of gross national product. In other words—in relative terms, railways, including the Burlington, were falling behind other segments of the economy. More specifically within the field of transportation, the railway share of intercity freight traffic fell from 67.3 in 1945 to 58.4 in 1949, while the share of intercity passenger traffic (excluding private automobiles) fell from 74.3 to 48.6 percent. The second reason why the postwar revenue performance of the Burlington Lines was not nearly so promising as it looked at first glance was that operating expenses, in sharp contrast to operating revenues, did not simply remain at the wartime level. Instead they increased nearly fourteen and a half percent.

• INCOME AND FINANCIAL STATUS •

THE ACID TEST of the success or failure of any railway as a transportation machine (as distinct from a railway as an overall financial enterprise) is the amount of its net railway operating income. In this respect the position of the C. B. & Q. in relation to its nearest and most comparable neighbors had always been strong, and the postwar years—save for 1949—provided no exception. Even though, for example, total operating revenues on the C. B. & Q. had been less than those of the Milwaukee and only slightly ahead of those of the North Western, the C. B. & Q. had been able to carry through to net railway operating income almost a third more than either of them. Indeed, the most nearly comparable performance was that of the Rock Island, which, with the lowest total revenue of the four roads, ranked second in net railway operating income in 1946–48, and barely nosed out the Burlington for first place in 1949. The performance of the C. & S. and the Texas Lines in respect to net railway operating income was encouraging indeed after the sharp transition year 1946.

The translation of net railway operating income into net income depends primarily (though not exclusively) on the extent of other income, less deductions therefrom on the one hand, and on the amount of fixed charges payable on the other. In broad terms, this part of any railroad's performance reflects the status of its financial structure. So far as the C. B. & Q. was concerned, other income less deductions during the postwar years varied between 3.5 and 8.2 percent of net railway operating income. Whereas this represented no inconsiderable amount, it simply highlighted the fact that the C. B. & Q. as a financial enterprise depended primarily on its earnings as a transportation company and could not base its plans on income from other sources.

In sharp contrast, other income was of primary importance to the Colorado and Southern which, over the years, had financed all expansion in Texas except the original main line of the F. W. & D. C., and therefore received substantial rentals and interest payments from that area. In each of the four postwar years, its other income less deductions substantially exceeded its net railway operating income. By the same token, the situation was reversed for the Texas Lines, whose payment of rentals and interest to the C. & S. generally meant that its deductions from other income were slightly higher than that income itself.

The final major element in financial performance is interest on the funded debt, and this depends in turn on the management of that debt. The postwar years saw no major changes in debt structure throughout the system, but rather a consistent implementation of the major changes that had taken place on the C. B. & Q. and the C. & S. during the war years. In summarizing the situation on the C. B. & Q. as of the end of 1947, the president pointed out that in the six-year period 1942–47, inclusive, funded debt (including equipment obligations) had been reduced $69,936,251. Furthermore, fixed charges had been reduced from $9,658,151 in 1940 to $5,771,614 in 1947. Ironically, however, Railroad Retirement and Unemployment taxes over the same years rose from $2,691,033 to $7,753,312, an increase exceeding by $1,175,741 the decrease in fixed charges. Thus the effort of the company to lighten the burden of its fixed charges was more than offset by the impact of new taxes.

Except for 1949, net income of the C. B. & Q. throughout the postwar period continued to surpass by a wide margin that of its most comparable neighbors, but the company's dividend policy remained conservative. Payments of six dollars a share were made in 1946 and 1947, and in view of much better business in 1948, were increased to seven dollars in that year. In 1949, however, when a combination of unusual circumstances reduced C. B. & Q. earnings, the dividend was cut back to five dollars.

The Colorado and Southern Plan of Adjustment precluded the payment of any dividends during the period of interest modification, 1941–54. Available net income was allocated by the Plan first to the replenishment of working capital, then to the retirement of debt. Meanwhile, the F. W. & D. C. steadily reduced the outstanding principal of its note to the R. F. C.; both western companies reduced their equipment obligations. Thus, despite the mounting costs of doing business, all portions of the Burlington Lines turned in a creditable financial record during the postwar years. What was the outlook for the future?

• TRENDS OF THE TIMES •

CLEARLY, many major problems lay unresolved at the close of the immediate postwar period. As Budd told his stockholders in the spring of 1948, "in order to carry on a healthy business it is obvious that there must be more money left out of earnings after paying fair dividends than was necessary when labor and materials costs were so much lower than they are now. . . . Railway investors cannot be expected to continue putting up risk capital unless there is evidence of fair treatment in a way of permitting them to earn a reasonable return. Inability to obtain new money for the business inevitably would tend to a deterioration of plant that would be far more costly to the country as a whole than the cost of adequate rates and charges, which would insure the best of transportation. A consistent and constructive regulatory policy towards the railroads," he said, "is of national importance."[3]

As Budd pointed out a year later, however, this was by no means the whole story. The proportion of the total transportation of the country which the railroads were handling was decreasing, though he ventured the prediction that even in peacetime they would probably handle nearly two thirds of all freight and nearly ten percent of all travel, including that by private autos. Yet, he emphasized, past experience had made it clear that a much larger proportion of total traffic moved by rail in time of war. It was essential, therefore, that the government should avoid aiding railway competitors to such an extent that if a war emergency should arise, the railways might not be up to requirements.

[3] CB&Q, AR 1947, p. 16.

Indeed, of all the problems facing the railways, the matter of subsidized competition emerged more and more as the most serious threat. "We are in an age of what may be termed precision transportation," Budd told a Chicago audience early in 1949. "The replacement of the older types of machinery and equipment will take time, but the period required for the change depends almost entirely upon the policies of the Government, as manifested in Congressional legislation and in the administration of the laws. A fair and reasonably liberal policy, along the lines of the 1940 National Transportation Policy, administered in the same spirit, should afford an opportunity to earn sufficient revenues to carry out a reasonable program of maintenance and of gradual but constant and steady improvement of railroad properties. On the other hand, hostile legislation, or an unfriendly administration of the laws, particularly if coupled with undue favors to competing agencies of transportation, would retard, and might prevent, improvements in railroad facilities and services which are entirely feasible and will be made if not prevented by harmful legislation or administrative action. It rests with the public to decide what kind of railroad transportation it will have."[4]

Speaking before the Chicago Association of Commerce and Industry, Budd reached the following conclusion: "Should the financial future of the railroads become so unfavorable that private ownership cannot be continued, it will not be because railway management has failed, but because government has created a situation making it impossible for the major, and most efficient, transportation agency of the country to survive the inroads of subsidized carriers, the burdens of social experimentation, and the assumption of managerial functions by the government. In other words, the financial outlook for the railroads is a political question, rather than one of finance or operation."[5]

Deep and genuine concern over national policy, however, by no means induced an air of helplessness on the part of the railroads in general or the Burlington in particular. They were proud of their past achievements and hopeful for the future. Evidence of this attitude took tangible form in the Chicago Railroad Fair of 1948 and 1949. Sponsored by thirty-eight of the nation's leading railroads, it was designed to celebrate Chicago's railway centennial, to dramatize the role of the industry in transforming the country from a wilderness into productive agricultural and industrial areas, and to give promise of better things to come.

During the spring and early summer of 1948, preparations moved forward briskly. As a member of the committee in charge, Budd played an

[4] Budd, address before the Chicago Chapter of Chartered Life Underwriters, January 19, 1949, CB&Q/Pres.

[5] Budd: "Financial Outlook of the Railroads," Chicago Association of Commerce and Industry, Chicago, March 23, 1945; cf.: Budd: "Peacetime Trends in Transportation," Railway Business Association, Chicago, November 18, 1949, CB&Q/Pres.

energetic role in many phases of planning and execution; before long, several miles of rail were in place on the lakefront exhibition grounds. Each of the sponsoring railroads participated in an exhibit. Burlington's *Pioneer Zephyr* appeared four times daily in the pageant "Wheels A-Rolling," the focal attraction of the Fair; the company participated jointly with the Great Northern and the Northern Pacific in presenting entertainment typical of the Western Vacationland, featuring a rodeo, Old Faithful Geyser, stagecoaches, Indian tepees, and a diorama.

The Fair was a huge success. From the day it opened on July 20 until its close on October 3, it attracted 2,504,000 visitors. Indeed, so successful was it that by November the decision was made to repeat it on a larger scale in 1949 and to keep it open for a hundred days, from June 25 to October 2.

During the summer of 1949 the hopes of the railway sponsors were fully justified. This time 2,732,739 persons attended, and once again the little *Pioneer Zephyr* appeared in the pageant, which attracted 1,449,954 spectators. As in 1948, Burlington joined with the Northern Lines in the Vacationland exhibit, and in addition operated the "Deadwood Central" narrow-gauge railway within the fair grounds, which carried no less than 1,236,751 revenue passengers. The Fair not only paid for itself, but also reminded the millions who attended of the part the railways had played in building up the country and gave them a chance as well to inspect the latest motive power and equipment. Furthermore, everyone had a lot of fun.

Meanwhile, on February 12, 1949, the C. B. & Q. celebrated its own Charter Centennial at Aurora. That morning the Paramount Theater was thronged with prominent citizens of Aurora and Chicago who had come to witness a musical pageant depicting the history of the region from the time Chief Blackhawk and his Indian tribes left northern Illinois to the moment when Governor Augustus C. French signed the Aurora Branch charter on February 12, 1849. A novel touch was added by having officers and friends of the railroad appear in costume as members of the Illinois Senate of 1849; later on, these same "Senators," adorned with frock coats, top hats, and mustaches, posed on and around an old 4-4-0 diamond-stack locomotive spotted in the Aurora station.

At a luncheon at the Leland Hotel, civic and business leaders made brief remarks appropriate to the occasion, and Ralph Budd, after reviewing the long and intimate association of the Burlington with the city of Aurora, announced as a "birthday present" the broad-scale program already described for completely modernizing the company's commuter service. And as an example of Burlington's hopes as it entered its second century, he described in detail the new *California Zephyr*, soon to enter service. Later on during 1949, "Burlington Days" were celebrated at all major points on the system.

· CHANGE AT THE HELM ·

WHEN RALPH BUDD came to the Burlington, he found many elderly, albeit capable, men in senior executive positions. Consequently one of the basic policies of his administration was to bring in promising younger people; at the same time he suggested that, as a general rule, Burlington officers should retire at seventy. Thus it came as no surprise when, early in 1949, he announced that he would step down as president on August 31, the end of the month in which he would mark his seventieth birthday.

As might well have been expected, the directors, countless associates, and his many friends paid him sincere tributes for his contributions to the Burlington and to the industry. At the Railroad Fair, August 31 was designated as "Ralph Budd Day," and after a testimonial dinner attended by some 500 persons, there was a re-enactment, as part of the "Wheels A-Rolling" pageant, of that historic moment more than fifteen years earlier when the *Pioneer Zephyr* triumphantly completed its dawn-to-dusk run from Denver on the stage of "Wings of a Century." There could have been no more fitting climax of a distinguished railway career.

Dr. James G. Lyne, the scholarly and knowledgeable editor of *Railway Age* summed up what many felt: "The Burlington is and has been for many years one of the great institutions of the United States. It is such a great institution because it is the lengthened shadow of four of the greatest railroad men of all time—John M. Forbes, Charles E. Perkins, James J. Hill, and Ralph Budd." After a summary of the railroad's development and Budd's part in it, Lyne concluded: "Mr. Budd was educated as an engineer and had a distinguished career as such; and his engineering education and experience have been of great value to him as a railway executive; but his chief claim to fame is that he has been one of the most accomplished, progressive, and courageous administrators and business statesmen who have ever devoted their talents to railroading. The Burlington had long been a great railroad system when he became president of it, but the Burlington of 1949 mainly owes its position in the worlds of transportation and of business to its management during seventeen years of depression, war, and postwar difficulties by Mr. Budd. It is today principally the 'lengthened shadow' of Ralph Budd."[6]

For a man of Budd's vigor and intellectual curiosity, retirement was out of the question; it was simply a question of what he would do next. Franklyn B. Snyder, president of Northwestern University, offered him, early in 1949, a professorial lectureship with *carte blanche* to give such seminars as he desired in a wide range of fields including transportation, business and government, investments, western history, and business administration. Budd gave that invitation very serious thought, but did not

[6] *Railway Age*, Vol. CXXVI, No. 6 (February 5, 1949), p. 79.

accept it for the simple reason that he did not think he was qualified. Many of his friends who thought otherwise, and who knew of his gifts as a teacher, sought to persuade him to reconsider, but to no avail. Not long afterwards, Mayor Kennelly of Chicago invited Budd to serve as chairman of the Chicago Transit Authority. The job was no sinecure, for no subject was more touchy or troublesome than the hopelessly tangled public transit system of Chicago. But the challenge was one that Budd could not resist, and early in April he announced that he had accepted the new post. As far as the Burlington was concerned, Budd's decision to remain in Chicago and to continue serving on the board of directors was a source of great satisfaction, for it meant that his counsel would be available in what promised to be difficult years ahead.

As might have been expected, the man selected by the directors to succeed to the presidency was no stranger to the property. When his election was announced by the board on July 30, Harry C. Murphy was completing his thirty-fifth year of service with the company, the last four of them as vice-president in charge of system operations.

Murphy grew up in Eldora, Iowa, and was educated at the Iowa State College and the Armour Institute of Technology in Chicago. In 1914 he took his first job with the C. B. & Q., serving first as a clerk in the Accounting Department, then moving into the Engineering Department. After service as a pilot throughout World War I, he returned to the Burlington as division engineer at Centralia, and during the next fourteen years saw service on nearly every division of the railroad. Called to Chicago in 1933 as superintendent of safety, he became assistant to the executive vice-president in 1936, and three years later became assistant vice-president of operations, succeeding to the vice-presidency in 1945. Thus his years in Chicago coincided almost exactly with the period of Ralph Budd's administration. He had had an excellent opportunity to observe and participate in many a top-level decision taken during the depression, the war, and the difficult period of transition that followed.

When Harry C. Murphy was elected to the presidency, the board made two other significant appointments. James C. James, who had begun his service with the Burlington as local attorney at Aurora in 1914 and had served as vice-president and general counsel since 1938, was named executive vice-president. In addition to his service as a lawyer, James had proved himself a capable financier and had played a leading role in the Colorado and Southern debt adjustment plan of 1943 as well as in the major refinancing of the C. B. & Q. that took place during the war years. He therefore brought a variety of experience to the new administration. To succeed Murphy as vice-president of operations, the board elected Samuel L. Fee, who had entered Burlington service as a station helper at Knoxville, Iowa, in 1905. During the intervening years he had moved steadily forward from brakeman until, late in 1947, he became general manager of Lines West.

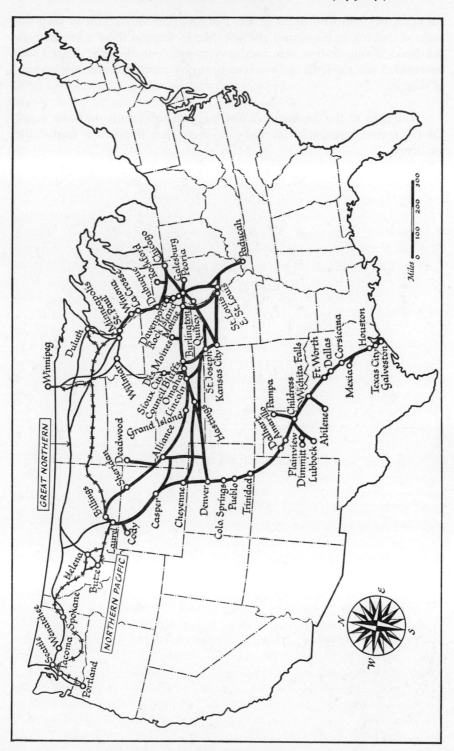

Burlington Route, 1963

An operating man from head to toe, Fee could be counted on to keep the railroad running at maximum efficiency. L. R. Capron, long a key man in the Budd administration, remained as vice-president of traffic. This, then, constituted the top-level team as the company entered its second century of service.

The story of the Burlington's first hundred years must speak for itself. Of the future, one could say only, in 1949, that it posed a formidable challenge.

PART V

Since 1949

Prologue to the
Epilogue

THE DEFINITIVE STORY of the Burlington since 1949 properly belongs to the historian of the company's second century. For one thing, events since then are so recent, historically speaking, that it is too soon to place them accurately in their true context; what, at the moment, seems to us of critical and potentially long-run importance may turn out to be a purely transient phenomenon; by the same token, what now appears trivial may prove to have abiding effects. Second, I know personally many of the men and women now working with the Burlington, both those who make decisions and those who carry them out. Objectivity, therefore, despite diligent effort, would be difficult to attain. Finally, the source records—notably, executive correspondence and memoranda—for the very recent years have neither been assembled and integrated nor made fully accessible. Consequently it is impossible as yet to marshal the evidence necessary to produce, as has been done for the period from 1849 to 1949, a comprehensive documented account from which a balanced summary may be distilled.

Under the circumstances, the most viable and forthright way to bring the story up to date would seem to be (1) to make clear what has just been said so that every reader will be fully aware that the following Epilogue is a preliminary treatment of the subject, and (2) to summarize, primarily on the basis of public sources now available, what appear to be the major developments of the past fifteen years.

In this task I have been helped immeasurably by my friend of long standing and former colleague at the University of Western Ontario, Dr. Donald L. McMurry, of Ithaca, New York. Using primarily the company's *Annual Reports,* he gathered together most of the basic facts for the pages that follow, leaving me to fill out and write the story from such notes and memoranda as I have. I am indebted to the present officers of the company, especially to President Harry C. Murphy, for their cooperation during this phase of the work.

R. C. O.

Epilogue

By the midpoint of the twentieth century, the colorful days of railway building on a grand scale had long since become history. With all major cities connected with each other and the fabled western frontier punctuated beyond recognition, no open spaces remained to challenge the aggressive instincts of rival railway empire builders. Yet the demands of a rapidly changing economy—characterized, for railways, by rising costs, intense competition from rival modes of transportation, and an outdated regulatory structure—and the breath-taking growth of automation posed challenges equal in intensity to those of earlier days.

• Plant •

One basic problem that faced the industry was how to rationalize the existing railway plant in view of these changing conditions. Two things were necessary: elimination of money-losing lines no longer needed by the public and radical improvement of those main arteries which had a vital and promising role to perform.

Continuing its well-established policy, the C. B. & Q., between the beginning of 1950 and the end of 1963, ceased operating 343 miles of unneeded and lightly patronized railroad. On the other hand, on main lines the company reduced curvatures, improved grades, upgraded ballast, increased protection against floods, and steadily increased the weight of rails. In 1961, for example, the 136-pound rail was adopted as standard for future main-line replacements. Parallel developments took place on the C. & S. and Texas lines.

Two of the most spectacular individual improvements were on the Chicago–Kansas City line that connected two of the most important gateways on the entire system. The first was the opening of the Centennial Cut-off, which sliced twenty-two and a quarter miles from the old route; as described in Chapter 28, this was accomplished at a cost of over $16 million by rehabilitating twenty-two miles of the old Carrollton branch and building 48.4 miles of brand-new line. This was the largest single new railroad built in the United States since the end of World War II. New fast freight schedules were inaugurated on October 28, 1952; on February 1, 1953, accelerated double-daily passenger service began operating over the new route. As *Railway Age* put it at the time: "It isn't too often these days that a railroad comes up with plans to double the service of an existing main-line passenger route. So when one does, and then adds that the trains will be completely new dome-streamliners, it is cause to sit up and take notice."[1] The two completely new *Kansas City Zephyrs* affording daily afternoon service between Chicago and Kansas City and the equally new, overnight *American Royal Zephyrs* represented the company's accumulated experience of over nineteen years in providing the ultimate in safety, comfort, and speed for Zephyr passengers. The fastest running time of passenger trains was cut from twelve hours twenty-five minutes over the old route to a minute less than eight hours over the new. This sort of "rationalization" approached a revolution.

The second development on this same route was the replacement in 1960 of the ninety-two-year-old span over the Mississippi at Quincy by a soaring high-level bridge. The original structure, one of James F. Joy's innumerable projects, had gone into service on November 9, 1868, as described in Chapter 6. The superstructure had been replaced in 1902, but aside from the strengthening of its tension members, the old bridge had remained virtually unchanged during its ninety-two years of hard service. Its rails were twenty-two feet above the normal level of the river, for which reason the drawspan had to be opened for river traffic on the average of from seven to ten times a day. Furthermore, as barge traffic on the river grew, there were increasingly frequent collisions with the bridge; in 1948 it was closed to rail traffic for three months after one pier had been struck by a line of barges being pushed by a towboat. When navigation interests complained that the bridge was becoming a hazard, the United States Corps of Engineers opened hearings at Quincy in 1952 to explore the sub-

[1] *Railway Age*, February 9, 1953, p. 71; see also *Modern Railroads*, February 1953, p. 111.

ject; on August 1, 1955, the Secretary of the Army ordered the railway to alter the existing bridge so as to provide 300 feet horizontal clearance and at least 63 feet vertical clearance. Rather than try to rebuild the existing structure, the railway elected to construct an entirely new one which, among other things, would permit a desirable change in the river channel and improve the railroad's alignment between Quincy and West Quincy, Missouri.

The new river crossing was located 500 feet upstream from the old bridge. Its fourteen spans measured 2,501 feet in length and provided the ample clearances for navigation specified by the federal government. Two shorter bridges, a 716-foot span over Quincy Bay, and another 296-foot bridge over Illinois Highway No. 7, completed the project. Total cost was approximately ten million dollars, of which the federal government provided some $2,400,000 to reimburse the company for changes required for the benefit of navigation; the railroad paid the rest. Service over the new structure began on October 21, 1960, and on November 11, President Harry C. Murphy presided over the official dedication. At the close of his remarks he announced that the railroad was donating to the City of Quincy a fifty-acre tract on Bay Island for development as a recreational area, as well as the railroad's old bridge connecting the island with the mainland. Referring to this, the editor of the *Quincy Herald Whig* observed that "the C. B. & Q. does things well—and does good things, too."[2]

Both the Centennial Cut-off and the new Quincy Bridge were outstanding improvements, but they were merely symbolic of what was going on from one end of the system to the other. Sometimes changes were made simply to accommodate the government. On the Denver–Billings line, for example, completion of the Boysen Dam by the Bureau of Reclamation necessitated the relocation at government expense of twelve miles of line and construction of a 7,100-foot tunnel, the longest on the system. Completion of the work was observed with appropriate ceremonies on August 5, 1950, and operations over the relocated line began on September 15.

In 1927 the Burlington was one of the first railways to adopt centralized traffic control. From that time on, this system was steadily expanded. By 1955 all single-track sections on the Chicago–Denver line were so equipped, and the company reported at the end of 1957 that about 1,500 miles of track had this advanced type of signaling. The board on December 4, 1963, authorized the further extension of CTC between Montgomery and Galesburg involving 242.80 track miles. Meanwhile, beginning in 1951, the C. B. & Q. began to install cab signals. Later on in the decade, the company began installing two-way radios in engine cabs and cabooses and on passenger trains so that engineers and conductors could talk not only with each other but also with train dispatchers or way-station

[2] *Quincy Herald Whig*, November 13, 1960.

operators wherever wayside radios were available, as on all principal lines. By 1963 the C. B. & Q. had equipped 448 locomotives and 468 cabooses with two-way radios, and was planning to continue such installations.

All these improvements increased the speed and quantity of the traffic that could be safely moved over the railroad. But the time between the delivery of freight to the company and its receipt by the consignee depended in part, as always, upon the adequacy and efficiency of terminal facilities, as well as on the speed with which it moved over the road. Consequently, modernization and innovation of freight houses and yards were a constant necessity. At Chicago, for example, Freight House No. 10, completed in 1950, was enlarged four years later and extended again in 1960 especially to provide adequate docks for the growing piggyback business. A completely new freight house was built in Minneapolis in 1953, another at Kansas City in 1960. The latter, 709 feet long, with over 100,000 square feet of space under one roof, cost $1,750,000. It was especially equipped for piggyback operations, and included 116 docks for trailers and for the handling of less-than-carload lots.

At the same time, yards such as those at Lincoln were steadily improved. One outstanding development was the transformation in 1957–58 of the flat yard at Cicero into a completely automatic hump yard utilizing electronically controlled retarders and the most modern switching and signaling equipment. When completed, this 2.3-mile long yard with its 93 miles of track had room for 5,777 cars and could classify as many as 3,600 a day, at the rate of five a minute. As a result, the average car moved through the new yard about three and a half hours faster than before; furthermore, it was calculated that operating economies would result in a return on this investment of approximately ten percent after taxes.

Along with the improvement of its yards, the Burlington modernized its shops as necessary to service new types of power and equipment. As the Diesel-electric locomotive completed its conquest of the beloved steam engine, the company supplemented its original facilities for servicing this new type of power by establishing additional Diesel terminals at West Quincy, Denver, Lincoln, and St. Joseph. Meanwhile, in 1957, the timber-treating plant at Galesburg was substantially enlarged and the plant at Sheridan, Wyoming, which had been in disuse for some time, was retired. Two years later the cleaning operations of the Burlington Refrigerator Express Company were transferred from Omaha to the more centrally located Pacific Junction. These changes were typical of many designed to increase efficiency on the system.

Despite the fact that freight traffic provided the most important source of income for the Burlington, as for any railway, many improvements to the plant were made exclusively for the benefit of the traveler by rail. New and modern passenger stations were completed at Ottumwa in 1951 and at Hannibal and West Quincy in 1954. Five years later the venerable union depot at St. Joseph, then over ninety years old, was replaced by a smaller but far more efficient structure. Additional facilities for the complete servicing and maintenance of Zephyr trains were established in 1957 at Denver, where they could serve trains operating on both the C. B. & Q. and the C. & S.–F. W. & D. lines.

• Motive Power and Cars •

THE MOST FUNDAMENTAL and obvious change in motive power on the Burlington after 1949 was the continued substitution of Diesel-electric locomotives for steam. What began as a bold experiment in 1934 gathered headway throughout that decade and during the 1940's. As of December 31, 1949, the roster of Burlington locomotives included 739 steam engines, 247 Diesel road engines, and 146 Diesel switchers, together with three gas-electric units still in service. But by the end of 1953 all passenger trains in regular service and about ninety-five percent of the freight trains were pulled by Diesels; at the end of 1963 the C. B. & Q.'s roster included only seven steam engines, 506 Diesel road locomotives, and 178 Diesel switchers. This total of 691 locomotives of all types was in contrast to 1,135 at the end of 1949. But the change-over to dieselization meant that the average tractive power per locomotive had increased, over the same period, from 55,601 pounds to 63,382 pounds. The same trends emerged on the C. & S.–F. W. & D.

Obviously the historic iron horse was becoming a museum piece. In 1961 the company donated three steam locomotives as permanent exhibits at Quincy, Burlington, and Galesburg, and in 1962 it donated four more for exhibition purposes at St. Joseph, Sheridan, Douglas, and Alliance. Two of those remaining continued to do yeoman service as "working exhibits" at the head end of steam fan tours. As a matter of fact, the company's nationally known *Pioneer Zephyr* became a museum piece itself. May 26, 1959, marked the twenty-fifth anniversary of its non-stop dawn-to-dusk run from Denver to Chicago; during its quarter century of service it had carried more than a million passengers and traveled about 3,200,000 miles. Just a year later it was presented, with appropriate ceremony, for permanent exhibition to Chicago's Museum of Science and Industry.

Whereas the total number of freight-train cars in the Burlington's fleet did not vary a great deal between the end of 1949 and the end of 1963, there was an increasing trend toward cars for special purposes. Boxcars, which made up about half the fleet, included such new features as damage-free equipment and doors fourteen feet wide to facilitate the mechanical loading of lumber and other building materials. In 1962, new, insulated boxcars appeared, equipped with polyurethane foam, a new moisture-proof, fire-resistant, and infestation-proof material of very high insulating efficiency. As piggyback operations became increasingly popular, flatcars assumed a new look too. Some were used for the increasing piggyback operations and were especially adapted to carry truck trailers. Others had bulkheads at the ends, designed to hold in place building materials such as wallboard and plaster board. Still others were fitted out with multi-level racks that could carry more than one tier of automobiles or tractors. Gondola cars, commonly used to carry iron and steel, were turned out with movable covers and bulkheads to protect such shipments. A good many of the newer, covered hopper cars were of the Air-Slide variety, designed especially for the handling of bulk flour and sugar; unloading was accomplished by a combination of gravity and air pressure. In July 1963 Burlington took delivery of 200 jumbo-size hopper cars for carrying coal from Illinois, Missouri, and Wyoming. These 100-ton cars, equipped with roller bearings, were the largest in service on the system and established the company in the coal-hauling business as a true low-cost carrier. As had been the case for many years, most of these new freight cars were built at the company's shops in Havelock; some special-purpose equipment, however, was purchased from outside manufacturers.

As always, the Burlington had a large number of service cars to carry such items as ballast, ties, and other materials for road work or construction, as well as the usual complement of wrecking and derrick cars. The total number of these service cars on the C. B. & Q., however, declined from 5,105 at the end of 1949 to 3,785 at the end of 1963, partly because of the increased efficiency of the cars themselves, partly because of the growing use of motorized off-track work equipment.

In passenger service, there was a slight decline in the number of baggage, express, and mail cars, but an increase in passenger-carrying cars, accompanied by a tremendous improvement in quality. In 1952 alone, for example, thirty-one new stainless-steel, sleeping, coach, dining, parlor, and mail and baggage cars were put into service. Vista-Dome cars were steadily added to almost all long-distance Zephyrs that did not already have them.

Meanwhile, on October 28, 1956, another Burlington "first" was recorded when Slumbercoaches went into service on the completely new *Denver Zephyrs*. These cars provided the coach passenger with a private room by day and a roomette type of bed for the night, with private toilet facilities and ample baggage space. Passengers paid only a coach railway fare plus a modest occupancy charge for the room. These Slumbercoaches each had twenty-four single and eight double rooms, thus providing accommodations for forty passengers. As the company hoped, these cars attracted passengers from chair cars without diverting them from Pullman cars. In 1963 the Vista-Dome *Denver Zephyrs* carried 34,042 passengers in the Slumbercoaches alone; this represented an average occupancy of 83.6 percent per car trip. By then the Northern Pacific–Burlington's *North Coast Limited* also carried a Slumbercoach. Following Burlington's lead, such major passenger carriers as the New York Central and the Baltimore and Ohio put cars of a similar type on several of their premier trains.

These improvements in long-distance passenger-carrying cars were matched by the introduction in August 1950 of stainless-steel suburban cars of the gallery type. By January 1951, thirty were in service, and others were added, to bring the total to sixty by the fall of 1957. By 1965 additional gallery cars, thirty-four in number, will be added, thus converting the entire suburban fleet to this type of modern equipment.

· LABOR RELATIONS AND PERSONNEL ·

PLANT AND EQUIPMENT are, in a sense, the tools that produce transportation service; highly skilled men and women are required, both in the ranks of management and labor, to use them efficiently. Furthermore, labor and management have to work together harmoniously; this is especially essential on a major railway such as the Burlington, for if the wheels stop turning, even for a day, not only those directly involved but also the public at large inevitably suffer. During the post-1949 period, two developments in particular made it extremely difficult to keep labor relations on an even keel.

An outstanding characteristic of these years was the trend, as in all highly industrialized nations, toward automation. New inventions, such as those in electronics, increasingly made it possible to perform more work per man-hour. On the C. B. & Q., for example, the average number of employees during 1950 was 30,076; by 1963 it had fallen to 21,038, a decrease of twenty-eight percent, even though the amount of freight and passenger transportation produced had increased. There were comparable declines in personnel on the C. & S. and the F. W. & D.

On the other hand, over the same span of time, payroll costs rose rapidly. On the C. B. & Q. they increased 26.5 percent, from $105 million to $133 million. Whereas wages in 1950 amounted to 40.6 percent of C. B. & Q. 's income dollar, they took 50.1 percent of it in 1963, or, if payroll taxes are included, 54.3 percent. The situation on the western subsidiaries was similar. Not only that, but, as the chart shows, hourly wage rates on the C. B. & Q. also increased far more rapidly than either material prices or, more to the point, revenue per ton-mile or per passenger-mile.

Consequently, two opposing, yet perfectly understandable, forces were set in motion. Organized labor, represented by national unions, sought to increase wages and other benefits, as they long had, and also to perpetuate jobs that technology was rendering unnecessary. On the other hand, management, pressed as never before by competition from other types of carriers, regulated more stringently than non-rail competitors, and faced with mounting costs and taxes, perforce made effective use of these technological improvements—specifically, to reassign or reduce the work force accordingly.

In this power struggle, which centered inevitably on wages and feather-

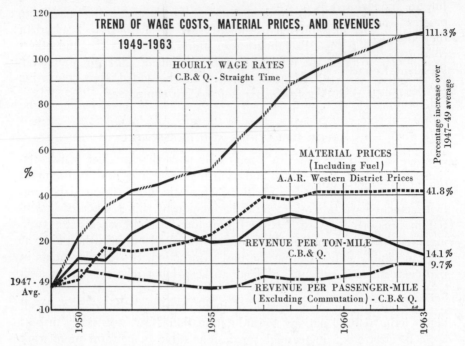

bedding, developments on the Burlington simply reflected what was taking place in the industry at large; as was true during both world wars, and in respect to all federal legislation, wages and working contracts, as well as interstate rates, continued to be determined primarily on a national basis.

One major change took place in 1959 when the carriers met union requests for wage increases and other benefits with counter proposals which contemplated basic changes in the rules covering the basis of pay and assignments for various operating personnel, notably firemen on road freight and yard Diesels, and for the abolition of various rules and practices requiring a stipulated number of employees in road or yard crews.

The complex details of this situation defy summation. Suffice it to say that a presidential commission, appointed to make recommendations regarding rule changes, reported on February 28, 1962, supporting much of what the carriers demanded; specifically, it recommended elimination of firemen on other than steam locomotives in freight and yard service; firemen with less than ten years of service were to be separated in July 1962, the others by natural attrition. It recommended that the individual roads negotiate on the matter of the composition of crews, with a provision for binding arbitration in case of disagreement. The commission urged recognition of management's right to make technological changes, and offered various other solutions to the complex problems that had been presented to it. When the operating unions refused to accept these recommendations, the National Mediation Board attempted to mediate, but on

July 16, 1962, closed its docket on the case after having failed to make any progress whatsoever. On the next day the carriers notified the unions that they intended to put into effect the recommendations of the presidential commission. A series of developments followed, including a plea from President Kennedy that negotiations be resumed and a decision by the United States Supreme Court that the recommendations of the presidential commission were valid under the Railway Labor Act. Finally, in the summer of 1963, a nationwide strike of the operating unions was prevented only when Congress, reluctantly, passed a law requiring (1) compulsory arbitration of the principal issues at stake (the use of firemen on road freight and yard Diesels and the consist of crews) and (2) further negotiation of other outstanding issues.

When, in respect to the first requirement, the arbitrators on November 26, 1963, upheld the carriers and provided for generous severance pay for the few men who would actually be let go, the unions voiced their disagreement. Some of them filed suit, claiming that the award was invalid and that the Act of Congress under which it had been made was unconstitutional. The United States Court of Appeals rejected these claims on February 20, 1964, and late in April the Supreme Court refused to review the matter. Thereupon, effective May 7, the railroads began to give effect to the arbitration award. Meanwhile, in respect to the second provision, a crisis arose on April 8 when the operating brotherhoods, without warning, struck on the Illinois Central over the remaining unsettled issues in the operating rules dispute. As a result of this action, the nation's railroads served notice that they planned to make the carriers' original rules proposals of 1959 effective on April 10. The unions responded with the threat of a nationwide strike, whereupon, on April 9, 1964, President Johnson intervened. Both parties to the dispute accepted the services of presidential mediators, and on April 22 it was announced that agreement in principle had been reached; final settlement in writing was achieved on June 25. Under it, among other provisions, employees received certain fringe benefits such as paid holidays and expenses while away from home; the railroads gained a moratorium through January 1, 1968, on increases in mileage rates of pay for road-service employees. It was also agreed to submit various minor unresolved issues to further negotiation.

The fact that newspapers and public attention naturally focused on issues such as this tended to obscure the basic truth that normally, year in and year out, labor and management collaborated effectively in the common task of producing the best rail transportation possible. After all, that was the only way to assure the future of any railroad and of everyone who worked for it, regardless of position.

During the post-1949 period, all sorts of personnel activities were shared by *all* employees of the Burlington. The long-established Relief Department, to which an overwhelming majority of employees belonged, and to which they contributed on a monthly basis, continued to disburse funds in the form of death and disability benefits; total payments for 1950–62, inclusive, exceeded ten million dollars. All Burlington employees were also covered by the Railroad Retirement Act and the Railroad Unemployment Insurance Act. The cost of retirement and survivor benefits continued to be shared equally by the company and the employees; the taxes to pay unemployment, sickness, and maternity benefits were assumed entirely by the railway.

Various "Burlington family" groups, distinguished by location, age, or special purpose, flourished. Early in 1937, a handful of employees had organized a Chicago Terminal Credit Union. Its membership, then 658 (including Ralph Budd), had expanded to 2,921 by the fall of 1963; loans outstanding to members exceeded half a million dollars. The Veterans Association, organized in the fall of 1920, had grown to 5,327 members when it met for its annual reunion at Denver in the fall of 1963; there were then thirty-four chapters from one end of the system to the other. Its counterpart, the Ladies Auxiliary, organized early in 1925, had thirty-two chapters and 4,139 members by the end of 1963.

Various company publications, some old and some new, were of interest to all Burlington personnel. In 1947 the C. B. & Q. *Annual Report* appeared for the first time with a glossy, illustrated cover. Thereafter, in increasing tempo, succeeding reports modernized their internal format, expanded their contents, added striking graphic material, and, in 1958, began to include colored photographs. In 1964 the company's 1963 *Annual Report* won *Financial World*'s bronze Oscar-in-industry in competition with other railroads with comparable gross revenues. In 1960 the *Safety News* was incorporated into a larger quarterly, the *Burlington Bulletin*, profusely illustrated and carrying all sorts of system news and special items. The Passenger Department's quarterly *Zephyr* kept everyone up to date on new trains, facilities, tours, and special events. And, of course, every Burlington employee shared a common interest in publications that marked high points in company history. In the fall of 1953, the present writer's *Gulf to Rockies*, which tells the story of the C. & S. and the F. W. & D. C. up to 1899, was published by the University of Texas Press. In 1956 the Harvard University Press released John T. O'Neil's *Policy Formation in Railroad Finance: Refinancing the Burlington, 1936–1945*; and in the same year Harvard also published Donald L. McMurry's *The Great Burlington Strike of 1888*. *Steam Locomotives of the Burlington Route*, by Bernard Corbin and William Kerka, published by Thomas D. Murphy of Red Oak, Iowa, appeared in 1960. David Morgan's *Diesels West! The Evolution of Power on the Burlington* came off Kalmbach's press in 1963.

There was a common interest too in the countless celebrations held from time to time across the system to mark specific events. The seventy-fifth anniversary of the Burlington *Fast Mail*, for instance, was marked by a banquet of Burlington and Post Office representatives in Chicago on March 11, 1959, followed by a series of special events in Omaha and Council Bluffs. David P. Morgan, the editor of *Trains*, wrote a brief history of the famous train, which the company published. In the fall of 1963, to cite another random example, Casper celebrated fifty years of Burlington service when a gold-painted steam locomotive brought a twelve-car special to the city for a whole day of jollification.

On a more sobering note, 2,458 company employees entered military service during the Korean War. Twelve died in the conflict; of those who were discharged from service by the end of 1953, more than ninety percent returned to their jobs on the railway.

Although inevitably there were changes within the directorate and in top management during the fourteen years from the end of 1949 to the end of 1963, there was a strong element of continuity. John M. Budd and Robert S. Macfarlane, presidents of the Great Northern and the Northern Pacific, respectively, replaced their predecessors, Frank J. Gavin and Charles E. Denney, on the board. However, four of the other seven members, including Harry C. Murphy, were still serving as directors in 1964. All three vice-presidents who were serving at the end of 1949 were living in retirement at the end of 1963: J. C. James, executive vice-president and general counsel, was replaced in 1952 as general counsel by Eldon Martin, who became a vice-president in 1954. L. R. Capron, vice-president in charge of traffic, was replaced in 1958 by Guy R. Glover; and Samuel L. Fee, vice-president of the Operating Department, by E. L. Potarf in 1959. The effect of these and other changes, however, was more apparent than real because throughout the post-1949 period, Burlington pursued its long-standing policy of filling vacancies from within its own ranks. Officers of the C. B. & Q. named from 1949 through 1959, for instance, had served the company at the time of their appointments from fifteen to fifty-four years, the average being just under thirty-six years.

From 1949 on, of course, Harry C. Murphy served as president and chairman of the executive committee not only of the C. B. & Q., but also of the C. & S., and of the Texas Lines. Locally in the West, E. G. Wesson, vice-president of the C. & S., remained as the highest ranking officer in Denver until his retirement in 1962, when he was replaced by J. W. Terrill. At Fort Worth, R. Wright Armstrong, as vice-president, presided over the Texas companies until the end of 1962, when he was succeeded by E. L. Simmons.

• SERVICE AND TRAFFIC: FREIGHT •

FROM THE END OF 1949 through the end of 1963, the Burlington spent a gross of more than $430 million to improve plant and equipment, an average of more than $30 million a year. The result was vastly increased efficiency in the handling of freight and passenger traffic. In respect to the former, for example, gross ton-miles handled per train hour on the C. B. & Q. by the end of 1962 had increased 55.9 percent over the average for 1947–49. Freight-train speeds increased. To cite an isolated but meaningful index, net ton-miles per freight-car day increased from 988 during 1961 to 1,100 in 1962. And during 1962 Burlington inaugurated a new fast freight schedule for a meat train from Omaha to Chicago which carried refrigerated cars, refrigerator trailers, and containers on flatcars. This train made the run in less than ten hours at a speed comparable to that of the *Nebraska Zephyr* and arrived in Chicago in time to connect with the fast freights of the eastern railroads; the net result was to cut from twelve to twenty-five hours from the previous schedules for fresh meats traveling from Omaha to the eastern seaboard.

Trailer-on-flatcar service (TOFC), commonly called "piggyback," was inaugurated on the Burlington in 1941, but for many years, as on other railroads, developed very slowly. Even in 1952, only 150 trailers were carried, but the number rose to over 800 in 1954 and then skyrocketed to a peak of 56,331 in 1960, at which point it leveled off. As the *Annual Report* of 1959 expressed it: "The Burlington believes the future of TOFC service is almost unlimited, and that it represents the most effective method not only to regain business previously lost to highway truckers, but also to prevent further erosion of this traffic."[3] In 1960 a variation of the piggyback appeared in the multi-level rack car for carrying two or three tiers of automobiles or trucks and farm tractors. These were an immediate success: the company carried 3,500 carloads of new automobiles in 1961 and 5,515 in 1963.

Back in 1935, Burlington, through a wholly owned subsidiary, had begun operating trucks, and because this step had been taken prior to the effective date of the Motor Carrier Act, the C. B. & Q. then acquired valuable "grandfather rights" that enabled its truck lines to develop into one of the major operations in the nation. In 1963 Burlington Truck Lines, Inc., operated over more than 9,800 route miles; its vehicles covered 15,661,627 miles in intercity traffic and 3,039,125 miles in pick-up and delivery service in fifty-three cities. Some of this service was of a general nature, in competition with independent truck lines; some was coordinated with Burlington rail movements. In 1963, as a case in point, B. T. L. delivered 6,789 loaded trailers for TOFC shipment over the Burlington.

But simply to provide plant and facilities for carrying freight was not enough, and never had been. In view of the ever present competition from other railways and other types of carriers, Burlington had constantly to generate new sources of business. This, indeed, was a primary obligation of the Traffic Department. Because the two largest sources of the company's

[3] CB&Q, AR 1959, p. 10.

freight traffic from the standpoint of revenue were (1) manufactures and miscellaneous and (2) products of agriculture, special efforts were made in those directions.

The long-standing policy of establishing industrial districts was pushed vigorously during the post-1949 period, and especially from 1953 onward. In that and every successive year the company purchased land for the establishment of new districts or for the enlargement of old ones. By 1963, purchases totaling over 2,500 acres had been made along Burlington tracks from Illinois to Colorado and Wyoming. In some of these districts the company built streets, installed utilities, and leased sites to industries, laying industrial tracks to give them access to the Burlington. At North Kansas City, for example, the extensive Paseo Bridge Industrial District was enlarged, and new streets and utilities were installed. At Aurora, 600 acres were cleared for development. The number of new industrial leases issued by the C. B. & Q. increased each year, from 401 in 1949 to 761 in 1963.

In addition to its industrial districts, Burlington owned land suitable for plant locations at many other points, and offered such land for sale. A brochure published in 1954 and widely distributed contained aerial photographs, maps, and information about numerous parcels of land of this sort suitable for industrial development. In addition, the company cooperated with chambers of commerce, industrial committees, and other civic groups interested in the attraction and development of new industries that could be served by the railroad.

Encouragement of agriculture was an old story for the Burlington. After all, in 1963 states served by the system produced sixty-eight percent of the nation's corn crop, forty-seven percent of the wheat, sixty-one percent of the soybeans, forty-nine percent of the hay, forty-seven percent of sorghum grain, thirty-two percent of the sugar beets, twenty-five percent of the dried beans, and fifteen percent of the potatoes; the company was as interested in the success of these crops as were the farmers. Accordingly, it continued to cooperate with the United States Soil Conservation Service, the United States Reclamation Service, and other federal and state agencies devoted to the improvement of agriculture through a variety of means, including the development of irrigation projects. The result of these joint efforts was spectacular. In Nebraska, for example, the 4,000 new wells completed during 1956 furnished enough water to irrigate 250,000 acres of semi-arid land; by 1963, 24,372 wells produced enough to irrigate 2,687,000 acres. The consequent increase in agricultural production meant, of course, more traffic for Burlington. The company also worked with young peoples' organizations such as the 4-H clubs and the Future Farmers of America to organize corn-producing contests, and with business groups, farm organizations, and agricultural colleges to promote better farming methods.

The character of the freight traffic carried by the three major components of the Burlington Lines, measured in terms of revenue produced, reflected no startling changes over the period 1949–63, inclusive. Manufactures and miscellaneous continued to account for roughly two fifths of system-wide freight revenues. Products of agriculture supplied nearly a quarter of C. B. & Q. freight revenues, with products of mines in third place. On the C. & S., products of mines maintained their rank as the second most important revenue producers, with products of agriculture in third place. On the F. W. & D., the front-ranking agricultural products increased in importance, with manufactures and miscellaneous not far behind.

TABLE I

BURLINGTON LINES
PERCENT OF TOTAL FREIGHT REVENUE BY COMMODITY GROUPS

		Products of agriculture	Animals and products	Products of mines	Products of forests	Manufactures & misc.	Forwarder traffic	Less-than-carload freight
C. B. & Q.	1949	23.71	7.58	17.24	6.15	37.91	1.78	5.64
	1963	22.66	6.35	15.02	7.03	43.12	4.24	1.58
C. & S.	1949	16.41	4.81	26.90	8.13	41.13	——	2.62
	1963	13.29	2.82	26.48	9.36	47.06	.19	.80
F. W. & D.	1949	41.06	2.65	7.44	4.95	39.33	1.84	2.73
	1963	44.09	1.51	6.20	4.60	41.56	1.13	.91

It is worth noting that, as always, the C. B. & Q. was less dependent on any one category of traffic than either of its western subsidiaries. This reflected not only the greater geographical extent of the C. B. & Q., but also the larger diversity of its sources of traffic. An additional development, relevant to the performance of the F. W. & D. after 1950, deserves mention: on June 1, 1950, the Fort Worth and Denver City Railway and the Chicago, Rock Island and Pacific Railroad jointly leased all of the property of the Burlington–Rock Island not previously under lease to those companies (that is, everything south of Waxahachie). Each of the lessor companies thereupon extended its joint freight and passenger service all the way from Fort Worth and Dallas to Houston, and its freight service on to Galveston. After June 1, 1950, therefore, a portion of *both* revenues *and* expenses formerly accounted for by Burlington–Rock Island was included in the revenues and expenses reported by the Fort Worth and Denver.

Table II reflects the fact that despite competition, freight business, measured according to revenue ton-miles, increased on all portions of the system. The rise of 15.7 percent on the C. B. & Q. was roughly comparable to the 18.1 percent rise over the same period for all Class I railroads. Freight revenues forged ahead also, increasing more rapidly than the amount of traffic on both the C. B. & Q. and the C. & S., and less rapidly, because of local conditions, on the F. W. & D. In the case of freight revenues, the 18.6 percent rise on the C. B. & Q. was slightly more than the 15.6 percent increase reported for all Class I railroads over the comparable span of time.

TABLE II

BURLINGTON LINES
FREIGHT TRAFFIC AND REVENUE

	C. B. & Q.		C. & S.		F. W. & D.	
	Ton-Miles*	Revenue†	Ton-Miles*	Revenue†	Ton-Miles*	Revenue†
1949	15,250	$179.8	911	$11.2	1,066(x)	$15.0(x)
1963	17,646	213.3	979	13.2	1,380(y)	17.8(y)

* Revenue ton-miles only, in millions.   † Millions
(x) Includes Wichita Valley Ry.
(y) Includes Wichita Valley and a portion of former B.–R. I.

· SERVICE AND TRAFFIC: PASSENGER ·

THE COMPANY'S ATTITUDE toward passenger service was concisely summarized in the *Annual Report* for 1956: "The Burlington believes in the future of railroad passenger service. We are confident that with the growth of our nation the railroads will enjoy a volume of traffic that will enable a continuance of good, fast, comfortable day and night service between centers of population."[4] Suiting action to words, the company left no stone unturned in an effort to recapture business from buses, airplanes, and private automobiles by improving equipment and schedules, reducing fares, engaging in vigorous sales promotion, featuring special tours, and generally enlivening traffic by rail.

When the first Slumbercoaches were introduced on the new *Denver Zephyrs*, for example, in October 1956, through service of that train was extended to Colorado Springs; at the same time the equipment on the *Texas Zephyrs* was greatly improved. Meanwhile, in the fall of 1953, Burlington began promoting student educational trips; by June 1954 it had carried some 22,000 young people on excursions. The number more than doubled the next year, and during 1963 the company carried the amazing number of 122,274 students. Nor were these the only special tours. The company's few remaining steam locomotives were recruited for steam fan excursions; in 1960, to pick a year at random, a dozen special trains of this sort carried some 6,000 passengers. Other special excursions included historic tours, camera-fan tours, off-season vacation tours, scenic trips along the Mississippi River, and baseball and football specials.

Efforts to secure more passenger business were unremitting. Sales teams canvassed the key cities in Burlington territory, conducting door-to-door campaigns; early in 1963, as a case in point, two dozen men and

[4] CB&Q, AR 1956, p. 13.

women in fur caps and red coats, wearing Burlington insignia, descended on St. Paul and Minneapolis businessmen, calling personally on some 3,000 of them in four days. Small wonder that late that year Burlington was honored by the Midwest Travel Writers Association for having performed the most effective travel-promotion job by a common carrier in 1963.

The success of these efforts was reflected in the fact that in 1963 the C. B. & Q. increased its share of the western rail passenger market for the eleventh consecutive year. The 9.8 million revenue passengers carried in 1949 increased to 10.8 million in 1963, a rise of 10.2 percent, which contrasted sharply with the decline registered by all Class I railways over the same period. Meanwhile, revenue passenger-miles on the C. B. & Q. moved ahead from just over 757 million to more than 800 million. Indeed, C. B. & Q. passenger revenues from 1960 on were higher than at any time since the World War II bulge, and this despite the fact that both the average amount of C. B. & Q. mileage offering passenger train service and the number of passenger train miles decreased during 1949–63 by approximately one third. And in five of the seven years 1957–63, the percent of increase of suburban revenue was greater than that of the regular passenger service. To put it in capsule form, quality service where it was most wanted clearly proved more attractive to the public and more justifiable economically than indiscriminate quantity service.

Although neither of Burlington's western subsidiaries reported any such spectacular performances, the decline in revenue passenger-miles on the C. & S. from 1949 through 1963 was only about half of the national decline; revenue passenger-miles on the Fort Worth and Denver fell off even less. Of course, neither freight nor passenger traffic accounted for all of the business or operating revenues of the Burlington. But they did account, in 1963 as in 1949, for about eighty-eight percent; the balance came from hauling mail and express, performing various switching operations, and the like.

One factor, as always, played an important part in every sort of transportation undertaking: safety. The Burlington continued its efforts to train its employees to avoid accidents both on and off the job and to warn the public about dangerous practices. During the 1950's the National Safety Council gave a series of awards to particular subdivisions of the C. B. & Q. such as the Denver Terminal, the Aurora Car Shop, the West Burlington Diesel Shop, the Special Agents Department, the Havelock Store, and the Eola Reclamation Plant. In 1961, for the sixth time in seven years, the Council gave the C. B. & Q. its Public Safety Award in recognition of the company's outstanding safety program for its employees and the general public. The Burlington Truck Lines received two Certificates of Achievement in 1961 from the National Safety Council, and in the next year five more fleet safety awards, including those from the National Safety Council and the American Trucking Association. These awards and the safety records that earned them were one indication of the condition of the system's plant and equipment, the efficiency of its operations, and the caliber of its personnel.

• RATES AND REVENUES •

WHAT ANY RAILROAD COLLECTS for performing transportation service is determined, roughly speaking, by multiplying what it transports by the rates and fares it charges. Thus, in the post-1949 years, how much the Burlington could (within limits prescribed by the various regulatory authorities) and should (as a matter of competitive policy) charge was, as always, a matter for constant thought and experimentation. After granting a small interim increase in freight charges in 1952, the Interstate Commerce Commission took action the following year which resulted in an estimated authorized increase for the Burlington of about thirteen and a half percent. Again, after granting various small increases in 1956, the I. C. C. the following year permitted increases of between nine and twelve percent and suggested that if these were inadequate to offset mounting wages, the railroads should ask for further moderate selective increases, which, in most cases, were authorized.

To generalize about rates in respect to any particular railway system is virtually impossible. Unless a maximum rate fixed by the authorities also happens to be the legal minimum rate, a railroad is not obligated to charge the maximum permissible amount, and does not do so whenever it believes a lower rate will attract enough additional volume to produce higher net revenues than could be obtained from making the full charge. Often, indeed, in order to meet non-rail competition, a considerable segment of the railway industry seeks relief from rates it feels are arbitrarily high. A notable example was the Kokomo case involving rates on iron and steel. Various companies, including the Burlington, asked that certain minimum rate requirements fixed in 1945, when competitive conditions were much different, be removed. But first the I. C. C. and then a federal court decided, in 1957, that such relief should be denied. "The effect of this action," Murphy wrote in the C. B. & Q. *Annual Report* for 1957, "is to preclude our meeting the rates of other transportation agencies without needlessly sacrificing revenue on traffic between points where there is either no carrier competition or [where] competition is not sufficiently severe to warrant competitive rate reductions."[5] The same *Report* indicated that the company was constantly reviewing rates with the idea of making adjustments where desirable to meet competition; the same thought was repeated in the *Report* for 1962. As a Granger system, Bur-

[5] CB&Q, AR 1957, p. 11.

lington was particularly concerned with grain rates and, to meet trucker competition, with the provision of carload rates on bulk commodities. Because of the bewildering factors involved, it is virtually impossible to measure the overall effect of rate policies, but it is significant, perhaps, to note, as indicated in the chart on page 564, that on the basis of the 1947–49 average, C. B. & Q. revenue per ton-mile rose approximately twenty-eight percent by 1953, dipped below nineteen percent in 1955, exceeded thirty percent in 1958, and stood at 14.1 percent in 1963.

Although there was no general increase in coach passenger fares between 1950 and early 1957, there were modest piecemeal rises between selected points served by the Burlington, and substantial rises in Pullman charges. During 1957 the Burlington and other western carriers obtained a basic five percent increase for both coach and first-class passengers; coach fares were increased in 1960 and 1961; meanwhile Pullman charges advanced moderately. C. B. & Q. suburban rates were advanced in 1953, 1957–58, 1960, and 1962, but as during those years commuter service had undergone a revolutionary improvement, there was virtually no public opposition to these rises. After long hearings, mail rates were substantially advanced in 1950 and again in 1953, 1957, 1959, and 1960. Parallel increases were permitted in express rates.

The rate pattern on the C. & S. and the F. W. & D. was similar, although inevitably different in detail. As the C. & S.–F. W. & D. *Annual Report* put it in 1957, for example: "The railroads, faced with ever-increasing costs, found it necessary to petition the Interstate Commerce Commission for additional increases on December 23, 1957. The petition deviated from the usual pattern of increase petitions in that it did not request horizontal increases, but treated commodities in an individual manner. No increases were requested on certain commodities particularly susceptible to truck competition."[6]

In the difficult year 1949, total operating revenues on the C. B. & Q. were just under $218 million, but from 1950 through 1962 achieved something of a plateau ranging between $245 million (1950) and $278 million (1953); for 1963 they stood at $262 million. Between 1949 and 1963, inclusive, total operating revenues on the C. & S. ranged from a low of $13.2 million (1949) to a high of $16.6 million (1951); for 1963 they stood at $15.9 million. On the F. W. & D. (including Wichita Valley revenues and, after June 1, 1950, a portion of former B.–R. I. revenues), total operating revenues, which were $17.8 million in 1949, varied between $22.3 million (1950) and $26.7 million (1959); in 1963 the company took in $21.9 million. Operating revenues for the Burlington Truck Lines increased every year from 1953, when they were $5.8 million, to 1963 when they reached $16.6 million.

[6] C&S–FW&D, AR 1957, pp. 7–8.

• EXPENSES AND INCOME •

As INDICATED ABOVE, the largest item of expense for all components of the Burlington system has been, and increasingly so since 1949, wages. To single out and describe the various increases in pay and fringe benefits granted during 1950–63, inclusive, would require a separate chapter; here it must suffice to repeat that on the C. B. & Q. alone the payroll in those years mounted from $105 million to $132 million, even though the labor force shrank by twenty-nine percent. In 1963 wages and payroll taxes together took 54.3 percent of the income dollar.

As usual, the second largest item of operating expense on all parts of the system was materials and supplies. The outcome of the continual battle to control expenses is reflected in the operating ratio. Until the mid-50's, the various components of the Burlington usually had a better showing (that is, a lower ratio) than the average for all Class I railways; since then only the F. W. & D. has generally done better than the average, the C. B. & Q. has roughly equalled it, and the C. & S. has not done so well. The operating ratio, of course, represents the relation of railway operating expenses to railway operating revenues; what is left over is called "net revenue from railway operations."

The two largest items that must be paid from this net revenue before arriving at net income are taxes and interest on the funded debt. Total taxes paid by the C. B. & Q. exceeded $26 million in 1949, reached a peak of over $41 million in 1951, and then started a definite, though irregular, downward trend to slightly under $23 million in 1963. The pattern of total taxes paid by the C. & S. and the F. W. & D. was similar over the same years. The decrease in these totals was caused primarily by two important factors: (1) the decline in taxable income on which income taxes are paid and (2) various government rulings affecting the amortization and depreciation of certain equipment. The effect of this second factor was to decrease income-tax liability and increase net income during the amortization period; after that period, however, the effect was reversed during the life of the property affected. On the C. B. & Q. during 1950–61, inclusive, net income benefited from this arrangement to the extent of over 35 million dollars, but beginning in 1962, with amortization exhausted, the effect was an increase in income-tax liability while net income was decreased by an equivalent amount. Under the same arrangement, C. & S. income taxes were reduced and net income increased through 1962, but thereafter the situation was reversed. The F. W. & D. exhausted its amortization in 1958, and consequently, beginning in 1959, its taxes were higher and its net income lower. Under a somewhat similar arrangement effective in 1954, all Burlington companies elected to adopt permissible accelerated depreciation practices which, in effect, deferred certain tax liabilities and increased net income for the time being. Shorter amortization periods, provided for under guidelines for depreciation, effective in 1962, augmented the effect of the 1954 ruling.

Although the net effect of these rather technical arrangements was to reduce federal income-tax payments for all three companies, payroll taxes virtually doubled during 1950–63. On the C. B. & Q. alone, for example, unemployment taxes rose from slightly over half a million in 1954 to almost $4 million in 1963; meanwhile, retirement taxes moved up moderately from $6.4 million to $7.2 million. Again, the pattern was similar on the western subsidiaries.

State and miscellaneous taxes continued to be a substantial burden. On the C. B. & Q. they represented about a quarter of the entire tax burden in 1950, nearly half of it in 1959, and about thirty-four percent in 1963. The company considered part of this local taxation unfair and excessive and made continued efforts to obtain relief. As the result of successful litigation in Illinois, for example, the C. B. & Q. up to the end of 1963 recovered over $4.8 million in refunds covering discriminatory *ad valorem* taxes assessed during the tax years 1958–61, inclusive.

In each of the four years 1950–53, taxes paid by the C. B. & Q., incidentally, were more than three times the amount paid in dividends to stockholders. In 1954–63 they were between two and two and a half times as much, except for 1960, 1962, and 1963, when they were slightly less than twice as much.

On the C. B. & Q., unmatured mortgage debt outstanding in the hands of the public at the end of 1949 amounted to slightly over $152 million. It jumped to over $171 million the next year, when the company sold bonds, partly to redeem some then outstanding and partly to meet capital expenditures incurred in building the Kansas City cut-off. But after 1950 mortgage debt declined steadily; in 1958 the General Mortgage was paid off, and at the end of 1963 the figure stood at approximately $120 million. Meanwhile, however, equipment obligations increased as the C. B. & Q. continually improved its rolling stock. Obligations of this sort rose from about $30 million in 1949 to slightly over $100 million in 1963. Thus total interest charges on the C. B. & Q., which stood at $5.6 million in 1949, moved to a peak of $7.5 million in 1961 and dropped slightly to $7.49 million in 1963.

The debt situation of the western subsidiaries was altered radically by a far-reaching corporate rearrangement and financial refunding in 1952. A preliminary step was taken in 1951, when the charter of the Fort Worth and Denver City Railway was amended, permitting it, in effect, to take over all the lines in Texas (except the half interest in the Burlington–Rock Island) which had previously been owned by the Colorado and Southern. At the same time the name of the company was changed to the Fort Worth and Denver Railway. In 1942, Colorado and Southern Lines mortgage debt had exceeded $53 million; a decade later this sum had been

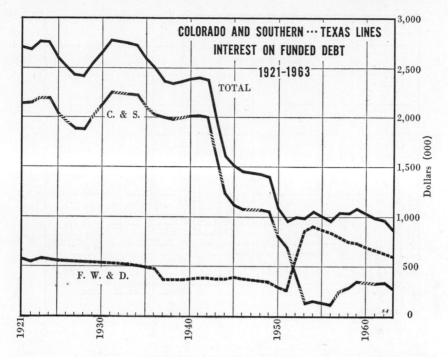

COLORADO AND SOUTHERN ··· TEXAS LINES
INTEREST ON FUNDED DEBT
1921-1963

reduced, in spectacular fashion, to $17 million. In that year the federal court in Denver permitted the C. & S. to terminate its Plan of Adjustment. Thereupon the renamed Fort Worth and Denver purchased from the C. & S. all stock and obligations of the seven Texas subsidiaries, which were forthwith merged into the F. W. & D. Thus, the Colorado and Southern Railway owned and operated all of the system property outside of the State of Texas, while the Fort Worth and Denver owned and operated all the Texas lines except the Burlington–Rock Island. The C. & S. continued to own one half of the B.–R. I., but according to an agreement effective at the beginning of 1951, the operation of that property rotated thereafter on a five-year basis between the Rock Island and the Fort Worth and Denver. In sum then, the former nine companies comprising the Colorado and Southern Lines were reduced to two, with the F. W. & D. responsible for operations in Texas, the C. & S. for those elsewhere.

So far as funded debt was concerned, these developments meant that interest charges, which stood at slightly over a million dollars on the C. & S. in 1949, fell drastically as of 1953; although they increased gradually thereafter as additional equipment was purchased, they stood at about a quarter of a million in 1963. On the F. W. & D., on the other hand, interest charges of approximately one third of a million in 1949 mounted sharply in 1953–54, but then decreased steadily to about two thirds of a million in 1962. This shifting of the debt burden was to be

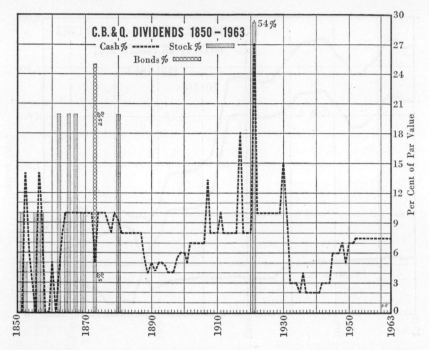

C.B. & Q. DIVIDENDS 1850–1963
Cash % -------- Stock % ▨▨▨▨
Bonds % ✗✗✗✗✗✗✗

fully expected in view of the fact that the C. & S. owned far less mileage after the 1952 changes than before, whereas the F. W. & D. expanded its ownership. The notable fact was that the combined interest of the two companies fell from $1.4 million in 1949 to less than a million in 1963.

During the post-1949 period, net income on the C. B. & Q. varied between a low of $12.5 million in 1960 and a high of $33.8 million in 1950. In 1951–56, inclusive, there was something of a plateau when net income each year was in the $20 million bracket; during 1957–61 it ranged in the "teens," but it climbed above $20 million in 1962 and 1963. The amount of capital stock of the C. B. & Q. remained unchanged throughout the period. The dividend of five dollars paid in the difficult year 1949 was increased to seven dollars in the next two years and to $7.50 a share in 1952–63; 1961, incidentally, was the one hundredth consecutive year in which the C. B. & Q. paid a dividend. The company's retained income increased from $243 million in 1949 to $351 million in 1962.

Under the C. & S. Plan of Adjustment approved in 1943, most of the net income of the C. & S. had to be used for debt reduction. Consequently not until 1952, when the Plan terminated, was any net income available for the payment of dividends. In that year, two dollars was paid on the company's first preferred stock, the first payment of any kind on C. & S. stock since 1931. The next year, with net income exceeding two million dollars, the company was able to pay four dollars on the first preferred, four dollars on the second preferred, and a dollar on the common stock;

similar payments were made through 1958. In 1959–61, inclusive, with net income below $900,000, the company reduced payments on the common to twenty-five cents while continuing the four-dollar payments on each of the preferred issues. C. & S. net income for 1962 and 1963 recovered somewhat, and dividend payments were held to the same scale as during the previous four years.

Net income of the F. W. & D. ranged between $1.4 million and $2.3 million during 1949–54, but fell more than fifty percent during the next four years and decreased even more in 1959–61. The low point was a net income of only slightly over $50,000 in 1960. In 1962, net income recovered to slightly over a quarter of a million dollars, but in 1963 the company reported a deficit of $25,084. Virtually all F. W. & D. stock continued to be held by the C. & S.

• REGULATION •

THE TRANSPORTATION ACT OF 1958 was the only general law affecting railways passed by Congress during the period under review. Among its provisions was a new rate-making rule under which rates of a carrier were not, as a general practice, to be held to a particular level in order to protect the traffic of any other mode of transportation. The I. C. C., under certain conditions, was given power to make the final determination on discontinuance or change of operation of unprofitable passenger trains in both interstate and intrastate service, a function formerly exercised exclusively by state regulatory bodies. And provision was made for guaranteed loans to railroads in serious financial condition. The entire railroad industry was encouraged by this Act and also by the repeal, on August 1, 1958, of the federal tax of three percent on freight charges.

The ten percent tax originally designed to discourage passenger travel during World War II was finally repealed in November 1962. Unlike many eastern railroads, the Burlington passed along this saving to its patrons. Meanwhile, in April 1962, President Kennedy sent to Congress a message on transportation. The President urged that all forms of transportation be viewed as interlocking parts of the whole, that each segment be given equal opportunity to compete with other segments, and that transportation subsidies be reduced or abolished by establishing user charges so that true economic costs would be reflected in rates and fares assessed by all forms of transportation. As Murphy pointed out in the C. B. & Q. *Annual Report* for 1962: "If followed by appropriate legislation, this message could prove to be of historic significance from a railroad viewpoint . . . adoption of these sound principles could be a renaissance in the railroad industry."[7] President Johnson later echoed the views of his predecessor. But time alone could tell how effective these measures, both on the books and in prospect, would prove.

[7] CB&Q, AR 1962, p. 39.

· THE OUTLOOK ·

IN THE LIFE OF ANY GREAT RAILWAY SYSTEM, plans for the future are fully as important as current performance. On July 16, 1960, the C. B. & Q., the Great Northern, and the Northern Pacific made a joint public announcement that they would seek authority to consolidate into a new corporation, subsequently called the Great Northern Pacific & Burlington Lines, Inc., to operate the properties of the three constituent companies and also to operate, under lease, the Spokane, Portland and Seattle Railway. The C. & S. and the F. W. & D. would continue to operate their own properties, but as subsidiaries of the new parent corporation.

The stockholders of all three applicant companies overwhelmingly approved this merger project early in 1961, and hearings before an I. C. C. examiner began in the fall of that year. The proponent companies stressed the facts that consolidation would provide faster freight service, better car supply, wider routing with better transit and diversion privileges, and more capital for modernization and improvement. During the hearings that took place in 1961–62, countless views were heard throughout the western territory; briefs in the case were filed early in January 1963. No railroad company filed a brief in opposition, although both the Milwaukee and the North Western requested the I. C. C. to impose certain conditions if unification was approved. The Railway Labor Executives Association opposed the merger; the companies proposing it maintained that "the best prospect for stable employment lies in approval of the proposed merger."[8]

On August 24, 1964, I. C. C. Examiner Robert H. Murphy approved the plan, providing, however, for certain traffic and other benefits for the North Western and the Milwaukee, including access of the latter to Portland, Oregon. He estimated that savings resulting from the merger would amount to $39.9 million annually, and suggested that the I. C. C. retain jurisdiction in the case for five years after approval to permit applications from other smaller roads for inclusion.

Here matters stood when this book went to press. Whatever the outcome of this particular proposal, the Burlington, 115 years after its beginning as the humble Aurora Branch, was still very much in business, still ready to face whatever the future might bring.

[8] CB&Q, AR 1961, p. 27.

Around the Circle,
Chapter Bibliographical Notes,
Selected Bibliography,
and Index

Around the Circle

So MANY GOOD PEOPLE have lent their hands, heads, or hearts—often all three—to help me put this book together over the last fifteen years that it is literally impossible to list them all. Some I have named specifically here; to them and to all the others who did me a good turn, my most hearty thanks.

As implied in the Foreword, this book owes its existence to Ralph Budd. Had it not been for his unfailing confidence, to say nothing of his active assistance in countless ways, I might easily have become discouraged and given up what, at times, seemed an impossible task. And if my wife and family had not been willing, over and over again, to let "the book" take priority in our everyday life, I could never have finished it. To these, above all, my humble and everlasting gratitude.

Special thanks for unique contributions are due the late Mrs. Edward Cunningham of Boston, who, in 1943, gave me the extraordinarily rich collection of her father's (C. E. Perkins) papers described in the Bibliography; until her death in 1961 she maintained her lively interest in this undertaking. Donald L. McMurry, as indicated in the Prologue to the Epilogue, did a herculean job in assembling the data from the *Annual Reports* for the original Epilogue; on earlier occasions, he ferreted out information on Perkins in general and the strike of 1888 in particular, while he was writing his classic monograph on that subject, extended my finding list of Burlington materials, assembled the preliminary long-draft Bibliography, read critically virtually all the manuscript, and gave me mature advice at every stage of the proceedings. Mrs. William F. Reece (Ardis Miller) of Watervliet, Michigan, after reading the early chapters of the long draft, helped me gain new insights into the relative roles of the early promoters. William Catton, then a graduate student at Northwestern and now of Middlebury, Vermont, and Mrs. Geoffrey Parsons (Elsbeth Bedell) and Miss Carmen Wessner, then of Manchester, Vermont, worked successively in making an indispensable finding list of my voluminous Burlington notes and memoranda. Miss Wessner also drew scores of basic charts and graphs. Herbert Werner, one-time student at Northwestern, supported by a grant from the Newberry Library, prepared a calendar of the Perkins Letterpress books which has proven an indispensable key to those treasures. Alan P. McGowan, a graduate student at the University of Western Ontario, helped tremendously in distilling the long draft for what appear here as chapters 15 through 29. Most recently Donald C. Bogle, a graduate student at the University of Western Ontario, has struggled manfully with the back-breaking job of compiling the Index and of helping me run down elusive details required for the final revision of the text, footnotes, Chapter Bibliographical Notes, and Bibliography; in these chores I have had most timely assistance from my wife and from Miss Anne Askew of London. Without the stout aid of all these good people, it would have taken far longer to complete this book.

The list of scholars and experts who have given me specific and substantial help is a long one: my long-time colleague at Northwestern, Howard F. Bennett, made available his special study of the Hannibal and St. Joseph, and read my pages concerning it; the Misses Beulah and Helen Budd of Claremont, California, and Robert R. Budd of Austin, Texas, contributed information about Ralph Budd; Thomas and Rosamond Cochran of Radnor, Pennsylvania, supplied important leads and made penetrating comments on the entire pre-1900 period; Frank E. Day, one-time colleague at Northwestern, let me read his study of Burlington townsites; Gerald Eggert of College Park, Maryland, lent me his excellent thesis on Richard Olney; Wallace Ferguson of London, Ontario, offered helpful ideas about handling the Chapter Bibliographical Notes and Bibliography; Charles E. Fisher of Waban, Massachusetts, gave me specialized information about Burlington motive power; Charles N. Glaab of Kansas City, Missouri, lent me access to the studies he and R. Richard Wohl compiled concerning Kansas City; Julius Grodinsky, while working on his *Iowa Pool* and *Jay Gould*, sent me countless copies and excerpts of source material relevant to my work, and read parts of the long draft; Robert S. Henry of Alexandria, Virginia, shared with me his vast knowledge about railways in wartime and read parts of the long draft; Ralph and Muriel

Hidy of Belmont, Massachusetts, read various chapters critically, especially those dealing with inter-railway relations and finance; Philip Holden of New York lent me important papers concerning his father, Hale Holden; C. Clyde Jones of Manhattan, Kansas, passed along many a clue concerning the company's agricultural development work; William Miller of Redding, Connecticut, appraised shrewdly a chapter on Iowa and Nebraska; Irene D. Neu of Bloomington, Indiana, sent me dozens of pertinent excerpts from the Corning Papers; John T. O'Neil of Evanston, Illinois, gave me the benefit of his special knowledge of the Burlington's refinancing of 1944–45 and checked my version of it; Bessie L. Pierce, of Chicago, let me use her vast collection of statistics on the growth of Chicago.

In addition, the following have supplied helpful bits and pieces of elusive information: Robert Athearn of Boulder, Colorado; Lucius Beebe of Virginia City, Nevada; Robert V. Bruce of Reading, Massachusetts; David T. Gilchrist of Washington, D. C.; David A. Hill of Chicago; Charles J. Kennedy of Lincoln, Nebraska; Thomas LeDuc of Oberlin, Ohio; Richard Lowitt of New London, Connecticut; William J. Petersen of Iowa City, Iowa; Harry L. Pierce of Syracuse, New York; M. C. Poor of Denver, Colorado; Leonard F. Ralston of Cortland, New York; George Van Santvoord of Bennington, Vermont; and D. W. Yungmeyer of Chicago.

Many of my graduate students who, over the years, have worked on Burlington or Perkins records have ferreted out details that either have found their way into this book or have sharpened my understanding of particular events: Donald C. Bogle, Robert J. Clark, David P. Gagan, Douglas A. Lawr, Donald MacKay, Alan P. McGowan, and James G. Snell of the University of Western Ontario; Frank E. Ashton, Alvin F. Jankowski, Richard Jenkins, C. Clyde Jones, Edgar E. Swanson, Eric Waugh, and Sherman Warso of Northwestern University; and Kenneth Wood of Burr and Burton Seminary. I am also indebted to T. M. Davis of the University of Nebraska, Gerald G. Eggert of the University of Michigan, John H. Hobart of Yale, A. Grant Holt of Amherst, and John E. Pixton, Jr., of the University of Chicago for letting me refer to their theses prepared at the institutions named. The subjects of these various contributions are listed under the names of the authors in the Bibliography.

In a more general way, the following people have made various thought-provoking suggestions as to balance, approach, and emphasis: Alfred D. Chandler, Jr. of Baltimore; Arthur H. Cole of Cambridge, Massachusetts; Frank P. Donovan of Minneapolis; Joe B. Frantz of Austin, Texas; Paul W. Gates of Ithaca, New York; Carter Goodrich of New York City; Codman Hislop of Dorset, Vermont; Leland Jenks of Wellesley Hills, Massachusetts; Arthur M. Johnson of Cambridge, Massachusetts; Donald L. Kemmerer of Champaign, Illinois; Edward C. Kirkland of Thetford Center, Vermont; Alfred Lief of New York City; Frederick Merk of Belmont, Massachusetts; David P. Morgan of Milwaukee; Fritz Redlich of Cambridge, Massachusetts; John F. Stover of West Lafayette, Indiana; George Rogers Taylor of Amherst, Massachusetts; and Harold F. Williamson of Evanston, Illinois.

My debt to the entire Burlington family is a great one; certainly this book could never have been carried through without their help. President Harry C. Murphy, like his predecessor Ralph Budd, assured me of his lively interest and confidence throughout. For acting, successively, as liaison men in respect to matters large and small, I owe sincere thanks to Richard T. Cubbage, Julius J. Alms, and most recently to Wilbur K. Bush, who helped so much in the final critical stages. For routing and handling, expeditiously and in high good humor, particular business with the President's office, I shall always be most grateful to John W. Cooper and B. A. Henry.

Over the years—and sometimes on very short notice—many present or one-time members of the Burlington family have supplied essential pieces of information: Mrs. Edith Alden, J. J. Alms, R. Wright Armstrong, Donald Ashton, Carl Bick, James F. Blair, Ralph Budd, William Burke, W. K. Bush, H. C. Clark, J. W. Cooper, Albert Cotsworth, Jr., R. T. Cubbage, Frank T. Darrow, Dale Ellis, S. L. Fee, Karl W. Fischer, H. L. Ford, Mrs. Irene Gross, H. H. Hasselbacher, B. A. Henry, Robert L. Hoyt, Russell B. James, H. W. Johnson, Dr. R. B. Kepner, Carl Krohl, Val Kuska, John Lamson, Walter McFarland, Arthur D. McLane, Miss Velma McPeek, Harry T. Mann, Henry Meinhardt, A. W. Newton, E. L. Potarf, John L. Rice, A. M. Rung, Andrew C. Scott, C. A. Smith, R. C. Smith, P. L. Smithburg, John Trent, Bert Vickery, O. O. Waggener, Robert D. Walker, O. E. Ward, and J. T. Williamson.

For drawing the charts and preparing rough drafts of the maps my thanks go to Edward Hain; and to George Burkhardt and E. A. Graham, for the difficult task of helping to re-check each map. A. M. Rung assembled for me scores of appropriate photographs from which the final selections could be made; he also went to great pains to produce the jacket illustration. Warmest thanks! For reading parts or all of the manuscript critically, I am indebted to Julius Alms, Ralph Budd, Wilbur K. Bush, Richard T. Cubbage, W. N. Ernzen, Guy R. Glover, J. C. James, F. L. Kartheiser, Eldon Martin, H. C. Murphy, E. L. Potarf (whose amazingly sharp eyes deserve special mention), A. M. Rung, and John T. Williamson. Nor can I forget those Burlington people who, from one end of the country to the other, have smoothed my path—and given me encouragement— in all sorts of ways: persons such as Joseph Brennan, W. L. Copenhaver, Floyd Crabbe, Miss Avis Cramer, W. L. Durway, Arthur Fortier, Fred Johnson, Miss Beatrice McDonald, Miss Elsie Miller, Harold Mortvedt, Miss Helen O'Connor, Nile Ogden, Carl Plagemann, Miss Antoinette

Slocik, N. Stockhammer, H. H. Urbach, Walter Wennman, and E. G. Wesson. Fully mindful of the frailty of human memory, I want to thank all those others who so willingly lent a hand here and there but whose names escape me at the moment.

Many others in the field of railroading have supplied both information and advice. At the Association of American Railroads in Washington, I often called upon Carlton J. Corliss, Robert S. Henry, Herbert McLaury, J. Elmer Monroe, Julius Parmelee, and Thomas Sinclair. David I. Mackie of the Eastern Railroads Presidents Conference in Jersey City forwarded timely information, as did James G. Lyne and Joe W. Kizzia of *Railway Age*. At the Denver and Rio Grande Western Railroad, G. A. Aydelott, John Evans, Wilson McCarthy, and Jackson Thode were uniformly helpful. C. W. Moore of the Great Northern and W. R. Moore of the Union Pacific helped me track down elusive details, while at the Western Pacific Warren Brown, Gilbert Kneiss, and Fred Whitman answered promptly my various inquiries, as did Nelson Trottman of the Chicago and North Western.

Any author is inevitably dependent upon the cooperation of librarians and their staffs. The principal libraries consulted are listed in the Bibliography, and at all of them I received cordial assistance. I owe special thanks, however, to Stanley Pargellis, long-time head of the Newberry Library and hence custodian of the Burlington archives deposited there, and to his successor, Lawrence Towner. At the Baker Library Arthur H. Cole, Donald T. Clark, and Laurence Kipp in turn placed every conceivable facility at my disposal. At the Bureau of Railway Economics Library in Washington, Elizabeth Cullen and, more recently, H. L. Eddy, answered fully and quickly my many requests. At the State Museum Library in Denver, Mrs. Dolores Renze has given me great help over the years, as has William Petersen from his post at Iowa City. Closer to my two homes, Willis Wright and Don Cary have helped me verify data at the Williams College Library, while in London, Ontario, James J. Talman, librarian of the Lawson Memorial Library, his assistant John McLaughlin, and Miss Anne Sexton have provided special care for the Burlington notes and the Cunningham–Overton records now on deposit there.

Specific thanks go to the Harvard University Press for permission to reprint, from John T. O'Neil's *Policy Formation in Railroad Finance: Refinancing the Burlington, 1936–1945* (Cambridge, 1956), the table that appears on page 508.

It is difficult to express adequately how much I appreciate the long and hard work put in by the imposing group of conscientious young people who have typed the manuscript in its many stages. Their cheerfulness as well as their competence added a bright touch to the whole undertaking. My lasting thanks to Miss Sally Ambrose, Mrs. Frank Bryan, Mrs. Russell Grimes, Mrs. Mary Hoffman, Mrs. Milton King, Mrs. Bruce

McLeod, Mrs. Geoffrey Parsons, Mrs. Lois Richardson, Mrs. Sidney Roberts, Miss Sheila Stacy, Mrs. Christine Waller, Mrs. Cecil Weston, Mrs. Perry Zavitz, and, for last-minute help, to Miss Diane Dawson, Miss Sue Morton, and Wayne Snyder.

While this book was being written, I have been teaching at various institutions, except during 1959–61. Accordingly, I am indebted to those in charge for so arranging my schedules that I could keep this project moving: at Northwestern, Deans Homer B. Vanderblue, Ernest Davies, and Richard Donham; at Burr and Burton Seminary, Headmaster E. H. Henry; at Williams College, Summer Institute, President J. P. Baxter III; and at the University of Western Ontario, Dr. Donald G. G. Kerr, head of the History Department at Middlesex College, and Dr. G. Alan Wilson, Director of Graduate Studies.

I must add a word about the skilled men and women at Knopf's. Over a span of more than a dozen years, Herbert Weinstock has given me the benefit of his superb editorial advice and the support of his unfailing enthusiasm. Sidney R. Jacobs and his assistant Bruce Fitzgerald have adeptly handled production matters and arranged for Mrs. Anita Karl to draw the maps. William A. Koshland made it a pleasure to conduct business with the firm. And from beginning to end Alfred A. Knopf has assured me of his lively interest in this book. No author could ask for more.

Finally, my wife and Mrs. Perry Zavitz have helped me immeasurably over the last high hurdle of proofreading; they were ably assisted by Glenn Cooper, A. M. J. Hyatt, Hugh Johnston, and Mrs. Peter Lawson. And perhaps I should repeat, once again, and on behalf of these good people, that responsibility for whatever shortcomings this text may have rests solely with me.

R. C. O.

Chapter Bibliographical Notes

THESE NOTES INDICATE, in brief form, the major sources, both primary and secondary, that were most frequently consulted in the preparation of each chapter. Under *Primary*, railway company records are listed first in alphabetical order; government sources, correspondence and interviews, and periodicals, follow in that sequence. *Secondary* sources are arranged alphabetically according to author or (if no author is given) work. Names of authors of books stand alone; authors of articles are followed by (A), of pamphlets by (P), of releases by (R), of speeches by (S), and of unpublished manuscripts by (UM). If an author has written more than one work, a shortened title of the item referred to has been added unless the reference is to all his works. Complete titles of all works cited will be found in the Bibliography, on pages 601–623. A key to the abbreviations used below appears at the end of the Note on Documentation, on pages xxi–xxiii.

• CHAPTER 1 •

Primary: AR (C&NW, 1865; G&CU, 1850; MC, 1851, 1854; MSo, 1850);
Harvard College Library, "Colton Manuscript"; ORB (AB, NC);
Aurora Beacon (1850); *Chicago Daily Democrat* (1850); *Chicago
Daily Journal* (1850).
Secondary: Burgess, G. H., and Kennedy, M. C.; BW; Carlson, C. F.; Carter,
C. F.; Casey, R. J., and Douglas, W. A. S.; CH; Clark, D. E.; Corliss,
C.; Daniels, W.; DH; Gates, P. W.; Haney, L. H.; Hargrave, F. J.;
Harlow, A. F.; MacGill, C.; Merk, F.; Million, J. W.; Nevins, F. J. (P);
Newton, A. W. (A): "Early History. . . C. B. & Q." (and UM); Pear-
son, H. G.; Riegel, R. E.; Robbins, R. M.; Sanborn, J. B.; Smalley,
E. V.; Stevens, F. W.; Stevens, W. E.; Thompson, S.; Towner, A.;
Warner, P. T.

• CHAPTER 2 •

Primary: Harvard College Library, "Colton Manuscript"; ORB (BMI,
CMT, NC); United States: *Congressional Globe* (1851–2); Federal
Coordinator of Transportation; Burlington *Daily Telegraph* (1851–2);
Macon Weekly Argus (1868).
Secondary: Antrobus, A. M.; Bennett, H. F. (UM); Calkins, E. E. (A);
CH; Chapman, C. & Co.; Cole, C.; Corliss, C.; Daniels, W.; Donald-
son, T.; Gates, P. W.; Haney, L. H.; Hungerford, E.: *B and O*;
Salter, W.; Sanborn, J. B.; Stratton, H. J. (A); Thompson, S.; Wilson,
B. H. (A).

• CHAPTER 3 •

Primary: AR (MC, 1854); CB&Q/Sec; EC; GM; ORB (AB, BMI, CMT,
C&A, CB&Q, HSJ, NC); Burlington *Daily Telegraph* (1852); Burling-
ton *Weekly Telegraph* (1852).
Secondary: Albion, R. G. (A); Baldwin, W. W. (P): "Making of the
Burlington"; Bennett, H. F. (UM); Bogart, E. L. (A); BW; Casey,
R. J., and Douglas, W. A. S.; CH; Dixon, F. H. (A); DH; Hargrave,
F. F.; Harlow, A. F.; Hughes, S. F., ed.; Kirkland, E. C.: *Men, Cities,
and Transportation*; MacGill, C.; Nevins, F. J. (P); Pearson, H. G.
(also A); Peterson, W. J. (A); Salter, W.

• CHAPTER 4 •

Primary: AR (BMI, 1858–61; C&A, 1854; CB&Q, 1855–65; CMT, 1855,
G&CU, 1855–6; HSJ, 1855–9; MC, 1862); CB&Q/N; CB&Q/Sec;
CNB, EC; ORB (BMI; C&A; CB&Q; CMT; HSJ); United States:

Congressional Globe (1855–6); Burlington *Daily Telegraph* (1852); Burlington *Weekly Hawk-Eye and Telegraph* (1856, 1858–9); *Monmouth Atlas* (1855); *Quincy Daily Whig and Republican* (1861).

Secondary: Antrobus, A.; *BW*; Casey, R. J., and Douglas, W. A. S.; *CH*; Cunningham, E. P.: *Owl's Nest*; *DH*; Donaldson, T.; Emerson, E. W.; Gates, P. W.; Goodwin, C. (A); Hebard, A. (A); Hedge, T.; Henry, R. S.; Holbrook, S.; Hughes, S. F., ed.; Marshall, J.; Mott, F. L. (A); Nevins, F. J. (P); Newton, A. W. (A): "Chicago and Aurora Railroad"; Pearson, H. G.; Peterson, W. J. (A); Starr, J. W.; Thompson, S.; Wilson, B. H. (A).

• CHAPTER 5 •

Primary: AR (BMI, 1861–5; C&A, 1854–6; CMT, 1855; CB&Q, 1858–65); CB&Q/N; CB&Q/Sec esp. H. W. Johnson to E. C. Wright, Oct. 28, 1946; *CH*; *DH*; EC; ORB (BMI, CB&Q); United States: Commissioner of General Land Office, AR, 1864; Department of Commerce: *Historical Statistics*; Federal Coordinator of Transportation; 48th Congress, Second Session, Senate Executive Document #40 (1885); *Chicago Daily Drovers Journal* (1940); *Quincy Daily Whig and Republican* (1861–2).

Secondary: Agnew, R. J. (UM); Anderson, W. H.; Bennett, H. F. (UM); Billington, R. A.; Black, R. C.; Bogle, D. C. (UM); Buck, P.; *BW*; Casey, R. J., and Douglas, W. A. S.; Cole, A. C.; Corliss, C.; Derleth, A.; Gates, P. W. (A); Grant, U. S.; Haskell, H. C., and Fowler, R. B.; Henry, R. S.; Hidy, M. (A); Holbrook, S.; Hughes, S. F., ed.; Hungerford, E.: *B and O*; Josephson, M.; Merk, F.; Myers, M. (A); Nevins, A.; Nevins, F. J. (P); Overton, R. C. (A): "Westward Movement"; Parmelee, J. H. (A); Paullin, C. O.; Perkins, J. R.; *Poor's Manual*, 1888; Quiett, G. C.; Robbins, R. M.; Taylor, G. R.; Trottman, N.; Weber, T.

• CHAPTER 6 •

Primary: AR (BMI, 1864–8; CB&Q, 1865–9; HSJ, 1870); CB&Q/N; CB&Q/Sec; *CH*; *DH*; DRB (BMN); EC; GM; ORB (BMI, CB&Q); PLB; Burlington *Daily Hawk-Eye* (1869); *Nebraska Herald* (1869); *North Missouri Courier* (1867).

Secondary: Baldwin, W. W. (P): "Making of the Burlington," "Some Features"; Bennett, H. F. (UM); *Biographical Directory of Railway Officials*, 1887; Bogart, E. L. (A); *BW*; Casey, R. J., and Douglas, W. A. S.; Chanute, O., and Morison, G.; Clarke, T. C.; Corliss, C.; Cunningham, E. P.: *CEP and EFP*; Davis, E. O.; Davis, T. W. (A): "Lines West"; Dixon, F. H. (A); Flint, H. M.; Grodinsky, J.: *Iowa*

Pool; Haskell, H. C., and Fowler, R. B.; Marshall, J.; Masterson, V. V.; McConkey, M. C. (UM); Merritt, W. W.; Neu, I. (A); Nevins, F. J. (P); Olson, J. C.: *Morton*; Pearson, H. G. (A); *Poor's Manual*, 1870–1, 1882, 1885; Reichman, A. (A); Stennett, W. H.; Trottman, N.; Waters, L. L.; White, H. K.

• CHAPTER 7 •

Primary: AR (BMN, MSo, 1876; CB&Q, 1865–75, 1879; HSJ, 1870–1); CB&Q/N; CB&Q/Sec esp. H. W. Johnson to E. C. Wright, Oct. 28, 1946; *CH*; EC; *GM*; ORB (CB&Q, HSJ); PLB.
Secondary: Beard, E. S. (A); *BW*; Cochran, T. C.; Cunningham, E. P.: *CEP and EFP*; Grodinsky, J.: *Iowa Pool*; Olson, J. C.: *Morton*; *Poor's Manual*, 1881, 1888; Stover, J. F.; Swanson, E. E. (UM); Thompson, S.; Throne, M. (A): "Grange in Iowa."

• CHAPTER 8 •

Primary: AR (CB&Q, 1868–75); CB&Q/N; CB&Q/Sec esp. H. W. Johnson to E. C. Wright, Oct. 28, 1946; *CH*; *DH*; *GM*; IC/N; JFJ; ORB (CB&Q); PLB; *Boston Daily Advertiser* (1875); *Boston Evening Transcript* (1875); Chicago *Inter-Ocean* (1875); *Chicago Tribune* (1875).
Secondary: Cochran, T. C.; Derleth, A.; Grodinsky, J.: *Iowa Pool*; Harlow, A. F.: *Road of the Century*; Harrington, G. B. (P); Pearson, H. G.; Stockder, A. H. (UM).

• CHAPTER 9 •

Primary: AR (CB&Q, 1875–80); CB&Q/N; CB&Q/Sec; *CH*; *GM*; ORB (CB&Q); United States: ICC Valuation Docket #44 (19   ); 94 US 113 (1877); 94 US 161 (1877); *Boston Daily Advertiser* (1875); Chicago *Inter-Ocean* (1875); *Chicago Tribune* (1875).
Secondary: Bruce, R. B.; *BW*; Cochran, T. C.; Davis, T. M. (UM); Derleth, A.; Grodinsky, J.; Harlow, A. F.: *Road of the Century*; Hughes, S. F., ed.; McMurry, D. L. (UM); Morgan, D. P. (P); Overton, R. C. (A): "Charles E. Perkins"; Pearson, H. G.; *Poor's Manual*, 1888; Swisher, C. B.

• CHAPTER 10 •

Primary: AR (CB&Q, 1877–81, 1896); C&S/Sec; CB&Q/Sec esp. H. W. Johnson to E. C. Wright, Oct. 28, 1946; *CH*; *DH*; ORB (CB&Q).
Secondary: *Biographical Directory of American Railway Officials*, 1887;

Brayer, H. O. (A); *BW*; Davis, T. M. (A): "Building the Burlington"; Grodinsky, J.; *GTR*; Overton, R. C. (UM); Poor, M. C.; *Poor's Manual*, 1888; Trottman, N.

• CHAPTER 11 •

Primary: AR (CB&Q, 1881–8; CM&StP, 1887; HSJ, 1881–2); CB&Q/N; CB&Q/Sec; *CH*; *DH*; *GM*; ORB (CB&N, CB&Q, HSJ); PLB; RCO; Sets B, C, M, Y; Chicago *Inter-Ocean* (1886); *Chicago Times* (1886); *Dubuque Daily Times* (1886); *St. Paul Pioneer Press* (1886).
Secondary: *Biographical Directory of Railway Officials*, 1887; Bogle, D. C. (UM); Cochran, T. C.; Davis, T. M. (UM); Grodinsky, J.; *GTR*; Hayes, W. E. (A); Hobart, J. H. (UM); Marshall, J.; McMurry, D. L.; *Poor's Manual*, 1888; Pyle, J. G.; Sharfman, I. L., *ICC*; Waters, L. L.

• CHAPTER 12 •

Primary: AR (CB&Q, 1876–88; Chicago Board of Trade, 1883); CB&Q/N; CB&Q/Sec esp. H. W. Johnson to E. C. Wright, Oct. 28, 1946; *GM*; ORB (CB&Q); PLB; PVB; RCO; Set M; *Chicago Times* (1888); Interviews with J. C. James (1939–45).
Secondary: Baldwin, W. W. (P): "Some Features"; *Biographical Directory of Railway Officials*, 1887; *BW*; Corbin, B. G., and Kerka, W.; Corliss, C. J. (P); Eggert, G. G. (UM); Hayes, W. E. (A); Henry, R. S.; McMurry, D. L.; Morgan, D. P. (P); Overton, R. C. (P): *Milepost 100*; Railway and Locomotive Historical Society (P); Scudder, M. L. (UM); Sharfman, I. L.: *ICC*; Swanson, E. E. (UM); Waters, L. L.; Westmeyer, R. E.

• CHAPTER 13 •

Primary. AR (CB&Q, 1888–1901); Car 200 Log Books, C–O; CB&Q/N; CB&Q/Sec; *CH*; *GM*; ORB (CB&Q); PLB; PVB; RCO; Set M; United States: ICC Finance Docket #12964 (1922); *Boston Daily Advertiser* (1889); *Daily Hawk-Eye* (1891); *St. Louis Globe–Democrat* (1894).
Secondary: Corbin, B. G., and Kerka, W.; Dawes, C. G. (A); Eggert, G. G. (UM); Gillette, E.; *GTR*; Holmes, G. W. (P); Pixton, J. E. (UM); Railway and Locomotive Historical Society (P); Stockder, A. H. (UM); Swisher, C. B.; Trottman, N.; Wallace, J. F. (S); Wood, K. (UM).

• CHAPTER 14 •

Primary: AR (CB&Q, 1900–07); CB&Q/Sec esp. H. W. Johnson to E. C. Wright, Oct. 28, 1946; GM; ORB (CB&Q); PLB; RCO; Set X; United States: ICC Valuation Docket #134 (1927); *Boston Herald* (1901); Burlington *Gazette* (1901); *Daily Hawk-Eye* (1901); *Chicago Chronicle* (1901); *Chicago Times Herald* (1901); *Chicago Tribune* (1901).

Secondary: Kennan, G.; *Poor's Manual*, 1914; Pyle, J. G.; Stockder, A. H. (UM); Swanson, E. E. (UM).

• CHAPTER 15 •

Primary: AR (C&S, 1900–15; CB&Q, 1901–16; GN, 1906–09); CB&Q/N; CB&Q/Pres esp. File #1065; CB&Q/Sec; CH; C–O; GM; ORB (C&S); RCO; Correspondence from R. Budd (1961), K. F. Burgess (1955), V. Kuska (1948), W. J. Lahr (1955) to R. C. Overton; Interview with H. J. Hasselbacher (1948); United States, Department of Commerce: *Historical Statistics;* ICC Finance Dockets #12964 (1922), #16456 (1949); *Daily Hawk-Eye* (1908, 1909, 1910); *Colorado Springs Evening and Sunday Telegraph* (1909); *Denver Post* (1908); *Monmouth Atlas* (1855); *Natrona County Tribune* (1913); *Railway Age* (1914, 1930); *Traveller's Railway Guide* (1903).

Secondary: *Biographical Directory of Railway Officials*, 1906, 1922; BW; Delano, F. A. (A); Derleth, A.; Hungerford, E.: *Daniel Willard;* Jones, C. C. (UM); Kuska, V. (R): "Big Horn," "Shoshone"; Mc-Murray, T. S. (UM); *Moody's*, 1912; Olson, J. C.: *Nebraska;* Overton, R. C. (A): "Ralph Budd"; *Poor's Manual*, 1900, 1914, 1919; Pyle, J. G.; Railway and Locomotive Historical Society (P); Reed, S. G.; Sharfman, I. L.: *ICC;* Snyder, C.; Swanson, E. E. (UM); Wattles, G. W.; Westmeyer, R. E. (UM); Williamson, J. T., and Annable, L. F. (UM).

• CHAPTER 16 •

Primary: AR (C&S, 1916–19; CB&Q, 1912–20; ICC, 1916–18); CB&Q/Emp; CB&Q/Pres esp. File #1045; ORB (CB&Q); Interview with Velma McPeek (1949); United States: *Congressional Record* (1917); Department of Commerce: *Historical Statistics;* Railroad Administration, Bulletin #4 (1918); 243 US 332 (1917).

Secondary: AAR (R): "Railroads in This Century," "Lest We Forget"; *Biographical Directory of Railway Officials*, 1922; Derleth, A.; Elliott, H.; Hines, W. D.; Jones, H. E.; Miller, S.; *Moody's*, 1938; Morison, S. E., and Commager, H. S.; Sharfman, I. L.: *American Railroad Problems;* Staples, H. L., and Mason, A. T.

• CHAPTER 17 •

Primary: AR (CB&Q, 1922–30); CB&Q/Pres esp. Files #1027, #1065; CB&Q/Sec; *DH*; Hale Holden Papers; Correspondence from R. Budd to Overton (1952, 1955, 1957); United States: ICC Finance Docket #12964 (1922); 61 ICC 455 (1921); 76 ICC 508 (1923); 159 ICC 524 (1929); 162 ICC 37 (1930); 259 US 214 (1922); *Chicago Tribune* (1928); *Kansas City Times* (1928); *New York Herald-Tribune* (1929); *Railway Age* (1931); *St. Louis Globe–Democrat* (1928); *Traffic World* (1928).

Secondary: AAR (P): "Transportation in America"; Daggett, S. (A); Dearing, C. L., and Owen, W.; Derleth, A.; Hines, W. D. (A); Leonard, W. N. (also A); Lodge, H. C.; Meyer, B. H.; *Moody's*, 1921; Parmelee, J. H.; *Poor's Manual*, 1919, 1935; Sharfman, I. L.; Stringer, H. E. (P).

• CHAPTER 18 •

Primary: AR (C&S, 1922–32; CB&Q, 1920–30, 1956); CB&Q/Sec; CB&Q/Traffic; FW&DC/Sec esp. Files #1494, #1835; Hale Holden Papers; PLD (1924–30); United States: 59 ICC 391 (1920); 134 ICC 52 (1927); 257 US 585 (1922); Correspondence from R. Budd (1955), J. W. Cooper (1955), C. J. Huhn (1955), J. T. Williamson (1947) to Overton; *Chicago Tribune* (1924); *Dallas Morning News* (1926); *The New York Times* (1957).

Secondary: AAR (P): "Statistical Record, 1921–53"; Bader, R. E. (A); *Biographical Directory of Railway Officials*, 1922; Elliott, H. (S); Henry, R. S.; Holden, H. (S): "Burlington in Nebraska"; Jones, C. C. (A): "Agricultural Policy"; Jones, H. E.; Metzman, G. (P); *Moody's*, 1929; Morison, S. E., and Commager, H. S.; Overton, R. C. (P): *Milepost 100*; *Poor's Manual*, 1924; Sharfman, I. L.: *ICC*; Smidl, O. (S); Swanson, E. E. (UM); Waggener, O. O.

• CHAPTER 19 •

Primary: AR (C&S, 1930–2; CB&Q, 1888, 1929–33; ICC 1932); CB&Q/Sec esp. H. W. Johnson to E. C. Wright, Oct. 28, 1946; CB&Q/Pres; FW&DC/Sec; PLD (1929–33); United States: Federal Coordinator of Transportation *Reports* (1934–6); 178 ICC 539 (1931); 179 ICC 215 (1931); Correspondence from R. Budd (1958), J. W. Cooper (1955), V. Kuska (1948), J. B. Lamson (1957), B. R. Willhite (1949), J. T. Williamson (1948) to Overton; Interview with R. Budd (1954); *Collingwood Standard* (1932); *Pampa Advocate* (1932); *The New York Times* (1930); *Railway Age* (1957).

Secondary: AAR (R): "Deteriorating Railroad Situation"; Bollinger, E. T. (A); Brayer, H. O. (A): "Colorado Railroads"; Budd, R. (S) to Inland Daily Press Association (A): "Light-weight Diesel-Electric Trains"; CB&Q, Comptroller's Office (R); Hough, H. W. (A); Metzman, G. (P); Overton, R. C. (A): "Ralph Budd"; Poor, M. C.; *Poor's Manual*, 1930, 1935; Reck, F. M.; Reed, S. G.; Upshaw, H. C. (A).

• CHAPTER 20 •

Primary: AR (CB&Q, 1928, 1933–40, 1956); PLD (1933–42); United States, Department of Commerce: *Historical Statistics*; Correspondence from R. Budd (1959), P. W. Gates (1958), O. O. Waggener (1959) to Overton.

Secondary: Bining, A. C.; Healy, K. T.: *Economics of Transportation*; Henry, R. S.; Kirkland, E. C.: *History of American Economic Life*; *Moody's*, 1943; Morison, S. E., and Commager, H. S.; Olson, J. C.: *History of Nebraska*.

• CHAPTER 21 •

Primary: AR (CB&Q, 1934–41, 1956); CB&Q/Pres esp. File #1062; CB&Q/Traffic; FW&DC/Traffic; PLD (1933–40); Correspondence from J. J. Alms (1958–9), R. Budd (1952, 1958–9), A. C. Cotsworth (1952, 1958), B. A. Henry (1954), H. F. McLaury (1960), E. C. Shafer (1950) to Overton; Interviews with R. Budd (1954, 1958–9), V. McPeek (1952); *Traffic World* (1934).

Secondary: Budd, Ralph (S): "Diesel Locomotives at Work"; Curtice, H. H. (S); Henry, R. S.; Kettering, C. F. (A); Lemly, J. H.; *Moody's*, 1938; Overton, R. C. (A): "Ralph Budd"; Reck, F. M.; Sharfman, I. L.: *ICC*; Waters, L. L.

• CHAPTER 22 •

Primary: AR (CB&Q, 1933–41; ICC, 1933); *CH*; PLD (1935–41); United States, Board of Investigation and Research: "Public Aids to Domestic Transportation"; ICC: "Railroad Abandonments"; 228 ICC 277 (1938); Correspondence from J. W. Barriger (1959), R. Budd (1958), R. B. Kepner (1947) to Overton; Interviews with R. Budd (1954, 1958).

Secondary: AAR (P): "Highway Motor Transportation," "Railroad Transportation, A Statistical Record 1921–57"; Automobile Manufacturers Association (P); Cullen, E. O. (P); Daggett, S.; Dearing, C. L., and Owen, W.; Donovan, F. P.; Hale Charts; Healy, K. T. (also A); Lemly, J. H.; *Moody's*, 1936, 1938, 1943; *Poor's*, 1935; Sharfman, I. L.: *ICC*; Stauffer, F. B. (A); Westmeyer, R. E.; Williams, E. W.

Chapter Bibliographical Notes

• CHAPTER 23 •

Primary: AR (CB&Q, 1933–41); CB&Q/Sec; PLD (1933–41); United States: 73rd Congress, Second Session, and 74th Congress, First Session, Reports of Federal Coordinator (1934–6); 74th Congress, Second Session, and 75th Congress, First Session, Investigation of Executive Agencies (1936–7); Department of Commerce: *Historical Statistics*; 295 US 330 (1935); 300 US 515 (1937); Correspondence from R. Budd (1958) to Overton.

Secondary: AAR (P): "Transportation in America," "What Is Public Aid to Transportation?," "Railroad Transportation: A Statistical Record, 1921–53"; Dearing, C. L., and Owen, W.; Dewey, R. L. (A); Healy, K. T.; Jones, H. E.; Kaufman, J. J. (A): "Government Intervention"; Morison, S. E., and Commager, H. S.; National Mediation Board; Sharfman, I. L.: *ICC*; Swisher, C. B.; Westmeyer, R. E.; Wilson, G. L., ed.

• CHAPTER 24 •

Primary: AR (C&S, 1906, 1929–42, 1957); C&S; RCO Notebook on Debt Adjustment Plan of 1941; C&S/Sec; CB&Q/Law; FW&DC/Sec; United States: District Court for Colorado (1943); ICC Finance Docket #12460 (1939); 240 ICC 637 (1939); Correspondence from R. Budd (1951), R. T. Cubbage (1951, 1960) to Overton; Interviews with R. Budd (1951, 1959); *Fort Worth Star-Telegram* (1939–40); *Houston Chronicle* (1940); *Houston Press* (1940); *Rocky Mountain News* (1940); *Wall Street Journal* (1941).

Secondary: Committee . . . to Oppose Removal of the F. W. & D. C. Headquarters (P); *Moody's*, 1933, 1938, 1943; *Poor's*, 1909, 1914, 1935; Reed, S. G.

• CHAPTER 25 •

Primary: AR (CB&Q, 1931–41, 1957); CB&Q/Sec; GM; PLD (1933–42); United States, Department of Commerce: *Historical Statistics*; Correspondence from R. Budd (1957–9), R. T. Cubbage (1959) to Overton; Interview, R. Budd (1954).

Secondary: Cochran, T. C.; *Moody's*, 1938, 1943; O'Neil, J. T.; *Poor's*, 1900, 1935; Swanson, E. E. (UM).

• CHAPTER 26 •

Primary: CB&Q/Pres; PLD (1940–2); United States: Office of Defense Transportation; Correspondence from R. Budd (1959–60), C. G.

Dawes (1942), R. S. Henry (1959) to Overton; Correspondence between R. Budd and F. D. Roosevelt (1941).

Secondary: AAR (P): "Railroad Transportation, A Statistical Record, 1921–57," "Railroads of the United States in Two Wars," "Trends in Railroad Operations"; American Railway Car Institute (P); Ashton, F. E. (UM); Budd, R. (A): "Transportation on the Home Front" (also S), ten during 1940–42; Jones, H. E.; Kemmerer, D. L., and Jones, C. C.; Latham, E.; *Moody's*, 1946; Overton, R. C. (A): "Ralph Budd"; Roosevelt, E., ed.; Sherwood, R. L.; Wilson, G. L., ed.

• CHAPTER 27 •

Primary: AR (C&S, 1939–45, 1958; CB&Q, 1940–5); C&S/Sec; CB&Q/Law; CB&Q/Op; CB&Q/Pres; CB&Q, RCO Journal of Relief Department (1943–5); CB&Q/Traffic; ORB (CB&Q); PLD (1940–6); United States: Civil Aeronautics Board, Docket #922 (1946); Department of Commerce: *Historical Statistics*; ICC Finance Docket #14426 (1944); 257 ICC 129 (1943); Correspondence from R. Budd (1959) to Overton; Interviews with E. Alden (1953), R. Budd (1954), H. H. Hasselbacher (1948), V. McPeek (1953); Burlington *Zephyr* (1942–5); *Railway Age* (1943).

Secondary: AAR (P): "Trends in Railroad Operation"; Budd, R. (A): "93 Billion Ton Miles"; Daniel, H. (A); Gray, C. R.; Holt, A. G. (UM); Jankowski, A. F. (UM); Jenkins, R. (UM); Jones, H. E.; Latham, E.; Lewis, L. (A); Matthew, A. P. (A); *Moody's*, 1943, 1946; O'Neil, J. T.; Overton, R. C. (A): "Scholars Get Access," "The Lexington Group"; Parmelee, J. H. (S): "Transport Regulation"; Transportation Association of America (P): "Stop Unfair Taxation"; Warso, S. (UM); Wiprud, A.

• CHAPTER 28 •

Primary: AR (C&S, 1945–9; CB&Q, 1945–50; CB&Q/Op; CB&Q/Pres; ORB (CB&Q); PLD (1945–9); United States, Department of Commerce: *Historical Statistics* and Supplement; District Court for the Northern District of Illinois (1949); ICC *Ex Parte* #168 (1948); ICC Finance Dockets #15365 (1947), #16456 (1949); Nebraska Supreme Court (1940, 1950); Correspondence from R. Budd (1960), R. T. Cubbage (1959–60), G. R. Glover (1959), O. O. Waggener (1959) to Overton; Interviews with R. Budd (1954), H. H. Hasselbacher (1948), O. H. Schmidt (1959); Burlington *Zephyr* (1944–9); *New York Times* (1947); *Railway Age* (1948); *Railway Progress* (1948).

Secondary: AAR (P): "Trends in Railroad Operations," "Railroad Transportation, A Statistical Record, 1921–57"; Allen, F. L.; Beebe, L.; Brétey,

P. R. (A); Dulles, F. R.; Ford, N. (A); Henry, R. S.; Jones, C. C. (A): "Survey of Agricultural Development" (also UM); Kemmerer, D. L., and Jones, C. C.; Kuska, V. (S): "Railroads Are Interested," (P) "Railroads to the Rescue"; Lemly, J. H.; *Moody's*, 1939, 1950, 1953; Plowman, E. G. (S); Tigrett, I. B. (P).

• CHAPTER 29 •

Primary: AR (C&S, 1945–9; CB&Q, 1945–9, 1952, 1959); CB&Q/Law; CB&Q/Op; PLD (1945–9); United States: District Court for Colorado (1948–9); Correspondence from R. Budd (1949), R. T. Cubbage (1951) to Overton; Correspondence between R. Budd and F. B. Snyder (1949); Interview with R. Budd (1954); Burlington *Booster* (1949); Burlington *Zephyr* (1949); *Railway Age* (1960); *Time* (1949).
Secondary: AAR (P): "Transportation in America"; Alderman, S. S. (P); Budd, R. (S) before Chartered Accountants: "Financial Outlook," "Peacetime Trends"; Dearing, C. L., and Owen, W.; Dulles, F. R.; Fort, J. C. (P); GTR; Jones, H. E.; Lyne, J. G. (A); Mackie, D. I. (P); Overton, R. C. (P): *Milepost 100* (also A) "Ralph Budd"; Parmelee, J. H. (P): "Railroad Situation," "Rebuttal," "Review of Railway Operations"; Prince, G. S. (P); Truman, H. S.

• EPILOGUE •

Primary: AR (C&S, 1949–63; CB&Q, 1947–63); Burlington *Booster* (1960); Burlington *Bulletin and Safety News* (1963); Burlington *Zephyr* (1963); CB&Q, RCO Supplementary Notebooks for 1949–64; PLD (1950–64); Correspondence from R. T. Cubbage (1964), E. L. Potarf (1964), A. M. Rung (1964) to Overton; American Short Line Railroad Association: *Weekly Information Bulletin* (1949–64); *Ithaca Journal* (1962); *Minneapolis Tribune* (1963); *Modern Railroads* (1953); *The New York Times* (1962); *Quincy Herald–Whig* (1960); *Wall Street Journal* (1963).

Selected Bibliography

THE COMPLETE BIBLIOGRAPHY of the parent "long draft" from which this book is distilled contains a full description of every primary source consulted, and an extensive list of secondary works, including background material. To give all this information here would take an excessive amount of space and go far beyond the reasonable needs of all but specialists. Hence I have simply summarized the nature and location of key source materials, and in respect to both primary and secondary sources have included only those which (1) are "standard" in the sense that anyone wishing to investigate Burlington history should refer to them, and (2) were used specifically in this book.

PRIMARY SOURCES

· BURLINGTON LINES RECORDS ·

Company archives constitute by far the most important source of material for this history. The archives of the Chicago, Burlington & Quincy Railroad, its predecessors, and its constituent companies are located principally in Chicago. At the Burlington Lines headquarters, 547 West Jackson Boulevard,

Chicago, Illinois 60606, the Secretary's Office contains, for the period 1849 to date, the corporate minutes and associated documents of all companies that have been or are now part of the C. B. & Q. as well as contracts and special files concerning directors, officers, particular facilities, and special events. The Secretary's Office also has, of course, complete sets of *Annual Reports*, appointment circulars, and other printed documents of permanent consequence. When the C. B. & Q. Valuation Report (131 ICC 1) was being prepared, Vice-President W. W. Baldwin compiled a single-volume *Corporate History* (1921) listing corporate and construction details of every company that eventually became part of the C. B. & Q.; he also gathered all charters and pertinent legislation relating to these companies and published them, with introductory comments, in his three-volume *Documentary History* (1928–29). These books, listed under "Baldwin" below, are essential for unraveling and understanding Burlington history. The master copies in the Secretary's Office contain notations of errata and addenda. C. B. & Q. executive and departmental correspondence since 1901, together with supporting memoranda, briefs, reports, statistics, maps, charts, and illustrations, are in the various departmental offices in the same building: Employment, Executive, Law, Operating, and Traffic. Serious scholars who desire access to any of the records described above should apply to the Secretary of the C. B. & Q.; material of a public and current nature may be obtained from the Director of Public Relations.

Executive and departmental correspondence, together with supporting material, for the C. B. & Q., its predecessors and constituent companies, prior to 1901 was deposited by the company in 1943 in the Newberry Library, 60 West Walton Street, Chicago, Illinois 60610. This material is listed in the 374-page *Guide to Burlington Archives in the Newberry Library, 1851– 1901* (Chicago, 1949), compiled by Elizabeth Coleman Jackson and Carolyn Curtis. Access to the records listed should be sought from the librarian of the Newberry Library.

There are also important C. B. & Q. records, some dating from the earliest days of the company and its predecessors, in company offices at such major on-line points as Aurora, Galesburg, Burlington, Omaha, St. Joseph, Kansas City, Lincoln, Denver, and St. Paul. The Lines West and the Agricultural and Colonization Department records at Omaha, and the Aurora Laboratory records, for example, are of particular importance to historians. Applications for access should be addressed to the Secretary of the C. B. & Q.

Records of the Colorado and Southern Railway from 1899 to date are located principally either at that company's headquarters in the C. A. Johnson Building, 17th and Glenarm streets, Denver, Colorado 80202, or in the Union Station, Denver. Included are the Receiver's records of the Union Pacific, Denver and Gulf Railway and of the Denver, Leadville and Gunnison Railway (both immediate predecessors of the C. & S.) for the period 1893–98, as well as a manuscript copy of T. S. McMurray's undated history of the C. & S. prepared when the company's Valuation Report (134 ICC 581) was being compiled.

Application for access should be made to the Secretary of the C. & S. Records of C. & S. predecessor companies for the period 1861–93 are located in the general headquarters of the Union Pacific Railroad, 1416 Dodge Street, Omaha, Nebraska 68102. Application for access should be routed through the Secretary of the C. & S.

Records of the Fort Worth and Denver Railway (prior to 1952 the Fort Worth and Denver City Railway) from 1898, when almost all earlier records were destroyed in the general office fire, to date, as well as the records of the Wichita Valley Railway and other Texas subsidiaries, are located principally in the F. W. & D. headquarters in the Fort Worth Club Building, Fort Worth, Texas 76102. For access, apply to the Secretary of the F. W. & D. Records of the Burlington–Rock Island Railroad (owned jointly by the C. & S. and the C. R. I. & P.) were originally in Houston; for present whereabouts and accessibility, apply through the Secretary of the F. W. & D.

· SOURCES IN POSSESSION OF THE WRITER ·

These materials fall into three general categories:

(1) Notes, documents, subject memoranda, interviews, unpublished manuscripts, statistics, photographs, maps, and approximately 800 letters pertaining to Burlington history collected during 1934–64. All items except transcribed source notes for 1849–79 are catalogued.

(2) The Cunningham–Overton collection of Charles E. Perkins material, given to the writer in 1943 by Mrs. Edward Cunningham, daughter of C. E. Perkins. This collection is described in *The Guide to the Burlington Archives in the Newberry Library, 1851–1901,* on pages 331–4.

(3) Approximately 2,000 items of background material collected during 1934–64. All items are catalogued by subject and author.

Categories (1) and (2) are currently housed in the Lawson Memorial Library, University of Western Ontario, London, Canada; (3) is at Manchester Depot, Vermont.

· MANUSCRIPTS AND PAPERS ·

Ralph Budd Papers, in possession of the family. Correspondence, reports, memoranda covering the period 1899–1962.

"Colton Manuscript," a memorandum from Chauncey S. Colton to C. E. Perkins, sometime between 1877 and 1881. In Western Historical Collection, Harvard College Library. Reprinted in BW, pp. 506–15.

Erastus Corning Papers, in Albany Institute of Art and History. Includes letters pertinent to the Forbes Group 1846–72.

"Cunningham Notebooks," in possession of the Cunningham family. Looseleaf notebooks of letters and memoranda by and about C. E. Perkins, mostly copies or excerpts from C–O, q.v.

Grenville M. Dodge Papers, State Historical Building, Des Moines, Iowa.
Voluminous indexed collection of Dodge Papers, including letterpress
books, maps, diaries, account books for 1851–1916.

John Evans Papers, State Museum, Denver, Colorado. Correspondence, official
documents, speeches, and photographs covering the period 1837–97.

Hale Holden Papers, in possession of the family. Reprints of speeches and
some correspondence pertinent to the Burlington for the period
1914–29.

Illinois Central Archives in the Newberry Library, Chicago. Described in
*Guide to the Illinois Central Archives in the Newberry Library, 1851–
1906,* compiled by Carolyn Curtis Mohr, Chicago, 1951.

James F. Joy Papers in Burton Historical Collection, Detroit Public Library.
Voluminous collection covering Joy's life, 1810–96.

"McConkey Manuscript," an unpublished "Manuscript Biography of James F.
Joy" in Michigan Historical Collections, Ann Arbor.

Frank Trumbull Papers, in possession of the family. Genealogical information,
reprints, and some correspondence pertinent to the C. & S. and its
predecessors, 1893–1908.

John Van Nortwick Papers, in possession of the family. Clippings, some manuscript reports, and a few letters pertinent to the early history of the
Burlington, 1848–65.

• OTHER COLLECTIONS •

Baker Library, Harvard Graduate School of Business Administration, Boston,
Massachusetts.
Extensive collection of railway *Annual Reports,* engineering surveys,
assorted circulars, and early guidebooks.

Library of the Bureau of Railway Economics, Washington, D. C.
Voluminous collection of railroad reports of all kinds, and complete
files of leading railway journals.

Burlington Public Library, Burlington, Iowa.
Newspaper files relating to the area and to the Burlington Lines.

Burton Historical Collection, Detroit Public Library, Detroit, Michigan.
Reports and articles relating to James F. Joy, together with important
correspondence.

Colorado State Historical Society Library, Denver, Colorado.
Contemporary pamphlets, photographs, and newspapers, many dealing
specifically with the C. B. & Q., the C. & S., and the C. & S.'s
predecessors and subsidiaries.

John Crerar Library, Chicago, Illinois.
Extensive reports, primarily of a technical nature, on all Chicago railroads, including the Burlington and its principal neighbors.

Deering Library, Northwestern University, Evanston, Illinois.

Includes the "Fowle Collection" of pamphlets relating to early midwestern railways.

Denver Public Library, Denver, Colorado.

The Western Collection contains contemporary pamphlets, newspapers, prints, and photographs.

Engineering Societies Library, New York, N.Y.

Railroad reports and pamphlets.

Fort Worth Public Library, Fort Worth, Texas.

Contemporary newspapers, prints, and photographs.

Harvard College Library, Cambridge, Massachusetts.

Particularly useful complete collection of government documents and reports. Includes the "Colton Manuscript."

Iowa Historical Society Library, Des Moines, Iowa.

Extensive files of Iowa newspapers.

Minnesota Historical Society Library, St. Paul, Minnesota.

Valuable Collection of Minnesota newspapers.

Nebraska State Historical Society Library, Lincoln, Nebraska.

Includes fourteen scrapbooks of newspaper clippings about the Burlington and Missouri River Railroad; largest collection of Nebraska newspapers.

Omaha Public Library, Omaha, Nebraska.

Pamphlets on Nebraska, and files of various Omaha newspapers.

United States General Land Office, Washington, D. C.

Original correspondence between the Land Office and the Hannibal and St. Joseph and Burlington and Missouri River companies; Receiver's accounts, maps, plats, and patents of all Burlington grants.

United States National Archives, Washington, D. C.

Miscellaneous documents referring to the Burlington land grants; materials on the Office of Transportation Commissioner (1940–41).

Warren County Library, Monmouth, Illinois.

Valuable file of early Illinois newspapers.

NOTE: For more detailed information on material pertinent particularly to the Burlington's land-grant period, see Bibliography in *BW*, pp. 541–55. For further detailed information concerning the C. & S. and the F. W. & D. between 1861 and 1899, see Bibliography in *GTR*, pp. 385 94. Note especially "Guide to the Location of Source Material" in *BW*, pp. 545–7.

• GOVERNMENT DOCUMENTS •

Federal: Executive and Legislative

Civil Aeronautics Board, Docket No. 922 (Burlington Transportation Co. helicopter application), 1946.

Commissioner of the General Land Office, *Annual Report*, 1864.

Congress, 48th, 2nd Session, Senate Executive Document No. 40, *History of the Railway Mail Service: A Chapter in the History of the Postal Affairs of the United States*, Washington, 1885.

—— 73rd, 2nd Session, Senate Document No. 119, *First Report* of the Federal Coordinator of Transportation, Washington, 1934.

—— 73rd, 2nd Session, Senate Document No. 152, *Second Report* of the Federal Coordinator of Transportation, Washington, 1934.

—— 74th, 1st Session, House Document No. 89, *Third Report* of the Federal Coordinator of Transportation, Washington, 1935.

—— 74th, 1st Session, House Document No. 394, *Fourth Report* of the Federal Coordinator of Transportation, Washington, 1936.

—— 74th, 2nd Session, Senate Resolution 217 (*re* select committee to investigate executive agencies, esp. *re* a proposed Department of Transportation), February 24, 1936.

—— 75th, 1st Session, Senate Report No. 1275, "Investigation of Executive Agencies of the Government," 1937.

—— 75th, 3rd Session, House Document No. 583, "Immediate Relief for the Railroads," 1938.

—— 79th, 1st Session, House Document No. 159, "Public Aids to Domestic Transportation," 1945.

Congressional Globe, 32nd Congress, 1st Session (*re* Hannibal and St. Joseph land grant), 1851–2.

Congressional Record, Vol. 56 (*re* World War I railways), 1917.

Department of Commerce, Bureau of the Census: *Historical Statistics of the United States, 1789–1945*, Washington, 1949.

—— Bureau of the Census: *Continuation to 1952 of Historical Statistics of the United States, 1789–1945*, Washington, 1954.

Federal Coordinator of Transportation: *Aids to Public Transportation*, 4 vols., Washington, 1940.

National Mediation Board: *Administration of the Railway Labor Act by the National Mediation Board, 1934–1957*, Washington, 1958.

Office of Defense Transportation: *Civilian War Transport: A Record of the Control of Domestic Traffic by the Office of Defense Transportation, 1941–1946*, Washington, 1948.

Railroad Administration, Bulletin No. 4, 1918.

Statutes-at-Large: Vol. 39 (Army Appropriation Act, Aug. 29, 1916).

—— Vol. 41 (Transportation Act of 1920, Feb. 28, 1920).

—— Vol. 48 (Railroad Retirement Act, June 27, 1934).

—— Vol. 54 (Transportation Act of 1940, Sept. 18, 1940).

Federal: Judicial

(A) UNITED STATES SUPREME COURT

94 U.S. 113 (1877), *Munn v. Illinois*

94 U.S. 155 (1877), *C. B. & Q. R. R. v. Iowa*

169 U.S. 466 (1898), *Smyth v. Ames*

169 U.S. 466 (1898), *Smyth v. Smith*

169 U.S. 466 (1898), *Smyth v. Higginson*

230 U.S. 352 (1913), *The Minnesota Rate Cases*

243 U.S. 332 (1917), *Wilson v. New* (*re* Adamson Act)

257 U.S. 585 (1922), *Wisconsin Railroad Commission v. C. B. & Q. R. R.*
   (*re* Wisconsin passenger fares)

259 U.S. 214 (1923), *Consolidation of Railroads* (*re* merger proposals)

295 U.S. 330 (1935), *Railroad Retirement Board v. Alton Railroad Company* (*re* 1934 Railroad Retirement Act)

300 U.S. 515 (1937), *Virginian Railway Co. v. System Federation No. 40*
   (*re* Railway Labor Act as amended in 1935)

315 U.S. 373 (1942), *ICC v. Railroad Labor Executive Association* (*re*
   employees effected by abandonments)

(B) CIRCUIT AND DISTRICT COURTS

Circuit Court for the District of Nebraska, *Higginson et al. v. Chicago, B. &*
   Q. R. Co. (*re* Nebraska Maximum Rate Law), Nov. 1894.

District Court for Illinois, *Asabel Enigh v. C. B. & Q. R. R. Co.* (*re* purchase
   of stock in Aurora Branch), Nov. 1860.

District Court for the Northern District of Illinois, *C. B. & Q. R. R. Co.*
   v. Illinois Commerce Commission et al. (*re* discontinuance of trains
   #51 and #52), 1949.

District Court for Colorado, Orders of the Court (*re* refinancing of the
   Colorado and Southern Railway), March 1943.

——— Orders of the Court (*re* excess profits of Colorado and Southern
   Railway), 1948–9.

Interstate Commerce Commission

Annual Reports for 1916, 1917, 1918, 1933, 1935.

Bureau of Transport Economics and Statistics: "Railroad Abandonments,
   1920–1943," Washington, 1945.

Docket No. 12964 (*re* consolidation of railroads), 1922.

Ex Parte No. 168 (status of transportation), 1948.

Finance Docket No. 12460 (*re* lease of F. W. & D. C. by C. & S.), 1939.

——— No. 14426 (*re* protection of employees in Mt. Ayr–Grant City abandonment), 1944.

——— No. 14668 (*re* protection of employees in Mt. Ayr–Grant City abandonment), 1945.

——— No. 14979 (*re* protection of employees in Mt. Ayr–Grant City abandonment), 1946.

——— No. 15365 (*re* negotiations with G. M. & O. for direct Kansas City
   line), 1947.

———— No. 16456 (*re* lease of Kansas City and Brookfield for direct Kansas City line), 1949.

Reports:

59 I.C.C. 391 (1920) (*re* Wisconsin passenger fares)

63 I.C.C. 455 (1921), "Consolidation of Railroads"

76 I.C.C. 508 (1923) (*re* Southern Pacific–Central Pacific merger)

134 I.C.C. 1 (1927) (Burlington Valuation Docket)

159 I.C.C. 524 (1929) (*re* consolidation of railroads)

162 I.C.C. 37 (1930) (*re* Great Northern Pacific merger)

178 I.C.C. 539 (1931) (*re* railway adjustment to truck competition)

179 I.C.C. 851 (1931) (*re* Railroad Credit Corporation)

228 I.C.C. 277 (1938) (*re* dismemberment of M. & St. L.)

240 I.C.C. 637 (1939) (*re* lease of F. W. & D. C. by C. & S.)

257 I.C.C. 129 (1943) (*re* competitive bidding on refinancing)

257 I.C.C. 700 (1944) (*re* protection of employees in Mt. Ayr–Grant City abandonment)

Valuation Docket No. 44 (1918) (of Chicago, Milwaukee, St. Paul & Pacific R. R.).

State: Judicial

Nebraska Supreme Court, *In re Application of the Chicago, Burlington & Quincy Railroad Co.*, Case No. 32706 (1950) (*re* reduction of service).

———— *C. B. & Q. R. R. Co. v. Nebraska State Railway Commission et al.*, 295 N. W. 389 (1940) (*re* reduction of service).

• NEWSPAPERS AND PERIODICALS •

American Short Line Railroad Association: *Weekly Information Bulletin*, 1948–64

Association of American Railroads: *Information Letter*, 1959–64

———— *Railway Digest of Developments and Comments*, 1949–63

Aurora Beacon, 1850

Boston Daily Advertiser, 1875, 1889

Boston Evening Transcript, 1875

Boston Herald, 1901

Boston Journal, 1865

Brookfield Gazette, 1869

Burlington *Booster*, a publication of the C. B. & Q. Booster Club, 1949–61

Burlington *Bulletin*, a publication of the C. B. & Q. Public Relations Department, 1960–4

Burlington *Zephyr*, a publication of the C. B. & Q. Passenger Department, 1942–64

Burlington *Daily Hawk-Eye*, 1869, 1891, 1901, 1908–10, 1912

Burlington *Daily Telegraph*, 1851–2
Burlington *Gazette*, 1901
Burlington *Weekly Hawk-Eye and Telegraph*, 1856, 1858–9
Burlington *Weekly Telegraph*, 1852–3
Chicago Chronicle, 1901
Chicago Daily Democrat, 1850
Chicago Daily Drovers Journal, 1940
Chicago Daily Journal, 1848, 1850
Chicago Daily News, 1948–9
Chicago *Inter-Ocean*, 1875, 1886
Chicago Republican, 1865
Chicago Times, 1886
Chicago Times Herald, 1901
Chicago Tribune, 1875, 1886, 1901, 1924, 1928, 1947
Collingwood Standard, 1932
Colorado Springs Evening and Sunday Telegraph, 1909
Dallas Morning News, 1926
Denver Post, 1908
Dubuque Daily Times, 1886
Fort Worth Star-Telegram, 1939–40
Hannibal Daily Messenger, 1859
Houston Chronicle, 1940
Houston Press, 1940
Ithaca Journal, 1962
Kansas City Times, 1928
Macon Weekly Argus, 1868
Minneapolis Tribune, 1963
Monmouth Atlas, 1855
Natrona County Tribune, 1913
New York Herald Tribune, 1929
The New York Times, 1930, 1947–8, 1957, 1962
North Missouri Courier, 1867
The Pampa Advocate, 1932
Quincy Daily Whig and Republican, 1859, 1861–2
Quincy Herald–Whig, 1960
Railway Age, 1914–64
Railway Progress, 1948–53
Rocky Mountain News, 1940
St. Louis Globe–Democrat, 1894, 1928
St. Paul Pioneer Press, 1886
Traffic World, 1928–60
Wall Street Journal, 1941, 1963
West Chicago Press, 1949

SECONDARY WORKS

• Books •

Allen, Frederick Lewis: *The Big Change*. New York, 1953.

Anderson, George L.: *General William J. Palmer, A Decade of Railroad Building, 1870–1880*. Colorado Springs, 1936.

Anderson, William H.: *Taxation and the American Economy*. New York, 1951.

Antrobus, Augustine M.: *History of Des Moines County, Iowa*. Chicago, 1915.

Baker, Ray S.: *Woodrow Wilson*, Vol. 6. New York, 1937.

Baldwin, William W.: *Corporate History of the C. B. & Q. Railroad Company and Affiliated Companies*. Chicago, 1921.

————: *Documentary History, C. B. & Q. Railroad Company*, 3 vols. Chicago, 1928–9.

Beebe, Lucius: *Mixed Train Daily*. New York, 1947.

Billington, Ray A.: *Westward Expansion: A History of the American Frontier*. New York, 1949.

Bining, Arthur C.: *The Rise of American Economic Life*. New York, 1949.

Black, Robert C. III: *The Railroads of the Confederacy*. Chapel Hill, 1952.

Bruce, Robert V.: *1877: Year of Violence*. Indianapolis, 1959.

Buck, Paul H.: *The Road to Reunion, 1865–1900*. Boston, 1937.

Burgess, George H., and Kennedy, Miles C.: *Centennial History of the Pennsylvania Railroad Company*. Philadelphia, 1949.

Carlson, Carl Frederick: *Aurora, Illinois: A study in Sequent Land Use*. Chicago, 1940.

Carter, C. F.: *When Railroads Were New*. New York, 1909.

Casey, Robert J., and Douglas, W. A. S.: *Pioneer Railroad: The Story of the Chicago and North Western System*. New York, 1948.

Chanute, Octave, and Morison, George: *The Kansas City Bridge*. New York, 1870.

Chapman, Charles and Co.; *History of Knox County, Illinois*. Chicago, 1878.

Clark, D. E.: *The West in American History*. New York, 1937.

Clarke, Thomas Curtis: *An Account of the Iron Railway Bridge Across the Mississippi River at Quincy, Illinois*. New York, 1869.

Cochran, Thomas C.: *Railroad Leaders, 1845–1890: The Business Mind in Action*. Cambridge, 1953.

Cole, Arthur C.: *The Irrepressible Conflict*. New York, 1934.

Cole, Cyrenus: *A History of the People of Iowa*. Cedar Rapids, 1921.

Corbin, Bernard G., and Kerka, William F.: *Steam Locomotives of the Burlington Route*. Red Oak, Iowa, 1960.

Corliss, Carlton J.: *Main Line of Mid-America*. New York, 1950.

————: *Trails to Rails*. Chicago, 1937.

Cunningham, Edith Perkins: *Owl's Nest*. Boston, 1907.

Cunningham, Edith P., ed.: *CEP and EFP-Family Letters and Reminiscences, 1865–1907*. Portland, Maine, 1949.

———, ed.: *Charles Elliott Perkins and Edith Forbes Perkins: Family Letters, 1861–69*. Boston, 1949.

Daggett, Stewart: *Principles of Inland Transportation*. New York, 1941.

Daniels, Winthrop: *American Railroads: Four Phases of Their History*. Princeton, 1932.

Davis, E. O.: *The First Five Years of the Railroad Era in Colorado*. Denver, 1948.

Dearing, Charles L., and Owen, Wilfred: *National Transportation Policy*. Washington, 1949.

Derleth, August: *The Milwaukee Road: Its First Hundred Years*. New York, 1948.

Donaldson, Thomas: *The Public Domain*. Washington, 1884.

Donovan, Frank P., Jr.: *Mileposts on the Prairie: the Story of the Minneapolis & St. Louis Railway*. New York, 1950.

Dulles, Foster Rhea: *The United States Since 1865*. Ann Arbor, 1959.

Elliott, Howard: *The Truth about the Railroads*. Boston, 1913.

Emerson, Edward W.: *Life and Letters of Charles Russell Lowell*. Boston, 1907.

Faulkner, Harold U.: *American Economic History*. New York, 1943.

Flint, Henry M.: *The Railroads of the United States: Their History and Statistics*. Philadelphia, 1868.

Fowler, Richard B., and Haskell, Henry C.: *City of the Future: The Story of Kansas City, 1850–1950*. Kansas City, 1950.

Gates, Paul W.: *The Illinois Central Railroad and Its Colonization Work*. Cambridge, 1934.

Gillette, Edward: *Locating the Iron Trail*. Boston, 1925.

Ginger, Ray: *The Bending Cross, A Biography of Eugene Victor Debs*. New Brunswick, 1949.

Grant, U. S.: *Personal Memoirs of U. S. Grant*, Vol. II. New York, 1886.

Gray, Carl R., Jr.: *Railroading in Eighteen Countries*. New York, 1955.

Grodinsky, Julius: *The Iowa Pool*. Chicago, 1950.

———: *Jay Gould: His Business Career, 1867–1892*. Philadelphia, 1957.

Hafen, Leroy R., ed.: *Colorado and Its People*. Denver, 1948.

Haney, Lewis H.: *A Congressional History of Railways in the United States to 1850*. Madison, 1908.

Hargrave, Frank F.: *A Pioneer Indiana Railroad*. Indianapolis, 1932.

Harlow, Alvin Fay: *The Road of the Century*. New York, 1947.

———: *Steelways of New England*. New York, 1946.

Haskell, Henry C., and Fowler, Richard B.: *City of the Future: The Story of Kansas City, 1850–1950*. Kansas City, 1950.

Healy, Kent T.: *The Economics of Transportation*. New York, 1940.

[611]

Hedge, Thomas: *Charles Elliott Perkins*. Boston, 1931.

Henry, Robert S.: *This Fascinating Railroad Business*. Indianapolis, 1942.

Hines, Walker D.: *War History of American Railroads*. New Haven, 1928.

Holbrook, Stewart H.: *The Story of American Railroads*. New York, 1947.

Hughes, Sarah Forbes, ed.: *Letters and Recollections of John Murray Forbes*. Boston, 1899.

Hungerford, Edward: *Daniel Willard Rides the Line*. New York, 1938.

————: *Men of Erie*. New York, 1946.

————: *The Story of the Baltimore & Ohio Railroad, 1827–1927*, 2 vols. New York, 1928.

Jones, Harry E.: *Railroad Wages and Labor Relations, 1900–1952*. New York, 1953.

Josephson, Matthew: *The Robber Barons*. New York, 1934.

Kemmerer, Donald L., and Jones, C. Clyde: *American Economic History*. New York, 1959.

Kennan, George: *E. H. Harriman, A Biography*, 2 vols. Boston, 1922.

Kennedy, Miles C., and Burgess, George H.: *Centennial History of the Pennsylvania Railroad Company*. Philadelphia, 1949.

Kirkland, Edward C.: *A History of American Economic Life*. New York, 1941.

————: *Men, Cities and Transportation, A Study in New England History, 1820–1900*. Cambridge, 1948.

Latham, Earl: *The Politics of Railroad Coordination*. Cambridge, 1959.

Lemly, James H.: *The Gulf, Mobile and Ohio: A Railroad That Had to Expand or Expire*. Homewood, Illinois, 1953.

Leonard, William N.: *Railroad Consolidation under the Transportation Act of 1920*. New York, 1946.

Lodge, Henry Cabot: *Daniel Webster*. Boston, 1883.

MacGill, Caroline: *History of Transportation in the United States before 1860*. Washington, 1917.

McMurry, Donald L.: *The Great Burlington Strike of 1888: A Case Study in Labor Relations*. Cambridge, 1956.

Marshall, James: *Santa Fe: The Railroad That Built an Empire*. New York, 1945.

Masterson, V. V.: *The Katy Railroad and the Last Frontier*. Norman, 1952.

Merk, Frederick: *Economic History of Wisconsin during the Civil War Decade*. Madison, 1915.

Merritt, W. W.: *A History of the County of Montgomery*. Red Oak, Iowa, 1906.

Meyer, B. H.: *History of the Northern Securities Case*. Madison, 1906.

Miller, Sidney: *Railway Transportation*. Chicago, 1924.

Million, John W.: *State Aid to Railways in Missouri*. Chicago, 1896.

Morgan, David P.: *Diesels West! The Evolution of Power on the Burlington*. Milwaukee, 1963.

Morison, Samuel E., and Commager, Henry S.: *The Growth of the American Republic, 1865–1942*, 2 vols. New York, 1942.

Nevins, Allan: *The Emergence of Modern America.* New York, 1932.

Olson, James C.: *History of Nebraska.* Lincoln, 1955.

———: *J. Sterling Morton.* Lincoln, 1942.

O'Neil, John T.: *Policy Formation in Railroad Finance: Refinancing the Burlington, 1936–1945.* Cambridge, 1956.

Overton, Richard C.: *Burlington West: A Colonization History of the Burlington Railroad.* Cambridge, 1941.

———: *Gulf to Rockies: The Heritage of the Fort Worth and Denver–Colorado and Southern Railways, 1861–1898.* Austin, 1953.

Parmelee, Julius H.: *The Modern Railway.* New York, 1940.

Pearson, Henry G.: *An American Railroad Builder: John Murray Forbes.* Boston, 1911.

Perkins, J. R.: *Trails, Rails and War: The Life of General G. M. Dodge.* Indianapolis, 1928.

Poor, M. C.: *The Denver, South Park and Pacific.* Denver, 1949.

Pyle, J. G.: *Life of James G. Hill,* 2 vols. New York, 1917.

Quiett, Glenn Chesney: *They Built the West.* New York, 1934.

Reck, Franklin M.: *On Time: the History of Electro-Motive Division of General Motors Corporation.* Chicago, 1948.

Reed, S. G.: *A History of the Texas Railroads.* Houston, 1941.

Riegel, Robert E.: *The Story of Western Railroads.* New York, 1926.

Robbins, Roy M.: *Our Landed Heritage.* Princeton, 1942.

Roosevelt, Elliott, ed.: *F. D. R., His Personal Letters, 1928–45.* New York, 1950.

Sage, Leland: *William Boyd Allison.* Iowa City, State Historical Society, 1956.

Salter, William: *Life of James W. Grimes.* New York, 1876.

Sanborn, John Bell: *Congressional Grants of Land in Aid of Railways.* Madison, 1899.

Sharfman, I. L.: *The American Railroad Problem: A Study in War and Reconstruction.* New York, 1921.

———; *The Interstate Commerce Commission,* 5 vols. New York, 1931–7.

Sherwood, Robert E.: *Roosevelt and Hopkins.* New York, 1950.

Smalley, Eugene V.: *History of the Northern Pacific Railroad.* New York, 1883.

Snyder, Carl: *American Railways as Investments.* New York, 1907.

Staples, Henry L., and Mason, Alpheus T.: *The Fall of a Railroad Empire.* New York, 1947.

Starr, John W., Jr.: *Lincoln and the Railroads.* New York, 1927.

Stennett, W. H.: *Yesterday and Today: A History of the Chicago & North Western Railway System.* Chicago, 1910.

Stevens, Frank W.: *Beginnings of the New York Central Railroad.* New York, 1926.

Stevens, W. E.: *The Northwest Fur Trade, 1763–1800*. Urbana, 1928.

Stover, John F.: *American Railroads*. Chicago, 1961.

Swisher, Carl B.: *American Constitutional Development*. Boston, 1943.

Taylor, George Rogers: *The Transportation Revolution, 1815–1860*. New York, 1951.

Thompson, Slason: *A Short History of American Railways*. Chicago, 1925.

Towner, Ausburn: *Our County and Its People: A History of the Valley and County of Chemung*. Syracuse, 1892.

Trottman, Nelson: *History of the Union Pacific: A Financial and Economic Survey*. New York, 1923.

Truman, Harry S.: *Memoirs of Harry S. Truman*, 2 vols. Garden City, 1955.

Van Oss, S. F.: *American Railroads as Investments*. New York, 1893.

Warner, Paul T.: *The Locomotives of the Chicago, Burlington & Quincy Railroad*. Philadelphia, 1936.

Waters, L. L.: *Steel Rails to Santa Fe*. Lawrence, 1950.

Wattles, Guerdon W.: *Autobiography of Guerdon Wallace Wattles*. New York, 1922.

Weber, Thomas: *The Northern Railroads in the Civil War, 1861–1865*. New York, 1952.

Westmeyer, Russell E.: *Economics of Transportation*. New York, 1952.

White, Henry Kirke: *History of the Union Pacific Railway*. Chicago, 1895.

Williams, Ernest W., Jr.: *The Regulation of Rail-Motor Rate Competition*. New York, 1958.

Williamson, Harold F., ed.: *The Growth of the American Economy*. New York, 1951.

Wilson, G. Lloyd, ed.: *Selected Papers and Addresses of Joseph B. Eastman . . . 1942–1944*. New York, 1948.

Wiprud, Arne C.: *Justice in Transportation*. 1945.

• Articles and Chapters •

Albion, Robert G.: "Robert Bennet Forbes," *Dictionary of American Biography*, Vol. VI. New York, 1931.

Bader, Robert E.: "The Curtailment of Railroad Service in Nebraska, 1920–1941," *Nebraska History*. Vol. XXXVI, No. 1 (March 1955).

Beard, Earl S.: "Railroad Regulation in Iowa," *Iowa Journal of History*. Vol. 51, No. 1 (January 1953).

Bogart, Ernest L.: "James Frederick Joy," *Dictionary of American Biography*, Vol. X. New York, 1933.

Bollinger, Edward T.: "Denver West, to Salt Lake," *Railroad Magazine*. Vol. 43, No. 4 (September 1947).

Brayer, Herbert O.: "History of the Colorado Railroads," in *Colorado and Its People*, Leroy R. Hafen, ed. Denver, 1948.

Brétey, Pierre R.: "Modern Technology as Aid in Reducing Operating Costs of Railroads," *The Analysts Journal*. Vol. 8, No. 2 (March 1952).

Budd, Ralph: "The Future of Transportation," *The Reviewing Stand*. Vol. 3, No. 8 (June 18, 1944).

———: "Light-Weight Diesel-electric Trains," *Civil Engineering*. Vol. VIII, No. 9 (September 1938).

———: "93 Billion Ton-Miles," *Army Transportation Journal*. Vol. II, No. 3 (April 1946).

———: "Transportation on the Home Front," *Civil Engineering*. Vol. XII, No. 9 (September 1942).

Calkins, Earnest Elmo: "Genesis of a Railroad," Illinois State Historical Society, *Transactions for the Year 1935*. Springfield, 1936.

———: "Some Early Railroad History," letter to the editor, *Wall Street Journal*. July 30, 1943.

Cochran, Thomas C.: "Did the Civil War Retard Industrialism?" *Mississippi Valley Historical Review*. Vol. XLVII, No. 2 (September 1961).

Daniel, Hawthorne: "American Railroad Men in India," *Official Organ*, Railroad Yardmasters of North America. Vol. VI, No. 8 (October 1945).

Davis, Thomas M.: "Building the Burlington through Nebraska—A Summary View," *Nebraska History*. Vol. XXX, No. 4 (December 1949).

———: "Lines West! The Story of George W. Holdrege," *Nebraska History*. Vol. XXI, No. 1 (March 1950).

Dawes, Charles G.: "Bank Wrecking and Salving," *Saturday Evening Post*. Vol. 175, No. 12 (September 20, 1902).

Delano, Frederick A.: "Perkins of the Burlington," *Appleton's Magazine*. Vol. XI, No. 3 (March 1908).

Dewey, Ralph L.: "The Transportation Act of 1940," *American Economic Review*. Vol. 31, No. 1 (March 1941).

Dixon, Frank Haigh: "Erastus Corning," *Dictionary of American Biography*, Vol. IV. New York, 1930.

Ford, Nancy: "A Break for the Commuters," *Railway Progress*. Vol. V, No. 7 (September 1951).

Frazee, George: "An Iowa Fugitive Slave Case," *Annals of Iowa*. Third series, Vol. VI, No. 1 (April 1903).

Gates, Paul W: "The Homestead Act in an Incongruous Land System," *American Historical Review*. Vol. XLI, No. 4 (July 1936).

Goodwin, Cardinal: "The American Occupation of Iowa, 1833 to 1860," *Iowa Journal of History and Politics*. Vol. XVII, No. 1 (January 1919).

Harteson, Robert W.: "Transportation, Achilles Heel of National Security," *Political Science Quarterly*. Vol. LXXIV, No. 1 (March 1959).

Hayes, William E.: "The Great Rock Island Route," *Rock Island Lines News Digest*. Vol. 11, No. 10 (October 1952).

Healy, K. T.: "Transportation Since World War I," in *The Growth of the American Economy*, Harold F. Williamson, ed. New York, 1951.

Hebard, Alfred: "The Original Survey of the C. B. & Q. R. R. Line," *Annals of Iowa*. Third series, Vol. VI, No. 3 (October 1903).

Hidy, Muriel: "The Capital Markets," in *The Growth of the American Economy*, Harold F. Williamson, ed. New York, 1951.

Hines, Walker D.: "The Relationship of the Burlington Great Northern–Northern Pacific to the Federal Railway Consolidation Law," *Harvard Business Review*. Vol. I, No. 4 (July 1923).

Hough, Henry W.: "Dave Moffat's Dream," *Railroad Magazine*. Vol. 43, No. 4 (September 1947).

Jones, C. Clyde: "The Burlington Railroad and Agricultural Policy in the 1920's," *Agricultural History*. Vol. 31, No. 4 (October 1957).

———: "A Survey of the Agricultural Development Program of the Chicago, Burlington & Quincy Railroad," *Nebraska History*. Vol. 30, No. 3 (September 1949).

Kaufman, Jacob J.: "Government Intervention in Railroad Labor Disputes," *Current Economic Comment*. Vol. 20, No. 3 (August 1958).

———: "Grievance Arbitration in the Railroad Industry," *Labor Law Journal*. Vol. 9, No. 3 (March 1958).

Kettering, Charles F.: "Future Unlimited," *Saturday Evening Post*. Vol. 230, No. 46 (May 17, 1958).

Leonard, William N.: "The Decline of Railroad Consolidation," *Journal of Economic History*. Vol. IX, No. 1 (May 1949).

Lewis, Lucia: "This Is Ralph Budd," *Chicago Daily News*. March 6, 1954.

Lyne, J. G.: "Mr. Murphy Audits Railroad Efficiency," editorial, *Railway Age*. Vol. 148, No. 26 (June 27, 1960).

Matthew, Allan P.: "Defects in Railway Labor Act and in Practices Thereunder Can and Must be Remedied," *Traffic World*. Vol. 105, No. 2 (January 9, 1960).

Mott, Frank Luther: "James Handasyd Perkins," *Dictionary of American Biography*, Vol. XIV. New York, 1931.

Murphy, Harry C.: "Cost—Rail vs. Truck, Barge," *Railway Age*. Vol. 148, No. 26 (June 27, 1960).

Myers, Margaret: "The Investment Market after the Civil War," in Williamson, Harold F., ed. *The Growth of the American Economy*, New York, 1951.

Neu, Irene: "The Building of the Sault Canal, 1852–1855," *Mississippi Valley Historical Review*. Vol. XL, No. 1 (June 1953).

Newton, A. W.: "The Chicago and Aurora Railroad," *Bulletin* No. 76. Railway and Locomotive Historical Society, Boston (March 1949).

———: "Early History of the Chicago, Burlington & Quincy Railroad in Illinois," *Bulletin* No. 74, Railway and Locomotive Historical Society, Boston (October 1948).

Overton, Richard C.: "Charles Elliott Perkins," *The Business History Review*. Vol. XXXI, No. 3 (Autumn 1957).

———: "The Lexington Group," *Special Libraries*. Vol. 36, No. 8 (October 1945).

————: "Ralph Budd, Railroad Entrepreneur," *Palimpsest*. Vol. XXXVI, No. 11 (November 1955).

————: "Scholars Get Access to Burlington Records," *Railway Age*. Vol. 116, No. 9 (February 26, 1944).

————: "Scholars Get Access to Burlington Records," reprinted in *Bulletin of Business Historical Society*. Vol. XVIII, No. 3 (June 1944).

————: "The Westward Movement since the Homestead Act," in *The Growth of the American Economy*, Harold F. Williamson, ed. New York, 1951.

Overton, Richard C., and Budd, Ralph: "Chicago Becomes the Nation's Railway Capital," *Journal of the Western Society of Engineers*. 75th Anniversary Edition (December 1944).

Parmelee, Julius Hall: "Albert Fink," *Dictionary of American Biography*, Vol. VI. New York, 1931.

Paper Makers' Chemical Corporation: "Batavia, Illinois, and Van Nortwick Family," *Superior Facts*, Ralph M. Shell, ed. Vol. 5, No. 11 (May 1932).

Pearson, Henry G.: "John Murray Forbes," *Dictionary of American Biography*, Vol. VI. New York, 1931.

Petersen, William J.: "The Burlington Comes," *Palimpsest*. Vol. XIV, No. 11 (November 1933).

Reichman, Albert: "The History of Bridge Development," *Journal of the Western Society of Engineers*. 75th Anniversary Edition (December 1944).

Remey, J. T.: "William F. Coolbaugh," *Annals of Iowa*. Third series, Vol. VII, No. 6 (July 1906).

Stauffer, Fred B.: "If you Can't Lick 'Em . . . ." *Railway Progress*. Vol. 7, No. 8 (November 1953).

Stratton, H. J.: "The Northern Cross Railroad," *Journal of the Illinois State Historical Society*. Vol. XXVII, No. 2 (July 1935).

Throne, Mildred: "The Grange in Iowa, 1868–1875," *Iowa Journal of History and Politics*. Vol. 47, No. 4 (October 1949).

————: "Streamliners in Iowa," *Palimpsest*. Vol. XXXII, No. 6 (June 1951).

Upshaw, H. C.: "Now, just look at the Panhandle!" *Transportation*. No place, no volume, no date—apparently 1932.

Wilson, Ben Hur: "Burlington Westward," "Planked from Burlington," "From Planks to Rails," *Palimpsest*. Vol. XVI, No. 10 (November 1935).

• UNPUBLISHED MANUSCRIPTS •

(In possession of the writer, unless otherwise indicated)

Agnew, Robert J.: "Albert Fink." Paper delivered at American Historical Association, Washington, D. C., December 28, 1952. In possession of its author.

Ashton, Frank E.: "Development of Centralized Traffic Control . . . ." Seminar Thesis, Northwestern University, 1950. In possession of its author.

Bennett, Howard F.: "The Hannibal and St. Joseph Railroad and the Development of Northern Missouri, 1847–1870." Doctoral Dissertation, Harvard University, 1950. In possession of its author.

Bogle, Donald C.: "Charles E. Perkins: His Interest and Involvement in Politics, 1865–1907." Seminar Thesis, University of Western Ontario, 1964.

Chicago and North Western Railway: "Historical Background of the Chicago and North Western Railway." Manuscript Memorandum, Chicago, 1936. In C&NW/Sec.

Clark, Robert J.: "John Murray Forbes, Charles Elliott Perkins, and the Board of Directors of the Chicago, Burlington & Quincy Railroad." Seminar Thesis, University of Western Ontario, 1964.

Davis, T. M.: "George Ward Holdrege and the Burlington Lines West." Master's Thesis, University of Nebraska, May 26, 1939. In possession of its author.

Eggert, Gerald G.: "Richard Olney, Corporation Lawyer and Attorney General of the United States, 1835–1895." Doctoral Dissertation, University of Michigan, 1960. In possession of its author.

Gagan, David P.: "The Railroads and the Public, 1870–1881: A Study of Charles Elliott Perkins's Business Ethics." Seminar Thesis, University of Western Ontario, 1964.

Hobart, John H.: "The History of the Chicago, Burlington and Northern Railroad." Seminar Thesis, Yale University, 1945.

Holt, A. Grant: "Development of Air Lines in the United States with Emphasis upon Integrating with Surface Transportation Today." Seminar Thesis, Amherst College, 1946.

Jankowski, Alvin F.: "Labor Protection in Railroad Abandonments: Grant City—Mount Ayr Abandonment Case." Seminar Thesis, Northwestern University, 1946.

Jenkins, Richard: "The Community in Railroad Abandonments: Mount Ayr–Grant City Case." Seminar Thesis, Northwestern University, 1946.

Jones, C. C.: "Agricultural Development Work of the Chicago, Burlington & Quincy Railroad Company." Doctoral Dissertation, Northwestern University, 1954. In possession of its author.

Lawr, Douglas A.: "Charles E. Perkins and the Far Northwest, 1880–1900." Seminar Thesis, University of Western Ontario, 1964.

MacKay, Donald: "The Chicago, Burlington and Northern: A Case Study in Strategy 1883–1887." Seminar Thesis, University of Western Ontario, 1964.

McConkey, M. C.: "Manuscript Biography of James F. Joy," 1933. In Michigan Historical Collections, Ann Arbor, Michigan.

McGowan, Alan P.: "Robert Harris and the Burlington: A Business Career." Seminar Thesis, University of Western Ontario, 1964.

McMurray, T. S.: "The Colorado and Southern Railway History." No date. In C. B. & Q. and C. & S. Secretary's Offices.

McMurry, D. L.: "Beginnings of the Relief Department." Manuscript memorandum, 1947.

Newton, A. W.: "Aurora Branch Railroad Company: First Depot and Its Successors." Manuscript Memorandum, Chicago, 1940.

———: "Memorandum concerning the Origin of Place Names on the Burlington." Memorandum for CB&Q/Sec. April 15, 1945.

Overton, Richard C.: "The Kansas City Story: A History of the Burlington's Interest in Providing Chicago–Kansas City Service, 1852–1952." Manuscript Memorandum, 1952.

Pixton, John E., Jr.: "Charles Dawes and the Nebraska Freight Rates Fight." Master's Thesis, University of Chicago, 1951. In possession of its author.

Scudder, M. L.: "History of Strike of Engineers and Firemen on the Chicago, Burlington & Quincy R. R., 1888." Manuscript prepared for C. E. Perkins, 1888. In C–O; copies also in CB&Q/Sec.

Snell, James G.: "Railway Regulation as Seen through the Eyes of C. E. Perkins, 1870–1907." Seminar Thesis, University of Western Ontario, 1964.

Stockder, A. H.: "The Burlington, Northern Pacific and Great Northern Systems: A Study of the Development of Their Corporate and Inter-Corporate Structures." Manuscript Report prepared for Columbia University, 1930.

Swanson, Edgar E.: "Financing a Railroad: the Chicago, Burlington & Quincy." Seminar Thesis, Northwestern University, 1949.

Warso, Sherman: "The Mount Ayr, Iowa, to Grant City, Missouri, Abandonment Case." Seminar Thesis, Northwestern University, 1946.

Waugh, Eric: "Burlington Colonization Activities in the British Isles in the 1870's." Seminar Thesis, Northwestern University, 1954.

Williamson, J. T., and Annable, L. F.: "History of the Relief Department of the C. B. & Q." July 1, 1948. CB&Q/Emp.

Wood, Kenneth: "The Log of Car 200." Seminar Thesis, Burr and Burton Seminary, 1960.

• Pamphlets, Speeches, and Releases •

Alderman, Sidney S.: "The Competition of Subsidized Commercial Air Transport." No. 3, Comment on Senate Resolution #50. Washington, 1950.

American Railway Car Institute: *Statistics: Car Building and Car Repairing.* New York, 1946.

Association of American Railroads (Washington), Bureau of Railway Economics: "Trends in Railroad Operations." December, 1957.

———: "The Deteriorating Railroad Situation." January, 1958.

———: "Growth of Railway Mileage in the United States, by States and by Years." 1945.

———: "Highway Motor Transportation." August, 1945.

———: "Lest We Forget." Series of speeches at Washington Union Station. April 26, 1940.

———: "Railroad Transportation, a Statistical Record, 1921–1953." 1954.

———: "Railroad Transportation, a Statistical Record, 1921–1957." 1958.

———: "Railroads 100 Years Old 1845–1945." 1948.

———: "Railroads in This Century." 1947.

———: "Railroads of the United States in Two Wars." 1947.

———: "Transportation in America." 1947.

———: "What Is Public Aid to Transportation?" October, 1940.

Baldwin, W. W.: *Some Features in the History of the Burlington Road.* Chicago, 1906.

———: *The Making of the Burlington.* Reprint from *Professional Engineering Magazine.* Chicago, 1920.

Budd, Ralph: Address before the Chicago Chapter of Chartered Life Underwriters. Chicago, January 19, 1949.

———: Address before the National Association of Shippers' Advisory Boards. Chicago, June 19, 1941.

———: "Diesel Locomotives at Work." Address before the Newcomen Society. New York, October 28, 1957.

———: "Financial Outlook of the Railroads." Remarks before the Chicago Association of Commerce and Industry. Chicago, March 23, 1945.

———: Address before the Inland Daily Press Association. Chicago, February 16, 1932.

———: "How the Mechanical Engineer May Contribute to the National Defense." Address before the American Society of Mechanical Engineers. New York, December 4, 1941.

———: "The Importance of Co-operation." Address before the American Short Line Railroads. Chicago, July 14, 1941.

———: "A Nail for the Iron Horse's Shoe." Address to the National Association of Railroad and Utilities Commissioners. St. Paul, August 26, 1941.

———: "The Nation's Defense Transportation Resources." Address before the Southern States Industrial Council. Birmingham, December 10, 1941.

———: Nationwide Radio Address from Station WRC (NBC). Washington, October 3, 1940.

———: "Peacetime Trends in Transportation." Address before the Railway Business Association. Chicago, November 18, 1949.

————: "Some Experiences in Washington." Address before the Commercial Club. Chicago, January 31, 1942.

————: "Transportation for National Defense." Address before the Veteran's Association of the Burlington Lines. Des Moines, September 27, 1941.

————: "The Ups and Downs of Transportation." Address before the American Mining Congress. Cincinnati, May 1, 1941.

C. B. & Q., Comptroller's Office: "History of Acquisition of Stock Ownership in . . . the G. M. & O." Chicago, 1955.

Committee Organized to Oppose the Removal of the Fort Worth & Denver Headquarters From Fort Worth and the Closing of the Shops At Childress: "Burlington Blitzkreig Against Texas." Fort Worth, 1940.

Corliss, Carlton J.: "The Day of Two Noons." Washington, 1959.

Cullen, Elizabeth O.: "Trailers on Flatcars—Piggybacks; Memorandum Listing Materials on History of Service, 1926–1953." Washington, 1953.

Curtice, Harlow H.: "Pattern for Technological Progress." Address at the Annual Dinner of the American Institute of Consulting Engineers. New York, November 27, 1956.

Daggett, Stuart: *Railroad Consolidation West of the Mississippi River.* University of California *Publications in Economics.* Vol. III, No. 2, 1933.

Davis, C. McD.: "Current Problems of the Railroad Industry." No. 12, Comment on Senate Resolution #50. Washington, 1950.

Elliott, Howard: Remarks at Dallas. June 1, 1925.

Fort, J. Carter: "Transportation Conditions and National Transportation Policy." No. 1, Comment on Senate Resolution #50. Washington, 1950.

Hale, H. E., Consulting Engineer: "Hale Charts for 1946." New York, 1946.

Harrington, George B.: "Coal Mining in Illinois." Newcomen Address. Princeton, 1950.

Holden, Hale: "The Burlington in Nebraska." Address delivered in Omaha. January 29, 1925.

————: Speech at Dallas. June 1, 1925.

Holmes, George W.: "Since 1871: A Short History of the First National Bank of Lincoln, Nebraska." Newcomen Address. Princeton, 1951.

Kuska, Val.: "The Burlington and Big Horn Basin" Omaha, 1959.

————: "The Burlington Railroad Played Part in the Big Horn Basin and Shoshone Project Development." Omaha, 1959.

————: "Railroads Are Interested in Development and Prosperity of their Territories." Speech before South Dakota Agricultural Coordinating Committee. Huron, South Dakota, July 10, 1953.

————: "Railroads to the Rescue," in *In All Its Fury.* Brochure of the January 12, 1888, Blizzard Club. Omaha, March, 1958.

Loomis, Daniel P.: "Railway Labor Legislation." No. 10, Comment on Senate Resolution #50. Washington, 1950.

Mackie, David I.: "The Highway Freighter Problem." No. 4, Comment on Senate Resolution #50. Washington, 1950.

Metzman, Gustav: "Frederick Ely Williamson, 1876–1944, A Railroader." Address to the Newcomen Society. New York, December 8, 1949.

Monroe, J. Elmer: "A Review of Railway Operations in . . . ." (Published annually, 1945 to date; for earlier versions, see under Parmelee, Julius H.) Washington, 1955, to date.

Morgan, David P.: *Fast Mail: the First 75 Years.* Chicago, 1959.

Murphy, H. C.: "Coordination of Rail and Highway Services." Address before the Western Society of Engineers. April, 1939.

Nevins, F. J.: *Seventy Years of Service.* Chicago, 1922.

Overton, R. C.: *Milepost 100.* Chicago, 1949.

————: *The First Ninety Years.* Chicago, 1940.

Parmelee, Julius H.: "The Railroad Situation, 1950." No. 2, Comment on Senate Resolution #59. Washington, 1950.

————: "Rebuttal and Supplemental Statements of the Association of American Railroads." No. 14, Comment on Senate Resolution #50. Washington, 1950.

————: "A Review of Railway Operations in . . . ." (Published annually, 1945–53; for continuation, see under Monroe, J. Elmer.) Washington, 1946–54.

————: "Transport Regulation in Peace and War." Fort Eustis, Va., March 26, 1954.

Plowman, E. G.: "Peacetime Transportation Overcapacity and its Effects." Address in Birmingham, Alabama. February 16, 1960.

Prince, Gregory S.: "Federal Policy Relating to Inland Waterway Transportation." No. 5, Comment on Senate Resolution #50. Washington, 1950.

"Proceedings of Conferences Between Presidents of Railroad Lines West of Chicago and St. Louis and Representatives of Banking Houses held at No. 219 Madison Avenue, New York, January 8 and 10, 1889." New York, 1889.

"Railroads and Their Relations to the Public . . . . A Colloquy between a Farmer, a Government Official and a Railroad Superintendent." Chicago, 1875.

Railway and Locomotive Historical Society: *Locomotives of the Chicago, Burlington & Quincy Railroad, 1855–1935.* Boston, 1936–7.

Smidl, Otto: "Reminiscences." Speech in Chicago. December 27, 1956.

Stringer, Henry E.: "The Regional Shippers Advisory Board, a Synopsis." AAR Stencil #80854. Washington, 1951.

Tigrett, I. B.: "My Railroad Saga." Address to the Newcomen Society, Princeton. February 20, 1952.

Transportation Association of America: "Stop Unfair Taxation on Transportation of Persons and Property." Chicago, 1957.

Waggener, O. O.: *Western Agriculture and the Burlington*. Chicago, 1938.
Wallace, J. F.: "History of the St. Charles Air Line in Chicago, 1852–1902."
    Chicago, April 26, 1902.

· REFERENCE WORKS NOT CITED ELSEWHERE ·

Association of Western Railways: *Railroad Facts*. Chicago, 1955–62.
Automobile Manufacturers Association: *Automobile Facts and Figures*. Detroit,
    1935–55.
———: *Motor Truck Facts*. Detroit, 1947.
Biographical Directory of Railway Officials of America. Chicago, 1887, 1906.
    New York, 1922.
Container Corporation of America: *World Geographic Atlas*. Chicago, 1953.
Eastern Railroad Presidents Conference: *Yearbook of Railroad Information*.
    New York, 1949–60.
Moody's Railroads. New York, 1888–1946.
Moody's Transportation. New York, 1953, 1958.
Official Guide of the Railways. New York, 1949–63.
Paullin, Charles O.: *Atlas of the Historical Geography of the United States*.
    Washington, 1932.
Poor's Manual of the Railroads of the United States. New York, 1870–1 to
    1935.
Rand McNally: *Commercial Atlas and Marketing Guide*. New York, 1928.
Traveller's Railway Guide. Chicago, 1903.
Who's Who in Railroading. New York, 1914–64.
World's Almanac. New York, 1960, 1962.

Index

RICHARD C. OVERTON, Professor of United States History at the University of Western Ontario (London), was born in Montclair, New Jersey, in 1907. He was educated at Montclair Academy, The Hotchkiss School, Williams College (A.B., A.M. in Economics), and Harvard University (A.M. and Ph.D. in History); then served on the staff at the last three and as an instructor in history at Amherst College (1936–38) before spending some time (1939–45) with the Burlington as an Executive Assistant, Research Director, and Superintendent of the Relief Department. From 1945 to 1954 he was a Professor of Business History at Northwestern University (Evanston, Illinois). From 1955 to 1960, he was a Master in History at Burr and Burton Seminary (Manchester, Vermont); since 1961 he has held his present appointment. Mr. Overton, who is married and who has two sons and a daughter, has his permanent home at Manchester, Vermont. His other books have been: *Burlington West: A Colonization History of the Burlington Railroad* (1941) and *Gulf to Rockies: The Heritage of the Fort Worth & Denver–Colorado & Southern, 1861–1898* (1953); he has contributed frequently to historical and railroad periodicals.

A NOTE ON THE TYPE

THIS BOOK is set in *Electra*, a Linotype face designed by W. A. DWIGGINS. This face cannot be classified as either modern or old-style. It is not based on any historical model, nor does it echo any particular period or style. It avoids the extreme contrasts between thick and thin elements that mark most modern faces, and attempts to give a feeling of fluidity, power, and speed.

W. A. Dwiggins (1880-1956) was born in Martinsville, Ohio, and studied art in Chicago. In 1904 he moved to Hingham, Massachusetts, where he built a solid reputation as a designer of advertisements and as a calligrapher. He began an association with the Merganthaler Linotype Company in 1929, and over the next twenty-seven years designed a number of book types for that firm. Of especial interest are the Metro series, Electra, Caledonia, Eldorado, and Falcon. In 1930, Dwiggins first became interested in marionettes, and through the years made many important contributions to the art of puppetry and the design of marionettes.

Composed, printed, and bound by The Haddon Craftsmen, Inc., Scranton, Pennsylvania. Photographs reproduced and lithographed by The Murray Printing Co., Forge Village, Mass. Typography and binding design by Guy Fleming. Maps drawn by Anita Karl.